Police
Operations

Kären M. Hess

Henry M. Wrobleski

Police Operations

Kären M. Hess

*Normandale Community College
Bloomington, Minnesota*

Henry M. Wrobleski

*Normandale Community College
Bloomington, Minnesota*

West Publishing Company

St. Paul   New York   Los Angeles   San Francisco

Artwork: Table 8–1, Figures 5–3 and 14–1 by Rolin Graphics.
All other illustrations by Alice Thiede, Carto Graphics.
Composition: Carlisle Communications
Copyediting: Luana Richards
Cover image: PhotoResource/Bob Cunningham
Indexing: Christine M. Hess
Text design: John Edeen

WEST'S COMMITMENT TO THE ENVIRONMENT

In 1906, West Publishing Company began recycling materials left over from the production of books. This began a tradition of efficient and responsible use of resources. Today, up to 95 percent of our legal books and 70 percent of our college and school texts are printed on recycled, acid-free stock. West also recycles nearly 22 million pounds of scrap paper annually—the equivalent of 181,717 trees. Since the 1960s, West has devised ways to capture and recycle waste inks, solvents, oils, and vapors created in the printing process. We also recycle plastics of all kinds, wood, glass, corrugated cardboard, and batteries, and have eliminated the use of styrofoam book packaging. We at West are proud of the longevity and the scope of our commitment to our environment.

Production, Prepress, Printing and Binding by West Publishing Company.

Library of Congress Cataloging-in-Publication Data
Hess, Kären M., 1939–
    Police operations / Kären M. Hess, Henry M. Wrobleski.
        p.   cm.
    Includes index.
    ISBN 0-314-00926-4
    1. Police. 2. Police—United States.   I. Wrobleski, Henry M.,
1922– . II. Title.
HV7921.H47   1992
363.2—dc20   92-10983
                                                        CIP

About the Authors

Kären M. Hess

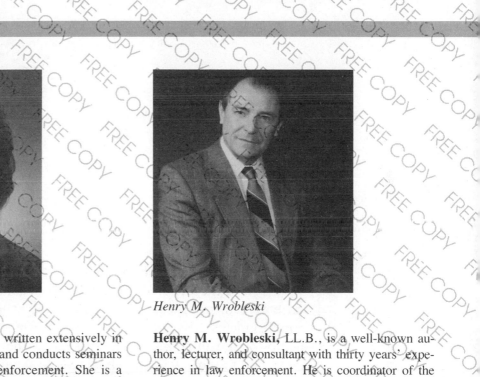

Henry M. Wrobleski

Kären M. Hess, Ph.D., has written extensively in the field of law enforcement and conducts seminars on communications in law enforcement. She is a member of the English department at Normandale Community College as well as the president of the Institute for Professional Development. Dr. Hess is a graduate of the University of Minnesota where she concentrated on educational psychology and instructional design.

Henry M. Wrobleski, LL.B., is a well-known author, lecturer, and consultant with thirty years' experience in law enforcement. He is coordinator of the Law Enforcement Program at Normandale Community College as well as Dean of Instruction for the Institute for Professional Development. Mr. Wrobleski is a graduate of the FBI Academy.

DEDICATION

Dedicated to the hundreds of thousands of uniformed law enforcement officers, past and present, whose accomplishments have made such a difference in the quality of life in communities throughout the United States and to those who are about to join them.

Contents in Brief

Contents

SECTION I
The Basics Behind Effective Police Operations   *1*

CHAPTER 1
Police Operations in Context: The Structure Behind the Scene   *3*

CHAPTER 2
Communications: The Foundation of Police Operations   *35*

List of Figures

List of Tables

List of Acronyms

AARP	American Association of Retired Persons	DNA	Deoxyribonucleic Acid
ACT	Awareness of Crime in Texarkana	DOT	Department of Transportation
A.D.	Alzheimer's Disease	DRE	Drug Recognition Expert
AFIS	Automated Fingerprint Identification System	DRT	Drug Recognition Technician
AI	Accident Investigator Artificial Intelligence	DUI	Driving Under the Influence
AIDS	Acquired Immuno Deficiency Syndrome	DUIL	Driving Under the Influence of Liquor
ALF	Animal Liberation Front	DWI	Driving While Intoxicated
AR	Accident Reconstruction	EEOC	Equal Employment Opportunity Commission
ATB	Auto Theft Bureau	EMS	Emergency Medical Services
ATF	Alcohol, Tobacco, and Firearms, Bureau of	EOC	Emergency Operations Center
AVL	Automatic Vehicle Locator	FAA	Federal Aviation Administration
BAC	Blood-Alcohol Concentration	FEMA	Federal Emergency Management Administration
BAQ	Breath-Alcohol Equivalent	GIS	Geographic Information System
CAAI	Computer-Assisted Accident Investigation	HAZMAT	Hazardous Materials
CAD	Computer-Aided Dispatching Coronary Artery Disease	HBV	Hepatitis B
CALEA	Commission on Accreditation for Law Enforcement Agencies	H.E.L.P.	High-Intensity Emergency Lighting Plan
CARS	Computer-Assisted Reconstruction System	HGN	Horizontal Gaze Nystagmus [test]
CAT	Combat Auto Theft	HIV	Human Immunodeficiency Virus
CEP	Community Empowerment Policing	HM	Hazardous Materials
CHD	Coronary Heart Disease	HUD	Housing and Urban Development, U.S. Department of
CHEMTREC	Chemical Transportation Emergency Center	IACP	International Association of Chiefs of Police
CHP	California Highway Patrol	ICMA	International City Management Association
CISD	Critical-Incident Stress Debriefing	ILA	International Listening Association
CPC	Child Protection Center	INS	Immigration and Naturalization Service
CPED	Crime Prevention through Environmental Design	LETIN	Law Enforcement Training and Information Network
CSO	Community Service Officer	MDT	Mobile Data Terminals Mobile Display Terminals
DAIP	Domestic Abuse Intervention Project	NAACP	National Association for the Advancement of Colored People
DARE	Drug Abuse Resistance Education		
DEA	Drug Enforcement Administration Drug Enforcement Agency	NABS	Neighborhood Action Base Station

NCADV National Coalition Against
Domestic Violence
NCIC National Crime Information
Center
NCPI National Crime Prevention
Institution
NET Narcotics Enforcement Team
NHTSA National Highway Traffic Safety
Administration
NIJ National Institute of Justice
NRT National Response Team
NTSB National Transportation Safety
Board
OFP Order for Protection
OJJDP Office of Juvenile Justice and
Delinquency Prevention
OSHA Occupational, Safety, and Health
Act
Occupational, Safety, and Health
Administration
PAS Preliminary Alcohol
Screening

PETA People for the Ethical Treatment of
Animals
PHA Public Housing Authority
POP Problem-Oriented Policing
PTS Police Traffic Services
PTSD Posttraumatic Stress Disorder
PWC Personal Watercraft
QUAD Quick Uniform Attack on
Drugs
SA Special Agent
SWAT Special Weapons and Tactics
[teams]
TAAR Traffic Accident Analysis and
Reconstruction
TDC Traffic Direction and Control
TREVI Terrorism, Radicalism, Extremism,
and Violence International
UCR Uniform Crime Reports
U.S.C.A. United States Code Annotated
VOA Voice of Animals

List of Cases

Foreword

Police Operations is a well-researched, comprehensive, and up-to-date text that covers all major aspects of policing. It deals with what law enforcement leaders and researchers feel are the most critical issues facing law enforcement in the 1990s. A theme running throughout *Police Operations* is that the motivated, professional uniformed officer can make a tremendous difference in how citizens are "served and protected."

The authors focus attention on what could be rather than on what has been in the past. They emphasize what the police responsibility is, the constitutional and statutory constraints under which police function, and how the tasks to be performed can be accomplished responsibly and humanely within these constraints. Relevant landmark Supreme Court cases affecting police operations are presented throughout the text, giving students an understanding of case law and police procedures under varying circumstances.

Students are challenged to apply the information contained in each chapter to application exercises, critical thinking problems, and discussion questions. These exercises, problems, and questions underscore the complexity of policing and the need for knowledge, skill, and common sense in carrying out police operations. With such a base, police officers of the future will be able to find new ways to deliver police services fairly, equitably, and effectively. They can, indeed, reshape approaches to some of the critical problems confronting law enforcement and may become the change agents of the future.

The authors are to be congratulated on writing a text that not only covers all the basics of police operations, but does so in a way which students should find both interesting and challenging.

Donald J. Clough
Bloomington Police Department President,
Minnesota Crime Prevention Association

Acknowledgements

We would like to thank Pam Reierson, media specialist, for her valuable assistance in research for this text and Christine Hess for her expert data entry, indexing, and preparation of the Instructor's Manual. We would also like to thank Waldo Asp for creating the *Exercises in Critical Thinking* found at the end of each chapter.

In addition, thanks are due to the reviewers of the manuscript for their careful reading and constructive suggestions: James S. Albritton, Marquette University; Michael B. Blankenship, Memphis State University; W.D. Braddock, Boise State University; David L. Carter, Michigan State University; Floyd W. Liley, Jr., Mansfield University; Neal W. Lippold, Waubonsee Community College; James Malcolm, College of Lake County; James L. Massey, Northern Illinois University; Carroll S. Price, Penn Valley Community College; Chester L. Quarles, University of Mississippi; B. Grant Stitt, University of Nevada at Reno; and Gary W. Tucker, Sinclair Community College. The content of the text is ultimately, however, the sole responsibility of the coauthors.

Finally, thanks to our editors at West Publishing, Robert J. Jucha, Diane Colwyn, Tom Hilt, and Peggy Brewington for their outstanding advice, support, and encouragement. Thanks, too, to copyeditor Luana Richards, whose eye for detail was valuable to this text.

Kären M. Hess
Henry M. Wrobleski

Preface

Welcome to *Police Operations*. This text presents the fundamentals of what policing is all about. The basic reason modern society has police departments is summarized in the classic statement of police sociologist Egon Bittner*: "Something-ought-not-to-be-happening—about-which-something-ought-to-be-done-NOW!" This text goes beyond this reactive approach (which will always be an important part of policing), however, by also incorporating the techniques of proactive policing. Proactive policing is perhaps best illustrated in *community policing,* where law enforcement enters into a partnership with the citizens and organizations in a community to take steps to make the community safer for all. For such a partnership to work, law enforcement agencies must have carefully thought-through policies and procedures for dealing with crime and violence both reactively and proactively. Community policing also emphasizes the need for individual officers on the street to be creative in their approaches to problems and to work with citizens as they solve these problems.

The first section of *Police Operations* discusses the basics behind effective police operations, including the context in which services are provided and the skills required to provide these services. Law enforcement officers must be thoroughly familiar with the citizens they are sworn to "serve and protect" as well as with the constitutional restraints within which they must operate. They must be proficient in communications skills as well in as the numerous profession-specific skills required in law enforcement: conducting stops and frisks, making arrests, searching crime scenes and suspects, investigating crimes, and assisting victims.

Section II of *Police Operations* discusses the personal side of law enforcement—what officers need to know about protecting themselves from being sued, about acting not only legally but ethically as well, and about maintaining their physical and emotional well-being so they can continue in their chosen profession.

Section III discusses actual operations law enforcement officers must undertake to get the job done. Approaches to patrol, traffic, crime and violence, domestic disputes, juveniles, gangs, the drug problem, and to working with others are examined within the context of our changing society.

Police Operations is designed to help you understand and remember the fundamentals of what policing is all about. Each chapter begins with a list of "Do You Know" questions that will get you thinking about the most important concepts

*From "Florence Nightingale in Pursuit of Willie Sutton: A Theory of Police," pp. 17–44, in *The Potential for Reform of Criminal Justice,* H. Jacob, ed. Beverly Hills, Calif.: Sage Publications, 1974, p. 30.

contained in the chapter. As you read the chapter, you'll find answers to these questions, highlighted. Each chapter also includes a summary of the key concepts. Be forewarned, however! Do not be like the lazy student who thinks a text has three parts: the front cover, the back cover, and the summaries. If you read only the summaries, you are not likely to understand or recall the content. Remember, not only your livelihood but your life is on the line in this demanding and rewarding profession. Begin your habits of self-discipline now. The summaries are intended as a *review*. The text is designed to give you *triple-strength* learning IF you (1) think about the questions at the beginning of the chapter before you read, (2) read the chapter thoughtfully for in-depth answers to these questions, and then (3) read and reread the summary.

To further strengthen your learning experience, the text includes terms you should know, discussion questions, application exercises in which you create policies and procedures related to the content of each chapter, and critical thinking exercises. Professional law enforcement officers should be able to create reasonable, legal, ethical, and effective policies and procedures for the most common situations encountered in law enforcement. In addition, they should be able to approach each situation as a unique experience, perhaps requiring a more creative approach. Law enforcement officers must have good critical thinking skills. It is the intent of this text to provide a balance of both.

Kären M. Hess
Henry M. Wrobleski

The Basics Behind Effective Police Operations

Police operations deals with what officers in the field do as they "serve and protect". To fulfill their responsibilities, law enforcement officers have been given great power. This power has been entrusted to them by the people they serve and is defined by the laws of the land, state, and municipality.

This section presents an overview of police operations beginning with the context in which those services are provided. The society served, the laws it has enacted, the individuals entering law enforcement, and the police organization itself have undergone great changes in the past decade. Today's law enforcement uses mission statements, value statements, goals, objectives, policies, procedures, and regulations to provide a basic structure within which officers normally function. Since law enforcement deals with such diverse problems, officers must also expect to use discretion while safeguarding the constitutional rights of people in the community (Chapter 1).

Law enforcement as a profession demands that its officers be multifaceted and well-rounded. Officers must understand the complex communications process and the barriers that often exist within the process itself and within our diverse society (Chapter 2).

Officers must also be skilled in making field inquiries, interviewing, and interrogating, and they must know how to do so while protecting the constitutional rights of victims, suspects, and witnesses (Chapter 3). Officers must record the information they have obtained into effective, reader-friendly reports, and they must know how to use the various records available (Chapter 4). Finally, officers need several profession-specific skills. They must understand and become skilled at conducting stop and frisks, making arrests, conducting searches, and participating in undercover operations, all without violating anyone's constitutional rights (Chapter 5).

POLICE OPERATIONS IN CONTEXT: THE STRUCTURE BEHIND THE SCENE

CHAPTER **1**

INTRODUCTION

Just what do police officers do? What skills must they possess and in what ways does the community rely on their services? Historically, police officers have been viewed as law *enforcement* officers. As noted by Cumming et al. (1965, p. 12): "The policeman's role in an integrative system is, by definition and by law, explicitly concerned with controlling—keeping the law from being broken and apprehending those who break it—and only latently with support." And yet, as noted by Reiss (1971, p. 63) over twenty years ago:

> *Many citizens consider the function of the police in everyday life to extend beyond their law enforcement and peace-keeping roles. The lower classes, in particular, call upon the police to perform a variety of services. They depend upon police assistance in times of trouble, crisis, and indecision. . . . Such roles of assistance are as much a police function as are coercive roles of authority.*

A more recent view of what constitutes police operations is offered by Greene and Klockars (1991, p. 273): "The question of what police do, day in and day out, is the subject of a variety of 'conventional wisdoms.' There are visions of police as crime fighters, social workers, peacekeepers, street-corner politicians, traffic controllers, and recorders of important social events. Each is associated with an interpretation of what actually does and, often, what ought to constitute police work." Greene and Klockars (p. 274) suggest that police operations may include the following:

- *Law enforcement interventions such as making arrests, enforcing the traffic code, and conducting criminal investigations.*

Do You Know

- What police operations is? What it includes?
- How our society has changed?
- How our law enforcement officers have changed?
- What community policing is?
- How the police organization has changed?
- What participatory leadership is?
- What a mission and a mission statement are?
- What the relationship is between goals and objectives?
- How policies and procedures differ? Why they are important?
- How a regulation differs from a policy? From a general order?
- What police discretion is?
- What problems are associated with discretion?
- What positive contributions discretion makes?

- *Handling situations and people.*
- *Resolving citizen-defined "something-that-ought-not-to-be-happening-about-which-something-ought-to-be-done-now" occasions.*
- *Acting as change agents.*
- *Serving as street-corner politicians.*
- *Being problem solvers.*

Police operations refers to those activities conducted in the field by law enforcement officers as they "serve and protect." Operations include patrol, traffic, investigation, and general calls for service.

No matter what priorities a law enforcement agency may have, certain basic police operations will be found.

Before looking at specific police operations and the skills required to perform them effectively and efficiently, it is important to understand the *context* in which these operations occur. Although police operations have changed little over the last hundred years, the public served and the laws enacted by that public, the officers providing the services, the community involvement, and the police bureaucracy itself have changed and will continue to change. Effective police operations in the 1990s and beyond must consider these changes.

A Changing Public and Society

Some trends to be dealt with are described by McCord and Wicker (1990, pp. 29–30):

- The U.S. population is aging. In 1996, the first wave of "baby boomers" will turn 50, marking the start of a "senior boom" in the United States. By 2020, one in every four Americans will be 55 or older.
- The minority population is increasing rapidly. By the year 2000, 21 percent of American children will be black or Asian. When the projections for white Hispanic children are added, the minority figure for children increases to 34 percent.
- Immigrants account for an ever-increasing share of the U.S. population and workforce. Legal immigration during the 1980s has accounted for an average of 570,000 people per year. In addition, one estimate holds that the number of *illegal* aliens is growing at a rate of 100,000–300,000 a year.
- The number of single-parent households is likely to increase.
- The United States is becoming a bifurcated society with more wealth, more poverty, and a shrinking middle class. The gap between the "haves" and the "have nots" is widening.

Our society is becoming older and has more minorities, more immigrants, and more single-parent households while the gap between the rich and poor widens.

These trends underscore the need for those in the criminal justice field to be culturally sensitive to the public they serve, especially those who work as directly with that public as police officers do. Going beyond statistics, the Tofflers (1990, pp. 2–3) present a vivid prediction of what the future might hold:

We are witnessing the massive breakdown of America as we knew it and the emergence of a strange new 21st-century America whose basic institutional structures have yet to be formed. . . .

America-As-We-Knew-It—the one we grew up in . . .—was an industrial America. . . .

This Smokestack America has since been battered by the most accelerated technological revolution in history. Computers, satellites, space travel, fiber optics, fax machines, robots, bar coding, ...

The new complexity of everyday life affects everyone, and the passing of Smokestack America has left millions of middle-class Americans stranded and disoriented. Expecting one kind of life, they find themselves plunged into another, frustrated and future shocked.

The Tofflers (p. 3) suggest that it is "witless to assume that millions of poor, jobless young people—not part of the work-world culture and bursting with energy and anger—are going to stay off the streets and join knitting clubs." They further note that the American family has become "fractured" by these radical changes in technology and that this has had "a massive impact on law enforcement." There are more singles and loners, more homeless people and drifters, all highly mobile, with few support systems. The Tofflers suggest:

More and more individuals are being freed from the social constraints that kept them on the straight and narrow. These individuals are multiplying, and that fact alone suggests further social turbulence in the years ahead.

America of the 1990s is vastly different from America even fifty years ago.

We all know that law enforcement is society's second line of defense. Crime, drug abuse, and sociopathic behavior generally are first held in check by social disapproval—by family, neighbors, and co-workers. But in change-wracked America, people are less bonded to one another, so that social disapproval loses its power over them.

It is when social disapproval fails that law enforcement must take over.

Indeed, the people and the communities served by the criminal justice system are drastically different from the past. All individuals working within the criminal justice system must become sensitive to these differences. As noted by Metts (1985, p. 35), the police officer of the future "will need to be flexible enough to deal with many divergent ethnic and social groups. There will be few easy answers in tomorrow's diverse and protean society."

Another major change affecting police operations is the type of officer performing them.

A Changing Law Enforcement Officer

Historically, law enforcement has attracted young white men out of the military. These men frequently had a high school education or less. This is no longer true. Many people entering the field have no military experience. As Tafoya (1990, p. 15) notes:

Until about fifteen years ago, most police recruits were men who had served in the Armed Forces. These men were accustomed to unquestioned response to command. Today, however, few of the young men and women entering law enforcement have such experience. They often ask questions that are unsettling to traditionalist managers, who often believe that people need to be coerced, controlled, and threatened.

In addition, women and minorities are being actively recruited, and educational standards are being progressively raised. According to Metts (1985, p. 31): "Future police officers will be extensively trained and qualified professionals. . . . Tomorrow's professional cop will have to be educated and educable. As a minimum requirement, a bachelor's or master's degree in the social sciences will be needed. . . . Administrators will care less about marksmanship and physical size and more about mental capacity and diplomas."

Another change in today's police officers is likely to be in their value systems. As noted by Donald C. Witham, Chief, Strategic Planning Unit of the FBI (1991, p. 30):

Decades ago, workers were interested primarily in higher pay, opportunities for advancement and fair treatment. . . . By contrast, today's workers embrace the values of "expressive success." They want a job that interests them, encourages the development of their abilities and potential, offers them opportunities to be creative, and allows them a voice in the decision-making process.

*Today's police recruits include fewer people with military
backgrounds and more women and minorities. New recruits
have more education and place more value on job satisfaction
than on material rewards. They are also expected to perform
more diverse operations.*

In addition to having different backgrounds and values from the "traditional"
police recruit, police officers now are often called on to perform operations well
beyond what has been traditionally provided. According to Siegel (1990, p. 119):

*Law enforcement agencies have traditionally been charged with maintaining
public order, enforcing the criminal law, preventing and detecting crime, and
apprehending and arresting criminal suspects. As our society has evolved,
new and complex functions have been required of police officers. Today, law
enforcement agencies work actively with community leaders to prevent
criminal behavior; they divert juveniles, alcoholics, and drug addicts from the
criminal justice system; they participate in specialized crime prevention
projects such as drug awareness projects in local schools; they resolve family
conflicts; they facilitate the movement of people and vehicles; and they
provide social services, such as preserving civil order on an emergency basis,
finding shelter for the homeless, and helping those with special needs.*

*Because of these expanded responsibilities, greater professionalism is required of
police officers. The officer must not only be technically competent to investigate
crimes and make an arrest but must also be aware of the rules and procedures
associated with arrest, apprehension, and investigation of criminal activity. The
police officer must be in possession of a wide variety of skills, from using
technological advances such as computers to developing the proper contacts with
social service agencies in order to give aid to an abused or homeless child.*

Officer involvement with the community is very apparent in the preceding description of operations that are likely to be performed by today's police officers.
Indeed, another change has been the greater involvement of communities in making
their neighborhoods safer.

A Change in Community Involvement

Many individuals involved in law enforcement are advocating greater community involvement, including neighborhood or community policing. Commissioner Lee P.
Brown, New York City Police Department (1991, p. 23), for example, suggests that:

*Neighborhood policing, in all of its many applications, is the key to
success. . . . The landscape of society has changed and will continue to
change. Unless the providers of services to the community change as well,
they risk being swept aside and consumed by the rising tide of change.*

Community policing puts officers in close contact with citizens on their beat.

Neighborhood policing is also commonly referred to as *community policing* and is being adopted by many police departments across the country.

Community policing *empowers citizens to help local law enforcement provide safer neighborhoods. It usually includes an emphasis on foot patrol.*

Community policing usually assigns specific officers to specific neighborhoods and actively involves them in helping the neighborhood solve its problems. It is proactive and often includes increased emphasis on foot patrol. According to Trojanowicz and Bucqueroux (1990, p. 5):

> *Community policing is a new philosophy of policing, based on the concept that police officers and private citizens working together in creative ways can help solve contemporary community problems related to crime, fear of crime, social and physical disorder, and neighborhood decay. The philosophy is predicated on the belief that achieving these goals requires that police departments develop a new relationship with the law-abiding people in the community, allowing them a greater voice in setting local police priorities and involving them in efforts to improve the overall quality of life in their neighborhoods. It shifts the focus of police work from handling random calls to solving community problems.*

Community policing may look like the older, traditional forms of law enforcement systems centered on foot patrol. However, as noted by Horne (1991, p. 24): ''Contemporary community policing is more than just 'old wine in new bottles.' It is really a new way of thinking about policing, suggesting that police officers are creative, intelligent individuals who can do more than just respond to incidents. By working with the people who live and work in the area, they can both identify the underlying problems and determine the best strategy to solve those problems.''

This is very similar to the conceptualization of community-oriented policing (COP) suggested by Vaughn (1991, p. 35) who says:

Community-oriented policing is not a program. Community-oriented policing is a philosophy, a style, and a method of providing police service and managing the police organization. It is value based and involves long-term institutional change. . . .

With a much broader focus on problem identification, analysis, and utilization of systematic problem-solving techniques, coupled with strong community partnerships, it is possible to find more effective long-term solutions to persistent crime problems.

The philosophy behind community-oriented policing is explained by Wilson and Kelling (1982) who suggest that crime and social disorder are ''inextricably linked'' (p. 31). They used the term **broken windows** as a metaphor to describe the deterioration of neighborhoods. Broken windows that go unrepaired make a statement that no one cares enough about the quality of life in the neighborhood to bother fixing things that need repair. According to Greene (1989, p. 361): ''The general thesis is that declining social relations within communities open them to criminal invasion. A strong policing program emphasizing order maintenance and community/police interaction can support neighborhood social relations, thereby providing some hedge against social decay and ultimately crime.''

Community policing goes much further than traditional community relations programs or neighborhood watch programs, although it often includes these components. Community policing means that officers get to know the citizens in their assigned areas—those who are law-abiding and those who are not. It means they listen to the citizens and treat them as a business treats its customers. As noted by Brown (1991, p. 20):

In the past, police administrators have assumed they were the experts and therefore knew what police services the community needed and how these services should be provided. To a large extent, however, it is the citizens themselves who know best what the community's problems are and how they can be solved. They are on the front lines. They are the ones who know the pain of victimization, who see relatives and friends die at the hands of criminals, who clearly understand that one does not have to be a police officer to know what actions should be taken.

Community policing capitalizes on people's natural tendency to subscribe to the NIMBY (Not In My Back Yard) philosophy. The closer to home police can get their message, the more likely they are to enlist community support. According to Trojanowicz and Carter (1990, p. 11):

Community policing offers an important new tool to help heal the wounds caused by crime, fear of crime, and disorder. In one community that might mean a community police officer recruiting elderly volunteers from a senior center to help immigrant youths become more fluent in English. This offers the hope that those retirees will overcome their fears, while at the same time enhancing a young person's opportunity to perform well in school and on the job. . . .

It would be naive to suggest that community policing is a panacea that can heal all the wounds in any community. But it has demonstrated its ability to make people feel safer and improve the overall quality of community life. Today's challenge is to find new ways for law enforcement to contribute to make the United States a place where all people have an equal chance to secure a piece of the American dream for themselves and their children.

Given the changing needs of the public, the new type of person entering law enforcement, the growth of new services, and increased community involvement, it is logical that the bureaucracy directing police operations must also change.

A Changing Police Bureaucracy

A basic principle of Sir Robert Peel, often called the father of modern policing, was that the police must be organized militarily. The military model of the Metropolitan Police of London (established in 1829) was adopted in the United States and has been the model for our police departments since that time. This model is now being questioned by many, partially because of the changes in police recruits and the trend toward community policing.

Metts (1985, p. 35) predicts that: "Tomorrow's police agencies will little resemble today's rigid military-like models. The role of the police will be more 'caretaker' and service delivery in nature, and less 'lock 'em up.' "

Another advocate of a need for change in the traditional police bureaucracy is Commissioner Brown, (1991, p. 20), who says: "The old ways of making decisions and delivering police services and programs will no longer suffice." Brown (p. 21) contends: "Police chiefs must facilitate a change in the organizational structure of their agencies. They must move away from the paramilitary model and adopt an appropriate corporate model that will result in a flattening of the organization." This flattening of the organizational structure means having fewer management and supervisory positions and more officers. These officers will be better trained to act independently while providing more field services—that is, police operations. Nees (1990, p. 263) predicts that in the future: "Management, supervision, and officers will develop a partnership. The line between management and officer ranks will become less clear." The management's span of control will also become wider.

Witham (1991, p. 30) also suggests: "The traditional paramilitary orientation of law enforcement cannot obscure the fact that times, people, and jobs have changed dramatically." The police bureaucracy is also changing; as Nees (1990, p. 257) notes:

We have lived through the "blue power" movement of the 1960s and 1970s. That movement left a wide gap between managers and employees, and many administrators are still learning how to listen and respond to employees. Those who fail in this and do not involve employees in planning will not survive in the 21st century.

The police bureaucracy should become less militaristic and should move toward a team approach to providing services. This includes participatory leadership.

Most people no longer depend on the authority or professed wisdom of people in places of position, power, and influence, preferring to make up their own minds and take responsibility for their own actions. They no longer allow somebody "above" them to dictate their opinions or control their actions. They are more independent and more willing to make their own judgments and decisions and accept the consequences.

The few people who had nearly all the power now have less, and the great number who had little or none, now have more. Children have more in relation to parents. Employees have more relative to employers. And police officers have more relative to that of their sergeants, lieutenants, and the chief.

In the view of most experts in human behavior, the change is positive. As noted almost a decade ago by William Walsh, professor of criminal justice at Pennsylvania State University (1983, p. 26):

> *Law enforcement managers, by the nature of their role and occupational experience, are to a great extent task-oriented. Police emphasis on quick response to calls for service and the authority expected of them by the public tend to reinforce their concern for tasks. Public as well as private sector managers are rewarded or penalized according to how well they accomplish organizational activities.*
>
> *Yet, it should always be remembered that organizational goals and objectives ultimately depend on the willingness of the personnel required to carry them out.*

Walsh suggests that police managers can be classified as "after-the-fact" supervisors because they are usually not present when officers perform their duties. Walsh warns that a police manager who does not recognize this and who attempts to "lead from a position of total authority and direction will often earn the contempt and disrespect of his officers. The willing performance of these officers is dependent on his ability to influence them in a positive manner at all times."

The change is from authoritarian leadership to a leadership style that focuses on teamwork. This style is often called *participatory leadership*. Buchholz and Roth (1987, p. 25) describe the differences between the two approaches in Table 1.1.

TABLE 1.1
Authoritative v. Participative Leadership Styles

Authoritative Leader		Participative Leader	
Approach	Results	Approach	Results
■ Mandate (tell) ■ Compliance (have to) ■ Time ■ Produce	■ Communication is downward; little upward communication ■ Position power ■ Tell-oriented ■ People do things because they "have to" ■ People put in their time but energy decreases ■ People produce to standard	■ Influence (tell and ask) ■ Commitment (want to) ■ Time and energy ■ Produce and perform	■ Greater upward and lateral communication ■ Personal power ■ Tell- and ask-oriented ■ People do things because they "want to" ■ People put in their time *and* their energy ■ People perform more than "just the expected"

Source: Adapted from *Creating the High Performance Team*, Steve Buchholz and Thomas Roth, ® John Wiley and Sons, Inc., 1987, p. 25. Reprinted by permission of John Wiley & Sons, Inc.

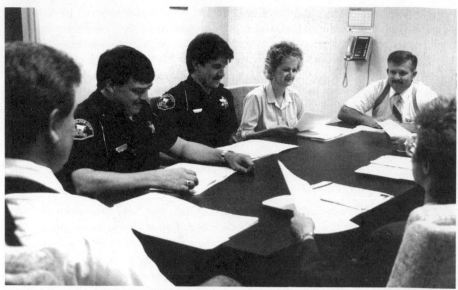

Participatory leadership allows input on important decisions from the rank-and-file officer. Teamwork is essential to accomplishing the department's mission.

Participatory leadership *allows officers to influence decisions affecting them and seeks to form a cohesive team.*

Participatory leadership is usually highly motivating to all members of the team. This change in leadership style is supported by Couper and Lobitz (1988, p. 81):

We must take a fresh look at this new model of leadership to complement the current movement in our field to community-oriented and problem-solving policing. We must shift from telling and controlling the men and women we work with to developing and enhancing them. We must ask their input before making critical decisions that affect them. We must make a commitment to ask them about policing strategies in the community, and actually listen to their answers. We must stop reacting to incidents and begin solving problems. We must permit risk-taking and tolerate honest mistakes in our agencies in order to encourage creativity and achieve innovation. We must try to experiment. We must avoid, whenever possible, the use of coercive power within our organizations. We need to permit ideas to "bubble up" within the organization and encourage development of the skills and abilities of the talented men and women who now police our nation's streets. If we learn nothing else about police organizational change, let us remember that when change is implemented from the top of the organization, either by coercive force or without real employee input, it will surely fail.

In other words, in progressive police departments, the role of rank-and-file officers is elevated significantly, with their input being critical in decision making. It is further expected that rank-and-file officers will be in close contact with the citizens they serve and can therefore reflect citizen concerns as decisions are made.

More and more departments are turning to the team concept as the most effective way to set and achieve their goals. Therefore, this text provides a chance to engage in some thought-provoking, critical thinking about important issues in police operations. To do so effectively requires an understanding of the basis for police operations. The functions undertaken by law enforcement officers should not be viewed as isolated activities, but rather as part of a master plan to accomplish the mission of the law enforcement agency.

Mission and Values

Work should be meaningful. Officers who see themselves as serving an important function will be more productive and more satisfied in their profession than those who feel no sense of mission.

---

*An agency's **mission** is its reason for existence, its purpose. It is often embodied in a **mission statement**.*

Mission statements should be short, believable, easy to understand, easy to remember, and widely known. Some common mission statements from the business world are familiar to most people:

- *We bring good things to life.* (General Electric)
- *All the news that's fit to print.* (New York Times)
- *The quality goes in before the name goes on.* (Zenith)
- *To serve and protect.* (Law enforcement agencies throughout the country)

Many businesses and law enforcement agencies go further than a slogan in articulating their purpose. Consider the following examples:

- The Charlotte Police Department is committed to fairness, compassion, and excellence while providing police services in accordance with the law and that are sensitive to the priorities and needs of the people.
- The mission of the Houston Police Department is to enhance the quality of life in the City of Houston by working cooperatively with the public and within the framework of the United States Constitution to enforce the laws, preserve the peace, reduce fear, and provide for a safe environment.

Mission statements are often accompanied by the set of values on which they are based. These values must be shared by members of the department and the public served, or they will be meaningless. Ideally, these values also are consistent with the overall cultural values of the state and the nation. As noted by Barker and Carter (1991, p. 34):

The process of inculcating values cannot be coercive, rather it must be consensual. To be effective it is a long-term process which integrates ethics, the departmental mission, professional responsibility, fairness, due process, and empathy. A department which attempts to coerce values will meet with little success.

The values underlying the Charlotte Police Department mission statement can be stated as follows. The Charlotte Police Department:

- Believes that the protection of life and property is our highest priority.
- Will respect and protect the rights and dignity of all persons and conduct all citizen contacts with courtesy and compassion.
- Will strive for excellence in its delivery of police services and will utilize training, technology, and innovation to achieve that goal.
- Recognizes its interdependent relationship with the community it serves and will remain sensitive to the community's priorities and needs.
- Will enforce the law impartially throughout the community.
- Recognizes the individual worth of each of its members.

Such value statements enhance officers' feelings of worth and importance and lend significance to the daily routine of police operations. See Table 1.2 for similar values set forth by the Houston Police Department.

TABLE 1.2
The Values, Guiding Principles and Mission of the Houston Police Department

Values

The Values, Guiding Principles and Mission of the Houston Police Department are as follows:

- *Preserve and Advance Democratic Values* We shall uphold this country's democratic values as embodied in the Constitution and shall dedicate ourselves to the preservation of liberty and justice for all.
- *Improve the Quality of Community Life* We shall strive to improve the quality of life through the provision of quality and equitable services.
- *Improve Quality of Work Life* We shall strive to improve the working environment for the department's employees by engaging in open and honest communication and demonstrating a genuine concern for one another.
- *Demonstrate Professionalism* We shall always engage in behavior that is beyond ethical reproach and reflects the integrity of police professionals.

Guiding Principles

- Life and individual freedoms are sacred.
- All persons should be treated fairly and equitably.
- The role of the police is to resolve problems through the enforcement of laws—not through the imposition of judgement and punishment.
- The neighborhood is the basic segment of the community.
- Because law enforcement and public safety reflect community-wide concern, the police must actively seek the involvement of citizens in all aspects of policing.
- The fundamental responsibility of the police is provision of quality service.
- The department's employees are its most valuable asset.
- Employee involvement in departmental activities is essential for maintaining a productive environment.
- Employees should be treated fairly and equitably and recognition of basic human dignity and as a means of enriching their work life.

Departmental Mission

The mission of the Houston Police Department is to enhance the quality of life in the City of Houston by working cooperatively with the public and within the framework of the United States Constitution to enforce the laws, preserve the peace, reduce fear and provide for a safe environment.

Values such as these will be stressed throughout the text. Sometimes the values are integrated into the mission statement as done by Chief David Couper of the Madison, Wisconsin, Police Department.

We have developed a mission statement that attempts to capture the values that "drive" and direct our organization. WE BELIEVE IN THE DIGNITY AND WORTH OF ALL PEOPLE. WE ARE COMMITTED TO:

- *Providing high-quality, community-oriented police services.*
- *Protecting constitutional rights.*
- *Problem solving.*
- *Teamwork.*
- *Openness.*
- *Planning for the future.*
- *Providing leadership to the profession.*

We are proud of the diversity of our workforce which permits us to grow and which respects each of us as individuals, and we strive for a healthful workplace (Madison Police Department Newsletter, December 26, 1986).

Mission statements and value statements are important to law enforcement agencies and should be the driving force behind police operations. They are, however, only the starting point. The next step is to develop goals and objectives that will accomplish the mission and to then decide what specific tasks must be undertaken to accomplish the goals and objectives.

Goals, Objectives, and Tasks

Goals may vary from one police department to another, but they usually focus on the following:

- To preserve the peace.
- To protect civil rights and civil liberties.
- To prevent crime.
- To enforce the law.
- To provide services.
- To improve the quality of life in the community.

The National Advisory Commission on Criminal Justice Standards and Goals (1973, p. 49) states: "One of the most pressing and challenging duties of police department executives is establishing goals and objectives toward which all personnel of the police department should be directing their efforts." Although the words *goals* and *objectives* are often used interchangeably, most authorities agree that a goal is a more general term, referring to a broad, nonspecific desired outcome such as those listed above. Goals are usually long range. Objectives, in contrast, are more specific outcomes, usually with a listing of specific tasks and a timetable attached.

Goals are broad, general intentions. Objectives are specific activities to accomplish goals.

The distinction between goals and objectives is clarified in the California Council on Criminal Justice's *A Guide for Criminal Justice Planning:*

Goal—A statement of broad direction, a general purpose of intent. A goal is general and timeless and is not concerned with a particular achievement within a specified time period.

Objective—A desired accomplishment which can be measured within a given time and under specifiable conditions. The attainment of the objective advances the system toward a corresponding goal.

Goals give purpose to what may appear to be relatively unimportant tasks. Words carved in 1730 in a church in Sussex, England, proclaim:

A vision without a task is but a dream, a task without a vision is drudgery, a vision and a task is the hope of the world.

Consider, for example, the difference in perspective in the following three bricklayers. In response to the question, What are you doing? the first bricklayer replies, "I'm making $15 an hour laying these stupid bricks." The second replies, "I'm building a wall." And the third says, "I'm part of a team that's building a cathedral so people can worship."

Common goals *are* important to team building. The characteristics of a team with a common purpose are summarized in Table 1.3.

Consider the difference in attitude between those police officers on the dog shift who see the drug pusher just arrested as nothing more than an annoyance and those who believe they have helped make the neighborhood safer, perhaps even saving a life.

Specific objectives or individual tasks in isolation may seem to accomplish little, but in combination they provide the direction needed to achieve the broad goals sought by the department.

How are objectives accomplished? Usually police departments establish policies that cover specific tasks that must be undertaken in basic police operations. They then create procedures to accomplish these tasks.

Policies

Goals and objectives are more easily achieved with written policies guiding the police department's activities.

TABLE 1.3
A Team with a Common Purpose v. a Team with No Common Purpose

Common Purpose	No Common Purpose
Works beyond money only; works for a cause	Works for money only
Finds satisfaction in work	Finds satisfaction only outside of work (often while *at* work)
Important to put in time *and energy*	Important to put in time
Important to know how their contribution adds to the organization	Not sure or doesn't have high interest in how their contribution adds to the organization
Describes work in terms of outcomes	Describes work in terms of activity

Adapted from *Creating the High-Performance Team* by Steve Buchholz and Thomas Roth. New York: John Wiley & Sons, Inc., 1987, p. 63. Reprinted by permission of John Wiley & Sons, Inc.

Some common definitions of policy for the operational level of a police department are as follows:

- The broad guidelines for management action that have been formulated by members of the top management are known as *policies*. They are an attempt to coordinate and promote uniformity in the conduct of the business and in the behavior of employees (Plunkett, 1983, p. 41).
- Policy consists of principles and values which guide the performance of a department's activity. Policy is not a statement of what must be done in a particular situation, rather, it is a statement of guiding principles which should be followed in activities which are directed toward the attainment of departmental objectives (National Advisory Commission, 1973, p. 53).

A ***policy*** *is a guiding principle or course of action.*

A policy is a statement of principles that guide decisions. For example, our country's foreign policy guides our diplomats in their negotiations with foreign powers just as the axiom "Honesty is the best policy" guides the conduct of most of us.

Policies not only provide guidance, they help maintain organizational control and ensure accountability within an organization. They also provide a basis for fair discipline. The importance of written policies was stressed almost two decades ago by the National Advisory Commission on Criminal Justice Standards and Goals (p. 54):

Every police executive should have available written policies in those areas of police operations in which guidance is needed to direct the department's officers toward the attainment of the department's goals and objectives. These written policies should be in those areas in which directions are needed, including:

- *General goals and objectives of the department.*
- *Administrative matters.*
- *Community relations.*
- *Public and press relations.*
- *Personal conduct of employees.*
- *Personnel procedures and relations.*
- *Specific law enforcement operations with emphasis on such sensitive areas as the use of force, the use of lethal weapons, and arrests, search and seizure, and custody.*
- *Use of support services.*

The Policy Process

As noted by More and Shipley (1987, p. v):

Development of policy usually requires study and research, often into law enforcement activities that may not have been researched by another law enforcement agency. . . .

Most smaller police departments do not employ formalized planning units for obvious reasons of costs and manpower limitations. Therefore, policies are not articulated and frequently are left to chance. Even in small police departments, however, policies should *not* be left to chance. They don't just happen. They must be thought through and written down.

The process undertaken in developing policies can be divided into a series of distinct but interlocking steps. The first step is identifying the need for a policy. This may result from court decisions, new legislation, citizen complaints, or research findings related to crime, social problems, or existing field practices.

Once a need for a policy has been identified, the problem is referred to some specific departmental unit to undertake an initial study of the need. In larger police departments this is usually a planning and research unit. Input from the rank-and-file officers and citizens is vital at this point in the process. The findings of this unit are then submitted to the staff of the police department.

The next step is to obtain the input of others who might be directly affected by the policy, including neighborhood advisory committees, the prosecutor's office and staff, judges and corrections personnel, and juvenile authorities. In many police departments insurance companies are also consulted because they determine the cost of civil liability insurance and their company lawyers will represent the police in many litigations. At this point the chief of police should have sufficient information to share with appropriate department personnel and to formulate a policy.

Once the policy is formulated, it must be made known. Individuals within the community might be informed via direct mailing or through neighborhood advisory committee meetings. Police personnel are usually advised at roll call, through general orders, or through training manuals.

It is up to field personnel to implement the policy. Implementation is greatly enhanced by careful statements of the procedures to be followed for each policy. How well the policies are being implemented will be controlled through supervision and inspection. A procedure for developing policies is summarized in Figure 1.1.

No policy should ever be considered ''cast in stone.'' All policies should be periodically reviewed and evaluated. As circumstances change, policies should also change. New legislation or new social problems may dictate a change in policy. Once the decision is made to review a policy, the policy will be put through the same cycle it went through when the initial need was recognized.

Many field officers are conscious of the need for addressing particular problems, but, as noted, some police departments' semimilitary natures tend to stifle suggestions or the addressing of major problems by rank-and-file officers. One way to overcome this is to have supervisors and managers use a participatory leadership style, encouraging discussions about field problems from those in a position to correct them.

In addition to the difficulty of getting field officers to participate in policy making, another difficulty exists with the communications between the police department and the courts (National Advisory Commission, 1973, p. 25):

> *The greatest impact upon the police policies and actions have come from the courts, but the courts are rarely concerned about the effects their decisions will have on police authority. They are rarely structured to provide significant guidance to officers in the infinite variety of complex situations that might in some way be affected by a particular court decision.*

Police chiefs and supervisors cannot establish goals, objectives, and policies in a vacuum. *All* police officers, particularly those in the field, can contribute to

FIGURE 1.1
Formulation and Execution of Police Policy
Source: Adapted from *The Task Force Report: The Police.* President's Commission
on Law Enforcement and Administration of Justice, 1967, p. 26.

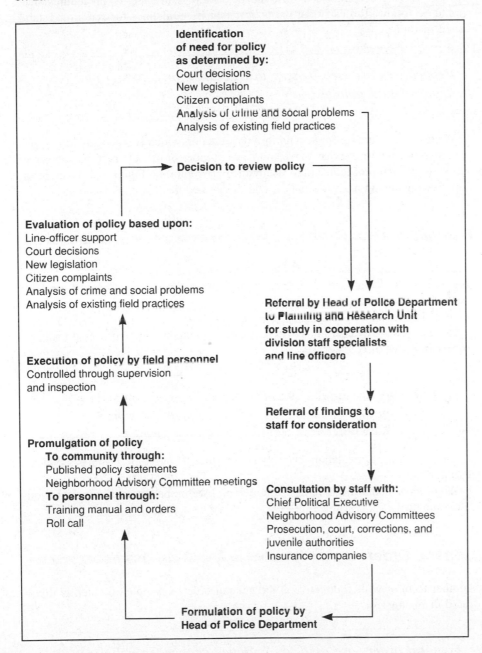

understanding problems and can assist in developing policies and procedures. Officers in face-to-face contact with members of the community are usually the most informed about problems in the field and potential solutions. These officers, in turn, will better identify and understand problems through direct contact and discussion with representative members of the community.

Procedures

To accomplish goals and objectives, policies need to be developed and put in writing. Having accomplished this, the next step is to identify procedures that should be followed to carry out the policy, that is, guidelines for action or established methods.

Procedures are step-by-step instructions for carrying out departmental policies.

Written procedures promote a uniformity of action which is especially important for ongoing calls for service or when a large number of officers perform the same services. Written procedures may also reduce civil liability. Figure 1.2 illustrates a directive containing a goal, a policy, and the procedures for implementing it.

Regulations

Regulations and procedures are similar and have the same intent—to guide conduct. Regulations are ''mini-laws'' or rules that are put out by a lower level of government, for example, a municipality or a police department. These orders have the force of law for those people under their jurisdiction.

Regulations are to a certain extent restrictive in that they force officers to adhere to certain codes of conduct.

Regulations are rules governing the actions of employees of the municipality, including police department personnel.

Like procedures, regulations should be in writing. Figure 1.3 illustrates a typical regulation.

Regulations help officers in decision making by eliminating discretionary action in certain areas.

General Orders

Another form of written directive is the general order, a sample of which is illustrated in Figure 1.4.

General orders are used to announce changes in policies, procedures, or regulations.

General orders can be written or verbal. Verbal orders, however, should be confirmed in writing as soon as possible. As the name implies, general orders direct or announce official acts of permanent duration, usually announcing a change of some sort. Such orders are often incorporated into a policy and procedure manual.

FIGURE 1.2
Sample Goal, Policy, and Procedure Directive
*Numbering is optional. It provides good continuity as well as an easy recall
reference.

Mytown Police Department   Date Issued: 01-01-92
                                                  Page 1 of 1

Procedure Directive No. 92-0001

Effective Date: 01-01-92
Subject: Community Service Officer in Service Operations

Goal:

To provide community service officers with uniform procedures for in-service operations.
The procedures will document community service officer (CSO) activities and provide
reference material for a CSO training manual. The CSO in-service operation is new. As
the CSO's tasks expand, additional procedures will be added to this directive.

Policy:

Community service officers will respond to calls only when directed by the dispatcher,
supervisor, or by the patrol officer's request. Community service officers will notify
dispatch immediately when observing any criminal or suspicious activity. Community
service officers will not respond to any call, emergency or not, as an emergency vehicle.

I. Responding to Calls

    A. When a CSO is responding to a call at the same time as a patrol officer, the CSO
    will stop or slow down to allow the patrol officer to arrive on the scene first. This
    will prevent a CSO from entering into a situation which is or could become
    dangerous.

    B. When a CSO is directed to a call where a patrol officer is not assigned or which a
    patrol officer has requested a CSO to handle, the CSO will call for assistance in any
    of the following circumstances:

        1. Any situation which the CSO determines on arrival as being dangerous or which
        could escalate into a dangerous situation.

        2. Any situation where a criminal violation has taken place and a suspect is still on
        the scene, leaving the scene, or likely to return to the scene.

        3. Any situation in which the CSO has not had training, experience, or feels unable
        or not equipped to handle.

II. Reports

    A. Turn in all reports, including daily logs, to the report basket in the squad room
    unless otherwise specified.

    B. A supervisor will review and approve all reports and handle accordingly.

    C. A supervisor will place the CSO's daily report in the administrative in-basket.

John J. Doe
Chief of Police

FIGURE 1.3
Sample Regulation

Mytown Police Department   Date Issued: 07-05-92
                                            Page 1 of 1

Procedure Directive No. 92-097

Reference: Procedure Directive 89-132 dated 05-10-89
Effective Date: 07-05-92
Subject: Police Uniforms—Name Plate Placement

Effective 07-05-92 all officers will wear over their left breast pocket on their shirts or in the case of a jacket or winter coat, over their left breast, a name plate containing the officer's name. These will be issued to each officer so that citizens may easily identify an officer. Removing the name plate or covering it with a jacket, whether intentional or not, will not be tolerated.

_____

John J. Doe
Chief of Police

FIGURE 1.4
Sample General Order

Mytown Police Department   Date Issued: 05-01-92
                                            Page 1 of 1

General Order No. 92-01

Effective Date: 05-01-92

<u>PURPOSE:</u>

This order modifies Procedure Directive 89-189, dated 12-14-89. All individuals booked for the misdemeanor charge of shoplifting who are not juveniles and who reside within a 25-mile radius of the court may be remanded to themselves upon signing the guaranteed court appearance.

_____

John J. Doe
Chief of Police

Guidelines for Writing Goals, Policies, and Procedures

As with any other type of administrative writing, goals, policies, and procedures should be clearly written. Consider the following guidelines:

- Use short, simple words, avoiding police jargon.
- Use short, simple sentences: 10–15 words.

- Use short paragraphs: 2–3 sentences.
- Use lists when possible.
- Use active verbs (say *Clean the gun daily* rather than *The gun should be cleaned daily*).
- Use illustrations and diagrams for clarification.
- Have three or four individuals read and evaluate the goal, policy, or procedure.

Most important, *keep things simple*. Avoid the tendency to *impress* rather than to *express* as illustrated in the story of the young boy who was asked to go to the chalk board and write the answer to 2 + 2 = and he wrote 4.00000.

A Caution

Goals, policies, procedures, regulations, and general orders all help to make police departments efficient and effective. They are extremely important and deserve care in development and periodic evaluation. It must always be remembered, however, that not everything can be anticipated. Further, for every rule an exception usually can be found. Too many rules can be detrimental.

As noted by Delattre (1989, p. 45): "Trying to make a rule for everything demeans our ability to apply our intelligence. When a bureaucracy becomes rule-bound, it is like a person who is muscle-bound; it can do less because it lacks flexibility." This flexibility is vital to law enforcement and results in the necessity for officers to use discretion.

Discretion

Delattre (p. 45) notes that: "Police are granted discretion because no set of laws and regulations can prescribe what to do in every possible circumstance. The possibilities are too numerous for us to have rules for everything that may happen."

According to Oran (1985, pp. 98–99), discretion is "1. the capacity to act intelligently and prudently. 2. the power to act within general guidelines, rules, or laws, but without either specific rules to follow or the need to completely explain or justify each decision or action."

Discretion is the ability to act or decide a matter on one's own.

In his analysis of discretion, Black (1983, p. 262) suggests that:

If visitors from another planet, anxious to learn our ways, asked us to explain how our police behave, perhaps the most unhelpful thing we could do for them would be to hand them a copy of our legal code and say, "Our police enforce these laws." What would make this bit of bad advice so terribly unhelpful is its failure to recognize the enormous range of police discretion, which, far more than legal codes, shapes the way our police behave. It must be emphasized that there are many areas in which the police exercise discretion and make discretionary decisions that profoundly affect the quality of community life.

Police departments use discretion when they decide to write policies for some areas and not others. They use discretion when they decide whether to thoroughly investigate a citizen's complaint against a police officer.

Individual police officers also use discretion daily when they decide to take certain actions or not. Pratt (1981, p. 46) notes that:

We seem convinced that purely objective, impartial, nondiscretionary actions are wanted and required by the public we serve. Yet we all know full well that such ministerial, nondiscretionary enforcement is impossible and always has been.

The simple fact is, police officers must make and do make literally millions of discretionary decisions every day, all across this land. We could not operate otherwise. A policy of full enforcement is both undesirable and unachievable. . . .

The typical officer on the street exercises discretion by overlooking minor and insignificant violations. He opts for individual warning and advice where he feels it is warranted or would be more productive than an arrest. . . .

These are discretionary decisions made daily in most police departments. They are necessary exercises of discretion if the officer is to do his job. Such decisions are the very essence of the exercise of professionalism by police.

Siegel (1990, p. 119) also notes: "The police officer's duty requires discretion in dealing with a variety of situations, victims, criminals, and citizens. The officer must determine when an argument becomes disorderly conduct or criminal assault; whether it is appropriate to arrest a juvenile or refer him or her to a social agency; or when to assume that probable cause exists to arrest a suspect for a crime."

Discretion *must* be allowed for several reasons. One reason is that the law *overreaches*. It seldom states exceptions that might arise. Black (1983) uses the example of traffic violations to explain the reason for and importance of discretion. Although a highway may have a posted speed limit of 55 mph, drivers exceeding this limit may have very good reasons for doing so, such as a volunteer firefighter on the way to a fire, an undercover police officer tailing a car, a parent taking a seriously injured child to the hospital, or a man taking his wife who is in labor to the hospital. Technically these people are speeding, but should they be given tickets? The law overreaches in each of these instances.

A second reason discretion must be used according to Black (p. 264) is that in some cases the law may be "amply served by not enforcing it. Consider the following appeals, apologies, and explanations from motorists clocked at 50 mph in a 35 mph zone:

- I'm sorry officer, I've just come from my mother's funeral and I'm very upset.
- I'm sorry officer, I just got fired from my job.
- I'm sorry officer, I've never in my life been stopped before. I think I'm going to faint. (Thud.)
- I'm sorry officer. The kids are yelling and the wife was screaming. I'm upset.
- I'm sorry officer. I haven't ever received a parking ticket in my life. I teach driver education at Central High School."

Police officers use discretion continuously. This officer will decide if a citation is appropriate.

In these instances, officers might decide that a ticket was not needed or could have more serious consequences than intended.

A third reason for discretion, according to Black is that police officers are well aware of the fact that most people will lie to avoid getting a ticket. Consequently, police officers must not only decide if the "excuse" justifies not giving the driver a ticket, they must also decide if the person is probably telling the truth.

Police officers use discretion in every traffic stop they make. It is completely up to them whether they issue a ticket or not. And, being only human, sometimes their real reason for giving the ticket cannot be told to the driver. As noted by Black (p. 265), police officers might refuse a plea for leniency, but would be highly unlikely to say any of the following:

- Sorry, but I've got a quota of arrests to make.
- Sorry, but the city depends on traffic fines for revenue.
- Sorry, but I don't like people like you.
- Sorry, but I don't think your excuse is good enough.
- Sorry, but I don't believe you.

Rather than saying any of these potentially truthful reasons, most police officers will respond with something like, "I don't make the laws, I just enforce them," or "Tell it to the judge."

Discretion and Ethics

"Discretion is a good thing and it is a necessary element of the law," says Pollock-Byrne (1989, p. 83), "but it also leads to a greater dependence on individual ethical standards in place of rules and laws." One study (Williams, 1984, p. 4) found that police do not make arrests in 43 percent of all felony cases and in 52 percent of all misdemeanor cases. Pollock-Byrne (1989, p. 83) notes that:

Unethical police behavior often arises directly from the power of discretion. Because police officers have the power to select and entrap suspects, they can also make that decision unethically, such as by taking a bribe in return for letting a suspect go. Since they have the power to decide how best to conduct an investigation, they may decide to use this power to entrap and select suspects in a biased or otherwise unfair manner rather than by probable cause.

Problems with Officer Discretion

Feldberg (1989, pp. 148–149) cites three major problems associated with officer discretion:

Problems associated with officer discretion include:

- *Inconsistency*
- *Unpredictability*
- *Lack of accountability*

Discretion lets officers treat different people differently. This may be seen as discrimination and, in fact, sometimes is. Some officers are harder on minorities or on men or on juveniles. This may be conscious or unconscious discrimination, but it does make for inconsistent enforcement of the laws.

Discretionary actions may also confuse citizens because they are not sure how they will be treated from one situation to the next; discretion can be unpredictable. For example, one traffic officer may allow up to 5 mph over the speed limit before stopping a motorist. Another may allow 10 mph. The driver who gets a ticket for exceeding the limit by 5 mph when the driver who is going 10 mph over the limit does not get a ticket will see the situation as unfair.

According to Cohen (1985, p. 29), however, fairness can also refer to "just deserts," which argues that to be treated fairly, people should get the treatment they deserve, regardless if it is different from one person to the next.

The third problem of discretion, lack of accountability, arises when supervisors cannot predict or control their officers' behavior when the officers are acting on their own. According to Feldberg (1989, p. 149):

Officer autonomy stems from many factors. The great bulk of patrol work cannot be planned with great efficiency; most patrol officers are given their daily workload by a dispatcher, one incident at a time, in response to citizen requests for service.

Positive Aspects of Officer Discretion

Although discretion can present serious problems, it is an absolute necessity. It makes enforcement of our laws *equitable,* that is, humanistic, considering the spirit of the law rather than the letter of the law.

Discretion also allows police officers to grow morally and professionally as they make their decisions. As noted by Bailey (1989, p. 149): "A patrol officer's experience of decision making with a variety of situations, settings and clienteles can expand the officer's intellectual horizons and prepare him or her to govern others with a sense of fairness, rather than with arbitrariness or excessive zeal." Discretion also gives officers a sense of control over their jobs which are, for all practical purposes, primarily reactionary.

---

*Discretion allows for equitable enforcement of our laws and
for police officers to grow morally and professionally.*

Most officers appreciate the chance to work through a citizen's problem from beginning to end. They also appreciate the acknowledgement that they have something to contribute in the form of expertise, imagination, and creativity as well as problem-solving ability. Further, as Cohen (1985, p. 30) notes: "Discretion is for many officers the most interesting—if confusing and at times anxiety provoking— aspect of their work. Using discretion wisely is ethically challenging; using it well allows an officer to invoke sanctions against those who he or she thinks deserve punishment and to forgo them for those who do not."

The importance and permanence of discretion in police work is described by Cohen (pp. 33–34):

The use of discretion is the inventive cutting edge of daily police work. By using it, officers express their autonomy and individuality in people management and problem solving. It also can become the license behind which some officers shield their lack of knowledge of rules and procedures, or their willingness to cut corners in the performance of their work. Police administrators are learning to balance their efforts to limit discretion within the bounds of acceptable behavior (i.e., assuring that officers do not blatantly discriminate nor act overly tolerantly toward violations of the law) with efforts to encourage creative use of discretion to solve chronic police problems, do justice to individuals, and meet community standards of public order.

---

*A major challenge facing law enforcement is finding the
balance between clearcut goals, policies, and procedures, and
the use of discretionary actions.*

Two factors must be kept in mind: (1) the primary goals of the department and (2) maintaining a balance between a need for clear policies and procedures and the accompanying need for discretion when exceptions arise. In addition, officers will be called upon to use critical thinking skills in performing police operations.

Discretion and Critical Thinking Skills

To use discretion wisely, police officers need to develop their critical thinking skills. Critical thinking includes a broad range of skills such as problem solving, identifying perceptions, generating concepts from observations, applying concepts to police problems, designing systematic plans of action, and approaching problems of society from several different perspectives. As a result of learning to think critically, students and future police officers will:

- Learn to use their diverse backgrounds and those of others to resolve problems in society in a more effective, acceptable manner.
- Learn specific ways to move from lower-order to higher-order thinking skills.
- Be better prepared to enter the world of police work and further their existing or future careers.

Summary

Police operations refers to those activities conducted in the field by law enforcement officers as they ''serve and protect.'' Operations include patrol, traffic, investigation, and general calls for service. Those engaged in police operations must take into consideration the important changes that have been occurring.

Our society is becoming older, has more minorities, more immigrants, and more single-parent households, while the gap between the rich and poor widens. Our law enforcement officers have also changed. Today's police recruits include fewer people with military backgrounds and more women and minorities. New recruits have more education and place more value on job satisfaction than on material rewards. They are also expected to perform more diverse operations.

Another change is the trend toward community policing. Community policing empowers citizens to help local law enforcement provide safer neighborhoods. It usually includes an emphasis on foot patrol. Yet another change is anticipated in the police bureaucracy itself. The police bureaucracy should become less militaristic and should move toward a team approach to providing services. This includes participatory leadership. Participatory leadership allows officers to influence decisions affecting them and seeks to form a cohesive team.

Not only should those in law enforcement understand the context in which police operations are performed and the changes that have occurred, they should also understand the foundation for these operations. Most law enforcement agencies are guided by a mission. An agency's mission is its reason for existence, its purpose. It is often embodied in a mission statement. This mission is accomplished most effectively by clearly stated goals and objectives.

Goals are broad, general intentions. Objectives are specific activities to accomplish goals. How these objectives are to be carried out is frequently described in policies and procedures. A policy is a guiding principle or course of action, whereas procedures are step-by-step instructions for carrying out department policies. Regulations are rules governing the actions of employees of the municipality, including police department personnel. General orders are used to announce changes in policies, procedures, or regulations.

Officers need to follow policies, procedures, and regulations, but they also need to use discretion. Discretion is the ability to act or decide a matter on one's own. Discretion is not without its problems, including the potential for inconsistency, unpredictability, and lack of accountability. Nonetheless, discretion allows for equitable enforcement of our laws and for police officers to grow morally and professionally.

A major challenge facing law enforcement is finding the balance between clearcut goals, policies, and procedures, and the use of discretionary action.

Application

General Directions.   When you complete each chapter, you will be asked to apply the information in developing suggested policies and procedures appropriate for your area. Appendix A contains a form you can use.

Write a policy for writing policies, that is, what should policies be written for.

Then write at least five procedures to be used when writing policies. You may want to refer to the guidelines listed on pages 22–23.

An Exercise in Critical Thinking

General Directions.   At the end of each chapter you will also be presented with exercises in critical thinking. These exercises are based on actual decisions of state appeals courts or state supreme courts throughout the country. Read each situation carefully. Then consider the alternative responses given and select the *most logical* statement based on what you have read in the chapter.

Criminal sanctions may be imposed on a person who intentionally obstructs, hinders, or prevents the lawful execution of any legal process, civil or criminal, or apprehension of another on a charge or conviction of a criminal offense or obstructs, resists, or interferes with a peace officer while the officer is engaged in the performance of official duties. Police officers need to use discretion as they carry out department policies and procedures.

On September 4th, State Trooper Richard Berg was on routine patrol when he stopped a vehicle driven by Carl Lundberg because of a traffic violation. Trooper Berg arrested Lundberg for breach of the peace and placed Carl in the back seat of Berg's squad car. Carl's brother, Allen Lundberg, went to the scene of the arrest and without identifying himself got into his brother's car with the apparent intention of driving it away from the scene.

Trooper Berg exited his vehicle, approached the as-yet-unidentified individual, and asked him to exit the vehicle and leave the scene. Only after Allen Lundberg left the car did he identify himself as the suspect's brother. Trooper Berg asked Allen to leave the scene, but Allen persisted in questioning Trooper Berg as to why he could not take the vehicle from the scene to avoid having it towed. Trooper Berg continued to insist that Allen leave the scene.

The verbal sparring continued to escalate to the point that several individuals in the parking lot of a shopping mall across the street had their attention drawn to the argument. Various witnesses testified that Lundberg yelled obscenities at Trooper Berg, "leaned over and pointed to his buttocks," and gave Trooper Berg "the finger." Witnesses also testified that Trooper Berg physically turned Lundberg around and "gave him a shove towards the parking lot," at which point Lundberg "kind of turned around and came close to hitting Trooper Berg's arm." That is when Trooper Berg told him he was under arrest.

1. While Trooper Berg was dealing with Allen Lundberg, Carl Lundberg (who was in the back of the squad car) managed to cause $500 damage to the interior of the vehicle by kicking the door.
   a. This demonstrates that sometimes sticking to policies and procedures is not worth the trouble that is caused, for the general public will not accept impersonal execution of procedures.
   b. Officers need to understand the reasoning behind operations and to be able to explain them to citizens, thereby possibly avoiding violent actions and breaches of the peace.
   c. In this case there was insufficient evidence to support a criminal conviction for obstructing legal process.
   d. Mere words (regardless of tone, loudness, agitation, and choice of words) cannot be used as a basis for a disturbing the peace charge.
   e. Only Carl Lundberg's actions should be prosecuted. Allen Lundberg should be released.
2. Officer involvement with the community would have helped Trooper Berg in what way?
   a. Witnesses might corroborate the yelled obscenities and other actions by Lundberg and Trooper Berg's responses.
   b. Some community members could talk the Lundbergs into cooling off and could also assist Trooper Berg in physically escorting Allen away from the scene to prevent the escalation of anger.
   c. Many would enjoy the power and authority of becoming ''assistant officers'' with the rights of enforcing the law as well as the status of being called an officer and a gentleman.
   d. Fair, compassionate, and excellent police service is only possible when responsibilities are not piled on one individual.
   e. With expanded opportunities for misconduct, more eyes are needed to keep watch for undesirable activity.

Discussion Questions

1. What purposes do goals serve in a police department?
2. What do you consider to be *the* most important goal for a police department?
3. What are the advantages of having written policies?
4. Do you feel that value statements are necessary?
5. Who should be involved in policy development?
6. Do you view discretion as more of an advantage or a disadvantage for police officers?
7. Have you observed police discretion in operation?

Definitions

Can you define the following terms?

broken windows metaphor	objective
community policing	participatory leadership
discretion	police operations
general order	policy
goal	procedure
mission	regulation
mission statement	

Bailey, W. G., ed. *The Encyclopedia of Police Science*. New York: Garland Publishing, 1989.

Barker, Thomas and Carter, David L. *Police Deviance*. 2d ed. Cincinnati, Ohio: Anderson Publishing, 1991.

Black, Donald. "Police Discretion: Selective Enforcement." In *Thinking about Police: Contemporary Readings,* Carl B. Klockars, ed. New York: McGraw-Hill, 1983.

Brown, Lee P. "Policing in the '90s: Responding to a Changing Environment." *The Police Chief,* (March 1991): 20–23.

Buchholz, Steve and Roth, Thomas. *Creating the High-Performance Team*. New York: John Wiley and Sons, 1987.

Cohen, Howard. "Authority: Limits of Discretion." In *Moral Issues in Police Work,* Frederick Elliston and Michael Feldberg, eds. Totowa, N.J.: Rowman and Allanheld, 1985, pp. 27–41.

Couper, David C. and Lobitz, Sabine H. "Quality Leadership: The First Step Towards Quality Policing." *The Police Chief* (April 1988): 79–81.

Cumming, E., Cumming, I., and Edell, L. "Policeman as Philosopher, Friend, and Guide." In *Social Problems,* 1965.

Delattre, Edwin J. *Character and Cops—Ethics in Policing*. Lanham, Md.: University Press of America, 1989.

Feldberg, Michael. "Discretion." *The Encyclopedia of Police Science*. W. G. Bailey, ed. New York: Garland Publishing, 1989.

Greene, Jack R. "Police and Community Relations: Where Have We Been and Where Are We Going?" In *Critical Issues in Policing: Contemporary Readings,* Roger G. Dunham and Geoffrey P. Alpert, eds. Prospect Heights, Ill.: Waveland Press, 1989, pp. 349–365.

Greene, Jack R. and Klockars, Carl B. "What Police Do." In *Thinking About Police: Contemporary Readings,* 2d ed., Carl B. Klockars and Stephen D. Mastrofski. New York: McGraw-Hill, 1991.

Horne, Peter. "Not Just Old Wind in New Bottles." *The Police Chief* (May 1991): 24–29.

Leonard, V. A. *Fundamentals of Law Enforcement: Problems and Issues*. St. Paul, Minn.: West Publishing, 1980.

McCord, Rob and Wicker, Elaine. "Tomorrow's America: Law Enforcement's Coming Challenge." *FBI Law Enforcement Bulletin* (January 1990): 28–32.

Metts, James R. "Super Cops: The Police Force of Tomorrow." *The Futurist* (October 1985): 31–35.

More, Harry W. and Shipley, O. R. *Police Policy Manual—Operations*. Springfield, Ill.: Charles C. Thomas, 1987.

National Advisory Commission on Criminal Justice Standards and Goals. *The Police*. Washington, D.C.: U.S. Government Printing Office, 1973.

Nees, Hal. "Policing 2001." *Law and Order* (January 1990): 257–264.

Oran, Daniel. *Law Dictionary for Nonlawyers*. 2d ed. St. Paul, Minn.: West Publishing, 1985.

Plunkett, W. Richard. *Supervision: The Direction of People at Work*. 3d ed. Dubuque, Iowa: Wm. C. Brown, 1983.

Pollock-Byrne, Joycelyn M. *Ethics in Crime and Justice: Dilemmas and Decisions*. Pacific Grove, Calif.: Brooks/Cole Publishing, 1989.

Pratt, C. E. "Discretion, the Essence of Professionalism." *Law and Order* (October 1981): 46–50.

President's Commission on Law Enforcement and Administration of Justice, Task Force Report. *The Police*. Washington, D.C.: U.S. Government Printing Office, 1967.

Reiss, A. J., Jr. *The Police and the Public*. New Haven, Conn.: Yale University Press, 1971.

Siegel, Larry J., ed. *American Justice, Research of the National Institute of Justice*. St. Paul, Minn.: West Publishing, 1990.

Tafoya, William L. "The Future of Policing." *FBI Law Enforcement Bulletin* (January 1990): 13–17.

Toffler, Alvin, and Toffler, Heidi. ''The Future of Law Enforcement: Dangerous and Different.'' *FBI Law Enforcement Bulletin* (January 1990): 2–5.

Trojanowicz, Robert and Bucqueroux, Bonnie. *Community Policing, A Contemporary Perspective*. Cincinnati, Ohio: Anderson Publishing, 1990.

Trojanowicz, Robert C. and Carter, David L. ''The Changing Face of America.'' *FBI Law Enforcement Bulletin* (January 1990): 6–12.

Vaughn, Jerald R. ''Community-Oriented Policing . . . You can Make It Happen.'' *Law and Order* (June 1991): 35–39.

Walker, Samuel. *Sense and Nonsense about Crime: A Policy Guide*. Monterey, Calif.: Brooks/Cole Publishing, 1985.

Walsh, William. ''Leadership, A Police Perspective.'' *The Police Chief* (November 1983): 26.

Williams, Gregory. *The Law and Politics of Police Discretion*. Westport, Conn.: Greenwood Press, 1984.

Wilson, J. Q. and Kelling, G. ''The Police and Neighborhood Safety: Broken Windows.'' *Atlantic Monthly* (March 1982): 29–38.

Witham, Donald C. ''Environmental Scanning Pays Off.'' *The Police Chief* (March 1991): 26–31.

COMMUNICATIONS: THE FOUNDATION OF POLICE OPERATIONS

CHAPTER *2*

INTRODUCTION

Police officers get most of the information they need by talking to people. Regardless of how much physical evidence they obtain at a crime scene, they will have to get information from many people as well. And, they must communicate with each other. Communications skills are critical to every aspect of effective police operations.

Communications are all around us. We are continuously bombarded by spoken and written messages, yet most people give little thought to what the communications process consists of, nor are they trained in communicating effectively.

Effective communications can produce several positive outcomes and can be used to:

- *Inform*
- *Motivate*
- *Persuade*
- *Reassure*
- *Diffuse*
- *Negotiate*
- *Guide*

In contrast, ineffective communications can result in confusion, false expectations, wrong conclusions, negative stereotypes, frustrations, anger, hostility, aggression, and even physical confrontations.

Police officers routinely communicate in every facet of their jobs, not only when they interview and interrogate individuals, but also in their interactions with the public, with coworkers in their department, and with professionals in other fields. Officers may also testify in court and fulfill public speaking assignments, especially those for school-age children and youth.

Do You Know

- What positive outcomes effective communications can produce?
- What the communications process consists of?
- What feedback is?
- What common barriers exist in the communications process?
- What nonverbal factors are important in communications?
- What the average speaking speed is? Listening or "word processing" speed?
- What skills are needed in active listening?
- What special communications problems law enforcement officers may encounter?
- When slurred speech may *not* be the result of intoxication?

The Communications Process

The communications process on the surface is rather simple, but when the variations in each component of the process are considered, it is exceedingly complex, as diagrammed in Figure 2.1.

---

*The **communications process** consists of one source sending a message to be received by another source.*

The Sender

Many attributes of the sender can color that sender's message; these include age, sex, intelligence, education, personal biases, life experiences, and vocation. The

FIGURE 2.1
The Communications Process
Source: Adapted from *The McGraw-Hill 36-Hour Management Course,* Lester R. Bittel, 1987, p. 160. Reprinted with permission from McGraw-Hill Publishing Company.

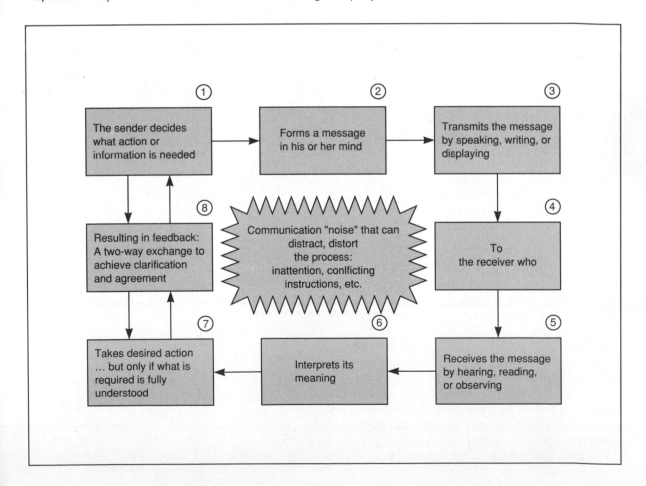

sender's purpose will also affect the message. Why is the person communicating? To offer information? To persuade someone of something? To get someone to take a specific action?

When police officers communicate, it is important that they understand *why* they send the messages they do. Sometimes they are attempting to establish rapport. Sometimes they are trying to calm a hysterical victim of a violent crime. Other times they are trying to extract information from a hostile person. The purpose behind the communication should be clearly understood by the sender if that communication is to be effective.

The Message

The message can be written or spoken. *And* it can be verbal or nonverbal. Most messages consist of some form of words surrounded by nonverbal factors. In our society we are in fact P.O.W.s—that is, prisoners of words. We attach specific meanings to words, and these meanings are not always the same as those attached by others to the same words. For example, consider the common word *strike*. What comes to mind? Police officers might associate it with assault. But it takes on entirely different meanings in the context of playing baseball, fishing, bowling, panning for gold, or negotiating a labor contract.

When a person asks another person if he can pick her up, this can easily have at least two different meanings. Sometimes lack of understanding can be quite humorous, as in the words of a young boy whose mother started to roll up the car window and almost "decaffinated" him. Other times, lack of understanding can be devastating.

Police officers must be aware of ethnic, cultural, and sexual differences in language and must avoid using terms that might be viewed as derogatory, for example, calling a woman "girl."

Spoken messages are common in police work. Police officers give directions, ask questions, relay information over their radios, and may give talks to citizen groups. Often, these spoken messages are conveyed amid confusion and a multitude of distractions. Noise levels may be high. Distances may be involved.

Written messages are also common in police work. Officers write field notes, primarily as reminders to themselves of information they obtain. They write reports based on these field notes to communicate the facts of an incident to others. They may also write letters, memos, and other types of messages for a variety of purposes. Effective written communication is discussed in Chapter 4.

Content, whether spoken or written, is of great importance to police officers. As noted by the International Association of Chiefs of Police or IACP (1985, p. 45), police officers must be careful to:

- Distinguish fact from opinion.
- Gather sufficient and reliable evidence.
- Avoid generalizations and haste.
- Be wary of superlatives and misleading statistics.
- Be careful with comparisons.
- Guard against non sequiturs.
- Guard against *post hoc ergo propter hoc.*

A **non sequitur** is something that doesn't follow or make logical sense. For example, to think, "He is a doctor, therefore he must be smarter than me, a cop," is not necessarily true. ***Post hoc ergo propter hoc*** literally means, "after which, therefore because of which." It is another type of faulty thinking. The best known example of this is probably the reasoning of the person who says, "I washed my car, so obviously it rained." Just because one event follows another does not mean that the first event caused the second. This is also known as the **illusionary correlation effect.** Messages must be clear and must avoid faulty thinking if they are to communicate well.

Common barriers to communication include:

- *Using confusing words to explain or describe.*
- *Judging others' statements as "black" or "white."*
- *Using abstract rather than concrete words.*
- *Confusing facts with inferences, opinions, and conclusions.*

The Receiver

Many of the same attributes influencing the sender of messages also influence those who receive the messages, including age, sex, intelligence, education, biases, past experience, vocation, and purpose for listening.

If the message is written, it is important that the receiver of the message be able to read and understand it. Literacy should *not* be taken for granted. People with limited reading skills are usually embarrassed to admit this deficit and will try to conceal the fact that they cannot read. Police officers must be on guard for this when they communicate through writing.

If the message is spoken, it is important that the receiver of the message be a good listener. Yet this skill is lacking in many people, including many police officers. They hear, but they do not actively listen. Consequently, many messages are misinterpreted or not received at all. Active listening is discussed later in this chapter.

Understanding the Message

Simply because a written or spoken message has been conveyed one should not assume that it has been understood. To illustrate this, think of the sender of the message as having a "blue" outlook on the world and the receiver as having a "yellow" outlook on the world. This message is very likely to be neither blue nor yellow, but a shade of green. That is why one-way communication can be extremely dangerous.

One-Way v. Two-Way Communications

Most written messages are one-way; that is, the sender writes the message, and it is relayed in some manner to the receiver who reads it. If the receiver of the message communicates back to the sender, this is two-way communication because feedback has taken place. Feedback is critical to effective communication.

Feedback is some indication that a message is or is not understood. It is how an individual or group responds to a message.

In a face-to-face conversation this can take the form of an affirmative nodding of the head (message understood) or a puzzled look (message not understood). Police officers should watch for such feedback when they talk with people, and they should also provide such feedback to those with whom they talk. Much feedback is nonverbal. Indeed, much communication is nonverbal.

Nonverbal Communications

Police officers' physical appearance—the uniform, gun, nightstick, handcuffs—convey a loud message, a message of authority before they ever say a word. This can be intimidating to many people. A harsh look can add to the intimidation; a smile can weaken or even dispel it. Officers should be aware of the nonverbal messages they send and use them to their advantage. They should also be aware of the negative response they will receive if they have an officious manner, a disrespectful attitude, or use inappropriate facial expressions such as a sneer.

Likewise, police officers should be alert to the nonverbal messages conveyed by those with whom they communicate. As noted by the IACP (1985, p. 48):

Although language is the main device through which people communicate, nonverbal cues often tell more. . . . As you try to understand what another person is saying (and thus to predict what that person is going to do next), look for the hidden cues.

Nonverbal communications involve eye and facial expressions, posture, gestures, clothing, tone of voice, proximity, and touch.

Eyes are among the most expressive parts of people's bodies. Consider the power of a simple wink. Eyes can reveal whether someone is happy, sad, excited, interested, tired, confused, sick, or perhaps lying. An entire science has sprung up around eye movements and what they can tell about individuals. People usually have very little control over the messages sent by their eyes.

Facial expressions, such as smiles, frowns, grimaces, scowls, pouts, or raised eyebrows, convey loud messages, as do flushed cheeks and perspiration. *Posture* also conveys messages. A person standing erectly with arms folded and feet apart conveys authority. A person slouching conveys a different message. *Hand gestures* can confirm or contradict what a person is saying and can even take the place of words. For example, a hand held out in protest can stop someone from speaking further, while a hand behind the ear can cause a speaker to increase volume.

Clothing conveys messages too but must be very carefully interpreted. Millionaires have been known to dress shabbily. Generally, however, it is accepted that

Bad News Bear. The sight of a police officer approaching your vehicle may cause severe stress, especially if you have been speeding.

clothes make a definite statement. Many books, such as *Dress for Success*, are available on using clothes to make positive statements about oneself.

Tone of voice as well as pitch and rate can tell much about the person speaking. A high pitch and rapid rate can reveal nervousness or anxiety. *Proximity* can reveal if a person feels comfortable or threatened. In the United States, we tend to stand eighteen inches to two feet away when talking. Standing closer is usually perceived as either intimate or threatening (perhaps both). Standing farther away than about four feet usually shows lack of interest or concern for the person being talked to. In some cultures, however, the comfort zone is much smaller, a fact police officers should be aware of when talking with individuals with different ethnic backgrounds.

Touch in our culture also conveys messages, although not as much in many other cultures. A handshake, a pat on the back, or an arm around a shoulder can show personal care and concern.

Findings about nonverbal communication based on extensive research by Evans (1990, p. 95) are presented in the following list. These findings use data from over 1,000 interviews conducted by the director of the National Training Center of Polygraph Science in New York City and Evans' own observations as a member of the New York State Police.

Body Cues of Respondent

- **Head Position**
  - *Tilted:* Cooperative, interested, probably truthful.
  - *Jutting forward, no tilt, jaw up:* Angry, aggressive, stubborn.
  - *Chin on chest, no tilt:* Depressed, bored, probably lying.

- **Eyebrows**
  - *Both raised with mouth partly open:* Surprised, truthful.
  - *One raised:* Confused, skeptical, probably truthful.
  - *Squeezed together and lowered:* Angry, worried, confused.
- **Eyes**
  - *Breaks eye contact* (1–2 seconds is common): Suddenly tensed, probably lying. May not resume eye contact until new subject is discussed.
  - *Looks at ceiling and blinks:* Just decided to confess.
  - *Pupils fully dilated:* High degree of emotional arousal, probably lying.
  - *Closes eyes:* Trying to mentally escape, probably lying.
  - *Narrows eyes:* Looking for trouble, anticipating the worst.
  - *Squints:* Tense, distrusting.
  - *Rapid blinking:* Dehydrated, nervous, probably lying.
- **Mouth**
  - *Smiling:* Most misleading of gestures. Most liars know enough to smile to cover up an unpleasant situation. When left alone, however, most liars stop smiling and sit tensely, while most truthful subjects will have ''Mona Lisa'' smiles and sit relaxed. *Real smile:* Usually the lower and upper teeth are seen, cheeks are lifted and the eyes are crinkled—probably truthful. *Faked smile:* Only the upper teeth are seen.
  - *Swallows the lips:* Feels about to confess—''swallowing'' the lips stops the confession.
  - *Dry mouth:* Very nervous, probably lying.
- **Shoulders**
  - *Slumped:* Depressed, probably lying.
  - *Forward:* tense.
  - *Back, sitting straight up:* Alert, proud, probably truthful.
- **Elbows**
  - *Away from the body:* Relaxed, probably truthful.
  - *Close to the body:* Tense, probably lying.
- **Hands**
  - *Cover both eyes:* Trying to mentally escape, probably lying.
  - *Over the mouth:* Does not want to talk, probably lying.
  - *On chin:* Deep thinking, probably truthful.
  - *Thumb and first finger form ''L,'' with thumb under chin:* Antagonistic.
  - *Touch or rub nose while talking:* Probably lying.
  - *Preen hair:* Attracted to interviewer.
  - *Comb hair with fingers spread apart:* Worried, undecided.
  - *Scratch top or back of the head:* Confused.
  - *Hit forehead with open palm:* Something suddenly remembered.
  - *Clasped together, holding back of head:* Confident, probably truthful.
  - *Woman makes curls with her hair:* Probably truthful.
  - *Arms tightly crossed in front of chest:* Confident, defensive, uncooperative, probably lying.
  - *Lint-picker, dress-smoother:* Tense, probably lying.
  - *Wipes hands on clothing to remove excess perspiration:* Very tense, probably lying.
  - *Form a fist:* Antagonistic, defiant.
  - *On hips:* Arrogant, antagonistic, aggressive.
  - *Clasped in front of body:* Great fear, holding back information, probably lying.

□ *Steepling* (tips of fingers touching): Confident, dominant, probably truthful.
□ *Arms resting on legs, head down:* Has given up, will confess.
□ *Crossed fingers:* Defensive, probably lying.
□ *Exhibits palms:* Cooperative, truthful, considers interviewer a friend.
□ *Snaps fingers:* Remembers something, probably truthful.

■ *Note:* A confident, assured person uses his hands comfortably to emphasize words and avoids touching the face or head, gestures that betray uncertainty.

■ **Legs:** (gender related)
□ *Men with crossed legs:* Defensive, probably lying.

■ **Feet**
□ *Moves feet beneath the chair:* Tense, probably lying.
□ *Moves feet to a forward position:* Relaxed, probably truthful.
□ *Tucks one foot underneath the other leg:* Timid, truthful.(Reprinted with permission from *Law and Order Magazine*).

Any single factor may be misleading, but in combination, a trained observer can often learn much from nonverbal cues. A current book on body language is Paul Ekman's *Telling Lies*. Body language is often used extensively in the art of interrogation. In fact, Anhorn (1991, pp. 31, 33) says, "I consider myself a bilingual person, if understanding body language counts for anything. Evasive eyes and nervous hands are danger signals." Paying attention to such signals may save an officer's life. On a more mundane level, paying attention to nonverbal clues can also improve listening skills.

Listening

Two men were walking along a crowded sidewalk in a downtown business area. Suddenly one exclaimed, "Listen to the lovely sound of that cricket!" But the other could not hear. He asked his companion how he could detect the sound of a cricket amidst the din of people and traffic. The first man, who was a zoologist, had trained himself to listen to the voices of nature, but he did not explain. He simply took a coin out of his pocket and dropped it on the sidewalk, whereupon a dozen people began to look about them. "We hear," he said, "what we listen for." Bhagwan Shree Rajnessh, The Discipline of Transcendence.

Listening is, indeed, a critical skill in law enforcement. Listening is necessary for effective verbal communication and results in a better understanding of people and in increased cooperation from them. Research has shown that 40 percent of the total time devoted to communication is spent in listening, 35 percent in speaking, 16 percent in reading, and 9 percent in writing (Burley-Allen, 1982, p. 2).

Says communications expert Elaine Thomas (1987, p. 99): "Of all the communications skills we use daily, we spend the most time listening." The importance of listening is attested to by the creation of the International Listening Association (ILA) in 1980 and by the publication of their journal beginning in 1987. According to Montgomery (1981, p. 65): "We listen more than we do any other human activity except breathe." He goes on to note, however, that "Listening is the most neglected and the least understood of the communications arts."

Too often people simply hear, but they do not listen. Why? A large part of the problem is the difference between the speed at which people speak and that at which they can process information.

People can speak about 150 words per minute. People can listen to over 450 words per minute.

Further, as noted by the IACP (1985, p. 48): "A speaker rarely can speak faster than 200 words per minute, whereas, he probably can think at least 1,000 words per minute." It is commonly said that people can think four times faster than they can talk. It is this lag time that can be devastating to listening effectiveness. Lag time allows the mind to wander, to daydream, to formulate arguments, and to attend to the person rather than to the message being conveyed.

This hazard was recognized by listening expert Dr. Ralph Nichols (1957) over thirty years ago when he said: "Not capitalizing on thought speed is our greatest single handicap. The differential between thought speed and speech speed breeds false feelings of security and encourages mental tangents. Yet, through listening training, this same differential can be readily converted into our greatest asset." Nichols suggests ten questions to test listening skills. Answer *yes* or *no* to each of the following:

1. Do you try to make others think you are listening to them whether you are or not?
2. Are you easily distracted from what a person is saying by outside sights or noises?
3. Do you take notes on what a person is saying?
4. Can you usually assess the quality of what a person will say by his appearance or how he says it?
5. We know that a person thinks four times as fast as another person talks. Do you use this excess time to think about other things (your reply?) while still maintaining the central idea about what is being said?
6. Are you receptive to facts and figures rather than concepts and ideas in a speech?
7. Do certain words or phrases "turn you off" so that you cannot listen clearly to what is being said?
8. If you do not understand or are annoyed by what a speaker is saying, do you question the speaker or try to figure it out in your own mind?
9. Do you try to avoid hearing something that you believe would take too much time and trouble to figure out?
10. If you ever decide that a speaker is not going to say anything worthwhile, do you "tune out" and think about other things?

Each *no* scores 10 points. A score of 80 is excellent.

Levels of Listening

Burley-Allen (1982, pp. 10–11) describes three levels of listening:

- *Level 3.* Listening in spurts, half listening, and quiet, passive listening. Often the person at this level is faking listening.

- *Level 2*. Hearing sounds and words, but not really listening. This level is dangerous because misunderstanding may occur since the listener is barely concentrating on what is said.
- *Level 1*. Active listening. At this level people refrain from evaluating the speaker's words and place themselves in the other's position—attempting to see things from that person's point of view.

Active Listening

According to Burley-Allen (p. 11):

> *Active listening requires that you listen not only for the content of what's being spoken but, more importantly, for the intent and feelings of the message as well. This is done while showing both verbally and nonverbally that you are truly listening.*

Active listening is critical to effective interviews and interrogations.

***Active listening** is concentrating on the message as well as on the intent and feelings of the message and involves:*

- *Attending skills.*
- *Encouragement or motivational skills.*
- *Reflecting skills.*

These Minneapolis Police Department cadets *appear* to be listening intently. Notice the body language of each cadet and draw your own conclusions.

The following guidelines can improve listening:

Attitudinal

- *Be interested in the person and the message. Be empathetic. Show you care.*
- *Be less self-centered.*
- *Resist distractions.*
- *Don't let personal biases turn you off.*
- *Prepare to listen. Clear your mind of other things.*

Behavioral

- *Be responsive in posture and facial expressions.*
- *Offer encouragement.*
- *Look at the other person.*
- *Don't interrupt.*
- *Take notes.*

Mental

- *Ask questions.*
- *Don't change the subject*
- *Listen for ideas, not just facts. Separate facts from opinions.*
- *Attend to content, not delivery. Look for main points.*
- *Avoid jumping to conclusions. Stay with the speaker, trying not to jump ahead. Draw only tentative conclusions.*
- *Concentrate. Work at listening, especially when the material is difficult or complex.*
- *Use excess listening time to summarize the speaker's main ideas. But do not plan your response.*
- *Keep your mind open and your emotions in check. Don't judge.*
- *Periodically clarify what has been said.*
- *Pay attention to body language.*

Listening is a skill, just as speaking, reading, and writing are. Listening can be improved by practicing. It should never be taken for granted. Neither should it be taken for granted that what is heard will be remembered. If the information received is important, it should be written down, as discussed later in the chapter.

Special Problems in Communicating

As our society becomes more diverse, it often also becomes more difficult for officers to effectively communicate with those they are sworn "to serve and protect." As noted by Sharp (1991, p. 95): "Roughly two-thirds of the departments responding recently to a poll focusing on language barrier problems indicated that they encounter difficulties from time to time."

*Special problems in communicating include understanding
individuals who speak little or no English or who have
disabilities or diseases, including blindness, deafness, epilepsy
and Alzheimer's disease, that may impair their ability to
communicate.*

Sharp (1991, p. 95) suggests "A cardinal maxim affecting police work is that
emergencies can happen anywhere, at any time. All emergencies are bad. They
grow worse when the responders and victims do not speak the same language."

Communicating with Non-English-Speaking Individuals

According to Sharp (p. 99): "There are currently between 12 and 22 million non-
English-speaking people living in the United States. Another 40 million visit the
country every year. Immigration quotas will account for 800,000 more entering
each year." How can this challenge be met?

One obvious way is to recruit bilingual officers. Another is to compile a list of
bilingual citizens in the community. This is easiest in large cities and those that have
colleges and universities. Legal problems may arise, however, if confidential information is involved.

A third way is to train officers to speak a second language. This is expensive but
has a high payoff. Hinkle (1991) suggests, however, that traditional language
classes are not necessarily effective because they include writing and "polite"
conversation. This is not what police officers need. Rather, says Hinkle (pp. 41–
42): "What police need to master is a small number of phrases with specific
application to street situations so that control can be maintained as long as is
necessary, or until the arrival of someone fluent in the target language."

Another approach to the language-barrier problem is to subscribe to the *language
line*. This is a translation service offered by AT&T that provides direct interpretation
for police and other emergency service units responding to calls. According to *Law
Enforcement News* (1990, p. 3), the service is capable of providing translation for
over 140 languages from Swahili to Sanskrit. Subscribers are given cards listing all
languages the service can translate, written so non-English-speakers can read the
name of the language in their native script and point to it enabling the subscriber to
connect with the right translator. The service is available twenty-four hours a day,
seven days a week.

Communicating with Individuals with Disabilities or Conditions Affecting Speech

Some disabilities are very obvious: paralysis and blindness, for example. Other
disabilities, however, are not immediately apparent. Likewise, many conditions or
diseases that impair speech are not immediately apparent and may be mistaken for
intoxication.

The visually impaired comprise over 11.5 million individuals according to the National Society to Prevent Blindness (Zehring, 1990, p. 33). When interacting with people who are blind, police officers should not only identify themselves, but should offer to let the person feel their badge as well. Police departments might also want to consider developing a program such as that used in Mesa, Arizona. The goals of this educational program, says Zehring (p. 33) are "to teach blind students how to seek help when lost, how to use the 911 system, and how to identify a police officer." The Mesa department adapted the Stranger Danger and the Officer Friendly program to meet the needs of visually impaired elementary school children. At the secondary level, the curriculum includes safe money handling and making purchases. Secondary-level students are also taught how to protect themselves if attacked and the dangers of drugs and alcohol. Says Zehring (p. 35): "These programs received local media attention and have been very good for police community relations. More importantly, the programs have helped Mesa's visually impaired students."

The hearing impaired are among those with "invisible" handicaps. Police officers will interact more effectively with citizens who are hearing impaired if they understand that most deaf people are not good lip-readers nor are they good readers. In addition, the speech of individuals who have been deaf since birth may sound garbled and even unintelligible.

The speech of a person who has been deaf since birth may be mistaken for intoxication.

Dr. King (1990, pp. 98–100), director of deaf education at the University of Southern Mississippi, states: "Deaf people communicate differently, depending on the age at which the person became deaf, the type of deafness, language skills, speech and speech-reading abilities, intelligence, personality, and educational background." He notes that, for police officers who find themselves needing to communicate with a deaf individual, the key is to determine how that particular person communicates and use whatever combination of techniques are needed to help communication. He offers the following suggestions:

1. Get the person's attention. Gently tap a shoulder, wave, or call out loudly yet respectfully.
2. Make sure the person understands the topic of discussion.
3. Speak slowly and clearly, but do not overenunciate or overexaggerate words. This makes lip-reading difficult, if not impossible. Speak in short sentences.
4. Look directly at the person.
5. Do not place anything in your mouth when speaking. Pencil chewing or smoking make lip-reading more difficult.
6. Maintain eye contact. This conveys the feeling of direct communication.
7. Avoid standing in front of a light source.
8. Don't hesitate to communicate by paper and pencil. Keep the message simple.
9. Use pantomime, body language, and facial expressions.
10. If possible, learn sign language. Even basic signing can overcome barriers.

11. Do not assume the person has understood the message just because he nods his head.

Many of these suggestions would also work for non-English-speaking people.

King (p. 100) also suggests that, when possible, the services of a qualified, certified interpreter be used. Each police department should obtain a list of such interpreters, usually available from local or state organizations providing services to the hearing impaired. When an interpreter is used, King suggests the following (p. 100):

1. Treat the interpreter as a professional.
2. Provide good lighting.
3. Speak directly to the deaf person, not to the interpreter. The interpreter is not a part of the conversation; he is there only to act as the channel through which communication flows.
4. Remember that the interpreter will be a few words behind the speaker.
5. Permit only one person to speak at a time.
6. Speak clearly and in a normal tone when using an interpreter. Try not to rush.

People with epilepsy may also present communication problems for law enforcement officers. The following discussion is based on *Epilepsy: A Positive ID,* from the Epilepsy Education Program of the University of Minnesota. The program stresses the need for greater human understanding and sensitivity toward "people with epilepsy" (*not* "epileptics").

Epilepsy is a disorder of the central nervous system in which a person tends to have recurrent seizures. A **seizure** is a sudden, uncontrolled event or episode of excessive electrical activity in the brain. It may alter behavior, consciousness, movement, perception, and sensation.

There are many types of seizures. A seizure isn't always a stiffening and jerking of the body. Seizures may alter behavior, level of consciousness, perception, or the senses. Seizures can be classified as absence seizures, simple partial seizures, complex partial seizures, or generalized tonic clonic seizure.

Absence seizures (formerly called *petit mal*) are often mistaken for daydreaming or staring and can occur up to 100 times a day or more.

Simple partial seizures consist of changes in motor function or sensations *without* accompanying alterations in consciousness. They may be characterized by stiffening or jerking in one or more extremities, a strange feeling in the stomach, tingling, or an alteration of taste or smell.

Complex partial seizures involve impairment of consciousness and may last from a few seconds to several minutes. Behaviors that may occur during this type of seizure include incoherent speech, glassy-eyed staring, aimless wandering, chewing or lip-smacking motions, and picking at clothing. The person may be confused or need to rest after a seizure. This type of seizure may be mistaken for a drug- or alcohol-induced stupor. A person having a complex partial seizure will have a fairly prompt return of their faculties (within several minutes) whereas a drunk or high person will not. Table 2.1 summarizes the differences between an epileptic seizure and drug and alcohol abuse symptoms.

A complex partial seizure can look like street drugs or alcohol at work.

TABLE 2.1
Epileptic Seizure or Drug/Alcohol Abuse?

Complex Partial Seizure Symptoms*	Drug and Alcohol Abuse Symptoms*
Chewing, lip-smacking motions	Not likely
Picking at clothes	Not likely
Should regain consciousness in 30 seconds to 3 minutes, except in the rare case of a complex partial status (when seizure continues)	A drugged or drunk person will not recover in 3 minutes or less
No breath odor	A drunk will smell like alcohol
Possibly wearing an epilepsy ID bracelet or tag	Not likely

*Symptoms common to complex partial seizures and drug or alcohol abuse: Impaired consciousness, incoherent speech, glassy-eyed staring, aimless wandering.

Source: Adapted from *Epilepsy: A Positive ID*. Reprinted with permission from Epilepsy Education Program, University of Minnesota, 1990.

The Epilepsy Education Program of the University of Minnesota suggests that police officers who encounter someone who might be experiencing a complex partial seizure check for medical alert bracelet or tag and smell their breath for alcohol. If it is a seizure, appropriate first aid should be administered.

Generalized tonic (stiffening) *clonic* (jerking) *seizures* (formerly called *grand mal* seizures) are what most people commonly associate with epilepsy. These seizures may last a few seconds to several minutes and may result in loss of consciousness, falling, stiffening and jerking (hence, the name *tonic clonic*), tongue biting (sometimes), drooling, and loss of bowel and bladder control (sometimes). Appropriate first aid should be administered promptly.

The Epilepsy Education Program stresses that first responders need to be able to recognize seizures, administer the proper first aid procedures, and be responsive to the sensitivities and pride of people with epilepsy. The incorrect handling of a seizure can be embarrassing for the person having the seizure and can make the first responder potentially liable.

Alzheimer's disease should also be considered by law enforcement officers who are communicating with elderly individuals who appear to be intoxicated.

---

*An individual with **Alzheimer's disease** may have slurred, incoherent speech resembling intoxication.*

If Alzheimer's disease is suspected, officers should follow these suggestions of the Alzheimer's Disease Association (1987):

- Look for an ID bracelet or other identification.
- Avoid lectures or confrontation. They will not work with these people, and they are likely to make things worse.
- Keep communication simple. Speak softly and slowly.
- Identify yourself and explain what you are or will be doing, even if it is obvious.
- Use distraction to end inappropriate behavior. Sometimes just your presence will accomplish that.

- Maintain eye contact when speaking.
- Try to maintain a calm atmosphere. Alzheimer's patients are prone to "catastrophic reactions" which you want to avoid.
- During a catastrophic reaction, Alzheimer's patients often lash out, verbally and physically, at people who try to help them.
- Avoid restraints if possible. Physical restraints are almost certain to cause a catastrophic reaction.

Summary

Effective communications can produce several positive outcomes. It can be used to inform, guide, reassure, persuade, motivate, negotiate, and to diffuse. The communications process consists of one source sending a message to be received by another source. Feedback is some indication that a message is or is not understood. It is how an individual or group responds to a message.

Common barriers to communication include using confusing words to explain or describe, judging others' statements as "black" or "white," using abstract rather than concrete words, and confusing facts with inferences, opinions, and conclusions.

Communications includes both the words used as well as nonverbal factors. Nonverbal communications involves eyes and facial expressions, posture, gestures, clothing, tone of voice, proximity, and touch.

Of the time spent communicating, the majority is devoted to listening. People can speak about 150 words per minute, but can listen to over 450 words per minute. This results in lag time which can be a problem unless active listening is used. Active listening is concentrating on the message as well as on the intent and feelings of the message. It involves attending skills, encouragement or motivational skills, and reflecting skills. Listening is important in the various types of communicating officers do with the public, including field inquiries, interviews, and interrogations.

Special problems in communicating include understanding individuals who speak no English or who have disabilities or diseases that impair their ability to communicate. The speech of individuals who have been deaf since birth or who have epilepsy or Alzheimer's disease may be mistaken for intoxication.

Application

As head of the public relations department, you have noticed an increase in complaints against officers who have mistaken a disability or physical problem as intoxication. Officers have no guidelines on how to determine whether what appears to be alcohol- or drug-induced intoxication is alcohol- or drug-induced intoxication.

Instructions Use the form in Appendix A to write a policy regarding communicating with individuals who *appear* to be under the influence of alcohol or drugs.

Exercises In Critical Thinking

The factual basis for stopping a vehicle need not arise from an officer's personal observation, but may be supplied by information acquired from another person. This information must be accurately communicated from reliable sources. Probable cause for an arrest *is something more than mere suspicion, but less than evidence which would sustain a conviction. Probable cause is based on a reasonable police officer standard and a careful consideration of the situation and the officer's sources of information, observations, training, and experience. The collective knowledge of the police force is pooled and imputed to the arresting officer for the purpose of determining sufficient probable cause for arrest.*

On April 13, Joel Powell's car was stopped, and he and a companion were arrested a few miles away from, and a few minutes after, the burglary of a supper club. The burglary had been reported by an eyewitness whose descriptions of the event and the car involved were transmitted by radio to area police officers. Powell's car matched the description of the car in which the burglars left the scene. It was also traveling in the same direction on the same road. After Powell and his passenger had been taken into custody, the car was sealed, towed, and searched. It contained two bank bags with about $500 in currency and coin, later identified as property of the club, and various tools, including pry bars, malls, tire irons, and a hacksaw.

1. Must the factual basis for stopping a vehicle arise from the officer's personal observation?
   a. Six factors must be taken into account:
      1. The particular description of the offender or the vehicle in which he fled.
      2. The size of the area in which the offender might be found.
      3. The number of persons about in that area.
      4. The known or probable direction of the offender's flight.
      5. Observed activity by the particular offender.
      6. Knowledge or suspicion that the offender has been involved in other criminality of the type presently under investigation.

      Not all of these factors were clearly or completely communicated, so the stop is not supported.
   b. When stopping a vehicle, officers must have a warrant when they do not personally observe a felony being committed.
   c. Arresting officers may rely on any communicated information when a possible felony is to be investigated.
   d. The basis for stopping a vehicle may be supplied by information acquired from another person as well as other law enforcement officials.
   e. Arresting officers must have personal knowledge of the facts constituting probable cause.

On January 10, a Minneapolis police officer applied for a warrant to search an apartment in Los Angeles for cocaine, crack/cocaine, and drug paraphernalia. The affidavit supporting the application stated:

An informant, who has proven to be reliable in the past and whose information has resulted in the arrests of drug dealers and the seizure of narcotics, told your affiant that he had been in Barbara Jane Leake's apartment within the past 72 hours and there he saw the hand-to-hand transfer of crack/cocaine for money.

2. Has sufficient information been communicated for a warrant to be signed?
   a. A warrant will be issued, but only if exact amounts of money and cocaine are stated, and only if the name of the informant is given.

   b. Because of the informant's past accuracy and because of the officer's recent personal knowledge of incriminating conduct, a warrant will be issued.
   c. Hypercritical and hypertechnical examination of the affidavit will result in the trial court granting Leake's motion to suppress.
   d. A magistrate will need corroboration—a second witness to verify the informant's reliability.
   e. A magistrate will not accept hearsay evidence in an affidavit.

Discussion Questions

1. When you communicate with another person, are you aware of whether that person is really listening? How can you tell?
2. Have there been instances when you have conveyed a message and you know that the person does not understand you? What symptoms did the person have that gave you this feeling?
3. What do voice inflections tell you about the other person's communications to you?
4. Do you feel that the average citizen with whom you communicate is going to understand any legal language that you may use to describe an offense?
5. How effective are you at listening? What areas do you need to improve?
6. What language barriers would you be likely to encounter in your community?
7. Are you better at speaking or writing? Why do you believe this occurred?

Definitions

Can you define the following terms:

active listening
communications process
epilespy
feedback
illusionary correlation effect

non sequitur
nonverbal communication
post hoc ergo propter hoc
seizure

References

Alzheimer's Disease and Related Disorders Association. *Victim, Not Criminal: The Alzheimer Sufferer.* Chicago, Ill.: Alzheimer Association, 1987.
Anhorn, Guy. "The Suburban Cop Shuffle." *Law and Order.* (March 1991): 31–34.
Burley-Allen, Madelyn. *Listening: The Forgotten Skill.* New York: John Wiley and Sons, 1982.
Epilepsy Education Program. *Epilepsy: A Positive ID.* Minneapolis, Minn.: University of Minnesota, 1990.
Evans, Daniel D. "Caught in a Lie." *Law and Order* (August 1990): 95.
Hinkle, Douglas. "Language Barriers and the Police." *Law and Order* (March 1991): 38–42.
International Association of Chiefs of Police. *Police Supervision.* Arlington, Vir.: IACP, 1985.
King, J. Freeman. "The Law Officer and the Deaf." *Police Chief* (October 1990): 98–100.
Law Enforcement News. "Parlez-Vous *Miranda* Warnings? Language Line Gives Police Gift of Gab." (September 30, 1990): 3.

Montgomery, Robert L. "Are You a Good Listener?" *Nation's Business* (October 1981): 65–68.

Nichols, Ralph G. "Listening is a 10-Part Skill." *Nation's Business* (July 1957).

Sharp, Arthur G. "Are We All Speaking the Same Language?" *Law and Order* (July 1991): 95–99.

Strother, Deborah Burnett. "On Listening." *Phi Delta Kappan* (April 1987): 625–628.

Thomas, Elaine. "Listen Well and Profits Will Tell." *Successful Meetings* (May 1987): 99–100.

Zehring, Timothy. "New Insights for the Visually Impaired." *Law and Order* (December 1990): 33–35.

COMMUNICATIONS IN THE FIELD: GETTING AND GIVING INFORMATION

CHAPTER 3

INTRODUCTION

A tremendous amount of time is spent communicating during police operations. In fact, according to Klockars (1985, p. 145), "The police officer's most important tool is his mouth." Officers continuously give and receive information, some related to crime, some not. Although much of the information officers receive may seem quite irrelevant to the law enforcement mission, it is important to the person conveying the information and should be treated accordingly. Officers who listen empathetically to citizens' concerns will do much to promote public relations, to enhance the department's image, and to foster true community policing.

If they are truly "to serve and protect," officers must listen to their "clients." As noted by Couper and Lobitz (1988, p. 79): "We must start to pay attention to the new ideas and trends coming out of America's businesses." They suggest:

> Our business is policing, our customers are the citizens within our jurisdiction, and our product is police service (everything from crime fighting and conflict management to safety and prevention programs). . . .
>
> We must listen to our customer—our citizens—in new and more open ways. We must stop reacting to incidents and begin solving problems.

Officers should remember that the majority of their communicating time should be spent listening rather than speaking. Skillfully phrased questions can elicit a wealth of information. Active listening can greatly enhance the quality of the information obtained. This is true whether the communication

Do You Know

- What a field inquiry is? An interview? An interrogation?
- How field inquiries, interviews, and interrogations differ?
- What a primary victim is? A secondary victim?
- What the cognitive interview technique is?
- Whether officers can act on information supplied by an informant regarding criminal activity? The precedent case?
- What would make a confession inadmissible in court?
- What "totality of circumstances" includes?
- What restriction on interrogations resulted from *Escobedo v. Illinois*?
- What rights are granted suspects in *Miranda v. Arizona*?
- What forensic hypnosis is?

involves a brief stop, a formal interview or inter-rogation, or communication with other officers in the field. One frequent type of communication is the field inquiry.

The Field Inquiry

The field inquiry basically involves asking questions of a person or persons, usually because the officers' suspicions are aroused. It is not an arrest but certainly could lead to one.

A *field inquiry* is the unplanned questioning of a person who has aroused a police officer's suspicions.

Police officers undoubtedly notice over the years that the relationship between themselves and citizens becomes extremely sensitive at times. Citizens may take sides, especially for a particular cause, or may be set against a cause, and police officers frequently get caught in the middle. Take the abortion issue, for example. Police officers are drawn into pro-life or pro-choice demonstrations that are, by their very nature, tension-building and difficult. Other sensitive situations involve fights, arguments, domestic violence, arrests, and situations where officers are placed in the position of disciplinarian.

Recognize that each situation is different. Officers cannot develop one "stock" approach that will work every time. Officers must be able to cope with emotion-charged people and potentially explosive situations. This means police officers must be very skillful at handling people and dealing with various situations.

Detaining a person for questioning is another important police function that easily generates hostility since people instinctively resent restriction of their free-dom. Officers must be flexible individuals with many faces and approaches. Offic-ers must be aware of their own strengths and weaknesses. In almost every use of their authority, to a certain extent, they must control people. When officers' requests are reasonable and necessary, those involved will usually comply.

Some inquiries will be brief and simple. Others will be extremely complex. The object is to obtain information. Some people, witnesses or complainants, seem to want to air their grievances to officers and will go out of their way to be helpful. Others may be uncooperative.

According to Payton (1986, pp. 289–291), field inquiries or interviews serve four basic functions: (1) to develop information and informants, (2) to identify individuals, (3) to develop suspects, and (4) to prevent crime. Field inquiry cards such as illustrated in Figure 3.1 should be completed for every stop made.

The principles of inquiry or interviewing are the same in virtually every situa-tion. To be successful in obtaining information, officers must have a clear idea of what they need to learn in each particular situation. The simplest way to do this is to think in terms of six key questions: who, what, where, when, how, and why.

To a certain extent, officers can evaluate the people they seek information from by listening to what they say. Watch for clues that indicate honesty, frankness, and openness. Does the person talk freely and willingly? Or does the person seem to attempt to hold back information? Watch body language. Watch for nervousness,

FIGURE 3.1
Sample Field Interview Card
Source: Police Field Operations, 2d ed., Thomas F. Adams, 1990, p. 188.
Reprinted with permission of Prentice, Hall, Englewood Cliffs, N.J.

OR. No.	FIELD INTERROGATION CARD	DATE & TIME

NAME (LAST NAME FIRST)	NICKNAME

RESIDENCE ADDRESS	RESIDENCE PHONE

CLASSIFICATION	DRIV (X)	PASS (X)	PED (X)

LOCATION OF OCCURRENCE	PLACE OF BIRTH

SEX	DESCENT	AGE	DATE OF BIRTH	HEIGHT	WEIGHT	HAIR	EYES	COMPLEXION

MARKS, SCARS, TATOOS, ETC.

CLOTHING WORN

YEAR AND MAKE OF CAR	BODY TYPE	COLOR(S)	LICENSE NO.	YEAR

SUSPECT'S BUSINESS ADDRESS (PH. NO. & SHIFT) (IF JUVENILE, NAME OF SCHOOL & GRADE)

NAME OF PERSONS WITH SUSPECT AT TIME OF INTERROGATION

REASON FOR INTERROGATION

DISPOSITION

OFFICER(S), REPORTING (LAST NAME AND SERIAL NUMBER)	DIVISION	DETAIL

Sometimes the most casual conversation may produce important information about neighborhood problems.

excessive perspiration, fidgeting, or signs of a dry mouth. Do not rely totally on the information obtained, particularly from a witness who is going to testify in court. It may fit your view of the case, but if the information may discredit your witness in court, seek other corroborating evidence. Once you have your information, test it for completeness. Is it all the information you need? Have you filled the gaps?

Some police officers use a simple chart such as that illustrated in Figure 3.2. Don't forget to be alert to signs that the conversation might be deteriorating—for example, a flushed face, loud voice, clenched fists, shaking or twitching, and rapid breathing.

The Interview

The interview is another important type of routine communication used by police officers. It differs from the field inquiry in that it is usually planned in advance for some specific purpose.

---

*An **interview** is the planned questioning of a witness, victim, informant, or other person with information related to an incident or case.*

Police officers interview witnesses, victims, informants, and others almost daily. To be effective, their interviews should be based on specific goals and objectives.

Witnesses—The Lifeblood of Every Criminal Case

A **witness** is a person other than a suspect who is asked to give information about an incident or another person. The witness may be a victim, a complainant, an

FIGURE 3.2
Sample of an Information Summary Chart

Statement of Witness	Statement of Others	Officer Observations	Physical Evidence
Says complainant provoked attack Has nothing good to say about complainant. May have a bias.	Jones says that complainant is a nerd and is provocative Suspect has problems with emotions	Victim had abrasions on face and arms Suspect highly emotional	2" x 2" x 4' board used by suspect in attack Bloody shirt of victim

accuser, a source of information, an observer of an occurrence, a scientific specialist who has examined physical evidence, or a custodian of official documents.

The typical witness is a layperson, unskilled in investigation techniques and unfamiliar with legal or police terminology. As a result, witnesses tend to offer confusing generalities from which it is difficult for police officers to form a definite picture or even to establish one useful peculiarity. Consequently, police officers are forced into situations where they must assist the witness, with the possibility that errors will result from suggestions made by the officer.

When police officers investigate an incident, they routinely seek out all the witnesses they can find. A crime of violence puts witnesses in shock. People who witness violent crimes and are relatives, friends, or spouses of the victim are usually overwhelmed by the tragedy of the crime. Often such witnesses become additional or secondary victims of the original incident and need victim services as much as the actual primary victim. Here police departmental policy and manuals are relevant in suggesting ways to calm and reassure emotional witnesses.

---

*A **primary victim** is one who actually is harmed. A **secondary victim** is one who is not actually harmed but who suffers along with the victim—a spouse or parent, for example.*

Frederick et al. (1990, p. 106) note that many witnesses to, and victims of, violent crime suffer from **posttraumatic stress disorder,** or **PTSD,** which they define as "a reaction to a violent event that evokes intense fear, terror, and help-lessness." They (p. 106) stress: "Police officers are often the first contact victims have following a traumatic encounter. The importance of police interaction with victims cannot be underestimated." Effective interviewing of victims not only helps obtain the needed information but also helps the victim's future mental and emotional well-being.

Frederick et al. (pp. 106–109) suggest several victim/witness intervention techniques:

- Display composure.
- Try to put the victim at ease. . . . "I'm here with you."
- Give honest and accurate information.
- Remove the victim temporarily from a stressful situation.
- Begin interviewing and questioning the victim only after establishing psychological and physical equilibrium. . . . Insensitive questioning can compound the trauma . . . [and] has been reported by some victims to be worse than the initial trauma.
- Proceed with a clear and unambiguous plan.
- Contact and meet with available relatives and friends.
- Make use of the victim's personal resources.
- Encourage physical activity if appropriate.
- Supply suitable advice and direction.
- Adapt to the needs of the victim, taking into account verbal facility, social background, age, sex, and the like.

When officers interview witnesses, they must take an accurate statement of what the witness saw, smelled, or heard. Officers must also evaluate the credibility of witnesses on a number of such intangible factors as their ability to articulate, their intelligence, their opportunity to observe, state of sobriety, stress at the time of observation, and similar factors.

Officers must ask themselves, Is the witness believable? Officers must note in their reports what witnesses say and the notes must be accurate. Spellings of names should be checked. Addresses and phone numbers should be repeated back to the witness as should any numbers. Whenever possible, officers should get the statements of witnesses in writing. A witness's statement should be read back to the witness to be sure it is accurate. Later, if the case goes to trial, witnesses can read their statements before giving testimony to refresh their memories. Before testifying in court, officers should ask witnesses to correct any omissions or errors in the statement. This can help to avoid any damage on cross-examination by the defense attorney.

Police officers should assure themselves that the witnesses they interview can and will testify. Ask yourself, Is the witness competent to testify? Will the witness assert any privilege at the trial not to testify? **Privileged information** is information that need not be divulged to the police or the courts. According to Oran (1985, p. 238), it is "the *right* and *duty* [of the witness] to withhold information because of some special status or relationship of *confidentiality*." Two kinds of privileges exempt witnesses from testifying: absolute and conditional. These privileges are granted for reasons of public policy unrelated to any reliability of the information involved.

An **absolute privilege** means no exceptions. If the witness claims the privilege not to testify about some protected information or evidence because of some special relationship, the testimony cannot be received. For example, conversations about social, business, and personal affairs are often private and privileged, including communications between physicians and patients, lawyers and clients, husbands and wives, or others under a special obligation of fidelity and secrecy.

A **conditional privilege** usually is the "official information privilege." An example of this would be the privilege asked of the court in not disclosing the identity of an informant. Some privileges occur only rarely in criminal cases, while others are of major importance and therefore occur frequently.

The Cognitive Interview Technique

Fisher (1990, p. 1) describes the cognitive interview technique used by the Metro-Dade Police Department in Florida. This technique tries to put witnesses and victims mentally at the scene of the crime by using:

> *several mnemonic [memory] techniques aimed at encouraging more "focused retrieval." These include allowing the interviewee to do most of the talking; asking fewer short-answer questions and more open-ended ones; allowing more time for the witness to answer; avoiding interruptions as the witness gives details; and encouraging the witness to report all details, no matter how trivial.*

---

*The **cognitive interview technique** puts witnesses mentally back at the scene of an incident and encourages them to tell the whole story without interruption.*

According to Fisher (p. 1), robbery detectives who used this technique were able to obtain nearly 50 percent more information from their subjects.

The Informant

An **informant** is a human source of information in a criminal action whose identity must be protected. There is no quarreling with the use of informants in police operations. Due to an informant's residence, occupation, associates, or lifestyle, certain people are in a better position than police officers to obtain information relevant to a particular crime.

Police officers have a recurring problem that will periodically act as a stumbling block to a successful search or arrest. That is, can they rely on an informant's statement to justify a search or an arrest? The main problem officers are faced with is, how reliable is the informant? The test of the "reasonably cautious man" seems to be quite obvious in that one would not believe Person A had committed a crime merely because the officer received an uncorroborated, anonymous phone call saying Person A had committed the crime. There are also serious problems of reliability with known informants. People who act as informants are sometimes not the most reliable members of the community and may themselves be engaged in criminal conduct. Many may be narcotic users or marginal criminals. Police are used to getting information, often false, from people who have been arrested and hope to get favorable treatment by talking. Some paid informants will make up stories just to get paid.

Nevertheless, reliable information is often received from informants. There are difficulties in determining what information is reliable but even information from anonymous sources should not be ignored. Such information, however, must be further investigated before a decision to arrest can be made. Such investigation should certainly include the prior reliability of the informant. An attempt should be made to corroborate the informant's information either by surveillance or personal observations. The suspect's background should also be checked. Payton (1986, p. 289) notes: "The importance of informants is seldom stressed because most officers are afraid to let it be known that about 50–60 percent of all major crime is solved through the use of police informants."

The legal right of officers to act on reports of criminal activity received from an informant was established in Adams v. Williams (1972).

Acting on a tip by an informer whom the officer knew, Sergeant Connolly approached Williams' parked car and asked him to open the door. When Williams rolled down the window, Connolly reached into the car and seized a loaded handgun from Williams' waistband—precisely where the informant had said it would be. Williams was then placed under arrest for unlawful possession of the pistol, and a subsequent search incident to arrest produced heroin and other contraband.

Williams was convicted in a Connecticut court for illegal possession of the handgun found during the "stop and frisk" encounter, as well as for possession of the heroin discovered during the full search incident to his weapons arrest. After his conviction was affirmed by the Supreme Court of Connecticut, Williams unsuccessfully sought habeas corpus relief in both the United States District Court of the District of Connecticut and the Court of Appeals (2d Cir.). However, on rehearing, the Court of Appeals reversed the conviction, finding that the search and seizure were unlawful.

Williams contended in his appeal to the United States Supreme Court that the initial seizure of the pistol, on which rested the later search and seizure of other weapons and narcotics, was not justified by the informant's tip to Sergeant Connolly. Williams claimed that, without corroboration of the tip, the police officer's actions were unreasonable under the standards set forth in *Terry v. Ohio*.

The Supreme Court stated that, in applying the *Terry* principles to the case, they believed Sergeant Connolly acted justifiably in responding to the informant's tip. He knew the informant, who had provided him with information in the past. In reaching their conclusion, the Supreme Court rejected Williams' argument that reasonable cause for a stop and frisk can be based only on the officer's personal observation rather than on information supplied by another person. Informant's tips, like all other clues and evidence coming to police officers on the scene, may vary greatly in their value and reliability.

Under the circumstances surrounding Williams' possession of the gun seized by Sergeant Connolly, the arrest on the weapons charge was supported by probable cause, and the search of his person and of the car incident to that arrest was lawful. The fruits of the search were, therefore, properly admitted at Williams' trial. The contrary conclusion of the Appeals Court was in error and was reversed.

The *Terry* opinion reflects a standard of *reasonableness* which relates to searches for weapons that is quite different from standards for other searches. Actually, the reasonableness standard established was *reason to believe* rather than the more common *probable cause to believe*. The Court did, however, carefully note that a "search in absence of probable cause to arrest must be strictly circumscribed by the exigencies of the situation."

The use of informants raises some ethical questions such as the following:

- Is it ethical to allow informant involvement in on-going criminal activity to keep the source of information available?
- Is it ethical to pay informants for their information?The

The Interrogation

The terms *inquiry, interview,* and *interrogation* are often confused. In police terminology, *inquiry* usually refers to conversations held with citizens during routine patrol. This is also called a field inquiry, field interview, or even a field interrogation, depending on what is discussed.

The *interview,* as just discussed, is a planned questioning of witnesses to, or victims of, crimes; informants; and others having information about an incident.

---

*An **interrogation** refers to the questioning of hostile witnesses and suspects from whom officers try to obtain facts related to a crime as well as admissions or confessions.*

As this officer interrogates a woman involved in a domestic dispute, what tactical error is evident?

Interrogation is as old as history itself. As recorded in *The Book of Acts* nearly 2,000 years ago, the Apostle Paul was taken into custody by the Romans after a riot in the temple at Jerusalem. The Roman tribune, anxious to know why the people had rioted against Paul, commanded that he should be examined by scourging, meaning interrogated by whipping. Under Roman law most witnesses could be tortured to make them give evidence. But certain classes of people such as full citizens, soldiers, certain ranks of nobility, children under fourteen, and pregnant women were exempted from torture by law.

Paul, a full citizen of Rome, evidently knew his civil rights. He asked the centurion guarding him if it was lawful to whip a Roman who had not been given a trial? The officer, startled by this question, reported it at once to the tribune. This high official came to Paul and asked if he was a Roman. Paul answered, ''I was born free.'' The Roman tribune was certain Paul spoke the truth, for the penalty for falsely claiming citizenship in the Roman Empire was death. On hearing this conversation between Paul and the tribune, those who were to examine Paul went away, and the next day Paul was set free.

Except for this elementary form of due process enjoyed by a few privileged Roman citizens, the concept of due process in criminal interrogation was unknown during the early centuries of Western civilization. Criminal law was enforced by the inquisitorial system, in which torture was a distinguishing feature. The government used various forms of torture to extract confessions, including the rack, the screw, the wheel, and red pepper (India). The objective of interrogation was to obtain a confession, and the end justified the means. If a person confessed, that confession was taken as adequate proof that the person committed the crime and vindicated the methods used to get it. There was virtually no due process in criminal interrogation. The test of admissibility of a confession was whether the prisoner said the words.

By the early 1700s, torture was officially abolished in Anglo-Saxon law, and elementary due process appeared in criminal interrogation. By the late 1700s, a confession was made inadmissible as evidence if it had been obtained by physical coercion such as beating, threats, or promises. A new standard was first clearly stated by the English courts in 1783:

*A confession forced from the mind by the flattery of hope, or by the torture of fear, comes in so questionable a shape when it is to be considered as the evidence of guilt, that no credit ought to be given to it, and therefore it is rejected (*The King v. Warickshall*).*

By the time of the American Revolution, it was established in English and American law that a confession or admission induced by torture, threats, or promises was inadmissible in evidence as inherently untrustworthy, involuntary, or both. Due process was placed in the Fifth Amendment to our Constitution as part of the Bill of Rights.

In 1944, the Supreme Court broadened the federal definition of due process to exclude from evidence not only confessions obtained by beating, threats, and promises, but also those obtained under conditions which were ''inherently coercive,'' even though there had been no beatings, threats, or promises.

Confessions obtained by force or under ''inherently coercive'' conditions are inadmissible in court.

The Court measured what is or is not inherently coercive by reviewing the "totality of circumstances" in each case where the admissibility of the confession was at issue.

Circumstances That Make Up the "Totality"

Each of the following circumstances has been considered an important part of the "totality" in decisions reached by the United States Supreme Court.

- *Age.* A minor may not properly be questioned for as long or as intensely as an adult. The lower the age, the more closely the courts scrutinize police conduct during the interrogation.
- *Mentality.* Police interrogation must be in proportion to the mental condition of the person being questioned.
- *Education.* The permissible limits of interrogation vary according to the educational level of the person being questioned.
- *Nationality.* The nationality of the person being interrogated or even the national origin of a naturalized citizen may be an important circumstance, particularly where the person is to some degree unfamiliar with the customs or the language of the United States.
- *Criminal Experience.* The police have wider latitude in questioning an experienced criminal than is permitted in the case of a person who has little or no criminal background.
- *Reasons for the Arrest.* Police failure to advise the person arrested of the charge against him has been mentioned in cases where the confession was held to be void.
- *Basic Necessities.* The extent to which the police did or did not allow the person under interrogation to have a proper amount of sleep, food, and clothing is a relevant circumstance.
- *Interrogation.* Each of the various aspects of the actual interrogation may become an important circumstance:
  - Number of questioners. The total number of interrogators should be kept as low as reasonably possible.
  - Total elapsed time. The longer the period of questioning, the greater is the tendency of the courts to view the confession with suspicion.
  - Relay questioning. Continuous questioning by officers working in relays is frowned upon.
  - False inducements to confess. A false statement encouraging the person to confess may invalidate a confession.
  - Visitors. Police denial of an arrested person's request to see a lawyer, relative, friend, or to call a person to seek legal advice may be viewed as a deliberate obstruction of justice.
  - Preliminary hearing. A delay in the date set for the preliminary hearing that is beyond the limit permitted by state law is an important consideration.
  - Warning of rights. Whether the interrogating officers did or did not first warn the person of his constitutional rights is important.
  - General police conduct. Police conduct toward the arrested person in general, even that occurring after the confession has been obtained, is scrutinized by the courts for such light as it may shed on the question of whether the confession was obtained by fair or deceptive means.

Totality of circumstances includes an individual's age, mentality, education, nationality, and criminal experience. It also includes the reasons for the arrest, how the suspect was advised, whether basic necessities were provided during interrogation, and the methods used in the interrogation.

The totality of circumstances rule has not been interpreted to mean that the presence of any one of these circumstances (or any particular combination of them) requires that the confession be held void for lack of due process. The judgment varies according to the number and severity of the circumstances. For cases in which unfavorable circumstances are not too great, the confessions have been upheld in U.S. courts.

The Downward Movement of the "Fundamental Fairness" Doctrine

Malloy v. Hogan (1964) involved a convicted gambler, William Malloy, who, during a Connecticut state investigation of gambling activities, refused to answer questions about his prior arrest and conviction "on the grounds that it may tend to incriminate me." The court held Malloy in contempt and ordered him jailed until he cooperated. The United States Supreme Court, however, reversed this action, saying that Malloy's Fifth Amendment rights against self-incrimination had been violated.

Most Americans are familiar with the scenario of the witness who invokes the constitutional privilege against self-incrimination based on the Fifth Amendment provision that "No person . . . shall be compelled in any criminal case to be a witness against himself." The privilege against self-incrimination is applicable to the states through the Fourteenth Amendment, although some states have similar protections in their constitutions as well.

Prior to *Malloy v. Hogan,* convictions in state courts based on alleged involuntary confessions were subject to appellate review under the due process clause of the Fourteenth Amendment. These courts also used the totality of circumstances in reviewing cases. In *Blackburn v. Alabama* (1960), the confession given by Blackburn, charged with robbery, was ruled inadmissible and his conviction reversed. Not only was there evidence that he was insane, he was interrogated by sheriff's personnel for eight to nine hours in a small room with as many as three officers present at once, and the confession was "composed" by a deputy sheriff.

For many years, a "voluntary" confession was admissible as long as it was deemed "trustworthy" or "probably true." When it came to evaluating the reliability of a confession under the totality of circumstances test, the courts usually looked to the circumstances in which the confession was obtained. These included the defendant's age, mental state, physical condition, prior criminal offenses, etc., as well as the methods of interrogation used by the police (police methods test) and the time and place of the interrogation.

Over a period of time, police began to make greater use of psychological techniques, which usually made proof of the voluntariness of a confession difficult. In many courts, the dispute as to the voluntariness of a confession usually resulted in a "swearing contest" between the defendant and police interrogators, and the courts invariably would resolve the dispute in favor of the police, erasing any doubts in the mind of the defendant as to whose side the court was on.

Another landmark case affecting the admissibility of confessions was *Escobedo v. Illinois* (1964). Escobedo allegedly murdered his brother-in-law. He engaged the services of a lawyer while at the station house but was not allowed to speak to him while in custody. He was interrogated for several hours and was never advised of his constitutional rights. He made several statements that were incriminating and which were admitted at his trial. He was convicted of murder and appealed his case. The Supreme Court reversed his conviction and held that "when the process shifts from investigatory to accusatory—when its focus is on the accused and its purpose is to elicit a confession—our adversary system begins to operate, and . . . the accused must be permitted to consult with a lawyer."

The Escobedo *decision held that, when a person accused of committing a crime is being interrogated, such a person has a right to have an attorney present.*

The *Escobedo* decision is important in that it indicates a shift in the Supreme Court's focus from the traditional totality of circumstances and voluntariness tests on the admissibility of confessions to the Sixth Amendment right to counsel. The court held that the right to counsel attaches at "critical stages" of the criminal process and that police interrogations is one such stage.

The Miranda *Decision*

The best known case related to interrogation is *Miranda v. Arizona* (1966). In this case, twenty-three-year-old Miranda was arrested and interrogated about a rape and kidnapping. He confessed to the crimes, but he had not been told of his rights because police assumed that, since he had been arrested before, he was aware of his rights. The Court ruled (in a 5–4 split) that the officers erred in not informing Miranda of those rights again, saying:

> *The Fifth Amendment privilege is so fundamental to our system of constitutional rule and the expedient of being given an adequate warning as to the availability of the privilege so simple, we will not pause to inquire in individual cases whether the defendant was aware of his rights without a warning being given. Assessments of the knowledge the defendant possessed, based on information as to his age, education, intelligence, or prior contact with authorities, can never be more than speculation; a warning is a clear-cut fact.* (Miranda v. Arizona)

The decision in *Miranda* was the culmination of a shift by the Court from the traditional voluntariness test to an elaborate set of procedural safeguards designed to prevent the police from circumventing due process protections. In essence, what the Court said in *Miranda* was:

- The suspect has the right to remain silent.
- If the suspect gives up the right to remain silent, anything that the suspect says can be used in a court of law against him.

**FIGURE 3.3
A Miranda Warning Card**

Statement of Miranda Rights

1. You have the right to remain silent.
2. Anything you say can and will be used against you in a court of law.
3. You have the right to talk to a lawyer and have him present with you while you are being questioned.
4. If you cannot afford to hire a lawyer, one will be appointed to represent you before any questioning, if you wish.
5. You can decide at any time to exercise these rights and not answer any questions or make any statements

- The suspect has a right to speak to an attorney and to have an attorney present when being questioned by the police.
- If the suspect cannot afford one, an attorney will be appointed to represent the suspect *before* questioning begins.

Miranda v. Arizona *established the suspect's right to remain silent, to talk to an attorney, and to have an attorney present during any questioning, the attorney to be provided free if a suspect cannot afford one.*

In the *Miranda* case, the Supreme Court held that these appropriate warnings are required *prior to custodial interrogation* and "custodial" was defined as referring to the situation of a person who is "in custody" (under arrest) or *otherwise deprived of his freedom of action in any significant way.*

Many officers carry with them a card with the **Miranda warning** printed on it, clearly spelling out the suspect's rights, as illustrated in Figure 3.3. They can then read it verbatim to suspects.

Of importance is whether the suspects understand each of the rights the officer reads to them. If, for example, a suspect speaks only Spanish, the warning might be read from a card bearing the warning in Spanish or from a card bearing the Spanish warning with pronunciation and translation (Figure 3.4).

In our culturally diverse society, officers must be cautious in dealing with suspects who are not familiar with the American legal system, its culture, or its language.

Another important facet of the *Miranda* decision is whether suspects are willing to give up these rights and talk to the police. If they do so, a signed waiver should be obtained. Look at the waiver form illustrated in Figure 3.5. Figure 3.6 shows a combined warning/waiver version in Spanish.

Arresting officers might note that it may not be necessary to give a suspect the Miranda warnings if the officer does not intend to question or otherwise interrogate the suspect, known as the *silent approach*. According to del Carmen (1987, pp. 266–268) the Miranda warnings are not normally required in the following nine instances:

- No questions asked. [This is not an interrogation.]
- General questioning at the crime scene.
- Questioning witnesses.
- Volunteered statements.
- Statements made to private persons, for example, friends, cellmates.
- Questioning in an office or place of business.
- Stop and frisk cases.
- Before a Grand Jury.
- Noncustodial interrogations by a probation officer.

FIGURE 3.4
A Miranda Warning Card in Spanish
Courtesy of Douglas P. Hinkle.

ADVERTENCIA ANTES DE TOMAR CUALQUIER CONFESION HABLADA O ESCRITA		
English	Spanish Translation	Approximate English Sound Equivalents
Before we ask you any questions, you have to understand your rights.	Antes que le hagamos cualquier pregunta, usted tiene que comprender sus derechos.	AHNtays kay lay ahGAHmos kwakKYAIR prayGOONta, oosTAY I YAI nay kay kowmprenDAIR soos dayRAYchos.
You have the right to remain silent.	Usted tiene el derecho de guarder silencio.	oosTAY TYAYnay el dayRAYcho day gwanDAR seeLAYNsyo.
Anything you say can be held against you in a court of law.	Lo que diga puede usarse contra usted en la corte.	Lo kay DEEga PWAYday ooSARsay KOWOtra cosTAYd ain lah KORtay.
You have the right to talk to a lawyer and have him present with you while you are being questioned.	Usted tiene el derecho de hablar con un abogado y de tenerlo presente con usted mientras le hacemos preguntas.	oosTAY TYAYnay el dayRAYcho day ahBLAR kown oon obbowGODdo ee day tenNAIRlo praySENtay kown oostAY MYENtrahs lay ahSAYmos prayGOONtas.
If you cannot afford to hire a lawyer, one will be appointed to represent you before any questioning, if you wish.	Si usted no tiene medios para contratar un abogado, la corte le asignará uno antes que le hagamos preguntas, si así lo desea.	see oosTAY no TYAYnay Maydios PAHra kowntrotTAR oon obbowGODdo, lah KORtay le ahsignaRAH oono AHNtays kay lay ahGAHmos prayGOONtas, see ahsee lo desSAYyah.
You can decide at any time to exercise these rights, and not answer any questions nor make any statements.	Usted puede optar en cualquier moment a emplear estos derechos, y así negarse a contestar preguntas o hacer declaraciones.	oostay PWAYday owptar ain kwahlKYAIR moMENto ah aimplayYAR AIStos dayZRAYchos ee ahSEE nayGARsay a kowntesTAR prayGOONtas. o ahSAIR dayklaraSYOWnays.
Do you understand what I have just read to you?	¿Comprende usted lo que acabo de leerle?	kowmPRENday oosTAY lo kay ahKOBbo day layYERlay?

FIGURE 3.5
A Miranda Waiver Form

STATEMENT

TIME_____DATE_____PLACE_____

_____ , being _____

I, the undersigned,_____

years of age, state that I live at _____

in the_____of _____ , that I have been warned and

advised by_____ , a person who has identified himself

as_____ , that (1) I have the right to remain silent; (2) I have the

right to refuse to answer any one or all of the questions put to me; (3) anything I say may be used against me in court; (4) I have the right to talk to a lawyer of my own choice and ask his advice before being questioned, and to have him present with me during the questioning; (5) if I cannot afford a lawyer and want one, a lawyer will be provided for me; (6) if I decide to answer questions now without a lawyer present I still have the right to stop answering at any time; and (7) if I wish, I may stop answering at any time until I talk to a lawyer.

I further state that I am willing to answer questions and make a statement; that I do not want a lawyer; that I understand and know what I am doing; that no promises or threats have been made to me and no pressure or coercion of any kind has been used against me. I therefore make this statement of my own free will.

_____

FIGURE 3.6
A Combined Miranda Warning and Waiver Form in Spanish

INTERROGATORIO: NOTIFICACIÓN DE LOS DERECHOS

Antes de hacerle pregunta alguna, Ud. debe entender lo que son sus derechos.

Ud. tiene el derecho de mantener silencio.

Cualquier cosa que Ud. diga, puede ser usada en su contra en un tribunal.

Ud. tiene el derecho de consultar con un abogado para que le aconseje antes de que le hagamos las preguntas. También, Ud. tiene derecho a la presencia del abogado durante el interrogatorio.

Si Ud. no puede pagar los gastos de un abogado, se le asignará uno antes de iniciarse el interrogatorio, si así lo desea Ud.

Si Ud. decide contestar las preguntas ahora sin la presencia de un abogado, Ud. todavía tiene el derecho de terminar de contestar en cualquier momento. Ud. tiene también el derecho de interrumpir las contetaciones en cualquier momento hasta consultar con un abogado.

RENUNCIA A LOS DERECHOS.

He leído esta declaración de mis derechos y entiendo lo que son. Estoy dispuesto a hacer una declaración y a contestar las preguntas. No quiero que esté presente un abogado en este momento. Tengo conciencia de lo que hago. No se me han hecho ni promesas ni amenazas y no se ha ejercido presión alguna en mi contra.

Firmado:

There is evidence that some suspects do not fully appreciate the significance of their rights and quickly waive the Miranda warnings because they are eager to tell "their side of the story." This often turns out to be very damaging to them because of their unfamiliarity with legal procedure and their liability under criminal law. For example, a suspect may say, "I only drove the car. My partner shot the bank teller." Many suspects will find it difficult to tell an arresting officer that they "don't understand their constitutional rights." Even though Miranda warnings are straightforward and appear to be easily comprehensible, a suspect may feel foolish admitting to an officer that he does not understand the Miranda warnings.

Many suspects will interrupt a police officer who is reciting the Miranda warning with, "Yea, knock it off. I know my rights." Officers must remember that the legal implications of the Miranda warning are complex, as evidenced by the hundreds of lower court decisions trying to interpret the case. As noted by Bates (1989, p. 90): "When an officer recites Miranda, he should be reminded of a country free from capricious persecution. This requires affirmative faith in investigative ability and confidence that in the long run, justice will prevail."

Recent pronouncements by the Supreme Court making further interpretations and further elaborations on the *Miranda* decision have been relatively scarce.

The courts have consistently suggested remedial action for police officers in the form of more instruction on the law of confessions. They stress that interrogations of persons under arrest ought to be shorter and more productive. They advise officers to place greater stress on scientific evidence and less on confessions. Finally, they advise the elimination from each interrogation or interview of all unnecessary factors in the ''totality.'' Though totality of circumstances has to a certain extent been replaced by the fundamental fairness doctrine and procedural safeguards, courts still use both in evaluating due process and confessions.

Whether officers are seeking to obtain a confession or seeking to comfort the victim of a crime, certain techniques can make interviews and interrogations more effective.

Interviewing and Interrogating Techniques

Interviews and interrogations should be structured around the investigatory elements of the incident or crime. The need for careful planning and advance preparation cannot be overstated. In a preliminary interview at a crime scene, officers have extremely limited time for such planning. Consequently, they need to know their priorities in advance. They should obtain as much information as possible, identify and locate the offender(s), and broadcast the information or alert other officers and departments about the offense and identity of the offender(s).

Follow-up interviews can be more carefully planned and structured. Evans (1990, pp. 91–94) offers ten suggestions for making interviews more effective. Most of the suggestions would work equally well during interrogations.

1. *Select the location of the interview yourself.* Friendly witnesses may be interviewed in their homes or offices, but, almost without exception, suspects and unfriendly witnesses should be removed from familiar surroundings. . . .

   When possible, the interview room should be small, with window blinds closed. The walls and furnishings should be solid, placid colors. There should be no pictures on the walls or other objects in the room that could distract the subject. Think safety; remove from the room scissors and other items that could be used as weapons.

   The subject's chair should be low to the floor and comfortable. Your chair should be slightly higher, facing, and within two feet of the subject's chair.

2. *Start with friendly small talk.* Small talk builds rapport with the subject and helps establish avenues of approach. This is a good time to observe the subject's ''truth-telling'' body language. . . . After the opening conversation, the Miranda warning must be given if the subject is a criminal suspect. . . .

3. *Create a feeling of reciprocity.* Providing token gifts, such as drinks of water or allowing the subject to smoke, puts that person in debt. . . .

Police officer taking a missing person report from a nursing home staff member.
Detailed information is critical.

Subjects should NOT be offered coffee. Caffeine is both a physical and mental stimulant and delays the onset of fatigue. . . . Hunger and thirst are counterproductive and tend to interfere with the interview process.

4. *Use deception sparingly.* [Too much may constitute coercion.]

5. *Listen carefully and empathize.* A subject should be encouraged to tell the story in his own words, thus increasing the chance that he will supply totally new information. . . . Don't interrupt the subject's story. It may never be told again. Be empathetic and reassuring.

Exceptions to an empathetic approach are sociopaths and most professional criminals. . . . Successful interviews with sociopaths often entail challenging their egos with such statements as, This is nothing, tell me how shrewd you really are.

To get professional criminals to talk, you often must convince them that there is sufficient evidence to prove their guilt.

6. *Help subjects to recall events.*

7. *Choose your questions wisely.* . . . Questions should be short, confined to one topic.

8. *Point out conflicts.*

9. *Be observant for signs of lying.* . . . Deceptive subjects often hesitate to gain more time to develop a lie. They use con words, such as "I swear to God," "Honestly," and "Believe me," to make their lies sound more believable.

10. *Be conscious of body language.*

Additional advice on conducting interviews and interrogations is provided by Wrobleski and Hess (1990, p. 307):

- Prepare for each interview in advance if time permits. Know what questions you need to have answered.
- Obtain your information as soon after the incident as possible. A delay may result in the subject's not remembering important details.
- Be considerate of the subject's feelings. If someone has just been robbed, seen an assault, or been attacked, the individual may be understandably upset and emotional. Allow time for the person to calm down before asking too many questions. Remember that when emotions increase, memory decreases.
- Be friendly. Try to establish rapport with the subject before asking questions. Use the person's name; look at the person as you ask questions; respond to the answers.
- Use a private setting if possible. Eliminate as many distractions as you can, so that the subject can devote full attention to the questions you ask.
- Eliminate physical barriers. Talking across a desk or counter, or through a car window, does not encourage conversation.
- Sit rather than stand. This will make the subject more comfortable and probably more willing to engage in conversation.
- Encourage conversation. Keep the subject talking by:
  □ Keeping your own talking to a minimum.
  □ Using open-ended questions, such as ''Tell me what you saw.''
  □ Avoiding questions that call for only a ''yes'' or ''no'' answer.
  □ Allowing long pauses. Pauses in the conversation should not be uncomfortable. Remember that the subject needs time to think and organize thoughts. Give the subject all the time needed.
- Ask simple questions. Do not use law enforcement terminology when you ask your questions. Keep your language simple and direct.
- Ask one question at a time. Allow the subject to answer one question completely before going to the next question.
- Listen to what is said and how it is said.
- Watch for indications of tension, nervousness, surprise, embarrassment, anger, fear, or guilt.
- Establish the reliability of the subject by asking some questions to which you already know the answers.
- Be objective and controlled. Recognize that many persons are reluctant to give information to the police. Among the reasons for this reluctance are fear or hatred of police, fear of reprisal, lack of memory, or unwillingness to become involved. Keep control of yourself and your situation. Do not antagonize the subject, use profanity or obscenity, lose your temper, or use physical force. Remain calm, objective, and professional.

The type of individual being interviewed or interrogated will influence the questioning session.

Terminology

According to Pena (1986, p. 206), police officers should not use police terminology when interviewing or interrogating people because it will increase the ''incriminating atmosphere'' of the questioning. He suggests words to avoid and appropriate substitutes for them:

Avoid	Better to Use
murder	death
mayhem	injury
robbery	property taken
burglary	entered
rape	have sex
assault	scuffle
kidnap	move
conspiracy	arrangement
embezzle	use
life imprisonment	some time

Phrasing Questions

The questions police ask have an impact on people and cases. Evidence shows that the phrasing of questions can definitely influence answers. In one study, for example, observers who were asked, How tall was the basketball player? estimated his height to be about 79 inches. Those asked, How short was the basketball player? responded with an estimate of about 69 inches.

Wells and Loftus (1982) have shown that altering information after the event can influence recall. Witnesses who were asked How fast were the cars going when they *hit, bumped, collided, smashed* each other? gave increasingly higher estimates of speed according to the increasing violence implied by the verb.

In another experiment, subjects were asked either Did you see a broken headlight? or Did you see the broken headlight? one week after observing an unbroken headlight. Those queried with *the* answered in the affirmative twice as often as those queried with *a*. Other research indicates that misleading information has its greatest effect on memory if it is stored very soon after the initial perception of the critical event.

Obviously, the police and others need to be concerned with how questions are asked. To minimize the inadvertent biasing of memory, witnesses should give an uninterrupted narration before being asked specific questions. Interrogation should also take place as soon as possible so that misleading information from various sources does not become part of the remembered event.

Police officers must also be aware of the importance of using follow-up questions to reduce or eliminate confusion and to clarify statements that seem to contradict previously stated facts.

Forensic Hypnosis

Another assist to interviewing and interrogation is forensic hypnosis. Forensic hypnosis differs from clinical hypnosis in that it involves establishing facts for judicial purposes as opposed to alleviating distress and pain. Forensic hypnosis is valuable when it provides police officers with information that otherwise would not be remembered.

Forensic hypnosis *seeks to establish facts for judicial purposes.*

This information may lead to other competent evidence that can be independently corroborated. Abuse is possible, however, as was recognized in *United States v. Adams* (1978). The Court stated:

> *We are concerned that investigatory use of hypnosis on persons who may later be called upon to testify in court carries a dangerous potential for abuse. Great care must be exercised to insure that statements after hypnosis are the products of the subject's own recollections, rather than of recall tainted by suggestions received while under hypnosis.*

Hypnotic memory, like other memory states, is susceptible to distortions and errors in recall. Furthermore, hypnosis cannot retrieve information not initially encoded.

In addition, hypnosis does not guarantee truth. Individuals can simulate hypnotic trances that can deceive even highly experienced hypnotists. Some people can also willfully lie even when in deep hypnosis. Willful lying is not the only major concern, however. Far more troublesome for the courts in cross-examination is the witness who believes that hypnosis reveals the truth and is convinced that his memory is now accurate.

Hypnotized people are hypersuggestible and hypercompliant. Consequently, they are susceptible to leading questions and cues from police and others. Because of their wish to please the hypnotist and his associates, witnesses may create plausible but inaccurate pseudomemories. It is difficult to separate accurately recalled information from that suggested or invented. For these reasons, most of the scientific community agrees that information gathered through hypnosis is not necessarily reliable. Unfortunately, in at least one case, a defendant has been convicted primarily on hypnosis-based testimonial evidence (*Quaglino v. California*, 1977).

Internal, Spoken Communications

Police officers rely not only on information from witnesses, informants, and suspects but also on information provided by headquarters and other officers. Much of this information is relayed via radio rather than face to face, necessitating careful pronunciation and lots of feedback.

Accuracy is critical in police work, so officers should spell any words that might be misunderstood or spelled incorrectly, especially names and addresses. Such spelling is most effective if done in the phonetic alphabet used by most police departments.

A	Adam	N	Nora
B	Boy	O	Ocean
C	Charles	P	Paul
D	David	Q	Queen
E	Edward	R	Robert
F	Frank	S	Sam

G	George	T	Tom
H	Henry	U	Union
I	Ida	V	Victor
J	John	W	William
K	King	X	X ray
L	Lincoln	Y	Young
M	Mary	Z	Zebra

If the spelling of a name is the "normal" spelling, this can be stated, for example, "Smith, normal spelling." But if the name is spelled *Smythe,* it should be spelled out.

Another way to enhance clarity of communication is to use the twenty-four hour clock rather than conventional time (A.M. and P.M.). This is also referred to as **military time.** It begins at midnight with 0000. The first two digits refer to the hour and the last two digits refer to the minutes. Usually the word *hours* follows the time designation. For example, ten minutes after midnight would be 0010 hours, while 3:15 A.M. would be 0315 hours. Noon is 1200 hours. From that point on, twelve is added to each hour so that one o'clock in the afternoon becomes 1300 hours. It continues full circle this way, with midnight also being called 2400 hours, depending on department policy.

Twenty-Four Hour Clock

Morning		Afternoon	
Midnight	= 0000	1 PM	= 1300
1 AM	= 0100	2 PM	= 1400
2 AM	= 0200	3 PM	= 1500
3 AM	= 0300	4 PM	= 1600
4 AM	= 0400	5 PM	= 1700
5 AM	= 0500	6 PM	= 1800
6 AM	= 0600	7 PM	= 1900
7 AM	= 0700	8 PM	= 2000
8 AM	= 0800	9 PM	= 2100
9 AM	= 0900	10 PM	= 2200
10 AM	= 1000	11 PM	= 2300
11 AM	= 1100	Midnight	= 2400
Noon	= 1200		

Pagers

Some departments are relying more on pagers than on radio for their internal communication. The traditional pagers use a beep or tone that alerts the officer to call headquarters or a phone number displayed on the pager. More advanced pagers alert the officer by a tone or by a soft vibration and display a digital message. According to Bubin (1991, p. 23): "Messages of up to 80 characters can be received on the liquid crystal displays of the new units, and they will store up to 426 characters." Bubin (p. 24) notes: "With alphanumerics, officers can communicate with each other with far less chance of interception." In addition, says Bubin (p. 25): "It gives the agents' informants access to them without having to engage the police communication system, which can be easily monitored."

Photophones

Another advance in internal communications is the photophone, being used by the Royal Canadian Mounted Police. The system works with a videocamera connected to a computer and a telephone. According to Harman (1991, p. 28), the system ''can transmit and receive high-resolution color or gray-scale images of fingerprints, mug shots, suspect travel documents, bank notes, handwriting samples, ballistics, and other forensic evidence.'' It uses standard telephone lines and operates wherever there is a power source and a telephone.

Other Means of Internal Communications •

Many departments also use cellular phones, voice-scrambler systems, and mobile digital terminals for internal communications.

Summary

Effective communications in the field are critical to successful police operations. These include field inquiries, interviews, and interrogations as well as internal communications.

A field inquiry is the unplanned questioning of a person who has aroused a police officer's suspicions. An interview is the planned questioning of a witness, victim, informant, or other person with information related to an incident or case. A primary victim is one who actually is harmed. A secondary victim is one who is not actually harmed but who suffers along with the victim—a spouse or parent, for example.

The cognitive interview technique puts witnesses mentally back at the scene of an incident and encourages them to tell the whole story without interruption. The legal right of officers to act on reports of criminal activity received from an informant was established in *Adams v. Williams* (1972).

An interrogation refers to the questioning of hostile witnesses and suspects from whom officers try to obtain admissions or confessions. Facts related to a crime as well as confessions obtained by force or under ''inherently coercive'' conditions are inadmissible in court. Whether confessions are inadmissible often depends on the totality of circumstances, including the suspect's age, mentality, education, nationality, and criminal experience. Also included in the ''totality'' are the reasons for the arrest, how the suspect was advised, whether basic necessities were provided during interrogation, and the methods used in the interrogation.

The *Escobedo* decision held that, when a person accused of committing a crime is being interrogated, such a person has a right to have an attorney present. Suspects' rights during interrogation were established in *Miranda v. Arizona*. This landmark case established the suspect's right to remain silent, to talk to an attorney, and to have an attorney present during any questioning, the attorney to be provided free if the suspect cannot afford one. Forensic hypnosis seeks to establish facts for judicial purposes.

Application

As the lieutenant in charge of the uniformed patrol officers, you have been notified by a local judge that the courts have noticed in your officers' reports a considerable reduction in their ability to conduct meaningful inquiries. Information which would be of utmost importance to the court is often omitted.

Instructions   Use the form in Appendix A to write a policy for conducting field inquiries and recording information gathered on a field inquiry form.

Keep in mind the purposes of field inquiries, such as discovering evidence of a crime, preventing potential criminal activity, checking people for warrants, follow-up reporting, and investigating suspicious behavior.

Make sure officers know that a field inquiry report is available. Make up a 3 × 5 field inquiry card complete with pertinent information. Emphasize the officers' responsibility to complete this report properly.

Exercises in Critical Thinking

Interrogation methods must follow a doctrine of fundamental fairness, and procedural safeguards are to be used in ensuring due process. The totality or entirety of circumstances will be the basis for most court decisions.

Shortly after midnight on September 29th, Deputy Sheriffs Patrick Medure and Harold Sande interviewed an inmate, Anita Krueth, at the county jail. Krueth revealed that (1) she had received and taken various drugs at a residence belonging to Kim Morgan, (2) others used drugs at the residence, (3) Morgan sold the drugs, and (4) people were referred to Morgan to buy drugs.

Based on that information, a magistrate issued a search warrant, and police observed the Morgan residence for twelve hours before they saw Morgan drive up and enter the residence. The police then executed the search warrant. Police discovered a large amount of cocaine stuffed in Kim's pants, and the trunk of Kim's car contained a duffel bag containing a scale, razor blades, and nicotinamide.

At the omnibus hearing the following week, Krueth's defense attorney testified that Krueth had denied making the statements listed above and had claimed the police coerced her into talking with them. She told her attorney that the deputies threatened to take away her child and to cause trouble for her husband.

Deputy Medure testified that Krueth had made all the statements recorded in the search warrant. He testified that Deputy Sande gave Krueth a cigarette because she asked for one. He denied threatening her children and husband, although he admitted Krueth could have "inferred" that her husband would not be charged if Krueth cooperated.

Deputy Sande testified that he and Deputy Medure had used a "good guy—bad guy" interrogation technique that required Medure to leave the room occasionally. He testified that while he had been in the room he heard Krueth make six of the statements on the affidavit. Sande admitted telling Krueth that if she did not cooperate, her husband might be the one "caught with the bag."

1. In conducting the interview, could either deputy have made an error? Which of the following items could be problems?
   a. The time (after midnight) and the place (in a room at a jail).
   b. The technique used (good guy—bad guy).
   c. Providing gifts (such as a cigarette).
   d. Use of deception (threatening her children and husband).
   e. Use of friendly small talk and letting a subject tell her story in her own words.
   f. No mistake was made.

2. Because of the interrogation method, what would void the search warrant?
   a. Containing material omissions of fact would void a search warrant.
   b. This warrant contains insufficient probable cause.
   c. One deputy leaving the room could bring questions about the other's testimony.
   d. The lack of an in-camera hearing to determine the reliability of the informant.
   e. Lack of disclosure of the informant's identity to establish reliability.
3. Courts will judge the results of interrogation based on:
   a. The totality of the circumstances and in a light most favorable to the state.
   b. The character and apparent sincerity of the witness's testimony.
   c. Total lack of coercive interrogation so that the officers' testimony cannot be doubted.
   d. Whether the interviewed subject was given a Miranda warning.
   e. Whether the subject said she understood her constitutional rights.

About 7:30 P.M. on July 24, a man approached a police cruiser parked on 8th Avenue near 42nd Street and told the two officers that he had just been robbed on 43rd Street between 7th and 8th Avenue. He pointed to a group of three people, two females and one male, walking across the nearby intersection and said, "Those are the ones who robbed me."

The officers got out of their cruiser and pursued the trio. They arrested two suspects, but one female vanished into the crowd. Arrested were Jennifer and Danny McGuire. A search of the suspects revealed that the male was carrying $127 in cash and a quantity of cocaine. The female had a knife in her purse. At the precinct station the officers questioned the victim and the suspects. The victim, Edward Stoner, said he was on his way to buy some theater tickets when he was approached by the female who escaped into the crowd. She asked him if he wanted to buy drugs, and he declined. The male suspect said he had a gun in his pocket and told the victim to hand over all his money. The first female took the money and walked away, accompanied by the male and another female. The victim then went to find the police to report his loss.

4. You are the senior patrol officer.

   a. What would be your next step?
   b. What procedures would you follow to complete this investigation?
   c. What pertinent questions must you ask the victim and the suspects in the incident?
   d. Who would you interview first? List questions you would ask the victim of the crime and questions you would ask the suspects.
   e. Are there circumstances you must consider as an important part of the "totality of circumstances"? If so, what are they?

Discussion Questions

1. Review the circumstances that make up "totality." Which one of these would you be most concerned about if questioning a juvenile who had just committed a heinous crime?
2. Correctional institutions frequently use a punishment and reward system, such as offering incentives like cigarettes for good behavior, to control inmates. Do

you see any objections to using the same system to get an individual to confess to a crime? Explain your position.

3. In a nighttime situation, you confront a suspicious man walking in an elite neighborhood. You stop to question the man, but he refuses to even give his name. What are you going to do? Elaborate and justify your decision.

4. How would you warn a suspect of his rights if, while you were interviewing this person, he suddenly said, "I committed the crime"?

5. What do you think is a reasonable amount of time to interrogate a suspect to get a confession? Clarify your answer.

6. Explain the differences between interviewing and interrogating.

7. How would you go about opening an interview to establish rapport?

Definitions

Can you define the following:

absolute privilege	military time
cognitive interview technique	Miranda warning
conditional privilege	post-traumatic stress disorder (PTSD)
field inquiry	primary victim
forensic hypnosis	privileged information
informant	secondary victim
interrogation	totality of circumstances
interview	witness

References

Bates, Robert B. "More than a Preliminary Ritual: A Modern Police View of *Miranda*." *Law and Order* (August 1989): 86–90.

Bubin, Chris. "Law Enforcement Discovers Pagers Fill Communication Niche." *Law and Order* (February 1991): 23–26.

Couper, David C. and Lobitz, Sabine H. "Quality Leadership: The First Step Towards Quality Policing." *The Police Chief* (April 1988): 79–84.

del Carmen, R. V. *Criminal Procedure for Law Enforcement Personnel*. Monterey, Calif: Brooks/Cole Publishing, 1987.

Evans, Daniel D. "10 Ways to Sharpen Your Interviewing Skills." *Law and Order* (August 1990): 90–94.

Fisher, Ronald (interview). "It's What You Say and How You Say It: Interview Style Pays Off." *Law Enforcement News* (February 14, 1990): 1, 6.

Frederick, Calvin J., Hawkins, Karen L., and Abajian, Wendy E. "Beyond the Call of Duty? Victim/Witness Intervention Techniques." *The Police Chief* (October 1990): 106–110.

Harman, Alan. "Photophone." *Law and Order* (February 1991): 28–30.

Inbau, Fred E., Reid, John E., and Buckley, Joseph P. *Criminal Interrogation and Confessions*. 3d ed. Baltimore, Md.: Williams and Wilkins, 1986.

Klockars, Carl B. *The Idea of Police*. Newbury Park, Calif.: Sage Publications, 1985.

Oran, Daniel. *Law Dictionary for Nonlawyers*. 2d ed. St. Paul, Minn.: West Publishing, 1985.

Payton, George T. *Patrol Procedure*. San Jose, Calif.: Criminal Justice Services, 1986.

Pena, M. S. *Practical Criminal Investigation*. 2d ed. Sacramento, Calif.: Custom Publishing, 1986.

Wells, Gary L. and Loftus, Elizabeth F., eds. *Eyewitness Testimony: Psychological Perspec-*
tives. Cambridge, Mass.: Harvard University Press, 1982.
Wrobleski, Henry M. and Hess, Kären M. *Introduction to Law Enforcement and Criminal*
Justice. 3d ed. St. Paul, Minn.: West Publishing, 1990.

Cases

Adams v. Williams, 407 U.S. 143, 92 S.Ct. 1921, 32 L.Ed.2d 612 (1972).
Blackburn v. Alabama, 361 U.S. 199, 80 S.Ct. 274, 4L.Ed.2d 242 (1960).
Escobedo v. Illinois, 378 U.S. 478, 84 S.Ct. 1758, 12 L.Ed.2d 977 (1964).
The King v. Warickshall, i Leach 263, 168 Eng. Rep. 234 (K.B. 1783).
Malloy v. Hogan, 378 U.S. 1, 84 S.Ct. 1489, 12 L.Ed.2d 653 (1964).
Miranda v. Arizona, 384 U.S. 436, 86 S.Ct. 1602, 16 L.Ed.2d 694 (1966).
Quaglino v. California, Sept. 20, 1977.
United States v. Adams, 581 F.2d 193 (9th Cir. 1978).

REPORTS AND RECORDS: ESSENTIAL AIDS TO POLICE OPERATIONS

CHAPTER 4

INTRODUCTION

Writing good reports is one of the most important skills law enforcement officers can possess. However, as noted by Hess and Wrobleski (1991, p. 1):

Most people enter law enforcement for the activity and excitement it offers, for the challenge of solving crimes, and for the chance to help others. They often do not realize the amount of paperwork involved—they think of themselves as law enforcement officers, not "pencil pushers." And then the rude awakening: For almost every official action law enforcement officers take, they must write a report.

Sergeant David Martens, training officer for the Minneapolis Police Department Cadet Academy, tells his recruits: "Police officers are gun-carrying secretaries." In fact, officers will use their pens and pencils much more often than their guns or handcuffs.

As noted by Dacy (1991, p. 66): "The offense and incident reports you take are the memory of the department. They may provide helpful information long after a particular case or incident has been disposed of."

How well officers write can make a significant difference in their career advancement. According to Miller and Pomerenke (1989, p. 66):

While officers are trained extensively in legal processes, human relations, and specific technical procedures, they are evaluated largely on their communication skills. The criminal justice system places great significance on accuracy, clarity, and thoroughness of the written report. Sometimes

Do You Know

- What are the characteristics of effective field notes?
- What purposes written police reports serve?
- What reader-friendly writing is?
- What two factors most directly affect readability?
- Who are likely audiences of police reports?
- What are the characteristics of effective police reports?
- What is the basic content of a police report?
- What basic writing principles should be followed in police reports?

it seems that the written report is more important than the substantive action that the officer takes in the field.

Indeed, as emphasized by Dacy (1991, p. 34): "The reports we write are the fangs of law en-forcement, the teeth that 'take a bite out of crime.' The pen is a vital tool in our profession, as essential as the gun or the baton."

The Importance of Field Notes

Effective field notes are the basis for all manner of reports and for further investigation of cases and incidents. They should be taken as soon as possible after the incident and should be contained in some sort of notebook. Most police officers prefer loose-leaf notebooks because they are easily organized, and notes can be removed and used as needed for writing reports or for testifying from in court.

Effective field notes are:

- *Accurate*
- *Brief*
- *Clear*
- *Complete*

The ABCs of effective field notes are accuracy, brevity, clarity, and completeness. Accuracy is assured by repeating information back, spelling names, verifying numbers, and so on. Brevity is accomplished by omitting the articles *a, an,* and *the;* by omitting all other unnecessary words, and by using common abbreviations. Be careful with abbreviations, however, as they are often misunderstood. For example, to most people in the 1990s, P.C. refers to a personal computer. To most police officers, however, it refers to probable cause or penal code. Context often helps make the meaning obvious. Abbreviations commonly used in field notes are summarized in Table 4.1.

Clarity includes legibility. Notes that cannot be deciphered a few weeks later because of sloppy handwriting are worthless. A clear picture of what happened during an incident or at a crime scene depends on careful, complete notes. The notes should contain answers to six basic questions: who, what, where, when, why, and how. This is as true of misdemeanors as of felonies. Prosecutors contend that many police officers suffer from the **felony syndrome;** that is, they obtain complete information only on felony cases, deeming these to be "real" cases. Misdemeanors are given much less time or attention. To the people involved, however, every incident or crime is important. Further, many more civil suits against police officers and departments arise from misdemeanor cases than from felony cases. Stokes et al. (1991, p. 5) offer the following notetaking tips:

Use a notebook which is easy to carry around (3 ¾" × 6 ¾" is a good size). A loose-leaf notebook is best because it is easy to organize, you can remove and add pages, and it looks more professional in court. Keep it full of blank paper and well-organized. You may want to use index tabs to separate

TABLE 4.1
Abbreviations Commonly Used in Law Enforcement Notes

Abbreviation	Term	Abbreviation	Term
A&A	Assisted and advised	Memo	Memorandum
AKA	Also known as (alias)	M.O.	Modus operandi
A/O	Arresting officer	NATB	National Automobile Theft Bureau
APB	All points bulletin		
Arr.	Arrest	N/B	Northbound
Asst.	Assistant	NCIC	National Crime Information Center
Att.	Attempt		
BAC	Blood alcohol content	NFD	No further description
		NMN	No middle name
Capt.	Captain		
CBA	Cleared by arrest	OID	Operation identification
CJRS	Criminal justice reporting system	P.C.	Penal code
		PIN	Permanent identification number
Co.	County		
Comp.	Complainant		
		Rec'd	Received
Def.	Defendant	R/F	Right front
Dept.	Department	R/O	Reporting officer
Dist.	District	ROA	Referred to other agency
DMV	Department of Motor Vehicles	R/R	Right rear
DOA	Dead on arrival	S/B	Southbound
DOB	Date of birth	Sgt.	Sergeant
DOT	Direction of travel	Subj.	Subject
DUI	Driving under the influence of alcohol	Susp.	Suspect
		S/w	Station wagon
DWI	Driving while under the influence of alcohol	UCR	Uniform Crime Reports
		UTL	Unable to locate
E/B	Eastbound	V.	Victim
GOA	Gone on arrival	Vict.	Victim
		VIN	Vehicle identification number
Hdqtrs.	Headquarters		
HWY	Highway	Viol.	Violation
I.D.	Identification	W&R	Warned and released
Inf.	Informant	W/B	Westbound
Insp.	Inspector	Wit.	Witness
Juv.	Juvenile	WFA*	White female adult
		WFJ*	White female juvenile
L/F	Left front	WMA*	White male adult
Lic.	License	WMJ*	White male juvenile
L/R	Left rear		
Lt.	Lieutenant	2drHT	Two-door hardtop

*The "W" indicates the race. It is also appropriate to substitute "B" for Black,
"O" for Oriental, "H" for Hispanic, "I" for Indian.

Source: Adapted from *For the Record: Report Writing in Law Enforcement,* 3d ed, Kären M.
Hess and Henry M. Wrobleski, 1991, p. 159. Reprinted with permission of Innovative
Systems, Inc., Shelter Cove, Calif.

*sections: offense reports, follow-up, arrests, wanted and missing persons,
stolen cars, and so on. Remove the notes when they've served their purpose
and file them by case number.*

*Write legibly. Other people may rely on your notes in investigating the case.
And you don't want to waste time later on trying to figure out what you've
written.*

Field notes are the basis for incident reports. Officers' listening skills are also critical.

Identify the notes with your name, the date, and the case number. You may work on several different cases in any one day. It is important to identify what notes belong to what case. Do this on each page of notes.

Record all relevant facts as you get them. Don't wait until later to write down information; you may forget some important details. Obviously, you won't write down everything that is said, but you should write down anything which might be important. A good rule of thumb is; When in doubt, write it down.

Check spelling, numbers, and dates as you record them. Accuracy requires that you verify all spelling, numbers, and dates as they are recorded. This can be done simply by repeating them aloud as you write them down and getting verification from the subject.

Use freehand sketches if the situation calls for it. Sketches can help to clarify a scene or a situation. They can also aid your memory as you are writing your report.

Omit words such as a, an, *and* the, *and use common abbreviations, but do not devise your own shorthand. To take notes rapidly, it is necessary to omit some words and to use abbreviations. You should not devise your own*

Field notes provide the basis for reports. Without good notes, officers cannot effectively perform one of their most important tasks, writing reports.

Written Reports

Police officers write many kinds of reports, including incident reports, continuation or supplemental reports, arrest reports, property and inventory reports, vehicle reports, missing-persons reports, bias-motived crime reports, police pursuit reports, and accident reports. Police reports serve many important purposes.

Reports are used to:

- *Permanently record facts.*
- *Provide details of a criminal incident to be used in a follow-up investigation.*
- *Provide a basis for prosecution.*
- *Provide data for federal and state crime reporting systems.*
- *Document the past and plan for future services.*

It has been frequently said that a good report is more important than a good arrest. Cases can be made or lost on the officer's report alone. In addition, officers are often judged by their reports. A shoddy report makes the reader question the officer's intelligence, education, or competence—or perhaps all three.

Unfortunately, many police reports are extremely poor. According to Rutledge (1986, pp. 19–21), former police officer and currently a public prosecutor:

It's not enough for you to be good at apprehending criminals—you've also got to be good at helping me with my job of convicting them, by giving me a report I can use against the guy you've busted, instead of the other way around.

You can't take much satisfaction in arresting criminals if you can't get a complaint filed, or make the right charges stick, just because you're no good at writing a report. Like it or not, as long as you're a cop, you're going to be a writer. And no matter how good you are in the field, you're not going anywhere if too many of your arrests wind up getting thrown out by the D.A. or the jury.

Got the picture by now? Writing reports is a crucial part of your job. And the problem is, the way we've always done it has created a lot of unnecessary problems—for you, for me, and for the community we work for.

In discussing problems with police reports, Dacy (1991, pp. 35, 64) suggests:

The main failing of most police reports is that they sound like police reports. They are coldly clinical; they often are clouded with pompous police jargon;

A written record is made of all official actions taken. Many departments use pre-printed forms for this purpose.

and to the layman, they are confusing. Worse, they may not include all of the elements of the offense charged. They may be inaccurate, incomplete, vague, and opinionated.

The most common problems in police reports include the following:

- Illegibility.
- Unfamiliar abbreviations.
- Confusing or unclear sentences.
- Missing information, such as elements of the crime.
- Missing work addresses and phone numbers.
- Extreme wordiness and overuse of police jargon.
- Written over letters or numbers.
- Missing or incomplete witnesses' names and addresses.
- Use of assumptions.

Pomerenke (1991, p. 39) offers the following example of a typical police report:

R/P informed R/O that VI found apt. entered. A/O and S/O assisted R/O at scene. COMPL/VI(w/f 25yoa 8/15/1945 dob) was taken to Mercy Hosp. TOT was 1135 hrs. VI's veh was transported by TCR.

She suggests: "No other profession uses so much jargon and so many acronyms in reports that must be read by people outside the profession. . . . Many readers, frustrated and confused, ultimately conclude that law enforcement reports are incomprehensible."

Rutledge (p. 150) gives another example of how police reports are typically written:

On the above date and time, Reporting Officer responded to the referenced location in regards to an area check. It should be noted that upon pulling adjacent to the south boundary fence of Lincoln Elementary School, which is situated at the above-described location, Reporting Officer observed two male subjects, later identified as Suspects No. 1 and No. 2, to be emerging from the heavy dense fog which had blanketed much of the city on this particular night and time.

The preceding report is certainly not very easy to follow. The constant references to information contained elsewhere, *above, referenced, above-described,* the extremely long second sentence, and the use of the third person, *Reporting Officer,* are not considered reader-friendly writing.

Reader-friendly writing *avoids police jargon and communicates in plain, simple language. It is written as it would be spoken, and it considers its audience.*

Readability

Effective police reports are *readable.* They allow the reader to concentrate on what happened rather than on figuring out what the writer is saying. According to Beckley (1984, p. 19), "People who have studied the readability of various pieces of writing agree that two things are vital. One is the length of the sentences. The other is the length and familiarity of the words."

Readability *results from two factors: using short sentences and short, familiar words.*

This does *not* mean that writing will end up sounding like, "Dick sees Jane." It does mean rewriting a sentence such as the following (Rutledge, 1986, p. 169): "It should be noted that a male white juvenile subject, identified as subject Dick, in fact visually observes a female white juvenile subject, identified as subject Jane." Rutledge says he'd prefer "Dick sees Jane" anyday. So would most readers. And that's who reports are written for.

The Audience

A basic premise of effective writing is that it is reader-based. However, as noted by Beckley (1984, p. 7): "Written English has a strong tendency to serve the ego of the writer rather than the interests of the reader." All too frequently, writers try to *impress* their readers rather than to *express* their ideas clearly. They equate big words and long sentences with big brains and extensive education. WRONG. Reader-based writing avoids the tendency to impress.

Dacy (1991) identifies four different audiences for whom police reports are written: the supervisor, investigators assigned to the case, the district attorney, and jurors.

The audience for police reports includes other officers, supervisors, other professionals within the criminal justice system, and laypeople such as insurance investigators and social workers.

Miller and Pomerenke (1989, p. 67) identify three audiences for police reports: "horizontal, vertical, and external." The **horizontal audience** is fellow officers on the same level in the organization and holding similar positions. The **vertical audience** is officers higher up in the agency who use the report as a basis for further action or for decision making. This includes supervisors who approve each report and detectives who may act on the report.

The **external audience** includes "the news media as well as insurance companies, service agencies, judges, juries, lawyers, and the interested public" (p. 68). It can also include coroners, parole officers, child welfare agencies, and social workers. As noted by Miller and Pomerenke (p. 68), "The external audience can judge an entire organization on the basis of a report."

The Content of Effective Reports

Many law enforcement agencies use report forms such as those found in Appendix B, Forms 1, 2 and 3. If the department uses report forms that include boxes and blanks to be filled in, they should *all be filled in,* using *N/A* if information is not applicable or *UNKNOWN* if the information is unknown.

Officers who have hard-to-read handwriting should type the narrative portion of their reports if possible. If this is not possible, they should print them. Information should be organized into chronological paragraphs. Double spacing between paragraphs will help improve readability and clarity.

The basic content of a police report includes an introduction, the body, and a conclusion. The information answers the questions who, what, where, when, why, and how.

The first paragraph should set the stage—time, date, and offense: "On 09-25-92 at 1355 hours I responded to a call of vandalism at Acme Hardware, 123 Main Street. I arrived at 1400 hours and talked to the clerk, JOHN DOE." Most departments are now using the **first person** *I* rather than the **third person** *this officer*. Many departments also capitalize all proper names.

The second paragraph should summarize the information provided during the interview: "DOE said that . . . ." If more than one person is interviewed, the information obtained from each should be in separate paragraphs.

Following the interview information, a paragraph should be written to describe the actions taken by the officer. The final paragraph should bring closure to the report, telling briefly the disposition of the case or incident.

Characteristics of Effective Reports $\blacksquare\blacksquare\blacksquare\blacksquare\blacksquare\blacksquare\blacksquare\blacksquare\blacksquare$ 93

CHAPTER 4
*Reports and Records:
Essential Aids to
Police Operations*

Good reports have the same characteristics as good field notes in addition to several other characteristics.

Effective reports are accurate, brief, clear, complete, legible, objective, grammatically correct, and correctly spelled.

Reports should be checked for **conclusionary language**—that is, nonfactual language that contains assumptions. Among the most common problems here are making statements about what someone can or cannot do. For example, it is a conclusion to write in a DWI report "The man *could not* touch his finger to his nose." The factual report would instead say "The man *did not* touch his finger to his nose." Even clearer, however, would be to say, "The man touched his left cheek rather than his nose."

Another common problem is the phrase "signed by" as in "The check was signed by John Doe." Unless the report writer saw John Doe sign that check, the report should read, "The check was signed John Doe." The little word *by* can get an officer into a lot of trouble on the witness stand.

Other problems arise when officers write about someone's state of mind, for example, saying a person is *nervous, frightened, uncooperative, belligerent*. These are all conclusions on the officer's part. The report should contain facts that lead to the conclusions. For example, rather than saying a person is nervous, describe the person's appearance and actions: "The man began to tremble, he began to perspire heavily, and his voice wavered. He repeatedly glanced over his shoulder at the door."

Rutledge (1986, pp. 110–111) offers the following description of how conclusionary language can pose difficulties for officers and prosecutors:

> *I once got into a drunk driving trial where, according to the arresting officers, the defendant had "repeatedly refused" to take a chemical test. The defendant was named Sanchez, and at trial he insisted, through a court interpreter, that he neither spoke nor understood any English. His defense that he couldn't possibly refuse an English-language request when he couldn't even understand it sold well with the jury, especially after the officer had to admit that he didn't recall exactly how or in what specific words the defendant had "refused" a test. The cop couldn't live with his conclusionary report. Neither could I. The defendant lived with it very comfortably, and he owed his acquittal directly to the same officer who had arrested him. Ironic?*
>
> *We would have been much better off if the cop had never used the conclusionary word "refused," but had instead married the defendant to his own words! The report could have helped the prosecution, instead of the defense, if it had been written like this:*
>
>> *After I explained the need to take a chemical test, SANCHEZ said, in Spanish-accented English, "Screw you, cop . . . I ain't taking no test, man. Why don't you take it yourself?" I told him he had to take a test or his license would be suspended. He said, "I don't need no license to drive*

*man, . . . I know lots of people drive without a license. You ain't scared
me man, and I ain't taking no stupid test . . . I'll beat this thing, too.''*

*See the difference? Not a single conclusion or interpretation. The reader gets
to ''hear'' the same things the writer heard. The officer could have lived with
something like that—the defendant couldn't.*

The same thing goes for these conclusionary interpretations:

- *He denied any involvement in the crime.*
- *She consented to a search of the trunk.*
- *Both waived their rights per Miranda.*
- *He admitted breaking into the car.*
- *He confessed to four more burglaries.*

Table 4.2 illustrates conclusionary language and what should replace it in effective
police reports.

Reports should be written in the **active voice,**—that is, the subject should name
who did the action, for example, ''My partner found the evidence.'' Unfortunately, many reports say instead, ''The evidence was found.'' *Who* found the
evidence is not clear and may not be remembered a few months after the report
was written.

TABLE 4.2
Conclusionary Language and Substitutes

You can't live with these	. . . so use these, instead	You can't live with these	. . . so use these, instead
indicated		angry	
refused		upset	
admitted		nervous	
confessed		excited	
denied		happy	when you're
consented	a verbatim or	unhappy	attributing these to
identified	approximate	intentional	someone else,
waived	quotation	accidental	identify the source
profanity	of what was said	attempted	of your conclusions
threatening		heard	
obscene		saw	
evasive		knew	
unresponsive		thought	
deceptive			
assaulted		matching the	
attacked		description	
accosted		suspicious	
confrontation		furtive	
escalated	a factual account	strange	
struggle ensued	of who did what	abnormal	the reasons for
resisted		typical	your belief that
battered		uncooperative	these apply
intimidated		belligerent	
bullied		combative	
forced		obnoxious	
		abusive	
		exigent	

Source: Adapted from *The New Police Report Manual,* Devallis Rutledge, 1986,
pp. 135–136. Reprinted with permission of Custom Publishing Company, Costa Mesa, Calif.

In addition, reports should use specific, **concrete language** rather than abstract terms. Rather than writing "tall," police officers should write "approximately 6'5"." Being specific does not mean being wordy. Wordy phrases frequently found in police reports include the following:

- square in shape
- red in color
- shrugged his shoulders
- pointed his finger

- month of February
- small in size
- nodded her head
- blinked her eyes

Effective reports are **concise** and to the point. As noted by the IACP (1985, p. 49): "While a report should be complete, it must not ramble and repeat. Completeness and brevity are not mutually exclusive. So long as it answers the five critical questions—who, what, when, where, and how [and a sixth critical question if known—why]—a report can be brief, complete, and accurate."

The report should be read from the perspective of someone who knows nothing about what happened or about police terminology. It should be written this way because it could be read not only by other law enforcement officers and agencies, including supervisors, but also by municipal, county, or state administrators; court personnel; other governmental agencies; members of the media; and even private citizens. Reports should present a clear, complete picture for all such readers.

Effective reports are also written in the past tense and in chronological order. They use verbs rather than nouns when possible, avoid sexist language, and can "stand alone."

It is imperative that report writers stay in the **past tense** because if the case comes to trial several months later, the officer will not know if the statement is still true. For example, visualize an officer who writes in an offense report: "Johnson lives at 123 Main Street and works for the XYZ Company." The defense attorney is likely to ask the officer if Johnson still lives there. The officer probably wouldn't know and would have to say so. The next question would probably be about whether Johnson still works for the XYZ Company and again the officer would have to say, "I don't know." Each time an officer has to say "I don't know," the officer's credibility is weakened. If the sentence in the report had been written in the past tense, the problem would not have happened.

It is also important that narration in an incident report be in **chronological order**— that is, that it start at the beginning and go straight through to the end of what happened, like telling a story. It includes what the writer knows at the time the report is being written. This means that if the writer knows the suspect's name, it should be used the first time the suspect is mentioned even though the suspect was not identified immediately. It is ineffective to say "later identified as Charlie Jones."

Officers' writing should be forceful and authoritative. One way to accomplish this is to use verbs rather than nouns. Do not *conduct an investigation*, rather, *investigate*. Do not *carry on a conversation*, rather, *converse,* or better yet, *talk*.

Effective reports also avoid sexist language. If *Mr.* is used with male names, *Ms.* should be used with female names. Use substitutes for *-man* and *-men* word endings, for example firefighter and police officer. Do not add an *-ess* to designate a woman. For example, Jane Doe is the author (*not* authoress) of a best-selling novel.

Effective reports should be able to "stand alone"—that is, they should make sense without the reader having to refer "above" or elsewhere for information. Rather than writing "On the above date at the above time," simply give the date and time in the narrative portion of the report.

Finally, reports should be carefully proofread to make certain that all names, addresses, phone numbers, and investigative facts are accurate, that the report is punctuated correctly, and that all words are spelled correctly. Don't rely on a spell-check. It cannot catch certain common errors. For example, one police report contained the sentence, "The toe truck was called." Although those reading it found it to be humorous, the officer who wrote it certainly did not.

Taping and Dictating Reports

Some police departments have their officers tape their reports or use a dictating machine. According to Kelly (1990, p. 50), "Dictating and transcribing reports can save patrol time—and money—for your department." Kelly's police department (Fort Collins, Colorado) has used dictating "successfully for over 15 years, generating savings well in excess of $1 million" (p. 49).

Similar impressive results were experienced by the Warwick Police Department in Rhode Island. As noted by Chief Blanchard (1990, p. 53):

The gain in productivity over the first six months of the system's operation [digital dictation system] is dramatic—perhaps even sensational. The key statistic: report preparation that once took a patrol officer roughly 1 hour each shift now takes only 20 minutes, and the detective who once needed approximately 3.5 hours per day for file searches, paper preparation, travel time, etc., can pick up any touch-tone phone and complete the same tasks in about 45 minutes. Between January 2 and July 1, 1989, total man-hours spent preparing reports has been reduced by more than 73 percent. . . .

Equally important is the fact that officers can maintain much higher visibility in the field since they are not compelled to spend so much of their time making out reports.

Computer-Assisted Report Entry

Some police departments are using word processing packages for report writing, and others are going even further and using computer-assisted police report entry systems. One such system, called CARE, leads officers through preformatted screens and questions. According to Lieutenant George (1990, p. 46), CARE coordinator for the St. Louis County Police Department in Missouri, implementation of CARE has accomplished five major goals:

1. Freeing officers to spend more time on patrol by reducing report-writing and notification times. . . . Written police reports that once took up to seven days for processing are now ready in minutes.
2. Improving the quality, accuracy, and timeliness of police reports and management reports by standardizing the collecting of information and creating a centralized on-line data base.

This California Highway Patrol Officer produces highly professional reports. Computes have made report writing much more efficient.

3. Providing citizens and county police officers with a convenient, efficient, round-the-clock police reporting service.
4. Improving the availability and timeliness of police report information by electronically processing, aggregating, distributing, and filing these documents.
5. Improving detective follow-up investigation procedures by providing the investigative officer with complete information in a shorter period of time.

Records

Computerization of records has also been of tremendous help to police operations. According to Sandona (1989, p. 71), the Arcadia Police Department's computerized records management system is used "to not only automate police report indexing operations but also for tracking field interview cards, controlling temporary overnight parking permits, handling case assignments, and providing complete office automation capabilities." Sandona (p. 73) also notes:

> *The computerized records management system provides a tremendous increase in the amount of indexing information available for our use. The system also makes it possible to achieve a vast increase in the quality of the information in terms of its completeness, integrity, accuracy, and security.*

> *The speed of finding information is also greatly increased. We can now search thousands of records in a matter of seconds.*

Leedy (1991, p. 79) describes the computerized records management system used by the St. Petersburg Police Department in Florida: "With our present computer

An Austin, Texas, officer checks for warrants. Records are essential to police operations.

system, we are able to research by name, address, telephone number, offense number, vehicle tag, property number, property description, and serial number.'' He notes that the system ''can find a name mentioned in only one supplement out of 10,000 in seconds. Under the old system we had to read each report to find the person.''

Computerized records systems also make it possible for individual patrol officers equipped with a computer in their vehicles to identify vehicles they are following and to obtain more complete information on individuals they have identified. The immediate availability of such information greatly enhances the officers' safety in the field.

Summary

In addition to verbal communications skills, police officers also need effective writing skills for both field notes and reports. Effective field notes are accurate, brief, clear, and complete.

Reports are used to permanently record facts, to provide details of a criminal incident to be used in a follow-up investigation, to provide a basis for prosecution, to provide data for federal and state crime reporting systems, and to document the past and plan for future services.

The basic content of a police report includes an introduction, the body, and a conclusion. The information included answers the questions who, what, where, when, why, and how. Reports should be reader-friendly, that is, readable and audience focused. Readability results from two factors: using short sentences and short, familiar words.

The audience for police reports includes other officers, supervisors, other professionals within the criminal justice system, and laypeople such as insurance investigators and social workers.

Effective reports are accurate, brief, clear, complete, legible, objective, grammatically correct and correctly spelled. Basic writing principles to be used in police reports include using paragraphs; using the first person and active voice; eliminating conclusionary language; using specific, concrete language; and eliminating wordiness. Effective reports are also written in the past tense and in chronological order. They use verbs, avoid sexist language, and can "stand alone."

Application

It has been brought to your attention, as a first-line supervisor, that some officers are filing their field notes and other officers are destroying them after they have written their report. Opinions differ on whether officers should retain their field notes, but within an individual law enforcement agency, all officers should follow the same procedure.

Instructions   Using the form in Appendix A, write a policy regarding the retention of field notes. The rationale behind the policy should be clear and convincing.

An Exercise in Critical Thinking

Accurate, brief, clear, and complete reports are necessary for follow-up investigations, prosecution, and data for future services. Basic writing principles are essential for the successful administration of justice, since court decisions rest on the accuracy of documents offered as exhibits. Reports need to provide sufficient evidence to find a defendant guilty beyond a reasonable doubt.

On August 4, Leroy Deloch was arrested on an unrelated charge. Before entering the county jail he was pat searched. Next he was booked into the facility. As part of the booking procedure, his clothes and personal property were confiscated. He was given jail clothes and placed in a holding cell for several hours. After that he was photographed, fingerprinted, and questioned.

The final step in the booking procedure was the strip search. Deputy Robert Nielson wrote a report about this procedure. First, Nielson wrote that he made a "visual check of the strip-search room before Deloch entered." Nielson reported that "the room was free of contraband at that time." Next, Nielson wrote that he "brought Deloch into the room and instructed him to begin disrobing." When Nielson asked Deloch to "take off his pants," Deloch sat down on a bench to comply. As Deloch handed Nielson the pants, Nielson saw "him making a whisking motion with his left hand." Nielson wrote that "it appeared that Deloch pushed something off the back of the bench with his left hand." Nielson wrote that "he immediately looked under the bench and discovered three packets of what turned out to be crack/cocaine."

1. Nielson's writing is flawed because
    a. The visual check of the room must specify what was in the room in addition to what was not.

    b. Some reference as to where Deloch got the three packages seems obviously omitted.

    c. An exact description of how Deloch gave Nielson the pants is necessary.

    d. A "whisking motion" is too vague.

    e. Deloch's name must be spelled correctly.

2. Nielson's writing can be improved by:

    a. Using shorter words and phrases that will be familiar to a jury.

    b. Giving more specific information such as the exact amount of cocaine.

    c. Writing more forcefully and authoritatively to be more convincing.

    d. Adding more descriptive words and phrases to give a more vivid report.

    e. Changing tense to write only in the past tense.

Discussion Questions

1. What are the ABCs of effective field notes?
2. What are the value of field notes?
3. How would you rectify a situation where an officer is having problems with writing incident reports?
4. What are some positive outcomes of good incident reports?
5. What would be the equivalent of nonverbal communication in a written report?
6. On a scale of one to ten, with ten being the most efficient, how do you rate yourself as a writer? What would you have to do to reach ten?
7. When you are making an incident report, is it better to dictate it to a secretary, write the report out in long-hand, or type the report yourself? What are the advantages and disadvantages of each?

Definitions

Can you define these terms?

active voice	first person
chronological order	horizontal audience
concise	past tense
conclusionary language	readability
concrete language	reader-friendly writing
external audience	third person
felony syndrome	vertical audience

References

Beckley, John L. *The Power of Little Words*. Fairfield, N.J.: The Economics Press, 1984.

Blanchard, Wesley. "Digital Dictation a Boon for Warwick." *The Police Chief* (March 1990): 53.

Dacy, Joe II. "Taming the Paper Tiger." *Police* (January 1991): 34–35, 64–68.

George, Dennis. "Computer-Assisted Report Entry: Toward a Paperless Police Department." *The Police Chief* (March 1990): 46–47.

Hess, Kären M. and Wrobleski, Henry M. *For the Record: Report Writing in Law Enforce-ment.* 3d ed. Shelter Cove, Calif.: Innovative Systems, 1991.

International Association of Chiefs of Police. *Police Supervision.* Arlington, Vir.: IACP, 1985.

Kelly, Patrick T. "Increasing Productivity by Taping Reports." *The Police Chief* (March 1990): 49–50.

Leedy, Leonard W. III. "ACISS." *Law and Order* (June 1991): 75–79.

Miller, Myron and Pomerenke, Paula. "Police Reports Must Be Reader Based." *Law and Order* (September 1989): 66–69.

Pomerenke, Paula J. "Jargon Dangers in Law Enforcement." *Law and Order* (March 1991): 39

Rutledge, Devallis. *The New Police Report Manual.* Costa Mesa, Calif.: Custom Publishing, 1986.

Sandona, Rick. "Arcadia Police Find a Cost-Effective Way to Computerize Records Man-agement System." *Law and Order* (August 1989): 71–74.

Stokes, Floyd T., Hess, Kären M., and Wrobleski, Henry M. *Outline Guide for Writing Law Enforcement Reports.* Shelter Cove, Calif.: Innovative Systems, 1991.

OPERATIONAL SKILLS: PERFORMING WITHIN THE LAW

CHAPTER **5**

INTRODUCTION

The basic skills discussed in this chapter—stopping and frisking, arresting, and searching—may be needed in a variety of situations. Not only are these skills used often, they are strictly governed by law and usually by department policies and procedures as well.

Police officers are expected to be familiar with the basic rules of criminal procedure. It is not the intent of this text to go into the details of any of these basic rules but rather to remind the reader of their critical importance in police operations. Chapter 3 discussed the importance of obtaining information legally. This chapter focuses on making legal arrests and searches as well as on conducting legal undercover operations.

Law enforcement officers must maintain a balance between "freedom to" and "freedom from."

In a democracy such as ours, law enforcement has the awesome responsibility of assuring that citizens have freedom *to* live, remain free, pursue happiness, and to have due process of the law. Law enforcement has also been charged with protecting society—that is, giving citizens freedom *from* crime and violence as well as *from* unreasonable search and seizure by law enforcement. In other words, police officers must strike a balance not only between rights of individuals and those of our country but also between the rights of law-abiding citizens and criminals. They must *act* to fulfill their responsibilities, but always within the constraints

Do You Know

- What sort of balance between freedom and order police officers must maintain?
- What two amendments restrict arrests and searches?
- What a stop and frisk involves?
- What constitutes an arrest?
- When officers may arrest someone?
- What probable cause is?
- Why understanding and making legal arrests are critical?
- How substantive and procedural criminal law differ?
- How to arrest someone?
- What the Exclusionary Rule is and its relevance to police operations?
- How much force can be used in making an arrest?
- When handcuffs should be used in conjunction with an arrest?
- When a search can be conducted?
- How a search conducted with a warrant is limited?
- When a search warrant is *not* needed?
- How to search a person? A building?
- When and where to expect booby traps?
- When undercover assignments might be necessary?
- What entrapment is and how it can be avoided?

of the law. Guarantees against unlawful arrests and searches are found in the Fourth and Fifth Amendments of our Constitution.

The Fourth and Fifth Amendments to the Constitution restrict arrests and searches.

The Fourth Amendment provides that:

The right of the people to be secure in their persons, houses, papers and effects, against unreasonable searches and seizures, shall not be violated, and no warrants shall issue but upon probable cause, supported by oath or affirmation, and particularly describing the place to be searched, and the persons or things to be seized.

The Fourth Amendment protects the fundamental right to privacy which lies at its core. Its guarantees extend to arrest warrants as well as to search warrants. It does *not*, however, prohibit arrests or searches without a warrant.

The Fifth Amendment provides that no person shall be "deprived of life, liberty, or property without due process of law." Both the Fourth and Fifth Amendments should be kept in mind throughout this text, and, indeed, throughout your career.

Stop and Frisk

Law enforcement officers are expected to stop and question people acting suspiciously. Such an activity is *not* an arrest, so the Miranda warning need not be given. If officers stop someone for questioning (a field inquiry) and the officers believe the person may be armed, the officers can also pat down their outer clothing for weapons. This action *is* considered a search.

A **stop and frisk situation** *is one in which law enforcement officers:*

- *Briefly detain a suspicious person for questioning (this is* not *an arrest),*
- *And if officers reasonably suspect the person to be armed, are allowed to pat the person's outer clothing (this* is *a limited search for weapons).*

The right to stop and frisk suspicious people was established in the landmark case of *Terry v. Ohio* (1968). The *stop* in a stop and frisk must be based on a reasonable suspicion that the person stopped is about to be or is actually engaged in criminal activity. Among the most common reasons for a stop are the following:

- The person doesn't "fit" the time or place.
- The person is acting strangely.
- The person is known to associate with criminals.
- The person is loitering.
- The person runs away.
- The person is present at a crime scene.
- The area is a high-crime area.

A Minnesota State Trooper conducting a stop and frisk. The patdown must be restricted to a protective search for weapons.

The **stop** may be all that occurs, it may lead to a **patdown,** or it may progress to an arrest, depending on the information received.

The **frisk** in a stop and frisk, conducted for the officers' safety, must also be based on a reasonable suspicion that the person is armed. Perry (1984, p. 45) suggests considering the following points when deciding to conduct a patdown or frisk:

1. The nature of the suspected criminal activity, and whether a weapon would be used.
2. Your situation—are you alone, or has assistance arrived?
3. The number of subjects and their emotional and physical state (angry, fighting, intoxicated, etc.).
4. The time of day and geographical surroundings.
5. Prior knowledge of the subject's reputation and/or any police record he may have that you have knowledge of.
6. The sex of the subject or subjects encountered.
7. The behavior and ability of the subjects.
8. The circumstances as they present themselves to you at the time and as you evaluate them.

The frisk cannot extend to a search for evidence. If, however, the stop turns into an arrest, then a more thorough search can be conducted, as discussed later in this chapter.

Although stop and frisk falls far short of an actual arrest and a full-blown search, it is *not* to be taken lightly. As the Court said in the *Terry* decision:

It is simply fantastic to urge that such a procedure [stop and frisk], performed in public by a police officer, while the citizen stands helpless, perhaps facing a wall with his hands raised, is a "petty indignity."

And, as noted, the stop might escalate into an arrest, depending on the specific circumstances.

Legal Arrests

Making an arrest is one of the most important and extreme steps law enforcement officers take in their daily duties. The frequency of its occurrence, the nonserious nature of many offenses for which arrests are made, the poor character of many people subjected to it and their lower socioeconomic status, must never lull officers into forgetting the lofty place arrest holds in our law. The police responsibility in arrests is clearly described by Ferdico (1985, p. 670):

> *The power of arrest is the most important power that law enforcement officers possess. It enables them to deprive a person of the freedom to carry out daily personal and business affairs, and it initiates against a person the process of criminal justice, which may ultimately result in that person being fined or imprisoned. Since an arrest has a potentially great detrimental effect upon a person's life, the law provides severe limitations and restrictions on the law enforcement officer's exercise of the power of arrest.*

Arrest Defined

The common meaning of *arrest* is simply "to stop." In a cardiac arrest, for example, the heart stops beating. Its meaning in the context of law enforcement is also generally known, that is, to seize and hold in jail or prison. The legal definition of *arrest* is somewhat narrower, as stated in Oran's *Law Dictionary for Nonlawyers* (1985, p. 26):

An **arrest** *is "the official taking of a person to answer criminal charges. This involves at least temporarily depriving the person of liberty and may involve the use of force."*

When Arrests Can Be Made

An arrest can legally be made:

- *With an arrest warrant.*
- *Without an arrest warrant:*
  - *a. When any offense (felony or misdemeanor) is committed in an officer's presence.*
  - *b. When officers have probable cause to believe a person has committed a felony and no time is available to obtain a warrant.*

The Fourth Amendment stresses the importance of having an arrest warrant when making an arrest (or conducting a search). The courts have, nonetheless, recognized other circumstances in which an arrest can be legally made.

In the presence does not refer to proximity, but rather to the officer's senses — that is, what the person making the arrest perceives through his or her senses.

Basic to lawful arrests is the concept of *probable cause*. Oran (1985, pp. 239–240) explains it this way:

Probable cause. *The fact that it is more likely than not that a crime has been committed by the person whom a law enforcement officer seeks to arrest. An officer's* probable cause *to conduct an arrest depends on what the officer knew* before *taking action.*

An often-quoted definition of probable cause is from *Brinegar v. United States* (1949):

Probable cause exists where the facts and circumstances within the officers' knowledge, and of which they had reasonably trustworthy information, are sufficient in themselves to warrant a man of reasonable caution in the belief that an offense has been or is being committed.

The law's ideal is for arrests to be made under an arrest warrant where a neutral magistrate or judge stands between the person to be arrested and the arresting officer and calmly determines that probable cause exists for the arrest. But the law also recognizes that the practical necessities of keeping the public peace frequently demand that law enforcement officers make arrests without a warrant. Despite this admitted necessity, the courts will not relax the fundamental requirement of probable cause for arrest. Without this requirement, law-abiding citizens might be left to the mercy of police officers' whims. The courts have made it clear that the requirements of arrest without a warrant are as stringent as those where warrants are obtained.

Under the common law of England, peace officers were authorized to arrest without a warrant both felons and people reasonably suspected of being felons. This was not only a right, it was also a duty. If they neglected it, officers could be punished.

Today, when officers arrest without a warrant in a felony, the courts assume the officers are acting in good faith. But subjective good faith alone is not enough. Officers must also meet the objective test of probable cause by establishing that the arrest was made on reasonable grounds.

No precise formula for determining probable cause exists that can be applied to every case. Probable cause for arrest must be determined from the individual facts and circumstances of each case. Officers must have a reasonable ground for belief of guilt before action is taken. Probable cause, according to Harr and Hess (1990, pp. 128–129) can be either observational (what the officer sees) or informational (what the officer is told).

Observational probable cause includes suspicious conduct, being high on drugs, associating with known criminals, the existence of a criminal record, running away, presence in an unusual place or at an unusual time, presence in a high-crime area, presence at a crime scene, failure to answer questions, failure to provide identification, providing false information, and physical evidence. The more factors present, the greater is the probable cause.

Informational probable cause consists of communications from official sources such as wanted posters, statements from victims, and information from informants.

The Importance of Legal Arrests

Americans treasure their freedom. President Carter once observed: ''America did not invent human rights. In a very real sense, it is the other way around. Human rights invented America.'' Immigrants flooded to America for the freedom it offered. Freedom has historically always figured prominently:

Of great importance to the public is the preservation of this personal liberty: for if once it were left in the power of any, the highest, magistrate to imprison arbitrarily whenever he or his officers thought proper . . . , there would soon be an end to all other rights and immunities.—Blackstone, Commentaries, Book 1, Chapter 1.

Sir William Blackstone was the first professor of English law at Oxford University in 1758. His Oxford lectures were collected, polished, and published in four monumental volumes that set forth all the rules and regulations decreed by the English kings. Blackstone divided these laws into four areas: rights of persons, rights of property, private wrongs (torts), and public wrongs (crimes). His Commentaries on the Laws of England explained in simple language the common law of England up to that time.

Because arrests deprive individuals of their freedom, it is crucial that law enforcement officers are understanding, humane, and skilled at making *lawful* arrests.

Understanding, humanism, and skill in making arrests is critical because:

- *Fundamental rights to personal liberty and privacy are involved.*
- *The law of arrest is strict and technical.*
- *Arrest is often the first step in criminal proceedings.*
- *Illegal arrests may taint crucial evidence of guilt.*
- *Police performance quality is judged by arrests.*
- *Arrests may lead to civil suits and criminal prosecution of officers.*
- *Arrests may endanger officers' lives.*

An arrest that may seem particularly brutal and inhumane can bring about immediate and violent community reaction as in the 1965 Watts riot.

Arrests Involve the Fundamental Rights to Personal Liberty and Privacy.

In every arrest, the right to personal liberty is involved. This is the fundamental right to come and go or stay when or where one may choose—the so-called right to freedom of locomotion. This right is embodied in the common law of England and is protected by our state constitutions and the U.S. Constitution.

Although the essential nature of the right to personal liberty cannot be denied, it is, nevertheless, not absolute. It is limited by the fact that people do not live in a vacuum, isolated from others. Their survival demands that they live and work in a society whose well-being is also vital. Therefore, when people commit offenses against society's law, their right to personal liberty can be restrained for the common good. In other words, they can be arrested, and their arrest is justified if made according to due process of law. The power of arrest is inherent in the right of society to defend itself. From the beginning, it has been recognized that offenders may be arrested on a criminal charge and be detained for trial even though they may ultimately be proved innocent of wrongdoing.

The law of arrest represents an effort to achieve a balance between the right of a person in a free society to enjoy liberty, and the right of society to protect itself against crime and criminals. Thus, law considers at one and the same time the rights of individual citizens and those of the community.

The Law of Arrest is Strict and Technical.

It severely limits the power of apprehension. It was formulated in England during the seventeenth and eighteenth centuries when conditions were far different from today. The professional police officer was unknown, and the fate of those arrested for crimes was fraught with danger.

In that era, people arrested on serious charges were rarely granted bail. Prisoners awaited court action in jails that were pestholes of disease and corruption and where the dreaded jail fever was common. They were kept in irons for the jailers' safety. If they escaped from the easily breached lockups, their wardens were held personally responsible. Because the jails were run for profit and fees were charged for almost every incident of prison life, a poor person was in desperate straits.

This state of affairs led to the development of arrest laws that greatly restricted the right to arrest. The courts made it clear that arrests were to be made only on the basis of a warrant issued by a magistrate. The courts wanted a judicial official to stand between the people being arrested and those doing the arresting. The courts recognized the need to arrest without a warrant, but they spelled out the conditions under which such arrests could be made.

For example, they clearly distinguished between arresting without a warrant for a serious felony and arresting without a warrant for a minor misdemeanor. Arrest for a misdemeanor without a warrant was limited to offenses committed in the arresting person's presence. Arrest for a felony without a warrant was not so limited. Obviously, there was less justification for arresting people without a court order for minor offenses and subjecting them to the attendant dangers than for serious offenses which affected the whole community.

The ironclad law of arrest has survived the conditions that brought it about. Modern statutes and decisions have remedied some technicalities of former times, but the old common law still controls many areas of arrest despite the arrival of professional police officers and vastly improved detention facilities and procedures. Legislatures and judges have hesitated to change concepts and procedures where the rights to personal liberty and privacy loom so large.

Arrest Is Often the Frst Step in Criminal Proceedings. In the community's timeless attempt to keep the public peace through its criminal law, arrest by police officers is often the first step in criminal proceedings against wrongdoers. The vital need to maintain law and order frequently requires that officers make arrests without warrants. Despite the law's ideal that a warrant be issued by a magistrate or court before an arrest, there is often no time in actual practice to apply for a warrant. The arrest must be made "now or never."

Because police officers' duty on many occasions demands that they arrest people without the protection of a warrant, officers must know both the substantive and procedural criminal law of their jurisdiction.

Substantive law *deals with content or* what *behaviors are considered crimes.* ***Procedural law*** *deals with process or* how *the law is applied.*

Substantive law defines the elements of crimes and the punishments for each crime. For example, premeditation is an element in first degree murder and the punishment if convicted might be life imprisonment or even death. Crimes and their punishments are decided by elected bodies such as Congress and state legislatures.

Procedural law governs how the law is enforced and is of perhaps greater importance to law enforcement officers than substantive law. As noted by Calvi and Coleman (1989, pp. 7–8):

> *Terms like* kangaroo court *and* railroading *a defendant indicate that our system of law is also concerned about fundamental fairness. Consequently, we guarantee everyone, especially those charged with criminal offenses,* ***due process of law.*** *We make this guarantee because our system of constitutional government is based upon the idea that there are limits to governmental power and that even those in authority must adhere to the rule of law. We wish to prevent government from acting toward us in an arbitrary fashion, and so we believe that even a person charged with the most heinous crime is entitled to "have his day in court" governed by a set of preordained rules of fairness. Thus, we guarantee the accused the right to remain silent before his accusers, the right to a trial by jury, and the right to counsel. Even after conviction, the Constitution protects the condemned person from cruel and unusual punishment.*

Procedural law tends to be more controversial than substantive law. Although some laws are controversial (for example, those governing "victimless crimes" such as prostitution, gambling, and use of marijuana), other laws such as whether criminals should "get off" because of a technicality are even more controversial. It seems to many people that the criminals have all the rights and that the rights of victims are ignored. This is in large part because, as noted by Calvi and Coleman (pp. 7–8), the framers of our Constitution:

> *. . . had firsthand experience with a tyrannical government and believed that, in the long run, it was better to risk letting the guilty go free than to risk creating an arbitrary and tyrannical government. Even though most citizens*

will never need the protection of the Bill of Rights, it is also true that it is better to have them and not need them than to need them and not have them. Understanding this fact does not necessarily make it acceptable to many people, however, and so the debate over how much "process" is due to those accused of crime will undoubtedly continue.

111
CHAPTER 5
*Operational Skills:
Performing Within
the Law*

Laws concerning crimes and arrest are complicated, and officers are allowed no margin of error in deciding whether the conduct, when not committed in the officers' presence, constitutes a felony and thus justifies arrest without a warrant. At one time, determining whether an offense was a felony or a misdemeanor was not difficult. The inherent seriousness or nonseriousness of the offense served as the guide. But this is no longer true. Legislatures have created felonies which are not inherently serious and misdemeanors which are. Officers must know the law.

The law will justify officers' actions if they proceed on the basis of probable cause or reasonable grounds. Yet, when they arrest without a warrant, they are charged with the responsibility of exercising good judgment in hectic, fluid situations where mistakes are bound to occur.

Illegal Arrests May Taint Crucial Evidence of Guilt.   Although illegal arrests will not immunize defendants against criminal prosecution, they may lead to the inadmissibility of crucial evidence of guilt. Physical evidence obtained by search and seizure incident to an illegal arrest, for example, recovered stolen property or burglary tools, will be considered tainted and therefore suppressed under the Exclusionary Rule.

---

*The **Exclusionary Rule** established that the courts cannot accept evidence obtained in illegal searches and seizures, regardless of how relevant the evidence is to the case (Weeks v. United States, 1914).*

Likewise, verbal evidence, such as incriminating statements obtained in the immediate aftermath of an illegal arrest, may be barred from the jury's consideration.

If officers are not aware that they are violating someone's constitutional rights, they are said to be acting in **good faith,** and the Exclusionary Rule may not apply. According to Harr and Hess (1990, p. 243):

The good-faith exception often comes into play when officers are executing arrest or search warrants. If such warrants are later found to be invalid, the evidence obtained while executing the warrants is still admissible because the officers were acting in "good faith."

The Quality of Police Performance Is Judged by Arrests.   The community's judgment of the quality of its police department frequently turns on the actions of officers in the more visible, dramatic areas of responsibility such as apprehending felons. The public pays much less attention to officers' performance in the less colorful fields of police endeavor even though extensive time and effort are necessarily required, for example, directing traffic or conducting daily patrol operations.

Arrests May Result in Civil Suits or Criminal Prosecutions.   An arrest may lead to a civil suit against the officers in state court for false arrest. It may also lead to a civil suit for deprivation of civil rights in federal court under an old post–Civil War federal statute, now codified as 42 U.S.C.A. § 1983. The hazard of lawsuits against police officers is discussed in detail in Chapter 6.

An arrest may also lead to a criminal prosecution against the officers for assault and battery on the grounds that an inordinate amount of force was used or to a criminal charge in federal court for deprivation of civil rights. The courts are conscious of the problems of law enforcement officers in this phase of their duty. For example, in the federal case of *Kozlowski v. Ferrara* (1954) the judge said:

> *The courts should bend every effort to insure the fearless and effective administration of the law by protecting their enforcement officers from vindictive and retaliatory damage suits. . . . Otherwise, as Judge L. Hand cautioned . . . to submit officials "to the burden of a trial and to the inevitable danger of its outcome, would dampen the ardor of all but the most resolute, or the most irresponsible, in the unflinching discharge of their duties."*

As noted by Allard (1991, p. 71): "Courts have traditionally recognized a 'bright line' between officer safety and a citizen's Fourth Amendment rights with officer safety afforded the judicial weight." This is in large part due to the danger inherent in making arrests.

Arrest is Extremely Dangerous and Sometimes Life-Threatening for Police Officers.   Arrests put police officers in jeopardy every time they take this drastic step. The peril exists not only with hardened criminals where possible violence is an obvious, ever-present concern, but also with people who don't have criminal records. Ordinary people often lose all sense of emotional and mental balance when arrested. They can react to their loss of freedom and the danger to their reputation in unexpected ways and may resist fiercely rather than submit to the command of the apprehending officers. Arrest is the antithesis of personal liberty, and people will instinctively give up almost everything else to preserve it. According to Connor (1989, p. 98): "At least 30 percent of these assaults [on police officers] occurred during the actual process of arrest."

Procedures for Making Legal Arrests ▰▰▰▰▰▰▰

The actual arrest is usually made by an officer stating to a person, "You are under arrest for. . . ." The person being arrested should be told clearly—not in police jargon or legalese—the reason for the arrest. Officers should always be on guard when making arrests. As noted, people can react violently to being arrested, even individuals who appear to be meek and incapable of violence.

Depending on the circumstances, the person may first be handcuffed for the officers' safety. The arrested person should be searched for weapons and destructible evidence, as discussed later in this chapter. If the arrested person is to be questioned, the Miranda warning must be given before any questions are asked.

In a typical arrest situation officers should:

- *Announce the arrest and the reason for it.*
- *Handcuff the person if warranted.*
- *Search the person arrested for weapons and evidence.*
- *Give the Miranda warning if questions are to be asked.*

As noted by Perry (1984, p. 51):

There are two types of arrests, easy and difficult. The difficult type [makes the] arrest a fight with scuffling, face punching, screaming, and violence. There are many officers who can single-handedly take a simple, insignificant arrest and turn it into a full-blown riot. Far too often they are overaggressive, insulting, badge heavy, or arrogant.

The Use of Force in Making an Arrest

If the person being arrested offers no resistance, *no* force should be used in making the arrest.

Guidelines for use of force when making an arrest:

- *No resistance—no force.*
- *Resistance—use only as much force as necessary to overcome resistance.*
- *Threat to officer's life—use deadly force.*

Figure 5.1 presents a continuum for the use of force, that is, the escalation from nonexistent force to extraordinary force. Connor (1991, p. 30) suggests that the "critical concern for safety must focus beyond the actor (suspect) and more directly upon the actions of the individual."

The Use of Handcuffs in Making an Arrest

Many law enforcement agencies have a policy stating: "In the interest of officer safety, all persons arrested and transported shall be handcuffed." This policy has been called the **mere handcuff rule.** According to Allard (1991, p. 69): "A 'mere handcuff' rule conflicts with the Fourth Amendment's 'objective reasonableness' standard for use of force as recently expressed by the U.S. Supreme Court in *Graham v. Connor.*" Handcuffing *is* a form of force. Allard (pp. 69–70) notes:

Police officers are trained and required to employ reasonable apprehension techniques and exhaust every reasonable means of apprehension before resorting to the use of force of any kind. The use of force must be necessary and in response to resistance offered. . . .

FIGURE 5.1
A Continuum in the Use of Force
Source: Adapted from "Use of Force Continuum: Phase II," by Greg Connor, *Law and Order* (March 1991): 30. (Reprinted with permission of *Law and Order Magazine*.)

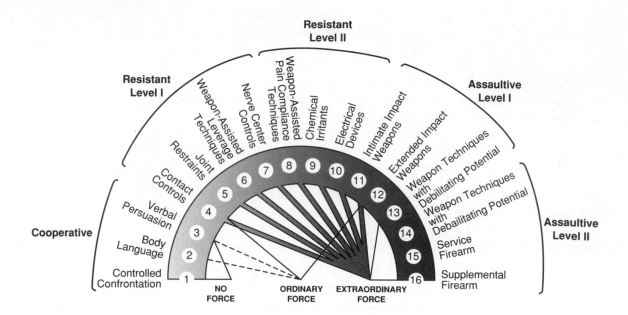

Handcuffing procedures must be judged from the perspective of the reasonable officer on the scene, rather than motivated by a predetermined use of force mandated in a policy statement.

Whether an arrested person should automatically be handcuffed while being transported is controversial. Officer discretion may be advisable.

To automatically handcuff every suspect arrested may leave the officer and the department open to a charge of objectively unreasonable handcuffing and a lawsuit. Discretion might be used with the very young, the very elderly, and with the physically disabled, always remembering, however, that even such individuals can pose a threat to officers' safety.

In some instances, handcuffing is vital to protecting an officer's life. As noted by Connor (1989, p. 98): "Arrest environments are varied and at times may lend themselves to potential violence." He notes that 84 percent of assaults against police officers during an arrest situation are committed by the suspect using feet, hands, and fists.

Using Forcible Entry to Arrest

The right of law enforcement officers to use force to enter a building to make an arrest is almost 400 years old:

In all cases where the King is a party, the Sheriff if the doors be not open may break the party's house, either to arrest him, or do other execution of the King's process, if otherwise he cannot enter. But before he breaks it, he ought to signify the cause of his coming and to make request to open the doors. (Semayne's Case, 5 Coke, 91B (1603).

The use of forcible entry to arrest was firmly established early on in common law, even though a fundamental liberty of people includes protecting their homes. This is expressed in the maxim, Every man's house is his castle. The home as a sanctuary and place of refuge is embodied in the Fourth Amendment to the Constitution and in state constitutions and protects homes against unjustified invasion.

Forcible entry was considered obnoxious under common law, not only because it breached the natural right to undisturbed habitation, but also because it caused terror and threatened a breach of the peace by the possibility of resistance. Its violent character produced shock, fright, and dismay to those within a home. It was also dangerous to those breaking in as they might be injured as trespassers. For those reasons, it was generally considered better to wait for another opportunity when violence and danger could be avoided.

However, common law also recognized that circumstances often demand immediate arrests and that, accordingly, a house may sometimes have to be forcibly entered. This necessity is recognized by the maxims, No one can have a castle against the King, and The King's keys unlock all doors. Individual rights must yield to public necessity.

Thus, the power to arrest with or without a warrant carries with it in common law an important privilege. This privilege allows an officer to enter into the possession of another—that is, a place of residence—for the purpose of making an arrest *if* the person sought is within, or *if* the officer reasonably believes this person to be within.

Officers making a forced entry. Such entries may be authorized by a no-knock search or arrest warrant.

Included within this power is not only the right to break open the outer doors of a house to make an entrance, but also the right to break open the doors of different rooms within the house to make a thorough search.

But even under common law, officers' authority to break the doors of a house to arrest was eventually drastically limited. It had to be shown that officers had reasonable cause to break and enter to arrest. They had to justify such extreme and drastic actions.

As a general rule, before crossing the threshold of a house in such emergency cases, officers must identify themselves, make known their purpose, demand admittance, and be refused. This requirement is frequently embodied in statutes. Such notice is consistent with the presumption of innocence and lessens the danger arising from ambiguous conduct, bad information, mistaken identity, and other practical hazards of everyday police work. It makes clear to those within a dwelling what the object of the breaking is and prevents them from justifiably considering it an aggression to be resisted.

Generally, such an announcement and demand are not required where there is no need. One example is when the facts make it clear that the officer's purpose is known. Another is when such an announcement and demand would frustrate the arrest or increase the peril of either the officer making it or those within.

If forcible entry is justified, the breaking must be done with the least amount of destruction. Only the slightest force is necessary to constitute a breaking. For example, pushing open a closed door constitutes forcible entry.

The forcible entry of a home is a sensitive area in law enforcement. Often officers will not do so unless a serious crime or other extreme emergency is involved, and they *know* the subject is within. If a delay can be justified, they may choose to not use such extreme force, even in situations where state law may allow it.

The Use of Deadly Force in Making Arrests

Using deadly force is perhaps the hardest decision a law enforcement officer faces. The use of such force is prescribed by state and federal statutes and basically requires that deadly force be used only in self-defense or in the defense of another. According to Harr and Hess (1990, p. 137): "The only justification for use of a deadly weapon is self-defense or protecting the lives of others." This view is also expressed by Ferdico (1985, p. 91): "Except in cases of self-defense, the officer is *never* justified in using firearms or other deadly force to effect an arrest for a misdemeanor. *The rule is that it is better that a misdemeanant escape rather than a human life be taken.*"

Until 1985, it was legal in many states for officers to use deadly force to prevent a felon from escaping. The "fleeing felon" rule was invalidated by a Supreme Court ruling in *Tennessee v. Garner* (1985). As noted by Farber and Manak (1986, pp. 151, 153):

In March, 1985, the U.S. Supreme Court initiated what must be viewed as a new era in the law of deadly force in the United States. Deadly force utilized to prevent the escape of suspected felons, the Court concluded, may not be used unless it is necessary to prevent the escape and the officer has probable cause to believe that the suspect poses a significant threat of death or serious physical injury to the officer or others. . . .

*A department which does not immediately review—and, if necessary,
rewrite—its policy on the use of deadly force to conform with Garner is
potentially playing with a firestorm of civil liability.*

If a felon is fleeing and an officer believes that felon is a significant threat to
himself or others, the officer should shout a loud warning, "Stop or I'll shoot!"
before firing. The warning should be loud enough that, in addition to the fleeing
felon, *everyone* who might be a witness to both the fleeing and the use of deadly
force would hear the warning. As noted by Aaron (1991, p. 67): "A witness who
did not hear the police warn the subject may eventually become a witness against
them."

Legal Searches

The Fourth and Fifth Amendments also restrict police officers in when they can
search and for what. As with an arrest, searches usually should be conducted with
a *warrant*. Procedures for obtaining and executing search warrants vary by locality,
but generally search warrants may be issued for the following reasons:

- The property was stolen or embezzled.
- Possession of the property is a crime.
- The property is in the possession of someone with intent to use it to commit
  a crime.
- The property was used in committing a crime.
- The items tend to show that a crime was committed or that a specific person
  committed the crime.

Three principal justifications have been established by the courts for the right to
search.

A search may be legally conducted if:

- *A search warrant has been issued.*
- *Consent is given.*
- *It is incidental to a lawful arrest.*

Search Warrants

Ideally, all searches would be conducted with a search warrant. To obtain a search
warrant, officers appear before a magistrate and explain why they believe evidence
might be found at a certain location (their probable cause). If the magistrate believes
that probable cause exists, he or she will issue a search warrant such as that in
Appendix B, Form 4.

As with an arrest warrant, officers seeking to search premises under the authority
of a search warrant can break down a door to gain admittance if they are denied
entrance. Even with a search warrant, however, the search must be limited.

A search conducted under the authority of a search warrant must be limited to the area specified in the warrant and for the items described in the warrant.

Exceptions to the Search Warrant Requirement

Bruce (1990, pp. 100–107) says that although "the general rule is that every search must be based on a warrant," ten basic exceptions to this rule are important to law enforcement officers. (Some of these exceptions have already been discussed.)

Ten exceptions to the search warrant requirement are:

1. *execution of an arrest warrant*
2. *frisks*
3. *incident to arrest*
4. *automobiles*
5. *consent*
6. *plain view*
7. *abandoned property*
8. *open fields*
9. *inventory*
10. *exigent circumstances*

Arrest Warrant Execution.   Officers can search for a suspect in the suspect's home to execute an arrest warrant if they have probable cause to believe the suspect is there. This exception applies to *only* the suspect's home. They cannot conduct a search of any other residence or location even though they have the arrest warrant. For other locations, a search warrant is required.

Frisks.   *Terry v. Ohio* established that officers can conduct a patdown of an individual they have stopped if they believe the person is armed and dangerous. This is a protective search for weapons only.

Search Incident to Arrest.   *Chimel v. California* (1969) established that officers can search a person they have arrested for weapons and for evidence. The search must be limited to the area within the arrested person's immediate control, sometimes referred to as the person's "wing span." The Court said:

When an arrest is made, it is reasonable for the arresting officer to search the person arrested to remove any weapons that the latter might seek to use to resist arrest or effect an escape.

It is entirely reasonable for the arresting officer to search for and seize any evidence on the arrestee's person in order to prevent its concealment or destruction and the area from within which the arrestee might gain possession of a weapon or destructible evidence.

The area within a person's control includes women's purses, chairs suspects are sitting in at the time of arrest, and the entire interior of an automobile if the person is in a car at the time of the arrest. (The trunk is not included in this exception.) *New York v. Belton* (1981) decided that the interior of an automobile could be searched after a passenger was arrested.

Automobile Exception.   *Carroll v. United States* (1925) established that, because automobiles are mobile, officers may search them without a warrant if they have probable cause to believe the car contains evidence of a crime. This is the only exception where officers can search without a warrant even if they have time to get one. Probable cause alone supports the warrantless search. This exception includes the car's trunk as well as suitcases within the trunk if the officers have probable cause to believe they contain evidence. Further, this exception applies to all kinds of motorized vehicles. *California v. Carney* (1985) declared that this exception applied to mobile campers.

Consent.   The consent must be voluntary, and it must be given by a person who has the authority to do so. No threats can be used. The officers do not need to identify themselves as law enforcement officers. The consent can be withdrawn at any time during the search. Landlords cannot give consent to allow their tenants' apartments to be searched.

Plain View.   If officers are performing their duties and come across evidence or contraband that is easily seen—that is, it is in **plain view**—they may seize it. Officers can use a flashlight, provided they have a right to be at the location in the first place. The question of whether officers using binoculars or telescopic devices can seize evidence they discover under the plain view exception is controversial.

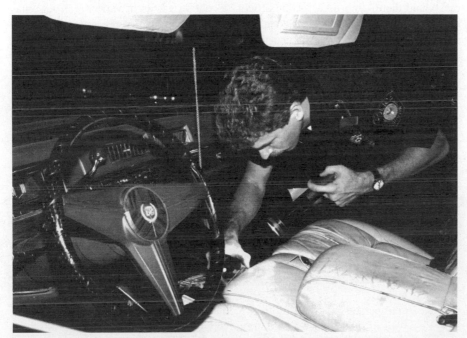

Officer searching a car for drugs after arrest of the driver. Such searches must be thorough and systematic.

Some courts have allowed it; others have not. *Florida v. Riley* (1989) authorized the use of a helicopter flying over a residence at 400 feet so that marijuana plants that could not have been seen from the street could be observed.

Abandoned Property. This applies to anything an individual throws away, including bags or purses discarded while being chased by the police. In *California v. Greenwood* (1988), the Court upheld the right of officers to search through an individual's garbage that had been placed on the curb. Some states, however, are more restrictive. New Jersey and Hawaii, for example, prohibit police from going through garbage without a warrant (*Law Enforcement News,* 1990, p. 4).

Open Fields. The house and the area immediately surrounding it, called the **curtilage,** cannot be searched without a warrant. The curtilage is basically a person's yard and is protected by the Constitution. Open fields, however, are not. *Oliver v. United States* (1984) states that open fields are not protected by the Constitution and that, even if they are posted with ''No Trespassing'' signs, police can search them without a warrant. In this case, police were headed for a marijuana patch.

Inventory. Most police departments will automatically conduct an inventory of impounded vehicles. Three justifications for such an inventory are noted by Bruce (1990, p. 106): ''First, an inventory protects the property of the owner; second, it protects the law enforcement agency against claims that property in its possession has been lost or stolen; third, it allows the police to discover any potential danger that may exist because of property in their possession.'' Inventorying must be a standard department procedure for this exception to be used.

Exigent Circumstances. An **exigent circumstance** occurs when an emergency exists and there is no time for the officers to obtain a search warrant. That is, the evidence could be destroyed or gone by the time they obtained the warrant. This is a frequently used exception and also the most difficult to justify. Says Bruce (p. 107): ''The more serious the crime, the more likely the courts are to recognize the situation as a true emergency justifying a search based on exigent circumstances.''

Procedures for Legally Searching People

The least intrusive search is a patdown or frisk of a person's outer clothing as a protective search for weapons. In the case of arrest, the search is more thorough and also includes a search for weapons. In either type of search, however, certain basic guidelines should be followed:

- Handcuff the person if warranted.
- Always be on guard. Keep yourself at arm's length from the person being searched.
- Keep the person facing away from you.
- Be aware of where your service revolver is and keep it as far from the suspect as possible.
- Be systematic. Be thorough.

- When patting down or searching females, use the back of the hand in the breast and crotch area.

When searching a person, handcuff if warranted, be on guard, be systematic, be thorough. Keep the person under control, preferably off balance.

The FBI and most police departments have a policy that individuals to be searched are handcuffed first for officer safety. Payton (1986, pp. 343–344) suggests that officers control suspects by grasping the back of the suspect's shirt or belt with their left hand and then beginning the search with their right hand on the person's right side using the following order of search:

1. Wrist, fingers, arms, and armpits.
2. The hair and neck. If the person has a hat, remove it from the rear.
3. The torso (chest, stomach, sides, and back, including clothes).
4. The belt and waist area.
5. The groin and crotch. Many officers are a little squeamish about doing this; yet this is a favorite hiding place. You have only your life to lose.
6. Legs, ankles, socks, and shoes. Look inside the edges of the shoes. Have the suspect lift one shoe at a time to inspect the bottom.
7. If the suspect has a hat, step back and look at it inside and under the band. Be careful that the suspect does not take advantage of this distraction.

This procedure is repeated with the left hand searching the left side while the right hand maintains control of the person being searched.

If more than one suspect is to be searched, all except those currently being searched should be ordered to lie on the ground, facing away from the person being searched. If two officers are at the search scene, one conducts the search while the other officer stands guard.

Conducting Strip Searches

Strip searches are much less commonly conducted and should be conducted only after considering the following factors which, according to Summers (1991, p. 55), ''have been approved by various courts as acceptable for conducting strip searches.''

1. The reasons for the search.
2. The nature and seriousness of the offense.
3. Whether the individual arrested has a criminal record.
4. Whether there is reasonable suspicion to believe the individual is carrying contraband, drugs, weapons, etc.
5. The length of time the individual may stay in custody.
6. Whether the individual will be held alone or with others.
7. Whether the individual resisted arrest or was violent.
8. Whether the individual has a known history of violence, contraband, or drugs.
9. Whether the individual is a danger to himself or others.

Summers (p. 55) suggests the following guidelines for all strip searches:

1. The search should be conducted by officers of the same sex as the individual being searched.
2. Officers of the opposite sex should not be allowed in the room where the search is being conducted, except in cases of overriding security concerns.
3. Privacy from outside observation must be guaranteed. The use of modesty screens may be considered to preserve the individual's dignity while disrobing, even though the individual will be observed and the clothes thoroughly searched.
4. To preserve the individual's dignity, officers conducting the search should refrain from making any references to the individual's body while conducting the search.
5. The searching officers should inquire as to whether there are any medical conditions or other factors that may affect the search.
6. Strip searches should never be conducted randomly or at the whim of an officer, but rather pursuant to specific guidelines established by the agency.
7. The arrest of an individual does not justify a strip search without the existence of reasonable suspicion.
8. Written documentation of the search should be completed and retained. The documentation should include the reasons for the search, the demeanor of the arrestee during the search, any unusual occurrences, and the results of the search.

Procedures for Legally Searching Buildings

Officers must often search buildings in response to either an alarm or a call from a citizen. Such searches are fraught with danger and require extreme caution. Perry (1984, p. 129) suggests five key elements in building searches: "A quick safe response, visual containment, adequate assistance, careful planning, and proper search technique."

Officers arriving at a building to search it should arrive as quietly as possible to preserve the element of surprise. To make certain that no one escapes from within the building, observation posts should be set up and maintained while the search is being conducted. A thorough search depends on having enough officers to not only visually contain the building but also to thoroughly and systematically search the inside.

The building search itself must be carefully planned. If time permits, the owner of the building should be contacted to learn as much as possible about its layout and possible hiding places. The number of floors including basements and attics should be determined. Usually one door is selected as the entry/exit door for the search team. In some instances, however, officers enter the front and back of the building simultaneously.

Once inside the building, to avoid shooting other officers, all officers must know what each is doing. Each should have a clear assignment and carry it out. A system of communication should be established to maintain contact. Should a suspect be located, assistance should be called for immediately. The search should continue, however, as more than one suspect might be in the building.

As officers search the building, they should use proven techniques. For example, when entering a room or a building, look into the structure from both sides of the doorway without exposing any more of the body than necessary. Always keep low and move rapidly. If the building is dark, know how to use a flashlight without becoming a target. According to Perry (pp. 135–136):

> *The preferred method for using the flashlight is to use it as sparingly as possible and hold it backhanded in the non-gun hand. Keep it in front of the body, moving it side to side while scanning an area. This technique also provides a stable shooting platform with gun and light coordinated.*

One of the most dangerous aspects of searching a building is when officers come to a *corner*. An armed suspect could be around that corner. Brelje and Krause note (1989, p. 97) that *mirrors* and *periscopes* can be invaluable but that they must be small enough to be easily carried. A 3 ½″ by 6″ plastic-backed visor mirror fits into a uniform pocket and works well for building searches. Mirrors take practice to use because everything is backward. Periscopes eliminate this disadvantage. In addition, with a periscope, officers can stay farther behind their cover. Be aware, however, that using either may draw fire.

When searching a building,

- *Arrive quickly and quietly.*
- *Set up containment positions around the building.*
- *Make sure enough personnel is available.*
- *Plan carefully. Set up an entry/exit point, learn the interior layout, assign personnel to cover each area.*
- *Use proper search techniques.*

Using K-9s in Searches

Dogs (known in the profession as K-9s) can be invaluable in conducting searches for suspects, evidence, drugs, and bombs. Spurlock (1990, p. 91) summarized the results of a Michigan study for the city of Lansing:

> *A single K-9 team was able to complete building searches seven times faster than four officers working together to search the same building. And while the dog team found the hidden suspects 93 percent of the time, the human officers found [them] only 59 percent [of the time].*

According to Frawley (1989, p. 115), a renowned expert on human scent, Dr. Koster, has determined that a dog is capable of recognizing an odor 10 million times better than a human can. Frawley suggests that if no suspect is identified at the scene of a crime, but evidence is found, police can collect the scent by wrapping the item in gauze for about 20 minutes and then putting the gauze in a glass storage jar. Frawley also (p. 117) notes: ''In his experiments, Brigadier de Bruin has stored the scent of police officers from his department in glass bottles for three years. The dogs are still identifying the correct individual using this evidence.''

A K-9 sniffing for drugs. Dogs can be of extreme value in police operations.

Avoiding Booby Traps

It is unlikely that officers will encounter booby traps during their searches of people or buildings, but the possibility is always there.

Booby traps are most likely to be encountered in searches involving drugs or paramilitary political extremists.

Lesce (1990, p. 56) suggests that officers dealing with drug smugglers or marijuana growers should beware of booby traps and alarms serving three purposes: ". . . [O]ne is to warn the proprietor that someone is approaching. Another is to impede access, such as a police search or raid. A third is to slow or stop a police pursuit."

Alarms can be simple or complex. A string attached to a bell or a can of stones can serve as a simple alarm. Of more concern, however, are booby traps designed to maim or kill. Lesce (pp. 57–58) describes several such traps, including pits dug into the ground containing spikes, punji sticks, fire bombs, and the like. Locations can range from open fields to desk drawers. Figure 5.2 illustrates some common locations for booby traps.

Lesce (p. 59) urges officers to recognize where booby traps are likely to be to avoid becoming victims. When outdoors, be wary of trails and gullies. When indoors, be wary of cabinets, closets, and even furniture. Lesce suggests some telltale signs of booby traps:

FIGURE 5.2
Common booby traps
Source: "Booby-Trap Awareness," by Tony Lesce, *Law and Order* (October 1990): 57. (Reprinted with permission of *Law and Order Magazine*.)

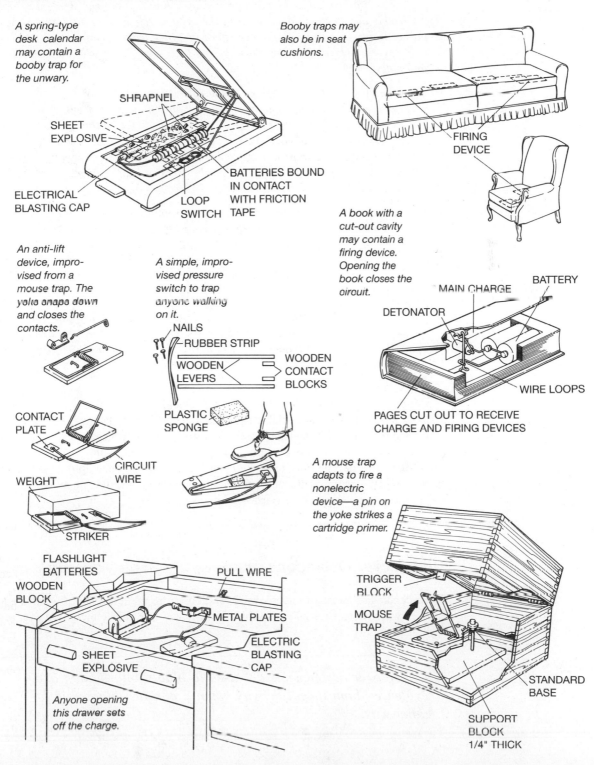

A spring-type desk calendar may contain a booby trap for the unwary.

SHRAPNEL
SHEET EXPLOSIVE
ELECTRICAL BLASTING CAP
LOOP SWITCH
BATTERIES BOUND IN CONTACT WITH FRICTION TAPE

Booby traps may also be in seat cushions.

FIRING DEVICE

A book with a cut-out cavity may contain a firing device. Opening the book closes the circuit.

An anti-lift device, improvised from a mouse trap. The yoke snaps down and closes the contacts.

A simple, improvised pressure switch to trap anyone walking on it.

NAILS
RUBBER STRIP
WOODEN LEVERS
WOODEN CONTACT BLOCKS

CONTACT PLATE
PLASTIC SPONGE
WEIGHT
CIRCUIT WIRE
STRIKER

MAIN CHARGE
BATTERY
DETONATOR
WIRE LOOPS
PAGES CUT OUT TO RECEIVE CHARGE AND FIRING DEVICES

A mouse trap adapts to fire a nonelectric device—a pin on the yoke strikes a cartridge primer.

FLASHLIGHT BATTERIES
WOODEN BLOCK
PULL WIRE
METAL PLATES
SHEET EXPLOSIVE
ELECTRIC BLASTING CAP

TRIGGER BLOCK
MOUSE TRAP
STANDARD BASE
SUPPORT BLOCK 1/4" THICK

Anyone opening this drawer sets off the charge.

First is location. Be very suspicious and watchful around any road, trail, gateway, or doorway leading into a suspect area.

Another is physical evidence. Obviously, if you see a wire stretched across a path, you'll be cautious. Monofilament fishing line is a danger sign. Also look for freshly dug earth. A depression in the ground suggests recent digging. A pile of leaves in a particular spot, where no other leaves are on the ground, may conceal a trap. Probing ahead of you with your baton will disclose pits and holes.

Anything out of place or artificial is cause for an extra look. A sheet of cardboard or newspaper on the ground might cover a pit. A nail, piece of pipe, length of wood, or anything else artificial on the ground may be a sinister signal. Be especially careful if you see anything that seems to compel you to pick it up and examine it, such as a weapon. When uprooting a marijuana plant, watch for razor blade slivers in the stalks.

If you come to a structure or a boat, circle around and observe it carefully before approaching. Look inside before entering. Don't open any doors, windows, or drawers without making sure that it's safe. Be especially wary of any wire you see running into a light socket. Once inside, don't turn on any light switches or other appliances until a technician has checked them out and pronounced them safe. . . .

Don't overlook the possibility that suspects may have booby-trapped themselves. Some types of suspects, such as outlaw bikers and drug dealers, conceal needles, razor blades, and fish hooks in their clothing to injure any officer searching them. This is why it's wise to use a miniflashlight to probe suspects' clothing.

Officers who do come upon a booby trap should carefully assess the situation. Usually it is best to call a specialist to disarm the booby trap. If this is not possible, officers might disarm it themselves—from a distance. An officer alone should not attempt this since he or she could be seriously injured and require help.

Suspects are not the only ones who can use trickery to accomplish their ends, however. Law enforcement, too, can be quite covert in specific situations, particularly those involving undercover assignments.

Undercover Operations

Most people are aware of undercover operations from the television programs and movies where detectives take on a false identity and infiltrate some group engaged in illegal activity.

Undercover assignments are used to obtain information and evidence about illegal activity when it can be obtained in no other way.

Because undercover assignments are dangerous, they are usually reserved for those situations where other investigative techniques have failed. A person working undercover must eat, sleep, and breathe the assumed identity. No identification other than the cover identification is carried. Communication with the police department is risky and carefully planned. Plans are also made for what the undercover officer is to do if the criminal operation is "busted" and how the officer will end the relationship.

One danger of using undercover operations is that officers may become what they start out only pretending to be. Another danger of using undercover operations is the potential for a charge of entrapment.

Entrapment

According to Klein (1980, p. 532):

The U.S. Supreme Court first recognized and applied the entrapment defense in Sorrells v. United States, *287 U.S. 435 (1932) case. A federal prohibition agent visited the defendant while posing as a tourist and engaged him in conversation about common war experiences. After gaining the defendant's confidence, the agent asked for some liquor, was twice refused, but upon asking a third time, the defendant finally capitulated, and was subsequently prosecuted for violating the National Prohibition Act.*

Speaking for the Court, Chief Justice Hughes said that the defendant should have had the defense of entrapment available. This defense prohibits law enforcement officers from instigating a criminal act by persons "otherwise innocent in order to lure them to its commission and to punish them."

Klein (p. 206) further notes that:

No police agency can be effective unless it utilizes the services of undercover agents. There is an old cliché that a detective is as good as his informant and no more. The courts have recognized this need; however, they have placed certain restrictions on its use where other fundamental rights are infringed upon by undercover agents.

Entrapment *is an action by the police (or a government agent) persuading a person to commit a crime that the person would not otherwise have committed.*

Gardner (1989, pp. 162–163) discusses the following three historic Supreme Court cases defining entrapment.

- *Sherman v. United States* (1958). A government informant and the defendant met in a doctor's office where they were both being treated for narcotics addiction. After several accidental meetings, the informant asked the defendant for a source of narcotics, stating that he was not responding to treatments. The defendant tried to avoid the issue but the informant continued to ask for narcotics, stating that he was suffering. In holding that the informant "not only enticed the defendant into carrying out an illegal sale but also to returning to the habit of use'' and that this was entrapment, the Court reversed the conviction of the defendant.

- *United States v. Russell* (1973). An undercover narcotics agent worked his way into a group manufacturing "speed" by offering to supply them with an essential ingredient that was difficult to obtain. . . . After seeing the drug lab, the undercover agent was told the defendants had been producing the illegal drug for seven months. After the agent supplied the essential ingredient, the agent received half of the finished batch of speed in payment. A month later, another batch of speed was made, and the agent obtained a search warrant. Defendant Russell's sole defense was entrapment. In holding that the participation of the narcotics agent was not entrapment, the Supreme Court stated:

> The illicit manufacture of drugs is not a sporadic, isolated criminal incident, but a continuing, though illegal, business enterprise. In order to obtain convictions for illegally manufacturing drugs, the gathering of evidence of past unlawful conduct frequently proves to be an all but impossible task. Thus, in drug related offenses, law enforcement personnel have turned to one of the only practicable means of detection: the infiltration of drug rings and a limited participation in their unlawful present practices. Such infiltration is a recognized and permissible means of apprehension; if that be so, then the supply of some item of value that the drug ring requires must, as a general rule, also be permissible. For an agent will not be taken into the confidence of the illegal entrepreneurs unless he has something of value to offer them. Law enforcement tactics such as this can hardly be said to violate "fundamental fairness" or [be] "shocking to the universal sense of justice."

- *Hampton v. United States* (1976). An informer arranged two separate, unlawful heroin sales by the defendant to undercover law enforcement officers. A government witness testified at the trial that the defendant supplied the heroin, but the defendant testified that he received the heroin that he sold to the agents from the informer. The defendant also claimed that he believed the substance to be a "nonnarcotic counterfeit drug which would give the same reaction as heroin." On appeal to the U.S. Supreme Court, the defendant argued that the jury instruction should have been given because, when the government itself supplies narcotics, the defendant is a victim of illegal government entrapment. In affirming the defendant's conviction, the Court held that a successful entrapment defense required that the defendant not have the criminal intention until implanted by the government agent.

Entrapment charges can be avoided by not enticing a person to do something illegal. Simply witness the illegal acts that are committed.

Public agents and informants acting on behalf of the police may also commit entrapment.

Nonpolice Undercover Informants

Nonpolice informers who operate in undercover roles may be involved only in passive observation. They can be used to vouch for and introduce sworn police undercover agents to a suspected group or persons and then should be dropped from the investigation. They may also play an active role in the criminal activities of those on whom they are informing. Only a small fraction of informers ever testify in court, although the information they provide may be offered to the magistrate to obtain warrants for arrests, searches, wiretaps, or electronic surveillances.

Some informers go beyond giving information obtained in their natural environment and use disguises and infiltrations. The environment is deceptively shaped to elicit information. For example, an informant is placed in a suspect's cell as a cellmate in the hope confidences will be transmitted. Other examples are an agent posing as an employee to infiltrate a factory in response to problems such as employee thefts or the police posing as reporters seeking comments from political and social activists.

Known tactics whose legality is questionable include planting informers in a group organized for the legal defense of an activist facing serious criminal charges or having a police officer dressed as a clergyman visit an arrested person in jail. Another common, and often significant, tactic is the "front," such as a cocktail lounge or a neighborhood used-property store set up for a sting operation or specifically created by the police for intelligence purposes.

Once a person has begun to inform, the threat of exposure becomes a factor. Allegiances may shift or become more intense. A criminal who becomes overzealous and tries to play the role of supercop may jeopardize a whole operation. Or, informants may become double agents—that is, clever informants experienced in deception who manipulate and control their police contact, rather than the reverse. Because undercover work is complex, it has both positive and negative aspects. Assessing them is difficult. Little research can be done because of the covert nature and the suspiciousness of the courts and civil rights advocates.

Undercover operations can offer information not otherwise available. No question, the police cannot be everywhere. They must rely on inside information or tips, particularly where there is no easily identifiable victim or witnesses and where highly skilled criminal activities are involved. Audio recording or video filming a crime is often feasible in undercover operations. This is a surer form of evidence and is more difficult to manipulate than verbal testimony. Undercover practices are costly and susceptible to abuse and unintended consequences. Therefore, they should be used for only serious offenses when alternative means are not available and then only under careful monitoring.

Summary

While conducting police operations involving arrests and searches, law enforcement officers must maintain a balance between "freedom to" and "freedom from." The Fourth and Fifth Amendments to the Constitution restrict arrests and searches.

A stop-and-frisk situation is one in which law enforcement officers briefly detain a suspicious person for questioning (this is *not* an arrest) and, *if* the officers suspect the person is armed, they are allowed to pat the person's outer clothing (this *is* a limited search for weapons).

An arrest is "the official taking of a person to answer criminal charges. This involves at least temporarily depriving the person of liberty and may involve the use of force." An arrest can legally be made with an arrest warrant when any offense (felony or misdemeanor) is committed in an officer's presence or when officers have probable cause to believe a person has committed a felony and no time is available to obtain a warrant. Probable cause refers to a situation where it is more likely than not that a crime has been committed by the person whom a law enforcement officer seeks to arrest. An officer's probable cause to conduct an arrest depends on what the officer knew before taking action.

Understanding, humanism, and skill in making arrests are critical because arrest involves fundamental rights to personal liberty and privacy, the law of arrest is strict and technical, arrest is often the first step in criminal proceedings, illegal arrests may taint crucial evidence of guilt, the quality of police performance is judged by arrests, arrests may lead to civil suits and criminal prosecution of officers, and arrests may endanger officers' lives. An illegal arrest may result in evidence being excluded under the Exclusionary Rule. The Exclusionary Rule established that the courts cannot accept evidence obtained in illegal searches and seizures, regardless of how relevant the evidence is to the case (*Weeks v. United States,* 1914).

To make lawful arrests, officers must know both substantive and procedural law. Substantive law deals with content or what behaviors are considered crimes. Procedural law deals with process or how the law is applied.

In a typical arrest situation officers should announce the arrest and the reason for it; if warranted, handcuff the person; and then search the person arrested for weapons and evidence. The person should be given the Miranda warning if any questions are to be asked. Use of force when making an arrest is always an issue. If there is no resistance, no force should be used. If resistance occurs, use only as much force as necessary to overcome the resistance. If a threat to an officer's life exists, the use of deadly force is authorized in most departments. Handcuffing may be considered to be use of force. Whether an arrested person should automatically be handcuffed while being transported is controversial. Officer discretion may be advisable.

A search may be legally conducted if a search warrant has been issued, consent is given, or it is incidental to a lawful arrest. A search conducted under the authority of a search warrant must be limited to the area specified in the warrant and for the items described in the warrant. Ten exceptions to the search warrant requirement are:

1. execution of an arrest warrant
2. frisks
3. incident to arrest
4. automobiles
5. consent
6. plain view
7. abandoned property
8. open fields
9. inventory
10. exigent circumstances

When searching a person, handcuff if warranted, be on guard, be systematic, be thorough. Keep the person under control, preferably off balance. When searching a building, arrive quickly and quietly, set up containment positions around the building, make sure enough personnel is available, and plan carefully. Set up an entry/exit point, learn the interior layout, and assign personnel to cover each area. Use proper search techniques. When searching, be alert for booby traps. Booby traps are most likely to be encountered in searches involving drugs or paramilitary political extremists.

Undercover assignments are used to obtain information and evidence about illegal activity when it can be obtained in no other way. Such assignments run the risk of charges of entrapment. Entrapment is an action by the police (or a government agent) persuading a person to commit a crime that the person would not otherwise have committed. Entrapment charges can be avoided by not enticing a person to do something illegal. Simply witness the illegal acts that are committed.

Application #1

You are a Bigtown patrol officer. You notice that transporting and booking a person arrested as a misdemeanant takes from one to three hours. This seems counterproductive because you are out of service during that time, are not available for other calls, and the arrested person will usually be released from jail in a short time, often even before you finish the reports. You feel that issuing a citation to the person without formal procedures of arrest and booking would more than serve the purpose and would release you for more important duties. You approach your sergeant and pose your recommendations to her. She asks you to "put it in writing."

Instructions   Use the form in Appendix A to make your policy and procedure. The policy will state the following:

> *The policy of the Bigtown Police Department for releasing persons from custody who have been arrested for a misdemeanor will change effective _____ (date). Any person cited for a misdemeanor whom the officer feels will appear in court as promised, may be given a written citation by the officer.*

- *When a Citation May Be Issued*. Give several circumstances or conditions that may exist whereby officers could issue a citation to such a person who also has no previous criminal record.
- *Justifications for not Issuing a Citation*. In completing this policy, you should insert what form is to be used when issuing a citation, what reports are necessary, and also that issuing a citation means suspects should be entered in the arrest log and assigned a log number and a case number. You should indicate what needs to appear in the citation notification form.

Application #2

Recently the courts have been critical of your police department's practice of stopping certain individuals on the street because they fit a certain profile of people often engaged in unlawful activity. These "investigative detentions" have been called "highly intrusive, offensive, and unnecessary by the courts." One judge called them discriminatory and stated they must cease: "They are unreasonable and in violation of constitutional protections, including the right of privacy."

Some stops have resulted in strip searches and the evidence found was declared to be inadmissible in the courts. You realize that these investigative detentions are happening because the police department has no policy for making field inquiries. The court has given you thirty days to produce a policy.

Instructions   Use the form in Appendix A to develop your policy and procedure. Consider the time of day, location, and circumstances that might justify officers' actions. Two Supreme Court cases provide guidelines: *Terry v. Ohio* (1968) and *Adams v. Williams* (1972). Keep in mind that investigatory stops are by their nature forcible and are, therefore, classified as seizures under the Fourth Amendment.

An Exercise in Critical Thinking

The U.S. Supreme Court has adopted the now classic standard for reasonable stops: In justifying the particular intrusion, the police officer must be able to point to specific and articulable facts which, taken together with rational inferences from those facts, reasonably warrant that intrusion.

At 7:40 A.M. on June 27, Officer Steve Sjerven was in the crossover preparing to turn south on Highway 65 to help the driver of an apparently disabled car. As he waited to turn, he saw a red pickup truck heading south on Highway 65 and made eye contact with the driver and sole occupant of the truck. The driver abruptly turned the truck right onto Tower Systems Road and appeared to immediately disappear. Not seeing the pickup truck or any dust that might be expected from a truck travelling down a gravel road, the officer concluded that the truck must have immediately pulled into a driveway. As the officer pulled up to assist the disabled car, he saw the pickup emerge and turn south onto Highway 65 —a very short time after having turned onto Tower Systems Road. Inferring that the driver had turned off Highway 65 to avoid him, the officer motioned the driver of the pickup to stop. The driver did so, identified himself as Mark Johnson, and admitted that his license had been revoked.

1. As the U.S. Supreme Court's decisions require only that an officer have a ''particular and objective basis for suspecting the particular person stopped of criminal activity,'' what is your judgment of Officer Sjerven's approach?
   a. Since Johnson's action can be explained as consistent with lawful activities, Officer Sjerven should not stop him.
   b. The officer's suspicion, though nothing more than a hunch, was later verified by the stop.
   c. Sjerven stopped Johnson on mere whim, caprice, or idle curiosity, and so should be disciplined for poor judgment in operational skills.
   d. Inferences and deductions might well elude an untrained person, but a trained police officer is entitled to draw inferences on the basis of ''all of the circumstances.''
   e. If the observed facts are consistent with innocent activity, then the stop is invalid.

Discussion Questions

1. The Fifth Amendment provides that no person shall be ''deprived of life, liberty or property without due process of law.'' What does this really mean? Explain your answer as if you were giving a lecture to a high school class.
2. Substantive law is concerned with the content of the law. In criminal law it defines what behaviors are illegal and imposes punishments for engaging in them. Name five types of behavior the law does not tolerate.

3. When officers make an arrest without a warrant, they act at their own peril and are allowed no margin of error. Why is it that the preceding statement seems to be so stringent?
4. Describe a good example of "reasonable grounds of suspicion."
5. What search situations are officers likely to find themselves in? How can they best prepare themselves?
6. What are some motivations for citizens to become informants?
7. Do the police commit entrapment when they make a "target of opportunity" by placing wrapped packages in an unlocked car in a shopping center parking lot?

Definitions

Can you define the following terms?

arrest	mere handcuff rule
curtilage	observational probable cause
due process of law	patdown
entrapment	plain view
Exclusionary Rule	probable cause
exigent circumstances	procedural law
frisk	stop
good faith	stop and frisk situation
informational probable cause	substantive law
"in the presence"	

References

Aaron, Titus. "Avoiding Jury Trials in Excessive Use of Force Suits." *Law and Order* (April 1991): 67–68.

Allard, Reginald Jr. "The Mere Handcuff Rule." *Law and Order* (April 1991): 69–72.

Brelje, Emery and Krause, Karl. "Fundamental Techniques for Building Searches." *Law and Order* (October 1989): 96–100.

Bruce, Theodore A. "The Ten Exceptions to the Search Warrant Requirements." *Law and Order* (October 1990): 100–108.

Calvi, James V. and Coleman, Susan *American Law and Legal Systems*. Englewood Cliffs, N.J.: Prentice Hall, 1989.

Connor, Greg. "Cover Cuffing." *Law and Order* (September 1989): 98–99.

Connor, Greg. "Use of Force Continuum: Phase II." *Law and Order* (March 1991): 30.

Farber, Bernard J. and Manak, James P. "Police Liability for Use of Deadly Force in the Wake of *Tennessee v. Garner*." In *Civil Rights Litigation and Attorney Fees Annual Handbook*, Vol. 2, by Lobel, ed. New York: Clark Boardman Company, 1986.

Ferdico, N. *Criminal Procedure for Criminal Justice Professional*. 3d ed. St. Paul, Minn.: West Publishing Company, 1985.

Frawley, Ed. "Police Service Dog Work in Holland." *Law and Order* (September 1989): 115–117.

Gardner, Thomas J. *Criminal Law Principles*. 4th ed. St. Paul, Minn.: West Publishing Company, 1989.

Harr, J. Scott, and Hess, Kären M. *Criminal Procedure*. St. Paul, Minn.: West Publishing Company, 1990.

Klein, Irving J. *Constitutional Law for Criminal Justice Professionals*. Belmont, Calif.: Duxbury Press, Division of Wadsworth, 1980.

Law Enforcement News. "NJ High Court Upholds Privacy of Curbside Trash," (July/August 1990): 4.

Lesce, Tony. "Booby-Trap Awareness." *Law and Order* (October 1990): 56–60.

Oran, Daniel. *Law Dictionary for Nonlawyers*. 2d ed. St. Paul, Minn.: West Publishing Company, 1985.

Payton, George T. *Patrol Procedure*. San Jose, Calif.: Criminal Justice Services, 1986.

Perry, Tim. *Basic Patrol Procedures*. Seattle, Wash.: Palladium Publications, 1984.

Spurlock, James C. "K-9." *Law and Order* (March 1990): 91–96.

Summers, William C. "Conducting Strip Searches." *The Police Chief* (May 1991): 54–56.

Cases

Adams v. Williams, 407 U.S. 143, 92 S.Ct. 1921, 32 L.Ed.2d 612 (1972).

Brinegar v. United States, 338 U.S. 160, 69 S.Ct. 1302, 93 L.Ed. 1879 (1949).

California v. Carney, 471 U.S. 386, 105 S.Ct. 2066, 85 L.Ed.2d 406 (1985).

California v. Greenwood, 486 U.S. 35, 36, 108 S.Ct. 1625, 1627, 100 L.Ed.2d 30 (1988).

Carroll v. United States, 267 U.S. 132, 45 S.Ct. 280, 69 L.Ed. 543 (1925).

Chimel v. California, 395 U.S. 752, 89 S.Ct. 2034, 23 L.Ed.2d 685 (1969).

Florida v. Riley, 488 U.S. 347, 109 S.Ct. 639, 102 L.Ed.2d 700 (1989).

Graham v. Connor, 109 S.Ct. 1865, 490 U.S. 386 (1989).

Hampton v. United States, 425 U.S. 484, 96 S.Ct. 1646, 48 L.Ed.2d 113 (1976).

Kozlowski v. Ferrara, 117 F.Supp 650 (S.D.N.Y. 1954).

New York v. Belton, 453 U.S. 454, 462, 101 S.Ct. 2860, 2865, 69 L.Ed.2d 768 (1981).

Oliver v. United States, 466 U.S. 170, 104 S.Ct. 1735, 80 L.Ed.2d 214 (1984).

Sherman v. United States, 356 U.S. 369, 78 S.Ct. 819, 2 L.Ed.2d 848 (1957).

Sorrells v. United States, 287 U.S. 435, 53 S.Ct. 210, 77 L.Ed. 413 (1932).

Tennessee v. Garner, 471 U.S. 1, 105 S.Ct. 1694, 85 L.Ed.2d 1 (1985).

Terry v. Ohio, 392 U.S. 1, 88 S.Ct. 1868, 20 L.Ed.2d 889 (1968).

United States v. Russell, 411 U.S. 423, 93 S.Ct. 1637, 36 L.Ed.2d 366 (1973).

Weeks v. United States, 340 F.2d 827 (10th Cir. 1965).

The Personal Side of Police Operations

Section I described the basic skills needed to perform the functions of today's law enforcement agencies in the context of a changing society. The need to protect the constitutional rights of all citizens, including those who commit crimes, was emphasized throughout Section I as was the need to act professionally.

This section examines the personal side of police operations even as it continues to stress the need for protecting the rights of others and for acting professionally. Today's officers face more civil liabilities than ever before (Chapter 6). Professional law enforcement officers must do more than simply stay within the law, however. They must ask not only, Is it legal? but also, Is it ethical? Given the great amount of discretion officers have, it is crucial that they select alternatives that are legally and morally acceptable to themselves, their colleagues, and the public they serve (Chapter 7).

Law enforcement officers need to maintain their physical and emotional well-being and to perform their roles safely. Law enforcement is not only a high-stress occupation, it is also a high-risk occupation. To perform at peak efficiency, indeed sometimes to stay alive, officers must be physically and mentally fit (Chapter 8).

IDAHO
DEPARTMENT
OF
LAW ENFORCEMENT

POLICIES AND

PROCEDURES

CIVIL LIABILITY: AVOIDING LAWSUITS IN A LITIGIOUS SOCIETY

CHAPTER 6

INTRODUCTION

"One element which policing has—increasingly—in common with other professions," say Scogin and Brodsky (1991, p. 41), "is the threat of lawsuits." In fact, they describe a new term which has come into being in the past few years: *litigaphobia* which refers to an excessive, irrational fear of litigation (combining *litigation* and *phobia*).

Law enforcement officers must act within the law. If they do not, they may be found criminally liable for misconduct under Title 18, Section 242, U.S.C.A., as well as under state criminal law. Most lawsuits against law enforcement officers, however, deal with civil matters. In carrying out their official duties, law enforcement officers must protect the constitutional rights of their public. The consequences of violating such rights in a criminal investigation as far as the criminal proceedings are concerned was discussed in Chapter 5. Actions in violation of a suspect's constitutional rights can cost a favorable decision. Additionally, the suspect can sue the police. Police operations also involve considerable discretion. This, too, can result in actions that are viewed as "not becoming a police officer" and thereby subject officers to civil lawsuits.

The United States has been called a **litigious** society—that is, its citizens are very likely to sue over any perceived wrong. As noted by Harr and Hess (1990, p. 76):

> Only naive or deluded police officers believe they will never be sued. The past two decades have produced an unprecedented increase in suits brought against the police. It is presently estimated that over 30,000 lawsuits are initiated against law enforcement annually. A decrease in this figure is unlikely.

Do You Know

- What Section 1983 is and how it affects police officers?
- What vicarious liability is?
- What the most frequent civil lawsuits against police involve?
- What the most common civil actions brought against supervisors, police departments, and municipalities are?
- What punitive damages are?
- What the most common defenses of police officers are?
- What are the six layers of protection against civil liability?
- How to minimize lawsuits?
- Whether officers can countersue?

Civil Liability—An Overview

When a person feels he has been wronged by someone, even though the action may not be a crime, he can sue. Such lawsuits are called **civil actions.** In civil law, the wrongdoing itself is called a **tort.** Sometimes an action is considered both a tort and a crime. For example, a person who strikes someone could be charged with assault (a crime) and sued for the assault (a tort). Individuals found guilty of a crime are *punished* by paying a fine and/or serving a jail or prison sentence. Individuals found guilty of a tort are made to make *restitution,* usually in the form of monetary payments.

Law enforcement officers are not immune from either criminal or civil lawsuits. As noted by Gallagher (1990a, p. 18):

What police officers do is inherently dangerous. They carry weapons that can injure and kill. They drive cars at high speeds. They must constantly enforce (and obey) laws, statutes, and ordinances, whose variety and intricacies confuse most people.

Yet, if an officer makes a mistake or if his actions lead to unnecessary injury, a lawsuit and an adverse judgment can follow. The results can be disastrous. In fact, the fallout from a major lawsuit can be damaging even if the lawsuit is won.

The estate of a Denver, Colorado, couple was awarded $800,000 as a result of their being killed by a vehicle being chased by an unmarked police vehicle. A New York man who was struck by a police officer's nightstick was awarded $3 million. A youth shot by the Detroit police in a looted store was awarded $1 million. In Richmond, California, the city, the police department, and two officers were ordered to pay $3 million to the families of the two black men the officers had shot and killed.

Law enforcement officers can be sued in just about every phase of police operations. Each time officers are sued, it exposes them to personal embarrassment in the community and on the job. It may result in possible job loss. It may mean financial ruin. Equally damaging is the undermining of respect for the rule of law when officers are found guilty. Although the increase in lawsuits is alarming, it is still true that most lawsuits against police officers can be traced to extremely poor judgment or malicious acts by one or more officers. Officers acting responsibly is a definite deterrent to any action against them.

Section 1983, the Civil Rights Act

Most civil lawsuits brought against law enforcement officers are based on Statute 42 of the United States Code, Section 1983, passed in 1871 after the Civil War and better known as the Civil Rights Act. This statute was designed to prevent the abuse of constitutional rights by officers who ''under color of state law'' deny defendants those rights. The Act states:

Every person who, under color of any statute, ordinance, regulation, custom, or usage, of any State or Territory, subjects, or causes to be subjected any citizen of the United States or other person within the jurisdiction thereof to the deprivation of any rights, privileges, or immunities secured by the

Constitution and laws, shall be liable to the party injured in an action at law, suit in equity, or other proper proceeding for redress.

Section 1983, the Civil Rights Act, *says that anyone acting under the authority of the law who violates another person's constitutional rights can be sued.*

This includes law enforcement officers. It now may also include their supervisors, their department, and even their municipality. According to McCoy (1984, p. 56): "The case law under 42 U.S.C.A. 1983 has evolved sufficiently so that a seamless web of liability . . . may be applied to defendants on each level of a police department's hierarchy." This is a concept known as *vicarious liability.*

Vicarious Liability

According to Oran (1985, p. 319), *vicarious liability* is the "legal responsibility for the acts of another person because of some relationship with that person, for example, the liability of an employer for the acts of an employee."

Vicarious liability makes others specifically associated with a person also responsible for that person's actions.

The vast majority of lawsuits naming supervisory officers are attempts to get to more, wealthier, and better insured defendants through vicarious liability. Suing every possible individual and agency involved creates a **collective deep pocket** from which astronomical judgments can be collected.

Until 1961, police officers, supervisors, departments, and municipalities were immune from civil lawsuits. This changed drastically when *Monroe v. Pape* (1961) held that individual line officers were liable for their actions under Section 1983. During the 1960s, patrol officers were the only police department personnel likely to be sued. *Monroe v. Pape* also established that police would not be liable if they acted in good faith. This defense allowed police departments to shift blame from their officers to their supervisors. The supervisors were immune from civil lawsuits or vicarious liability because they were not considered to be the patrol officers' employers.

In the 1970s, however, as noted by McCoy (1984, p. 57): "Failure to train patrol officers properly, or failure to supervise them so that they adhere to constitutional standards, are independent activities sufficiently negligent in themselves to bring supervisory personnel into the web of liability." Supervisors, however, were also afforded the good faith defense and were able to pass responsibility if they could point to a department or city policy they were enforcing, even if that policy was found to be unconstitutional. "I was only following orders," protected all involved until 1978. That year, in *Monell v. New York City Department of Social Services*, the Supreme Court ruled that municipalities that violated constitutional rights under local custom, policy, or practice, could be sued.

McCoy notes (p. 58): "The liability web was completed in *Owen v. City of Independence* [1980], which held that municipalities could not claim good-faith defenses to constitutional violations."

Common Charges Brought Against Police Officers

As noted, most cases being tried are based on Section 1983 alleging police violation of constitutional rights. More recently, several lawsuits have been brought for failure to protect or investigate. Addicks (1981, p. 180) notes two important distinctions in determining personal liability of city officers and employees for acts committed while on duty:

- Discretionary v. ministerial acts.
- Mis- or malfeasance v. nonfeasance.

Discretionary acts are those actions officers perform using their own judgment. Policies and procedures for the acts leave decisions up to the officers. If police officers are carrying out a duty requiring judgment, they cannot be liable for damages unless they are willfully or grossly negligent. Making arrests is an example of a discretionary act.

Ministerial acts have to do with the way the duty is to be performed. If officers fail to perform the duty as prescribed, they can be sued. If, for example, a department has a policy against shooting a gun from a moving squad car and an officer does so and injures someone, the officer can be sued.

Misfeasance or **malfeasance** refers to acts of misconduct, while **nonfeasance** refers to failure to take action. In the infamous Rodney King incident, officers participating in the beating might be charged with misfeasance in civil proceedings. Those who stood by and did nothing to interfere might be charged with nonfeasance.

The most frequent civil lawsuits against police involve false arrest or imprisonment, malicious prosecution, use of unnecessary force, brutality, wrongful death, failure to protect, and negligent service.

False Arrest or Imprisonment

The largest number of lawsuits are for false arrest and imprisonment and account for about 50 percent of all lawsuits filed. False arrest and false imprisonment are exceptionally vulnerable to lawsuits because such suits are filed with ease and can be filed as a group action.

False arrest and false imprisonment are almost synonymous under the law. Both are usually alleged against the officer.

Arrest is broadly defined as taking an individual into custody by physical or constructive restraint with the intention of charging the individual in a court of law (Chapter 5). Physical force need not be used to accomplish arrest or imprisonment.

The assertion that would be brought to the court's attention in such a lawsuit is that the officer lacked probable cause to arrest. An absolute defense in such a case is that probable cause *did* exist.

The courts look at two important factors when examining liability for false arrest: (1) the information known to the police officer at the time the arrest was made and (2) the reasonableness of the officer's action given all the circumstances at the time of the arrest.

A common problem area is when police officers respond to retail stores' calls for assistance in arresting a person suspected of shoplifting. Most agencies have standardized procedures requiring the apprehending store employee to make a formal citizen's arrest. In this case, a claim of false imprisonment may be filed against both the store and the police officer.

Malicious Prosecution

An area of liability closely associated with false arrest and imprisonment is malicious prosecution. **Malicious prosecution** is a proceeding instituted in bad faith without any probable cause in the belief that the charges against the defendant can be sustained. The cause of action in the civil suit is usually for damages suffered. This type of civil action arises most frequently when one citizen formally charges another citizen and the defendant is not successfully prosecuted.

Excessive Force or Brutality

The second largest number of civil actions against police officers are filed in the areas of excessive force or brutality. These suits can be the result of lawful or allegedly unlawful arrests and will usually name a supervisor as a defendant along with the officer(s) actually involved.

The specific allegations may be civil assault and battery. Assault refers to conduct which may result from a well-founded fear of imminent peril. Battery is the unlawful, hostile touching or shoving of another, no matter how slight. Some states have combined the two into a single charge of assault. In some instances, criminal charges may be brought as well. For example, if a police officer were to strike a handcuffed prisoner with his nightstick hard enough to shatter the bones in his face, the prisoner could bring a civil action *and* press criminal charges against the officer.

As a general rule, police officers should remember that any time officers use excessive force to make an arrest, citizens can use reasonable force to protect themselves. Many states hold that a person has a right to forcibly resist an unlawful arrest, using reasonable force. Other states say that people taken into custody or arrested must go peaceably and if they have any grievance as to treatment, they have civil recourse in court. Courts have held an officer liable for assault and battery if she strikes a defendant or uses an aerosol irritant on him because he talked back, or if an officer continues to beat on a defendant after he has stopped resisting.

Almost every state now has statutes which define the extent to which police officers can use physical force in specific situations. All officers should become thoroughly familiar with their state's statutes in this area.

Most states allow officers to use some physical force short of deadly force to make an arrest or prevent an escape. Officers may also use physical force, short of deadly force, to defend themselves.

The use of *deadly force* to make an arrest or prevent an escape is generally permitted only when:

- The crime committed was a felony involving the use or threatened use of imminent physical force against a person.
- The crime committed was an inherently dangerous felony such as kidnapping, arson, or burglary in a dwelling.
- The officer's life or personal safety was endangered in the particular circumstances involved.
- The person is an escapee from a correctional facility.

It is doubtful the court would uphold the use of deadly physical force in cases involving property crimes unless there was imminent danger to the officer or other individuals.

The use of physical force by police officers to prevent destruction of evidence is controversial. Generally, the force used must be reasonable under all circumstances. Deadly physical force is *never* permitted in preventing the destruction of evidence. Swallowing drugs in an arrest is an area where courts have not given police any guidelines. Cases have ranged from officers sticking their fingers down suspects' throats to officers taking suspects to hospitals to have emergency personnel give them enemas.

Handcuffing an arrested person who is not resisting the arrest has also been deemed excessive force in some instances, as discussed in Chapter 5.

Wrongful Death

Closely related to excessive force and brutality complaints is the area of wrongful death actions. Wrongful deaths can be caused either by intentional or negligent acts or by omissions of police officers. Intentionally inflicting fatal injuries causes the greatest number of wrongful death actions. Circumstances that lead to wrongful death suits include the following:

- Shooting an unarmed, fleeing misdemeanant.
- Shooting a fleeing felon where the felon could have been subdued without deadly force.
- Shooting any misdemeanant to effect an arrest.
- Shooting in self-defense of an actual or threatened attack when the attacker did not use great bodily force.

Negligent killings account for a much smaller number of deaths and usually arise in the following situations:

- Shooting to halt a motor vehicle and striking a passenger. (This practice has been regulated by most police departments by forbidding firing at a moving vehicle.)
- Accidentally shooting a bystander.
- Reckless firing of warning shots. (Many police departments forbid the firing of warning shots.)
- Poor aim when shooting to wound a suspect. (This includes accidentally striking a hostage or accidentally discharging a firearm, wounding or killing an innocent person.)

Officers participating in raiding parties, such as those making drug arrests, must act reasonably. Any lawsuits that may emanate from their actions will encompass all officers participating in the raid. The lawsuit can extend to the supervisors, the department, and the city itself.

Negligent Operation of a Vehicle

Another area of specific liability is the operation of a police vehicle. Liability in this particular area has increased dramatically in recent years. Police officers are charged with the same standard of care as the general public and are found liable under a straight negligence theory for the negligent operation of vehicles. Statutes allowing police officers to disregard stop signs and other traffic laws and cautions are now being interpreted by the courts to require officers to use reasonable care under existing circumstances. The requirement of reasonable care is particularly critical when ''hot pursuit'' is involved and the police vehicle being used is unmarked and lacks a siren and red lights. According to Payton (1986, p. 136),

> *Most states provide legal protection against civil liability when damage or injury results from an emergency response that is in the line of duty:*
>
> *1. Red light (or blue light) and siren are used.*
> *2. The officer is pursuing an actual or suspected violator*
> *3. It is a response to (but not from) a fire.*

Payton cautions: ''The above conditions do not excuse an officer from criminal liability if it can be shown that the officer was criminally negligent in his actions.''

An officer responding to a call of a crime in progress. Rapid responses and high-speed pursuits may result in lawsuits if injuries occur.

Failure to Protect

Another broad area of officer liability involves lawsuits alleging "failure to protect." This can take several forms, including failure to answer calls for help, failure to arrest, failure to investigate, and so on. Carrington (1989, p. 22) explains: "The 'public duty' rule . . . holds that law enforcement officers owe a duty to the public in general, but they owe no duty to specific individuals injured by crime *unless* a 'special relationship' has been created between the crime victim and the law enforcement authorities." Some such "special relationships" have been found to exist in the following circumstances.

General Failure to Protect.   Failure to protect can involve several types of situations. One of the most common is when a victim assumes the police will provide protection and then relies on that assumption. Publishing a 911 number, according to some courts, implies that the police will protect those who call that number. In *Delong v. County of Erie* (1983) a woman heard someone in her house, called 911, and was told help was on the way. She made no attempt to leave the house and was murdered while the police were responding to an incorrect address.

Failure to protect also occurs when the police tell a victim they will let the victim know when someone is released from custody or from prison and fail to do so. Failure to protect witnesses who have cooperated with police and whose cooperation brings them into contact with the suspects has also resulted in lawsuits. In *Schuster v. City of New York* (1958), a citizen spotted the infamous Willie Sutton and alerted the police, who arrested him. The citizen became a city hero but also began receiving threats against his life. The city refused to protect him, and he was murdered.

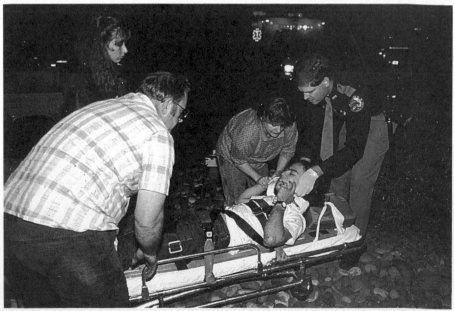

Deputy assisting at an accident scene. The public expects their law enforcement officers to help accident victims. Many courts also expect this.

Failure to Arrest or Restrain People Committing or About to Commit Violent Crimes. This is usually classed as an act of negligence. For example, an officer failed to get a drunken motorist off the road before causing a serious accident. Failure to arrest a person known to be dangerous when probable cause exists can also lead to suits for damages subsequently done by that person. In *Baker v. City of New York* (1966) the victim was made to share a waiting room with her estranged husband who was known to be violent. He shot her, and the city was held responsible.

Failure to Respond to Calls for Assistance. If police officers have reason to believe someone is in imminent danger, they must take action or face the possibility of a lawsuit. In *Thurman v. City of Torrington* (1984), the victim, an estranged wife who was beaten by her husband, received a $2.3 million award because the police had refused to act on her complaints.

Failure to Identify. At times, failure to identify oneself as a police officer before making an arrest can lead to liability on negligence theory. The liability would be for incurred damages or injuries that might have been avoided if the officer had given proper identification.

Failure to Investigate. According to Carrington (1989, p. 23): ''The courts, quite properly, have kept a 'hands-off' attitude towards the investigative stage of police work. . . . [H]owever, when a failure to investigate can be attributed to alleged racial motivations on the part of the authorities, courts—especially federal courts—will assume jurisdiction of the issues.'' This was established in *NAACP v. Levi* (1976).

Negligent Service

The past two decades have seen an increase in civil lawsuits claiming negligence by police officers, departments, and municipalities in providing traffic services. Kappeler and del Carmen (1989, pp. 25–30) state the following concerning liability in traffic-related services:

- Where a police officer or agency has actual or constructive knowledge of a potentially dangerous condition and fails to take reasonable action to correct the existing hazard, liability may be imposed.
- Where a police officer fails to warn oncoming traffic of a hazard and injury results, negligence may be found.
- Where a police officer takes control of a hazardous situation (a traffic accident scene, for example), the duty to warn can extend to third parties not directly involved in the initial accident.
- Police officers are not liable for failing to aid or assist endangered individuals. Failure of a police officer to render aid or assistance is not tortious [a civil offense] conduct. . . . [This is not true in some states.]

Some courts do hold police officers responsible for providing assistance at an accident scene. Other courts, however, contend that, although the police have a duty to help at an accident scene, officers become liable only after establishing a special relationship with the victim. This relationship can be established in at least three ways, according to Kappeler and del Carmen (p. 27):

First, once an officer begins to rescue someone, a special relationship may be established. The officer must then complete the rescue in a nonnegligent fashion even though there was no duty to rescue in the first place. . . .

Second, failure to take simple actions to reduce the risk of harm to an incapacitated individual may lead to liability. Failure of a police officer to summon or render medical aid or to transport an injured person from the scene of an accident has been considered a breach of duty by some courts. . . .

Third, liability may be found where an officer impedes medical aid or another's attempt at assistance. . . . An officer's presence at the scene of an accident can create a situation where others will not assist because of the officer's presence. . . . Compounding the problem is the fact that police officers often direct other drivers away from the scene of an accident, reducing the possibility that others will render aid.

Traffic-related incidents are not the only area in which charges of negligent service can be made. Recent cases suggest that the negligent administration of first aid by police officers can be the basis for an action in negligence in which either an act or an omission of the officer becomes the cause for complaint. In addition, some lawsuits have been filed in attempts to make an officer liable for not recognizing existing medical impairments. Though these cases are rare, officers should be aware of them. Most have not been successful, and many have centered around what appeared to be a drunken person and who was treated as a drunk, only to find that person was suffering a heart attack or having an epileptic seizure.

Other Areas of Civil Liability

Although the next areas to be discussed have produced limited litigation against police officers to date, officers should be aware of these possibilities for lawsuits.

Libel and Slander.   An action in this area is usually based on written (**libel**) or oral (**slander**) false statements that tend to humiliate and degrade a person in the esteem of others. These usually are known as *defamation of character* suits. These types of suits often pivot around statements made during arrests since much of the court process and testimony are privileged communications and should not be repeated by the police officers. Proving the truth of the statement is a defense to such actions.

Invasion of Privacy.   Invasion of privacy involves the wanton or malicious publication of a truthfully told act or event when the publicity is calculated to embarrass, ridicule, or shame the victim. Many states do not recognize this type of action. Police officers should be aware that this type of action is often disguised as an intangible loss under false arrest or imprisonment lawsuits.

Abuse of the Legal Process.   Actions in this area usually deal with the willful misapplication of the court process in an attempt to obtain a result not intended by law. An example is when an officer uses a valid search or arrest warrant to meet an objective not within the scope of the warrant. The claim is usually that the officer used the warrant as a cover for intended wrongdoing, use of excessive force, repressive conduct, or receipt of a bribe.

Cruel and Unusual Punishment.   This area usually deals with prisoners. It is the subject of much litigation currently and is of vital importance to officers who must house prisoners. Lawsuits have accelerated in this area due to the increased availability of the federal court system for such actions. The action is usually based on a negligence theory claiming that jailors have a duty to all prisoners to ensure their safekeeping and that the jail facility itself be safe. If jailors breach this duty by negligent acts or omissions, they are liable. Some specific areas where jailors have been held liable are as follows:

- Placing inmates in cells with other inmates known to be dangerous.
- Denial of, and failure to obtain, medical aid.
- Overlooking continued physical or sexual activity by prisoners.
- Unsanitary jail conditions.
- Allowing a kangaroo court in jail.

Charges Brought Against Supervisors and Cities

Some areas in which people have frequently attempted to hold supervisors and cities liable include:

- Negligent hiring of the officer(s).
- Failure to adequately train the officer(s).
- Failure to adequately supervise the officer(s).
- Negligent retention of the officer(s).

The two most frequent civil actions brought against supervisors, police departments, and cities are for failure to train and for failure to supervise.

City of Canton v. Harris (1989) established that a municipality *can* be held liable in a Section 1983 lawsuit because of a failure to properly train municipal employees. In this case, Harris was arrested and taken to the Canton police station. She fell twice during this stay, and when police asked if she needed medical attention, she gave an unintelligible answer. She was left lying on the floor, allegedly so she would not fall again. When she was released an hour later, her family took her by ambulance to a hospital. She was diagnosed as suffering from emotional ailments and put into the hospital. Subsequently, Harris sued the city for not providing adequate medical care. At issue was whether inadequate training can be the basis for suing the city under Section 1983. The Court said yes, but only under three specific conditions:

- The failure reflects a ''deliberate'' or ''conscious choice'' by the municipality.

- The inadequate training represents city policy.
- The identified deficiency in training must be closely related to the injury for which damages are claimed.

About the new legal landscape after the *Harris* case, del Carmen and Kappeler (1991, p. 12) note:

The Harris *case brings good news and bad news to potential plaintiffs. The good news is that for the first time the U.S. Supreme Court has ruled that cities and municipalities may be liable for inadequate training of police officers. The bad news is that most plaintiffs will find it difficult to meet the tough legal standard of "deliberate indifference" set out by the Court as the criterion for liability.*

Just what constitutes deliberate indifference is not at all clear from the *Harris* case, however, as noted by Alpert and Smith (1991, p. 23):

The Supreme Court's only substantive indication of what it may consider deliberately indifferent appears in a footnote to the text and targets the issue of the need to train officers in the use of deadly force against fleeing felons. . . . The clear statement from this note is that some training needs are "so obvious" that failure to train with respect to them shows deliberate indifference to constitutional rights.

Daane and Hendricks (1991, p. 26) suggest that failure-to-train suits are likely to become more common and that: "A well-planned training program can save vast amounts of money, especially now in this litigious society."

Legal Representation and Insurance Companies

Who pays for legal representation and for any awards that are made depends on many factors. If insurance coverage is available, it is the primary source of funds to pay the lawyers and any awards. Since many police departments, cities, and municipalities in the United States have insurance covering basic areas of police officer misconduct, this is often the responsible party.

If a police department does not have insurance coverage for the particular act of misconduct alleged, responsibility for legal representation as well as primary liability for any judgment returned generally falls on the police department or the political subdivision responsible for creating the police department. It must be noted, however, that a judgment against a police officer can be satisfied by confiscating the personal assets of the officer. Even where the police department or the political subdivision has been held jointly liable, it is possible that assets of individual officers may be seized. Police officers should know that if their conduct involves intentional misconduct or malicious acts, they are much more likely to be found personally liable.

Even where police departments are covered by insurance, officers should be familiar with the policy provisions because they can exclude coverage in many areas. Punitive damages, for example, are often excluded.

*Punitive damages refer to compensation awarded by a court
to a person who has been harmed in a particularly malicious
or willful way. The person who has done the harm is held
responsible for payment.*

The purpose of punitive damages is to serve as a warning to keep that sort of act
from happening again. It is not related to the actual cost of the injury or the harm
suffered. Officers might be heartened by the finding in *Cornwell v. City of Riverside*
(1990) which held that a city *can* pay the punitive damages assessed against its
employees. In this case, Cornwell brought a Section 1983 action against five Riverside police officers. The jury awarded Cornwell both general and punitive damages. When the City of Riverside attempted to pay the punitive damages assessed
against its officers, Cornwell refused, saying that such payment would not punish
the wrongdoers but would, rather, use tax dollars. The court disagreed, saying the
city could pay the punitive damages if it considered such an act to be in its best
interest.

Another area frequently not covered is the loss incurred from the misuse of a
motor vehicle. If law enforcement officers are found guilty of the negligent operation of their squad cars, the insurance company may not pay for any damages
sustained.

Often benevolent and fraternal police organizations will provide legal and other
support to officers in litigation.

Insurance Costs

Insurance premiums have risen sharply since cities have become liable. In some
cities, they have risen so much that the cities simply cannot pay them. Such cities
are extremely vulnerable because a large judgment or several smaller judgments
could monetarily cripple them.

The alternative, suggests McCoy (1984, p. 59), ''is for the municipality and its
police department to take decisive action to reduce the risk of adverse judgments.
Police administrators must prove that they have reviewed departmental policies and
that line officers are trained and supervised to keep within constitutional bounds;
such 'loss prevention' vigilance may persuade an insurer to provide liability coverage at comparatively affordable rates. In noninsurance terms, this means that
police administrators must deter departmental and officer misconduct.''

Defenses in Civil Lawsuits

In reviewing defenses in civil lawsuits against police officers and their superiors,
Thomas and Means (1990, p. 41) found that

> *The U.S. Supreme Court has repeatedly held that state and local government
> officials will not be held liable in lawsuits brought under Section 42 U.S.C.A.
> 1983 as long as they had an objectively reasonable belief in the lawfulness of*

their conduct. As the court itself has said, this immunity shields "all but the plainly incompetent or those who knowingly violate the law."

The normal defenses used by police officers, departments, and municipalities being sued are that:

- *They didn't intend to deprive the plaintiff of constitutional rights.*
- *They acted in good faith.*
- *They acted with what was considered reasonable judgment at the time and with valid authority.*

Reducing the Occurrence of Civil Lawsuits

Police officers and agencies can expect more rather than fewer lawsuits unless specific steps are taken. Ultimately, the risk of civil liability rests upon the individual actions of each police officer. Police departments can develop extensive policies and procedures to help assure that their officers act in a way that will deter civil lawsuits. As noted by Gallagher (1990b, p. 40): "Factors that decrease the chance of liability ultimately increase the agency's overall professionalism."

Gallagher has developed a *Six-Layered Liability Protection System* based on the analysis of major causes of lawsuits. His study also identified what many chiefs would want in place should a major incident occur.

The Six-Layered Liability Protection System *includes:*

- *Policies and procedures*
- *Training*
- *Supervision*
- *Discipline*
- *Review and revision*
- *Legal support and services*

Policies and Procedures.   At the base of the protection system are the department's policies and procedures. As Gallagher (1990b, p. 40) cautions, "The old maxim, falsely held by some chiefs, that you cannot be held responsible for a policy you don't have, is [no longer] operable."

He suggests using the "test of foreseeability" in formulating policies. Admittedly, no one can foresee every conceivable incident that might arise, but chiefs can look at crime and incident data and come to some conclusions about what officers should reasonably be prepared to deal with.

Training.   Training should include the basic rookie training as well as on-going in-service training and specialized training. Training must include the policies and procedures of the department; it must also include a continual updating on changes in laws that affect police operations. According to Gallagher (1990a, p. 20): "Provision should be made for on-going in-service legal training for all officers, covering court decisions, new statutes, and a brief review of the major high-risk, critical task policies."

Some departments are requiring college educations for their recruits. According to Mahan (1991, p. 282), when the requirement of the Dallas Police Department for forty-five semester hours of college credit with a "C" average was challenged as not being a *bona fide occupational requirement,* the court held in *Davis v. City of Dallas* (1979) that it was, indeed, related. The defendant's experts were able to establish a direct relationship between a college education and the superior performance of law enforcement officers.

Supervision. Supervisors must also be trained in the department's policies and procedures and be committed to implementing them. As noted by Gallagher (1990b, p. 41), "To avoid liability and achieve a high level of professionalism in a police department, it is impossible to overemphasize the importance of preparing and training supervisors for their roles as communicators and enforcers of policies. They must also be trained in management and leadership skills, with an emphasis on liability management and risk reduction."

Discipline. Discipline is possible if the first three components of the liability protection system are in place. Discipline can be viewed from both the positive and the negative sides. On the positive side, police departments should foster professional discipline within their officers; that is, they should encourage an atmosphere where officers act according to established policies and procedures. They should be able to say of their personnel, They are well-disciplined officers. On the negative side, officers who do not act according to established policies and procedures should be reprimanded (disciplined).

Review and Revision. Change is the only constant in our complex society. Chapter 1 described changes in the population being served, the changing role of police officers, and changes in the administration. In addition, laws at the local, state, and federal levels are continuously changing. Policies and procedures should be continuously reviewed and revised as needed. According to Gallagher (1990b, p. 43): "One of the reasons why police departments have been so severely hit by liability is that they have reacted either too slowly or not at all to the clear indicators that change must be effected. . . . To take more of the offensive against liability, change must occur as soon as possible."

Legal Support and Services. Lawsuits *will* increase against police officers, departments, and municipalities. According to Gallagher (1990b, pp. 43–44): "If there is one given, it is that law enforcement officers will find themselves in an increasingly legalistic environment. . . . Almost unanimously, police executives will agree that increases can be expected in all cases. Unfortunately, 90–95 percent of our law enforcement agencies will continue to conduct their business without experienced, available, and aggressive legal counsel; uniform, timely updates on legal issues and new court decisions; or relevant updates on new state statutes."

Police officers whose department provides the preceding layers of protection against civil liability and who take advantage of these layers will be much more likely to perform in a way that avoids civil lawsuits.

On a more personal level, del Carmen (1987, pp. 420–421) suggests specific ways law enforcement officers can minimize lawsuits:

1. Know and follow your department's manual or guidelines. If you do so, you will have a strong claim to a good faith defense.
2. Act within the scope of your duties.
3. Act in a professional and responsible manner at all times. When faced with a difficult situation, use reason instead of emotion.
4. Know the constitutional rights of your constituents and respect them.
5. Consult your legal consul or supervisor if you have doubts about what you are doing. Be able to document the advice given.
6. In sensitive cases, document your activities. Keep good written records.
7. Establish and maintain good relations with your community.
8. Keep yourself well informed on current issues and trends in civil and criminal liability cases.

To minimize lawsuits at a more personal level, law enforcement officers should:

- *Know and follow their department's guidelines.*
- *Stay in the scope of their duties.*
- *Always act professionally.*
- *Know and respect their constituents' rights.*
- *If in doubt, seek advice.*
- *Carefully document their activities.*
- *Maintain good community relations.*
- *Keep up to date on civil and criminal liability cases.*

The importance of documentation cannot be emphasized enough. Comprehensive incident reports are vital to defenses against civil suits. Videotaping traffic stops also provides officers with documentation of their actions, especially in cases involving DWI arrests.

Countersuits

In many instances, civil suits brought against law enforcement officers have either no basis or are frivolous. Some people consider the best defense to be a good offense and therefore sue the officer who arrested them, thinking it might put them in a better bargaining position.

Law enforcement officers and agencies can countersue if they are falsely accused of a civil offense.

Manak (1991), senior counsel for the Northwestern University Traffic Institute, describes a case involving Richard Hathaway, a Napa County, California deputy sheriff, who responded to a public drunkenness complaint at a convenience store. When he arrived, the deputy approached the suspect and asked the suspect to accompany him outside to discuss the problem. The suspect filed a brutality complaint against the deputy, claiming the deputy had grabbed him by the throat and physically dragged him out of the store. As noted by Manak (p. 15):

The Napa County Deputy Sheriff's Association undertook to assist Hathaway in his action. The evidence, obtained from a videotape taken by the convenience store security camera, showed that the deputy not only did not grab the offender by the throat, but held the door open for him when he exited the store. The trial judge awarded Hathaway $25,000 in damages as a result of the false accusations.'' (Richard Hathaway v. Troy Gilfuss)

Law enforcement officers can also sue even if they have not been sued. As noted by Manak (1989, p. 16):

Public safety personnel, be they prosecutors, firefighters, police, sheriff's deputies or emergency medical personnel, are entitled to the same right to recover for wrongful injury as any other citizen. In increasing numbers, public safety personnel are themselves becoming plaintiffs in lawsuits filed against individuals who assault them or otherwise put them in danger. And in a good number of instances, they are successful in recovering.

Summary

Section 1983, the Civil Rights Law, says that anyone acting under the authority of the law who violates another person's constitutional rights can be sued. Vicarious liability makes others specifically associated with a person also responsible for that person's actions.

The most frequent civil lawsuits against police involve false arrest or imprisonment, malicious prosecution, use of unnecessary force, brutality, wrongful death, failure to protect, and negligent service. The two most frequent civil actions brought against supervisors, police departments, and cities are for failure to train and for failure to supervise. Punitive damages refer to compensation awarded by a court to a person who has been harmed in a particularly malicious or willful way. The person who has done the harm is held responsible for payment.

The normal defenses used by police officers being sued are that they didn't intend to deprive the plaintiff of constitutional rights, that they acted in good faith, and that they acted with what was considered reasonable judgment at the time and with valid authority.

Gallagher's *Six-Layered Liability Protection System* includes policies and procedures, training, supervision, discipline, review and revision, and legal support and services.

To minimize lawsuits at a more personal level, law enforcement officers should know and follow their department's guidelines; stay in the scope of their duties; always act professionally; know and respect their constituents' rights; if in doubt, seek advice; keep good records of their activities; maintain good community relations; and keep up to date on civil and criminal liability cases.

Law enforcement officers and agencies can countersue if they are falsely accused of a civil offense.

Application #1

You are the administrative sergeant. The chief has sought your help in reducing the cost of insurance by establishing a clear policy and procedure for reducing the risk of civil liability.

Instructions   Using the form in Appendix A, write this policy and procedure. Include what areas are vulnerable to lawsuits and how officers can protect themselves in each area.

Application #2

Many criminals have led officers into situations where the officers become vulnerable to lawsuits. Many have also recovered awards under Section 1983. In a procedure bulletin, have the officers establish what they feel would be a good approach to avoid becoming trapped in a situation of this type and what reports would be necessary should the officer and the department be sued.

Exercises in Critical Thinking

The most frequent lawsuits against police officers involve false arrest, use of unnecessary force, malicious prosecution without probable cause, negligence, and failure to protect. The exigencies of a situation must be sufficient to allow a warrantless search. These factors are: (1) that a grave offense is involved, such as a crime of violence; (2) that the suspect is believed to be armed; (3) that there is a clear showing of probable cause to believe the suspect committed the crime; (4) that there is strong reason to believe the suspect is on the premises; (5) that there is a likelihood the suspect will escape if not swiftly apprehended; and (6) that although the entry may not be with consent, it must be peaceable.

In the early morning of September 20, Sergeant James Nichols and Officer John Peck gave chase to a suspect who had allegedly stolen thirteen cartons of cigarettes. Three additional officers from St. Paul and several Washington County sheriff's deputies were also involved in the chase. In total, an estimated twenty officers from six police agencies joined the twenty-mile chase and its aftermath. After pursuing the suspect from Minnesota across the state line into Wisconsin at speeds of up to 110 miles per hour, Michael Merten, Jr., 18, of St. Paul, was stopped. According to the officers, Merten attempted to resist arrest, and they punched, kicked, and struck Merten with their flashlights. Nichols described the beating as a ''thumping.'' Merten suffered bruises and head cuts that required fourteen stitches.

Hudson officer Edward Rankin reported that he saw a Washington County deputy use his flashlight to strike the head of Michael Newborg-Ordorff, another teenager riding with Merten, while the victim was pinned face down by several officers.

1. Despite nearly a year of investigations by the FBI, Merten's attorneys, police internal affairs units, and the Civil Service Commission, the officers

who actually did the beating have not been identified. Which of the following situations will result?

  a. Not one officer came forward to give a clear accounting of what took place, and therefore no disciplinary action or legal action will occur.

  b. Officer Rankin wrote, "It is this officer's opinion that there was an excessive amount of force used by numerous officers after the suspects were under control. There were so many officers at the scene with many different uniforms that I would be unable to identify any of the officers and what their particular involvement was." So no disciplinary action will be possible although the agencies involved may still have to pay a settlement.

  c. As the law provides for damages if officers stand by and do nothing to prevent the use of excessive force, damages must be paid by individual officers who will also receive disciplinary action.

  d. As the code of ethics calls for officers to support one another, no officer has to testify in such a way as to incriminate another.

  e. St. Paul police and the state patrol will be held responsible for compensating Merten, and disciplinary action will probably be taken against some officers.

On March 29, Sergeant Frank Zaruba arranged through an informant for the purchase of 3.5 grams of cocaine. Zaruba drove to the parking lot of a restaurant and met Merle Jones and Rolando "Jose" Espinosa. After negotiating the purchase, both Jones and Espinosa left to get the cocaine while Zaruba remained at the parking lot. Zaruba had not yet paid for the cocaine. Surveillance officers Nelson and Carter followed Jones and Espinosa and observed their vehicle park in front of 81 or 83 East King Street. Espinosa returned to his vehicle and gave something to Jones. Jones then came back to Zaruba's vehicle and gave him the cocaine. Both Espinosa and Jones were then arrested.

Because money had not been exchanged, the officers believed the source would be expecting payment. At this point, Carter told Sergeant Neil Nelson that it was his best guess that the source of the cocaine lived at 81 East King. Carter told Nelson that Espinosa went into a white house with an open porch and pillars, which 81 East King has and which 83 East King does not. Additionally, Carter believed that if a door had opened at 83 East King, he would have observed it, but he did not.

Nelson knocked on the door of 81 East King and Rolando Alayon answered the door. Nelson said that "Jose" had sent him up there with the money. At this point, Alayon frowned and glanced at the street. Sergeant Nelson pulled out the money and told Alayon that Espinosa had gotten into a fight and that was why he was delivering the money. Alayon then nodded his head but did not take the money or reply. During this encounter, the front door was partially open. Alayon began to close the door and open the screen door at the same time. Nelson then drew his gun and ordered Alayon to the floor. Nelson then stepped into the house and ordered two females to remain seated in the living room. Shortly after Nelson's entry, other surveillance officers entered the house with their guns drawn. A sweep of the house was performed to identify other occupants.

Nelson then asked Montanez if he could search the premises and Montanez orally agreed. Then Alayon also agreed to allow a search of the house.

  2. Was the warrantless search of the house supported by probable cause and exigent circumstances?

    a. No, for the only exigency which might have existed was created by the officers' own tactical decisions and actions.

b. Yes, because Carter said it was his best guess that the source of the cocaine was 81 East King.

c. Yes, probable cause existed because of Alayon's actions at the door.

d. Yes, because the officers did a reasonable job of surveillance and used good logic in deducing that Espinosa went into a white house with an open porch and pillars, which describes 81 East King but not 83 East King.

e. Yes, because Alayon frowned, glanced, nodded, and probably would have taken the money.

3. Was Alayon's consent to search voluntarily given?

a. Alayon's consent was voluntary if all the officers' guns were holstered when it was given.

b. A verbal statement is sufficient to define voluntary consent—and here we have two consents.

c. Under the totality of circumstances (a number of police with drawn guns and no attempt to secure a search warrant), no issue of consent can arise.

d. Because voluntariness of consent is a finding of fact made by the totality of circumstances, there are a sufficient number of factors in this case that combine to justify voluntary consent even though each single factor in isolation may not.

e. Although voluntariness of consent may not be true in this case, its lack will not hurt the prosecution of Alayon, and officers would never be held liable for similar actions.

Discussion Questions

1. Why are law enforcement officers being sued more frequently today than ten years ago?

2. Since public employees have mutual responsibilities, why aren't firefighters subjected to lawsuits like police officers are?

3. Have any misconduct lawsuits been filed against local police officers? Check with your police department and see what their history of civil lawsuits has been.

4. How much training is enough to avoid lawsuits under Section 1983? Explain your reasoning in the areas of firearms, search and seizure, and laws of arrest.

5. How could a Section 1983 action be brought where an officer in the locker room preparing for duty accidentally discharged his revolver, striking a custodian? What would be the justification for a lawsuit in this case?

6. In what areas of law enforcement should police officers be exempt from lawsuits, if any?

7. Who is responsible for seeing that officers are adequately protected from lawsuits under Section 1983?

Definitions

Can you define the following terms?

civil actions	discretionary acts
the Civil Rights Act	libel
collective deep pocket	litigious

malfeasance	punitive damages	**157** CHAPTER 6 Civil Liability: Avoiding Lawsuits in a Litigious Society
malicious prosecution	Section 1983	
ministerial acts	slander	
misfeasance	tort	
nonfeasance	vicarious liability	

References

Addicks, Mentor C. Jr. *Handbook for Minnesota Cities*. 4th ed. St. Paul, Minn.: League of Minnesota Cities, 1981.

Alpert, Geoffrey P., and Smith, William C. "Beyond City Limits and into the Woods: A Brief Look at the Policy Impact of *City of Canton v. Harris* and *Wood v. Ostrander.*" *American Journal of Police* X:1 (November 1991): 19–40.

Carrington, Frank. "Avoiding Liability for Police Failure to Protect." *The Police Chief* (September 1989): 22–24.

Daane, Diane M. and Hendricks, James E. "Liability for Failure to Adequately Train." *The Police Chief* (November 1991): 26–29.

del Carmen, Rolando V. *Criminal Procedure for Law Enforcement Personnel*. Monterey, Calif.: Brooks/Cole Publishing Company, 1987.

del Carmen, Rolando V. and Kappeler, Victor E. "Municipalities and Police Agencies as Defendants: Liability for Official Policy." *American Journal of Police* X:1 (November 1991): 1–17.

Gallagher, G. Patrick.
a. "Risk Management for Police Administrators." *The Police Chief* (June 1990): 18–29.
b. "The Six-Layered Liability Protection System for Police." *The Police Chief* (June 1990): 40–44.

Harr, J. Scott, and Hess, Kären M. *Criminal Procedure*. St. Paul, Minn.: West Publishing Company, 1990.

Kappeler, Victor E. and del Carmen, Rolando V. "Police Conduct at Accident Scenes: Avoiding Liability for Negligent Service." *The Police Chief* (September 1989): 25–30.

Mahan, Richard. "Personnel Selection in Police Agencies: Educational Requirements for Entry Level." *Law and Order* (January 1991): 282–286.

Manak, James P.
a. "The Law Enforcement Plaintiff: An Update." *The Police Chief* (March 1991): 15–16.
b. "The Police Plaintiff: Making the System Work for Law Enforcement." *The Police Chief* (September 1989): 16–19.

McCoy, Candace. "Lawsuits Against Police: What Impact Do They Really Have?" *Criminal Law Bulletin* (1984):56–60.

Oran, Daniel. *Law Dictionary for Nonlawyers*. 2d ed. St. Paul, Minn.: West Publishing Company, 1985.

Payton, George T. *Patrol Procedure and Enforcement Concepts*. 7th ed. San Rolando, Calif.: Criminal Justice Services, 1986.

Scogin, Forrest and Brodsky, Stanley L. "Fear of Litigation Among Law Enforcement Officers." *American Journal of Police* X:1 (November 1991):41–45.

Thomas, Bob, and Means, Randy. "The Qualified Immunity: How to Never Lose a § 1983 Lawsuit." *The Police Chief* (June 1990):41.

Cases

Baker v. City of New York, 25 A.D.2d 770, 269 N.Y.S. 2d 515 (1966).
City of Canton v. Harris, 489 U.S. 378, 109 S.Ct. 1197, 103 L.Ed.2d 412 (1989).
Cornwell v. City of Riverside, 896 F.2d 398 (9th Cir. 1990).

Davis v. City of Dallas, 483 F.Supp. 54 (N.D. Tex 1979).

Delong v. County of Erie, 60 N.Y.2d 296, 469 N.Y.S.2d 611, 459 N.E. 2d 717 (1983).

Monell v. City Department of Social Services, 436 U.S. 658, 98 S.Ct. 2018, 56 L.Ed.2d 611 (1978).

Monroe v. Pape, 365 U.S. 167, 81 S.Ct. 473, 5 L.Ed.2d 492 (1961).

NAACP v. Levi, 418 F. Supp. 1109 (D.D.C. 1976).

Owen v. City of Independence, 445 U.S. 622, 100 S.Ct. 1398, 63 L.Ed.2d 673 (1980).

Schuster v. City of New York, 5 N.Y.2d 75, 180 N.Y.S.2d 265, 154 N.E. 2d 534 (1958).

Thurman v. City of Torrington, 595 F. Supp. 1521 (D. Conn. 1984).

ETHICAL CONSIDERATIONS: A COMMITMENT TO DO THE "RIGHT" THING

CHAPTER 7

Law enforcement officers must not only act legally, as discussed in the last two chapters, they must also act ethically. Ethics has become a "hot topic" of the 1990s, in business, education, medicine, *and* law enforcement. *Ethics* is described by Oran (1985, p. 114) as "standards of fair and honest conduct; in particular, professional standards for lawyers and judges." Ethics involves integrity, doing what is considered just, honest, proper.

Ethics deals with standards of honesty, fairness, and integrity in behavior.

Ethics looks at human conduct in the light of **moral principles,** that is, set ideas of right and wrong. Moral principles can be established by individuals, set forth by a particular society or culture, laid down by a religious body or doctrine, or established by a given subculture. In most instances, an individual's moral principles derive from a combination of all of these. Further, in our pluralistic country, many differences exist in what is considered right and wrong.

Do You Know

- What ethics is?
- Whether ethical issues are usually absolute or relative?
- What a code of ethics is?
- How the police culture has been characterized?
- What gratuities are and how they relate to discussion of ethics in law enforcement?
- What the scandal-reform cycle is?
- What "common promise" ethics involves?
- What basic ethics tests can be used to assess behavior?
- How ethical behavior can be promoted?
- Who is most responsible for the ethics of a law enforcement agency?

Ethics—An Overview

Ethics also usually involves what is often referred to as a **conscience,** the ability to recognize right from wrong and to follow one's own sense of what is right. Some believe conscience is an innate moral sense, people are either born with it or not. Others believe it is a power acquired by experience, that is, it can be taught.

A further complexity is whether the issues addressed by ethics are absolute or relative. For example, is killing a human being always "bad" (absolute) or is it even "good" (relative) at times?

---

*An **absolute issue** is one with only two sides, the decision is "black" and "white." A **relative issue** is one with a multitude of sides, that is, varying shades of "gray" between the black and white, absolute sides.*

Ethics, then, involves looking at moral rules which are recognized by individuals with a conscience and are held to be either absolute or relative. What is considered ethical behavior by one individual may be considered highly unethical behavior by another individual. An example of this is the Hmong practice of adult males marrying very young girls. To the Hmong this is moral and right. To many Americans, this is immoral and wrong. Ethics *is* complex and presents serious challenges to those who seek to behave ethically. Consider, for example, which of the following ethical principles are behind how you behave:

- Do unto others as you would have them do unto you.
- Do what will accomplish my goal/vision in the most efficient manner.
- Do whatever you please so long as it does not cause harm to anyone else.
- Might makes right.
- Rule of "I am Third": Supreme Being, others, myself.

Although what people consider ethical behavior is highly personal, according to Klockars (1989, p. 427): "Some areas of human conduct or enterprise develop their own distinct ethics while others do not. There is no special ethics for grandparents, cooks, bus drivers, or college presidents even though all of them do important work and have the capacity to behave in morally exemplary or morally reprehensible ways in the course of doing so." He suggests that special codes of ethics are developed under the following conditions:

- The area has some special features making it difficult to bring under the domain of general, conventional ethics. Police, for example, can use force, even deadly force, and may lie and deceive people in their work.
- The area involves issues of concern not just to those who practice them, but to others. They involve moral controversy.
- The area involves certain types of misconduct that cannot, or perhaps should not, be controlled by other means.

Ethics in Law Enforcement

Law enforcement fits all three conditions, partly because of its great discretionary power. According to Pollock-Byrne (1989, p. 72): "Police are the initial decision makers in the criminal justice system. They are the enforcers of the law, but more important, they also have the power to define lawbreaking.'' Pollock-Byrne also notes that most police departments have a formal code of ethics, often framed and hanging on the wall. Such codes usually have at least three important themes:

- Justice or fairness is the single most dominant theme. Officers are not to take advantage of people or accept gratuities.
- The importance of the law and the police as tools of the Constitution is a second theme. Police behavior must be totally within the bounds set by the law.
- Police must at all times uphold a standard of behavior consistent with their public position.

---

*A **code of ethics** sets forth accepted standards of behavior for a profession.*

The Law Enforcement Code of Ethics, shown in Table 7.1, was adopted unanimously at the 98th Annual IACP Conference October 5–10, 1991. This conference also adopted unanimously the Police Officer Code of Conduct shown in Table 7.2.

TABLE 7.1
Law Enforcement Code of Ethics (From the International Association of Police Chiefs)

As a law enforcement officer, my fundamental duty is to serve the community; to safeguard lives and property; to protect the innocent against deception, the weak against oppression or intimidation and the peaceful against violence or disorder; and to respect the constitutional rights of all to liberty, equality and justice.

I will keep my private life unsullied as an example to all and will behave in a manner that does not bring discredit to me or to my agency. I will maintain courageous calm in the face of danger, scorn or ridicule; develop self-restraint; and be constantly mindful of the welfare of others. Honest in thought and deed both in my personal and official life, I will be exemplary in obeying the law and the regulations of my department. Whatever I see or hear of a confidential nature or that is confided to me in my official capacity will be kept ever secret unless revelation is necessary in the performance of my duty.

I will never act officiously or permit personal feelings, prejudices, political beliefs, aspirations, animosities or friendships to influence my decisions. With no compromise for crime and with relentless prosecution of criminals, I will enforce the law courteously and appropriately without fear or favor, malice or ill will, never employing unnecessary force or violence and never accepting gratuities.

I recognize the badge of my office as a symbol of public faith, and I accept it as a public trust to be held so long as I am true to the ethics of police service. I will never engage in acts of corruption or bribery, nor will I condone such acts by other police officers. I will cooperate with all legally authorized agencies and their representatives in the pursuit of justice.

I know that I alone am responsible for my own standard of professional performance and will take every reasonable opportunity to enhance and improve my level of knowledge and competence.

I will constantly strive to achieve these objectives and ideals, dedicating myself before God to my chosen profession . . . law enforcement.

TABLE 7.2
Police Code of Conduct

All law enforcement officers must be fully aware of the ethical responsibilities of their position and must strive constantly to live up to the highest possible standards of professional policing.

The International Association of Chiefs of Police believes it important that police officers have clear advice and counsel available to assist them in performing their duties consistent with these standards, and has adopted the following ethical mandates as guidelines to meet these ends.

Primary Responsibilities of a Police Officer

A police officer acts as an official representative of government who is required and trusted to work within the law. The officer's powers and duties are conferred by statute. The fundamental duties of a police officer include serving the community, safeguarding lives and property, protecting the innocent, keeping the peace and ensuring the rights of all to liberty, equality and justice.

Performance of the Duties of a Police Officer

A police officer shall perform all duties impartially, without favor or affection or ill will and without regard to status, sex, race, religion, political belief or aspiration. All citizens will be treated equally with courtesy, consideration and dignity.

Officers will never allow personal feelings, animosities or friendships to influence official conduct. Laws will be enforced appropriately and courteously and, in carrying out their responsibilities, officers will strive to obtain maximum cooperation from the public. They will conduct themselves in appearance and deportment in such a manner as to inspire confidence and respect for the position of public trust they hold.

Discretion

A police officer will use responsibly the discretion vested in his position and exercise it within the law. The principle of reasonableness will guide the officer's determinations, and the officer will consider all surrounding circumstances in determining whether any legal action shall be taken.

Consistent and wise use of discretion, based on professional policing competence, will do much to preserve good relationships and retain the confidence of the public. There can be difficulty in choosing between conflicting courses of action. It is important to remember that a timely word of advice rather than arrest—which may be correct in appropriate circumstances—can be a more effective means of achieving a desired end.

Use of Force

A police officer will never employ unnecessary force or violence and will use only such force in the discharge of duty as is reasonable in all circumstances.

The use of force should be used only with the greatest restraint and only after discussion, negotiation and persuasion have been found to be inappropriate or ineffective. While the use of force is occasionally unavoidable, every police officer will refrain from unnecessary infliction of pain or suffering and will never engage in cruel, degrading or inhuman treatment of any person.

Confidentiality

Whatever a police officer sees, hears or learns of that is of a confidential nature will be kept secret unless the performance of duty or legal provision requires otherwise.

Members of the public have a right to security and privacy, and information obtained about them must not be improperly divulged.

Integrity

A police officer will not engage in acts of corruption or bribery, nor will an officer condone such acts by other police officers.

The public demands that the integrity of police officers be above reproach. Police officers must, therefore, avoid any conduct that might compromise integrity and thus undercut the public confidence in a law enforcement agency. Officers will refuse to accept any gifts, presents, subscriptions, favors, gratuities or promises that could be interpreted as seeking to cause the officer to refrain from performing official responsibilities honestly and within the law. Police officers must not receive private or special advantage from their official status. Respect from the public cannot be bought; it can only be earned and cultivated.

Cooperation with Other Police Officers and Agencies

Police officers will cooperate with all legally authorized agencies and their representatives in the pursuit of justice.

An officer or agency may be one among many organizations that may provide law enforcement services to a jurisdiction. It is imperative that a police officer assist colleagues fully and completely with respect and consideration at all times.

TABLE 7.2 Continued

165

*CHAPTER 7
Ethical Considerations:
A Commitment to Do
the "Right" Thing*

Personal-Professional Capabilities

Police officers will be responsible for their own standard of professional performance and will take every reasonable opportunity to enhance and improve their level of knowledge and competence.

Through study and experience, a police officer can acquire the high level of knowledge and competence that is essential for the efficient and effective performance of duty. The acquisition of knowledge is a never-ending process of personal and professional development that should be pursued constantly.

Private Life

Police officers will behave in a manner that does not bring discredit to their agencies or themselves.

A police officer's character and conduct while off duty must always be exemplary, thus maintaining a position of respect in the community in which he or she lives and serves. The officer's personal behavior must be beyond reproach.

Source: The Police Chief, LIX: 1 (January 1992) p. 17. Reprinted from *The Police Chief* magazine, Volume LIX, No. 1, page 17, 1992. Copyright held by the International Association of Chiefs of Police, Inc., 1110 North Giebe Road, Suite 200, Arlington, VA 22201, USA. Further reproduction without express written permission from IACP is strictly prohibited.

The importance of ethics in police work is stressed by Pollock-Byrne (1989, p. 73):

> *Ideally, a set of ethics will help the officer make decisions in a lawful, humane, and fair manner. A code of ethics also helps to engender self-respect in individual officers; self-pride comes from knowing they have conducted themselves in a proper and appropriate manner. Further, a code of ethics contributes to mutual respect among police officers and helps in the development of an esprit de corps or a group feeling toward common goals. Agreement over methods, means, and aims are important to these feelings. As with any profession, an agreed-upon code of ethics is a unifying element and one that can help define the occupation as a profession, since it indicates a willingness to uphold certain standards of behavior.*

Often, however, the police department's formal code of ethics and its informal code of ethics are entirely different. The informal code of ethics results from what is commonly referred to as the police subculture.

The Police Subculture

Johnson and Copus (1981, p. 52) summarize the research on the police subculture as showing officers to be cynical, isolated, alienated, defensive, distrustful, dogmatic, authoritarian, with a poor self-image. The same general image is described by Scheingold (1984) who found three dominant characteristics in the police subculture:

- Cynicism—all citizens are viewed with suspicion, especially those who fit a certain type. Since [the police] regularly see people at their worst, [police]

come to view them as weak, corrupt, and dangerous. It comes to be a
"them v. us" mentality.

- Use of force at any perceived threat to their authority—any person who has
an "attitude" problem needs to be taught a lesson in humility. Force is both
expressive and instrumental—it expresses the officers' dominance, and it is
the most effective tool to keep people in line.
- A view of self as victim—police see themselves as victims of public
misunderstanding as well as of vindictive administrators.

---

*The police subculture has been characterized as cynical and
authoritative with feelings of victimization. It promotes a
"them v. us" mindset.*

This subculture has its own set of standards, often in direct conflict with the
formally stated code of ethics. Sherman (1982, pp. 10–19) summarizes these informal values:

1. *Discretion A.* Decisions about whether to enforce the law, in any but the
most serious cases, should be guided by both what the law says and who
the suspect is. Attitude, demeanor, cooperativeness, and even race, age,
and social class are all important considerations in deciding how to treat
people generally, and whether or not to arrest suspects in particular.
2. *Discretion B.* Disrespect for police authority is a serious offense that
should always be punished with an arrest or the use of force.
3. *Force.* Police officers should never hesitate to use physical or deadly force
against people who "deserve it," or where it can be an effective way of
solving a crime.
4. *Due Process.* Due process is only a means of protecting criminals at the
expense of the law abiding and should be ignored whenever it is safe to do
so.
5. *Truth.* Lying and deception are an essential part of the police job, and
even perjury should be used if it is necessary to protect yourself or get a
conviction on a "bad guy." Deceiving muggers into thinking you are an
easy mark and deceiving burglars into thinking you are a fence are proper
because there are not many other ways of catching predatory criminals in
the act.
6. *Time.* You cannot go fast enough to chase a car thief or traffic violator,
nor slow enough to get to a "garbage" call; and when there are no calls
for service, your time is your own.
7. *Rewards.* Police do very dangerous work for low wages, so it is proper to
take any extra rewards the public wants to give them, like free meals,
Christmas gifts, or even regular monthly payments (in some cities) for
special treatment.
8. *Loyalty.* The paramount duty is to protect your fellow officers at all costs,
as they would protect you, even though you may have to risk your own
career or your own life to do it. If you don't like it, quit—or get
transferred to the police academy. But never, ever, blow the whistle.

Although the preceding behaviors are overstated, they do exist in some form in some police departments and illustrate behaviors that would be considered unethical by most.

Unethical Behavior

"Police ethics involve a broad spectrum of behavior that includes not only corruption, but also malpractice, mistreatment of offenders, racial discrimination, illegal searching and seizures, [violation of] suspects' constitutional rights, perjury, evidence planting, and other misconduct committed under the authority of law enforcement" (Roberg, 1989, p. 125). This broad spectrum includes three basic forms of police malpractice according to Roberg (p. 1): legalistic, professional, and moralistic. Says Roberg (p. 126):

- Legalistic malpractice may also be referred to as police corruption, including misuse of police authority for personal gain, protecting illegal activities from police enforcement, and even receiving free meals or discounts.
- Professional malpractice can range from physical and verbal abuse of an individual to "conduct unbecoming an officer."
- Moralistic malpractice includes the discretionary powers of police officers, including consciously or unconsciously labeling and stereotyping certain types of individuals as good or bad.

There has always existed a concern about the control of the powers granted by the government to the police to use force. Where power exists, there also exists the potential to abuse that power. Unethical behavior, which in its extreme form is sometimes referred to as police corruption, is an exceedingly complex problem. As noted by Klockars (1983, p. 332): "Perhaps the most serious mistake one can make about police corruption, and it is a mistake that has been made often, is to assume that it is a simple matter. It is not."

Cohen (1986, p. 23) defines unethical behavior as *exploitation*—that is, "acting on opportunities created by virtue of one's authority for personal gain at the expense of the public one is authorized to serve."

As noted by Pollock-Byrne (1989, p. 83):

We often formally expect the police to enforce laws while informally encouraging them to ignore the same laws. . . . As long as the public gives such clear indications that it is willing to overlook many crimes, it is no surprise that the police are able to rationalize nonenforcement.

Police routinely deal with the seamier side of society, not only drug addicts and muggers, but middle-class people who are involved in dishonesty and corruption. The constant displays of lying, hiding, cheating, and theft create cynicism and threaten even the strongest code of ethics, especially when these behaviors are carried out by judges, prosecutors, superiors, and politicians. The following are some rationales that might easily be used by police to justify behavior.

- *The public thinks every cop is a crook—so why try to be honest?*
- *The money is out there—if I don't take it, someone else will.*

- *I'm only taking what's rightfully mine; if the city paid me a decent wage, I wouldn't have to get it on my own.*
- *I can use it—it's a good cause—my son needs an operation, or dental work, or tuition for medical school, or a new bicycle. . . (Murphy and Moran, 1981, p. 93).*

Gratuities

The formal law enforcement code of ethics disapproves of **gratuities,** material favors or gifts given in return for a service. However, many citizens feel there is nothing wrong with business giving freebies to a police officer, such as gifts or free admission. Many officers believe these are small rewards indeed for the difficulties they endure in police work. According to Pollock-Byrne (1989, p. 83): ''Gratuities seem to be part and parcel of a police officer's job.''

A controversial ethical issue involves whether police officers should accept gratuities and, indeed, whether the issue is absolute or relative.

Officer paying his check. Most departments do not allow their officers to accept "free lunches" or other forms of gratuities.

The question becomes—what gratuities are acceptable and under what circumstances—if any. Certainly gratuities are acceptable in many other professions. But in a profession involving great discretion, gratuities can be extremely problematic. They can give the appearance of preferential treatment, even if such preferential treatment does not exist.

Some officers take a very strong stand on this issue. Benson and Skinner (1988, pp. 32–33), for example, say: "Amazingly, many police officers, including police administrators, continue to justify 'harmless gratuities.' . . . As a police group, how are we molding the way others see us? What do our minor habits and routines say to others? What are we really—unequivocal, strong individuals or part-time moochers? . . . Any personal police gratuity is wrong, patronizing, and damaging." Benson and Skinner contend that such behavior should never be tolerated. They (p. 33) also suggest that, for officers to avoid gratuities with "tact and dignity," they follow three basic lessons:

- Vary your habits and places. Take breaks, eat meals, and fill out reports at different times and places.
- Develop a set response, without fanfare, for avoiding the offer of free coffee. Leave a tip at the table for the waitress, of course. But also know the price of coffee and, on your way out, leave that amount at the cash register, with or without a bill.
- Develop set responses for declining free or half-priced food. For example, you might say, "No, I feel much better paying the same as everyone else. But thanks for being thoughtful."

The River Cops

At the far end of the unethical spectrum is the behavior of seven young Hispanic Miami police officers hired during the early 1980s, nicknamed the Miami River Cops. Dorschner (1989, p. 264) notes: "They have been charged with big-time dope dealing, and three of them were charged with murder, which was altered to 'violating the civil rights' of the dead victims when the case was moved to federal court. In their trials, testimony has revealed that, while on duty, they would often frequent a couple of bars where dopers hung out or meet doper contacts in parking lots. At least one cop, according to testimony, used to have sexual intercourse with women in the back seat of his patrol car."

Why? Dorschner describes some of the reasons people gave (pp. 265–266). A former classmate of one of the River Cops said: "I really blame the system. They give these guys something like fourteen or sixteen weeks of training, and then they put them out there where they can make twice their salary just by turning their head the other way."

According to one of the commanders of the midnight shift: "Over time these individuals had changed a lot. . . . They had values they lost, for one reason or another." He blamed part of the change on the "ultrafirm discipline" of their supervisor, reprimanding for the smallest infractions. "The philosophy existing in that section was very damaging to young officers. . . . I think a lot of their self-pride and self-esteem was lost."

Others blamed it on lack of supervision. The sergeant in charge of the Hispanic officers group said: "Overall, I would have to place some of the blame on the supervisors. If you supervise a person right, you can't do half the s____ those River Cops did, or were alleged to have done."

The ultimate blame, however, must be placed on the individual officers. That is where all ethical decisions are made—individually, based on individual values.

Modes of Ethical Analysis

Robinette (1991, p. 42–47) describes four ways individuals might analyze the behavior of others, including police officers. First is the *expressive* mode of ethical analysis, the "bumper-sticker, t-shirt morality": American—love it or leave it! or Guns don't kill people—criminals do. Says Robinette (p. 43): "Such ethical analysis is adolescent at best and leads to mob tyranny at worst." The second mode of analysis is relying on *maxims,* folk wisdom such as the Golden Rule and sayings like, Honesty is the best policy.

A third mode is the *postethical analysis* or "after-the-fact judgment" which is modeled on the scandal-reform cycle.

The **scandal-reform cycle** occurs when the behavior of an organization is changed due to extreme pressure resulting from some negative behavior. It is reactive.

The scandal-reform cycle can be seen in operation in the reaction of the Los Angeles Police Department to the national public outcry over the beating of Rodney King, which was viewed on television across the country. According to Robinette (p. 42):

Injury examination during testimony in Simi Valley, California, in the trail of four Los Angeles officers charged with assault of Rodney King. Defense attorney, Michael Stone, left, points out an area of a model of a skull to Dr. David Dianetto, the second physician to treat Rodney King.

Typically police departments react to ethical issues and situations. The scandal-reform cycle is well documented and seems to be the norm for many departments. The cycle usually begins with some scandalous behavior by the police, which is then bruited about by the media. This leads to mounting public pressure on the department. The organizational response is a sort of fortressing, which further heats up the demand for inquiry.

"What is needed," continues Robinette (p. 42), "is proactive development and departmentwide acceptance of ethical standards of officer and organizational behavior." Such an approach would fit well with the fourth mode of analysis, that is based on the common promise police officers make when they become law enforcement officers. According to Robinette (p. 44):

---

*The **common promise** that all police officers make with their oath of office announces to the community that they are engaged in the bargain as agents, and from this bargain are derived five clear principles of fair conduct:*

- *Fair access for all members of the public.*
- *Respect for the public trust.*
- *A balance between enforcement efforts and the maintenance of order and security.*
- *Coordination and cooperation among all members of the criminal justice system.*
- *Objectivity in all dealings with the public.*

Basic Ethics Tests

Some questions, such as the question of gratuities, might appear to be black and white (absolute issues) to most, but many other ethical decisions police officers must make are not black and white at all but are instead varying shades of gray (relative issues). To arrest or not? To inform on someone or not? To lie to suspects to build a case? In such instances, the answer is seldom obvious.

How do police officers decide what is and is not ethical behavior? Benson and Skinner (1988, p. 33) suggest the following tests:

- *Test of common sense.* Does the act make sense or would someone look askance at it?
- *Test of publicity.* Would you be willing to see what you did highlighted on the front page of your local newspaper?
- *Test of one's best self.* Will the act fit the concept of ourselves at our best?
- *Test of one's most admired personality.* What would Mom, Dad, your minister, priest, or rabbi do in this situation?
- *Test of hurting someone else.* Will the act contribute to "internal pain" for someone?
- *Test of foresight.* What is the long term likely result?

Other considerations would be, Is it legal? and Is it fair?

Basic ethics tests include the tests of common sense, publicity, one's best self, one's most admired personality, hurting someone else, and foresight. Is it legal? Is it fair?

Many people believe that all behavior should be guided by the Golden Rule, Do unto others as you would have them do unto you. Other, more negative people, have coined the Silver Rule, Do unto others before they do unto you. A simple maxim set forth by Blanchard and Peale (1988, p. 9) might guide police officers when they wrestle with ethical decisions:

There Is No Right Way To Do A Wrong Thing.

Police officers have awesome powers over other people's lives. They must act legally and ethically to be true professionals and to be true to themselves as individuals. Fair and Pilcher (1991, p. 24) note:

Ethics ought to make our task easier. If we avoid oversimplifications, then our decisions are more likely to be the sort that we can explain to others because we will have understandable, defensible reasons for them. In fact, we will be better able to explain them to the audience closest to us—ourselves. . . .

We move naturally into ethics when we are called upon to explain what we think and what we do. Ethics then is accountability, or ''response-ability,'' that is, part of what distinguishes us from the other animals—being able to answer for what we do.

It has been said that there is no pillow as soft as a clear conscience.

The Role of the Police Department

The U.S. Department of Justice's Bureau of Justice Assistance and the International Association of Chiefs of Police (1991) suggest that police departments can assure ethical behavior among their officers through three processes:

- Thoroughly investigate applicants and hire only those whose values coincide with those of the department.
- Continuously reinforce integrity by ensuring that officers understand its importance in policing.
- Reduce the opportunity for human failure by creating an anticorruption environment using all legitimate positive and negative inducements.

To maintain departmental integrity:

- *Hire selectively.*
- *Assure that all officers understand the importance of integrity in policing.*
- *Create an anticorruption environment.*

To assure that police officers understand the importance of integrity in policing, these two agencies suggest the following policy (p. 33):

A department must develop a clear and precise statement of policy that defines the exact level of priority given to departmental integrity. This policy should be widely disseminated and incorporated into union contracts and association agreements.

The public demands that the integrity of police officers be above reproach. The dishonesty of any police officer may impair public confidence and cast suspicion upon the entire department. Succumbing to even minor temptations can destroy an officer's effectiveness and contribute to the corruption of others. An officer must avoid any conduct that might compromise his or her own integrity, or that of fellow officers or of the department.

Just as each officer is responsible to maintain the highest level of personal integrity, the department must develop and foster an environment where honesty will thrive. It is the policy of this police department to place the objective of enhancing and sustaining integrity at the cornerstone of all its policies and operations.

Ethical behavior within a law enforcement agency is ultimately the responsibility of each individual officer within that agency.

A law enforcement agency with a clearly stated mission and clearly stated values, as discussed in Chapter 1, is likely to foster ethical behavior. Other ways to improve law enforcement ethics include the following (Roberg, 1989, p. 128):

1. Improved selection and screening techniques for persons entering police service, and especially, those selected for leadership positions.
2. Increasingly stringent personnel requirements, such as advanced education and formal training including the encouragement of higher education for in-service police ethics.
3. Basic research and development in police organizations, goal setting, policies, techniques, and community attitudes toward the police.
4. Policy guideline formulation and training in policy application and practice within the department.
5. More control over discretionary decision making by police officers.
6. Facilitating the change of citizen perspectives of the police by developing supportive services within the community as well as within the department.
7. Increased review of police actions by independent agencies and media representatives knowledgeable of the police profession.

No matter what steps are taken by the department, however, as noted, the ultimate responsibility for ethical behavior lies with the individuals within the department. Fair and Pilcher (1991, pp. 24–28) suggest the following problem-solving guidelines:

1. Recognizing that a problem exists—the first, absolutely essential step and one that can be particularly difficult in ethics.

2. Problem identification—thinking and data gathering to understand just exactly what the problem is.
3. Creating alternatives—part of making the problem more specific is to create an array of alternative responses.
4. Evaluating the alternatives—the next phase in the problem-solving process.
5. Public justifiability of each of the alternatives—this does not mean to grab a megaphone immediately and tell them to the world, but rather to address the issue of whether the alternatives are the *kinds* of actions that a person could defend publicly.

As police officers carry out their assigned tasks and responsibilities, they must always consider both the legal and ethical implications that might be involved. Likewise, as you continue in this text, keep in mind the legal and ethical implications that might be involved in the specific police operations under discussion.

Summary

Police officers are concerned not only with acting legally so as to avoid civil lawsuits, but also with acting ethically. Ethics deals with standards of honesty, fairness, and integrity in behavior. An absolute issue is one with only two sides, the decision is black and white. A relative issue is one with many sides, that is, varying shades of gray between the black and white, absolute sides.

A code of ethics sets forth accepted standards of behavior for a profession. Sometimes existing alongside a formal code of ethics is an informal code resulting from the police subculture. This subculture has been characterized as cynical and authoritative with feelings of victimization. It promotes a "them v. us" mindset.

A controversial ethical issue involves whether police officers should accept gratuities and, indeed, whether the issue is absolute or relative.

Many police departments operate under the reactive scandal-reform cycle. The scandal-reform cycle occurs when the behavior of an organization is changed due to extreme pressure resulting from some negative behavior.

A starting point for evaluating whether the behavior of law enforcement personnel is ethical is to examine it in light of the common promise that all police officers make with their oath of office. This promise announces to the community that they are engaged in the bargain as agents, and from this bargain are derived five clear principles of fair conduct: Fair access for all members of the public, respect for the public trust, a balance between enforcement efforts and the maintenance of order and security, coordination and cooperation among all members of the criminal justice system, and objectivity in all dealings with the public.

Basic ethics tests include the tests of common sense, publicity, one's best self, one's most admired personality, hurting someone else, and foresight. Is it legal? Is it fair?

To maintain departmental integrity: Hire selectively, assure that all officers understand the importance of integrity in policing, and create an anticorruption environment. Ethical behavior within a law enforcement agency is ultimately the responsibility of each individual officer within that agency.

Two Ethical Challenges

Cohen and Feldberg (1985, p. 49) present two scenarios in Tables 7.3 and 7.4 to promote thoughtful consideration of common situations police officers encounter and the ethical issues involved in each.

TABLE 7.3
One Scenario: The Drunk Officer

You have been assigned to a special drunk-driving enforcement unit, and have been specially trained in administering the field sobriety test and in the use of the breathalyzer. Your state has also recently adopted a mandatory drunk-driving loss of license statute: If a driver is convicted of operating with a blood alcohol content of .1 percent, he is considered to be driving while illegally intoxicated and must lose his license for three months.

While patrolling around 11:00 P.M. on a clear, dry night along a main but lightly traveled road, you spot a vehicle pulling out of a restaurant parking lot that begins to weave across the road, change speeds erratically, and even stops in the middle of the road for a moment although there are no other cars around. You decide to stop the vehicle on probable cause to suspect operation by a drunk driver. You turn on your flashing lights, and when the driver finally stops, you ask him to step out of the car. He stumbles, falls, gets up again, and hands you what you think is his wallet. To your discomfort it is a case containing his shield, and you recognize the driver as a fellow officer with whom you graduated from the academy. He is off-duty, and tells you with slurred speech that his wife has just left him and is threatening to leave town with his three-year-old son. He starts to cry.

What should you do?
From the following list of possible responses, check the one(s) that would meet the ethical standards of good police work.

_____ 1. Administer the field sobriety test; arrest him if he fails.
_____ 2. Follow him home, since he lives less than a mile from the scene.
_____ 3. Put him in a taxi and tell him he can pick up his car keys at headquarters tomorrow.
_____ 4. Do not arrest him; drive him home, but report him to his immediate superior tomorrow.
_____ 5. Tell him he has put you in a terrible position, and that you will arrest him if you catch him driving drunk again.
_____ 6. Other_____

What if the situation were different?
1. Suppose that the officer in the original example is abusive to you instead of apologetic. He tells you to mind your own business and butt out of his private life. He also tells you that in his book, cops don't hassle other cops. Review responses 1–6. Which one(s) meet the ethical standards of good police work in this situation?
2. Suppose that instead of a fellow officer from your academy days, the officer you stopped was a high-ranking official in your department who makes it clear that your career is on the line if you report him. Review responses 1–6. Which one(s) meet the standards of good police work in this situation?

In the original example, the most important ethical consideration is:
_____ The offending officer's attitude.
_____ The mandatory arrest provision of the law.
_____ Loyalty to fellow officer.
_____ Equal treatment of all violators.
_____ The reaction of your fellow officers if you arrest your colleague.
_____ The seriousness of the offense.
_____ The consequences of the arrest for the officer himself.
_____ The consequences of the arrest for you.

The ethical standard most applicable to this example is:
_____ Fair access.
_____ Public trust.
_____ Safety and security.
_____ Teamwork.
_____ Objectivity.

Source: *The Police Chief* (January 1991): 49. Reprinted from *The Police Chief* magazine, January 1991, p. 49. Copyright held by the International Association of Chiefs of Police, Inc., 1110 North Glebe Road, Suite 200, Arlington, VA 22201, USA. Further reproduction without express written permission from IACP is strictly prohibited.

TABLE 7.4
Another Scenario: The Offer of a Gratuity

This scenario and others like it serve as useful discussion starters for experienced police officers attempting to identify the standards of conduct to which they have committed and personally clarifying the values that generate acceptable police behavior. The use of such scenarios by a knowledgeable and skilled instructor invariably results in lively, illuminating group analysis.

The dispatcher sends you to the scene of a single-car accident. When you arrive, you determine that the driver needs an ambulance and that the car is disabled. You ask the dispatcher to get you an ambulance and to send a wrecker to tow the car.

When the wrecker arrives, it is driven by the owner of a nearby garage. He starts to make friendly conversation as he hooks up the car. As he finishes hitching it and is about to drive off, he says to you, "Thanks for calling me on this one. I really appreciate it. Why don't you bring your own car to my place for a tune-up one of these days? I'll be real glad to give you one—on the house."

What should you do?
From the following list of possible responses, check the one(s) that would meet the ethical standards of good police work.
_____ 1. Tell him, "Thanks, I'll have to take you up on that as soon as I've got the time," but never take him up on the offer.
_____ 2. Tell him, "You're under arrest for trying to bribe an officer for future considerations."
_____ 3. Tell him, "That's really nice of you to offer, but I can't take credit for calling you. The dispatcher issued the call."
_____ 4. Accept his offer courteously in order not to alienate local business people.
_____ 5. Tell him that you are not his business partner and that you resent the suggestion that you work for him.
_____ 6. Report the offer to your supervisor.
_____ 7. Other_____

What if the situation were different?
1. Suppose that instead of a free tune-up, the garage owner offered you a "business proposition" of $15 for each call you referred to him? Review responses 1–7. Which one(s) meet the ethical standards of good police work in this situation?
2. Suppose that instead of a free tune-up, the garage owner said nothing but dropped a $20 bill on the seat of your cruiser? Review responses 1–6. Which one(s) meet the standards of good police work in this situation?

In the original example, the most important ethical consideration is:
_____ The size of the offer.
_____ The fact that an offer was made.
_____ The way the officer responds to the garage owner.
_____ The fact that the garage owner wants special access to the police.

The ethical standard most applicable to this example is:
_____ Fair access.
_____ Public trust.
_____ Safety and security.
_____ Teamwork.
_____ Objectivity.

Application #1

The chief of police has been receiving complaints from some citizens that squad cars meet at a certain time at Wong's Cafe, to eat breakfast, snacks, lunch, and sometimes dinner. He calls together three patrol officers, including you, and asks you to discuss the problem and come up with a policy and procedure to deal with it.

Instructions   This can be a simple policy which merely defines times when officers may eat, or it can also contain policies for what the department rules and regulations are regarding free lunches, coffee, and to what extent the department will tolerate gratuities, if at all. Include what the policy should be, what procedures should be implemented, and by whom.

Application #2

The chief of police has also been concerned about officers coming to him wanting advice about what to do when business people give them freebies such as boxes of candy, children's toys, bottles of liquor, and other items useful to the officer and family. The officers are concerned as to how much they can take, when they can take it, and whether they should report to the administration upon receipt. The chief asks a committee, of which you are a part, to develop a policy and procedure to clarify how officers are to respond to such freebies.

Instructions   Write a policy specifying the need for uniformity in accepting gratuities and gifts—*if* they are to be accepted at all. Include what can be accepted and under what circumstances. The policy may also simply specify that no gratuities can be accepted.

Exercises in Critical Thinking

Court decisions consider the issues of justice. Constitutional rights and legal precedence determine the decision of the court, and thus police action must be within the bounds set by law. The ethics of law enforcement, however, also includes the fair and respectful treatment of people. Police officers are not to take advantage of their position of power. Officers need to feel for and extend humane treatment to those who may be victimized by criminal actions. Considerate, sympathetic treatment of citizens is the key to an ethical commitment to do the right thing. Professionalism needs to include respect for the law and for others paralleled with self-respect and mutual respect for other law enforcement personnel.

In the early morning hours of August 18, Jacqueline McKone stepped outside her apartment and witnessed what she said was the uncalled-for arrest and beating of a young black man, twenty-one-year-old Dennis Cherry. McKone was a legal assistant in an attorney's office, completing course work to become a court reporter. She reported that four police officers held Cherry, and one, whom she identified as Ed Nelson, hit him. Cherry, she reported, had done nothing to attract the police or to resist their efforts to arrest him. The incident occurred more than a block away from the Convention Center where police had come to close down a dance.

Several officers, including Ed Nelson, tried to intimidate McKone as she stood watching the scene. She said to herself, however, that, I can't stop it, but I will watch this whole thing and report it. When Lieutenant Bruce Jones arrived on the scene, she approached him to report what she had witnessed.

1. When Lieutenant Jack Nelson arrived at the scene, what should have been his treatment of McKone?
   a. To tell McKone that the police were simply following arrest procedure and that, because she was not present at the beginning of the incident

or close enough to hear all that Cherry said to police, she could not be expected to understand what actually happened.

    b. First, to ask if she had been harmed; second, to apologize for what she had witnessed; and then to provide her with the information needed to contact civilian review.

    c. First, to interview the police officers who conducted the arrest, then to interview McKone, and then to explain to McKone that although Cherry denies it, the police say he tried to hit them, which justifies their treatment of Cherry.

    d. To ignore McKone other than to tell her that she can bring her views and testimony to the Police Civilian Review Authority.

    e. To gently remind McKone that it is not wise to offend local police, especially well-liked officers such as Ed Nelson and to point out that, if she calls the news media and files a complaint, she will get a series of hateful, racist responses accusing her of having a black boyfriend or of being a "nigger lover."

In June 1988, a police officer received information from a confidential, reliable informant. He had observed a film depicting a sixteen-year-old girl engaging in sex with a Rottweiller dog while at the home of Robert Bonynge. The officer applied for a search warrant for Bonynge's residence. The affidavit accompanying the application reiterated the information received from the informant and stated that the officer sought the search warrant "to seize any film involving child pornography and bestiality." The warrant permitted seizure of the following:

> *Pornography films involving female juveniles and a Rottweiller dog and any contraband that would violate the state statute governing the pornography laws. Any filming equipment and duplicating equipment. The affidavit was attached to the warrant.*

On June 16, the police executed the search warrant at Bonynge's residence. A police lieutenant observed the Rottweiller dog on the premises and numerous video cassettes, 8-millimeter movies, photographs, and magazines depicting sexual scenes involving young females, possibly juveniles. The officers seized hundreds of films and photographs, including several commercial videotapes of popular motion pictures. The officer stated that it was his experience that "obscene material is planted in the middle of what appears to be a commercial tape to make it difficult to locate."

  2. Were the videotapes seized in violation of Bonynge's Fourth Amendment rights?

    a. Yes, because the Fourth Amendment gives individuals the right to be free from unreasonable search and seizure and declares that warrants shall particularly describe the place to be searched and the person or things to be seized, and not all the videotapes were of pornographic subjects.

    b. Yes, because a warrant limits the discretion of the executing officers as well as gives notice to the party searched, and the materials seized were not described with sufficient particularity.

    c. No, because a warrant to search a residence gives rights to search all parts of that residence and seize any evidence found.

    d. Yes, because pornography is an ethical issue that must be left to individual discretion—no law or police action is appropriate.

    e. No, because the officers who swore out the affidavit also executed the search; they had the benefit of the more specific language of the affidavit.

3. Which of the following would be an unethical action?

    a. The temporary seizure of constitutionally protected material (in this case, of every film and videotape regardless of content).

    b. Providing a prior adversary hearing before authorizing the seizure of allegedly obscene material for the purpose of destroying it.

    c. Accepting gratuities from bookstores or commercial theaters involved in the distribution or exhibition of pornographic materials, and being loyal to fellow officers who accept gratuities.

    d. Varying the times when you take breaks, eating meals at different times and places, filling out reports at irregular times and places to protect yourself from temptation, and blowing the whistle on colleagues who routinely bend rules.

    e. Exercising discretion while extending due process to criminal suspects and victims alike (such as withholding the identity of the sixteen-year-old girl).

Discussion Questions

1. Is the practice of discretion by police detrimental to ethical behavior?
2. It is said that most people have a little larceny in their blood. Do police officers fit this saying? Might they have more than "a little" and be more larcenous because of their position?
3. Does the police subculture affect the ethical behavior of police officers?
4. Can ethical standards that apply to police officers be circumvented when it comes to apprehending drug dealers? If so, to what extent?
5. Do minor police misdeeds overlooked by supervisors lead to major corruption?
6. Blame in the River Cops situation was distributed in a variety of areas. What is the most likely reason the officers got into such serious trouble?
7. Is comparing police ethics to other professions such as medicine, law, and politics a fair analogy?

Definitions

Can you define the following terms?

absolute issue	gratuities
code of ethics	moral principles
common promise	relative issue
conscience	scandal-reform cycle
ethics	

References

Benson, Bruce L. and Skinner, Gilbert H. "Doughnut Shop Ethics: There Are Answers." *The Police Chief* (December 1988):32–33.

Blanchard, Kenneth and Peale, Norman Vincent. *The Power of Ethical Management*. New York: Fawcett Crest, 1989.

Cohen, Howard. "Exploiting Police Authority." *Criminal Justice Ethics* no. 2 (1986):23–31.

Cohen, Howard and Feldberg, Michael. *Ethics for Professional Policing*. Boston: Wasserman Associates, 1985.

Dorschner, John. "Police Deviance: Corruption and Controls," pp. 249–285. In *Critical Issues in Policing, Contemporary Readings,* Roger G. Dunham and Geoffrey P. Alpert, eds. Prospect Heights, Ill.: Waveland Press, 1989.

Fair, Frank K. and Pilcher, Wayland D. "Morality on the Line: The Role of Ethics in Police Decision-Making." *American Journal of Police* 10: 2 (November 1991):23–38.

Johnson, Charles and Copus, Gary. "Law Enforcement Ethics: A Theoretical Analysis," pp. 39–83. In *The Social Basis of Criminal Justice: Ethical Issues for the 80's,* F. Schmalleger and R. Gustafson, eds. Washington, D.C.: University Press, 1981.

Klockars, Carl B. "Police Ethics, Corruption and Conduct," pp. 427–428. In *The Encyclopedia of Police Science,* W. G. Gailey, ed. New York: Garland Publishing, 1989.

Klockars, Carl B. *Thinking About Police, Contemporary Readings*. New York: McGraw-Hill, 1983.

Murphy, Paul and Moran, Kenneth T. "The Continuing Cycle of Systemic Police Corruption," pp. 87–101. In *The Social Basis of Criminal Justice: Ethical Issues for the 80's,* F. Schmalleger and R. Gustafson, eds. Washington, D.C.: University Press, 1981.

Oran, Daniel. *Law Dictionary for Nonlawyers*. 2d ed. St. Paul, Minn.: West Publishing Company, 1985.

Pollock-Byrne, Joycelyn M. *Ethics in Crime and Justice, Dilemmas & Decisions*. Pacific Grove, Calif.: Brooks/Cole Publishing Company, 1989.

Roberg, Roy. ed. *Human Relations and Police Work*. Belmont, Calif.: Wadsworth, 1989.

Robinette, Hillary M. "Police Ethics: Leadership and Ethics Training for Police Administrators." *The Police Chief* (January 1991):42–47.

Scheingold, Stuart. *The Politics of Law and Order*. New York: Longman, 1984.

Sherman, L. "Learning Police Ethics." *Criminal Justice Ethics* 1: 1 (1982):10–19.

U.S. Department of Justice's Bureau of Justice Assistance and the International Association of Chiefs of Police. "Police Ethics: Building Integrity and Reducing Drug Corruption." *The Police Chief* (January 1991):27–41.

PHYSICAL AND MENTAL FITNESS AND OFFICER SAFETY: KEEPING FIT FOR DUTY

CHAPTER 8

INTRODUCTION

Police work has been characterized as long periods of devastating boredom punctuated by sporadic, relatively brief periods of utter terror. Much about the job unfortunately allows officers to become less physically and mentally fit than they were when they passed the rigorous pre-employment screening. Physical and mental fitness are fundamentally related: mental discipline is needed to maintain or improve physical fitness, and mental alertness requires physical fitness. Physical and mental fitness also affect stress levels and officers' responses to stress. Furthermore, physical fitness, mental fitness, and adaptability to the stresses of police work are all correlated with officers' safety on the job—in effect, their very lives may depend on such mental and physical preparedness.

Although this chapter discusses physical fitness, mental fitness, stress, and officer safety as separate topics, their interrelationship must be kept in mind. It is well illustrated in the "Pre-Quantico Kit" booklet in which the objectives of the FBI's fitness philosophy and program are described as follows (Slahor, 1990, p. 53):

1. To increase muscular strength, flexibility and cardiovascular endurance so as to assist the SA [Special Agent] in meeting the demands of the job.
2. To prevent cardiovascular disease and related ailments through early detection of danger signals.
3. To educate all employees of the FBI in the attainment and maintenance of personal wellness standards.
4. To establish a personalized wellness prescription for each SA.

Do You Know

- What physical fitness is?
- What the key indicators of physical fitness are?
- What police-specific physical skills are important?
- What job-related factors detract from police officers' physical fitness?
- What the criticality index is and what physical activity is seen as most important in police work?
- What constitutes an effective fitness program?
- What mental fitness is?
- What the major categories of stressors are for police officers?
- What burnout is?
- What the awareness spectrum is and where in that spectrum police officers should try to be?
- What the five Cs of basic tactics for survival are?
- What the three sides of the border patrol's survival triangle are?

5. To reduce incidence of lower back pain, obesity, high blood pressure, and other law-enforcement-related ailments.
6. To increase [officers'] ability to cope with the inherent stress-related ailments of the law enforcement profession through physical fitness and positive life-style modifications in order to enjoy life to the fullest.

Physical Fitness

The United States has become fitness conscious. Drive through almost any town and you can see joggers and runners, bikers and rollerbladers. Health clubs do a brisk business. Weight-loss programs have proliferated. Even McDonalds has joined the fitness fever by reducing the fat in their hamburgers. People strive to be fit.

Physical fitness is the body's general capacity to adapt and respond favorably to physical effort.

Physically fit police officers not only enjoy life more, but the demands of their work absolutely require that they be in top physical condition. Physical fitness may make the difference between success and failure on the job and sometimes may even make the difference between life and death. Furthermore, officers who are not physically fit are not prepared to adequately discharge their duties and may, as a result, be sued. Says Getz (1990, p. 44): "Trends in training due to litigation make it clear that cops are going to get healthier—in spite of themselves."

Getz (p. 45) cites the case of *Parker v. District of Columbia,* a case in which the jury awarded nearly half a million dollars to a man shot twice by a D.C. police officer during an arrest. The jury reasoned: "Had the officer been physically fit, . . . he might have overpowered the suspect instead of reaching for his gun. The officer 'simply was not in adequate physical shape' to do his job." This is not an isolated case. One study, says Getz (p. 45), found that 56 percent of police officers are overweight and that 86 percent of them do little or no exercise.

Many people evaluate fitness on the basis of appearance alone. Although personal appearance can give certain indications of fitness levels, what is going on inside is more important. The traditional image of fitness—the Charles Atlas physique—has given way to an image stressing endurance and stamina as the true indicators of fitness.

The prime indicators of physical fitness are endurance, balance, agility, flexibility, strength, power, and body composition.

Although many factors contribute to a well-conditioned body, the prime factor is the condition of the circulatory (cardiovascular) system upon which endurance or stamina depends.

185

*CHAPTER 8
Physical and Mental
Fitness and Officer
Safety: Keeping
Fit for Duty*

Officers during physical training. Fitness is essential to police operations.

Endurance or **stamina** is the capacity to continue exertion over prolonged periods as well as the ability to withstand pain, distress, and fatigue for extended periods. It applies to both cardiovascular or aerobic endurance as well as to muscular endurance. Cardiovascular disease is the leading cause of police disability retirement. Physical endurance is required in long-distance running, swimming, cycling, and wrestling.

Balance is neuromuscular control—the muscles and nerves working together to perform various movements. Poor balance results in poor body control and may cause the person to be accident prone. Closely related to balance is **eye-hand coordination,** critical to shooting skill.

Flexibility is mobility of the joints, the ability to "bend without breaking." A flexible person has a wide range of movement. The sedentary nature of police work can greatly contribute to a lack of flexibility.

Agility is the ability to react quickly and easily. Agility is needed to run an obstacle course, to jump or vault fences or barriers, to climb a ladder quickly, or to lie down and spring back up.

Strength and **power** imply toughness, durability, and vigor as well as the ability to exert force with the hands, arms, legs, or body. Hand and arm strength is needed to lift or pull heavy objects. Leg strength is needed to walk, run, and jump. Body strength is needed to support all movements of the arms and legs. Power is the explosive force which moves the body suddenly or which propels some object independent of the body.

Body composition refers to the ratio of fat to lean tissue in the body. Many police departments are now using body composition rather than height/weight charts in setting their physical standards. Excessive body fat not only hinders physical motion, it is a serious health risk for heart disease, diabetes, and stroke.

In addition to the preceding factors involved in physical fitness, several other physical factors are specifically related to how well police officers perform.

Motor skills important to police officers include coordination, speed, and accuracy.

Geier (1990, p. 52) suggests: "Motor skills are an important factor in a police officer's work. In fact, these may directly affect his survival in some instances. Motor skills, such as coordination and balance, are used in defensive tactics. Firearm proficiency is based on hand-to-eye coordination, balance, and accuracy. A foot chase involves speed and agility. Other motor skills can be readily observed in handcuffing techniques or police baton usage."

Self-Evaluation

A self-evaluation can reveal some startling things. Just because a person feels good or has no recognized illnesses or diseases does not necessarily mean they are physically fit. The tests in Table 8.1 can be used to conduct a self-evaluation for physical fitness.

Myths about Physical Fitness

People hold many misconceptions about physical fitness. Sometimes these are used as excuses to avoid getting back into shape.

Too Far Gone.   Many people feel that they are either too old or have physically deteriorated to such a degree that it is impossible to get back into good physical shape. This is not true. Regardless of age or how "far gone" a person is, if the person is organically sound, he or she can become fit through a well-structured physical training program.

Hard Work Will Kill You.   A rather common misconception is that the harder you work, the quicker you die. Not only is this false, just the opposite is true. People need to exercise regularly or they deteriorate. People "rust out" from inactivity far more than they "wear out" from hard physical work.

Any Kind of Exercise Is Good.   Again, this is simply not true. Different exercises and activities have varying degrees of value depending on their intensity, duration, and frequency. Short-duration exercising such as stretching or isometrics offers limited benefits. Likewise, an hour of racquetball, tennis, or softball every few weeks by a usually sedentary person not only offers limited benefits, it can be extremely dangerous. The most beneficial programs are those done regularly for at least twenty to thirty minutes and directed toward all aspects of total fitness.

No Pain, No Gain.   Although when people first begin exercise programs, they often experience some stiffness and soreness, usually such programs should not cause *pain*. This is not to imply, however, that getting and keeping physically fit is not hard work.

TABLE 8.1
Physical Fitness Self-Tests
Courtesy of the Federal Bureau of Investigation

CARDIOVASCULAR TESTS
Cureton's Breath-Holding Test

One simple and acceptable way of testing your respiratory capacity, which is related to circulatory fitness, is to step onto and off a chair, bench, or stool (approximately 17 inches high) for a period of 1 minute, and then see how long you can hold your breath. You should be able to hold it for at least 30 seconds. If you can't, it's an indication that your cardiovascular function has deteriorated below a desirable level.

Kasch Pulse Recovery Test (3 minutes)

This test can be performed by either sex and almost any age group. Only the infirm or the extremely unfit would find it too strenuous. You should not smoke for 1 hour or eat for 2 hours prior to taking the test. Also, you should rest for 5 minutes before taking the test.

EQUIPMENT: 12″ bench or stool, clock or watch with a sweep second hand

PROCEDURE
1. Start stepping onto and off the bench when sweep second hand is at 11.
2. Step 24 per minute, total 72.
3. Duration is 3 minutes.
4. Stop stepping when sweep second hand is again at 11, after three revolutions, and sit down.
5. Start counting the pulse rate when sweep second hand reaches 12 on the clock, using either the artery located inside the wrist or the carotid artery in the throat. Count every 10 seconds and record for 1 minute.
6. Total the six pulse counts for 1 minute and compare with the following scale:

Classification	0–1 Minute Pulse Rate After Exercise
Excellent	71–78
Very good	79–83
Average	84–99
Below average	100–107
Poor	108–118

Cooper's 12-Minute Walk/Run Test

NOTE: Persons over 30 years of age should not take this test until they have had a complete medical examination and have completed approximately 6 weeks in a "starter physical fitness program."

Find a place where you can run/walk a measured distance of up to 2 miles. A quarter-mile track at a local school would be ideal; however, a nearby park, field, or quiet stretch of road can be used. The test is quite simple—see how much of the 2 miles you can comfortably cover in 12 minutes. Try to run the entire time at a pace you can maintain without excessive strain. If your breath becomes short, walk until it returns to normal, then run again. Keep going for a full 12 minutes, then check your performance on the following scale:

Distance in Miles Covered in 12 Minutes

FITNESS CATEGORY	AGE			
	Under 30	30 to to 39	40 to to 49	50
Very poor	0 <1.00*	<.95	<.85	<.80
Poor	1.00 – 1.24	.95–1.14	.85–1.04	.80 – .99
Fair	1.25 – 1.49	1.15–1.39	1.05–1.29	1.00–1.24
Good	1.50 – 1.74	1.40–1.64	1.30–1.54	1.25–1.49
Excellent	1.75 +	1.65 +	1.55 +	1.50 +

*< Means less than

Continued on the next page

TABLE 8.1 (*Continued*)

BALANCE TEST

Stand on your toes, heels together, eyes closed, and your arms stretched forward at shoulder level. Maintain this position for 20 seconds without shifting your feet or opening your eyes (Figure A).

FLEXIBILITY TESTS

Trunk Flexion

Keep your legs together, your knees locked, bend at the waist, and touch the floor with your fingertips (Figure B).

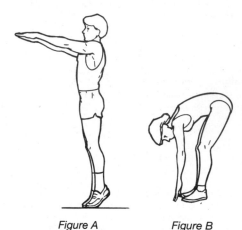

Figure A   *Figure B*

Trunk Extension

Lie flat on your stomach, face down, fingers laced behind your neck, and your feet anchored to the floor. Now raise your chin until it is 18 inches off the floor (Figure C).

Figure C

(*Note:* The average for men students at the University of Illinois is 12.5 inches.)

AGILITY TEST

Squat Thrusts

Standing, drop down to a squatting position, palms flat against floor, arms straight (Figure D). Next, with weight supported on the hands, kick backward so that your legs are fully extended. (Figure E). Immediately kick forward to the squatting position (Figure F) and stand up. You should be able to perform four in 8 seconds.

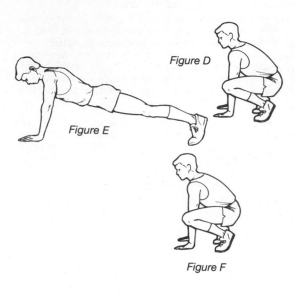

Figure D

Figure E

Figure F

STRENGTH TESTS

Pull-ups

Hang from a bar, hands slightly wider than shoulders, palms turned away, arms fully extended (Figure G). Pull up until your chin is over the bar (Figure H). Lower yourself until your arms are fully extended and repeat. You should be able to perform four pull-ups.

Figure G   *Figure H*

Continued on the next page

TABLE 8.1 *(Continued)*

Push-ups

From the front leaning rest position, hands slightly wider than the shoulders with fingers pointed straight ahead (Figure I), lower your body until your chest barely touches the floor (Figure J). Push up to the front leaning rest position, keeping your body straight. You should be able to perform fifteen push-ups.

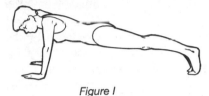

Figure I

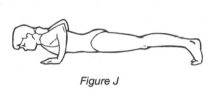

Figure J

Sit-ups

Lie on your back with your hands behind your neck, with your legs straight and free. Flex the trunk and sit up (Figure K), and then return to the starting position. You should be able to perform 25 sit-ups.

Figure K

POWER TESTS
Standing Broad Jump

From a standing position, jump as far forward as you can, landing on both feet (Figure L). Do not take a running start. The length of your jump should equal your height.

Figure L

Vertical Jump

Stand facing a wall, feet and chin touching wall, arms extended over the head. Mark the height of the hands on the wall. (A piece of chalk will do.) Now jump up and touch the wall as high as you can with one hand; use chalk (Figure M). Note the difference between the two marks on the wall. You should be able to perform a vertical jump of 18 inches or more.

Figure M

The Quick and Easy Way to Fitness.   Despite hordes of advertisements to the contrary, getting and keeping physically fit is hard work and requires commitment and discipline. It also takes time—weeks or months—to get into shape. Unfortunately, it takes much less time to get out of shape.

The Criticality Index of Physical Activities

Jordan and Schwartz (1986, p. 29) describe a *criticality index* developed by the New York City Police Department. The index was developed to assure that their physical performance testing program met Equal Employment Opportunity Commission (EEOC) guidelines. To determine how critical specific physical activities are to police officers, 452 officers were asked to indicate the frequency with which they performed each activity as well as the importance of each activity to the successful completion of police work. The frequency and importance were then multiplied to achieve the criticality index. The results are summarized in Table 8.2.

> The **criticality index** measures the frequency and importance of physical activities performed by police officers. Rated as the most critical activity is the ability to run up stairs.

Police officers are called on to perform many physical activities, yet many officers are not physically fit. Some of this may be inherent to the job. Says Mostardi et al. (1986, p. 32): "It's no secret that safety force employees are at a higher than normal risk for heart disease, based on such variables as high job stress, excessive cigarette smoking, poor diet, and the generally sedentary nature of their jobs. The net result is often myocardial infarction, leading to early retirement and reduced departmental efficiency."

TABLE 8.2
The Criticality Index of Physical Activities

Activity	Frequency	Importance	Criticality Index
Running up stairs	12.10	2.51	30.4
Physical restraint	7.39	2.07	15.3
Jumping—distance	4.73	2.77	13.1
Jumping—barrier	4.73	2.77	13.1
Lifting adult	4.53	2.56	11.6
Climbing a wall	4.10	2.56	10.6
Running	3.50	2.37	8.3
Dragging adult	2.85	2.74	7.8
Climbing fence	2.84	2.63	7.4
Nightstick defense	1.53	2.54	3.9

191

CHAPTER 8
Physical and Mental
Fitness and Officer
Safety: Keeping
Fit for Duty

Police work is often sedentary, involves irregular hours and rotating shifts, and may promote poor diets, excessive cigarette smoking and consumption of alcohol, and great amounts of stress.

Because of these factors, it is important that police officers engage in some sort of physical fitness training program.

Physical Fitness Training Programs

Because police officers often face situations involving physical restraint, self-defense, or foot pursuit, many police departments have set up both mandatory and voluntary physical fitness programs for officers.

Physical fitness programs are controversial. Some police administrators feel the police are being unfairly singled out in expectations of fitness. Nevertheless, it is obvious that law enforcement officers should maintain a high level of physical fitness. Not only is it desirable from the standpoint of being able to enjoy life to the fullest, for police officers, physical fitness is a necessity because of the frequency with which officers face situations that place great demands on their physical capacities.

What kind of program is instituted varies from department to department. Many departments do not have programs. In fact, Getz (1990, p. 45) reports on a study done in 1988 that found that "comprehensive health fitness programs are still the exception rather than the rule." According to the study, only about 25 percent of the country's police departments have a fitness program and health standards their officers must meet.

Often it is up to individual officers to institute their own programs. This is easier if the department at least provides space and some equipment. Geier (1990 p. 53) describes some activities police officers can engage in that can constitute a physical fitness program. He stresses that the activities should be of interest to the officer and be related to the successful performance of duty.

The first part of the program suggested by Geier is **aerobic training** aimed at the cardiovascular system. This can be biking, cross-country skiing, rowing, swimming, or walking. It can also include treadmills, stationary cycles, and rowing machines. Aerobic training should be done at least three times a week for a minimum of fifteen to twenty minutes. It should be preceded by a light warm-up and followed by a brief cool-down. Aerobic training can also incorporate **cross-training,** with an officer biking one day, running one day, and swimming one day.

Another important part of an exercise program is *strength training* or **anaerobic training.** Strength training helps maintain muscle tissue. Aerobic activities do little in this area. Geier (p. 53) stresses: "Preventing muscle loss is a crucial issue. After a person reaches physical maturity, some muscle cells shrink and others disappear altogether. Between ages 30 and 70, a person can experience a loss of up to 30 percent of the total number of muscle cells." Geier notes that preventing injury and improving physical capacity are also reasons to include strength exercises. Low-back problems are the second leading reason for early police retirements, and 80 percent of low-back problems are muscular.

In addition, an officer's physical abilities are frequently tested when restraining a violent suspect, pushing a disabled vehicle, or lifting an injured person. Among the methods available for building strength are free weights and machines, which usually rely on "progressive resistance," and resistance against one's own body weight, which usually relies on "progressive repetition." Resistance against one's own body weight includes push-ups, pull-ups, dips, and sit-ups.

Geier (p. 54–55) stresses that strength training should be varied yet balanced and should work all the large muscles of the body during a given week. He recommends strength training at least twice a week because studies show significant decreases in muscular strength occur after as little as 96 hours of inactivity.

Flexibility training is the third part of Geier's police-specific physical training program. This can be done as stretching in the warm-up and cool-down portion of aerobic or strength training. Stretching reduces muscle tension, improves coordination, and can prevent injuries. Each stretch should be held for approximately ten seconds. Breathing should be normal, and no bouncing should be done. It should *not* be painful. If a muscle is stretched to the point of pain, it is being stretched too far.

Speed training can be incorporated into the aerobic portion of the exercise. Geier (p. 55) notes that police officers will probably be older than the suspects they chase and that the officers will be further hindered by the twenty or more pounds of weight added by their gun belt and accessories. He also notes that more than speed is usually needed in a foot chase. *Agility* is often even more important. Agility can be practiced on an obstacle course or through drills such as those football players use. Jumping rope is another way to improve agility. *Eye-hand coordination* can be improved through racquetball, tennis, basketball, and softball. Martial arts training can improve an officer's power, flexibility, speed, and balance.

Geier (p. 56) concludes by stating: "The concept of police-specific physical training is similar to sport-specific physical training. . . . An officer should likewise train to win for the real-life encounters of the profession."

An effective physical fitness training program that is varied and of interest to the officer should include aerobic, strength, and flexibility training. It should be engaged in regularly for twenty to thirty minutes a day, at least three days a week.

Pulse-Rate Guidelines.   Most people take their pulse rate by placing two fingers on the carotid artery in the neck and counting the beats for ten seconds. They then multiply this number by six. Many experts suggest that the safe, effective pulse-rate range for individuals can be determined mathematically. First, subtract your age from 220. Multiply this by 70 percent for the lower limit and by 80 percent for the upper limit. For example, consider a thirty-year-old person.

$$220 - 30 = 190$$
$$190 \times .70 = 126$$
$$190 \times .80 = 152$$

The pulse-rate range during peak exercise for a thirty-year-old would be 126–152 beats per minute. Below 126 would not be accomplishing much, and above 152 might be dangerous. This, of course, is a general guideline and may vary depending on how physically fit the person is to begin with. The pulse rate should return to normal within a few minutes after exercising.

During exercise, **encephaloendorphins** are released by the brain. They are relaxants that can reduce stress and make people feel ''in control'' and energetic. In other words, physical fitness programs also promote mental fitness.

Additional Benefits

Besides the obvious benefits to individual officers, physical fitness programs tend to reduce absenteeism and sick time as well as early retirement. Insurance premiums may go down while productivity often goes up.

Fitness and Nutrition

Nutrition plays an important role in a person's overall fitness. According to Dr. Lopez (1991, p. 12):

> *Most officers realize the health dangers of their sedentary lifestyle; hours of boredom spent in the patrol car, at the desk, or on the street, are punctuated only by minutes of high-stress activity (such as a confrontation or a pursuit), or by meals. While such brief episodes of stress are dangerous, many don't realize that a quick meal of a double bacon cheeseburger, fries, and a shake can be just as bad for the heart.*

Dr. Lopez's advice is to eat low-cholesterol, low-fat foods to reduce the risks of coronary artery disease (CAD), sometimes called coronary heart disease (CHD).

Fast-food establishments offer quick, inexpensive meals, and late-night service.

Some basic guidelines for good nutrition are offered by Harrison-Davis (1989, p. 46):

- Eat a variety of foods in moderation.
- Get fit with regular aerobic activity.
- Eat less fat, saturated fat, and cholesterol.
- Eat whole grains, vegetables, and fruits.
- Eat less sugar and salt.
- If you drink alcoholic beverages, do so in moderation and don't drive when drinking.

Law enforcement officers trying to lose weight may face additional problems. As noted by Violanti (1985, p. 59): "An important problem for officers trying to lose weight is shift work. It is difficult to maintain proper eating habits when shifts continually change and the officer must eat away from home." Violanti (p. 58–60) offers the following suggestions:

- Eat your largest meal at the beginning of the night shift, not when you go off duty. This will give your body a chance to use up calories.
- Keep coffee consumption to a minimum. Caffeine lowers blood sugar levels and increases hunger.
- When eating in a restaurant, order "special." Tell the waitress that you want your meat broiled, that you don't want gravy, etc. Otherwise, you will get what the cook gives you—high-calorie extras.
- Do not read the menu. You should go into a restaurant knowing what you want. Menus are purposely designed to increase your hunger.
- Eat smaller meals when you work night shifts. This is necessary because you will most likely eat more meals in the same twenty-four-hour period (both during the shift and during the day when you are off duty).

Smoking, Alcohol and other Drugs, and Fitness

Smoking and the use of alcohol or other drugs should be eliminated. They adversely affect health. As noted by Chris Anonymous (1982, p. 13):

Alcoholism [or other drug abuse] doesn't happen overnight. Usually it's years in coming. But for many beleaguered cops the day does come when the bottle is their only escape from the hell-pits they patrol, their only way to hold on to some sort of sanity in a crazy, mixed-up, no-justice-ever world. Let a judge turn loose on a technicality the crook this cop caught red-handed, and he'll pacify his anger and frustration with a half-dozen belts of bourbon or vodka. Or let a younger and less experienced officer place higher on the promotional eligibility list, and he'll drown that sorrow in gin or Scotch.

Then the day comes when he doesn't want a drink, he needs one. It scares the stuffing out of him.

Officers with drinking or drug abuse problems should seek professional help from an employee assistance program or from organizations such as Alcoholics Anonymous.

Protecting the Back

195

CHAPTER 8
Physical and Mental
Fitness and Officer
Safety: Keeping
Fit for Duty

"Back-related injuries have reached epidemic proportions in the western world. Approximately 80 percent of the population will experience significant low-back pain at some point in life," asserts Stamps (1989, p. 39). Although back problems are common among law enforcement officers, they can be avoided and even prevented. Stamps (pp. 41–42) recommends the following, and these points are illustrated in Figure 8.1.

Correct Standing. Stand erect, with head high, eyes forward, chin tucked in, abdominal and buttock muscles firm, knees slightly bent, and toes straight ahead. Wear comfortable, low-heeled shoes. Stand with one foot up if standing for prolonged periods of time, and change position often.

Correct Walking. Walk tall, keeping head high, chin tucked in, pelvis forward, and toes pointed straight ahead. Wear comfortable shoes.

Correct Sitting. Sit in chairs low enough for you to place both feet flat on the floor. Sit firmly against the back of the chair, with chin tucked, chest back, and knees level with your hips. Protect your low back with a lumbar support or towel.

Correct Driving. Sit straight, with both hands on the wheel. Move the car seat forward to keep knees level with the hips. Protect your low back with a lumbar support or towel roll.

Correct Sleeping. A good night's sleep is paramount to a healthy, active lifestyle. Sleep on your side, with knees bent, or on your back, with a pillow under the knees. Use a firm mattress to help keep the spine in proper alignment.

Mental Fitness

Mental fitness is not as easily perceived or analyzed, but it is equally as important as physical fitness. As noted by Remsberg (1986): "Your day-by-day (sometimes minute-by-minute) contact with criminals, complainants, and citizens alike who are crying, cursing, bleeding, puking, yelling, spitting, biting, fighting, lying, dying, dead, drunk, doped, dirty, scared, scarred, angry, vengeful, irrational, evasive, outlandish, grieving, manipulative, taunting, demanding, defiant, cruel, neurotic, hopeless, and just plain crazy subjects your system to repeated onslaughts of disturbance." The result of such contacts can seriously affect police officers' mental fitness, as noted by Maslach and Jackson (1979, p. 59) who quote a New York City police officer as saying:

> *You change when you become a cop—you become tough and hard and cynical. You have to condition yourself to be that way in order to survive this job. And sometimes, without realizing it, you act that way all the time, even with your wife and kids. But it's something you have to do, because if you start getting emotionally involved with what happens at work, you'll wind up in Bellevue [psychiatric hospital].*

As noted by Reese (1982, p. 51)

> *[Law Enforcement officers] confront human beings who are emotionally charged and often at their worst. The officer must respond, on a routine basis, to situations others would consider emergencies. There is an image to*

FIGURE 8.1
Correct and Incorrect Posture Positions

Sleeping

Don't lie flat on your back; this arches the spine too much.

Don't Lie on your back with a high pillow.

Don't sleep face down.

Do support your knees if you lie on your back.

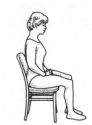

Do lie on your side with knees bent and pillow high.

Sitting

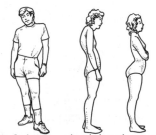

Don't leave your lower back unsupported when you sit.

Do sit straight with back supported and knees higher than hips.

Standing

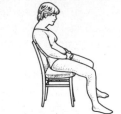

Don't let your back bend out of its natural curve.

Do stand upright with hips tucked and knees slightly bent.

Walking

Don't lean forward or wear high heels.

Do lead with chest; toes forward.

uphold, and one must become psychologically hardened in such emergencies. Officers are not allowed to show natural human emotions such as fear, anger, or sadness while doing normal duty.

Anderson and Bauer (1987, p. 381) concur: "After a person has been a law enforcement officer for a time, there are frequently some personality changes that take place that seem to be a means of defending the individual against the effects of potential and actual violence." Among the changes that can be seen in law enforcement officers are the following, described by Adlam (1982, pp. 344–345):

- Their level of self-confidence and assertiveness increases.
- A protective shell develops that insulates them from emotional upheavals caused by some of the dreadful experiences that they have had to undergo.
- Their attitude becomes more suspicious, cynical, distrustful, and skeptical.
- They become either more intolerant and bigoted or more broad-minded and compassionate.
- They support a traditionally masculine set of outlooks on the world.
- They become more manipulative with people.

Such changes indicate a problem with the officers' mental fitness.

***Mental fitness** refers to a person's emotional well-being, the ability to feel fear, anger, compassion, and other emotions and to express them appropriately. It also refers to a person's alertness and ability to make decisions quickly.*

Police officers' continued exposure to people in crisis and to violence can result in the following escalating mental stages (Minnesota P.O.S.T. Board, 1991, p. 105):

- Emotional distancing.
- Denial.
- Isolation.
- Agitation.
- Irritability.
- Depression.
- Anger.
- Blaming others.
- Relationship changes.
- Over- or underreaction to the job.
- Taking excessive risks on the street.

It is important that officers showing such emotional reactions should have programs available to help them deal with their feelings and to become more mentally fit.

Mental Fitness Programs

Although seldom called *mental fitness programs,* many police departments have established programs geared to helping their officers combat emotional problems. Such programs are absolutely essential. As noted by Depue (1981, p. 304), The single call that evokes an immediate response from every officer in the area is an "Officer needs help," call. Police rally to help their fellow officers in physical danger as in no other profession, perhaps because they all realize that someday the

*CHAPTER 8
Physical and Mental
Fitness and Officer
Safety: Keeping
Fit for Duty*

call could be for them. Police officers share a deep bond experienced by few other professions. Says Depue (p. 304), "This common identity and awareness of mutual problems may be a relatively untapped resource for dealing with the serious *personal* problems associated with the policing job as well as professional dangers."

According to Goolkasian et al. (1985, pp. 76–77): "While much recent research has identified specific stressors associated with police work, most stress program practitioners make the broad assumption that all personal problems and crises that render an officer unable to perform his work effectively—whatever their source—are considered to be legitimate concerns that warrant a response from the stress program." They note the following problems included in stress programs: post-shooting trauma; alcoholism; drug abuse; marital or other family difficulties; difficult relationships with fellow officers or supervisors; trauma associated with the catastrophic death of a child or spouse; debt management; gambling; issues associated with layoffs due to budget cuts; and adjustment to retirement.

Stress

Most people have a general idea of what **stress** is. Most people also perceive stress as negative, but this is not necessarily true. A certain amount of stress keeps people alert and functioning. Too much stress, however, can be incapacitating. In ancient China, the symbol for stress included two characters—one symbolizing danger, the other opportunity.

According to Hanson (1985, pp. xvii–xix): "Stress can be *fantastic*. Or it can be *fatal*. . . . Olympic records are not set on the quiet training tracks, but only with the stress of competition—in front of huge crowds. . . . Many people with sedate working lives actively seek stress in the form of parachuting, cliff climbing, downhill skiing, horror movies, or simply riding a roller coaster. Such stresses bring more joy into their lives."

Hanson (p. 19) suggests that the human body can be thought of as a "magnificent but outdated wooden battleship. . . . The problem is that many of our battleship's weapons are beautifully designed, but for the wrong war." Thousands of years before we became "civilized," our bodies were faced with simple survival for which either a "fight" or "flight" response was appropriate. In Table 8.3, Hanson (pp. 19–27) explains the anatomy of stress, what physical and psychological changes occur, how they were previously advantageous, and how they now become disadvantages.

In his classic work *The Stress of Life,* Dr. Hans Selye (1956) suggested that humans subjected to excessive stress undergo a "general adaptation syndrome" consisting of three distinct stages: alarm reaction, resistance, and exhaustion. In the first stage, *alarm reaction,* individuals perceive a threat to their safety or happiness. They recognize their inability to reach their personal/professional goals. The body releases stress hormones. In the second stage, *resistance,* individuals try to cope with the problem. The amount of resistance to the stressors increases, and bodily defense mechanisms are activated. In the third stage, *exhaustion,* individuals feel helpless and hopeless. Bodily resources are also exhausted, and people cannot adequately defend against the stressors.

The National Institute for Occupational Safety and Health have studied the effects of job stress on police officers for several years and have concluded (Depue, 1981, p. 305): "Police work becomes one of the few jobs which has a potent adverse effect on the total life of the worker. That is, the policeman's job affects his

199

CHAPTER 8
Physical and Mental
Fitness and Officer
Safety: Keeping
Fit for Duty

TABLE 8.3
The Anatomy of Stress

Natural response	Original benefit	Today's drawback
■ Release of cortisone from adrenal glands.	■ Protection from an instant allergic reaction or from a dustup with an attacking foe.	■ If chronically elevated, cortisone destroys the body's resistance to the stresses of cancer, infection, surgery, and illness. Bones are made more brittle by cortisone. Blood pressure can be elevated.
■ Increase of thyroid hormone in the bloodstream.	■ Speeds up the body's metabolism, thereby providing extra energy.	■ Intolerance to heat, shaky nerves to the point of jumpiness, insomnia, weight loss, and ultimately exhaustion or burnout.
■ Release of endorphin from the hypothalamus.	■ Identical to morphine, a potent pain killer.	■ Chronic, relentless stresses can deplete levels of endorphin, aggravating migraines, backaches, and the pain of arthritis.
■ Reduction in sex hormones—testosterone in the male and progesterone in the female.	■ Decreased fertility. In wartime, decreased libido made both partners' lives more bearable.	■ Obvious anxieties and failures when intercourse is attempted. Premature ejaculation in male; failure to reach orgasm in female.
■ Shutdown of the entire digestive tract. Mouth goes dry to avoid adding fluids to the stomach. Rectum and bladder tend to empty to jettison any excess load prior to battle.	■ Acts as a vital "self-transfusion" allowing person to perform superordinary feats of muscular power.	■ Dry mouth makes it difficult to speak with authority. The drawback of the "jettison response" is obvious.
■ Release of sugar into the blood, along with an increase in insulin levels to metabolize it.	■ Quick, short-distance energy supply.	■ Diabetes can be aggravated or even started.

Adapted from *The Joy of Stress* by Peter G. Hanson, (Kansas City, Missouri: Universal Stress Syndicate Company, 1985), 19–27.

own personal social life, his family's social life, his children's perception of him as a father, etc." The mental, emotional, and physical demands of the job can become so stressful that they can destroy officers' lives.

Sources of Stress

Many lists of stressors have been generated, including stressors specific to the police profession. Most of the stressors fall into four main categories, although some overlap exists.

Sources of stress for police officers include:

- *Internal, individual stressors.*
- *Stressors inherent to the police job.*
- *Administrative and organizational stressors.*
- *External stressors from the criminal justice system and the citizens it serves.*

Internal, Individual Stressors

Internal stressors vary greatly and can include officers' worries about their competency to handle assignments as well as feelings of helplessness and vulnerability. According to Victor (1986, p. 19), an especially pertinent source of stress today is "personal stress which may be generated by an officer's racial or gender status among peers, with consequent difficulty in getting along with individual fellow officers and in adjusting to group-held values not in accordance with one's own values, to perceptions of bias, and to social isolation."

Stress Related to Police Work

The police role itself is often vague and contradictory. Many people became police officers to fight crime, not to do social work. They are surprised to see how much "service" is actually involved in police work. They are also surprised to learn that their efforts are often not appreciated and that, in fact, their uniform is an object of scorn and derision.

The media presents an extremely distorted view of police work and police officers, resulting in unrealistic expectations by many citizens. Further, the distorted image is displayed over and over. Approximately one-third of regular television programming deals with some aspect of the criminal justice system. If a TV cop can solve three major crimes in an hour, why can't the local police at least keep prostitutes off the street or find the person who vandalized the school?

As Depue (1981, p. 306) states: "Except for general statements like 'enforce the law and maintain order,' the duties of the police officer depend upon such diverse factors as the oath of office, the law, court decisions, departmental policy, informal quota systems, the political climate, community pressures, common sense, and the personality of the chief of police."

Monthly shift rotations necessitate not only physical adaptations such as getting used to sleeping different hours, but also adaptations in officers' social and personal lives. O'Neill and Cushing (1991, p. 67) report on a study conducted by the Chicago Police Lieutenants Association on the impact of shift work on police officers: "If there is any conclusion that can be drawn from this study, it is that shift work is deleterious to the physical and psychological health of the individual and to the well-being of the organization." Other stressors inherent in police work, according to Goolkasian et al. (1985, pp. 4–5) include:

- The constant threat to officers' health and safety.
- Boredom, alternating with the need for sudden alertness and mobilized energy.

- Responsibility for protecting others' lives.
- Continual exposure to people in pain or distress.
- The need to control emotions, even when provoked to anger.
- The presence of a gun, sometimes even during off-duty hours.
- The fragmented nature of police work, with only rare opportunities to follow a case to conclusion or obtain feedback or follow-up information.

201

CHAPTER 8
Physical and Mental
Fitness and Officer
Safety: Keeping
Fit for Duty

Not to be forgotten are the stresses described by Victor (1986, p. 18), ". . . produced by real threats and dangers, such as the necessity of entering a dark and unfamiliar building, responding to a *'man with a gun'* alarm, and the pursuit of lawbreakers at high speeds." The stress induced by the fear and danger associated with police work is also emphasized by Russell and Beigel (1990, p. 353):

> *Whether police officers acknowledge it or not, police work involves dangerous acts that can provoke fear and lead to serious injury, disability, or even death. Although the actual frequency of these incidents is quite low in relation to number of police contacts throughout the country on any given day, the tension is still there because officers are aware from the beginning of training that there is no such thing as a routine stop.*

Administrative and Organizational Stressors

Many management practices and organizational factors can cause stress specific to law enforcement. Stress frequently arises from having to operate from a set of policies and procedures drawn up by individuals who do not have to carry them out. Seldom is the on-line officer's opinion on operational policies and procedures sought, even though it is the individual officer who must carry out these policies and procedures.

Lack of support from an administration when a questionable action is taken, the unavailability of needed resources, or the poor condition of equipment also causes stress for officers. Goolkasian et al. (1985, p. 5) cite the following as additional administrative and organizational stressors: ". . . [P]oor supervision, lack of administrative support for the patrol officer, lack of rewards for good job performance, insufficient training, inadequate career development opportunities, and excessive paperwork."

A similar list of management practices and organizational factors causing law enforcement stress is set forth by Ayres (1990, p. 81):

- Autocratic quasi-paramilitaristic model.
- Hierarchical structure.
- Poor supervision.
- Lack of employee input into policy and decision making.
- Excessive paperwork.
- Lack of administrative support.
- Role conflict and ambiguity.
- Inadequate pay and resources.
- Adverse work schedules.
- Boredom.
- Unfair discipline, performance evaluation, and promotion practices.

Stressors Related to the Criminal Justice System and Society

The criminal justice system and society at large can also induce stress in police officers. As noted by Goolkasian et al. (pp. 5–6), officers are often faced with:

- Lack of consideration by the courts in scheduling police officers for court appearances.
- Turf battles and lack of cooperation among individual law enforcement agencies.
- Court decisions that curtail individual officers' discretion or restrict the role of law enforcement.
- The perceived leniency of the courts.
- The premature release of offenders on bail or parole.
- Lack of public support and negative attitudes toward police.
- Distorted and unfavorable media accounts of incidents involving police.
- Inaccessibility and the perceived ineffectiveness of social services and rehabilitation agencies to which police must refer individuals.

As stated by one police officer (Conroy and Hess, 1992, p. 29):

> I think the crowning blow was to see that it's almost futile to go out there and do anything about it. Ya keep putting 'em away, and they keep letting 'em out. And then new people come along, and it just doesn't stop, and it will never stop.

The Relative Criticality of Individual Stressors

Individuals will vary as to how stressful certain events are perceived. The criticality of specific events within police officers' lives was studied by Sewell (1983, p. 113–114). Sewell developed a critical events scale listing 144 specific events and asked two sessions of the FBI National Academy to rank them from most to least stressful. The respondents included 500 officers from departments throughout the country. Sewell also surveyed a Virginia county police department for comparison. The results of his research are contained in Table 8.4.

According to Territo et al. (1989, p. 226): "Sewell's research indicated that the events requiring the greatest amount of adjustment were those relating to the categories of violence, threat of violence, personnel matters, and ethical concerns."

Effects of Stress

Goolkasian et al. (1985, p. 1) assert: "Unrelieved stress can result in high blood pressure, cardiovascular disease, chronic headaches, and gastric ulcers. It can lead to severe depression, alcohol and drug abuse, aggression and suicide. Stress affects officers' alertness, their physical stamina, and their ability to work effectively."

Police officers tend to have high rates of suicide, divorce, and alcoholism, often related to the stress of the job.

203

CHAPTER 8
*Physical and Mental
Fitness and Officer
Safety: Keeping
Fit for Duty*

TABLE 8.4
A Scale of Critical Life Events in Law Enforcement

Event	Value
1. Violent death of a partner in the line of duty	88
2. Dismissal	85
3. Taking a life in the line of duty	84
4. Shooting someone in the line of duty	81
5. Suicide of an officer who is a close friend	80
6. Violent death of another officer in the line of duty	79
7. Murder committed by a police officer	78
8. Duty-related violent injury (shooting)	76
9. Violent job-related injury to another officer	75
10. Suspension	72
11. Passed over for promotion	71
12. Pursuit of an armed suspect	71
13. Answering a call to a scene involving violent nonaccidental death of a child	70
14. Assignment away from family for a long period of time	70
15. Personal involvement in a shooting incident	70
16. Reduction in pay	70
17. Observing an act of police corruption	69
18. Accepting a bribe	69
19. Participating in an act of police corruption	68
20. Hostage situation resulting from aborted criminal action	68
21. Response to a scene involving the accidental death of a child	68
22. Promotion of inexperienced/incompetent officer over you	68
23. Internal affairs investigation against self	66
24. Barricaded suspect	66
25. Hostage situation resulting from a domestic disturbance	65
26. Response to "officer needs assistance" call	65
27. Duty under a poor supervisor	64
28. Duty-related violent injury (nonshooting)	63
29. Observing an act of police brutality	62
30. Response to "person with a gun" call	62
31. Unsatisfactory personnel evaluation	62
32. Police-related civil suit	61
33. Riot/crowd control situation	61
34. Failure on a promotional examination	60
35. Suicide of a fellow officer	60
36. Criminal indictment of a fellow officer	60
37. Improperly conducted corruption investigation of another officer	60
38. Shooting incident involving another officer	59
39. Failing grade in police training program	59
40. Response to a "felony in progress" call	58
41. Answering a call to a sexual battery/abuse scene involving a child victim	58

Continued on the next page

Table 8.4 *— Continued*

Event	Value
42. Oral promotional review	57
43. Conflict with a supervisor	57
44. Change in departments	56
45. Personal criticism by the press	56
46. Investigation of a political/highly publicized case	56
47. Taking severe disciplinary action against another officer	56
48. Assignment to conduct an internal affairs investigation on another officer	56
49. Interference by political officials in a case	55
50. Written promotional examination	55
51. Departmental misconduct hearing	55
52. Wrecking a departmental vehicle	55
53. Personal use of illicit drugs	54
54. Use of drugs by another officer	54
55. Participating in a police strike	53
56. Undercover assignment	53
57. Physical assault on an officer	52
58. Disciplinary action against partner	52
59. Death notification	51
60. Press criticism of an officer's actions	51
61. Polygraph examination	51
62. Sexual advance toward you by another officer	51
63. Duty-related accidental injury	51
64. Changing work shifts	50
65. Written reprimand by a supervisor	50
66. Inability to solve a major crime	48
67. Emergency run to "unknown trouble"	48
68. Personal use of alcohol while on duty	48
69. Inquiry into another officer's misconduct	47
70. Participation in a narcotics raid	47
71. Verbal reprimand by a supervisor	47
72. Handling of a mentally/emotionally disturbed person	47
73. Citizen complaint against an officer	47
74. Press criticism of departmental actions/practices	47
75. Answering a call to a sexual battery/abuse scene involving an adult victim	46
76. Reassignment/transfer	46
77. Unfair administrative policy	46
78. Preparation for retirement in the near future	46
79. Pursuit of a traffic violator	46
80. Severe disciplinary action to another officer	46
81. Promotion with assignment to another unit	45
82. Personal abuse of prescription drugs	45
83. Offer of a bribe	45

Continued on the next page

Table 8.4 — *Continued*

205

CHAPTER 8
*Physical and Mental
Fitness and Officer
Safety: Keeping
Fit for Duty*

Event	Value
84. Personally striking a prisoner or suspect	45
85. Physical arrest of a suspect	45
86. Promotion within existing assignment	44
87. Handling a domestic disturbance	44
88. Answering a call to a scene involving the violent nonaccidental death of an adult	44
89. Change in supervisors	44
00. Abuse of alcohol by another officer	44
91. Response to a silent alarm	44
92. Change in the chief administrators of the department	43
93. Answering a call to a scene involving the accidental death of an adult	43
94. Move to a new duty station	43
95. Fugitive arrest	43
96. Reduction in job responsibilities	43
97. Release of an offender by the prosecutor	41
98. Job-related illness	41
99. Transfer of partner	40
100. Assignment to night-shift duty	40
101. Recall to duty on day off	39
102. Labor negotiations	39
103. Verbal abuse from a traffic violator	39
104. Change in administrative policy/procedure	38
105. Sexual advance toward you by a citizen	37
106. Unfair plea bargain by a prosecutor	37
107. Assignment to a specialized training course	37
108. Assignment to stakeout duty	37
109. Release of an offender on appeal	37
110. Harassment by an attorney in court	37
111. Administrative recognition (award/commendation)	36
112. Court appearance (felony)	36
113. Annual evaluation	35
114. Assignment to decoy duty	35
115. Assignment as partner to an officer of the opposite sex	35
116. Assignment to evening shift	35
117. Assignment of new partner	34
118. Successful clearance of a case	34
119. Interrogation session with a suspect	33
120. Departmental budget cut	33
121. Release of an offender by a jury	33
122. Overtime duty	29
123. Letter of recognition from the public	29
124. Delay in a trial	28
125. Response to a "sick, or injured person" call	28

Continued on the next page

Table 8.4—*Continued*

Event	Value
126. Award from a citizen's group	27
127. Assignment to day shift	26
128. Work on a holiday	26
129. Making a routine arrest	26
130. Assignment to a two-man car	25
131. Call involving juveniles	25
132. Routine patrol stop	25
133. Assignment to a single-man car	25
134. Call involving the arrest of a female	24
135. Court appearance (misdemeanor)	24
136. Working a traffic accident	23
137. Dealing with a drunk	23
138. Pay raise	23
139. Overtime pay	22
140. Making a routine traffic stop	22
141. Vacation	20
142. Issuing a traffic citation	20
143. Court appearance (traffic)	19
144. Completion of a routine report	13

Source: From "The Development of a Critical Life Events Scale for Law Enforcement," by
J. D. Sewell in the *Journal of Police Science and Administration* 11:1 (1983),
pp. 113–114. Reprinted with permission of the International Association of Chiefs of Police,
Inc. 1110 N. Glebe Rd., Suite 200, Arlington, VA 22201, USA

Some authorities feel that police suicides are underreported because fellow officers are usually the first on the scene and may cover up the suicide to save the family further pain or embarrassment or for insurance purposes.

Whether police divorce and alcoholism rates are higher than those in other professions is open to question. It is known, however, that the police job does seriously interfere with officers' social and home lives, that many officers take their job home with them, that spouses worry about the officers' safety, and that rotating shifts makes normal social life difficult.

It is also clear that stress usually results in other forms of behavior changes. The Dallas Police Department has developed a list of fifteen common warning signs for stress (see Table 8.5). In addition, the Dallas Police Department has identified several job-related stressors and the likely immediate and long-term responses in the areas of personality, health, job performance, and home life (see Table 8.6).

Burnout

When stress continues unremitting for prolonged periods, it can result in the debilitating condition referred to as *burnout*. Daviss (1982, p. 10) notes:

207

*CHAPTER 8
Physical and Mental
Fitness and Officer
Safety: Keeping
Fit for Duty*

TABLE 8.5
The Fifteen Most Prevalent Stress Warning Signs

Warning signs	Examples
1. Sudden changes in behavior (usually directly opposite to usual behavior)	From cheerful and optimistic to gloomy and pessimistic
2. More gradual change in behavior but in a way that points to deterioration of the individual	Gradually becoming slow and lethargic, possibly with increasing depression and sullen behavior
3. Erratic work habits	Coming to work late, leaving early, abusing compensatory time
4. Increased sick time due to minor problems	Headaches, colds, stomachaches, etc.
5. Inability to maintain a train of thought	Rambling conversation, difficulty in sticking to a specific subject
6. Excessive worrying	Worrying about one thing to the exclusion of any others
7. Grandiose behavior	Preoccupation with religion, politics, etc.
8. Excessive use of alcohol and/or drugs	Obvious hangover, disinterest in appearance, talk about drinking prowess
9. Fatigue	Lethargy, sleeping on job
10. Peer complaints	Others refuse to work with the officer
11. Excessive complaints (negative citizen contact)	Caustic and abusive in relating to citizens
12. Consistency in complaint pattern	Picks on specific groups of people (youths, blacks, etc.)
13. Sexual promiscuity	Going after everything all of the time—on or off duty
14. Excessive accidents and/or injuries	Not being attentive to driving, handling prisoners, etc.
15. Manipulation of fellow officers and citizens	Using others to achieve ends without caring for their welfare

Source: Reprinted with permission of the Psychological Services Unit, Dallas Police Department.

[B]urnout—the costly and dangerous terminal phase of stress—is now claiming cops faster than it used to. . . . Burnout warps officers' attitudes, skews their judgment, impairs their reflexes, endangers their health, and saps their strength. . . .

According to experts, burnout is costing departments across the country immeasurable amounts of money and time and is robbing law enforcement organizations of their best officers.

Burnout *refers to a person who is "used up or consumed by a job," made listless through overwork and stress. The person experiences a persistent lack of energy or interest in his or her work.*

TABLE 8.6
Short-Term Chronic Reactions to Stress

Job-related stressors			
Administration	Inadequate resources	Job overload	Conflict values
Job conflict	Inequities in pay and job status	Responsibility for people	Racial situations
Second job	Organizational territoriality	Courts	Line-of-duty crisis situations
Inactivity		Negative public image	Job ambiguity
Shift work			

Immediate responses to stress			
Personality	**Health**	**Job Performance**	**Home Life**
Temporary increases in:	Temporary increases in:	Job tension	"Spats with spouse"
Anxiety	Smoking rate	"Flying off the handle"	Periodic withdrawal
Tension	Headaches	Erratic work habits	Anger displaced to wife and children
Irritability	Heart rate	Temporary decrease in workload	Increased extramarital activity
Feeling "uptight"	Blood pressure		
Drinking rate	Cholesterol level		

Long-term responses to stress			
Personality	**Health**	**Job Performance**	**Home Life**
Psychosis	Chronic disease states:	Decreased productivity	Divorce
Chronic depression	Ulcers	Increased error rate	Poor relations with others
Alienation	High blood pressure	Job dissatisfaction	Social isolation
Alcoholism	Coronary heart disease	Accidents	Loss of friends
General malaise	Asthmatic attacks	Withdrawal	
Low self-esteem	Diabetes	Serious errors in judgment	
Low self-actualization		Slower reaction time	
Suicide			

Source: Adapted from W. H. Kroes, *Society's Victim—The Policeman,* p. 66, 1976 by the Psychological Services Unit, Dallas Police Department. Reprinted with permission.

Unfortunately, burnout only happens to those who are initially "on fire" — that is, to enthusiastic, highly productive workers. As noted by Reese (1982, p. 52): "Burnout has been referred to as a disease of overcommitment, ironically, causing a lack of commitment." The result is an unproductive officer who simply puts in time, counting the days to retirement. According to Reese (p. 52), "When an officer fails to function at acceptable levels, the label 'an empty suit' is often applied. . . . This officer has, in essence, 'retired in place.' " Says Reese:

> *Burnout is a common affliction to those employed in the human services. The police profession, like many others, is laden with job-related pressures such as role overload, role confusion/conflict, and low job satisfaction. While being a helping service, officers rarely receive positive reinforcement from those they help or protect. They live life in "the high-speed lane," responding to calls ranging from domestic disturbances to homicides; child abuse to kidnappings. . . . The police cruiser may leave the "high-speed lane" but the officer remains there emotionally, burning out.*

The following stressors are listed by Reese (pp. 52–53) as contributing to officer burnout:

- Devaluing traditional police work.
- Perceived or actual lowering of the department's public image.

- Reduced manpower.
- Frequent rotation in supervisory personnel.
- Turnover in executive policy-making posts.
- Police unions.
- Specializations such as SWAT and undercover.
- Policies regarding deadly force.
- Adoption of affirmative action programs.
- Fluctuation in promotional policies and qualifications.
- Increased legal liabilities and civil suits.
- Failure to adopt psychological services programs for officers.
- Public scrutiny.
- Increased assaults on officers.
- Budget reversals.
- Limited range of income potential.
- Lack of mobility.
- Lack of control over intradepartmental transfers.

209

CHAPTER 8
Physical and Mental
Fitness and Officer
Safety: Keeping
Fit for Duty

As one officer put it (Conroy and Hess, 1992, p. 209), "I just couldn't go on. It seemed that there was nothing inside of me to keep me going. I couldn't look at one more dead body, one more abused child, or handle one more domestic fight. I'd just had it." Officers who are burned out are at extremely high risk of being injured or killed on duty because they are usually not safety conscious.

Reducing Stress

Many books and articles deal with stress reduction. Good nutrition and exercise can help. So can taking time for oneself, relaxing, meditation, going for a walk, or finding a hobby. Parker et al. (1989, p. 160) suggest:

Individual approaches to stress management include exercise, recreation, time management, and socializing with friends and family. Zen, transcendental meditation, and yoga have been found to reduce oxygen consumption, respiration rate, heart rate, and blood pressure, while systematic relaxation reduces muscle tension. Biofeedback techniques also appear to be helpful in reducing the side effects of chronic stress.

Russell and Beigel (1990, pp. 356–362) suggest the following to reduce the adverse effects of police work: "Anticipate the stressors; if possible, avoid them; practice for those that may be unavoidable; pay attention to diet and exercise; take private time to be alone; use relaxation techniques; get adequate sleep; think positively; and engage in positive self-talk."

Conroy and Hess (1992, p. 228) emphasize that stress management is a life-style:

Stress management doesn't just happen. To effectively reduce stress in your life, you must adopt a life-style conducive to managing stress. To force yourself to reduce stress can become just another stressor. If you force yourself to work out, meditate, or relax, it becomes just one more thing added to the pile of stress you already have. Therefore, it is important to practice the techniques discussed, but with patience. Realize that you may want to work out every day, but sometimes can't. Allow yourself a day off when necessary. . . .

Stress management is taking care of yourself. You can't take care of others unless you take care of yourself first!

Law enforcement departments should be as concerned with their officers' mental health as they are with their physical health and should offer some sort of employee assistance program for those officers needing help in this area. Professional counseling, peer counseling, police-spouse support groups, and the like can do much to improve the mental fitness of a law enforcement agency.

Officer Safety

A physically and mentally fit officer is in a much better position to perform effectively and to stay alive. But there is another aspect to officer safety that sometimes comes into play. After being in police work for a few years, officers often come to feel invincible. They have what is called the "it won't happen to me" syndrome. Although they see people all around them being victimized, such police officers refuse to believe that they can become victims themselves. This attitude lulls them into a false sense of security.

Most officers injured or killed in the line of duty could have either avoided the confrontation or minimized the injury had they been mentally prepared for the danger, alert, and trained in the proper survival techniques.

Remsberg (1986, p. 16) says: "Your mind is the most dangerous weapon you carry on patrol." He proposes an *awareness spectrum* for police officers that might save lives (see Table 8.7).

The **awareness spectrum** *describes an officer's level of awareness, ranging from condition white, environmental unawareness, to condition black, panicked/blacked out/perhaps dead. Ideally, officers will be at condition yellow: alert but relaxed.*

Part of being alert is being aware of objects that can pose a danger to police officers. Ottman (1987, pp. 22, 24) describes some everyday items that can be used as dangerous weapons:

TABLE 8.7
The Awareness Spectrum—Stages of Alertness

Stage	Definition
Condition white	Environmental unawareness
Condition yellow	Relaxed but alert
Condition orange	State of alarm
Condition red	Something *is* wrong
Condition black	Panicked/blacked out/perhaps dead

Source: Adapted from *The Tactical Edge: Surviving High-Risk Patrol* by Charles Remsberg, 1986, pp. 47–51.

211

CHAPTER 8
*Physical and Mental
Fitness and Officer
Safety: Keeping
Fit for Duty*

- Any newspaper or magazine, tightly rolled, can be converted into a baton.
- A ball point pen can kill as surely as any switch blade.
- A nylon headband, leather thong necklace, or elastic belt can be turned into a garrot.
- Wire hangers can be used to wrap around a neck and crush the windpipe.
- A set of keys is far more dangerous than brass knuckles when firmly locked between the fingers and jabbed into an officer's face or raked across exposed flesh.
- An open handcuff's ratchet teeth can cut an officer's hand to shreds.
- The lenses in a pair of sunglasses can be as deadly as a razor blade.
- A plastic drinking straw can be driven completely through a raw apple— or an officer's throat.

Ottman (pp. 22, 24) warns, "Commonly found items on nearly every homo sapiens of this planet may become offensive weapons under the right circumstances. By taking note of this fact and guarding carefully during prime resistance and escape conditions, you avoid being suckered into a deadly confrontation." He continues (p. 24):

*Bear in mind, we are not talking about the unique ability of television's
A-Team to convert a discarded washing machine and a book of matches into a
multiple-warhead rocket launcher capable of impacting rounds with computer
accuracy at 500 yards. Think rather in terms of picking up a rubber band and
paper clip and shooting someone's eye out from across a desk, setting
someone's newly sprayed hair on fire with two flashlight batteries touched
together in the fumes, or jabbing a toothpick into an unguarded eyeball. Now
you're thinking gutter tactics, and that is just what you're up against.*

The survival course developed for border patrol agents has components that are relevant to police operations as well. Smith (1990, pp. 110–111) describes some of the basic components:

*Effective training, therefore, must begin with effective mental conditioning.
Making an officer aware that he can be hurt in a situation falls far short of
conditioning the officer's thought process to recognize warning signs and
constantly think in terms of appropriate action or reaction in any situation.*

*Basic survival training . . . must be restricted to the teaching of "constants."
Constants are axioms which have broad application; they are procedural
steps for which there are no viable alternatives. An example of a constant
would be to establish sufficient distance between yourself and a suspect during
an interview to allow for reaction lag time. Another example of a constant is
to avoid exposing your weapon so as to not make it available to a suspect, or
not turn your back on a suspect. . . .*

The Border Patrol . . . built its course around a "survival triangle."

---

*The border patrol's **survival triangle** consists of:*

- *Mental and physical preparedness.*
- *Sound tactics.*
- *Weapon control.*

The survival triangle is illustrated in Figure 8.2. The focus of this chapter has been on the base of the survival triangle, physical and mental preparedness.

The second side of the survival triangle is sound tactics, which consist of the five "Cs": cover, concealment, control, containment, and communications. Effective, constant communications is the single thread that stitches all the pieces together.

The five Cs for survival tactics are cover, concealment, control, containment, and communications.

The third side of the survival triangle is weapons control, addressed through the following checklist:

1. Do you know the capabilities and limitations of yourself and each of your weapons?
2. Are your weapons clean and functional?
3. Are they loaded? How are they loaded? What type of ammunition are they loaded with? Does your partner know the answers to these questions?

FIGURE 8.2
Survival Triangle

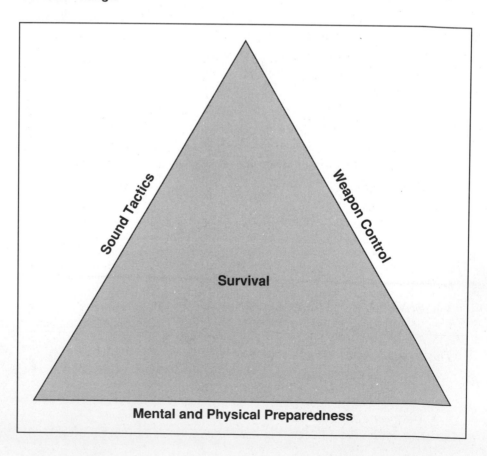

213

CHAPTER 8
*Physical and Mental
Fitness and Officer
Safety: Keeping
Fit for Duty*

A Los Angeles Police Department sniper practicing at the rifle range. Says Sniper Kessner, "I try to disregard that I'm going to have to take a life. I have to react to save a life."

4. Are your weapons immediately accessible to you? Or are they on the seat next to you where they might slide out of reach under your leg, or in the trunk, or the back seat? Close to you is not the same as accessible in a dynamic confrontation!

5. Do you practice constant forearm contact with your sidearm? (This is an excellent habit to acquire.)

6. Have you mastered a good technique for weapon retention?

7. Can you practice fire discipline?

8. Have you mentally prepared yourself to use your weapons? Lag time is a killer.

Protecting Against AIDS, Hepatitis B, and Other Infections

As noted by Lopez (1991a, p. 14): "Handling bleeding accident or assault victims, collecting bloody body parts and evidence, performing mouth to mouth resuscitation, patting down a junkie, and getting spat or vomited on are activities that are part of a police officer's job. These activities put officers at risk for AIDS, hepatitis B, and a number of other serious infections."

AIDS (Acquired Immune Deficiency Syndrome).
This infectious, fatal disease presents a challenge to law enforcement, especially given the many misconceptions and myths about it. Gates and Lady (1991, p. 45) stress using precaution whenever blood or body fluids are present: ". . . *all patients should be presumed to be infectious for HIV and other blood-borne pathogens.*" Although this policy was formulated for emergency and public safety workers, it applies equally to law enforcement officers.

Law enforcement officers should know how AIDS is *not* transmitted. The Center for Disease Control says that AIDS is not spread by sneezing, coughing, breathing, hugging, handshaking, sharing eating and drinking utensils, using the same toilet facilities, or other nonsexual contacts.

To protect against AIDS, officers who have any open sores, cuts, or scratches on their hands should wear gloves. All officers should wear gloves when handling body fluids such as blood and semen. Remember that such fluids may be mixed with other body fluids of the suspect or victim at a crime or accident site.

Hepatitis B (HBV).

This infectious disease is transmitted in many of the same ways as AIDS and can kill directly (1.3 percent of the time) or significantly increase the chances of getting cirrhosis and liver cancer. A series of three shots can protect against hepatitis B.

Other Infections.

As noted by Lopez (1991a, p. 14):

Cuts, scrapes, and puncture wounds can all get infected, and they're more of a threat when they're inflicted by people of dubious sanitary habits. Such wounds need to be washed and bandaged as soon as possible. Deep cuts and puncture wounds should be seen by a doctor. Any wound that turns red or tender needs immediate professional attention.

The *tetanus shot* is an important safeguard against infections and should be repeated every ten years. If, however, a deep or dirty wound is sustained, a tetanus shot should have been given within the last five years.

Officers can become infected from a human bite. If officers are bitten by a human, they should wash the wound immediately and then see a doctor for the appropriate antibiotics. If officers are bitten by an animal, they should impound the animal if possible and have it tested for rabies.

Summary

Physical fitness is the body's general capacity to adapt and respond favorably to physical effort. The prime indicators of physical fitness are endurance, balance, agility, flexibility, strength, power, and body composition. Motor skills important to police officers include coordination, speed, and accuracy. The criticality index measures the frequency and importance of physical activities performed by police officers. Rated as the most critical activity is the ability to run up stairs.

Police work is often sedentary, involves irregular hours and constantly changing work shifts, and may promote poor diets, excessive cigarette smoking and consumption of alcohol, and great amounts of stress. These factors can be offset by physical fitness training programs. An effective physical fitness training program that is varied and of interest to the officer should include aerobic, strength, and flexibility training. It should be engaged in regularly for twenty to thirty minutes a day, at least three days a week.

Mental fitness refers to a person's emotional well-being, the ability to feel fear, anger, compassion, and other emotions and to express them appropriately. It also refers to a person's alertness and ability to make decisions quickly. Mental fitness can be negatively affected by excessive stress.

Sources of stress for police officers include internal, individual stressors; stressors inherent to the police job; administrative and organizational stressors, and external stressors from the criminal justice system and the citizens it serves.

Burnout refers to a person who is "used up or consumed by a job," made listless through overwork and stress. The person experiences a persistent lack of energy or interest in his or her work.

Officer safety is another important aspect of keeping prepared for duty. The awareness spectrum describes an officer's level of awareness, ranging from condition white, environmental unawareness, to condition black, panicked/blacked out/ perhaps dead. Ideally, officers will be at condition yellow: alert but relaxed.

The Border Patrol's survival triangle consists of mental and physical preparedness, sound tactics, and weapon control. The five Cs for survival tactics are cover, concealment, control, containment, and communications.

215

CHAPTER 8
*Physical and Mental
Fitness and Officer
Safety: Keeping
Fit for Duty*

Application #1

You have noticed that many of your fellow officers have become nonproductive due to various activities affecting their morale. Many are stressed out, and the department has no program to assist them. You approach your supervisor and offer to discuss it with your colleagues and then develop a policy dealing with stress management. The policy should point out various types of stressors officers must cope with and various services available to help officers. It should also bring employee assistance programs to the attention of the officers. It should include how to contact an individual or a group for help. Consider such programs as Alcoholics Anonymous, marriage counseling, financial advisers, psychological counseling, and any others that are locally available. It should stress that officers may keep their contacts confidential and that no department interference will be generated that might impair or threaten an officer's job because that officer seeks assistance.

Application #2

Stress can lead to a variety of tragic situations such as a fellow officer being killed on the job. Most police departments have no next-of-kin-notification policies or any support or assistance policies for surviving spouses. Police departments can help their own officers as well as survivors when an officer is killed by establishing specific policies on how to proceed in the event of the death of a fellow officer. Research the problem and then develop a policy whereby procedures are spelled out in case of a death or other unanticipated tragedy. Having a policy concerning notification procedures, psychological services, and emotional support, will better prepare police officers to respond compassionately and effectively to those in need.

Application #3

You are the training officer for your department. The chief has also designated you to be the wellness officer and has asked you to develop a strictly voluntary physical fitness program. Use the form in Appendix A. For those who wish to participate in this wellness program, outline exercises they might do to improve their physical fitness. Include such exercises as aerobics, walking, jogging, and nautilus training, and list the benefits officers can derive from these and other exercises. Keep in mind that each officer has specific needs and that age and present physical condition should be considered.

An Exercise in Critical Thinking

Unexpected challenges and critical life events test the fitness of police officers. Mental fitness and physical fitness enable officers to cope with the variety of circumstances that occur in the line of duty. Endurance, balance, agility, strength, power, and body composition are requisite for doing a good job, while the ability to feel and express emotions appropriately reveals a person's mental fitness and emotional well-being. Officer survival consists of mental and physical preparedness as well as sound tactics and weapon control.

On July 14, at approximately 9:00 P.M. a state trooper received a message from the dispatcher that a probable drunken driver was traveling southbound on Highway 61 in a white Cadillac. The dispatcher did not know the identity of the person who called in the "tip." While driving north, the trooper thereafter observed a white Cadillac southbound on Highway 61, approximately 200 yards from his squad car. The Cadillac was traveling about 15 miles per hour with at least half the width of the car on the shoulder of the road. The trooper was able to walk over to the southbound lane and hold up his hand to stop the driver of the Cadillac for investigation.

The Cadillac stopped for approximately five seconds, then made a U-turn into a driveway, and reentered the northbound lane of Highway 61. While this turnaround was happening, several drivers passed by the trooper and told him that the Cadillac had been driving all over the road. The trooper ran to intercept the Cadillac, which by then had crossed over the centerline and was headed for the ditch. The Cadillac continued, traveling about ten miles per hour, into the ditch and headed for a steep embankment (a drop-off of about 30 feet) about 50 yards away.

1. If the trooper is in good shape, what should he do?
   a. Continue to hold up his hand to stop the Cadillac.
   b. Let the Cadillac continue in the ditch—sooner or later it will come to rest.
   c. Run alongside the Cadillac, try to reach in and turn off the ignition, or at least steer the vehicle in a safe direction.
   d. Shoot out the tires to make it impossible for the vehicle to continue.
   e. Try to verbally communicate with the driver in a nonthreatening, calming voice to help the driver become cooperative, and only as a last resort attempt to physically stop the vehicle.
2. The trooper discovers that the driver of the Cadillac is fellow trooper Vernon Francis. After being successfully stopped, Francis takes an alcohol concentration test which yields a result of more than .10. Now, what are the appropriate actions for the state trooper on duty?
   a. An arrest for aggravated drinking is appropriate.
   b. Both an arrest and a recommendation for counselling should be made.
   c. Francis needs to be shocked into understanding that his career is jeopardized, so the kindest treatment is to be as harsh with him as possible.

217

CHAPTER 8
*Physical and Mental
Fitness and Officer
Safety: Keeping
Fit for Duty*

d. In addition to the arrest, Francis should be dismissed from duty.

e. Criminal indictment of a fellow officer should be avoided out of loyalty, but a verbal warning (no written report) does need to be given.

Discussion Questions

1. Is peer counseling—"cops working with cops"—better for helping troubled officers than outside professional counseling?

2. Is there one best way to handle officers who have drinking problems? Explain.

3. One reason police officers are reluctant to seek therapeutic services is they fear their careers will be jeopardized. How can this obstacle be overcome?

4. Is it a good idea for every police department to have its own police psychologist? What are the advantages of in-house versus outside psychological assistance?

5. Are police officers confronted with the same stressful problems that everyone in society faces—that people such as firefighters, construction workers, business people, military personnel face?

6. Does the media create unnecessary stress for police officers in your community? If so, how?

7. How do police administrations contribute to the stresses of police officers?

Definitions

Can you define the following terms?

aerobic training	endurance
agility	eye-hand coordination
anaerobic training	flexibility
awareness spectrum	mental fitness
balance	physical fitness
body composition	power
burnout	stamina
criticality index	strength
cross-training	stress
encephaloendorphins	survival triangle

References

Adlam, K. R. C. "The Police Personality: Psychological Consequences of Being a Police Officer." *Journal of Police Science and Administration* Vol. 10 (1982): 344–349.

Anderson, Wayne and Bauer, Barbara. "Law Enforcement Officers: The Consequences of Exposure to Violence." *Journal of Counseling and Development*, Vol. 65 (March 1987): 381–385.

Anonymous, Chris. "You Need Help from Friends to Escape from the Bottle." *Police Magazine* (May 1982): 12–13.

Ayres, Richard M. *Preventing Law Enforcement Stress: The Organization's Role*. Bureau of Justice Assistance. Washington, D.C.: U.S. Government Printing Office, 1990.

Conroy, Dennis L. and Hess, Kären M. *Officers at Risk: How to Identify and Cope with Stress*. Placerville, Calif.: Custom Publishing Company, 1992.

Daviss, Ben. "Burnout." *Police Magazine* (May 1982): 9–15.

Depue, Roger L. "Turning Inward: The Police Officer Counselor." In *Stress and Police Personnel*, by Leonard Territo and Harold J. Vetter, eds. Boston, Mass.: Allyn and Bacon, 1981.

Gates, Daryl F. and Lady, Kenneth E. "Enhancing AIDS Awareness in Los Angeles." *The Police Chief* (March 1991): 44–47.

Geier, Michael J. "Training to Win: Police-Specific Physical Conditioning." *Law and Order* (September 1990): 50–56.

Getz, Ronald J. "You Can't Afford *Not* to Have a Fitness Program." *Law and Order* (June 1990): 44–50.

Goolkasian, Gail A.; Geddes, Ronald W.; and DeJong, William. *Coping with Police Stress*. National Institute of Justice, Washington, D.C.: U.S. Government Printing Office, 1985.

Hanson, Peter G. *The Joy of Stress*. Kansas City, Mo.: Universal Press Syndicate Company, 1985.

Harrison-Davis, Marvel. "Nutrition on the Go." *Emergency Medical Services* 18: 2 (March 1989): 46–58.

Jordan, David B. and Schwartz, Sam. "NYC's Physical Performance Testing Program." *The Police Chief* (June 1986): 29–30.

Lopez, Carl.
    a. "Cheeseburgers, Cholesterol, and Cops." *Law and Order* (May 1991): 12–14.
    b. "Protecting Yourself from AIDS, Hepatitis B, and Other Infections." *Law and Order* (January 1991): 14–15.

Maslach, Christina and Jackson, Susan E. "Burned-Out Cops and Their Families." *Psychology Today* (12) (May 1979): 59.

Minnesota P.O.S.T. Board. *Learning Objectives for Professional Peace Officer Education*. St. Paul, Minn.: Minnesota P.O.S.T. Board, 1991.

Mostardi, Richard A.; Porterfield, James A.; King, Steven; Wiedman, Kate; and Urycki, Stan. "Cardiovascular Intervention Among Police Officers: A Two-Year Report." *The Police Chief* (June 1986): 32–34.

O'Neill, James L. and Cushing, Michael A. *The Impact of Shift Work on Police Officers*. Washington, D.C.: Police Executive Research Forum, 1991.

Ottman, Jim. "Deft Death: Everyday Items Transform to Dangerous Weapons." *Police* (August 1987): 22, 24.

Parker, L. Craig, Jr.; Meier, Robert D.; and Monahan, Lynn Hunt. *Interpersonal Psychology for Criminal Justice*. 2d ed. St. Paul, Minn.: West Publishing Company, 1989.

Reese, James T. "Life in the High-Speed Lane: Managing Police Burnout." *The Police Chief* (June 1982): 49–53.

Remsberg, Charles. *The Tactical Edge: Surviving High-Risk Patrol*. Northbrook, Ill.: Calibre Press, 1986.

Russell, Harold E. and Beigel, Allan. *Understanding Human Behavior for Effective Police Work*. New York: Basic Books, 1990.

Selye, Hans. *The Stress of Life*. New York: McGraw-Hill, 1956.

Sewell, J. D. "The Development of a Critical Life Events Scale for Law Enforcement." *Journal of Police Science and Administration* 11:1 (1983): pp. 109–116.

Slahor, Stephenie. "Focus on Fitness: The FBI Way." *Law and Order* (May 1990): 52–55.

Smith, Paul M. "Survival Course for Border Patrol Agents." *Law and Order* (October 1990): 109–113.

Stamps, Janice L. " 'Back' to Basics." *Emergency Medical Services* 18: 2 (March 1989): 39–45.

Territo, Leonard; Halsted, James; and Bromley, Max. *Crime and Justice in America, A Human Perspective*. St. Paul, Minn.: West Publishing Company, 1989.

Territo, Leonard and Vetter, Harold J. *Stress and Police Personnel*. Boston, Mass.: Allyn and Bacon, 1981.

Victor, Joseph. "Police Stress: Is Anybody Out There Listening?" *New York Law Enforcement Journal* (June 1986): 19–20.

Violanti, John M. "Obesity: A Police Health Problem." *Law and Order* (April 1985): 58–60.

219

CHAPTER 8
Physical and Mental
Fitness and Officer
Safety: Keeping
Fit for Duty

Case

Parker v. District of Columbia, 850 F.2d 708, 109 S.Ct. 1339.

Getting the Job Done

It is in this section that most police operations books begin and end. But a law enforcement officer must never forget that the actual operations themselves are only half the job, just as they take up only half this text.

To perform police operations professionally, officers must always keep in mind the content of the first two sections. They must consider the context in which they operate—the citizens they serve as well as the colleagues with whom they work. Law enforcement officers are an integral part of this context, not a separate entity. They do not operate in a vacuum. Officers must use effective communications skills, including active listening skills. They must document their actions in well-written reports. They must be certain their actions are not only legal, but also ethical, and they must take care of themselves so they will be better able to take care of others.

With this solid foundation, you can now focus on the actual operations law enforcement officers perform. At the heart of police operations is patrol, often called the backbone of the police organization (Chapter 9). Activities conducted during patrol often include other functions performed by officers such as traffic enforcement (Chapter 10), dealing with crime and violence (Chapter 11), intervening in domestic disputes and violence (Chapter 12), interacting with juveniles (Chapter 13), controlling gangs and drug traffickers (Chapter 14), handling emergency situations (Chapter 15), and, of extreme importance, working with others both individually and in groups (Chapter 16). Effective law enforcement is a joint effort of all concerned.

PATROL AND CALLS FOR SERVICE: THE HEART OF POLICE OPERATIONS

CHAPTER 9

INTRODUCTION

Patrol has been one of the most widely discussed and controversial areas in law enforcement over the past several decades.

Patrol service has been described as the "backbone of the police department."

Theoretically, police patrol officers are the most valuable people in the organization. To a certain extent, all activity radiates from uniformed patrol officers. It is difficult to totally support such a concept, however, because salary, working conditions, and issues of authority seem totally unrelated.

Usually, the most complex, burdensome, and dangerous aspect of police service is performed by uniformed patrol officers. The work may be performed in an atmosphere emotionally charged with hostility—an environment that breeds distrust and danger—and in situations that require officers to be clergy, psychologist, therapist, or one of many other professionals who deal with human problems. Patrol officers are expected to be all things to all people. And while the officers may not always be able to contribute to the solution, they are at least expected to never contribute to the problem.

Considering all the ranks and specialized assignments in a police department, patrol responsibilities certainly are high in priority in terms of complexity, importance, and the need for a broad spectrum of knowledge. Yet most officers working at this very challenging level eventually seek promotion or transfer to higher status position with an increase in salary.

Do You Know

- How patrol is typically described?
- What organizational contradiction is embodied in the patrol function?
- What functions patrol typically performs?
- How crowds can be classified?
- How typical patrol shifts are organized?
- What *proportionate assignment* is?
- How the majority of patrol time is spent?
- What the Kansas City Experiment found?
- What directed patrol and problem-oriented policing are?
- What most affects the possibility of on-scene arrests?
- What two basic causes account for delays in calling for service?
- What differential police response strategies do?
- What kinds of patrol have been used and the advantages and disadvantages of each?
- What type of patrol has the most mobility and flexibility and is usually the most cost effective?
- What issues are involved in the one-officer v. two-officer squads issue?
- What issues should be addressed in a pursuit policy?

One reason the professionalization of law enforcement is slow in coming is because this condition exists. The fact is, the most crucial people on the law enforcement team are lowest on the totem pole. Police departments were created to provide service to the public. The department's ability to carry out its mission depends greatly on the uniformed patrol officers' capabilities.

The fact that patrol officers, those who actually accomplish the department's goals, are lowest in status and in pay results in a serious organizational contradiction.

According to Territo et al. (1989, pp. 160–161), police chiefs often say that patrol is the backbone of their agency, but they transfer the best and brightest officers out of patrol to other assignments. Territo et al. suggest, "This practice guarantees that the 'backbone' of the police department will be composed primarily of inexperienced officers and those who are average, or even below average, in ability and motivation."

The reasons given for the practice include the following. First, administrators might not truly believe in the importance of the patrol function. Second, they might not think that patrol is "sufficiently stimulating, or rewarding, or challenging enough to keep the best, brightest, and most able officers satisfied." Third, many officers want to be transferred because of the schedule. Patrol officers work nights, weekends, and holidays. Such schedules can be especially troublesome to married officers who have spouses with normal working hours. Further, as noted by Territo et al. (1989, p. 161):

The normal working day of a patrol officer is not filled with glamorous and exciting crime-fighting activities like those depicted on popular television programs. Instead, days are spent on routine patrol or performing noncriminal services for the public. However, in spite of this routine, the patrol officer's job is often far more dangerous than most people imagine. Patrol officers are the ones who are called to respond to crimes in progress or crimes that have just been committed. Such assignments increase the possibility that a criminal will still be at the scene of the crime or in the immediate area, thereby increasing the potential for physical and armed confrontation. Thus, the job of the patrol officer has been described as one consisting of both hours of boredom (especially on the midnight shift) and moments of terror. Patrol officers also spend much of their day in contact with the human dregs of our society. They have to deal with drunks who have soiled themselves but who still must be searched before being transported to jail; with teenage gangs who are arrogant, disrespectful, and openly contemptuous; with prostitutes, pimps, and petty thugs; and with child abusers.

Little wonder that patrol officers frequently find themselves stressed out both physically and psychologically. It is also understandable why so many seek transfers to other divisions or into management, not only to escape the hazards of patrol, but to have a better schedule, higher pay, and increased status both inside and outside the department.

This is unfortunate because highly competent patrol officers are crucial to the successful operation of every police department. As noted by Adams (1985, p. 1):

The uniformed patrol officer of the department is the personification of law enforcement in the United States. To many people in the community, uniformed patrol officers are the government or the establishment. To many, they alone are the criminal justice system, as the one judge they encounter becomes the courts. These are people who cannot see the mayor, or the council members, or the prosecuting attorney, or a judge. Patrol officers thus become the representatives of those individuals because they are highly visible. Most of the people served respect and consider field officers as their protectors. Others, however, see the uniformed officer as a nuisance, and still others look upon the officer as the enemy. It is the officer's responsibility to serve all members of the community with equal dedication and respect and with a sense of justice.

Adams notes that over 80 percent of the country's police agencies employ fewer than twenty officers. These departments have almost all their officers assigned to patrol, delegating additional special duties as needed. In a police agency with only one officer, that officer performs all roles from chief to records clerk, with the majority of the time spent serving a patrol function.

Patrol Functions

Every patrol division performs different tasks, although some are common to all. Patrol duties are not usually described in great detail, except when officers answer specific calls for service. "Routine" patrol means different things to individual officers, supervisors, and departments. For example, one officer on routine patrol may feel that if nothing is "happening," time can best be spent talking to citizens and getting to know the patrol areas. Another officer might feel the time should be spent looking into suspected gang activity. A third officer might feel this is the time to catch up on current events by reading the newspaper.

Kenney and More (1986, p. 9) note that the police "have a preventive and protective role as well as a peace-keeping function." Their presence is intended to deter crime and give citizens a feeling of being protected. Officers not only help reduce racial tensions in large city ghettos, they often conduct educational programs and provide help to "the down-and-out drunk, the mentally ill, street persons, or the naive patrons of vice activity who may be subjecting themselves to the risk of robbery or worse."

Among the important patrol functions are:

- *Responding to noncrime calls for service.*
- *Controlling traffic.*
- *Conducting preliminary investigations.*
- *Making arrests.*
- *Patrolling public gatherings.*
- *Providing community service.*

Responding to calls for service is an important function of patrol officers. Vetter and Territo (1984, pp. 156–157) suggest that:

Many of these calls involve possession and repossession of property, landlord and tenant disputes, property-line arguments, animal control, and noise at parties. Thus, patrol officers must be knowledgeable about the civil law as well as the criminal law. Even calls for service that are clearly civil in nature must be handled promptly and tactfully, because they can quickly escalate into violent confrontation between disputants or between a disputant and an officer. . . .

Patrol officers are frequently called upon to perform tasks not in their job descriptions. They are called upon to deliver babies, to give advice to families about marital problems and problems with adolescent children, to help people who have lost the keys to their homes or automobiles, to inform people about accidents and deaths, and to deliver blood from one hospital to another.

Between 80 and 90 percent of all calls for police service are of a noncriminal nature.

Whether police officers should spend time in such activities is controversial. And yet, proposals to eliminate what are basically social service functions fail to recognize the relationship between social-service-type calls and more serious crime. Kenney and More (1986, p. 11) stress that:

Domestic disturbances, for example, often culminate in a serious assault or a homicide. The down-and-out drunk is almost a certain victim of a theft if he is left to lie on the street and has any article of value on him. The street-walking prostitute may, in one sense, be primarily a social problem, but many streetwalkers regularly engage in arranging the robbery of their patrons as a supplement to their income.

In addition, police agencies are the only agency available for immediate help because of their twenty-four hour a day, seven-day a week, fifty-two weeks a year, including holidays, schedule.

Such availability is one reason the police are so often called on to intervene in *domestic disputes*. Such disputes usually occur at night and often involve people who have been drinking. Police officers are often expected to defuse such situations without making an arrest. And they are frequently called to the same scene time and time again. Such calls may lull officers into complacency, making them extremely vulnerable should a call that is normally just routine turn out to involve crazed weapon-wielding individuals. Dealing with domestic disputes is discussed in detail in Chapter 12.

Patrol officers also serve a *traffic* function by directing traffic, responding to traffic accident calls, issuing tickets for traffic violations, and the like. This important function is discussed in detail in Chapter 10.

Responding to calls about crimes in progress or recently committed and conducting the *preliminary investigation* is another important function of patrol officers. Since they are on patrol and readily available to respond, they are usually first on the scene. This is the type of call most officers consider to be ''real'' police work. On such calls, patrol officers are responsible for aiding injured victims, securing the scene, interviewing victims and witnesses, and arresting any suspects present at the scene. In smaller departments, patrol officers may also continue the investigation. In larger departments, the investigation may be turned over to the detective division. The investigative function is discussed in detail in Chapter 11.

Making arrests is one of the most awesome responsibilities of patrol officers, as discussed in Chapter 5. Officers have much discretion in this area, making decisions that can drastically change the future of a person engaged in unlawful activity. Officers can decide to arrest or not. Frequently a simple warning is the best alternative. Patrol functions are summarized in Table 9.1.

Not only do patrol officers deal with a wide variety of criminal and noncriminal situations, they often deal with several such situations within a very brief time. Kenney and More (1986, p. 7) contend that:

TABLE 9.1

227

CHAPTER 9
Patrol and Calls for
Service: The Heart of
Police Operations

Patrol Officer Functions

Function	Situations
Noncrime calls for service (80–90% of the calls)	Noise and party calls Domestic disturbances Landlord/tenant disputes Nuisance complaints
Traffic control	Traffic delays Pedestrian problems Accidents Traffic violations Drunken drivers
Preliminary investigations	Scene security Emergency first aid Evidence procurement Victim/witness statements
Arrests	Warrants Suspect transport Court testimony
Public gatherings	Sporting events Political rallies Rock concerts Parades Special events
Community service	Speeches and presentations Auto and home lockouts Babies delivered Blood transported Home/business security checks

[Patrol officers] are under constant pressure (especially in highly congested areas) to handle a volume of cases that is beyond their capacity, forcing them to develop 'shortcut' responses to run-of-the-mill situations. Because most of the patrol officers are the least experienced officers on the force, they lack adequate training with respect to some of the most complex social problems. And there has been little effort to provide individual officers with the guidelines which they require if they are expected to make more effective and judicious decisions in disposing of the incidents that come to the attention of the patrol officer.

The Peacekeeping Function

In addition to their enforcement function, patrol officers also serve an important peacekeeping function. And although this function occupies the majority of the officers' time, it is largely unrecorded and unaccounted for. According to More (1985, p. 26), "Police departments literally do not know and cannot explain how individual officers spend most of their time. When asked how they discharge the peacekeeping function, officers say they merely use common sense, although they admit that experience is valuable."

The public often misunderstands this function. When they see officers driving around simply observing the area, citizens often criticize the police for not chasing criminals or for not finding the ''jerks'' who ''ripped off'' their apartment when they were gone.

Further, the peacekeeping function is seldom included in police training. The tendency is to think that all officers need is a little common sense. Consequently, texts, manuals, and training sessions seldom include this important patrol function, leaving officers to ''play it by ear.''

Special Events

Many of the functions performed by patrol officers can also be required in handling special events. Patrol officers are often an essential part of large public gatherings including sporting events, rock concerts, parades, celebrations, and political rallies. The presence of uniformed patrol officers helps assure peaceful assembly and prevents unlawful actions. Patrol officers also help expedite the traffic flow of both vehicles and pedestrians.

According to Bessmer (1989, p. 29): ''Special events may be planned or spontaneous, known or unknown to the police in advance, likely or unlikely to generate criminal disorder.'' She notes that the San Francisco Police Department handled 731 special events in 1987, an average of two per day. Unfortunately, however, the events do not spread themselves out evenly, but rather tend to be concentrated on the weekends. Bessmer (p. 36) noted that special events management required 117,563 actual hours and cost the San Francisco Police Department over $4 million in 1987. This does not include the countless hours spent planning. For example, when Pope John Paul II visited San Francisco in 1987, the planning for his security began a year in advance. Field operations alone estimated that they spent almost 2,000 hours in planning.

Because of the heavy demand placed by special events on police resources, the San Francisco Police Department created an *Events Management Manual*. This manual classifies crowds into specific types and subtypes and prescribes appropriate police responses for each (Bessmer, 1989, pp. 29–30). Table 9.2 summarizes the specific subtypes of crowds and the appropriate police reaction to each.

Crowds may be classified as self-controlled, active, or explosive.

Officers may become involved in what have been called ''social revolution'' gatherings. As noted by Kenney and More (1986, pp. 10–11):

It is difficult, in policing such situations, to distinguish between legitimate and illegitimate group behavior and to balance the value of free expression against the risk of public disorder. The lines which must be drawn are difficult to determine and call for policy *decisions quite different from those made in traditional crimes like burglary.*

One trend is to hire off-duty patrol officers to perform the crowd-control function, particularly if the event is sponsored by private business or industry. This trend can be seen in the crowd-control management used by Busch Memorial Stadium in St. Louis. Their system uses thirty-six to forty officers, most of whom are off duty. Hoffmann (1990, p. 92) says they have ''possibly the most sophisticated security

TABLE 9.2
Appropriate Police Responses to Specific Subtypes of Crowds

Self-Controlled Crowds	Police Action
Tranquil (e.g., shoppers and commuters)	No police action
Apprehensive (e.g., crowd forms because of an unanticipated event like a bomb threat)	Provide accurate information
Exuberant (e.g., outdoor concert goers)	Monitor
Competitive (e.g., sporting event or labor dispute)	Monitor closely
Note: In all but the first case, an active police presence is assumed.	

Active Crowds	Police Action
Confused (e.g., traffic jam)	Give accurate information
Annoyed (e.g., a schedule event doesn't start on time)	Provide accurate information
	Monitor closely
	Prepare control tactics
Displaying horseplay (e.g., throwing frisbees in a sports stadium)	Take immediate action to stop small group horseplay
Protesting (e.g., during the visit of an unpopular head of a foreign state)	Contact leaders of protest
	Establish rules for behavior

Explosive Crowds	Police Action
Crazed but not malicious (e.g., something desirable offered on a first-come, first-served basis)	Provide accurate information
	Set rules
	Use firm control techniques
Panicked (e.g., a fire at a crowded event)	Provide information
	Use control techniques
	Give avenues of escape
Vicious pranks (e.g., anarchists and skinheads mixed in with a group demonstration)	Remove disturbers immediately or place under close surveillance
	Consider dispersing the entire crowd
Disorderly (e.g., rioters)	Use full crowd-control techniques

Source: Adapted from Sue Bessmer. "Law Enforcement's Role in Special Events Management." *The Police Chief* (December 1989), pgs. 29–36.

system in all of major league baseball'' through a carefully balanced use of on- and off-duty police officers:

> Outside Busch Memorial Stadium, the police department stations ten to fifteen on-duty traffic safety officers to work stoplights and handle pedestrian crosswalks before and after each game. To supplement these officers, Civic Center employs nine off-duty but uniformed officers to direct traffic into parking garages and parking lots. During the games these officers patrol the parking areas for car prowlers. . . .

> Besides the stadium and parking details, two off-duty officers in plain clothes work a ticket-scalping assignment that averages two arrests a night. One off-duty officer works every game in soft-clothes for the stadium's beer vendor watching for minors attempting to buy beer.

Officers are given their assignments in a special police room on the ground floor behind the box seats. In the room next to it is a room containing seventeen television monitors manned by a recently retired police officer. His office can zoom specially mounted cameras to exact seat locations and give detailed

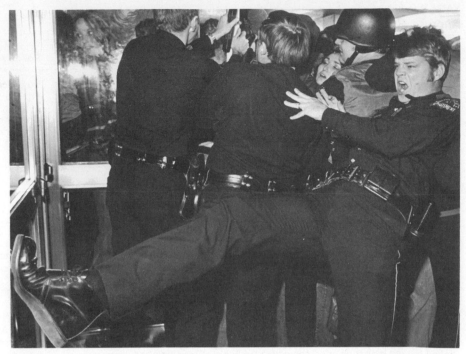

Dallas police officers holding back a crowd at a rock concert. Crowd control is an important peace-keeping function.

descriptions of troublemakers to officers on bleacher patrol or to ushers. The base for security operations is in the press box from which a recently retired ATF [Alcohol, Tobacco, and Firearms] special agent scans the stands with binoculars and directs calls for police and safety services.

Alternatives to hiring off-duty police officers also exist. Bessmer (1989, p. 36) suggests:

> *Congestion, not criminality, defines most crowded events. Volunteer police, reserves, or civilian police service officers could handle most such problems, including ensuring transit to emergency vehicles. Should a fight break out, a drunk become unruly, or a thief enjoy an embarrassment of victims, sworn personnel could be called just as they are routinely summoned in other situations.*

Patrol is, indeed, an essential function of law enforcement, yet its effectiveness is not always what it could or should be. Perhaps the most critical study of patrol as it is traditionally performed is the Kansas City Experiment.

The Kansas City Preventive Patrol Experiment

Although this classic study was conducted twenty years ago in 1972, it is still the most comprehensive study of the effects of routine patrol. In this experiment, fifteen beats in Kansas City were divided into three groups, each with five beats:

- *Group 1* Reactive Beats—no routine patrol, responding only to calls for service.

- *Group 2* Control Beats—maintained their normal level of routine preventive patrol.
- *Group 3* Proactive Beats—doubled or tripled the level of routine preventive patrol.

According to Kellings et al. (Klockars, 1983, p. 160), in the Kansas City Experiment: "The overwhelming evidence is that decreasing or increasing routine preventive patrol . . . had no effect on crime, citizen fear of crime, community attitudes toward the police on the delivery of police services, police response time, or traffic accidents."

The Kansas City Preventive Patrol Experiment found that increasing or decreasing routine preventive patrol had no measurable effect on

- *Crime*
- *Citizen's fear of crime*
- *Community attitudes toward the police on delivery of police services*
- *Police response time*
- *Traffic accidents*

Says Klockars (1983, p. 130), commenting on the findings of the Kansas City Experiment, "It makes about as much sense to have police patrol routinely in cars to fight crime as it does to have fire fighters patrol routinely in fire trucks to fight fire." Alternative approaches such as directed patrol and problem-oriented policing are currently being emphasized.

Directed Patrol and Problem-Oriented Policing

If a department's goals are clear, and if the department has kept accurate records on calls for service and on crimes committed in the community, then based on this data, patrol time should be effectively structured to provide the best service and protection possible. It is usually much more productive to have an officer's discretionary time directed toward accomplishing specific department objectives rather than expecting each officer to simply do his or her "thing." This is most commonly referred to as *directed patrol*.

Directed patrol *uses officers' discretionary patrol time to focus on specific department goals. These goals are often identified through* ***problem-oriented policing****—that is, grouping calls for service to identify specific problems.*

Problem-oriented policing, first formally introduced by Herman Goldstein in 1979, is based on twenty years of research. In this approach, police are trained to think not in terms of incidents, but in terms of problems. According to Goldstein (1990, p. 33): "In handling incidents, police officers usually deal with the most obvious, superficial manifestations of a deeper problem—not the problem itself." He contends that "incidents are usually handled as isolated, self-contained events. Connections are not systematically made among them, except when they suggest a common crime pattern leading to identifying the offender." What is needed, suggests Goldstein (p. 33) is a different approach—problem-oriented policing:

> *The first step in problem-oriented policing is to move beyond just handling incidents. It calls for recognizing that incidents are often merely overt symptoms of problems. This pushes the police in two directions: (1) It requires that they recognize the relationships between incidents (similarities of behavior, location, persons involved, etc.); and (2) it requires that they take a more in-depth interest in incidents by acquainting themselves with some of the conditions and factors that give rise to them.*

Directed patrol and problem-oriented policing are both forms of *proactive* patrol. The Kansas City Experiment's version of proactive patrol was to simply add more of the same kind of patrol. The results of their study might have been different had a variety of patrol techniques, shift arrangements, and methods of patrol been studied rather than simply increasing the number of patrol officers.

Patrol Techniques

Increasing or decreasing the number of officers engaged in unstructured random patrol appears to have limited effect, as demonstrated in the Kansas City Experiment. As noted by the International Association of Chiefs of Police (1985, p. 100):

> *Recent studies and field experiments by police departments indicate that other approaches may enhance the effectiveness of patrol. Different patrol techniques have been used in a number of police departments to increase productivity. A patrol force can undertake preplanned activities to accomplish specific patrol objectives. This concept is in sharp contrast to routine patrol where calls for assistance largely determine a department's daily activity.*

> *Structured, or preplanned, patrol activities can functionally replace the random preventive patrol, which usually composes 40 percent of an officer's tour.*

Harrison (1991, p. 67) suggests, "Years from now, we may fondly look back at the patrol tactics of today. The concept of random patrol will probably be relegated to the stories recounted to rookies and grandchildren. *'Really? You just drove around all day with no idea where the crooks were? No way. . . .'*" Changes in techniques may also necessitate changes in how patrol units are assigned.

Shift and Area Assignments

Patrol shifts typically divide the twenty-four-hour period into three eight-hour shifts. One common division is 7 A.M. to 3 P.M., 3 P.M. to 11 P.M., and 11 P.M. to 7 A.M.

(the dog shift). The municipality served by the police department is typically divided into geographic areas that depend on the personnel available for patrol.

Many departments rotate shifts and areas or both. Other departments assign permanent shifts, areas, or both, feeling this allows officers to become more familiar with their assignment and, consequently, more effective in patrolling.

How the shift and area new officers are assigned depends on the philosophy of the supervision. Some departments assign rookies to high-crime areas and "fast" shifts to help them to learn their new job more rapidly and to assess their performance. Other departments assign their rookies to the slowest shifts and the lowest crime areas to allow them to ease into their new job in a more relaxed atmosphere.

Two basic forms of shift scheduling are used. The first assigns equal numbers of patrol officers to each of the three shifts. The second assigns officers based on anticipated need. A study conducted by the Chicago Police Lieutenants Association (O'Neill and Cushing, 1991, p. 52) found that, in a typical city, almost half the calls for service (45 percent) were in the third shift, from 4 P.M. to midnight; 22 percent were in the first shift between midnight and 8 A.M.; and 33 percent were in the middle shift from 8 A.M. to 4 P.M. The study also noted that: "With equal staffing, little time is spent on routine or directed patrol during the third watch." Officers could do little more than answer calls during this shift.

As departments become more proactive, many are using *proportionate assignment,* which considers not only the number of calls, but many other factors as well.

In **proportionate assignment,** *area assignments are based on the data available from requests for service. No patrol beat area should be larger than the area a responding car can cover in three minutes or less.*

Proportionate assignment takes into account the amount of crime occurring in various areas, the severity of the crime, the population density, routes to the areas, and any special problems that might be involved such as large segments of non-English-speaking citizens. Assignments are made so that in normal circumstances police can respond in three minutes or less.

Response Time

Patrol effectiveness is frequently measured in **response time,** the time elapsed from when the need for police arises and when they arrive on the scene. One obvious reason for rapid response is the opportunity to apprehend a person engaged in criminal activity. However, as stressed by Klockars (1983, p. 130): "Police currently make on-scene arrests in about 3 percent of the serious crimes reported to them. If they traveled faster than a speeding bullet to all reports of serious crimes, this on-scene arrest rate would rise to no higher than 5 percent."

Spelman and Brown replicated the citizen-reporting component of the Kansas City Experiment response time analysis. They found (1991, p. 164): "In the cities we studied, however, *arrests that could be attributed to fast police response were made in only 2.9 percent of reported serious crimes.*" They attribute this low response-related arrest rate in large part to the fact that 75 percent of all serious crimes are **discovery crimes;** that is, they are completed before they are discovered. This is in direct contrast to **involvement crimes** where the victim and suspect confront each other. Spelman and Brown (p. 164) concluded:

These outcomes unequivocally support conclusions reached by the Kansas City, Missouri, Police Department in its 1977 study of police response to serious crimes: that citizen-reporting time, and not police response time, most affects the possibility of on-scene arrests, and that, when citizens delay in reporting crimes, efforts to reduce police response times have no substantial effect on arrest rates.

Citizen-reporting time affects the possibility of on-scene arrests more than does police response time.

Spelman and Brown (p. 165) note that the average citizen reporting time for involvement crimes ranges between 4 minutes and 5.5 minutes or between 28 and 47 percent of the total response time. ''When citizens delay even a few minutes, the suspect has usually left the crime scene and no on-scene arrest is likely.'' They suggest two primary reasons for such delays.

Citizens delay calling the police because of decision-making problems or problems in communicating with the police.

Spelman and Brown (pp. 165–166) suggest three basic decision-making problems that result in citizens not calling the police immediately:

- Citizens sometimes want first to verify that a situation does indeed involve a crime; that is, they try to resolve *ambiguity* in the situation.
- Sometimes citizens take actions to help themselves *cope with problems the crime has created* for them, for example, leaving the scene, talking with someone else to enlist support, chasing the suspect, or taking care of a physical injury.
- Most citizens experience *conflict* as to whether or not to call the police, and they try to avoid making immediate decisions.

After citizens decide to call the police, they may encounter other problems: no phone available, not knowing what number to call, or not being able to communicate clearly with the person receiving the call. The sources of delays in calling the police and how these delays might be reduced or eliminated are illustrated in Figure 9.1.

Response time is also increased when the department does not have enough patrol officers available for such duty at any particular time. Although response time is important, Spelman and Brown (p. 163) suggest, ''Rapid police response may be unnecessary for three out of every four serious crimes reported to police.'' Nonetheless, citizens *expect* a rapid response when they call. This expectation could be modified, however, as suggested by Sumrall et al. (1981, p. 36): ''There is some indication that citizens, if informed of police department procedures, will accept responses other than the immediate appearance of sworn officers.'' In other words, the response may not be immediate and it may not have to be made by a sworn

FIGURE 9.1

Potential Increases in Response-Related Arrests as a Result of Removing Each of Several Important Causes of Delay

Source: Adapted from "Response Time," by William G. Spelman and Dale K. Brown, p. 167. In *Thinking about Police: Contemporary Readings,* 2d ed. by Carl B. Klockars and Stephen D. Mastrofski, eds., McGraw-Hill, New York, 1991. Reprinted with permission of McGraw-Hill, Inc.

	ARRESTS PER PRESENT RESPONSE TIME	ADDITIONAL ARRESTS WITH DECREASED RESPONSE TIME
		Police make about 29 response-related arrests per thousand serious crimes reported

DECISION-MAKING DELAYS

If ambiguity delays were eliminated:		+2 The police would make 31 arrests per thousand crimes
If coping activities were never taken:		+2 31 arrests per thousand crimes
If there were never a need to resolve conflict:		+19 48 arrests per thousand crimes
If all decision-making delays were eliminated:		+25* 54 arrests per thousand crimes

COMMUNICATIONS-ACCESS PROBLEMS

If phone were always available:		+1 30 arrests per thousand crimes
If the phone number were always known:		+3 32 arrests per thousand crimes
If the complaint taker were always cooperative:		+2 31 arrests per thousand crimes
If all communications problems were eliminated:		+8* 37 arrests per thousand crimes

Even if all reporting delays could be eliminated, no more than 70 crimes per thousand could result in response-related arrest.

* The total is more than the sum of the individual savings because of the nonlinear nature of the relationship between reporting time and arrest.

235

officer. Many police departments are implementing differential police response strategies.

> ***Differential police response strategies*** *vary the rapidity of response as well as the responder based on the type of incident and the time of occurrence.*

Usually, if a crime is in progress, the response will be immediate and made by a sworn officer. If it is proximate, that is, recently committed, response to the call may be expedited, that is, put ahead of other, less urgent calls. If the incident is "cold," that is, it happened several hours before, the response may be "as time permits" or even by appointment.

Differential police response strategies replace the traditional "first-come, first-served" and as-fast-as-possible response. The most common alternatives used in differential response strategies are summarized in Figure 9.2.

FIGURE 9.2
Example of Completed Differential Response Model
Source: *Differential Police Response Strategies,* by Raymond O. Sumrall, Jane Roberts, and Michael T. Farmer, p. 49. Police Executive Research Forum. Reprinted by permission of *PERF,* 1981.

TYPE OF INCIDENT/TIME OF OCCURRENCE

RESPONSE ALTERNATIVES			MAJOR PERSONAL INJURY			MAJOR PROPERTY DAMAGE/LOSS			POTENTIAL PERSONAL INJURY			POTENTIAL PROPERTY DAMAGE/LOSS			MINOR PERSONAL INJURY			MINOR PROPERTY DAMAGE/LOSS			OTHER MINOR CRIME			OTHER MINOR NON-CRIME		
			IN-PROGRESS	PROXIMATE	COLD	IN-PROGRESS	PROXIMATE	COLD	IN-PROGRESS	PROXIMATE	COLD	IN-PROGRESS	PROXIMATE	COLD	IN-PROGRESS	PROXIMATE	COLD	IN-PROGRESS	PROXIMATE	COLD	IN-PROGRESS	PROXIMATE	COLD	IN-PROGRESS	PROXIMATE	COLD
SWORN	IMMEDIATE		X	X	X	X			X	X					X			X									
	EXPEDITE										X	X				X					X			X		
	ROUTINE						X	X										X			X					
	APPOINTMENT						X	X										X			X					
NON-SWORN	IMMEDIATE																									
	EXPEDITE		X	X	X																					
	ROUTINE																									
	APPOINTMENT																									
NON-MOBILE	TELEPHONE						X	X				X	X					X	X			X		X	X
	WALK-IN																									
	MAIL-IN																									
	REFERRAL																						X	X	X
	NO RESPONSE																									

Another important variable affecting response time and patrol effectiveness is the method of patrol used.

Methods of Patrol

The types of patrol police departments use varies, depending on local needs. Most jurisdictions use some form of foot patrol in combination with automobile patrol. Areas whose jurisdiction includes coast lines or major waterways will probably also use boat patrols. Those whose jurisdictions are immense may rely on air patrol. Those whose jurisdictions include rugged country may use special-terrain vehicles. Those in the northern states may use snowmobiles.

Methods of patrol include foot, automobile, motorcycle, bicycle, golf car, horse, air, water, special-terrain vehicle, and K-9-assisted.

Foot Patrol

Foot patrol is the oldest form of patrol. Its primary advantage is close citizen contact. According to the National Neighborhood Foot Patrol Center at Michigan State University's School of Criminal Justice (Trojanowicz and Bucqueroux, 1990):

Foot patrol is an exercise in communication, an attempt to develop rapport between the officer on the beat and the citizens he or she serves.

Foot patrol officers constantly interact with the community. They instruct citizens in crime prevention techniques and link them to available governmental services. They are catalysts of neighborhood organizations. . . .

Motorized patrolling has proved ineffective in certain key areas. Crime rates continue to rise, and even in areas where they are not high, vagrants, abandoned cars, and groups of juveniles on the street create an impression that the environment is violent and uncontrollable.

Another advantage of foot patrol is that it can be proactive rather than reactive, seeking to handle neighborhood problems before they become crimes.

Foot patrol is not without its disadvantages however. It is relatively expensive and limits officers' ability to pursue suspects in vehicles as well as their ability to respond rapidly to calls for service in another area. Many studies show that, although increasing the number of police officers on foot patrol may not reduce crime, it does increase citizens' feelings of safety.

Automobile Patrol

Automobile patrol reverses the advantages and disadvantages of foot patrol. Unlike officers on foot, officers in squad cars can pursue suspects in vehicles and can respond rapidly to calls for service in another area. They can also transport the equipment needed to process crime scenes as well as the suspects they have arrested. They can patrol a larger area in less time, or the same area as an officer on foot, but more frequently. The radio gives them instant communications with headquarters.

Communication with the citizenry, however, is greatly reduced. As noted by Conroy and Hess (1992, p. 120), "You're encapsulated in this [squad] car, and you're driving along. Usually the windows are rolled up because you're moving. So you're in this *steel cocoon*, pretty isolated from the outside world." In addition, the physical act of driving requires much of the officers' attention, diverting it from attention to subtle signs that criminal activity may be taking place.

A further obvious disadvantage is that automobiles are restricted in the areas they can access. In spite of these disadvantages, automobile patrol continues to be a mainstay of the patrol division.

Automobile patrol has the greatest mobility and flexibility and is usually the most cost-effective method of patrol.

Research on the effectiveness of the automobile patrol in preventing crime suggests that crimes prevented by a passing squad car are usually committed as soon as the police have gone. Nonetheless, as Hale (1981, p. 90) argues:

> *It is likely that the automobile will continue to be the dominant form of transportation for the patrol officer in the foreseeable future. . . . The automobile should be regarded as only one form of patrol, even though a dominant one. Other forms of patrol can be combined with automobile patrol to increase the overall effectiveness and scope of the police patrol function.*

One-Officer v. Two-Officer Patrol Units.

Whether automobile patrol should have one or two officers per vehicle is a controversial issue. Arguments can be made for either approach. One-officer units are more cost effective from a personnel point of view, allow for twice the coverage and twice the power of observation. In addition, officers riding alone may be more careful and also more attentive to what is happening around them since they have no one to distract them by conversation.

Two-officer units are more cost effective in the number of patrol vehicles required and may increase officer safety. Some unionized departments' contracts stipulate that two officers be assigned to each patrol car. Some departments use two-officer units only in high-crime areas or only at night.

Efficient communication among one-officer units on patrol and a clear policy on when to call for backup is one way to increase the safety of single officers on patrol. Other ways include K-9-assisted patrol and the use of vehicle-mounted TV, discussed later in this chapter.

Police Emergency and Pursuit Policies.

Another controversial area associated with motor vehicle patrol is how police respond to emergency calls and whether they engage in high-speed pursuit of persons breaking the law. In a study of 296 Illinois municipal and county law enforcement organizations, the following information about police pursuit policies and the percentage of departments having such policies (in parentheses) was obtained (Auten, 1990, pp. 53–54):

1. Officers must consider the seriousness of the offense prior to initiating a pursuit and in deciding whether to continue a pursuit (93.6%).

2. Officers must consider their own safety and the safety of others prior to initiating a pursuit and in deciding whether to continue a pursuit (100%).
3. Officers must notify dispatcher or communications upon initiating a pursuit (93.2%).
4. A supervisor or superior officer must monitor an on-going pursuit (62.1%).
5. Officers have the responsibility to discontinue an on-going pursuit (85.1%).
6. Supervisors and/or superior officers have the authority to discontinue any on-going pursuit (83.4%).
7. Physical contact between vehicles—for example, ramming—during a pursuit is prohibited (68.9%).
8. Roadblocks are prohibited as a means of terminating pursuits (37.9%).
9. Supervisors and/or superior officers must authorize the use of roadblocks as a means for terminating pursuits (39.6%).
10. There is an absolute limit on the number of police vehicles permitted to become actively involved in a pursuit (49.8%).
11. "Caravaning" is specifically prohibited (45.1%).
12. Permission is required to join on-going, interagency pursuits (57%).
13. A written report is required of pursuit-driving operations (72.8%).
14. Pursuit-driving operations are limited to marked police vehicles (44.7%).
15. The use of firearms during pursuit-driving operations is prohibited (56.2%).
16. The use of occupant restraint devices is required (60%).

Issues that should be addressed in a pursuit policy include:

- *Number of units actively participating.*
- *Use of roadblocks to end pursuits.*
- *Use of firearms during pursuit.*
- *Use of intentional contact.*

Auten's research found that the majority of the pursuits begin with an officer seeing a traffic violation and that four out of every ten police pursuits result in an accident involving either the officer, the suspect driver, or a bystander. Arrests are made 70 percent of the time.

Approximately one-fifth of the departments surveyed did not have written guidelines for pursuit operations. As noted by Auten (1990, p. 54), "That approximately 20 percent of the departments would be absent such policy statements certainly places their employees, their unit of local government, and the administrator of the organization far out on the 'liability limb,' and demonstrates a lack of concern for the safety of all concerned." Civil liability as well as other types of liability can be greatly reduced by having a clearly stated pursuit policy that is known and adhered to by all patrol officers. Officer discretion, however, will continue to be critical in many pursuit situations and decisions.

Patrol Cars in the 1990s.   According to Brand (1990, p. 36): "With the ever-increasing fuel costs and the need for making budget dollars stretch to the fullest, the use of compact patrol cars is proving to be an alternative for large and small departments alike." These cars are not only economical (costing less to purchase and to operate), but have greater speed and superior maneuverability. Highway patrols in California, Minnesota, and Texas are using Ford Mustangs which have a top speed of approximately 140 mph and can accelerate from 0 to 60 in 6.64 seconds. The Toyota Camry and Chevrolet Camaro RS are also being used. The disadvantages of less space and a less comfortable ride are outweighed by economic advantages and superior performance.

Yates (1990b, p. 32) describes special-service vehicles available from Ford and Chevrolet, including station wagons and a special-service station wagon for police K-9 teams. Yates (1990a, pp. 26–29) also describes a unique program in Dearborn, Michigan, involving the police department and the Ford Motor Company, which is located there. Ford loans vehicles to police department personnel who then test their performance and durability on the job in a much more realistic way than track testing (p. 26): "Police departments operate vehicles twenty-four hours a day, seven days a week, fifty-two weeks a year, in the most severe service any vehicle is ever likely to face."

The program involves a Thunderbird Super Coupe, two Thunderbird LX models, two Mercury Cougar XR-7s, one Cougar LS, and a Lincoln Continental. Not only is the program good public relations, it also enhances the officers' image. As noted by Yates (p. 27):

> When a police officer in a Super Coupe drives up to talk to a group of young men, the car can be an ice breaker. The kids' attitude seems to be, A cop can't be all bad if he's driving a Thunderbird Super Coupe.

Safety Designs.   Many police departments use reflecting pressure-sensitive film rather than paint to mark their patrol vehicles. The film is less expensive, enhances image, and improves safety because of its greater visibility at night. In addition, it can be removed by a special process, making preparation for resale less costly. As noted in *Law and Order* (1990c, p. 39): "The police vehicle is truly a full extension of the police uniform and ranks equally in importance with the officer's personal appearance in reflecting . . . pride, respect, dependability, and professionalism."

Vehicle-Mounted TV.   Also increasingly popular are compact, high-resolution video cameras mounted by the rearview mirror of a squad car. These cameras can record whatever happens in front of the car through a wide-angle lens. The camera is turned on and off by the officer and is supplemented by a lightweight, wireless microphone worn by the officer. Many of these units are wired to operate automatically whenever the overhead flashing lights are activated. The cameras operate in very low light. A squad car's parking lights are sufficient.

The actual recording unit and tape are stored in a fireproof, bullet-resistant vault in the squad's trunk, inaccessible to suspects and officers alike. Therefore, any charges of tampering are avoided.

The cameras are used to document exactly what is said and done during a police stop, be it for a traffic violation or a DWI. Having such tapes helps officers write their incident reports and also assists in internal affairs investigations and in settling court cases rapidly. Often people who are stopped and are acting belligerently will change their attitude completely when they learn they are being videotaped. In addition, the tapes serve a valuable training purpose. (*Law and Order*, 1990d, pp. 55–57).

Computers—Mobile Data Terminals (MDT).   Increasingly, patrol cars are equipped with *mobile data terminals* (MDTs); these are computers that allow officers access to department files as well as to information from the National Crime

Information Center. As noted by Clede (1991, p. 71), officer safety is a primary reason many departments are going to MDTs: "An officer may quickly check a plate for wants and warrants before he stops or approaches a suspect car."

Harrison (1991, p. 67) also notes, "With the ever-increasing connectivity of computers, there will no doubt be an avalanche of potential aids to the way we patrol and respond by use of technology. Staying up to date and being flexible enough to see and use applications effectively is a mandate for this decade."

High-Intensity Emergency Lighting Plan (H.E.L.P.) Cars. New York City police have twelve emergency response lighting cars, each with ten aircraft landing lights that provide two million candle power of lighting. Halloran (1990, p. 24) notes that the lights can be adjusted in any direction. The purpose of these cars is to develop a program in which instant lighting is available for any emergency — blackouts, highway or aircraft accidents, or construction accidents.

Golf Cars. Two communities in Georgia use a very unconventional means of patrolling — E-Z Go golf cars. They began using the golf cars to deal with golfers driving their carts back and forth between the city's golf courses on trails intended for only pedestrians. Not only are the golf cars very maneuverable, they also allow for close contact with the public. The cars are also used for special events such as leading parades and monitoring road races. In addition, they have been found useful for the litter pickup performed by prison inmates (*Law and Order*, 1990a, pp. 49–50).

Parking Violation Vehicles. Another innovative, unconventional vehicle is the Dispatcher II. According to Revering (1990, p. 50), this is "just the right type of vehicle to enforce ordinances in congested downtown parking areas." It is similar to postal service right-hand-drive jeeps. The right-hand drive makes it easy to mark tires or to place tickets under windshield wipers. Made of fiberglass, it won't rust out.

Motorcycle Patrol

Most police departments have their motorcycles marked with the same insignia as their patrol cars. Motorcycle patrol has many of the same advantages as automobile patrol, especially in speed and maneuverability. Motorcycles have greater access than automobiles to some areas and are better suited to heavy traffic, narrow alleys, and rugged terrain.

Disadvantages include motorcycles' relatively high cost to operate, their limited use in bad weather; their inability to carry large amounts of equipment, evidence, or prisoners; and the danger involved in riding them. Proper protective clothing and helmets are a must. Motorcycles also offer patrol officers much less protection than a squad car should a person in a vehicle being pursued decide to start shooting. Nonetheless, their ability to maneuver through traffic and their ability to access areas squad cars cannot make them valuable patrol vehicles.

Bicycle Patrol

Bicycle patrol is growing in popularity. Bicycles are often used in parks and beaches and have many of the same advantages and disadvantages as motorcycles. They

Officers on motorcycle patrol. Motorcycles allow officers access to areas inaccessible to squad cars.

have the additional advantages of lower cost and a "stealth" factor. In Seattle, Washington, for example, bicycle officers use bikes to whip around corners and surprise drug dealers. Their twenty bicycle officers have averaged five times the number of arrests made by foot patrols in the downtown area.

According to Halloran (1990, p. 22), Miami Township, Ohio, has a special bicycle squad that uses 15-speed mountain bikes donated by the Huffy Company. The bikes use the same insignia as the patrol cars.

McLean (1990, p. 24) suggests: "Bike cops are the hottest new community relations players in town. More importantly, they're also proving to be potent crime controllers." He describes the success of the bicycle patrol in Tucson, Arizona: "In one eleven-month period, three Tucson bike cops made a whopping 1,886 arrests."

Like motorcycles, bicycles leave the patrol officer extremely vulnerable. Officers should have the proper safety equipment and follow all basic safety practices while on bicycle patrol.

Mounted Patrol

Mounted patrol is decreasing in the United States but is still used in some large cities for crowd and traffic control. Expense is one of the main disadvantages of mounted patrol. The greatest advantage is that an officer on horseback is much more effective at controlling a disorderly crowd than one on foot or in any kind of vehicle (other than a tank).

Mounted patrol is also valuable in search-and-rescue efforts in rural and wilderness areas. For example, when eleven-year-old Jacob Wetterling was kidnapped near his St. Joseph, Minnesota, home in October of 1989, mounted sheriff's deputies from six counties joined in the hunt for Jacob and his abductor. As noted by Hildreth (1990, p. 30), "At the peak of the search, 59 mounted deputies were

Seattle bicycles officers wait for a radio report of wants and warrants on an unidentified suspect in the Pioneer Square area. Bicycle patrol is becoming increasingly popular in the United States.

involved. The mounted searchers covered about 20 square miles a day.'' Despite these efforts, Jacob was not found.

Hildreth (pp. 30–31) says that mounted patrol members have often been called upon to:

- Assist in evidence searches at crime scenes.
- Round up straying cattle after a truck has tipped over.
- Search for lost children in tall corn or grass where men on foot would be ineffective.

Air Patrol

Air patrol is the most expensive form of patrol, but it is highly effective when large geographic areas are involved. For example, searching for a suspect, an escaped convict, a lost child, or a downed aircraft can all be accomplished most efficiently by air.

Small airplanes and helicopters are most often used along with police cars on the ground to conduct criminal surveillance as well as to control traffic. Aircraft not only report traffic tie-ups, but can also clock speeds of individual vehicles and radio the locations of the speeding vehicles to officers in patrol cars. In addition, they can reduce the hazards and costs associated with high-speed pursuits.

Helicopters are also valuable in rescue efforts during disasters such as fires in tall buildings, floods, and earthquakes. Police aircraft and helicopters are also a cost-effective way to transport prisoners long distances.

Los Angeles mounted police officer observing two unidentified women on Sunset Boulevard in the Hollywood area during a special patrol designed to help curb prostitution.

In addition to the high cost of buying, operating, and maintaining aircraft, other disadvantages include citizen complaints about the noise and about being spied on.

Water Patrol

Water patrol units are extremely specialized and are not in great use except in those areas with extensive coasts or a great deal of lake or river traffic.

Like aircraft, boats are expensive to buy, operate, and maintain. Further, those who operate them must have special training. Nonetheless, boats are the best means to effectively control violators of water safety regulations as well as to apprehend drug and gun smugglers. They are also valuable in rescue operations during times of flooding as well as in dragging operations for drowning cases.

The diversity of functions performed by water patrol units is seen in Hennepin County's water patrol. This Minnesota county has 104 lakes and three rivers, including a stretch of the Mississippi, for a total of 48 square miles of water throughout the county. Winter or summer, the water patrol is responsible for "search and rescue, routine patrol, buoying and marking, removal of navigation hazards, safety inspections, and accident investigation" (Hildreth, 1990, p. 32).

A new trend in water patrol is the use of personal watercraft (PWC). In the spring of 1990, Yamaha Motor Corporation began a loan program that over 70 public safety agencies participated in. Under the program, law enforcement agencies can obtain free use of Yamaha Water Vehicles during the boating season. These vehicles have a very shallow draft, high maneuverability, and stability. They are also easy to operate. The two models most frequently used are the WaveRunner LX, which

Water patrol officer watching for "No Wake" violations near a marina.

carries two people, and the WaveRunner III, which carries three people. The front compartment allows for storage of a ticket book, high-powered binoculars, and a portable breath test. Many are equipped with public-address systems, sirens, and lights.

In Miami Beach, Florida, officers using the personal watercraft find they can approach areas not accessible to their conventional patrol boats because of shallow water, low bridges, or other impediments.

The watercraft have been used in search and recovery, in recovering drowning victims, in deterring boating law violations including reckless operation and DUI violations, checking fishing licenses and catch limits, and in improved public relations. In Erie County, the WaveRunner III (*Law and Order,* 1990b, pp. 43–47):

> *. . . has proved extremely useful in rescue missions, particularly in "tight spots" caused by difficult weather conditions, rocks, reefs, or shallow water. It can be used to deliver a tow rope to a grounded craft, transfer occupants of a disabled vessel to safety, or investigate complaints made by people on local beaches.*

Special-Terrain Patrol

Police departments responsible for areas with extensive coastlines may also rely on jeeps or amphibian vehicles to patrol the beaches. This is also true of those departments whose jurisdiction includes miles of desert. Departments whose jurisdiction includes remote parts of the country may also use jeeps or all-terrain vehicles. Those who must patrol where snow is common frequently rely on snowmobiles. Special-terrain vehicles such as these are useful not only for routine patrol but also for rescue missions.

K-9-Assisted Patrol

The K-9-assisted patrol is becoming more popular, with even smaller departments beginning to establish K-9 units. Says Spurlock (1990, p. 91), "Along with mainframes and microchips, the small- to medium-sized police department shopping for the latest in cost-effective high-tech law enforcement might want to consider the four-legged, cold-nosed variety." Spurlock notes that:

> According to a Michigan study for the city of Lansing, a single K-9 team was able to complete building searches seven times faster than four officers working together to search the same building. And while the dog team found the hidden suspects 93 percent of the time, the human officers found [hidden suspects] only 59 percent [of the time] . . . a dog can also track a suspect or lost person through a field or wooded area more efficiently than a team of officers. The K-9 unit can also be used for controlling crowds, breaking up fights, recovering lost articles, or finding evidence discarded by fleeing suspects. And, yes, if the need arises, the dog will attack and subdue on command.

> "But he's not lethal," says Patrolman Gary Collins, a dog handler with the Kettering (Ohio) Police Department, speaking of his dog, Kris. "I can recall the dog. I can't recall a bullet."

Dogs are of great assistance in search and rescue as well as in smelling out drugs and bombs. In addition, they can provide protection for a one-officer patrol and are of great value in crowd control. As noted by Hale (1981, pp. 94–95): "Properly trained dogs are virtually fearless and totally loyal to their handlers. They also have a significant psychological effect on would-be troublemakers. Officers assigned to high-crime areas have little to fear with a well-trained canine at their side."

Dogs are used extensively in international airports to detect narcotics and bombs because of their keen sense of smell. As noted by Frawley (1989, p. 115), "A dog is capable of recognizing an odor 10 million times better than a human can."

According to Clede (1990, p. 83), a new breed of K-9 cops is being trained by Trooper Andrew Rebmann of the Connecticut State Police. These dogs are specially trained to find bodies and are extremely effective. In 1988, for example, Rebmann and his search dog Josie found a body in New Jersey that was buried between 1972 and 1974. And, as noted by Clede, "When the L'Ambiance Plaza construction collapsed in Bridgeport two years ago, Rebmann and Josie found all twenty-eight victims."

According to a survey researching which of nine breeds of working dogs might be best suited to police work (Goldstein, 1989, p. 39), the German shepherd is the most frequently used and highest scoring dog for police work (79 percent of those surveyed use only German shepherds). This is followed by black Labrador retrievers, giant schnauzers, Rottweilers, Doberman pinschers, Bouviers, Newfoundlands, Airedale terriers, and Alaskan malamutes.

The K-9 units are also an asset to public relations efforts. They can be used for demonstrations at state fairs or in local schools, showing how well trained and under control the animals are.

Like other forms of specialized patrol, K-9-assisted patrol has disadvantages. Most police dogs work with only one handler. Should that handler become ill, disabled, or be killed, the dog is of no use. Further, if a K-9 handler is wounded, his dog may not allow emergency personnel near the officer to help. To counter such problems, many departments are cross-training their dogs to work with two handlers.

Another difficulty is that K-9s, like most dogs, are territorial, and their handler and their K-9 cruiser are part of their territory. They may become aggressive without being told to do so if their handler or cruiser are approached by strangers.

As far as expense is concerned, the greatest expense is the training involved. The training usually takes ten to twelve weeks and can cost one to two thousand dollars per team, in addition to the officer's salary during this time. Often the dogs are donated. The other expense is modifying the patrol car, removing the back seat and replacing it with a platform. Some units are equipped with a radio-controlled door or window opener that allows the officer to release the K-9 from a distance. An alternative is for the officer to leave a back window rolled down so that the dog can get out of the car if called.

Eden (1990, p. 79) cautions that: "When a police department initiates a dog section, its vulnerability to law suits is automatically increased." He stresses (p. 82):

> *Dog handlers statistically get involved in more violent confrontations on the street than any other officer. They are more likely to come across armed offenders who have left crime scenes, and get called to every violent confrontation. They work more night shifts than most members, do more callouts from home, and spend literally hundreds of off-duty hours caring for and training with their K-9 partners.*

Combination Patrol

No single type of patrol or combination of patrol methods is best. Usually, the greater the variety of patrol methods available, the more effective a department will be. Which types of patrol to use will vary depending on the department's geographic makeup, the type of crimes occurring, the size of the department, the training of its officers, and its budget.

The United States Border Patrol, for example, must cover both land borders and coastlines in their efforts to stop unauthorized aliens and illegal drugs from entering the United States. As noted by Smith (1990, p. 109): "This mission is performed by agents on foot who track aliens through the Arizona desert as well as by high-speed boat pilots/agents on the Great Lakes."

Getting Ready for Patrol

Going out on patrol always involves some risk, no matter what method of patrol is used or what function is being performed. The California Commission on Peace Officers Standards and Training (P.O.S.T.) studied the violent deaths of forty-one patrol officers killed between 1980 and 1986. Their findings have relevance to how officers should prepare themselves for patrol duties. Eight specific findings and their implications are described by Garner (1990, pp. 80–82):

1. *Finding:* Victim officers were frequently older than their attackers. Six were murdered with their own firearms. *Implication:* **"To perform police work safely, officers must be in good physical condition regardless of age."**

2. *Finding:* Of those surveyed, 40 percent had between six and ten years of experience, were quite likely to become complacent, and thereby careless, at times. *Implication:* **"Officers must not permit their experience level to cause them to become sloppy or careless."**

3. *Finding:* A number of attacks were committed by subjects described as "suspicious persons in a stationary vehicle." *Implication:* **"Approaching a suspicious subject, particularly one in a vehicle, can be especially dangerous."**

4. *Finding:* In two-thirds of the attacks, at least two officers and only one suspect were involved. *Implication:* **"Officers must learn, and rehearse, the duties of the backup officer and carry them out faithfully."**

5. *Finding:* In 15 percent of the killings, the officer killed was shot either with his own weapon or one the offender obtained from another officer. In only one case did the suspect have a firearm of his own. *Implication:* **"Officers must learn, and practice, effective weapon retention techniques."**

6. *Finding:* Officers scored hits less than 50 percent when firing at suspects. Almost 40 percent said they had had no "realistic" firearms training. *Implication:* **"Officers must be proficient with their firearms under realistic, simulated combat-shooting situations."**

7. *Finding:* Many of the officers killed had cover available but did not use it. Almost 90 percent of the officers assaulted and *not* killed either used or tried to use cover during the attack. *Implication:* **"It is vital that officers learn the proper use of available cover."**

8. *Finding:* Over half the officers involved had prior knowledge that the call was potentially dangerous. A large percentage were aware that firearms were involved in the incident to which they were responding. *Implication:* **"Get all available information on each call, then exercise caution in devising a personal survival plan."**

Garner (p. 83) stresses that officers on patrol must also have "top-of-the-line personal firearms and leather gear, safe vehicles, quality body armor and reliable communications devices." Proper restraining devices such as handcuffs are also essential.

Summary

Patrol service has been described as the "backbone of the police department." The fact that patrol officers, those who actually accomplish the department's goals, are lowest in status and in pay results in a serious organizational contradiction.

Officers on patrol serve many functions. Among the important patrol functions are responding to noncrime calls for service, controlling traffic, conducting preliminary investigations, making arrests, patrolling public gatherings, and providing community service. Between 80 and 90 percent of all calls for police service are of a noncriminal nature. Patrol officers are often responsible for maintaining order with large groups of people. Crowds may be classified as self-controlled, active, or explosive.

The Kansas City Preventive Patrol Experiment found that increasing or decreasing routine preventive patrol had no measurable effect on crime, citizen's fear of crime, community attitudes toward the police on delivery of police services, police response time, or traffic accidents. Alternatives to increasing patrol efficiency include directed patrol and problem-oriented policing. Directed patrol uses officers' discretionary patrol time to focus on specific department goals. These goals are often identified through problem-oriented policing — that is, grouping calls for service to identify specific problems. Patrol may also be made more effective by modifying how assignments are made and using appropriate methods to patrol.

In proportionate assignment, area assignments are based on the data available from requests for service. No patrol area should be larger than the area a responding car can cover in three minutes or less. However, citizen-reporting time affects the possibility of on-scene arrests more than does police response time. Response time is often lengthened because citizens delay calling the police. They often do so because of decision-making problems or problems in communicating with the police. Differential police response strategies vary the rapidity of response as well as the responder, based on the type of incident and the time of occurrence.

Methods of patrol include foot, automobile, motorcycle, bicycle, golf cart, horse, air, water, special-terrain vehicle, and K-9-assisted. Automobile patrol has the greatest mobility and flexibility and is usually the most cost-effective method of patrol. Issues that should be addressed in a pursuit policy include the number of units actively participating, the use of roadblocks to end pursuits, the use of firearms during pursuit, and the use of intentional contact.

Application #1

The chief of the Mytown Police Department has been receiving numerous complaints from citizens and the mayor that imply that the patrol force and police department have not been functioning to their utmost efficiency. The citizenry cites considerable delays in police responses to both routine and emergency calls. The mayor has appointed a citizens' task force to study the problem and report back to the council. You are appointed by the chief to be the police department representative on the task force.

The task force has concluded that the patrol officers are overburdened with nonenforcement duties and that the lack of any policy in assigning response priorities has created a situation where patrol supervisors do not actually manage the activities of the patrol division. The task force recommends that a policy be developed so that uniformed supervisors can regain control over responses and manage the patrol officers' time.

The task force has designated you to provide a policy for their recommendation and for possible adoption by the department. The police would read, "It will be the policy of Mytown Police Department to assign priorities to calls for service and to institute a delayed response time system." They also want you to consider certain factors in setting priorities on incoming calls. The heart of any priority system will be the competence of the people who receive the calls and those who assign the response — in most departments, the dispatcher. Consider the following factors when making assignments:

- Which calls are emergencies?
- Which calls can be referred to other municipal or social agencies?
- Which calls can be handled by nonsworn personnel? Community services officers? Animal control officers?

- Can the call be one the person can mail in a report on (minor theft) or come in to the station to report the incident?
- Can response to the call be delayed?

Priority-One Calls.   The task force also wants you to list in the policy the types of calls that should be given first priority and that require an immediate response.

Need-for-Assistance Calls.   Priority-two calls include all calls requiring the officer to respond with an investigation, but which do not meet the criteria of a first priority call. The urgency of an investigation, the condition of victims, the personnel available, and the necessity to process the crime scene immediately are factors to consider.

Priority-Three Calls.   These calls have low-priority responses that can be handled when the demands for service are not as great. Use the form in Appendix A to write the policy.

Application #2

The local chamber of commerce has asked that you assign an officer to foot patrol in the business district because of numerous problems such as vandalism, shoplifting, boisterous conduct by young people, and general disruption of business because of gang activity.

You realize foot patrol is proactive, designed to prevent crime and deal with social problems before they become overtly criminal. The city council wants you to proceed, and they will add an officer to your department to provide this service.

Use the form in Appendix A to write a policy and procedure that would offer guidelines to an officer and satisfy the business community's request. Keep in mind that foot patrol is an important assignment with many advantages over automobile patrol: more person-to-person contact, high visibility, enhanced public relations, the potential to be proactive and solve problems, and increased community support.

Begin the policy with a statement of need. Consider that the officer, being highly visible, may need more supervision. Who will supervise the officer, and what will the officer's duties be while on foot patrol? Some type of communication with the officer while on duty must be established, and a system of assignment decided on. Decide what parameters would be useful to officers on foot patrol when they employ the directed-patrol approach and problem-oriented policing. List expectations for the officer's conduct and responsibilities while serving this important function.

An Exercise in Critical Thinking

Officers on patrol are mainly called to respond to noncriminal situations. During all patrol assignments, it is necessary to distinguish between legitimate and illegitimate behavior and to balance the rights of individual citizens against the risk of public disorder or criminal actions. In the 10–20 percent of calls to suspected criminal situations, officers must act reasonably and diligently, in a graduated, balanced step-by-step way. There must be reasonable suspicion to justify a limited investigation, and probable cause is necessary to justify an arrest.

At 2:04 A.M. on Friday, July 29, 1988, a burglar alarm went off at Prior Lake Marine, a business located on the outskirts of Prior Lake. Officer Andrew Ferderer of the Prior Lake Police Department, responding to the dispatcher's request at 2:07 for assistance in investigating a burglary in progress, drove toward the scene of the burglary. The only car he saw was a red 1983 Plymouth Horizon with three men in it proceeding on a residential street just two blocks from Prior Lake Marine and headed away from that area. Ferderer turned and stopped the car about a mile from the scene at approximately 2:15 A.M.

Ferderer waited until Officer Terrance Gliniany of the Savage Police Department arrived to assist, then approached the car on foot. Another officer arrived a short time later. The three men in the car were all in short-sleeved shirts and jeans and were sweating heavily (their bodies were literally "soaked with sweat"). Although it was a warm night, the heavy sweating was obviously inconsistent with the men having just been driving around in the car. Ferderer could see that the driver and the rear-seat passenger were wearing tennis shoes and that the front-seat passenger was barefooted. In fact, as Gliniany testified, the front-seat passenger's feet were muddy.

After telling the men in the front-seat to put their hands on the dashboard (a security precaution), Ferderer asked the driver, Terry Lee Theis, what he was doing in the area. He said he had stopped to "take a leak" and that he and Rolland Lee Moffatt and Gerald Joe Moffatt were on their way to New Prague to visit a friend. Ferderer asked who the friend was, and apparently no name was given. Ferderer told the men that there had just been a burglary in the area and that he was checking it out. He did not tell the men they were suspects.

A decision was made to separate the men from each other by placing them in separate squad cars. Ferderer did this by removing each man, one at a time, frisking him for weapons, and then placing him in a squad car.

After the three men were placed in separate squad cars, Officer Gliniany contacted Officer Brandt, who was with officers at the scene of the burglary, and asked Brandt if there were footprints at the scene. Brandt reported there were.

Under instructions radioed by a police sergeant at the burglary scene, the officers then told each of the two men with shoes to take off one tennis shoe. At this point, Theis said he asked one officer if he was under arrest, and the officer said, "No, you're being detained." One officer got the third tennis shoe, that of the barefoot front-seat passenger, by reaching in and removing it from the floor of the front-seat passenger side, where it was in open view. It was then about 2:45 A.M. Officer Randall Klegin of the Savage Police Department, who had been roused from sleep by a dispatcher at 2:20 A.M. five minutes after the stop, drove to the scene of the stop, arriving there about fifteen minutes after the shoes had been seized, picked up the three shoes, and drove them to the burglary scene. There he compared the distinctive treads of the tennis shoes, each a different brand, with the two different fresh tennis shoe footprints he found. He concluded that the pattern and size of each print were such that the prints must have been made by two of the men.

Ten to fifteen minutes after Officer Klegin picked up the shoes, Sergeant McColl contacted the officers, then placed handcuffs on the three men, told them that they were being taken into custody, gave them Miranda warnings, and impounded the stopped car. This occurred at 3:16 A.M., 61 minutes after the car was stopped.

Subsequently, a search warrant was obtained and the car was searched. Three pairs of gloves, a box of tools, a crowbar, and other items were found in the trunk.

1. Did the police violate the Fourth Amendment rights of Rolland and Gerald Moffatt and Terry Theis in stopping their car a short distance from the scene of a burglary?
   a. Prior to receiving a search warrant, neither the stop, the limited investigation, nor the seizing of shoes would be considered justified or proper.
   b. Police obtained probable cause to arrest shortly before 2:45 A.M., but prior to that time a stop would not be lawful.
   c. Observing the only car in the area moments after the report of burglary justifies stopping the vehicle.
   d. The observation that the three men were soaked with sweat and gave a lame reason for being in the area justified the stop.
   e. Actually, police have a justifiable right to stop any vehicle at any time as long as an officer has a hunch there is possible suspicious activity, so this stop was lawful.

2. Was the conduct of the police diligent and reasonable?
   a. There are no good reasons for placing each man in a separate squad car, and no such action should occur before they are given a Miranda warning and told they are under arrest.
   b. While conducting a limited investigation, officers must get all available information within half an hour, including any search. Further, confiscating the shoes so they could be taken to the burglary scene for comparison with footprints requires a warrant.
   c. Once the officers frisked for weapons and put the three men in the squad cars they converted what might have been a detention into an arrest for which there was no probable cause—no weapons were found.
   d. This was diligent and reasonable police action because of the small police department, the fact that is was a burglary investigation (not just a petty offense), there were three men involved, it was not in the interest of the police to release them quickly and thus allow them to get away with evidence of their guilt.
   e. The twenty-minute "bright line" rule by the American Law Institute, for the length of an investigative detention, makes this hour-long detention illegal.

Discussion Questions

1. Which of the following is the most complex objective of patrol: crime prevention, crime repression, apprehending offenders, or recovering stolen property?
2. What factors should be considered when using K-9-assisted patrol? What restrictions should be placed on such patrol?
3. Which is the most effective method of patrol for the 1990s: foot patrol, bicycle patrol, one-officer patrol vehicle, two-officer patrol vehicle, or some other method?
4. What factors should be considered in determining the most suitable patrol methods to use in a police agency? How do these factors affect the choice of patrol methods?

5. What are the relative strengths and weaknesses of foot patrol and automobile patrol? How can these two patrol methods be combined to enhance the effectiveness of patrol efforts?
6. Why does the patrol officers' behavior vary so widely from community to community?
7. How might the organizational contradiction embodied in the patrol function be reduced?

Definitions

Can you define the following terms?

differential police response strategies   problem-oriented policing
directed patrol   proportionate assignment
discovery crime   response time
involvement crime

References

Adams, Thomas F. *Police Field Operations*. Englewood Cliffs, N.J.: Prentice-Hall, 1985.

Auten, James. "An Analysis of Police Pursuit Policy." *Law and Order* (November 1990): 53–54.

Bessmer, Sue. "Law Enforcement's Role in Special Events Management." *The Police Chief* (December 1989): 29–36.

Brand, Loren. "Compact Patrol Cars." *Law and Order* (November 1990): 36–37.

Clede, Bill. "A New Concept in Police Cars." *Law and Order* (July 1991): 69–71.

Clede, Bill. "Search Dogs Locate the Hard-to-Find." *Law and Order* (June 1990): 83.

Conroy, Dennis L. and Hess, Kären M. *Officers at Risk: How to Identify and Cope with Stress*. Placerville, Calif.: Custom Publishing Company, 1992.

Eden, Bob. "K-9 Administration." *Law and Order* (June 1990): 79–82.

Frawley, Ed. "Police Service Dog Work in Holland." *Law and Order* (September 1989): 115–117.

Garner, Gerald W. "Preparing for High-Risk Patrol." *Law and Order* (August 1990): 80–84.

Goldstein, Debbie. "The New K-9s: International Watchdogs on the U.S. Beat." *Law and Order* (August 1989): 38–39, 43–44.

Goldstein, Herman. *Problem-Oriented Policing*. New York: McGraw-Hill, 1990.

Hale, C. D. *Police Patrol Operations and Management*. New York: John Wiley and Sons, 1981.

Halloran, James. "Vehicles for Very Special Uses." *Law and Order* (November 1990): 22–25.

Harrison, Bob. "Random Patrol: Days of Future Past?" *Law and Order* (July 1991): 65–67.

Hildreth, Reed. "The Modern Posse." *Law and Order* (June 1990): 30–33.

Hoffmann, John. "Baseball Cops." *Law and Order* (October 1990): 92–95.

International Association of Chiefs of Police. *Police Supervision*. Arlington, Va.: International Association of Chiefs of Police, 1985.

Kenney, John P. and More, Harry W. *Patrol Field Problems and Solutions*. Springfield, Ill.: Charles C. Thomas, 1986.

Klockars, Carl B. *Thinking about Policing: Contemporary Readings*. New York: McGraw-Hill, 1983.

Law and Order
    1990a. "Operation Golf Car." (November): 49–50.
    1990b. "Personal Watercraft: Wave of the Future for Marine Law Enforcement." (November): 43–47.

1990c. "Safety Designs." (November): 39–42.

1990d. "Vehicle-Mounted TV: A Patrol Officer's 'Silent Partner.' " (February): 55–57.

McLean, Herb. "Heat on the Pedals." *Law and Order* (December 1990): 24–29.

More, Harry W. *Critical Issues in Law Enforcement.* Cincinnati, Ohio: Anderson Publishing Company, 1985.

O'Neill, James L. and Cushing, Michael A. *The Impact of Shift Work on Police Officers.* Washington, D.C.: Police Executive Research Forum, 1991.

Revering, Andrew C. "Parking Violation Vehicle." *Law and Order* (November 1990): 50.

Smith, Paul M. "Survival Course for Border Patrol Agents." *Law and Order* (October 1990): 109–113.

Spelman, William G. and Brown, Dale K. "Response Time," pp. 163–167. In *Thinking about Police: Contemporary Readings,* 2d ed., Carl B. Klockars and Stephen D. Mastrofski, eds. New York: McGraw-Hill, 1991.

Spurlock, James C. "K-9." *Law and Order* (March 1990): 91–96.

Sumrall, Raymond O.; Roberts, Jane; and Farmer, Michael T. *Differential Police Response Strategies.* Washington, D.C.: Police Executive Research Forum, 1981.

Territo, Leonard; Halsted, James; and Bromley, Max. *Crime and Justice in America.* St. Paul, Minn.: West Publishing Company, 1989.

Trojanowicz, Robert and Banas, Dennis W. *The Impact of Foot Patrol on Black and White Perceptions of Policing.* Michigan State University, East Lansing, Mich.: National Neighborhood Foot Patrol Center, 1990.

Trojanowicz, Robert and Bucqueroux, Bonnie. *Community Policing, A Contemporary Perspective.* Cincinnati, Ohio: Anderson Publishing Company, 1990.

Vetter, Harold J. and Territo, Leonard. *Crime and Justice in America.* St. Paul, Minn.: West Publishing Company, 1984.

Yates, Tom.

1990a. "A Change of Pace." *Law and Order* (November 1990): 26–29.

1990b. "'91 Police Specials." *Law and Order* (November 1990): 32–33.

TRAFFIC: POLICING IN A COUNTRY ON THE MOVE

CHAPTER 10

INTRODUCTION

Will Rogers once commented, ''The only way to solve the traffic problems of the country is to pass a law that only paid-for cars are allowed to use the highway.'' Witticisms aside, the traffic problem in the United States is no laughing matter. As noted by Sweeney (1990, p. 48):

There were more than twice as many people killed in motor vehicle accidents last year than in homicides, and motor vehicle accidents claim one death every eleven minutes and an injury every eighteen seconds.

Besides the grisly death toll, there were 5,808,000 persons injured in 1988 (including 150,000 permanent impairments), 132,952,000 productive days lost to the nation's labor force, and an economic loss of $70.2 billion from motor vehicle accidents.

Public concern with this loss of lives and property has prompted the involvement of government agencies in highway safety programs at all levels. Local, state, and federal governments are continually passing new laws and spend tremendous amounts of money for this problem.

The United States is truly a nation on the move. Citizens feel it is their God-given right to drive cars and resent any limitations imposed on this ''right.'' At the same time, they also expect city and state governments to keep the roadways in good condition and the police to keep traffic moving. Besides simply keeping traffic flowing, officers involved in this important aspect of police work are also charged with helping at, and conducting investigations of, accidents involving vehicles. They must also deal with criminals who

Do You Know

- What six functional areas police traffic services includes?
- What the basic purposes of traffic enforcement are?
- Who is responsible for traffic enforcement?
- What syndromes are common in the driving public?
- What selective enforcement is?
- What the enforcement index is?
- What the number one problem of traffic enforcement is?
- What implied consent means to traffic enforcement?
- What steps have been taken to deter DWI?
- What a hazardous materials enforcement program should include?
- What the responsibilities of officers responding to the scene of an accident are?
- What ancillary services may be provided by the traffic division?
- What management functions are vital to effective police traffic services?

use vehicles in committing their crimes; this often involves high-speed chases as alluded to in Chapter 9. At the opposite end of the spectrum is law enforcement's responsibility to educate the driving public as to their responsibilities and the rules and regulations they must obey. Bufe (1989, p. 628) summarizes what is involved in traffic services:

> *Police traffic services (PTS) is one of the broadest areas of law enforcement. Nationally, more officer time is spent on PTS (including routine traffic patrol) than on any other activity. It is one of the key areas in which police practice both parts of the motto, To serve and protect. . . .*
>
> *The field of PTS faces difficulties in that it is not a glamorous part of law enforcement and often lacks a strong public mandate. People demand their right to drive and often resent police interference over what they consider*

trivial infractions. The PTS budget is also often the first to be cut. People fear crime more than crashes even though they are more likely to be involved in the latter.

Police traffic services (PTS) is divided into six functional areas:

- *Traffic law enforcement.*
- *Accident investigation and management.*
- *Traffic direction and control.*
- *Traffic engineering.*
- *Traffic ancillary services.*
- *PTS management.*

The six functions of traffic services listed by Bufe are also used by the Commission on Accreditation for Law Enforcement Agencies (CALEA) in their standards.

Traffic Enforcement

A primary responsibility of traffic services is the enforcement of the traffic rules and regulations of municipalities and states. Although many other agencies are involved in keeping traffic flowing on our streets and highways, it has been noted by Bufe (p. 621) that: "Enforcement is a unique police contribution. It is the keystone of the entire structure of PTS."

The two basic purposes of traffic enforcement are to control congestion and to reduce accidents.

This is the area the general public is most aware of and usually most critical of unless a driver under the influence of alcohol or other drugs is involved. Even many police officers do not regard traffic enforcement as "real" police work. According to many, writing traffic citations could be done by nonsworn personnel. And, indeed, nonsworn personnel are helpful in many areas such as parking violations.

The importance of traffic enforcement becomes clear when the relationship between it and accidents, public relations, and even crime is studied. As noted by Sweeney (1990, p. 50):

> *If we rededicate ourselves to bringing back the basics of traffic enforcement, we can not only make the 1990s a safer decade for all our citizens, but also reap dividends in improved public relations and more effective suppression.*

Sweeney (p. 48) suggests that, "Vehicles traveling on our highways have become the major pipeline for shipments of illegal drugs into and through the nation. . . . Cities with . . . more active traffic enforcement programs generally experience a lower rate of certain preventable crimes such as robberies and burglaries, because criminals shy away from a community where there is a high likelihood of being stopped and checked for a traffic violation."

In addition, law-abiding citizens who know that traffic laws are enforced are likely to comply with the laws more willingly. It is critical that traffic enforcement be conducted fairly and uniformly. Departments must have clear policies on when motorists should be stopped and on the appropriate action to take. As Bufe (1989, p. 621) says:

> *Enforcement must be uniform in its application.* Nothing is more damaging *to the police image than the suspicion that certain elements of the populations are "picked on" or victimized by enforcement action. The seriousness of the offense, the degree of violation, the conditions and circumstances surrounding the offense, and the available evidence should be the controlling factors to support the action.*

A Traffic Enforcement Unit

The prestige of a traffic assignment and its productivity may be enhanced by establishing a special traffic enforcement unit such as that instituted in Bloomington, Minnesota, a city of approximately 84,000. In the development and employment of the special unit, Officers Guthery, Frawley, and Orcutt (1989, p. 71) explained that it would:

- Consist of three officers.
- Work citywide.
- Not be for the investigation of accidents.
- Be primarily responsible for writing traffic citations.
- Not be assigned to routine patrol calls. The unit might, however, respond to medicals or felony-in-progress calls.
- Set its own shifts, including 10-hour shifts if desired.
- Set its own break times.
- Elect to take compensatory or vacation time as desired.
- Serve 6–8 weeks, after which a new group would rotate in.

No quota system was associated with the traffic enforcement unit (such systems are illegal in Minnesota). Instead, the officers set their own goals. During the first month in operation, the unit wrote more than 400 tickets, the second month more than 700, and the third month more than 800. Of these, only 1 percent went to court and only one case resulted in a "not guilty" verdict. As noted by Guthery et al. (p. 72), "The unit members are encouraged to write solid, quality tickets. They 'sell' the validity of the tickets by maintaining professional, courteous contacts."

In addition, the public's aid was enlisted. A local television station did a ride-along with a member of the unit, and coverage was provided by local newspaper and radio. Citizens were encouraged to report problem areas where enforcement might be needed. Many citizens volunteered their driveways for police radar setups.

In the first year of the program, 40 percent fewer accidents were reported; in the second year, 63 percent fewer accidents were reported. In addition to reducing accidents (the primary goal of the unit), over $45,000 in fine penalties were turned over to the city's general fund. An unexpected benefit has been the increased job

259

Chapter 10
*Traffic: Policing in a
Country on the Move*

Idaho State Trooper checks a trucker's license on Interstate 84. The trucking industry depends on patrol officers to keep traffic moving on our freeways.

satisfaction with a traffic assignment. Today, officers bid for the job. Besides instituting the traffic unit, the Bloomington chief of police also stressed the importance of traffic enforcement to all other members of the department.

Even if a traffic enforcement unit exists, traffic enforcement is the responsibility of all *officers.*

The Traffic Violator

Judging by the millions of traffic citations and parking tickets issued every year, operating a motor vehicle in compliance with all the laws is mastered by only a few motorists. Despite motorists' good intentions and their interest in community safety, hundreds of thousands of people violate traffic laws. The reasons range from "getting away with something," to disregard for traffic laws which impede drivers' freedom of movement, to daydreamers whose thoughts are far away from the responsibilities of driving a car.

Drivers who violate traffic laws are not necessarily refusing to conform to society's laws. Often they simply do not think. They represent a cross-section of the community—young and old, all occupations, races, national origins, both sexes. Traffic laws are enacted for the safety of all citizens and to discourage driving which causes congestion and accidents. Enforcement action is taken so our courts can evaluate the propriety of motorists' conduct and administer appropriate measures to prevent the recurrence of such violations.

Enforcement always has side effects. When people hear about someone who has been stopped and given a ticket, this is a reminder that compliance with traffic laws is expected. It is a graphic reminder to other motorists to pay strict attention to driving safely and properly.

Everyone has heard a friend or relative's sad tale about an unjust traffic ticket. Although most people respect the aims and efforts of police officers in traffic enforcement, they don't believe their minor infractions will be noticed or result in a ticket.

The I-won't-get-a-ticket syndrome is common among the driving public.

Traffic enforcement officers should realize that motorists dislike admitting their own failings and errors. Most motorists shield themselves from a realistic self-evaluation by attributing their mistakes to someone else such as the officer or another motorist, to something else like the road or weather conditions, or to an emergency situation. Rarely will motorists admit it was their own inattention or inability that caused the officer to notice their driving and issue the traffic citation.

Making the Stop

Any stop, even a routine traffic stop, should be made with caution. It should be made in a safe place, not necessarily the first available place. Dispatch should be notified of the stop and of the car's description and license number. After parking safely and leaving the light bar flashing, the officer should approach the car cautiously, standing clear of the driver's door which could be swung open unexpectedly.

It is up to the individual officer doing the enforcing to make the traffic contact as pleasant as possible. It should be an educational encounter for the driver, not a belittling or degrading experience. Motorists can be given information so they will be less likely to violate the law again. Studies have shown that many traffic stops by courteous, respectful officers have a positive affect on the citizens' perceptions of the police, even though a citation may be issued.

Police encounters with a citizen involving a traffic infraction will almost always be emotional. Most traffic violators display emotion: anxiety, remorse, fear, surprise, anger, or even hate. Reactions vary greatly. The first words officers say to violators set the tone for the rest of the contact. If officers are belligerent, the violators may be belligerent. If officers are pleasant, chances are the violators will be pleasant, but not always. Officers can anticipate with some certainty that the reaction of the violator will often be emotional.

Officers dealing with traffic violators should *never argue*. Motorists who want to debate their driving actions will never be convinced that they are wrong and that the officer is right. Officers should never try to justify the enforcement action to drivers. This only adds to the drivers' preconceived idea that the officer is wrong, prejudiced, or "just picking on them."

Officers have great discretion in the area of traffic enforcement. After making a stop, they usually do one of three things: (1) simply talk to the motorist and explain

261

Chapter 10
Traffic: Policing in a
Country on the Move

how they have violated the law, perhaps warning them verbally, (2) issue a warning ticket, or (3) issue a citation. It is the third action that causes motorists to become irate, often acting illogically. Motorists have been known to make ridiculous and profane statements, to tear up tickets, and to curse at officers out of frustration. Sometimes such behavior stems from the fear of being discovered as ''wanted'' by the police and of being arrested on the spot, which can happen with a good communications system.

If tickets are issued, it is the officers' responsibility to include enough information to successfully prosecute the offender. As noted by Bufe (1989, p. 622):

A traffic citation is of little use unless it results in a conviction. The judicial process sometimes dilutes the effect of the citation by plea bargaining, minimum sentences, or findings of ''not guilty'' because of a legal technicality. Enforcement agencies should provide rigorous training for officers to minimize the number of convictions lost as a result of some mistaken action or inaction on the part of the arresting officer. . . .

An officer who issues a traffic citation accepts the obligation to pursue that action through the courts by preparing evidence, obtaining witnesses, testifying, and performing the necessary functions to ensure a conviction.

Automated Citations

As noted by Parks and Skinner (1990, p. 36): ''The manual procedure of issuing parking citations and traffic tickets is as tedious as it is old. Ticket books, carbon copies, illegible scribbling and writer's cramp are all by-products of the handwritten citation.'' In addition, the information must then be shuffled, batched, and keypunched into the data processing equipment. All this takes time and increases the chances for error. It also decreases job satisfaction. Enter the handheld computer. According to Parks and Skinner (p. 44):

These computers can be used for parking citations, traffic tickets, field interviews, false alarm responses, abandoned vehicle or towing reports, and other short-form reports that require a field paper copy.

The handheld police computer is the ticket to the future, and only our imagination is required to advance them to the next generation.

Because the computer prompts the officers for the information to be entered, citations are much more complete. The computer prints out the citation for the motorist on the spot, and it is legible. The information is stored throughout the shift, to be downloaded into the main processing unit at the end of the shift. In addition, these handheld computers can store, and produce on command, lists of stolen vehicles and revoked driver's licenses.

Some handheld computers can read the magnetic stripe on the driver's license in the same manner as magnetic tapes are read on credit cards. This is being done in California.

The cities of Long Beach and San Diego, both of whom issue about 500,000 parking citations annually, are using handheld computers extensively. These cities based their selection on four criteria (Parks and Skinner, p. 39):

- Proven performance, with existing systems in place in other agencies.
- A lightweight single-unit-construction handheld computer and printer.

- The capability of issuing 300 citations on a single charge.
- Storage capacity for 30,000–40,000 license plates on a "hot list."

263

Chapter 10
Traffic: Policing in a
Country on the Move

With handheld computer use, tickets can be issued quickly and are legible and complete. In addition, the system can produce the daily logs which formerly required quantities of time and were tedious to complete. Such convenience has resulted in greater job satisfaction.

In Camden, New Jersey, handheld computers are being used to deal with **scofflaws**—drivers with at least three unpaid parking tickets. When officers issue a parking ticket, they are able to run a check on the license plate and determine whether other parking tickets are outstanding. If there are outstanding tickets, the officer calls in an impounding unit which puts a "boot" on one of the vehicle's tires so the vehicle cannot be moved before it can be towed to the impound garage. According to Pound (1991, p. 79): "The program generated approximately $250,000 in revenue from tickets, tow charges, and booting fees by the end of the third quarter of 1990. . . . As a result of the increase in revenue it generated . . . the computer system paid for itself within its first year of operation."

Selective Enforcement

Officers cannot possibly stop and ticket every traffic violator. And to do so would cause a citizen uproar. Consequently, most police departments rely on *selective enforcement*.

Selective enforcement assigns officers to areas identified as having large numbers of traffic violations or high-accident rates, or it focuses on enforcing certain regulations more vigorously citywide.

Saturating such areas usually results in a reduction of violations and accidents. Selective enforcement relies on accurate records and intelligent analysis of the data.

In Minneapolis, for example, a program called TACT—Top Accident Control Targets—is based on the finding that 23 percent of the city's traffic accidents occur on 2 percent of the street system. The program involves the police, public works, courts and prosecutors, the mayor and city council, the Minnesota Department of Public Safety, and the citizens of Minneapolis. It concentrates its existing resources where the problems are greatest, emphasizing the enforcement of laws related to speeding, drunk driving, signal and stop sign violations, improper turns, and unsafe driving practices. This program has reduced the yearly economic loss from traffic accidents from $42 to $27 million (TACT, 1984). This is an outstanding example of a joint effort to resolve a community problem, discussed in greater depth in Chapter 16.

The Enforcement Index

In addition to selective enforcement, many police departments use the *enforcement index*, a figure based on the ratio of tickets issued for hazardous driving violations and the number of fatal and personal injury accidents. The International Association of Chiefs of Police and the National Safety Council suggest that an index of between 1:20 and 1:25 is realistic for most cities.

---

*The **enforcement index** suggests that, for each fatal and personal injury accident, between twenty and twenty-five convictions for hazardous moving violations is effective traffic enforcement.*

For some cities, the ratio may be higher; for others, it may be lower. But the index provides a starting point for setting goals in traffic enforcement and evaluating the results.

Other Areas of Traffic Enforcement

In many states, traffic enforcement also includes enforcing truck weight limits, enforcing bicycle and pedestrian regulations, and regulating transportation of hazardous materials. Among its most important functions is DWI enforcement.

Drivers Under the Influence of Alcohol and Other Drugs

Whether the department calls them Driving While Intoxicated (DWI), Driving Under the Influence (DUI), Driving Under the Influence of Liquor (DUIL), or some other designation, those who do so are a critical problem for the community. "Drunken drivers kill more people every year than any other type of criminal," says Hoffmann (1990, p. 56). And Kent (1990, p. 54) states:

> *Drunk driving is a problem of staggering proportions in this country, affecting virtually all members of society. It is estimated that over 40 percent of all traffic fatalities each year are related to the use of alcohol. In addition, the National Highway Traffic Safety Administration (NHTSA) estimates that two out of every five people in the nation will be involved in an alcohol-related traffic accident at some time in their lives.*

> *To put these statistics in human terms, the National Transportation Safety Board reports that someone is killed every twenty minutes by an intoxicated driver.*

Schultz and Hunt (1983, p. 69) contend, "Besides the tragic loss of lives, the millions of dollars spent on the ensuing injuries and property damage make this offense [DWI] the number one traffic law enforcement problem."

Nationwide, DWI is the number one traffic law enforcement problem.

265

*Chapter 10
Traffic: Policing in a
Country on the Move*

Yet police officers frequently simply issue a ticket and perhaps write a brief report, making prosecution extremely difficult. Those who do write complete reports may become frustrated at how the prosecutor treats DWI cases. According to Hoffmann (1990, p. 58):

The ongoing practice of dealing away DWI cases frustrates officers—and leads to sloppy case preparation on the part of the officer who knows the case will be reduced anyway.

Some prosecutors hold that, if they didn't reduce DWI charges, they would have to go to trial on almost every DWI arrest, increasing their workload and taking time away from more important cases. . . .

Many prosecuting attorney's offices in metropolitan areas still treat DWI cases as just another traffic ticket. The arrest report is glanced over for the first time as the prosecutor walks into the courtroom or never read at all.

Such prosecutors are often up against defense lawyers who specialize in DWI and are able to successfully defend their clients, largely because of the prosecutor's lack of preparation or the lack of evidence in the arresting officer's report. The problem is compounded when the driver mixes alcohol and other drugs.

The Physical Effects of Alcohol

Schultz and Hunt (1983, p. 71) stress, ''The police officer must realize that, in driving offenses, the amount of alcohol or drugs ingested need not approach that which produces the condition known as drunkenness; rather the amount required is only that which impairs the normal faculties of the individual.''

Alcohol, a clear, odorless, colorless substance, acts as a depressant and an anesthetic. Beer, wine, and hard liquor contain alcohol, water, and other specific compounds that give them their distinctive taste and odor.

Alcohol is absorbed directly into the bloodstream and its level of concentration can be tested. The **blood-alcohol concentration (BAC)** represents the weight of alcohol in grams per milliliters of blood. A BAC of .08 represents 80 milligrams of alcohol per 100 milliliters of blood. States set specific blood-alcohol levels that are considered legally intoxicated, the most common being .10. The concentration can also be revealed through a breath test, called a breath alcohol equivalent (BAQ). The same percentage should be obtained from both the breath and the blood test. According to Schultz and Hunt (p. 71):

The rate of absorption varies somewhat from person to person and varies in the same person at different times. Alcohol passes into the blood stream within one or two minutes after consumption. Most alcohol is absorbed within fifteen minutes and nearly 90 percent within one hour. Nearly all alcohol is absorbed within an hour and a half. . . . Food in the stomach delays absorption.

Symptoms of Being "Under the Influence"

Most police officers are familiar with the common physical symptoms of the person under the influence of alcohol or drugs: slurred speech, bloodshot eyes, lack of coordination, staggering, smell of alcoholic beverage on breath or clothing, confusion, dizziness, nausea, exaggerated actions. Officers must be cautious, however, because many of these symptoms can be produced by medical conditions such as diabetes, epilepsy, heart attack, or a concussion.

Recognizing the Driver Who Is "Under the Influence"

Schultz and Hunt (p. 79) suggest that driving actions that tend to indicate a DUI suspect include:

- Unusually slow speeds.
- Slow-moving vehicle in left or passing lanes.
- Excessive speed for conditions or posted limits.
- Uncoordinated vehicular control including racing the engine, erratic starts and stops, weaving, failure to slow down properly for an intersection with a blocked view, and excessive maneuvering for a parking place.
- Employing turn signals when not preparing for a turn.
- Overtaking or attempting to overtake several cars at once.
- Sudden movements at the approach of police.
- Unlighted or lighted parked cars with engine running.
- Close following of vehicles at or near speed limits.
- Repeated use of horn in traffic.

Any one of these actions by itself may indicate only carelessness or haste, but a combination of such actions provides probable cause for an officer to stop the car. The officer must then determine whether the driver is "under the influence" or not.

Videotaping Drivers

Many police departments have made it standard practice to videotape individuals who are stopped for DWI. This does not violate the person's constitutional rights. In *Pennsylvania v. Muniz* (1990), the defendant was stopped, asked to perform some field sobriety tests which he failed, and was then arrested for DWI. He was taken into custody. At the station he was again asked to perform field sobriety test which were videotaped. He again performed poorly. When asked to take a Breathalyzer test, Muniz refused. He was given the Miranda warning; he waived his rights and admitted he was driving while intoxicated. At the trial, use of the videotape was objected to because it was taken before he was given the Miranda. The question before the Supreme Court was whether the police must give motorists suspected of DWI the Miranda warning before asking routine questions and videotaping them. The Court said, "No. The privilege against self-incrimination protects an accused from being compelled to testify against himself or otherwise provide the state with evidence of a testimonial or communicative nature, but not from being compelled by the state to produce real or physical evidence."

Even though it is not a violation of a person's constitutional rights, videotaping a DWI stop may not be in the best interests of the prosecution. Unless the suspect is "falling down drunk," the videotape may actually work in the suspect's favor.

Troehler (1991, p. 51) notes that the second set of tests is given up to thirty minutes later, that the suspect has had a chance to see what the tests involve and to reflect on how well or poorly the tests had been performed. In addition, once in the police station most suspects are subdued and quite cooperative. The station's environment is also more advantageous for performing the test: well lit, level ground, few distractions. Troehler (p. 52) concludes:

> *Accurate and concise officer's reports on standard formalized field sobriety tests, automated breath-test readings, and knowledgeable, accurate, and honest testimony from the officers involved should be all that is needed to convict a drunk driver. Too frequently juries and judges have ignored all of these and wrongly placed their faith entirely in videotapes.*

> *Too often an officer's word appears to contradict what a jury sees on videotape. This is not because the officer has embellished the facts. It is because the jury is untrained at detecting intoxication at levels as low as .10 BAC in a defendant viewed on a video monitor.*

Field and Chemical Tests for DWI

Common field tests to determine sobriety include the heel-to-toe straight line walk, the finger-to-the-nose test, a balance test, and reciting the alphabet from a certain letter to another letter.

One test used by some officers is the Horizontal Gaze Nystagmus (HGN) test. In this test, a thoroughly trained officer moves a pencil in front of a driver's face and watches the eyes. The trained officer can determine the motorist's level of intoxication from the manner in which the person focuses. According to Clede (1990, p. 58), the test is reliable, easy to test for, nonthreatening, and works with people who have physical handicaps. The disadvantages are that it takes about sixteen hours of training and officers must keep an accurate record documenting their experience and accuracy. In addition, some appellate courts have not allowed HGN to be admissible in court.

Chemical tests are also used. Many squads carry a portable breath analyzer to make a preliminary determination of intoxication level.

A new form of test, the preliminary alcohol screening (PAS) device, is being used by some departments, especially at sobriety checkpoints. The devices are small and portable and can display a BAC level after a person suspected of drunk driving blows into them. They will not, however, usually detect the driver who is under the influence of drugs.

Recognizing the Driver Under the Influence of Drugs

Zarraga (1991, p. 40) describes a study conducted by the University of Tennessee Medical Center on male drivers injured in vehicle accidents. This study found that 40 percent of the tested group had drugs other than alcohol in their system. This should not be surprising given the extremely serious drug problem in the United States. Often the symptoms of an individual impaired by drugs are very similar to those exhibited by an intoxicated person. This has given rise to a new speciality, the

267

Chapter 10
Traffic: Policing in a
Country on the Move

drug recognition expert (DRE) or **drug recognition technician (DRT).** These experts have over 80 hours of classroom training and 100 hours of field certification training in addition to passing rigorous written and practical tests. The drug recognition process these individuals use was developed by the Los Angeles Police Department in the 1970s.

As noted by Zarraga (p. 54): "A DRE may not always be able, in 100 percent of the cases, to provide by drug category the cause for impairment, but in nearly 100 percent of the cases he will be able to tell you that the person evaluated was or was not impaired at the time of the evaluation."

People suspected of being under the influence of drugs or of alcohol may be asked to take a blood, urine, or breath test. If they refuse, the consequences can be extremely negative because of the concept of implied consent.

Implied Consent

The implied consent law is based on the precept that driving an automobile is not a personal right but a privilege. Permission to drive a motor vehicle is given under whatever conditions and terms are considered reasonable and just by the granting state. Courts have uniformly upheld this principle.

In theory, no one is deprived of his or her constitutional rights by the implied consent law, nor is anything demanded of the driver that was not required before the law was enacted. The implied consent law gives drivers a choice:

If you wish to drive an automobile upon the public highways of this state, you shall be deemed to have consented to submit to certain prescribed circumstances and conditions (such as breath tests). If you fail to submit to such tests, your privilege to drive upon the highways of this state will be revoked.

---

*The **implied consent** law states that those who request and receive driver's licenses must agree to take tests to determine their ability to drive. Refusal will result in revocation of the license.*

Consequences of Being Convicted of Driving Under the Influence of Alcohol or Other Drugs

The costs of a DUI can become prohibitive. Loss of one's driver's license, increased insurance rates, attorney costs, loss of time at work, costs to reinstate one's driver's license, and legal fines all accumulate to what could be personal disaster.

Still, many consider the consequences of conviction in the United States to be too lenient. Some of the ways alcohol or drug impaired drivers are dealt with in other countries include:

- Australia—Names are published under the heading "Drunk and in Jail."
- England—One year in jail, one-year suspension of license, and $250 fine.
- France—One year in jail, loss of license for a year, and $1,000 fine.
- Norway—Three weeks in jail at hard labor, loss of license for one year. On second offense within five years, permanent loss of license.

269

Chapter 10
Traffic: Policing in a
Country on the Move

- Russia—Driver's license revoked for life.
- South Africa—Ten-year prison term, a fine of $10,000, or both, depending on the circumstances.
- Turkey—Drunken drivers are taken twenty miles out of town and forced to walk back under escort.

Programs to Deter DUI

People often say we need tougher laws, tougher judges, and frequent, continuous effective awareness campaigns to keep impaired drivers out of the driver's seat. Young people must be educated about the hazards of driving while high on pot, speed, cocaine, crack, or various other drugs used today for recreation, escape, and thrills.

Programs to deter DUI include passing laws, establishing sobriety checkpoints, using ignition interlocks, and having those convicted of DUI pay the bill.

Representative Legislation to Deter DWI

California passed several laws in 1989 aimed at deterring drunk drivers. The state has, according to Hannigan (1990, p. 51),

- Lowered the BAC for DUI from .10 to .08 percent.
- Lowered the BAC for DUI for commercial drivers from .10 to .04.
- Empowered peace officers to confiscate the driver's license of anyone arrested for DUI.
- Permitted the courts to add 48 hours to 90 days of jail time if a person convicted of a DWI had a passenger under age 14.
- Permitted the courts to sell the vehicle of any person charged with three or more misdemeanor DWIs or a felony DWI within seven years of a prior DWI conviction.

Sobriety Checkpoints

In addition to passing strict legislation, many states are using sobriety checkpoints. In *Michigan Department of State Police v. Sitz* (1990), the Supreme Court ruled that "Sobriety checkpoints are constitutional" because the states have a "substantial interest" in keeping intoxicated drivers off the streets and that the "measure of intrusion on motorists stopped at sobriety checkpoints is slight." The Court also cautioned against random stops, authorizing only well-conceived, carefully structured programs.

The California Supreme Court has outlined seven safeguards to assure that sobriety checkpoints are reasonable under the Fourth Amendment (Hannigan, p. 52):

1. The decision to establish a sobriety checkpoint, the selection of the site, and procedures for the checkpoint must be established by supervisory law enforcement personnel and not by an officer in the field.

At a sobriety checkpoint in El Toro, California, an officer instructs a driver to "Follow my finger with your eyes." Such checkpoints are legal in most states, but must meet strict guidelines.

2. A neutral formula must be used to determine which vehicles are to be stopped, such as every third, fifth, or tenth driver.
3. Primary consideration must be given to maintaining safety for motorists and officers with proper lighting, warning signs, and clearly identifiable official vehicles and personnel.
4. The location of the checkpoint must be determined by policy-making officials rather than by officers in the field. The sites chosen must have a high incidence of alcohol-related accidents and/or arrests and be consistent with safety considerations.
5. The checkpoint must have high visibility and display its official nature by signs, lights, and uniformed officers to reassure motorists that the stop is duly authorized.
6. Each motorist stopped should be detained only long enough for the officer to question the driver briefly and to look for signs of intoxication, such as alcohol on the breath, slurred speech and glassy or bloodshot eyes. If the driver does not display signs of impairment, he should be permitted to drive on without further delay.
7. Advance publicity must be given a sobriety checkpoint to reduce its intrusiveness and increase its deterrent effect.

Ignition Interlocks

Ignition interlocks are aimed at the major problem of recidivism in DWI. The NHTSA's research shows that DWI offenders have usually committed between 200 and 2,000 unapprehended drunk driving violations before their first arrest and that an estimated 60–80 percent of people with suspended licenses continue to drive (Kent, 1990, p. 54).

To combat this problem, the courts in Texas have begun ordering a ignition interlock device be put on offenders' vehicles. This is a device that the person must blow into and register a satisfactory BAC (usually .02 percent) before the car will start. To prevent someone other than the convicted DWI offender from using the system, a breath code is established. The Texas program provides installation, training in, and periodic mandatory inspection of the ignition interlock device.

As noted by Kent (p. 54), since 1986, sixteen states have passed laws enabling the use of ignition interlocks with DWI offenders, and in the past year another thirty states have passed similar laws. According to Kent (p. 55):

> To date [in the Texas program], nearly 5,000 DWI offenders have been ordered to enroll in the Guardian Interlock Responsible Driver Program and, of these, less than 2 percent have been rearrested for drunk driving while on the program. . . .
>
> In areas using the Guardian Interlock Responsible Driver Program, statistics reveal that the incidence of repeat DWI arrests has dropped by an average of over 80 percent for interlock users compared to offenders sentenced to other sanctions.

Paying the Bill

Another innovative approach to deterring DWI is being tried in San Jose, California, where drivers found guilty of DWI are being ordered to pay for the costs incurred. According to Slahor (1990, p. 90):

> The average amount charged to a drunk driver arrested is about $150, but there have been charges far below that—and a few close to the limit of $1,000. The amount is based on officer time and tests of blood/urine/breath which might be required.

The convicted person receives a bill along with a copy of the law authorizing it and is given thirty days in which to pay. Since January of 1988, about $330,000 has been collected.

Enforcement and Pursuit

A controversial area within traffic enforcement and patrol is whether officers should pursue motorists who refuse to stop when ordered to do so. Beckman (1989, p. 472) defines a *pursuit* as "an event involving a peace officer attempting to apprehend a suspect in a motor vehicle while the suspect is trying to avoid capture and is willfully failing to yield to the officer's signal to stop." The circumstance that caused the pursuit is called the *preceding event;* the circumstance that causes it to end is called the *terminating event.*

The primary question is whether such pursuits create more danger than the potential benefits from apprehending the fleeing suspect. The danger is not only to the pursuing officers and the pursued suspect, but also to innocent motorists and

271

Chapter 10
Traffic: Policing in a
Country on the Move

pedestrians who might happen to be in the path of the pursuit. Property damage is also frequent. According to Beckman (1985, p. 101):

The police community knows from its own experience that pursuits are synonymous with hazard. Dangers are inherent in pursuit driving. At its best, it can be a risky business. At its worst, it can be a menace to the people on the highways. This must be avoided at all cost. A 4,000-pound automobile traveling at 120 mph has almost two million pounds of energy. Every second that a high-speed chase continues will increase the chances for death, injury, or property damage.

Beckman (1989, pp. 470–471) reports on a study of forty city police departments and thirty-five sheriff's departments from various states in which 424 pursuits were analyzed. Among the results are the following:

- Long-distance, high-speed pursuits occurred primarily during the 0001–0400 time period. Drunk-driving arrests occurred primarily between 2001–0400.
- Property and injury accidents occurred throughout the various distance and time-duration categories. In other words, no pursuit speed, distance, or duration is particularly safe.
- Longer pursuits tended to result in felony charges.
- The majority of suspects (75 percent) were apprehended regardless of distance, time duration of pursuit, type of roadway, locale, environmental conditions, police speed, or suspect speed.
- In 70 percent of the cases where the officer quit and the suspect escaped, the officer had no backup.
- Wet road conditions increased risk of injuries to officers and others, but not to suspects.
- Suspects wanted for minor violations normally did not exceed 80 mph; those wanted for felonies did not exceed 100 mph.
- The most common preceding event was a vehicle-code violation based on the officer's personal observation.
- The most common terminating event was the voluntary stop, followed by collision and surrender.
- The voluntary stop termination usually resulted in booking for reckless driving or DWI.
- When police used any kind of forcible intervention (roadblock, ramming, boxing in), only three suspects escaped. Such intervention increases the capture rate, decreases the overall injury rate, and increases the suspect injury rate only slightly.
- The ratio of injuries is one per approximately seven pursuits, and the ratio of deaths is one per approximately thirty-five pursuits, with suspects being most vulnerable, other motorists second, and police officers third.
- Nearly half the pursuits were performed by a single police unit.
- Of the captured suspects, 94 percent were booked.

Beckman described the population as 96 percent male, 67 percent white, 45 percent aged twenty-one to thirty, 37 percent aged eleven to twenty. When interviewed, their primary reason for fleeing was to avoid arrest or because they feared the consequences for the event preceding the pursuit. Most stopped from fear of crashing. It is imperative that law enforcement agencies have clearly established pursuit policies in place.

Enforcement and Transportation of Hazardous Materials

273

*Chapter 10
Traffic: Policing in a
Country on the Move*

Another area that is often overlooked in the traffic enforcement areas is the transportation of hazardous materials. Hermann (1990, p. 20) points out that most traffic codes do not include dealing with the transportation of hazardous materials (HM or HAZMAT). He suggests that the logical starting point is to adopt federal hazardous materials transportation regulations at the state level. He also suggests the following components as critical elements in a hazardous materials enforcement program (pp. 20–24).

A hazardous materials enforcement program should consist of:

- *Terminal audits.*
- *Shipper and other audits.*
- *Road enforcement.*
- *Technical assistance and enforcement training.*
- *Emergency response.*

Not only should the police conduct periodic audits at the terminals of transporters of hazardous materials to assure compliance with regulations, they should also conduct periodic audits of those who pack the materials to be transported. Police should also conduct periodic inspections on the highway.

In addition, training classes should be made available to carriers and shippers as well as to other law enforcement agencies in the state. Finally, law enforcement should have clearly established emergency response plans should an accident involving hazardous materials occur. Dealing with such emergencies is discussed in Chapter 15.

Accident Management and Investigation

The driving public has an extremely poor perception of the risks involved in driving on our country's roads and highways.

---

*The an-accident-won't-happen-to-me syndrome is common
among the American driving public.*

When an accident does happen, people are frequently in shock or disbelief. They may be dazed or seriously injured. They may be hysterical. They may be belligerent. Officers called to or coming upon the scene of an accident have a dual responsibility.

At an accident, officers are responsible for:

- *Managing the scene, including protecting the scene, attending to injuries, keeping traffic moving, and restoring normal traffic flow.*
- *Investigating the cause(s) of the accident.*

Responding to an Accident Call

Officers called to the scene of an accident usually must proceed as rapidly as possible, treating it as an emergency. Once there they should park so as to protect the scene, but not so as to endanger other motorists coming on the scene. Once the scene is protected, the first responsibility is to attend to the victims. If injuries are serious, an ambulance or rescue squad should be called immediately. During this time one officer should be keeping the traffic moving.

Accident scene management is critical according to Bufe (1989, p. 623) "because the most severe results of an accident situation can occur after the initial collision has taken place." This can include: the injured not being properly or promptly cared for, other vehicles becoming involved in the accident, fires starting, hazardous materials leaking, or other matters that increase the probability of injury or property loss and increase congestion.

Sometimes problems arise at an accident scene when police, fire fighters, and emergency medical services (EMS) personnel converge on the scene. As stressed by Spurlock (1991, p. 79):

> *The last thing an accident or crime victim needs is to witness the EMS and police officers arguing among one another. This will not bolster confidence—a major factor in keeping a victim calm. Regardless of how an officer may feel about another department's actions during a particular situation, it is important to either work around them or to make known these concerns without resorting to raised voices and red faces, especially when it can be overheard.*

Spurlock gives as an example the frequent practice of fire fighters arriving on the scene with a fire truck that police officers feel is simply in the way. The police may, in fact, demand that it be moved because it is obstructing traffic. What they should realize, however, is that fire trucks are brought to accident scenes for two very specific purposes: (1) the equipment officers may need is already on the truck, and (2) the truck provides good traffic control, protecting the accident scene and those responding to it. Such cooperation is important enough that it is mandated by the National Accreditation Association. Any police department seeking accreditation from this agency must meet the following guideline: "Command staff meetings will be held with the fire department command staff to exchange information and coordinate the public safety efforts."

After victims have been tended to, officers should turn their attention to the accident investigation phase. This usually begins with taking statements from those involved and from any witnesses to the accident. It has been suggested that officers not ask bystanders if they are witnesses to the accident, because they might not want to get involved. A better question is, What did you see happen?

275

*Chapter 10
Traffic: Policing in a
Country on the Move*

After statements are taken, a physical examination of the vehicles involved and the scene is conducted. According to Badger (1990d, p. 16), "measurements are required in all serious personal injury accidents, spectacular or 'freak' accidents, violations of the law or where physical evidence is present to use in prosecution, and cases where a civil suit is imminent." He suggests that officers measure the approximate diameter of the **soilcake** (dirt and grime caked under the fenders which usually falls from the vehicle on impact and concentrates in a small, defined area on the road) as well as where the center of the vehicle is in relation to a reference point. They should also measure the location of skid marks, the final position of vehicle(s), roadway widths, distances to bridge abutments, utility poles, and the like.

Photographs and careful notes are also critical in most serious accident investigations. An accident investigator (AI) should have a camera and be skilled in its use. As noted by DuBois (1990, p. 15): "Cameras do not take pictures—people take pictures. When an author writes a best-seller, people don't ask what kind of typewriter he used." DuBois suggests using a 35 mm camera with a normal lens and a wide-to-telephoto zoom lens. Screw-in filters can be used for close-ups. A strobe is also extremely helpful. According to DuBois (p. 19): "Collisions involving fatalities, personal injuries, commercial vehicles, railroad crossings and pedestrian accidents should always be documented with photography."

He suggests photographing debris showing approximate point of impact, for example, broken glass; dirt from the underside of the vehicles; and tire imprints or skidmarks in soft material like mud, snow, and sand. Also, photographs should be taken of more permanent evidence: roadside objects, view obstructions, traffic signs, vehicular damage, road and tire marks, and the roadway environment. In addition, says DuBois: "It's not a bad idea at the first free moment to grab a few overall-scene photos of people standing around and of their parked vehicles. They

An investigating police officer inspects one of the vehicles involved in a traffic accident. Accident reconstruction has become a highly specialized science in its own right.

may be important witnesses—and someone may have a video camera that could provide a valuable tape later.''

One important piece of evidence that is frequently overlooked by AIs is the speedometer which, according to Ose (1989, p. 17), can be a simple, valid method to determine the speed of vehicles involved in heavy collisions:

In a severe collision with a fixed object the deceleration of the vehicle occurs in a very short period of time. The speedometer needle will usually strike the face of the odometer with great force, marking it at collision speed. This is also true for the striking vehicle in a head-on or T-bone collision. . . . In older vehicles, the needle will mark on the dirt on the face.

Ose gives as an example a drunken driver in the wrong lane of a four-lane roadway with no divider passing a driver in the proper lane:

As the drunk pulled out to pass, the driver [in the proper lane] looked at his speedometer. [The accident that resulted] was a multiple fatal with an oncoming pickup. The speedometer of the drunk's sedan was marked nearly precisely at the speed the eye witness stated.

This investigative aid is not of use in vehicles with digital odometers.

Another area that AIs should be aware of is the possibility of **hydroplaning.** Many investigators incorrectly attribute the cause of an accident to hydroplaning when the roads are wet. As explained by Badger (1990b, p. 19): ''When the tread of a tire is not adequate to channel all the water from under a tire, it hydroplanes. When hydroplaning, a tire actually rides upon the surface of water as a skier would behind a boat.''

Frequently, however, cars involved in accidents on wet pavements have not hydroplaned; they have simply lost traction or skidded. Most wet-road accidents happen during the first half hour after the rain begins according to Badger (p. 19). This happens because the rain brings the dust and road oil to the surface and mixes with it, causing a lubricant to form between the vehicle's tires and the pavement. This can happen even with tires that have a deep tread. Badger (p. 21) also notes: ''Wet roads, in and of themselves, do not cause accidents. Standing water or road wetness may contribute to the accident, but driver error is generally the chief factor.''

A number of follow-up activities should be completed in an accident investigation as noted by Bufe (1989, p. 627):

Every effort must be made to identify and apprehend drivers who leave the scene of accidents without fulfilling their legal responsibilities. Such drivers are a serious threat to the goals of traffic safety.

Persons involved in accidents must be provided information concerning their rights and responsibilities. This includes the completion of forms, the exchange of identifying information, and other matters specified by law. They also have the right to obtain information and avoid self-incrimination.

In minor accidents, the so-called fender benders, a thorough investigation is seldom required. Officers should make certain the drivers involved exchange insurance information and complete the required forms.

Some accidents, including those involving disabling injuries and fatalities, are often investigated by officers with specialized training using techniques beyond the scope of this text.

277

Chapter 10
*Traffic: Policing in a
Country on the Move*

Accidents frequently result in law suits, so careful documentation of all facts is important. In addition, accident-scene management and investigation may also be the target of lawsuits, with the officers involved, their department, and their city being named as defendants. Accurate, complete documentation not only helps should a lawsuit be initiated, but it also helps identify areas to be targeted for selective enforcement.

Accident Reconstruction

Accident reconstruction (AR) is a science in its own right, requiring training and experience. It has been greatly enhanced by the use of computer programs that assist in the reconstruction, called Computer-Assisted Reconstruction Systems (CARS). Programs available include TAAR (Traffic Accident Analysis and Reconstruction) and CAAI (Computer-Assisted Accident Investigation).

Because AR is highly technical, Badger (1990a, pp. 15–16) suggests that reconstructionists have a legal and ethical responsibility to prepare the prosecuting attorney and might do so using the following checklist:

1. Insist on a witness conference.
2. Establish rapport.
3. Provide the attorney with your qualifications.
4. Inform the attorney of your limitations.
5. Educate the attorney.
6. Provide the attorney with your reports, notes, etc.
7. Prepare the attorney for cross-examination of opposing experts.
8. Provide the attorney with a glossary of terms and suggested examination questions.
9. Notify the attorney of all real evidence in the case and provide suggestions for demonstrative evidence.
10. Emphasize your ethical obligations.

Pedestrian Accidents

In 1989, approximately 8,800 pedestrians were killed by motor vehicles. Most were children under age fourteen or elderly individuals over age sixty-five. Pedestrian accidents are very different from vehicle accidents and require different techniques. As noted by Bowes (1990, p. 17):

> *Pedestrians get thrown over, around and bounced off cars, making physical evidence difficult to locate and analyze. Pedestrians leave no skid marks to show the preimpact path of travel. Acceleration rates and velocities are difficult to find.*

He states that estimating the speed of the vehicle is impossible in a glancing or side impact or if the pedestrian is carried by the vehicle or vaulted onto the roof or windshield. Bowes presents the following general guidelines for estimating vehicle speed if none of the preceding conditions are present:

- 10 mph impact—surface cleaning or scuffing.
- 17 mph or greater—deformation of hood.
- 45 mph—gross vehicle deformation.
- 50–60 mph—dismemberment.

Photographs should be taken at all pedestrian accidents, including photographs of the victim, the vehicle involved, and the roadway.

Fake Accidents

Staged auto accidents are always a possibility. According to Rubin (1991, p. 21): "Of all claim dollars paid out nationwide in car insurance, 10–15 percent result from some form of fakery. In 1989, the total came to between $5.4 billion and $8.1 billion of the $54 billion in claims paid."

Ambulance-chasing personal injury mills include a "capper" or "runner" who spreads the word that anyone involved in an auto accident can come to their agency for help. Some accidents are arranged, as described by Rubin (p. 21):

In a typical accident case arranged by a ring, two cars containing only their drivers have a collision. But when the insurance claims are filed it turns out that four additional people, two in each car, say they were also occupants at the time of the accident. All six claim injuries require treatment by medics (doctors, chiropractors, osteopaths, or physical therapy practitioners) who are part of the ring.

Not all traffic involves enforcement or accidents. Much of it deals simply with keeping the traffic flowing smoothly.

Traffic Direction and Control

Traffic direction and control (TDC) is often part of an officer's responsibility at accident scenes. It can also be needed during emergencies such as natural disasters or civil disturbances.

More often, however, traffic direction and control is a planned assignment and may take place regularly at such places as schools before and after closing, major sporting events, parades, rush hour, and the like. Auten (1990, pp. 69–72) cites six primary responsibilities of officers in charge of traffic direction and control:

1. Regulate flow of traffic. Constantly assess vehicular and pedestrian traffic volume and keep it moving.
2. Control and assist turning vehicles. When possible, anticipate their movements.
3. Coordinate traffic flow with other intersections, whether controlled electronically or by other traffic officers.
4. Protect pedestrians. Watch for jaywalkers, pay particular attention to children and the elderly—talk with them, they may be impatient.
5. Assist people seeking information. Effectively dealing with such requests pays off in the long run. Have small maps available for distribution. If the answer will take time, direct the person out of the traffic flow.
6. Assist emergency vehicles. The best option is usually to stop all traffic and let the emergency vehicle select the most appropriate route.

Auten (p. 72) stresses that too often traffic control officers become complacent and careless in a hazardous environment:

. . . an environment where projectiles weighing a ton or more are being guided by individuals of unknown intellectual abilities and physical skills. . . .

Relax for a minute and you could become a hood ornament on a passing vehicle.

279

*Chapter 10
Traffic: Policing in a
Country on the Move*

Safety precautions include wearing Day-Glo vests and, at night, using a flashlight with a cone attached.

Traffic direction and control requires great skill in nonverbal communication. The tools officers use are normally their hands and eyes and a whistle. Seldom can verbal commands be issued. Officers get attention by short blasts on their whistles and by making eye contact with the driver. They provide direction with their hands, motioning the driver to stop, turn, or go straight ahead.

Officers engaged in traffic direction and control should plan carefully how best to position themselves, considering both their visibility to oncoming traffic and their personal safety. They must also consider how best to keep the traffic moving, including pedestrians, in the overall plan. Hand signals should be given at shoulder level or higher, slowly, and consistently. And, from a public relation perspective, it wouldn't hurt to smile.

The "Cruising" Problem

Since the 1950s, **cruising** has been a favorite pastime of teenagers. Cruising—driving around and around a predetermined, popular route, usually through the heart of a town or city—gives teenagers a chance to see who's going out with whom, what kind of cars other teenagers are driving; to pick up dates; and to spend their socializing hours in a relatively inexpensive way. When teenagers got out of hand in the 1950s and 1960s, police used existing curfew or loitering laws to send them home, easy to do in a small town.

By the 1970s, however, cruising had become a problem in major urban areas. Some cities passed cruising ordinances which prohibited a car from passing a specific point more than a certain number of times within a specific period.

In the 1980s, many cities, including Boise, Idaho, began experiencing a serious cruising problem that previous solutions failed to curtail. According to Worley (1990, p. 43):

> *By 1988, cruising, once viewed as an inconvenience, was considered by some to be intolerable. Reports of unacceptable activity ranged from citizen harassment, vandalism, and underage drinking, to littering and urinating in public. Businessmen tired of greeting Monday morning amid broken windows and littered parking lots. It was time for a change.*

The first step the Boise Police Department took was to survey the cruisers themselves and other police departments who had programs dealing with the problem. The survey of about 80 cruisers, ages nineteen to twenty-one, revealed the following (Worley, p. 43):

- Cruisers enjoyed the relatively unsupervised environment of the cruise, viewing it as a place to socialize, display driving ability, and to compare cars.
- They would not be receptive to alternatives such as teen centers or organized dances.
- They cited lack of public rest rooms and trash cans in the downtown area as reasons for some of their behaviors.
- They also asked for consideration of better lighting in parking lots and a supervised drag strip.

▪ Some 80 percent said their parents knew about and approved of their cruising. [Probably because most of the parents had done it themselves as teenagers.]

The survey from other police departments had a 52.6 percent response. Most departments had increased police presence in cruising areas. Some had instituted an alternative cruising area that did not conflict with the business area. The departments who seemed to have the best success, according to Worley (p. 44) were "those willing to accept something new. These cities felt that cruising was a community problem rather than just a law enforcement problem."

Based on the survey results, Boise's City Council held a public hearing on the topic to listen to citizens' concerns. The mayor appointed a task force that included cruisers to look at the problem. They came up with eight major recommendations (Worley, pp. 44–45):

1. Open a storefront police station in the cruise area.
2. Review existing noise ordinances. Purchase decibel meters to aid police in enforcing noise ordinances.
3. Reestablish a program of sentencing violators to community service.
4. Develop a juvenile citation to allow police to more quickly handle juvenile status offenders.
5. Increase street lighting and lighting in Capitol Park and designate the park as a focal point of cruise activity.
6. Create alternatives to cruising, such as car shows or street dances.
7. Appoint a standing advisory committee to help implement and monitor the recommendations.
8. Sanction a cruising area with many of the amenities thought necessary to the activity.

Six of the eight recommendations were implemented. Not implemented were the standing advisory committee (#7) and a sanctioned cruise area (#8).

Traffic Engineering

Traffic engineering is included within the scope of responsibilities of most traffic officers because they are in an excellent position to provide the city's traffic engineers with information about the roadways—where hazards exist, where accidents are occurring, etc. In some instances, traffic officers may be alerted to a situation that poses an immediate threat and requires some sort of protective measures until the hazard can be removed or corrected.

Traffic officers can be invaluable sources of information to the city's traffic engineers and should endeavor to keep this mutually beneficial relationship open. Officers' input to future roadway construction plans can help eliminate hazards and keep traffic flowing smoothly—primary goals of the traffic function of any police department.

Traffic Ancillary Services

Another important part of traffic services includes such *ancillary* services as educational programs on traffic and bike safety. These programs can be conducted through the schools, through civic groups, or through the police department itself.

Specific discussions on such topics as the dangers of drinking and driving, the use of seat belts, and driver's rights and responsibilities can be presented at schools or through news articles or speaker's bureaus. In addition, as noted by Bufe (1989, p. 625):

Police assistance is most welcomed by the motorist in situations where breakdowns, lack of information, or other problems occur that can interfere with a safe and efficient trip. Such help may include providing trip directions, obtaining gasoline or necessary supplies, or summoning specialized assistance for a variety of mechanical or medical problems.

281

Chapter 10
Traffic: Policing in a
Country on the Move

Ancillary traffic services include educational programs as well as providing assistance to motorists.

In large urban areas such assistance is often available through other public agencies or through privately owned travel clubs, but in small towns and rural areas, the police or sheriff's departments may be the only source of help available.

To avoid problems and citizen complaints, police departments should have clearly established policies on what and at what level ancillary traffic services will be provided. Such services must be equally available to all citizens within the department's jurisdiction.

Police Traffic Services Management

As with other areas of the police department, the traffic services division has important management functions that must be carried out.

Management functions vital to effective police traffic services include allocating resources, developing personnel, and providing information.

Allocating resources is sometimes difficult in the traffic services section because traffic services may be considered lower in priority than other areas such as those dealing with felonies. Citizens clamor if a serial murderer or rapist is on the loose. Citizens are largely unaware of traffic problems. In fact, should they be issued a traffic citation, they may criticize this use of their police resources. Why aren't officers out catching true criminals rather than wasting precious tax dollars telling basically law-abiding citizens how to drive?

A key to sound resource allocation is good data and sound analysis, as noted previously. This can lead to selective enforcement, placing resources where most needed and where they are likely to do the most good. And, incidentally, this can bring in the most dollars in fines.

Developing personnel is also sometimes difficult. First, the financial resources may not be there. Second, many police supervisors feel any officer can fulfill the traffic function with basic patrol training. As in other areas of police work, however, specialized training is often required, for example, in accident reconstruction or in investigating hit-and-run accidents.

Traffic Management and Community-Oriented Policing

In Reno, Nevada, the police department has used a community-oriented approach to modify its traffic management program. According to Weston (1991, p. 35): "As with community-based policing, the results of the new traffic program are not measured by watching the accident rate, or the number of citations issued by officers, or other numerical standards. Instead, the department looks for a measurement of citizen satisfaction."

Individual traffic officers are evaluated on the number of traffic service requests they successfully complete rather than on the number of tickets they write. A "Service Request Form" was developed to document traffic-related complaints and their disposition. Warning tickets are an important part of the management systems. Because of their Computer-Aided Dispatching (CAD) system, officers can easily check to see if a violator has had a previous warning. If so, a ticket is issued. The new approach is welcomed by officers and citizens alike.

Summary

Police traffic services (PTS) is divided into six functional areas: traffic law enforcement, accident investigation and management, traffic direction and control, traffic engineering, traffic ancillary services, and PTS management.

The two basic purposes of traffic enforcement are to control congestion and to reduce accidents. Even if a traffic enforcement unit exists, traffic enforcement is the responsibility of *all* officers.

The I-won't-get-a-ticket syndrome is common among the driving public. To combat this syndrome, selective enforcement is often used. Selective enforcement assigns officers to areas identified as having large numbers of traffic law violations or high-accident rates, or it focuses on enforcing certain violations more vigorously citywide. The enforcement index suggests that, for each fatal and personal injury accident, between twenty and twenty-five convictions for hazardous moving violations is effective traffic enforcement.

Nationwide, DWI is the number one traffic law enforcement problem. A key to detecting DWI offenders is the implied consent law which states that those who request and receive driver's licenses must agree to take tests to determine their ability to drive. Refusal will result in revocation of the license Programs to deter DUI include passing laws, establishing sobriety checkpoints, using ignition interlocks, and having those convicted of DUI pay the bill.

Another area traffic enforcement is concerned with is the transportation of hazardous materials. A hazardous materials enforcement program should consist of terminal audits, shipper and other audits, road enforcement, technical assistance and enforcement training, and emergency response.

The an-accident-won't-happen-to-me syndrome is also common among the American driving public. This results in countless accidents to which traffic officers must respond. At an accident, officers are responsible for managing the scene, including protecting the scene, attending to injuries, keeping traffic moving, and restoring normal traffic flow. Officers are also responsible for investigating the cause(s) of the accident.

Ancillary traffic services include educational programs as well as providing assistance to motorists. Management functions vital to effective police traffic services include allocating resources, developing personnel, and providing information.

Application #1

283

Chapter 10
Traffic: Policing in a
Country on the Move

The chief of police of Ourtown receives a letter from the prosecutor stating that a serious problem exists in prosecuting DWI cases. There is no uniformity of procedures. To correct this, a policy must be written and instituted to successfully prosecute cases and to reinstate the faith of the public in police work. This news comes as a shock to the chief who immediately asks you as supervisor of the traffic division to take charge. The chief emphasizes that this is a problem demanding immediate attention. DWI cases must be thoroughly investigated so offenders can be successfully prosecuted.

Instructions.   Use the form in Appendix A to write a procedure so officers who deal with DWI have direction, guidance, and technical information. Include ways of detecting a driver under the influence, probable cause for stopping, observing the driver's condition, questioning the driver, giving the necessary field tests, and invoking the implied consent law. Officers should mentally record the events as they occur as accurately as possible and make written notes at the earliest practical time. Witnesses should be interviewed to strengthen the case.

Application #2

Recent police chases in the state have aroused the interest of the media to the extent that they would like to interview you, supervisor of the traffic unit. A newspaper reporter has noted that three officers and five citizens have recently been seriously injured in automobile crashes as a result of police instigating chases for flagrant traffic violations. The reporter wants an explanation of the department's policy regarding high-speed chases. You realize the department has no pursuit policy and immediately call together your officers to state the problem: ''We need a police pursuit and response driving policy.''

Instructions.   Using the form in Appendix A, write a policy titled ''Police Pursuit and Emergency Response Policy.'' Keep in mind the purpose and objective of the procedure as you begin with the routine operation of the police vehicle under normal conditions and then determine:

- Definitions of calls for service, assistance, or emergency.
- When officers should be exempt from the preceding policy such as during emergency calls, when assisting other emergency vehicles. Also state when red lights and the siren should be used.
- Whether each pursuit should be individually authorized. If so, by whom?
- How radio should be used during a pursuit.
- How many patrol vehicles should be involved.
- What the spacing between units should be.
- Whether to use aerial surveillance. If so, when?
- A specific firearms policy for pursuit.
- Whether pursuit will be allowed outside jurisdictional limits.
- How long pursuit should continue and under what conditions for what type of violations.
- What considerations are involved when pursuing known felons.
- What supervisory responsibilities are during pursuit.
- Whether blocking or ramming of pursued vehicles should be allowed.

- Whether seatbelts are required. Helmets? Other protective devices?
- Any further procedures to promote safety.

Application #3

The chief of police of Myville notes in going through the policy and procedure manual that the policy covering procedures at accident scenes is outdated. A new policy and procedure is needed. A particular deficiency is that there is no priority in what officers should do at an accident scene. He calls his traffic officers to a special meeting and says he wants priorities implemented at the scene of an accident so all officers can be held accountable for their actions when responding to accident calls.

Instructions.   Use the form in Appendix A to make a policy for this particular problem. The policy should provide a uniform procedure for all officers handling traffic accidents. Title it "Traffic Accident Investigation." The policy and procedures should consider that accidents can involve injury or death, hit and run, drunken drivers, and property damage. List sequentially, in order of priority, what officers should do at an accident.

Exercises in Critical Thinking

The implied consent law states that those who request and receive a driver's license must agree to take tests to determine their ability to drive. Refusal can result in the revocation of the license. Probable cause exists where all the facts and circumstances warrant a reasonable person to believe that a suspect was driving or operating a vehicle while under the influence of alcohol. A Fourth Amendment seizure exists when an officer in some way restrains a citizen's liberty. If contact constitutes a seizure, an officer must have articulable suspicion.

At 9:39 P.M. on Wednesday, June 14, 1989, Minneapolis Police Officer Jesse Morse investigated a motor vehicle collision. Fire fighters extricated Janice Fae Kostecky from her vehicle, which had rolled over. One of the fire fighters who placed her in an ambulance informed Morse that she "reeked of alcohol." Morse did not speak to Kostecky or observe her closely at the scene of the accident. The other driver, who had a strong odor of alcohol on her breath, and several other witnesses indicated that Kostecky was not at fault for the accident.

Morse then spent fifteen to twenty minutes with Kostecky at her bedside in the emergency room. She admitted she "had something to drink." Morse detected a moderate odor of alcohol on her breath, but testified that his face was not close to hers. Morse also noted that her eyes were "glassy and runny-looking."

Morse concluded that Kostecky was under the influence of alcohol and arrested her for DWI. He read her the implied consent advisory and obtained a test which disclosed an alcohol concentration of .10 or more. Kostecky's driver's license was revoked pursuant to the implied consent law.

1. Does Officer Morse have probable cause to believe Kostecky was under the influence of alcohol?
   a. No, because the officer's questioning of Kostecky amounted to a limited seizure, requiring a particularized and objective basis for suspecting her of

285

Chapter 10
*Traffic: Policing in a
Country on the Move*

criminal activity, and the other driver and witnesses indicated that
Kostecky was not at fault for the accident.

b. Yes, because Kostecky told the officer she "had something to drink," the
officer detected a moderate odor of alcohol on her breath, and the officer
noted that her "eyes were glassy and runny-looking."

c. No, because merely "something to drink," a "moderate odor of alcohol,"
and "glassy and runny-looking" eyes are not sufficient for probable cause
to believe Kostecky was under the influence of alcohol.

d. Yes, because any reasonable suspicion that an officer might have will be
sufficient to believe someone involved in a traffic accident is under the
influence of alcohol.

e. No, because Kostecky was in a litter or bed in a hospital emergency room
and was not able to perform field sobriety tests.

Just prior to 1:00 A.M. on February 10, Officer Jeffrey Janacek stopped Frank
Joseph Pastuszak's vehicle for erratic driving. Pastuszak was 67 years old and
claimed to have various physical ailments. Officer Janacek detected signs of intoxication which Pastuszak claimed were due to his medical conditions. Pastuszak said
he did not consume any alcoholic beverages that evening. As Pastuszak became
belligerent and profane, Officer Janacek arrested him and took him to the police
station.

At the police station, Janacek told Pastuszak to empty his pockets. His response
was an obscenity. After again telling Pastuszak to empty his pockets and receiving
the same response, the officer told him that, if necessary, his pockets would be
emptied by force. Pastuszak then clenched his fists and raised his left hand. Officer
Janacek and another officer then forcibly subdued Pastuszak, in the process frac-
turing his ankle.

Immediately after Pastuszak was forced to the floor, the officers started a video
camera. Officer Janacek read the implied consent advisory, and when asked if he
understood the test, Pastuszak did not respond. When asked to take an Intoxilyzer
test, Pastuszak said, "I took one." When asked why he refused the test, Pastuszak
responded with another barrage of profanity.

The officers did not arrange for a blood sample to be taken when Pastuszak was
subsequently taken to North Memorial Hospital for surgery on his ankle.

2. Was Pastuszak reasonably justified in refusing to take an Intoxilyzer test?

a. Pastuszak failed to meet his burden of showing that he could not have
blown into the Intoxilyzer.

b. The physical pain of multiple medical problems, compounded by the pain
of a broken ankle, justified Pastuszak's behavior and refusal to take an
Intoxilyzer test.

c. The refusal to take an Intoxilyzer test places the burden of proof on the
officers to arrange for a blood sample at a hospital.

d. In the case of a senior citizen, officers should show respect even when
verbal belligerence and abuse are experienced. The use of force is not
justified in overpowering someone for a driving violation, even when he
refuses to be cooperative.

e. As there is no necessary reason for requiring Pastuszak to empty his
pockets, considering the violation was simply for erratic driving, he has
good reason for noncompliance. And without a blood test from the
hospital, the courts will believe his claim about medical problems and his
assertion that he did not consume any alcoholic beverages.

Discussion Questions

1. What should be the top priority in a traffic program? Justify your selection.
2. Your municipality has an ordinance stating that it is against the law to drink and drive. Obtain a copy of that ordinance and bring it to class. What is the legal limit for intoxication? Do you feel the legal limit justifies the penalty if one is convicted? Would you suggest some modifications in the law as you see it enforced?
3. Three tests are usually given to determine if a person is under the influence of alcohol while driving: a breath test, a urine test, and a blood test. From evidence that might be presented in court, which test would you favor if you were a police officer? What are the advantages and disadvantages in administering each test?
4. Is a pursuit policy justified in a police department, or should officers be allowed to make a discretionary decision to chase without the benefit of a specific policy?
5. Should officers expose those they are pursuing to hazardous roadblock conditions or be given permission to ram cars? If so, what restrictions should apply, if any?
6. Radar detectors used by motorists are a source of irritation to most traffic officers. Do you feel they should be declared illegal to possess and use?
7. Most warning tickets issued by officers are never formally recorded on a driver's record. Are such tickets an effective tool in obtaining compliance to traffic laws?

Definitions

Can you define the following terms?

BAC	implied consent
cruising	scofflaw
DRE or DRT	selective enforcement
enforcement index	soilcake
hydroplaning	

References

Auten, James. "An Analysis of Police Pursuit Policy." *Law and Order* (November 1990): 53–54.

Auten, James. "Traffic Direction and Control." *Law and Order* (May 1989): 69–72.

Badger, Joseph E.
   a. "Legal and Ethical Responsibilities of the Accident Reconstructionist." *Law and Order* (October 1990): 15–16.
   b. "Investigating the Hydroplane Phenomenon." *Law and Order* (June 1990): 19–21.
   c. "CARS Program User Friendly." *Law and Order* (April 1990): 15–16.
   d. "Mapping and Measurements for Scale Drawings." *Law and Order* (February 1990): 16–17.
   e. "Accident Reconstruction Computer Programs Reviewed." *Law and Order* (August 1989): 17–19.

Beckman, Erik. "High-Speed Chases," pp. 470–473. In *The Encyclopedia of Police Science*, W. G. Bailey, ed. New York: Garland Publishing Company, 1989.

Beckman, Erik. "High-Speed Chases," pp. 99–106. In *Police Management Today, Issues and Case Studies*, James J. Fyre, ed. Washington, D.C.: International City Management Association, 1985.

287

Chapter 10
Traffic: Policing in a
Country on the Move

Bowes, William B. ''Pedestrian Accident Investigation.'' *Law and Order* (November 1990): 17–18.

Bufe, Noel C. ''Traffic Services,'' pp. 621–628. In *The Encyclopedia of Police Science*, W. G. Bailey, ed. New York: Garland Publishing Company, 1989.

Clede, Bill. ''HGN.'' *Law and Order* (July 1990): 57–58.

Department of California Highway Patrol. *Pursuit Study.* Sacramento, Calif.: Department of California Highway Patrol, June 1983.

DuBois, Robert A.
a. ''Accident Reconstruction Photographics: Part I.'' *Law and Order* (August 1990): 15–16.
b. ''Accident Reconstruction Photographics: Part II.'' *Law and Order* (September 1990): 19–22.

Guthery, Tom; Frawley, Henry; and Orcutt, James. ''A Traffic Enforcement Unit.'' *Law and Order* (September 1989): 71–72.

Hannigan, M. J. ''California's Ongoing Battle Against DUI.'' *The Police Chief* (July 1990): 51–53.

Hermann, Stephen L. ''Developing a Hazardous Materials Enforcement Program.'' *The Police Chief* (December 1990): 20–25.

Hoffmann, John. ''DWI—Police and the Criminal Justice System.'' *Law and Order* (May 1990): 56–60.

Kent, Cynthia. ''Ignition Interlocks Help Deter Drunk Drivers.'' *The Police Chief* (April 1990): 54–55.

Ose, C. Dean. ''Skidmarks of a Different Sort.'' *Law and Order* (September 1989): 17–18.

Parks, Charles H. and Skinner, William. ''Handheld Police Computers: The Ticket to the Future.'' *The Police Chief* (April 1990): 36–44.

Pound, James S. ''Camden Uses Computers to Snare Scofflaws.'' *Today's Office* (May 1991): 76–79.

Rubin, Hal. ''Staged Auto Accidents: The Safest White Collar Crime.'' *Law and Order* (July 1991): 21–22.

Schultz, Donald O. and Hunt, Derald D. *Traffic Investigation and Enforcement*. Costa Mesa, Calif.: Custom Publishing Company, 1983.

Slahor, Stephanie. ''Drunken Drivers Footing the Bill.'' *Law and Order* (November 1990): 90–91.

Spurlock, James C. ''First Responder Conflicts . . . A Problem That Shouldn't Happen.'' *Law and Order* (May 1991): 77–79.

Sweeney, Earl M. ''Traffic Enforcement: Getting Back to Basics.'' *The Police Chief* (July 1990): 48–50.

''Top Accident Control Targets.'' Minneapolis, Minn.: Minneapolis Department of Public Works, Traffic Engineering Division, January 1984.

Troehler, Phillip. ''Video Recording for the Small Agency.'' *Law and Order* (June 1991): 49–52.

Weston, Jim. ''Community-Oriented Policing: An Approach to Traffic Management.'' *Law and Order* (May 1991): 32–36.

Worley, R. Mike. '' 'Cruising' in Major U.S. Cities and One City's Response.'' *Law and Order* (September 1990): 42–46.

Zarraga, Jose I. ''What's a DRE?'' *Law and Order* (June 1991): 40–56.

Cases

Michigan Department of State Police v. Sitz, 496 U.S. 444, 110 S.Ct. 2481, 110 L.Ed.2d 412 (1990). WL 78597, 1990.

Pennsylvania v. Muniz, 496 U.S. 582, 110 S.Ct. 2638, 110 L.Ed.2d 528 (1990).

CRIME AND VIOLENCE: RESPONDING TO THE CALL

CHAPTER 11

INTRODUCTION

The seriousness of crime and violence in the United States is graphically depicted in an article in *U.S. News and World Report,* "Dead Zones: Whole Sections of Urban America Are Being Written Off," (Moore, 1989, p. 20):

> *Like MASH units in war, overburdened war-zone police districts apply triage to crime reports, focusing mainly on murders and shootings and ignoring burglaries. Implicitly, if not explicitly, many have adopted a policy of crime containment rather than prevention. "Why not let the bozos shoot it out, then go in, pick up the bodies and arrest the winner?" says Cleveland Detective Doug Charney.*

Many Americans are afraid to leave their homes and apartments today for fear of crime. People in the city are haunted by and fearful of thoughts of being mugged on the street, assaulted, or being the victim of an armed robbery or rape. They fear that their worldly possessions could be lost with one swift action by a burglar during their absence. People feel vulnerable.

Serious crime tends to be concentrated in poorer neighborhoods, involving members of the lower socioeconomic strata of society, a disproportionate number of whom are members of minority groups. Poverty-infested neighborhoods, slums, and ghettos have a much higher proportion of crime, including crimes of violence. This leads to greater police observation and patrol of such neighborhoods which turns up crime and produces arrests. But crime is not confined to poorer neighborhoods; it can occur any where, any time.

Do You Know

- What the responsibilities of officers responding to a criminal action call are?
- What the preliminary investigation of a crime consists of?
- What A.F.I.S. is and how it helps solve crimes?
- What two forms of positive identification may be available in criminal investigations?
- What the chain of possession is?
- What role violence has played in our country's history?
- What civil disobedience is?
- What issues may lead to civil disobedience in the 1990s?
- How police departments should be prepared to deal with demonstrations and violence?
- How terrorists are usually classified and which group is increasing?
- What narcoterrorism is?
- What the Stockholm syndrome is?
- Who may make the best hostage negotiator?
- What the number one rule is when dealing with hostage situations, barricaded subjects, or attempted suicides?

How Crimes Are Classified

The FBI gathers statistics on reported crimes from law enforcement agencies throughout the country. They report the findings annually in their **Uniform Crime Reports (UCRs),** called *Crime in the United States*. In their UCRs, the FBI classifies crimes as **Part One** or **Part Two Index offenses,** with the Part One offenses consisting of the most serious crimes. These are further divided into crimes against persons and crimes against property. The four major **crimes against persons** are murder, assault, rape, and robbery. Of all crimes reported to police, crimes against persons usually have a high clearance rate because victims have a chance to see the offender or the victim knows the suspect. Robbery has the lowest clearance rate among the four because it usually is considered a "stranger" crime. The victim may possibly provide a description of the suspect, but seldom an actual identification.

The four **crimes against property** are burglary, larceny theft, auto theft, and arson. Crimes against property are known in police vernacular as "cold" crimes because rarely does the victim see the suspect, and the suspect is usually gone before the police arrive to investigate. Cold crimes can still provide police with substantial leads. Evidence left at the scene of the crime can be critical to convicting criminals.

Responding to Calls about Committed Crimes

Police expect to deal with reports of criminal activity. And such calls are likely to increase, as noted by Vaughn (1990, p. 71):

In 1987, the U.S. Justice Department's Bureau of Justice Statistics released a report that calculated what crime would be like in the future if it continued to escalate at the then current rate. The report indicated that the average twelve-year-old child stands an 83 percent chance of being the victim of a violent crime in his or her natural lifetime and over half will be victimized more than once. One in twelve females will be raped and one in two households will be burglarized at least once. . . .

Through 1989, we experienced a 191 percent increase in violent crime in the United States over the past two decades, and a 256 percent increase in both Part One and Part Two index crimes. Nearly 500,000 citizens died in criminal homicide events.

How police officers respond to calls about committed crimes depends on several important variables:

- What specific crime is involved?
- Is the crime still in progress?
- How many suspects are involved?
- Are weapons involved?
- Is there a danger to the public?
- Could a hostage situation develop?
- How many officers are needed to respond?
- How many officers are available?
- Where are they?

Sometimes answers to all these questions are available. More often, however, responding officers lack much of this information.

Responsibilities of officers responding to a call regarding a criminal act include:

- *Arriving as rapidly, yet as safely, as possible.*
- *Caring for any injured people at the scene.*
- *Apprehending any suspects at the scene.*
- *Securing the scene.*
- *Conducting a preliminary investigation.*

Whether the police arrive with red lights and sirens will depend on the nature of the information to which police are responding. The element of surprise may be important if the crime is believed to be still in progress. At other times, such as in assault cases, the siren may be desirable because it may frighten off the attacker. Each specific call must be assessed for whether the added speed of response available through the use of red lights and siren is an advantage. Recall the Kansas City Experiment which showed that rapid response time did not greatly improve chances of making an arrest at the scene. In addition, the more rapid the response, the greater the likelihood of an accident en route involving the responding squad or citizens who happen to be in the way.

The actual arrival may be fraught with danger; consequently, officers should approach cautiously, making use of cover if it is thought the suspect might still be at the scene. If the element of surprise is important, officers should have a system of hand signals to coordinate their arrival and approach to the scene.

The next two responsibilities, attending to injured persons and apprehending suspects at the scene, may occur in reverse order, depending on the situation. If the injuries are not life threatening and the suspect is considered dangerous, apprehending that suspect will take precedence over attending to the injuries. Usually injuries and suspects at the scene are considered emergency matters to be attended to first.

As soon as emergency matters are tended to, the primary responsibility of the police is to secure the crime scene. If more than one officer responds to the call, the scene can be secured immediately by one officer while the other officer handles any emergency situation. Sometimes securing the scene is as simple as closing a door, but other times it is more complex. In a bank robbery, for example, the entire lobby is usually secured and closed for business until the preliminary investigation is completed. Outdoor crime scenes are usually roped off or barricaded. Only those individuals with official business should be allowed into the crime scene.

In some departments, this is where the responsibilities of the responding officers end. They keep the scene secure until investigators or detectives arrive to conduct the investigation, especially in crimes such as murder. In other departments, the responding officers conduct the preliminary investigation and, perhaps, the entire investigation.

The Preliminary Investigation

The more information and evidence that can be obtained immediately after a crime has been committed, the better the chances of identifying the person responsible and successfully prosecuting the case. Usually the officers responding to the call are in the best position to obtain this information and evidence.

---

*The **preliminary investigation** of a crime involves on-the-scene interviews of victims and witnesses, interrogation of suspects, and a search of the scene itself.*

In larger departments, if a suspect is apprehended at the scene, interrogation is usually done at the police department by investigators who are experienced, trained interrogators. Interviewing and interrogating were discussed in Chapter 3. Remember that witnesses should be separated and their statements carefully recorded.

Some crimes solve themselves. The suspect is at the scene or is known or identified through information supplied through interviews. Officers must know the elements of each crime and what evidence will prove them.

Evidence left at the scene of the crime can be critical to convicting criminals. The use of informants and undercover agents can contribute greatly to the success of criminal investigations. Notably these have been used over time in narcotics trafficking and sting operations to recover stolen property and apprehend burglars, petty crooks engaged in shoplifting, and car prowlers.

Officers arriving at the scene are often responsible for recognizing and gathering evidence as part of the preliminary investigation. The complete investigation itself is the topic of an entire course, criminal investigation, and is beyond the scope of this text.

State troopers conducting an investigation. The crime scene has been clearly marked to preserve evidence.

Some crimes such as forgery, embezzlement, and credit-card fraud have no crime scenes and must be investigated using information provided by victims and others. Many crimes, however, do have crime scenes and physical evidence. The value of any physical evidence used in court to verify that a crime has been committed, to identify the person(s) who did it, and to obtain a conviction, often rests with the officers who arrive first at a crime scene. In most cases, the officers who protect and search a crime scene play a critical role in determining whether a case can be made.

The first officers to arrive on the crime scene automatically incur the critical responsibility of securing the crime scene from unauthorized intrusion or other contamination. Officers should consider any crime scene as highly dynamic and make the preliminary survey of the layout carefully. The crime-scene search is, in certain offenses, the most important part of the investigation. Crimes of violence often involve a struggle and may leave such evidence as blood or a weapon. In homicides, assaults, and burglaries, criminals contact the physical surroundings and may leave fingerprints, jimmy marks, or other evidence linking suspects to victims and crimes.

Experienced officers anticipate finding certain types of evidence in specific crimes. Crimes against persons, for example, frequently yield evidence such as blood, hair, fibers, fingerprints, and weapons. Crimes against property, in contrast, commonly yield evidence such as tool marks on doors, windows, safes, money chests, cash registers, and desk drawers as well as fingerprints.

Fingerprints are among the most common and useful evidence found at crime scenes because they are a positive form of identification. Finding latent prints has become especially important since the availability of *Automated Fingerprint Identification Systems (A.F.I.S)*. If latent prints are found, they can be entered into either the FBI's system, which contains millions of prints, or into a city's own system. The Miami Police Department, for example, has been using A.F.I.S. for ten years, and its criminal file contains almost 200,000 entries and more than that amount in the civilian file. According to Shonberger (1990, p. 87), since the system was installed, 1,380 latent identifications involving 1,073 burglaries, 140 robberies, 68 homicides, 29 sexual batteries, 29 auto thefts, and 45 "other" crimes, have been directly attributed to it. The system checks incoming prints against every print in the file and identifies a small number to manually check. It can cut the time needed to examine prints from what has sometimes been months or even years to a matter of minutes.

Shonberger notes that a number of cases have been solved by a **case tie** where a suspect in one crime is linked to other crimes by fingerprints (p. 87):

> *An example of this type of case tie occurred in April 1984. Latents were entered into the A.F.I.S. System under Case #1653109F. These latents identified a subject who was then manually searched and identified on eleven additional burglary cases.*

Latent prints not linked with a suspect are stored in the system and checked against individuals when they are arrested. In one instance, a suspect who was arrested for the first time in Miami had his prints run through the system and was identified in two cases entered into the system two months before. He was then manually searched and identified in over twenty cases in Miami.

*The **Automated Fingerprint Identification System, A.F.I.S.**, drastically reduces the time needed to identify latent fingerprints, by selecting a limited number of likely matches for the latent.*

In June of 1990, New York City "unveiled a $40-million automated fingerprint system that officials say will help them solve 10,000 crimes yearly by identifying latent fingerprints found at crime scenes in cases involving unknown suspects" (*Law Enforcement News,* 1990b, p. 4).

Dallas, likewise, has found A.F.I.S. to be of extreme value. In three months the system identified nearly 1,500 individual crime scene prints, 80 percent of which led to viable suspects. According to the supervisor who oversees the system (*Law Enforcement News,* 1990a, p. 5):

We've increased the number of crime-scene-print identifications by 340 percent per month. . . . During its first week of operation in July 1989, A.F.I.S. allowed Dallas police to identify a serial rapist who was later charged with thirteen rape/robbery offenses. Since then, A.F.I.S. has allowed police to finger suspects in 38 homicides, 33 rapes, 209 robberies, 680 burglaries, 145 auto thefts, 5 aggravated assaults, and 40 miscellaneous crimes.

Blood may be valuable as evidence in assaults, homicides, burglaries, hit-and-run cases, and rape. It is classified as A, B, AB, or O. Although blood cannot be used to identify a particular individual's race or sex, it can help *eliminate* suspects.

Hair from victims and suspects can be found on clothing, weapons, blankets, sheets, seat covers, and the undercarriage of vehicles. Microscopic examination can identify hair as human or animal, but it cannot be identified as coming from a specific person. Microscopic examination of hair can usually identify the person's race, but not the person's sex or age, except in the case of infants. Microscopic examination can also tell if the hair was pulled out forcibly and which part of the body it is from.

Blood, hair, and other body tissues and fluids can also be used in **DNA fingerprinting.** This technique analyzes the genetic sequence of DNA—the "blueprint of life." Whereas other tests of human tissues and secretions can only eliminate suspects, DNA can positively identify an individual, except for identical twins. While DNA fingerprinting has been heralded as a major breakthrough for criminal investigation, it is still not accepted by some courts. Researchers have used DNA fingerprinting to make identifications from a four-year-old bloodstain and from semen stains that were several weeks old.

Physical fingerprints and DNA fingerprinting are the two forms of positive identification available to investigators.

Bite marks are sometimes significant in child and adult abuse cases. Bite marks have individual characteristics that match the size and configuration of the teeth.

Marks on the body may last for several weeks. Bite marks may sometimes also be found in partially eaten food.

Shoe or tire impressions are often found where suspects hastily enter or leave a crime scene. Shoe and tire prints are of two types: contamination prints and impressions. Contamination prints are left when a shoe or tire has a substance such as dirt or blood on it which then leaves a print on a hard surface. Impressions are imprints left in soft surfaces such as mud or sand. Shoe or tire impressions can place a suspect at a crime scene.

Tool fragments may also be found at a crime scene and later matched to a broken tool in the possession of a suspect. *Tool marks* are most often found in burglaries and in malicious destruction of property crimes. They may be found on windowsills and frames, doors and frames, cash register drawers, file cabinets, and cash boxes. Tool marks are often left when windows have been forced open with screwdrivers or pry bars; when locks have been snipped with bolt cutters; or when safes have been opened with hammers, chisels, or punches. These tools leave marks that often can be identified as definitely as fingerprints.

Glass from windows, automobiles, bottles, and other objects is often used as evidence in assaults, burglaries, murders, and many other crimes. When a person breaks a window, tiny pieces of glass are usually found in the clothing, pant cuffs, pockets, or on the clothing's surface. Glass is excellent evidence because two pieces of glass rarely contain the same proportions of sand, metal oxides, or carbonates. In addition, police can usually determine whether the glass was broken from inside or outside a building by observing the fracture marks and the location of the fragments.

Paint is frequently transferred from one object to another during the commission of a crime. During burglaries, it may be chipped off surfaces. During hasty getaways, it may flake off automobiles. Paint has provided a strong link in the chain of circumstantial evidence because it can associate an individual with the crime scene. It can also eliminate innocent suspects.

Safe insulation can be identified microscopically by composition, color, mineral content, and physical characteristics. Particles of safe insulation or fireproof insulation on a suspects' clothing or shoes is a strong indication of guilt.

Fibers from clothing are often found where burglars crawled through a window or opening. Clothing fibers are also often found adhering to the fenders, grill, door handles, or undercarriage of hit-and-run vehicles. Fingernail scrapings and weapons may also contain fiber evidence. Examination of the fibers can identify the type of fabric: wool, cotton, rayon, nylon, and so on. Sometimes the type of garment from which the fibers came can be identified.

Documents may contain fingerprint evidence and may also be examined for handwriting characteristics or for typewriter or printer characteristics. If a document has been handwritten, experts can do a side-by-side comparison with the document and samples of the suspect's handwriting to determine if both were done by the same person. Testimony of handwriting experts has been accepted in our courts for several years. Documents produced on a typewriter or printer can be examined to determine the manufacturer, make, model, and age of the machine.

Firearms left at a crime scene may be traced to their owner through the serial number, the manufacturer's identification, or the dealer who sold the gun. Firearms may also contain fingerprints or other marks that could lead to identification. The weapon's make is usually determined by the barrel rifling, spiral grooves cut into the gun barrel in its manufacture. The rifling varies considerably from manufacturer to manufacturer.

A large part of the preliminary investigation centers around whether officers can obtain evidence that a crime has been committed and been committed by a particular person. Evidence may be the turning point as to whether a case can be made.

All preliminary investigations must be systematic and thorough. Finding some answers does not mean that all answers have been uncovered. Likewise finding some evidence does not mean that more may not exist. One is mindful of the question once considered the epitome of the obvious, Who's buried in Grant's tomb? Those who answer ''General Ullyses S. Grant'' are only half right. His wife, Julia, is buried with him. Professional police officers must get *all* the facts and information, not just the obvious.

When evidence is found, it must be carefully marked, (often with the officer's badge number), placed in a secure container, sealed, tagged, recorded in the officer's notebook, and as soon as practical, placed in the property or evidence room. It must be kept secure until it is needed for trial.

---

*The **chain of possession** documents who has had control of the evidence from the time it is discovered until it is presented in court.*

Any time evidence is taken from the property room, it must be signed for. When it is returned, it is examined to be sure that it has not been altered in any way.

Computers as Partners in the Fight Against Crime

The use of computers in identifying fingerprints has already been discussed. Computers also assist in other important ways. A department's own case information can be made immediately available to officers in the field through Mobile Display Terminals (MDTs). These same terminals can also access national data bases such as those of the National Crime Information Center (NCIC) in a matter of seconds.

Computers are being used to track stolen vehicles as well. Dealing effectively with auto theft is a major concern of most law enforcement agencies because the crime is so prevalent. According to the Michigan Automobile Theft Prevention Authority: ''If auto theft were an industry, it would rank 56th on the 1990 Fortune 500 list of the most profitable U.S. corporations.''

Automatic vehicle locators (AVLs) use satellites and small transmitters. Cars are equipped with a high-tech tracking device that can be tracked by police cars with special computers. In some systems, if a person drives off without deactivating the system, an alarm is sent. In other systems, the owner must notify police that the car has been stolen before they begin tracking it. Some systems include an alert service that allows motorists to signal police in case of an emergency. One system even allows police to shut off a stolen car's engine by remote control, a feature that would eliminate high-speed pursuit.

According to officials at one tracking device manufacturer (*Law Enforcement News,* 1990c, p. 4): ''Cars are found in an average of 90 minutes, and damage is reduced from an average of $6,000 to $500.'' During the four years one system has been operating in Massachusetts where 36,000 cars have been equipped with the system, approximately 1,000 have been stolen, and all but 43 have been recovered.

Computers are also being used in criminal investigations themselves. Artificial intelligence (AI) programs are being used in several police departments to structure investigations. Software can also help determine which cases are most likely to be cleared by arrest. As noted by Bock (1990, p. 96):

> Departmental data bases can be linked to artificial intelligence to help prioritize calls. The system can analyze the call based on previous history of the location and factor that information into priority assignment. . . .

> Personal Information Managers are an innovation that can help investigators gather, classify, and review all the bits of data that are part of an investigation. One of these programs, Lotus Agenda, lets the investigator enter bits of data as they are obtained. Later the officer can review the information in several ways at the touch of a couple of keys. Things can be looked at in chronological order, or according to what information is linked to certain individuals, or according to the descriptions different people gave of the same incident.

The Long Beach Police Department in California is using a new geographic information system (GIS) which allows officers to analyze certain crimes by type and location. As noted by Chief of Police Binkley (1991, pp. 142–143):

> Geographic analysis of crime—though an important part of our job—can be a tedious and cumbersome task. That is obvious to anyone who has stared at a wall map full of thousands of colored push pins! . . .

> The Long Beach GIS ties each crime report to the city's computerized mapping data base, enabling instant cross-checking and analysis to locate patterns in modus operandi, time of incident, and suspect description. . . .

> The Long Beach system has successfully targeted high-volume crimes typically associated with career lawbreakers, including robbery, burglary, auto theft, and auto burglary.

Computers can also be used to help cluster crimes and identify problems—the first step in problem-oriented policing, as discussed in Chapter 9.

Crime-Scene Units

Another aid in the fight against crime is the crime-scene unit. Since the majority of local police departments consist of fewer than twenty-five sworn officers, they seldom have the luxury of special teams of criminal investigators. In such cases, a crime-scene team consisting of patrol officers assigned crime-scene duty as a collateral duty is often of value. According to Glidden (1990, p. 54), "The primary goals should be collecting and preserving physical evidence, and completing all related reports, sketches, and photographs." Glidden also stresses (p. 55):

> A policy must be firmly set that gives the crime-scene unit administrative control over the crime scene. This normally means that only crime-scene unit personnel will be allowed in the crime-scene area. Such a policy prevents problems later when officers, senior to the crime-scene unit investigator, wish to enter the crime scene.

A mobile police station. Such facilities are often effectively used in neighborhoods with high crime rates.

The crime-scene unit, after a preliminary survey of the crime scene, determines the actual crime-scene perimeter and search area. They set the objectives of the search as well as the equipment and manpower needed and also develop a theory of the crime. In addition, they identify and protect transient evidence, and prepare a narrative description of the scene.

In some departments, after these functions are performed, the work of the crime-scene unit is complete, and the case is turned over to an investigative or detective division. In smaller departments, however, the crime-scene unit may conduct the entire investigation.

Mobile Police Stations

When specific sections of a city are crime-infested, police departments might also consider using a mobile police station. Called Neighborhood Action Base Stations (NABS), these facilities may help reduce crime and violence by their presence alone. One such station used in Aurora, Illinois, is an 8 × 33 foot mobile office building installed on property donated by the owner of a large apartment complex. It has two paneled offices, a rest room, and is equipped with heating and air conditioning, telephones, and a radio. The use of NABS trailers has met with resistence in some instances, with Aldermen demanding their removal.

Closely associated with the problem of crime is the problem of violence in our country. When violence occurs, police are expected to deal with it.

Violence

America has always been a relatively violent country. According to Blumenthal et al. (1972, p. 243), "Research brings out what is seldom openly avowed: that violence is a part of our unacknowledged value system."

*Violence has accompanied every stage of our country's
existence from its birth to the present and is often involved in
assuring law and order.*

The important role of violence in shaping our country is also acknowledged by Brown (1989, p. 23), "Apart from its role in the formation and preservation of the nation, violence has been a determinant of both the form and substance of American life." He goes on to note (p. 23):

*Violence has characterized the struggle of American groups in conflict from
the colonial period to the present. Group hostility has often escalated to the
level of violence in white–Indian wars, white–black confrontations, ethnic
rivalries, religious vendettas, agrarian uprisings, and the struggles of
laborers against industrialists. . . .*

*In one way or another, much of our nineteenth- and twentieth-century violence
has represented the attempt of established Americans to preserve their favored
position in the social, economic, and political order. . . .*

*Violence has formed a seamless web with some of the most positive events of
U.S. history: independence (the Revolution's violence), the freeing of the
slaves and the preservation of the Union (Civil War violence), land settlement
(white–Indian wars), the stabilization of frontier society (vigilante violence),
the social elevation of the farmer and the laborer (agrarian and labor
violence), and the preservation of law and order (violent law enforcement).
The patriot, the humanitarian, the nationalist, the pioneer, the landholder, the
farmer, the laborer, and the capitalist have all used violence as the means to
a higher end. . . .*

*Thus, as our nation approaches the twenty-first century, historical patterns of
violence survive and are deeply embedded in our heritage and habits.
Violence is strongly rejected for inclusion in the American creed, but so great
has been our involvement with it over the long sweep of American history that
violence has become a compelling, although unacknowledged, element in our
values and in our culture.*

Many feel that violence is becoming a way of life in the United States. Children, for instance, are taught to compete and win at all costs. Aggression is rewarded. Some of the nation's most violent criminal figures like Al Capone, John Dillinger, Jessie James, and Bonnie and Clyde have become popular folk heroes.

The dominant expression of violent behavior in the United States involves acts of *interpersonal* violence that occur nearly everywhere, every day. Domestic violence is a major challenge for law enforcement, as discussed in detail in Chapter 12. In addition, barroom brawls, street fights, beatings, slashing, stabbings, and shooting are the types of violent transactions that are most likely to require a police response. These "garden variety" acts of violence require police officers to possess excellent communications skills. They may also have to resort to violence themselves.

Police use of Violence and Deadly Force

The fact that the police have a monopoly on the *legitimate* use of force means they have the authority to impose themselves on conflicts as third-party agents of social control. Therefore, police–citizen encounters are *always* potentially coercive relationships. This is a particularly important contextual variable when considering the role of the police in controlling "typical" violent encounters. The dangers implicit in this for both the police and the citizens involved are thoroughly documented in research on violence.

Anderson and Bauer (1987, p. 382) suggest three levels of intervention:

First, there are low-level, relatively easily applied techniques to be used early in a confrontation (e.g., distraction, problem solving, and making clear to the citizen the long-term consequences of his or her behavior). . . . Second, the officer takes direct control of the situation, perhaps by giving an order (e.g., when several people are talking at once and he or she instructs them to keep quiet and take turns). Also, the officer may use more sophisticated verbal interventions that require additional training to use effectively (e.g., pacing an individual to a calm state by the use of body language and speaking rate and the disruption of anger by use of confusion techniques and imbedded suggestions). Finally, if these techniques fail, the officer may move to power techniques (e.g., threatening or physically subduing the offender).

During this third level of confrontation, police are sometimes forced to use violence against lawbreakers, including physical restraint, choke holds, blows from a nightstick, and sometimes, use of their firearms.

Violence and Civil Disobedience

Pick up the daily newspaper, turn on the radio or the television, and you will find civil disobedience occurring daily around the world. From the civil disobedience in South Africa against apartheid, to the need for self-autonomy of ethnic groups in Europe, to the demonstrations in Washington, D.C. against racism, aid for street people, and a more responsive government, society is filled with dissension and violence. And law enforcement officers are the ones called on to control or suppress these demonstrations.

Usually dissent will start with a simple protest for a cause that has confronted society for some time, for example, the pro-life/pro-choice controversy surrounding abortion. Most protests start out lawfully and are relatively peaceful demonstrations. However, when emotions become inflamed, legal barriers are crossed, and a classic civil disobedience situation develops. Nonviolent lawbreaking begins when participants are willing to be punished by the courts for their lawbreaking. From there demonstrators may become violent lawbreakers, frequently disregarding the rights of others.

The ultimate of this type of action is anarchy, chaos, revolution, and bloodshed. The police generally agree that nonviolent protest is one thing to contend with, but violent protest infringes on the rights not only of others, but of the police officers as well. This usually results in property damage, looting, personal injuries, and, in some cases, death. Sometimes even the mildest protest can lead to other groups demonstrating for other causes.

The purpose in most cases of civil disobedience is to protest some governmental or institutional policy. A civilly disobedient person breaks the law to prove a point. The act is done openly. A law is violated because people feel the law violates their sense of what is right. They are willing to accept punishment for their actions supporting their beliefs.

Civil disobedience consists of breaking a law to prove a point or to protest something.

For example, the production of war materials during peace time, the violation of the ecology, the construction of nuclear power plants, and the lack of government interest in housing street people are all causes that have brought about demonstrations in the past and that required the presence of police to control them.

The picture of civil disobedience in our society is relatively simple. People marching, conducting sit-ins, blocking entryways and exits, and carrying placards are rather nonthreatening. Strikes, emotionally charged pickets, pro-life and pro-choice demonstrations, however, can become very difficult for police to manage.

Riots caused by civil disobedience have been touched off by various police actions. In relatively mild protests and demonstrations, the presence of dogs, police officers' overreactions to demonstrators, and rumors can cause conflagrations.

Police move in to disperse and arrest demonstrators outside the Minneapolis Federal Building.

These are not in keeping with the traditional nonviolent view of civil disobedience the police have had over the years.

Is civil violence ever acceptable? Will it produce reforms or lead to repression, destruction of property, hostility, injury, and death? Whether civil disobedience is justified or unjustified, usually only the police can provide stability in such situations. Ironically, police actions often actually cause riots and violent protests to escalate.

Violent dissent seems to be on the increase, yet it is seldom defensible because it seldom succeeds in securing massive reform, especially where there are alternative ways to protest. Violence may bring quick recognition of a need in our society, but it seldom brings a quick remedy.

It should be remembered, however, that some of our greatest Americans, heroes nonetheless, were lawbreakers in their time. George Washington, Benjamin Franklin, John Adams, and Alexander Hamilton, were all civilly disobedient and considered traitors until success crowned their efforts.

An extreme desire for change often results in frustration and may be the reason for the radical switch in tactics. It can be seen in neighborhoods, on city blocks. Militancy and hatred spark riots. Violence seems to be a necessary way of life. People will not condemn the violence just because it seems to get faster results and, in fact, seems to be the only way to get results in some cases. Whether demonstrations are violent or nonviolent, police have been designated by our society as the correct vehicle for coping with the various kinds of demonstrations occurring in the 1990s. Vaughn (1990, p. 73) says:

Law enforcement will be significantly affected by an increasing level of social unrest in the United States over the next five years. Much of this unrest will be related to a resurgence of overt racism, fast-changing world events involving human rights concerns, environmental activism, a strong animal rights movement, and other moral issues including the pro- and antiabortion movement and the homeless population.

Issues leading to civil disobedience include:

- *Overt racism*
- *Human rights concerns*
- *Environmental concerns*
- *Animal rights movements*
- *Pro- and antiabortion conflicts*
- *The homeless population*

Vaughn (p. 73) also notes that: ''The tactics used by many protesters today are more sophisticated and difficult for the police to deal with.''

Racism.   Historically, the Ku Klux Klan has been the epitome of violent racism. However, other groups are now contending for this dubious title. In the 1980s, according to Brown (1989, p. 144):

Two events in New York City that illustrate the volatile mixture of crime and race in contemporary America are the wounding of four black youths by a white electronics specialist, Bernard Goetz, in a 1984 subway shooting and the 1986 killing of another black who was the victim of murderous behavior by young whites in the Howard Beach section of Queens.

In the 1990s, a group known as the Skinheads is posing a threat of violence against minorities of several types, including "people of color" whom they call "mud people." Says Christensen (1990, p. 73), "They hate just about everyone; especially blacks, Jews, gays, Asians, and Hispanics. . . . They are patriotic—in their own way. They believe the white man built America but the Jews and minorities are destroying it."

Skinheads get their name from their practice of shaving their heads, although some have let their hair grow out so as to not be so easily recognizable by police. Acting in groups, they attack ruthlessly, often beating their lone victims with baseball bats and stomping victims with their heavy boots, called "Doc Martens." They often display patches of American flags, German swastikas, and slogans such as "White Supremacy" and "WAR," an anachronism for White Aryan Resistance. According to Christensen (p. 75): "They are proud of what they are doing and, if an officer at least puts on the pretense of respecting them and appears interested in what they have to say, they will talk the officer's ear off."

Human Rights Concerns.   Violent civil rights protests swept the country in the 1950s and 1960s and are being heard again in the 1990s. Gay rights issues, the rights of individuals with communicable diseases such as AIDS, and the right to die are among the most hotly debated controversies.

Environmental Concerns.   "The nineties seem to be gearing up as the decade of environmental protests," says Fanton (1990, p. 92), "resulting in an increasing number of rural demonstrations and campaigns." Issues include nuclear waste disposal and logging v. forest preservation. Activist groups such as Earth First have forced not only municipal police, but also rural police, into thinking about dealing with protests and the unique circumstances they present.

One key problem with the rural protests and demonstrations is that most of the law enforcement officers who have to deal with them know the protesters. In Allegheny County, demonstrators protested over being investigated as a possible site for low-level radioactive waste. Sheriff Scholes commented, "When I see my friends and neighbors being arrested for a cause they believe so strongly in, to protect their county and their families, that's very difficult to deal with" (Fanton, p. 97). And Undersheriff Timberlake, recalling his days with the New York City Police Department concurred: "I had people spitting at me, cursing me, calling me 'pig,' and things like that—really raunchy type demonstrations. I'll tell you, I'll take any one of them over this type because of the fact that you know these are decent people you're dealing with."

Animal Rights Movements.   Campaigns to protect certain species of animals have been around for decades and are usually confined to fund-raising efforts and massive informational mailings. One group, however, the Animal Liberation Front (ALF) is, according to Hueston of the University of Arizona Police Department in Tucson (1990, p. 52), "one of the newest terrorist groups confronting law enforcement in the United States today." Hueston tells how, in April 1989, the ALF destroyed two animal research laboratories, a penthouse research center, and an off-campus office, causing $300,000 in damages and resulting in the university having to spend over $1 million in animal research protection.

Sprayed or hand-painted in red were slogans such as "Nazi Torture," "Nowhere is Safe," "You Can't Hide from the AFL," and "We Shall Return." The group was methodical and left no clues. They sent videotapes to the local television station that their own crew made of the destruction. The tapes were also transmitted via satellite from the headquarters of People for the Ethical Treatment of Animals (PETA) in Washington, D.C., by three major television stations.

The group did return, as promised, a year later to link up with Tucson's Voice of Animals (VOA) group. The treasurer and president of the VOA were arrested when found inside one of the new animal research construction sites.

According to Hueston (p. 53), the ALF has been associated with 85 break-ins since 1977, including a break-in which caused $3.8 million in damages to an animal research facility at the University of California at Davis. Given the seriousness of the threat of the ALF, Hueston suggests that law enforcement should push for legislation making attacks on any animal research facility a felony and for involving the FBI in such attacks, treating them as a form of terrorism. The FBI should gather intelligence on the ALF and maintain a hotline to help local police departments deal with any problems they encounter with this group.

Pro- and Antiabortion Conflicts.   Conflicts between pro-life and pro-choice groups are common and often make headlines as groups of pro-lifers seek to destroy abortion centers and pro-choicers seek to stop them. What may begin as a relatively peaceful march around an abortion center or clinic may rapidly escalate into a violent, destructive confrontation resulting in property damage and personal injuries. Political careers have been made and destroyed on this single issue. The courts have also become involved in the controversy. And police officers are likely to have their own views on this highly personal issue.

Responding to Demonstrations and Violence

A key to responding to demonstrations and violence is advance planning. Although police officers may not know exactly when they may need to intervene, they can anticipate what types of intervention might be needed depending on their specific locality. A police department responsible for a jurisdiction in which animal research is being conducted or in which an abortion clinic is located should be prepared for demonstrations that might turn violent.

To deal with demonstrations and possible violence, police departments should:

- *Assess their risks.*
- *Develop contingency plans.*
- *Have a call-out system for off-duty officers.*

Lieutenant Scott of the Colorado Springs Police Department (Mallory, 1990, p. 85) suggests the following as essential preparations for demonstrations:

- Have built-in plans, and exercise them periodically. The most important thing is to have a thought-out plan based on realistic capabilities.
- Don't overcomplicate the paper plans. Fancy stuff may not work.
- Use a phased response, and ask for more help before it's too late.
- Conduct continual risk assessment during the incident, so decisions can be made promptly.
- Have a call-out system.
- Have a mutual aid agreement with adjacent departments, and make sure it works.
- Always deal with equipment issues in advance. Don't wait until the equipment is needed, then start rounding it up.
- Have mass arrest kits ready. Include evidence envelopes, marking pens, camera equipment, and flex cuffs.
- Designate your first response units in advance.
- Conduct annual training of your cadre. Training should include crowd-control techniques, putting on gas masks, and working with K-9 units.

Police departments should know what emergency medical personnel might be available and how to contact them. Departments should also provide for prisoner handling and transportation. Some departments use a cross-arm carry to remove prisoners; others use stretchers. Videotaping the demonstration and the police response is usually a good idea to counter any claims of police brutality.

During demonstrations, police should use only as much force as is necessary to control the crowd. Fanton (1990, p. 97) cautions that officers should not act like John Wayne because that will tend to turn the crowd aggressive also and because "they're going to have their own John Wayne, and he might be bigger than your John Wayne."

If a demonstration gets big enough and violent enough, a jurisdiction may call on the National Guard for help. This request usually has to be made by the sheriff to the governor. The exception is cities of the first class (usually those having a population over 100,000 [Minn. Statute 410.01]). The Mower County Sheriff's Department sought and received help from the Minnesota National Guard when the strikers at the Hormel plant in Austin, Minnesota, turned violent.

Russell and Beigel (1990, p. 288) suggest the following code of conduct when dealing with civil disturbances and riots:

1. Remember that your most powerful weapons are psychological ones—patience, tolerance, good humor, tact, and the ability to set an example by your own conduct.
2. Remember that it is your uniform and your position as symbols of the establishment that cause some people to react negatively. Do not take threats, insults, or abuse personally.
3. Do not look on all situations as a challenge to your ability as a police officer.
4. Try to learn all you can about how a person functions in a group, especially under stress conditions.
5. Don't overestimate your endurance threshold.
6. Have faith in others. You are not alone.
7. Remember that all riots must end sometime and that then the task of restoring affected areas or people must begin. Therefore, do not do anything

during the stress of the disturbance that jeopardizes either you or the department's position in carrying out this task.

8. Remember that you are a professional law enforcement officer.

Sometimes individuals believe in a cause so strongly that they become terrorists. Although police officers are not as likely to have to deal with terrorists as they are with citizen groups demonstrating for or against a specific cause, the possibility always exists.

Terrorists

Terrorists are often classified as left- or right-wing, with the 1990s seeing a decline in left-wing terrorism and a marked increase in right-wing terrorism.

Although in our political system, democrats are usually referred to as being "leftist" and republicans as being more to the "right," Strentz (1990, p. 70) cautions that "left-wing and right-wing terrorist groups represent outrageous and illegal expressions of these diverse and legitimate political perspectives." Strentz summarizes the basic characteristics of right-wing and left-wing terrorists in Table 11.1.

Rightist groups include the American Nazi party, the Ku Klux Klan, the Aryan Nations, the National Socialist White Peoples party, the Covenant, the Order, and the Skinheads.

TABLE 11.1
Distinctions in Characteristics of Right-Wing and Left-Wing Terrorists

Characteristic	Right Wing	Left Wing
Radical political orientation	Nazi/fascist	Communist/socialist
View of government	Perfect—retain or revive	Perfectible—replace
View of government opposition	Illegitimate	Honorable
Desire for social change	None/reactionary	Revolutionary
Social class	Lower/middle	Lower/middle/upper
Leadership	Male-dominated	Egalitarian
Sex roles	Established/rigid	Unspecified
Marital status	Married	Single/divorced/separated
Group dynamics	Families/cults	Single coequals
Age	16–76	25–45
Education—members	High school	University
Education—leaders	High school/university	University
Religion	Fundamental protestant	Agnostic, atheistic
Criminal planning	Impulsive	Meticulous

Source: From "Radical Right v. Radical Left: Terrorist Theory and Threat," by Thomas Strentz, *The Police Chief,* August 1990, p. 73. Reprinted with permission of the International Association of Chiefs of Police, Inc., 1110 Glebe Road, Suite 200, Arlington, Virginia, 22201 U.S.A. Further reproduction without express written permission from IACP is strictly prohibited.

Leftist groups include the Symbionese Liberation Army (SLA), the May 19th Communist Organization, the Weathermen, the Black Panthers, and the Black Lib eration Army. Mullins (1990, pp. 44–45) states:

> *During the 1980s, the most active terrorist organizations in the United States were those of the far right. In the 1990s, the major internal threat will continue to be those organizations. In fact, we can expect their terrorist activities to increase significantly in the coming decade. The level of sophistication of those activities will also improve significantly.*

Because of this, Strentz (p. 75) suggests, ''Law enforcement must develop a solid understanding of [terrorist groups'] idiosyncrasies and adapt strategies accordingly in order to successfully investigate these aberrant organizations.

The 1990s will also experience *narcoterrorism,* defined by Mullins (1990, p. 45) as:

> . . . *the use of terrorists by drug cartels to attack those who would attempt to disrupt drug-related activities, and the involvement of terrorist organizations in the sale and distribution of drugs to further their organizational goals.*

Narcoterrorism includes hiring terrorists to protect the drug cartels as well as the sale and distribution of drugs by these cartels.

Narcoterrorism was used by the Medellin cartel when it hired the M-19 organization to assassinate twelve Colombian Supreme Court justices. As noted by Williams (1990, p. 47): ''The connection between Columbian terrorists and drug smugglers, with Cuban assistance to both groups, has been well documented. Other terrorist organizations that have been used by drug cartels include the Irish Republican Army and the Palestinian Liberation Organization.''

It should be noted, however, that some experts, including individuals with the DEA and the FBI feel narcoterrorism is nonexistent. They emphasize that terrorists are ideologically driven whereas drug traffickers are economically driven. This alternative viewpoint bears consideration.

The drug trade has also resulted in what Mullins (1990, p. 46) calls:

> . . . *a unique category of terrorist—the street gang. Over the past few years, we have seen a dramatic increase in street gangs using terrorist-type activities to establish dominance in drug territories and prevent interference from law enforcement. There has been a startling proliferation of terrorist-type weapons—automatic weapons, assault rifles, sophisticated explosive devices—among street gangs, as well as a reliance on urban guerrilla warfare techniques. In the 1990s, street gangs will become even more organized and vicious as they adopt and adapt the tools and techniques of terrorism into their daily operations. . . . Expect bombings, sabotage operations, and attacks on rivals, as well as on law enforcement personnel, to increase in frequency over the next decade.*

Dealing with street gangs and with heavily armed drug traffickers is the focus of Chapter 14.

If terrorist acts are committed in a jurisdiction, the investigative report should be made available to neighboring jurisdictions as well as to the FBI. In 1982, the FBI was designated the lead agency for investigating terrorism in the United States. Revell (1990, p. 67) suggests that "the strongest tools in the fight against terrorism are the exchange of vital information and mutual cooperation to achieve common goals."

Sessions (1990, p. 11), director of the FBI, notes that the FBI has "formed counterterrorism working groups to cover special events such as political conventions and major sporting events." The International Association of Chiefs of Police is also taking steps to counteract terrorism by the formation of its Committee on Terrorism. At the international level, the Terrorism, Radicalism, Extremism and Violence International (TREVI) organization is made up of representatives from several European countries who meet twice a year to discuss ways to deal with terrorism.

Another form of violence law enforcement officers must be prepared to deal with is the hostage situation. This can be associated with terrorist groups or with certain crimes.

Hostage Situations

When police respond to a call about a crime in progress or a terrorist group in action, they may encounter a hostage situation. Or, they may be called because of a hostage situation. Hostage takers may be criminals using bystanders as shields or bargaining tools, mentally unstable individuals, disorganized groups such as demonstrators who get out of hand, or terrorist groups. According to Stitt (1990, p. 21), "A hostage situation exists when one or more persons seize another person or persons by force and hold them captive against their will for the purpose of bargaining to have certain demands met by authorities." He further notes (p. 22):

The FBI and most domestic police departments divide hostage takers into four distinct categories. These categories are: (1) traditional (or criminal trapped at the scene of a crime or in the process of escaping from the scene of a crime), (2) terrorists, (3) prisoners, and (4) the mentally disturbed.

It is important to recognize which type of hostage situation is involved, because the negotiation process is directly affected. Stitt suggests the most dangerous hostage situation is usually one involving terrorists. Terrorists are usually willing to die for their cause and have little problem with killing others. The most prevalent and usually least dangerous hostage situation involves the mentally disturbed.

Stitt (p. 26) also describes five distinct strategies police frequently use in hostage situations:

1. Attack or assault without making any attempt to negotiate.
2. Neither negotiate nor assault, but attempt to wait out the hostage takers.
3. Negotiate, but do not make concessions to demands.
4. Negotiate and give in to demands.
5. Negotiate and lie about giving in to demands.

The first option is likely to result in deaths, as noted by a Rand Corporation study which found that 78 percent of hostages were killed when an assault took place. The second strategy has two advantages: (1) the police do not need to lie or use deceit, and (2) it is possible the Stockholm syndrome may occur.

Armed police officers wearing bullet-proof vests take up position behind a car outside a small branch of the Bankers Trust office being held up by a lone gunman. The gunman was holding six hostages and demanded ten million in gold and the release of several SLA members.

---

*The **Stockholm syndrome** refers to the process of transference, where hostages feel positive toward their captors and negative toward the police and the captors return these positive feelings.*

Stitt (p. 34) describes the three elements of the Stockholm syndrome as follows:

- Positive "feelings" from the hostages to their captor(s).
- Negative "feelings" toward authorities by both hostages and captor(s).
- Positive "feelings" returned by the captors to the hostages.

When this situation occurs, the likelihood of the hostages being harmed is greatly reduced. Sometimes, however, the hostages actually join their captors in their illegal or terrorist activities. This seemed to happen in the case of Patty Hearst, the newspaper heiress who was kidnapped and later photographed providing cover gunfire for her "captors" as they attempted a robbery.

The third alternative, negotiating without concessions, can buy time. Stitt suggests that sometimes it is wise to make small concessions to build a sense of trust. The fourth alternative, negotiating with concessions, according to Stitt (p. 28), "is not acceptable if the concessions made are major ones." Likewise, he feels (p. 29): "The fifth strategy, to negotiate and lie about giving in to demands, is certainly not condoned as a general approach to hostage situations."

If a strategy which involves negotiation of some type is selected, it is critical that someone skilled in hostage negotiations should be available to talk with the hostage holder. As suggested by Aradi (1989, p. 62), this may well be the police dispatcher who is already well-trained in police telecommunications. He notes the FBI course emphasis in hostage negotiation that "negotiators don't command; commanders don't negotiate." To have the person in command of the containment of the situation also conduct the negotiations is usually not the best approach. The commander at the scene should be able to devote full attention to the entire situation. In addition, if the hostage taker knows the negotiator is also the person in command, he knows he has the authority to grant requests. With the commander as negotiator, the advantage of stalling while waiting for authorization is lost.

The police dispatcher may make the best hostage negotiator.

Among other reasons for using the police dispatcher as hostage negotiator are the following (Aradi, p. 62):

- Manpower is at a premium.
- This person is a professional telecommunicator with critical telecommunications skills . . . accustomed to dealing with angry or hysterical callers.
- Initial contact may already have been made . . . when the individual calls the agency.
- Rapport may have been established during those initial contacts.
- Training can be more fully utilized. . . . Training material, manuals, notes, and helpful preplan forms are readily available in the communications center.
- There is no ego involved. . . . A dispatcher should have no delusions of authority and, as such, should not convey an authoritarian attitude.
- Contingencies are covered.

If the dispatcher is used as hostage negotiator, he or she should be relieved of all other duties while the negotiations are going on.

In hostage situations and also in some high-risk entries, some police departments have used **flashbangs.** A flashbang, according to Heal (1990, p. 18), is a generic term to describe:

Stun grenades, flashbangs, flash-sound diversionary devices, distraction devices, stun munitions, grenade simulators—the list goes on and on. Each refers to a device that explodes with a loud bang and emits a brilliant light. . . . .

Deputies have reported resounding success in the ability of these devices to disorient a potentially violent suspect. . . .

The ability to create a state of confusion and disorientation has profound tactical significance when appropriately exploited.

Heal suggests, however, that flashbangs not be used when the elderly or small children are a part of the situation because they may panic. Flashbangs may also create a lot of smoke, reducing visibility, and they may set off smoke alarms.

Maher (1989, p. 276) says that the number one rule applying to a high-anxiety situation is to *slow everything down*. The benefits of stalling for time include:

- Time to contain and isolate the scene is made available.
- The initial state of high emotion is given time to subside and rational thinking to return.

- As time passes, the lives of hostages become more secure as the holder realizes the value of their continued safety and is subjected to increasing awareness of them as persons, not pawns.
- Fatigue can set in and alertness will fade. (This will also affect negotiators, requiring the need for knowledgeable relief personnel.)

The number one rule in hostage situations is to slow things down.

Maher (p. 276) suggests, in addition to stalling for time, the following guidelines:

- Weapons are not negotiable—an obvious rule, but one that must be stressed. Anyone who surrenders a weapon is taking the chance of being killed with it.
- Negotiators should not substitute for hostages—a cardinal rule.
- Avoid lying—negotiations should be sincere attempts to bargain, with lies told only when absolutely necessary.
- Do not allow relatives, friends, neighbors, etc., to negotiate.
- Avoid deadlines, and do not grant outrageous demands.
- Do not converse with hostages as this increases their importance in the hostage taker's mind.
- A senior officer commands the scene—not the negotiator. Public safety, scene security, perimeter control, media liaison, and so on, must be outside the negotiation process.
- Gather intelligence on the subject as well as all others involved in the situation and the logistics of the scene.
- Negotiate in person when possible. Telephones or bullhorns are not as effective, but they are safer than face-to-face negotiations.

Many of the techniques used in hostage situations are also appropriate when responding to a situation in which an individual is barricaded or is threatening to commit suicide.

Barricaded Individuals and Suicide Attempts

Police departments need clear guidelines on how to handle life-threatening situations such as barricaded individuals and those who are threatening to commit suicide. Of prime importance are the lives of those involved. If no danger exists for the police or the public, it is often best to talk the situation out or simply wait it out.

The number one rule in barricaded individuals or suicide-attempt situations is to slow things down.

Russell and Beigel (1990) suggest the following guidelines for dealing with a suicide attempt or other crisis situations:

1. Assume the proper mental attitude.

2. Secure the scene and assess the threat to your own safety, the safety of others, and the safety of the suicide attempter. In securing the scene, try to keep as many people as possible away from the immediate action.
3. Introduce yourself and your organization, using name and title.
4. Give plenty of reassurance.
5. Try to determine the main theme. (Usually anger at someone or feelings of hopelessness.)
6. Comply with any requests if at all possible.
7. Remember that the person attempting suicide is in control.
8. After the crisis is over, reassure the attempters.

If officers respond to a successful suicide, they must secure the scene and conduct a thorough investigation, keeping in mind that, to many people, suicide is a stigma. Family members may hide or destroy evidence of a suicide, including a note that may have been left. Sometimes this is done so that insurance can be collected.

Dealing with Victims

Wherever there is crime and violence, there are victims. Part of the police responsibility is to deal effectively with these victims without becoming secondary victims themselves. A delicate balance between empathy and objectivity must be maintained.

Those who have been victimized will have varying physical and psychological reactions from their trauma: numbness, silence, withdrawal, denial, acceptance, fear, confusion, embarrassment, shock, anger, rage, loss of control, hysteria. Any of these are normal reactions to trauma.

Victims need to be made safe and to feel secure, to be able to release whatever emotions they are experiencing, to know what has happened, what their rights are, and what is likely to happen next.

When dealing with victims, police officers should attend to any physical injuries, assure their safety and assure them of their security, show genuine concern for their situation, listen attentively, and allow them to set the pace for questions. Police officers' questions should avoid jargon. After the needed information is obtained, officers should explain what assistance is available to the victim and arrange for any emergency assistance that might be needed. Many larger cities have crime-victim-assistance centers that can be of great help in such situations. Many states have victimization laws that provide financial assistance for certain expenses associated with being a victim. Police should be aware of such assistance if it is available.

According to Burnley, Director of the Office for Victims of Crime, U.S. Department of Justice (1990, p. 13):

The early 1980s were marked by increased public attention to the rights and needs of crime victims; passage of landmark federal legislation, the Victim Witness Protection Act of 1982 and the Victims of Crime Act of 1984, and increased advocacy at local, state, and federal levels.

Roberts (1990, p. 13) further notes:

After decades of neglect, crime victims are finally being recognized as a vulnerable and forgotten group of people who have rights and are in need of services. During the past ten years, as a result of federal, state, and local initiatives, a host of victim-service and witness-assistance programs have been developed. . . . Forty-four states have crime victims bills of rights. In addition, there are now several thousand programs to aid crime victims, including general victim-assistance centers, specialized services for elderly victims, and programs for victims of rape, domestic violence, and child sexual abuse.

Waller (1990, p. 139) emphasizes the importance of victims to police in criminal investigations and the need for their assistance and cooperation. He suggests that victims be treated as "privileged clients" and that police departments should follow the urgings of the International Association of Chiefs of Police (IACP) to establish procedures and train personnel to implement the "incontrovertible rights of crime victims." These rights include the following (IACP, 1983):

1. To be free from intimidation.
2. To be told of financial assistance and social services available and how to apply for them.
3. To be provided a secure area during interviews and court proceedings, and to be notified if presence in court is needed.
4. To be provided a quick return of stolen or other personal property when no longer needed as evidence.
5. To a speedy disposition of the case, and to be periodically informed of case status and final disposition; and, wherever personnel and resource capabilities allow, to be notified in felony cases whenever the perpetrator is released from custody.
6. To be interviewed by a female official in the case of rape and other sexual offenses, wherever personnel and resource capabilities allow.

Waller (1990, p. 140) suggests: "Research and common sense show that police leaders who implement the IACP Crime Victims Bill of Rights will achieve the police mission in ways no other reforms can. Implementing those rights will help victims in ways only the police can."

Summary

One major function of law enforcement is to respond when a crime has been committed. Responsibilities of officers responding to a call regarding a criminal act include arriving as rapidly, yet as safely, as possible; caring for any injured people at the scene; apprehending any suspects at the scene; securing the scene; and conducting a preliminary investigation.

The preliminary investigation involves on-the-scene interviews of victims and witnesses, interrogations of suspects, and a search of the scene itself. The use of A.F.I.S., an Automated Fingerprint Identification System, has greatly increased the importance of finding fingerprints at a crime scene. The A.F.I.S. drastically reduces the time needed to identify latent fingerprints, by selecting a limited number of likely matches for the latent. Physical fingerprints and DNA fingerprinting are the two forms of positive identification available to investigators. The chain of possession documents who has had control of the evidence from the time it is discovered until it is presented in court.

In addition to dealing with crime, police officers are also often called upon to deal with situations involving violence. Violence has accompanied every stage of our country's existence from its birth to the present and is often involved in assuring law and order. Violence often accompanies civil disobedience. Civil disobedience consists of breaking a law to prove a point or to protest something. Issues leading to civil disobedience include overt racism, human rights concerns, environmental concerns, animal rights movements, and pro- and antiabortion conflicts.

Although not encountered as often, police must also be prepared to deal with terrorist activity. Terrorists are often classified as left- or right-wing, with the 1990s seeing a decline in left-wing terrorism and a marked increase in right-wing terrorism.

To deal with demonstrations and possible violence as well as terrorist activity, police departments should assess their risks, develop contingency plans, and have a call-out system for off-duty officers. Narcoterrorism includes hiring terrorists to protect the drug cartels as well as the sale and distribution of drugs by these cartels.

Sometimes when police respond to a call regarding a crime or terrorist activity, a hostage situation develops. Again, contingency plans are vital. The Stockholm syndrome refers to the process of transference, where hostages feel positive toward their captors and negative toward the police and the captors return these positive feelings. The police dispatcher may make the best hostage negotiator. The number one rule in hostage situations as well as in situations involving barricaded individuals or those threatening to commit suicide is to slow things down.

Application #1

The chief of police of the Bigtown Police Department notices there is no policy or written procedure to guide patrol officers when they receive a call to a crime scene. Past analysis of reports indicates that many officers have made their own policy as to what their responsibilities are. No uniformity exists. The chief calls you, the head of the patrol division, in and instructs you to formulate a policy and procedure for all officers when responding to a crime.

Instruction.   Use the form in Appendix A to make the policy and procedure. The overall policy of how such calls are to be regarded and the specific procedures to be followed, including priorities, should be addressed.

Application #2

Excessive force factors that allow the police to use whatever discretion is necessary in certain situations and which situations are high on civic policy lists has changed very little since the Civil War. Whether force is used with updated technology, K-9s, fists, clubs, or firearms, community perceptions conflict as do the community values that must be addressed by policy makers in police departments.

Issues surrounding excessive force are filled with emotion, fear, entrenched assumptions, class-and-race-based suspicions, and virtually intractable value conflicts. The chief has been receiving citizen complaints that the police officers are brutal. The department has no policy on excessive force, and the chief asks you to develop one.

Instructions.   Use the form in Appendix A to write a procedure directive. Write it so officers who deal with the problem have the direction, guidance, and technical information they need. Write the policy first and then the procedures in which you cover specific instances of potential public disturbances, demonstrations, and other peacekeeping needs.

Remember that police must use force at times to protect themselves or their communities from dangerous individuals. Most of the force used will be in public and at night. Also remember the imminent threat to officers' or other people's lives will depend on the types of calls they receive—for example, calls to high crime areas, "man with gun" calls, disturbance calls, and the like. The FBI Uniform Crime Reports are a good resource.

Application #3

You are also asked to review the portion of the department's policy and procedure directive that refers to hostage negotiators. Make six procedures that would be likely to enhance hostage negotiations.

Instructions. Keep in mind who will call in the negotiator, who evaluates the negotiation process, what the negotiator does with the information received, and who decides when to either continue or suspend negotiations.

An Exercise in Critical Thinking

Officers responding to a call regarding a criminal act must first deal with the emergency situation, this includes deciding how to approach the scene. Second, officers must attend to injuries and possibly apprehend a suspect. The next responsibility is to secure the crime scene. Finally, it is the officers' responsibility to conduct investigation interviews and interrogation and to collect evidence.

In the early afternoon of July 3, Walter Skramstad recognized Officer John McArthur driving a police car ahead of him. Walter closed in on McArthur, allegedly to ask him whether there would be either a dance or a demolition derby during the holiday weekend. The testimony conflicts as to whether Skramstad tried to run McArthur off the road or flag him down. Thereafter, both cars pulled over to the side of the road. Officer McArthur maintains that Skramstad got out of his car with his fists clenched. Using profanity, Skramstad vehemently threatened McArthur. A scuffle ensued in which McArthur broke Skramstad's jaw. Officer McArthur subsequently arrested Skramstad.

After arriving at the Law Enforcement Center, Skramstad told McArthur, "The next time I come after you, I'll put you in intensive care. I'm going to kill you. I'm going to get your family. I know where you live." As a result of these events, Skramstad was charged with making terroristic threats.

1. If you were to back up Officer McArthur and you had approached the scene just as the scuffle broke out, what would be your first actions?
   a. Make careful observations so that you can collect physical evidence and record exactly what was said and done by both parties.
   b. Look to see if other witnesses might be present so that you could interview them for corroboration.

c. Secure the crime scene so that evidence is preserved and no one else gets involved.

d. Prepare to attend to the injuries each has sustained.

e. Arrive as rapidly, yet as safely, as possible, and assist in apprehending the suspect.

2. Approximately a week before this incident, Skramstad and McArthur met at a gas station where they engaged in a heated argument during which Skramstad challenged McArthur to a fight and threatened to ''get'' McArthur's family.

a. Because physical safety has been threatened, use of violence on July 3 is justified.

b. If Skramstad has a prior conviction for aggravated assault, an officer would have the right to shoot to prevent Skramstad's escape.

c. An officer should first threaten, then give an order and try other sophisticated verbal interventions, and finally resort to distraction so that suspects see the consequences of their behavior.

d. Because Skramstad operates in a John Wayne style, officers can best communicate with him in the same style.

e. Physical violence is not justified, and courts will not support officers who use violence in cases of threats like Skramstad's.

3. As testimony is conflicting about whether Skramstad tried to run McArthur off the road or flag him down to ask information, how might you proceed to gather evidence as part of the preliminary investigation?

a. Refer to departmental data bases to discover previous Skramstad incidents.

b. Call for a crime-scene unit to set the objectives, develop a theory of the crime, and prepare a narrative description of the scene.

c. Seek and interview witnesses.

d. Look for fingerprints, blood, hair, bite marks, shoe and tire impressions, tool fragments and marks, glass fragments, paint marks, fibers, firearms, and other tangible evidence.

e. Photograph the scene and draw diagrams to show the positions of cars and persons.

Discussion Questions

1. What forces spark violence in our streets?
2. Select a recent popular movie you have seen that contains scenes of violence. Compare your reactions with those of other students or critics if it was reviewed. Discuss its effects on the general population who may see it.
3. If violence is only a symptom, name some disease it may be symptomatic of.
4. Have you ever participated in a demonstration? If so, what was the cause? How did you feel about participating? Was it peaceful?
5. What is the nature of people and the environment that creates a climate for violence and murder?
6. Have there been any violent demonstrations in your community in the past few years? Were they handled well by the police?
7. Have there been instances of police use of deadly force in your community? If so, were they justified?

Definitions

Can you define the following terms?

Automated Fingerprint Identification
   System (A.F.I.S.)
case tie
chain of possession
civil disobedience
crimes against persons
crimes against property
DNA fingerprinting

flashbangs
narcoterrorism
Part One Index offenses
Part Two Index offenses
preliminary investigation
Stockholm syndrome
Uniform Crime Reports

References

Anderson, Wayne and Bauer, Barbara. "Law Enforcement Officers: The Consequences of Exposure to Violence." *Journal of Counseling and Development* 65 (March 1987): 381–384.

Aradi, Lester. "The Police Dispatcher as Hostage Negotiator." *The Police Chief* (November 1989): 62.

Binkley, Lawrence L. "Futuristic System Helps Long Beach Corner Career Criminals." *The Police Chief* (April 1991): 142–145.

Blumenthal, Monica D.; Kahn, Robert C.; Andrews, Frank M; and Head, Kendra B. *Justifying Violence: Attitudes of American Men*. Ann Arbor, Mich.: Institute for Social Research, University of Michigan, 1972.

Bock, Walter H. "Law Enforcement: The Next Ten Years." *Law and Order* (May 1990): 94–97.

Brown, Richard Maxwell. "Historical Patterns of Violence." In *Violence in America, Protest, Rebellion, Reform*, vol. 2, Ted Robert Gurr, ed. Newbury Park, Calif.: Sage Publications, 1989.

Burnley, Jane Nady. "Foreword." In *Helping Crime Victims: Research, Policy, and Practice* by Albert R. Roberts. Newbury Park, Calif.: Sage Publications, 1990.

Christensen, Loren W. "Hate Warriors." *Law and Order* (September 1990): 73–76.

Fanton, Ben. "Rural Demonstrations." *Law and Order* (November 1990): 92–97.

Glidden, Ronald C. "Establishing a Crime Scene Unit." *Law and Order* (June 1990): 53–55.

Heal, Sid. "Flashbangs: Effective Use of Diversionary Devices." *The Police Chief* (July 1990): 18–24.

Hueston, Harry R. "Battling the Animal Liberation Front." *The Police Chief* (September 1990): 52–54.

International Association of Chiefs of Police. "Crime Victims Bill of Rights." Board of Officers. Arlington, Vir.: International Association of Chiefs of Police, 1983.

Law Enforcement News
   1990a. "Fingering the Bad Guys: Dallas A.F.I.S. Gets Results." (October 31): 5.
   1990b. "New York Unveils A.F.I.S." (June 15/30): 4, 13.
   1990c. "Police Are Cautiously Hopeful as Use of Car-Theft Tracking Devices Grows." (June 15/30): 4.

Maher, George F. "Hostage Negotiations, pp. 274–277. In *Encyclopedia of Police Science*, W. G. Bailey, ed. New York: Garland Publishing, 1989.

Mallory, Jim. "Demonstrations." *Law and Order* (September 1990): 83–85.

Moore, Thomas. "Dead Zones: Whole Sections of Urban America Are Being Written Off." *U.S. News and World Report* (April 10, 1989): 20–32.

Mullins, Wayman C. "Terrorism in the '90s: Predictions for the United States." *The Police Chief* (September 1990): 44–46.

Revell, Oliver B. "Counter Terrorism: Planning and Operations." *The Police Chief* (August 1990): 61–67.

Roberts, Albert R. *Helping Crime Victims: Research, Policy, and Practice.* Newbury Park, Calif.: Sage Publications, 1990.

Russell, Harold E. and Beigel, Allan. *Understanding Human Behavior for Effective Police Work.* 3d ed. New York: Basic Books, 1990.

Sessions, William S. "Cooperative Efforts to Counter Terrorism." *The Police Chief* (August 1990): 11.

Shonberger, M. Frank. "Miami Police and A.F.I.S. Complete First Decade." *Law and Order* (November 1990): 85–89.

Stitt, B. Grant. "Ethical and Practical Aspects of Police Response to Hostage Situations," pp. 20–45. In *Issues in Justice: Exploring Policy Issues in the Criminal Justice System.* Roslyn Muraskin, ed. Bristol, Ind.: Wyndham Hall Press, 1990.

Strentz, Thomas. "Radical Right v. Radical Left: Terrorist Theory and Threat." *The Police Chief* (August 1990): 70–75.

Vaughn, Jerald R. "Three Emerging Issues Confronting Law Enforcement." *Law and Order* (November 1990): 71–73.

Waller, Irvin. "The Police: First in Aid?" Ch. 8, pp. 139–156. In *Victims of Crime: Problems, Policies, and Programs,* Arthur J. Jurigio et al., eds. Newbury Park, Calif.: Sage Publications, 1990.

Williams, David F., Jr. "The Skull and Crossbones Still Flies." *The Police Chief* (September 1990): 47–50.

Cases

Tennessee v. Garner, 471 U.S.1, 105 S.Ct. 1694, 85 L.Ed.2d1 (1985).

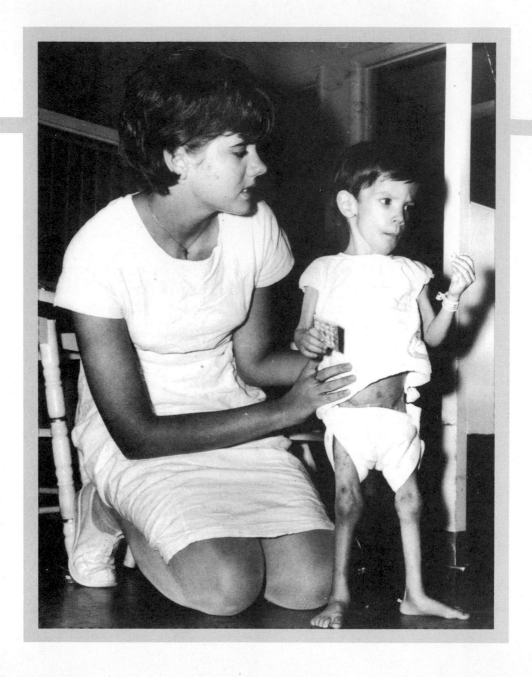

DOMESTIC VIOLENCE: TRAGEDY BEHIND CLOSED DOORS

CHAPTER **12**

INTRODUCTION

"The toughest thing about being a cop," says Behan, 1988, p. v), "is daily confronting the cruelty and abuse which family members inflict on one another. People tied by blood are supposed to have special reasons of love and loyalty to abstain from injuring, exploiting, or humiliating their kin." Traditionally, the American family has been viewed as a warm, loving place, with the father earning a living and the mother being a full-time homemaker. There was, however, a dark note lurking in the traditional notion, A man's home is his castle. To some, this notion included the right of men to discipline their wives and children in any way they saw fit, including physical punishment.

Times have changed. Many homes have single parents. Many other homes have both parents working. And most women no longer are willing to be subservient to men. It may well be that domestic violence has always existed, but that now women are speaking up about it.

In addition, the tensions of our complex society, the prevalence of drug and alcohol abuse, and the fact that people are living longer, often creating a strain on their children, also adds to the problem of domestic violence.

Children, the elderly, wives, husbands—in fact, anyone within a family unit—may be at risk of being a victim of domestic violence.

Sherman (n. d., p. 1) says that about one-fourth of all homicides and serious assaults are domestic and that, while hard to measure, " 'family' violence is probably the most widespread form

Do You Know

- Who is at risk of being a victim of domestic violence?
- What constitutes child abuse?
- How prevalent child abuse is?
- What constitutes elder abuse?
- How prevalent elder abuse is?
- What constitutes battering?
- How prevalent wife battering is?
- What the Minneapolis Experiment established?
- What law enforcement's responsibility is when domestic violence occurs?
- What the Tracy Thurman case established?
- How dangerous is police response to a domestic violence call?

of violence in the country and can occur in all social classes and income groups.''

People who live together usually form close relationships. They may also take their hurts and frustrations out on others within the family unit. As noted by Steinmetz (1988, p. xvi): ''The very nature of the family unit makes it fertile ground for tension and conflict. Closeness is likely to lead to friction; and the family is our most intimate and close-knit institution.''

It seems contradictory that the social unit people depend on for love and support can also foster violence. But this is true for thousands of homes. In fact, violence is often taught by parents who use physical force to discipline their children. Some parents even say, while administering a spanking or beating, ''This hurts me more than it hurts you.'' They truly believe that it is their responsibility to physically punish their children when they misbehave. Many parents also teach their children to defend themselves and to ''fight their own battles.'' Children come to learn that ''might makes right.''

Domestic violence knows no social bounds. It occurs in families of all socioeconomic and educational levels, although it is usually more likely to involve law enforcement at the lower levels. Domestic violence is often viewed by others, including those in law enforcement, as a family matter.

The President's Task Force on Victims of Crime (1982, pp. 49–50): says:

For those who live in a home where violence occurs, the pressures are tremendous. The assaults affect everyone in the house, not only the immediate victim, because of the ever-present threat of violence.

The decision to report this type of conduct to authorities is agonizing. The victim wrestles with feelings of fear, loyalty, love, guilt, and shame; often there is a sense of responsibility for other victims in the household. The victim also knows that reporting is a risk. All too often police or prosecutors minimize or ignore the problem and the victim is left alone to face an attacker who will respond with anger at being reported or incarcerated.

Victims often do not want to press charges and do not want the victimizer to be put in jail. They may not only fear retaliation, but also may not want to give up the income or the company of the abuser. All victims want is for the violence to stop. It seldom does, however. And, violence tends to be self-perpetuating. As Paisner (1991, p. 35) notes:

Violence is learned behavior. Children who have witnessed abuse or have been abused themselves are 1,000 times more likely to abuse a spouse or child when they become adults than are children raised in a home without violence.

Child Abuse

Why parents abuse their children is a perplexing question. Sometimes it is out of frustration. Sometimes it is from unrealistic expectations. Often abusing parents feel their children ''have it coming'' because of words or actions.

Closely related to physical abuse is child neglect. Parents who do not provide their children with the food, clothing, and nurturing they require are guilty of neglect. Such neglect can be just as damaging to the child as physical abuse. Frequently, child abuse and neglect occur together. Such children grow up with poor self-images and view the world as hostile and violent. As noted, these children tend to perpetuate this hostility and violence in their lives and, should they marry, within their future family.

Sexual abuse of children is another critical problem that must be dealt with by law enforcement. Sexual abuse is usually much less obvious than physical abuse.

Physical abuse of adolescents is not as common because they are more able to defend themselves or even to strike back. But psychological abuse can be even more devastating. Adolescence is a difficult time for many youth as they experience physical and emotional changes. Their emerging sexuality and growing independence can be extremely difficult to live with. They may become involved with drugs or alcohol. They may join gangs. At the same time, their parents may be entering middle age and facing their own personal crises.

As noted by Drowns and Hess (1990, p. 424), child abuse is: "Any physical, emotional, or sexual trauma to a child for which no reasonable explanation, such as an accident, can be found. Child abuse includes neglecting to give proper care and attention to a young child."

Child abuse *includes intentional physical, mental, or sexual trauma as well as the intentional neglect of the basic needs of the child.*

When parents become abusive to adolescents, the youth have an option not available to younger children—they can simply run away. Many become part of the homeless population and often turn to prostitution or crime to support themselves. Girls tend to run away from home more frequently than boys. This may be because they are not usually as strong physically and are therefore not able to strike back or defend themselves. In addition, they are more likely to be victims of sexual abuse. Finally, girls tend to mature faster than boys and are therefore better able to strike out on their own.

The Metropolitan Court Judges Committee Report (1986, p. 6) notes that:

. . . as many as four or five million children are neglected or physically or sexually abused each year, with an additional two million vulnerable as runaways or missing. . . .

Studies have indicated astounding correlations between child abuse and deviant behavior among violent juvenile delinquents and among adults who had committed violent crimes. Most violent criminals have been severely physically abused as children. . . . Those who experience violent and abusive childhoods are more likely to become child or spouse abusers than those who have not.

Four to five million children are abused or neglected each year.

The Police Response

When police are called about child abuse, their first responsibility is to the child. In many states, if it appears that the child is in danger, police may take that child into protective custody. Their next responsibility is to thoroughly investigate the situation. Interviews with family members, medical records, reports from welfare workers, interviews with neighbors can all help determine if a charge of child abuse is warranted. The interviews can also provide information as to whether the child can be returned to the home or placed in a foster home.

Police must be especially careful when charges of sexual abuse of children are involved. Such charges will destroy reputations, even if unfounded.

Police should also be alert to children who are present when adults are arrested. Often additional charges of *endangering children* should be made, and those children should also be taken into protective custody. Duvall (1991, p. 73) cites several recent examples of such rescue operations:

- A traffic officer making a Willful Fleeing/DUI arrest discovers small children inside the vehicle.
- A vice officer makes a deal for sex from a prostitute in her apartment, with her seven-year-old daughter present.
- A patrol officer makes an intox arrest of a female inside a bar and discovers her small infant asleep in the parked car during the dead of winter.

Duvall (p. 76) suggests: "In today's society, officers have to be alert to the many dimensions of criminal activity. A drug investigation, DUI arrest, or domestic dispute call could very well be the best thing to ever happen to a child if an alert officer remembers the child's future when charging the adult."

Cooperative Efforts

Cedar Rapids, Iowa, provides a model for investigating and treating child abuse cases. Their Child Protection Center (CPC) is operated jointly by the police de-

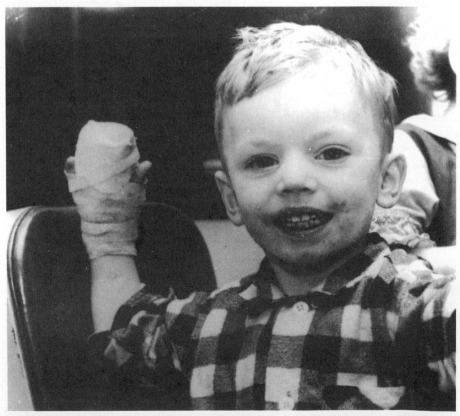

This young boy received second and third degree burns when his parents held his hand over their stove's gas flame to teach him not to turn on the stove. They were charged with cruelty to a child.

partment and St. Luke's Hospital. The center's medical personnel are trained in conducting exams and gathering evidence for the prosecution of abuse cases. An interviewing room is equipped with state-of-the-art videotaping equipment and also has a two-way mirror so officers and personnel from the Department of Human Services can observe the child being interviewed. As noted by Hinzman and Blome (1991, p. 24): "This cooperative interviewing process frequently spares the child from being interviewed repeatedly."

Abuse of the Elderly

The elderly may be as vulnerable to violence as children are. Plotkin (1988, p. 3) defines *elder abuse* as encompassing "physical and emotional abuse, financial exploitation, and general neglect."

Elder abuse *includes the physical and emotional trauma, financial exploitation, and general neglect of a person aged sixty-five or older.*

Just as it is difficult to understand how parents could abuse their children, it is difficult to understand how adult children could abuse their elderly parents. According to the Riverside Mental Health Services (1991, p. 7), certain situations put older adults at greater risk for being abused:

- The care needed may exceed the abilities of the caregiver.
- Unable to meet even their own basic needs (dressing, eating, toileting), the older adult may have to depend solely on a caregiver, making such care a twenty-four-hour a day responsibility.
- Some caregivers are incapable of caring for someone other than themselves because of youth, immaturity, chemical abuse, mental illness, or physical problems.
- Often caregivers may be forced into their role because they are dependent on the elder emotionally and financially.
- There may be a past history of family violence for the caregiver, abuse may be an acceptable way of dealing with stress, nonconforming behaviors, or control issues.
- Often caregivers do not have any relief from their responsibilities—no backup and no support.

Abuse of the elderly has received increasing attention as more cases come to light. Abuse of elderly parents who live with their children is very often unreported because the elderly parents either do not know who to report it to or are physically unable to report the abuse. They may, for example, be bedridden, with no telephone within reach and no visitors.

Roberts (1990, pp. 80–81) suggests the following reasons for nonreporting of elder abuse:

1. The feelings of guilt and shame at having raised children who are physically abusing them prevent many elderly victims from acting. They choose to suffer in silence rather than face the embarrassment of having others know.

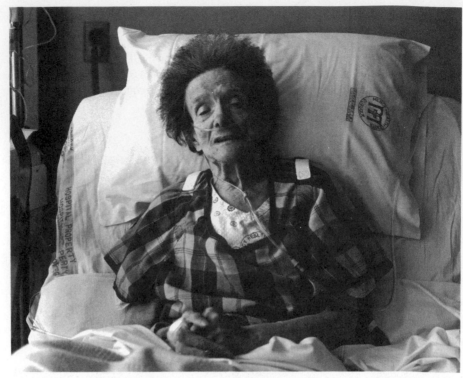

Thousands of elderly Americans are totally dependent on others for their care. This can cause family tensions and may result in elder abuse.

2. An elderly parent may fear that the adult child will retaliate with increased and more intense maltreatment if the abuse is reported.
3. An elderly abuse victim may fear that if he or she reports the abuse, the caretaker will be arrested and then incarcerated. The removal of the caretaker from the home could result in the victim being placed in a nursing home.
4. The most frequent victims of battering and neglect are aged 75 and older, and these persons are more likely to be disoriented, confused, impaired, and incapable of taking care of their own physical needs than their younger (65–74 years of age) counterparts. Some members of this age group are unaware of what is going on around them and are also unfamiliar with procedures for reporting elder abuse.
5. Victims of elder abuse do not report the abuse because of the hope that the most recent incident of abuse was the last one and that it will not be repeated.

Elderly residents in nursing homes have also been abused, physically and sexually, by caregivers and sometimes even by other residents. As with the elderly parents living with their children, nursing home residents may have no way to contact help.

Many other elderly people are not physically abused; they are simply neglected, deprived of all but the most basic necessities. According to Riverside Medical Center Mental Health Services (1991, p. 7): ''Currently some studies suggest that 500,000 to 2.5 million older persons (over age 65) are abused or neglected each year.''

The number of cases of elder abuse is probably between
500,000 and 2.5 million.

The Riverside Medical Center also notes:

- Only one in six cases are reported.
- Most victims of elder abuse are women. The typical victim is 75 years of age and physically and perhaps mentally dependent.
- The older the person, the higher the rate of being abused. Advanced age is often associated with physical and mental impairments and the older elderly are more vulnerable and less able to resist abuse.
- A relative, usually an adult child of the victim, is found to be the most common abuser.
- Abuse can happen anywhere, in any family, neighborhood, or nursing home.
- Literature suggests there are multiple causes of abuse and that most instances are not intentional and preconceived but are the result of the accumulation of stress and limited knowledge and resources for the person providing care.

The Police Response

The Police Executive Research Forum and the American Association of Retired Persons (AARP) conducted a joint study to investigate the police response to domestic elder abuse. Of the 200 agencies receiving the survey, 88 percent responded (Plotkin, 1988, pp. 20–26). Key finds of this survey include the following:

- Only 2 percent indicated elder abuse was a major problem, 54 percent indicated it was "somewhat of a problem," and 44 percent indicated it was "no problem."
- Of the agencies responding, 43 percent did not know how elder abuse cases came to their attention; of the remaining responding agencies, 12 percent of the cases were reported by concerned individuals, 11 percent by social service agencies, 9 percent by the elderly victim, 9 percent discovered while investigating a complaint or disturbance, and 2 percent by a family member (14 percent of the agencies had no reported cases).
- Nearly one-third of all departments surveyed were unaware of laws related to elder abuse and neglect, even though such governing laws existed in their state.
- Few departments had a means for distinguishing elder abuse from the more general crimes of assault, battery, and fraud.

The report recommends that domestic elder abuse be defined as a crime separate from assault, battery, burglary, murder, or some other category. This would accomplish two purposes: raise awareness of the problem and help outline a proper police response to the problem.

Physical evidence of assault or neglect is vital to establishing a charge of elder abuse. Often the victim is confused or unable to grasp what has happened. Victims often have impaired mental abilities or memories. In such instances, information provided by other people becomes extremely important.

If elderly victims live at home, all those who have contact with the victims should be interviewed. If elderly victims live with one of their children, all members of the family should be interviewed. If elderly victims live in a nursing home, other residents of the home as well as the care providers should be interviewed. The past record of the institution should be looked into, including any violations of licensing standards reported to the state department of human services or whatever agency issues licenses to nursing homes.

Cooperative Efforts

Cooperative efforts in this area are critical and can include social workers, mental health workers, elder protective services, hospital workers, shelters for the elderly, and transportation services. Rogers (1990, p. 81) suggests:

> *The protection and provision of services for victims of elder abuse and neglect should be the joint responsibility of a network of community agencies, including victim-assistance programs, family violence programs and shelters, police departments, visiting nurses' associations, in-home respite-care programs, hospital senior-care programs, and senior community centers.*

Battered Women

Often in a home where there is child abuse or elder abuse, there is also wife beating. Because marriage is such an intimate and complex relationship, it is especially at risk for violence when things go wrong. The same is true between couples who are not married but who are living together or have a relationship. But battering does not happen only in a marriage or relationship gone wrong; the battering may be inherent in the abuser's approach to any relationship.

***Battering** is the use of physical, emotional, economic, or sexual force to control another person.*

Battering is about power and control. It can take many forms, as illustrated in Figure 12.1. According to *Newsweek* (1990, p. 23), three to four million women are battered each year; every eighteen seconds a woman is beaten. More than one million women seek medical assistance for injuries caused by battering each year.

Three to four million women are battered each year.

Roberts and Roberts (1990, p. 187) suggest:

> *Battered women are usually subjected to a prolonged pattern of abuse coupled with a recent severe attack, so that by the time the victim makes contact with a shelter, she is generally in need of crisis intervention. Abused women are subjected to an extended period of stress and trauma, which results in a*

FIGURE 12.1
A Perspective on Battering
Source: Domestic Abuse Intervention Project, Duluth, MN. Reprinted by permission.

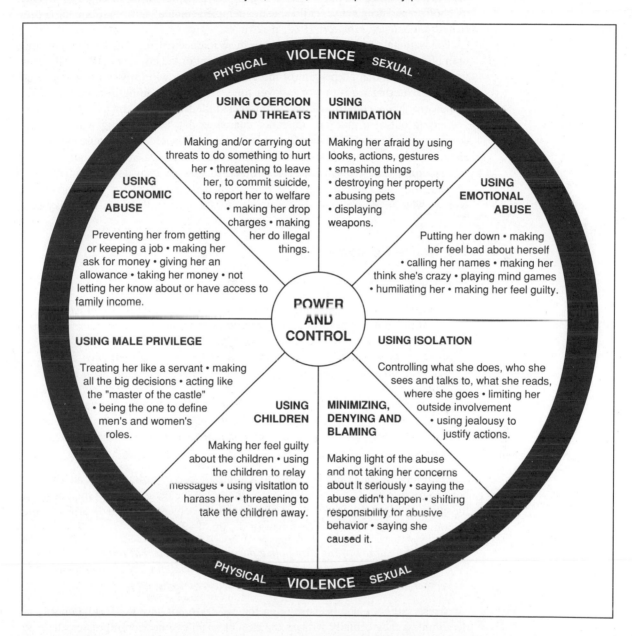

continual loss of energy. A battered woman is in a vulnerable position, and when a particularly severe beating takes place, or when other factors occur (e.g., the abuser starts to hurt the children), she may be thrust into a state of crisis.

Batterers are not only violent, most are extremely jealous, suspicious, and possessive. Most also have very traditional ideas about the relationship between men and women and may tend to isolate their wives or girlfriends from family and friends.

A five-year study at Yale-New Haven Hospital concluded that 40 percent of all injury-related visits to the hospital by women were the result of battering. The study also disclosed that battering was a major precipitating factor in cases of female alcoholism and drug abuse, child abuse, attempted suicide, and situational disorders (*Christian Science Monitor,* 1988, p. 24).

The National Coalition Against Domestic Violence (NCADV) cautions that children often witness the battering and that 60 percent of the boys who do so will grow up to batter and that 50 percent of the girls who do so will grow up to be battered women. Battering tends to worsen over time, sometimes ending in death. In 1986, 40 percent of all women homicide victims were killed by male relatives or boyfriends.

Getting out of a marriage does not guarantee that the battering will end. According to the Bureau of Justice Statistics figures, in 75 percent of spouse-on-spouse assaults, the victims were separated or divorced at the time of the assault.

Sometimes being battered drives women to kill the man doing the battering. Movies such as *The Burning Bed* have helped to publicize the predicament of women who are beaten by their husbands and the lengths to which they may go.

The Police Response

According to Parker et al. (1989, p. 113):

Intervention in family disputes has long been regarded by police officers as one of the more difficult and distasteful aspects of the job. There are a number of reasons for this view. Many officers consider dealing with family problems to be social work and thus beyond the realm of their own responsibilities and expertise. Officers are often uncomfortable with the intimate nature of the problems presented, or have marital problems of their own that are disconcertingly similar. Some feel that the battered spouse (usually a woman) must have stimulated the abuse in some way, or believe that a little slap here or there is an acceptable way to keep a wayward spouse in line.

Traditionally, the police response to a domestic call regarding wife battering has been to try to mediate the situation or to simply get the batterer out of the house for the night. Unless the police were threatened or actually assaulted, arrests were seldom made. According to Sherman (n.d., pp. 1–2):

In 1984, a survey of big city police departments found that only 10 percent encouraged officers to make arrests in domestic violence cases, while 40 percent still encouraged mediation and 50 percent had no policy at all.

Arrests are not made because often the police do not have the legal authority to do so unless they actually witness the assault or unless the victim presses charges. Only twenty-eight states allow police to make arrests for battering that they did not actually see themselves. And sometimes, making an arrest only adds to the violence as the batterer seeks to avoid being arrested.

In addition, such cases are often not prosecuted vigorously. Sometimes the victim changes her mind and refuses to cooperate with the police. As noted by Valentine (1985, p. 11):

Currently the criminal justice system's response to battering is ineffective. Police agree that prosecutors too often fail to convict; prosecutors agree that police seldom arrest; judges agree that sentencing alternatives fail to include effective rehabilitation services; and underneath it all, everybody claims that the victims are somehow to blame.

Over a decade ago, the Police Foundation published a monograph, *Domestic Violence and the Police: Studies in Detroit and Kansas City.* These studies reported that, during the two years preceding a domestic assault or domestic homicide, in over half the cases police had been called to the address of the incident at least five times before. In other words, as noted by James Q. Wilson: "Contrary to popular thought, opportunities do exist to combat domestic violence" (Police Foundation, 1977, p. 2).

Emotional abuse is also prevalent in many homes and can be just as destructive. Emotional abuse ranges from ignoring a wife or girlfriend to belittling and downgrading her, shouting at her, criticizing her in public, and the like. As with children who are mistreated, many women are both physically and emotionally abused.

The Minneapolis Experiment—The Domestic Abuse Intervention Project (DAIP)

In 1982, the National Institute of Justice (NIJ) and the Minneapolis Police Department conducted research on the problem of domestic violence. The majority of the victims were women beaten by their husbands, boyfriends, or former boyfriends; 80 percent of the victims had been assaulted by the suspect within the last six months. The majority of both victims and suspects were unemployed, in their early thirties, and were white. Minorities were disproportionately represented, however. Table 12.1 summarizes the characteristics of the victims and suspects included in the study.

TABLE 12.1
Characteristics of Victims and Suspects of Domestic Assault

The data is from initial interviews and police sheets; 205 cases were studied.

Relationship of suspect to victim	(%)	Unemployment		(%)
Divorced or separated husband	3	Victims		61
Unmarried male lover	45	Suspects		60
Current husband	35			
Wife or girlfriend	2	**Mean Age (years)**		
Son, brother, roommate, other	15	Victims		30
		Suspects		32
Prior assaults and police involvement	**(%)**	**Education (%)**	**Victim**	**Suspect**
Victims assaulted by suspect, last six months	80	Less than high school	43	42
Police intervention in domestic dispute, last six months	60	High school only	33	36
Couple in counseling program	27	More than high school	24	22
Prior arrests of male suspects	**(%)**	**Race (%)**	**Victim**	**Suspect**
Ever arrested for any offense	50	White	57	45
Ever arrested for crime against person	31	Black	23	36
Ever arrested on domestic violence statute	5	Native-American	18	16
Ever arrested on alcohol offense	29	Other	2	3

Source: From "The Minneapolis Domestic Violence Experiment" by the National Institute of Justice and the Minneapolis Police Department, 1982, p. 5. Courtesy of the Police Foundation.

The study examined three responses to domestic violence calls:

- Arrest the suspect.
- Give only advice to the suspect.
- Order the suspect to leave the premises.

Police were assigned a specific "designed treatment" to be used on each domestic violence call. Of those targeted for arrest, 99 percent were arrested; of those targeted to receive advice, 78 percent did receive only advice, and of those targeted to be ordered to leave the premises, 73 percent were sent away. The designed treatment and the treatment actually used are summarized in Table 12.2.

It is interesting to note that, in the designed treatments of "advise" and "separate," the delivered treatments were more dispersed. According to Sherman and Berk (1985, p. 123), an explanation for these results might be that ". . . mediating and sending were more difficult ways for police to control a situation. There was a greater likelihood that officers might have to resort to arrest as a fallback position. When the assigned treatment is arrest, there is no need for a fallback position."

Instances of repeat violence were looked at in two ways over a six-month period: (1) police records and (2) interviews with the victims. Figures 12.2 and 12.3 summarize the results of the six-month follow-up effort. Although the effectiveness of "advise" compared to "separate" is inconclusive from this study, the effectiveness of arrest is clear.

In the Minneapolis Experiment, arrest was clearly more effective than advice or sending the suspect away.

The results of this experiment do *not,* however, suggest that arrest is always the answer. Each case must still be looked at individually. Many cities did adopt this approach, dubbed the DAIP approach, to domestic violence, including New York

TABLE 12.2
Designed Police Treatment and that Actually Delivered in the Domestic Assault Cases Studied

	Delivered Treatment			
Designed Treatment	Arrest	Advise	Separate	
Arrest	98.9% N = 91*	0.0% N = 0	1.1% N = 1	29.3% N = 92
Advise	17.6% N = 19	77.8% N = 84	4.6% N = 5	34.4% N = 108
Separate	22.8% N = 26	4.4% N = 5	72.8% N = 83	36.3% N = 114
Total	43.3% N = 136	28.3% N = 89	28.3% N = 89	100% N=314

*"N" is actual number

Source: From "The Minneapolis Domestic Violence Experiment" by the National Institute of Justice and the Minneapolis Police Department, 1982, p. 4. Courtesy of the Police Foundation.

FIGURE 12.2
Police Records on Repeat Violence in 314 Cases Over a Six-Month Period
Source: "The Minneapolis Domestic Violence Experiment" by the National Institute of Justice and the Minneapolis Police Department, 1982, p. 1. Courtesy of the Police Foundation.

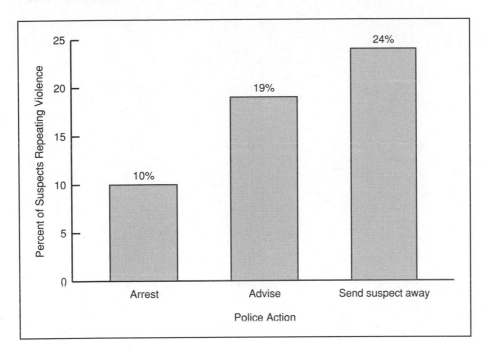

City, San Francisco, Houston, and Dallas. In October 1986, Connecticut passed Public Act 86-337 dealing with domestic violence (Parker et al., 1989, p. 115):

This Act reflects the Legislature's intent that domestic or family violence is no longer to be treated as a personal family matter, but is a crime and must be treated as such by the police, prosecution, and courts. If probable cause that a crime has occurred exists, the officer shall arrest the person suspected of committing the crime. Mandating arrests based on probable cause will insure that victims of family violence will be protected and the public will be informed that violence in the home is a crime and not to be tolerated.

Once on the scene, the officer is required by Public Act 86-337 to:

1. Assist the victim in obtaining medical treatment, if such is required.
2. Pursue an investigation to determine if a crime has occurred. Emphasis shall not be on mediation, but rather on determining if probable cause exists for an arrest.
3. Notify the victim of his/her rights to file an affidavit or warrant for arrest.
4. Inform the victim of the available resources, both at the local and state level in regards to support services, and the Criminal Injuries Compensation Board. The officer will give the victim an information card containing victims' rights and service phone numbers.

Public Act 86-337 requires that an officer's decision to arrest and charge shall not:

▪ Be dependent on the specific consent of the victim.

FIGURE 12.3
Victim Interviews on Repeat Violence in 161 Cases Over a Six-Month Period
Source: From "The Minneapolis Domestic Violence Experiment" by the National Institute of Justice and the Minneapolis Police Department, 1982, p. 4. Courtesty of the Police Foundation.

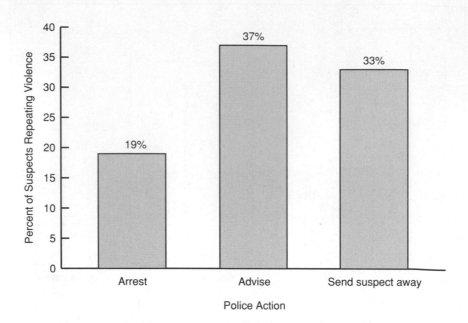

- Consider the relationship of the parties.
- Base the decision solely on a request by the victim.

According to Pence (1985), this approach has led to a decrease in domestic violence, a decrease in repeat calls, a decrease in police injuries on such calls, an increase in felony convictions, and an increase in victim satisfaction with the police and with the judicial system.

The Crime Control Institute surveyed police departments serving jurisdictions with populations of 100,000 and found an increase in proarrest policies (Paisner, 1991, p. 38). In 1984, 10 percent had such policies, compared with 46 percent in 1986. Benefits of proarrest policies include the following (p. 38):

- The victim begins to regain her self-confidence and seek help. . . .
- The assailant receives a message that his violent behavior is against the law, and that he will be treated accordingly. . . .
- The children in these violent homes benefit because they are often the overlooked victims. Since violence is learned behavior, it can also be unlearned. . . .
- Finally, the police also benefit. A strongly implemented proarrest domestic violence policy reduces repeat calls, which results in increased manpower availability. A police department's liability to multimillion-dollar damage awards in domestic violence cases will also decrease. On the street level, officers who have been trained to understand domestic violence will be less

frustrated by the actions of the victim and will no longer experience the feelings of helplessness they did when they could not make arrests.

Paisner (p. 38) concludes: "As more police departments become enlightened and proactive, and as more victims become aware of the support services available to them, the cycle of violence that is perpetuated throughout generations will slowly, but surely, begin to break."

It should be noted, however, that follow-up studies by Sherman tend to challenge his 1983 findings. According to Hodges and Brunswick (1991, p. 5A), an extensive study of 1,200 cases of domestic violence in a study in Milwaukee completed by Sherman in November 1991 shows that "mandatory arrests may exacerbate domestic battery." Sherman has begun to call for the repeal of mandatory arrest laws (p. 5A):

"This is not a matter of ideology," said Sherman, whose new study has aroused the ire of women's groups across the country. "We can't say for sure that mandatory arrests help battered women. But we can say for sure that in some cases it's going to backfire, especially among the unemployed."

He said his study shows that officers should be given latitude in deciding whether to make an arrest.

As is so often the case, discretion is always important.

Measures to Help Battered Women

Support groups, counseling programs, and shelters have been established throughout the country to help battered women. Laws have been passed to provide both temporary and permanent restraining orders, forbidding batterers to come anywhere near those they have assaulted. Such orders are sometimes ignored, however, and newspaper reports of women who have restraining orders being killed are all too common.

A two-frame editorial cartoon lampooned the effectiveness of such restraining orders. The first frame showed a man's fists, feet, a gun, a knife, and a baseball bat. The second frame showed a woman's hand holding a piece of paper containing the words *Restraining Order*.

More support is needed. One effective model is that of the Family Trouble Center, a cooperative venture between the Memphis Police Department and the community. The center offers anger management groups for batterers as well as crisis and support counseling for victims, mediation through contract, referral services to other agencies for protective shelter, alcohol and drug counseling, and community outreach. Center staff train police officers to use anger management techniques when responding to domestic violence calls. Officers also leave a Family Trouble Center warning and referral sheet on all such calls. This sheet, according to Stern (1991, p. 73), contains the following:

One side of the sheet addresses the abuser: "WARNING! You can be arrested for hitting or threatening another person with physical harm. . . . Get Help Now! Stop Your Illegal Behavior." (That wife beating is a crime and not an acceptable part of a man's duty to keep his wife in line still surprises a great number of offenders. In fact, only in 1977 did it become illegal in every state.) The reverse side is directed to the victim: "NO ONE HAS THE RIGHT

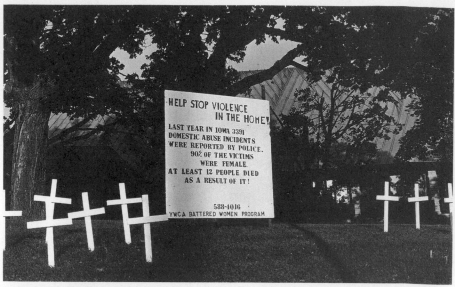

A woman's shelter in Iowa. Such shelters often also provide care for children and for abused husbands.

TO HARM OR THREATEN TO HARM ANOTHER PERSON. . . . Call for advice or shelter." Several agencies and choices of action are listed.

Husband Abuse

Although not as prevalent as wife battering, husband or boyfriend battering also exists. Some women are much larger and stronger than their husbands or boyfriends and may beat them at will. Others are physically inferior to the men in their lives, but the men, when hit, will not hit back. Further, women tend to use weapons as equalizers, therefore the physical harm may be greater. Husbands and boyfriends can also be emotionally abused through belittling, name-calling, ridiculing in public, and the like.

The Police Response

It is often difficult for police to believe that a woman can physically abuse a man. They may tend to downplay the seriousness of the call and may actually blame the man for being such a weakling or coward. As with any other assault, a woman battering a man must be investigated thoroughly. If probable cause exists to believe that an assault has occurred and that the woman did it, she should be arrested.

Trends in Responding to Calls about Domestic Violence

Legislative bodies have placed the burden of settling domestic disputes largely on the shoulders of the police. "The most vigorously pursued strategy to control violence in the home has been the criminalization of the domestic violence of-fenses," says Hamm (1989, p. 38). "During the 1980s, over half of the states around the country implemented policies to expand police powers by enacting probable cause, warrantless arrest legislation governing misdemeanor assault and battery." For example, as noted by Plotkin (1988, p. 35):

> *The policy of the Denver Police Department is to view all domestic violence complaints as instances of alleged criminal conduct. "Arrest, charging and taking custody of the suspect(s) involved, shall be deemed the most appropriate law enforcement response when officers determine that probable cause exists in domestic violence situations," [from the] Denver, Colorado, Domestic Violence Manual, 1986, and Denver Police Department Operations Manual.*

Other strategies which may also effectively address the problem include using protective and restraining orders and assuring that these orders are adhered to, providing family violence shelters, and establishing programs to rehabilitate those who commit domestic violence.

Brown (1988, pp. 271–273) examined police officers' operational styles in fam-ily violence incidents and found that experience was a key factor in whether officers made an arrest. Two other important factors were whether the officers were seeking promotion and how broad they felt their discretionary powers were.

Basically, the arrest decision hinges on how vulnerable the responding officers feel. The most vulnerable patrol officers, according to Brown (p. 272), are "those with less than five years experience, those who desire a promotion, and those who believe their discretion is severely limited by administrators." These patrol officers said they did not make an arrest because they did not have a signed complaint from the victim.

Effective Intervention in Domestic Disputes

The domestic dispute requires special skills, especially communications and nego-tiating skills, on the part of law enforcement. Family violence has a strong tendency to repeat, and officers are often called back several times—sometimes in the same evening. It also tends to escalate. Effective handling of the first few calls can greatly decrease the number of such calls.

In most crimes, the responsibilities of the responding officers are clear-cut: gather evidence supporting the elements of the crime, determine who is responsible, and make an arrest. Responsibilities in domestic violence calls are much less clear-cut. Often it is not at all obvious who is responsible. Frequently both parties are at fault, but the violence must still be ended. Even if one party is clearly to blame, it is usually a mistake for officers to take sides in a domestic dispute. They must maintain their objectivity. Responsibilities at the scene of domestic violence include the following:

- Stop the violence.
- Separate those in conflict.
- Administer medical assistance if required.
- Determine if assault has occurred.
- If no probable cause for an arrest exists, mediate the situation. Get them to talk it out, to stop shouting and fighting and to start talking and thinking about their situation.

- If mediation is not possible, order the abusive spouse out of the house.
- Suggest possible solutions and sources of assistance to the abused person.
- If probable cause supporting the crime of assault does exist, make an arrest.

Police officers responding to a domestic violence call are responsible for investigating it thoroughly as an assault and for making an arrest if probable cause exists.

After the abuser has been arrested and removed from the scene, a thorough investigation is needed, including comprehensive interviews with the victim and any witnesses. Obtain information about the frequency and intensity of the domestic violence as well as any previous police contacts. Photographs should be taken of injuries and of indications of the level of violence, such as tipped over or broken furniture, smashed objects, and the like. Any evidence of the violence should be properly collected.

Connor (1990, p. 66) suggests that domestic violence is not just a police problem, it is a societal problem. The police, however, "can and must become the advocate for action; they can be the most immediate and eminent agents for change." The approach Connor suggests is for police departments to develop a "model proarrest policy." That is, the assumption is made that police responding to a domestic call will plan to arrest the perpetrator of domestic violence if sufficient probable cause for arrest exists. As noted, in twenty-eight states, police officers can arrest for offenses not committed in their presence. More states are likely to adopt such legislation. Says Connor (p. 66):

> *Research indicates that an arrest tends to prevent further criminal behavior, reduces risks to officers as a result of incident reduction, reduces risks to the victim, encourages and supports the victim's perception of rights, initiates an increased opportunity for long-term, therapeutic treatment for those involved, and positions the officer in less likelihood of future civil litigation.*

"Failure to Protect" Lawsuits

According to Clede (1990, p. 68), in many states officers who have evidence that an assault has occurred have no choice but to make an arrest. He cites the Tracy Thurman case as largely responsible for this change in approach:

> *Tracy Thurman had complained before about her estranged husband, Charles (Buck) Thurman, enough that police apparently took an "oh, no, not again" attitude. For whatever reason, when Thurman was stabbed 13 times and kicked in the head in a violent attack by her husband on June 10, 1983, police response was seen by the jury as less than adequate.*

Thurman sued the police department for "failure to protect" and was awarded $2.6 million dollars. The department appealed and Thurman later settled out of court for $1.975 million. According to Bangham (1986, p. 52), the suit "heralded the end of the traditional law enforcement approach to domestic violence." The case resulted in the passage of the Family Violence Protection and Response Act in Connecticut. The message in the law is clear: domestic violence is a crime.

The Tracy Thurman case established that domestic violence is an assault rather than simply a family affair. Officers and departments can be sued for "failure to protect."

Since its passage, 60,000 arrests have been made under the law. Bangham (1986, pp. 52, 54) presents the following guidelines for investigating domestic violence cases:

1. The duty of the responding officer is to look for signs of probable cause.
2. Emphasis is not on mediation but rather on determining—through normal police investigative techniques—whether probable cause exists for an arrest. . . . If an officer arrives at the scene of a domestic assault and finds multiple injuries, a threatening spouse and a terrorized victim, it's clear that the situation presents a high degree of probable cause. If, however, there is no injury, the victim is uncooperative, and the offender has left the scene, there is a low degree of probable cause.
3. Apply established and recognized officer skills when investigating a domestic assault. Compassion must play a role.
4. The administration must establish a written arrest policy that mandates arrest when probable cause exists. . . . Finding probable cause usually takes less time than it does to mediate the crisis, and less time at the scene means less possibility of injury to the officer. The most important reason for adopting an arrest policy is that help can begin promptly for both the victim and the offender.
5. The decision to arrest should not rest with the victim. . . . The victim is unlikely to press charges for many reasons: she may fear for her life, her children's safety, or the loss of income.
6. Immediately remove the offender from the scene when probable cause is established.
7. Provide support for the victim. Give the victim a list of social service agencies to which she can turn for help, including shelters for battered women, welfare agencies, members of the clergy, counseling services, and women's help organizations.

The Danger of Domestic Calls

It is commonly thought that a domestic call can be one of the most dangerous calls police officers receive. Indeed, some calls are extremely dangerous, even fatal, for the responding officer(s). Connor (1990, p. 66) says: "In reference to frequency and intensity of actual as well as perceived danger to the police, no other call qualifies to the degree as that of a domestic complaint." He notes that according to FBI figures, 160 police officers have been killed in the last twenty years while intervening in domestic calls. However, as noted by Garner and Clemmer (1987, p. 2), "The notion that domestic disturbances are one of the most dangerous police assignments relies on the assumption that the FBI 'disturbance' category is in great part composed of *domestic* disturbance incidents. . . . *This assumption is wrong.''* They go on to note:

> *The widespread belief that domestic disturbances are particularly dangerous to the police is found to be without a sound empirical basis. . . . A careful review of the empirical evidence demonstrates that [domestic disturbances] account for less than 6 percent of all felonious deaths of police officers, less than one-third that commonly cited in the previous research.*

According to Sherman (n.d., p. 2), the belief that domestic calls are unusually dangerous is based on old FBI statistics that combine all types of disturbance calls and that new analysis presents a different picture:

> *A recent breakdown of those figures provided by the FBI showed that most police killed in disturbance calls were dealing with bar fights. The number actually killed in family quarrels was a much smaller fraction, and less even than the number of officers shot accidentally by other police officers. Thus, police face more danger from one another than from domestic calls.*

Data on police officer deaths for the twelve-year period from 1973 to 1984, summarized in Figure 12.4, show that robbery is the most hazardous call.

FIGURE 12.4
Officer Deaths: Separating Deaths from Domestic Disputes from Deaths from Other Disturbances
Source: From "Danger to Police in Domestic Disturbances—A New Look. (Research Brief) by National Institute of Justice, November 1986, U.S. Department of Justice, National Institute of Justice, Washington, D.C. p. 3.

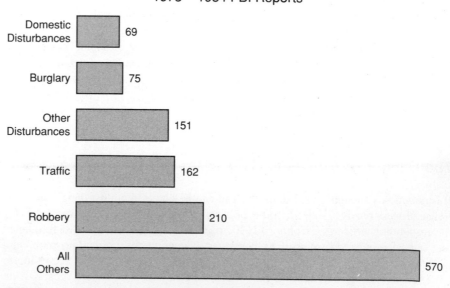

1973 – 1984 FBI Reports

Domestic Disturbances	69
Burglary	75
Other Disturbances	151
Traffic	162
Robbery	210
All Others	570

Number of Felonious Deaths

Brothers and partners of a Boston police officer killed in the line of duty during a drug bust serve as pall bearers at his funeral. Domestic calls can be equally hazardous for responding officers.

---

*Responding to a domestic violence call is hazardous, but not
as hazardous as is often thought.*

The fact remains, however, that at least 69 police officers lost their lives responding to domestic disturbance calls in the United States over the past decade (Garner and Clemmer, 1987).

A Change in Perspective

The traditional police perception that domestic violence calls are hazardous social work might be enlarged by looking at the positive results that could be accomplished. As suggested by Friedman and Shulman (1990, pp. 100–101),

> *Ironically, domestic violence may be more amenable to law enforcement and criminal justice intervention than most other crimes. It is ironic because domestic violence is a crime that has been avoided, devalued, and joked about by police, prosecutors, and judges. It is amenable because data and experience are showing that, unlike drug dealers, burglars, and muggers (criminals who are notorious recidivists), batterers may change their behavior in response to sanctions—warrants issued, arrests made, and jail time served. While the goals of sentencing—deterrence, rehabilitation, and retribution—elude the system for the most part, they appear attainable in*

domestic cases: offenders respond to arrests and jailing (specific deterrence), some abusers learn to be nonviolent (rehabilitation), and the victim feels justice is done (retribution). Therefore, rather than perceiving domestic cases as a millstone, criminal justice practitioners should perhaps view family cases—if treated as a crime and handled with special procedures—as cases that can burnish their image, and now the promise, not the frailties of the system.

Summary

Children, the elderly, wives, husbands—in fact, anyone within a family unit—may be at risk of being a victim of domestic violence. Child abuse includes intentional physical, mental, or sexual trauma as well as the intentional neglect of the basic needs of a child. Four to five million children are abused or neglected each year.

Elder abuse includes the physical and emotional trauma, financial exploitation, and general neglect of a person aged sixty-five or older. The number of cases of elder abuse is probably between 500,000 and 2.5 million.

Battering is the use of physical, emotional, economic, or sexual force to control another person. Three to four million women are battered each year. In the Minneapolis Experiment, police officers responding to domestic violence calls found that arrest was clearly more effective than advice or sending the suspect away. Police officers responding to a domestic violence call are responsible for investigating it thoroughly as an assault and for making an arrest if probable cause exists.

The Tracy Thurman case established that domestic violence is an assault rather than simply a family affair. Officers and departments can be sued for "failure to protect." Responding to a domestic violence call *is* hazardous, but not as hazardous as is often thought.

Application

As the officer in charge of the records bureau, you have noted an extraordinary amount of activity this past year in family violence. The officers' reports show that dispositions have been erratic and, in some cases, officers' actions have caused more serious violence. You bring this to the attention of the chief and other members of the department through their supervisors. You are instructed to get input for formulating a policy and procedures to handle family violence calls.

The statement of need should include the fact that family violence is a serious crime and that victims of such violence are not receiving the maximum protection that the law and those who enforce the law can provide. Write the need statement first.

Then state the purpose of the policy establishing procedures in family violence cases. Make sure the policy and procedures do not interfere with officers' individual discretion when it is needed. This should be stated in the policy.

In the procedures that follow, provide guidelines on how officers should proceed when the family dispute is a misdemeanor and how they should proceed when it is a felony. Cite the state law or city ordinance governing these procedures. Also state when an arrest should be made. If necessary, contact your local police department or sheriff's office for examples of a policy and procedures that would be useful as guidelines.

Exercises in Critical Thinking

343

CHAPTER 12
Domestic Violence:
Tragedy Behind
Closed Doors

> *At the scene of domestic violence, officers are to stop the violence, separate*
> *those in conflict, administer medical assistance if required, and determine if*
> *assault has occurred that justifies arrest. If no probable cause for arrest*
> *exists, officers are to mediate so that the fighting and shouting stops and the*
> *talking and thinking begins. If mediation is not possible, officers should order*
> *the abusive spouse out and suggest possible solutions and sources of*
> *assistance to the abused person.*

On November 22, Officers David Miller and Peter Kelly were called to investigate a disturbance of the peace at 1131 Selby Avenue, St. Paul, Minnesota, reported by Jeanne McDowell, a neighbor. In the past month, several domestic disturbances had been reported and investigated at this address, which officers know is the residence of Eddie and Donna Konkler.

While approaching 1131 Selby, the officers heard a loud male voice shouting obscenities, the sound of breaking glass, two loud thumps, and the muffled sounds of children crying. Officer Miller knocked loudly on the door and called out to Eddie. Eddie opened the door. He held a revolver in his right hand, and his breath smelled of alcohol. Donna was sitting on the floor leaning against a wall. She had a bloody nose and several red marks on her face. Broken glass was scattered around the room.

Officer Miller was successful in talking Eddie into relinquishing the revolver and in quieting him, but for fifteen minutes, Eddie and Donna continued shouting and cursing at each other and at the officers. During this time, Officer Kelly assisted Donna in stopping the bleeding, and she became subdued. Eddie continued his verbal abuse, so the officers requested that Eddie leave the house until he became calm. Eddie then told the police he was sorry and would not cause any more trouble. The officers gave suggestions for possible agencies that could help and suggested specific places where Donna could receive assistance if future repetitions of abuse were to occur.

1. What mistake did Officers Miller and Kelly make?
   a. Because of the cold weather in Minnesota, Eddie should not be removed from his residence; a firm warning and threat of arrest would be sufficient.
   b. Police should not approach a domestic disturbance by letting an abusive person know who they are. The abuser should not be given a chance to then draw a dangerous weapon.
   c. Police should not allow the parties to refuse to talk to one another—make the two stop fighting and shouting, and then insist that they talk and think about their situation so that mediation can bring about a solution to their problem.
   d. Repeated domestic abuse and an assault involving the display of a dangerous weapon justifies an arrest for second-degree assault.
   e. The officers should write out a ticket for disturbing the peace, but cases of domestic problems do not involve an arrest for criminal sexual conduct, kidnapping, terroristic threats, or second-degree assault.

William Mosby, age 34, had known the mother and family of N.D. for seven years. Immediately before the events in question, Mosby had lived with N.D.'s family for three weeks. At the end of the third week, N.D.'s mother gave permission for N.D. to go grocery shopping with Mosby while she went to work. After going to the cleaners, grocery store, and liquor store, Mosby took her back to the apartment building. There Mosby had N.D. scrub a shower stall. He gave her a robe to change into, saying he would wash her clothes with his laundry. N.D. reported that Mosby, who had been drinking beer, had N.D. sit on his lap. N.D. reported that Mosby said, "I want to have a baby by you." But N.D. said she was not ready for that. After taking a shower, Mosby came and stood naked in front of N.D. He then put on some boxer shorts, sat on the bed, and asked N.D. to comb his hair. Mosby then told her to lay down and asked if she "ever had a dicky before." He then put his finger in her vagina and touched her chest. N.D. began crying and Mosby slapped her, telling her to shut up, and tried to get the robe off. When she ran to unlock the door, Mosby told her to lock the door, or he was going to beat her. However, N.D. unlocked the door and ran screaming to the caretaker's apartment. The caretaker testified that Mosby, wearing only boxer shorts, came running after N.D. and asked the caretaker if he believed N.D. N.D. told the caretaker to look at her, opened the robe, and said, "Look at what I've got on." Mosby kept closing the door to the caretaker's apartment, and the caretaker kept opening it. A next-door tenant came and said she had called the police. Mosby looked excited, jumped up, and left the apartment building. The next-door tenant took N.D. to the tenant's apartment. N.D. threw up while there. The police let N.D. go home without being given a medical examination.

2. What is the responsibility of the police who arrive on the scene?
   a. Having made sure that physical violence has ceased, the police are responsible to advise the mother on her rights and responsibilities.
   b. Police should require the caretaker to notify them if Mosby returns and again causes trouble.
   c. Police must interview all witnesses, determine if there is a substantial basis for finding probable cause for criminal sexual conduct, procure an arrest warrant, and go out to search for Mosby.
   d. As no probable cause for arrest exists, mediate so that emotions can calm down, and help the mother and N.D. start talking about their situation by suggesting possible solutions and sources of assistance.
   e. Instead of letting N.D. go home without being given a medical examination, medical assistance should be sought.

3. Why are cases of domestic violence or criminal sexual conduct difficult to prosecute?
   a. Evidence is usually insufficient to establish beyond a reasonable doubt that one is guilty of domestic violence or criminal sexual conduct in either the first or second degree.
   b. Testimony is insufficient to establish sexual penetration.
   c. Victims have tendencies, due to emotional trauma, to fabricate charges resulting in evidence of dubious credibility which, upon close examination, is filled with discrepancies.
   d. Victims are fearful of future retaliation and continue to hope the offender will change his ways.
   e. Adult males are more believable than children or women.

4. If N.D.'s mother obtains an order for protection (OFP):
   a. The police can arrest Mosby even if he has done nothing to her or her child *if* he comes to her home after having been ordered to stay away, and she calls the police.

b. Mosby can have no further contact with the victim at her home but can make contact only at her place of work or other neutral ground.

c. Police can and should make an arrest only if additional assault or threat of bodily harm is made.

d. A police officer will be assigned to protect her for twenty-four hours.

e. It will be voided if she lets the abuser into her home or allows visitation with her children.

Discussion Questions

1. Before reading this chapter, did you know about the extent of family violence? If yes, what have you read, seen, or known about the problem?

2. It is said that children who are abused tend to become, in turn, abusive parents. Do you agree? Do you know of any examples to support or disprove this statement?

3. Although people tend to deplore brutality, most will tolerate and even expect a certain amount of force and violence. Why?

4. Are any marriages without violence? Any intimate relationships?

5. Do you think parents have the right to discipline their teenage children? What do you think about hitting, slapping, yelling, restricting youth to their rooms, imposing monetary penalties, and the like?

6. Much controversy exists in the schools regarding punishing children through the use of physical force. What is your position on allowing school officials to use physical force against students?

7. Do you feel violence is part of our value system in the United States?

Definitions

Can you define the following terms?

battering
child abuse
elder abuse

References

Bangham, LeRoy. "Domestic Violence: Too Late to Mediate." *The Police Chief* (June 1986): 52, 54.

Behan, Cornelius J. "Preface." In *A Time for Dignity: Police and Domestic Abuse of the Elderly* by Martha A. Plotkin. Washington, D.C.: Police Executive Research Forum, 1988.

Brown, Michael K. *Working the Street: Police Discretion and the Dilemmas of Reform*. New York: Russel Sage Foundation, 1988.

Bureau of Justice Statistics. *Preventing Domestic Violence Against Women*. Washington, D.C.: U.S. Department of Labor, 1988.

Christian Science Monitor. (July 15, 1988): 23–24.

Clede, Bill. "TV Spotlights Landmark Domestic Case." *Law and Order* (February 1990): 68–69.

Connor, Greg. "Domestic Disputes: A Model Proarrest Policy." *Law and Order* (February 1990): 66–67.

Drowns, Robert W. and Hess, Kären M. *Juvenile Justice*. St. Paul, Minn.: West Publishing Company, 1990.

Duvall, Ed., Jr. "Rescue Operations." *Law and Order* (March 1991): 73, 76.

Friedman, Lucy N. and Shulman, Minna. "Domestic Violence: The Criminal Justice Response," Ch. 5, pp. 87–103. In *Victims of Crime: Problems, Policies, and Programs*, A. J. Lurigio, W. G. Skogan, and R. C. Davis, eds., Newbury Park, Calif.: Sage Publications, 1990.

Garner, Joel and Clemmer, Elizabeth. *Danger to Police in Domestic Disturbances—A New Look*. Washington, D.C.: National Institute of Justice, 1987.

Hamm, Mark S. "Domestic Violence: Legislative Attitudes Toward a Coherent Public Policy," pp. 37–40. In *Journal of Crime and Justice* XII: 2, Cincinnati, Ohio: Anderson Publishing Company, 1989.

Hinzman, Gary and Blome, Dennis. "Cooperation Key to Success of Child Protection Center." *The Police Chief* (February 1991): 24–27.

Hodges, Jill and Brunswick, Mark. "Arresting Offenders May Hurt Victims of Domestic Violence, Professor Says." *Star Tribune* (December 19, 1991): 5A.

Metropolitan Court Judges Committee Report. "Deprived Children: A Judicial Response." Washington, D.C.: National Council of Juvenile and Family Court Judges, Office of Juvenile Justice and Delinquency Prevention, U.S. Department of Justice, 1986.

Newsweek. "Victims of Violence," July 16, 1990, p. 23.

Paisner, Susan R. "Domestic Violence: Breaking the Cycle." *The Police Chief* (February 1991): 35–38.

Parker, L. Craig; Meier, Robert D.; and Monahan, Lynn Hunt. *Interpersonal Psychology for Criminal Justice*. St. Paul, Minn.: West Publishing Company, 1989.

Pence, Ellen. *Criminal Justice Response to Domestic Assault Cases: A Guide for Policy Development*. Duluth, Minn.: Domestic Abuse Intervention Project, 1985.

Plotkin, Martha R. *A Time for Dignity: Police and Domestic Abuse of the Elderly*. Washington, D.C.: Police Executive Research Forum, 1988.

Police Foundation. *Domestic Violence and the Police: Studies in Detroit and Kansas City*. Washington, D.C.: Police Foundation, 1977.

President's Task Force on Victims of Crime. *Victims of Crime*. Washington, D.C.: U.S. Government Printing Office, 1982.

Riverside Medical Center Mental Health Services. "55 and Better." Riverside, Calif.: Publisher, 1991.

Roberts, Albert R. "Intervention with the Abusive Partner." In *Battered Women and the Families*, Albert R. Roberts, ed. New York: Springer Publishing Company, 1984.

Roberts, Albert R. *Helping Crime Victims: Research, Policy, and Practice*. Newbury Park, Calif.: Sage Publications, 1990.

Roberts, Albert R. and Roberts, Beverly S. "A Model for Crisis Intervention with Battered Women and their Children." Ch. 9, pp. 186–205. In *Helping Crime Victims: Research, Policy, and Practice*, Albert R. Roberts, ed. Newbury Park, Calif.: Sage Publications, 1990.

Sherman, Lawrence W. "Domestic Violence." In *Crime File Study Guide*, National Institute of Justice. Washington, D.C.: U.S. Government Printing Office, not dated.

Sherman, Lawrence W. and Berk, Richard A. "The Minneapolis Domestic Violence Experiment," pp. 118–131. In *Police Management Today: Issues and Case Studies*. Washington, D.C.: International City Management Association, 1985.

Sherman, Lawrence W. and Berk, Richard A. "The Specific Deterrent Effects of Arrest for Domestic Assault." *American Sociological Review* 49(April 1984): 261–72.

Steinmetz, Suzzane K. *The Cycle of Violence: Assertive, Aggressive and Abusive Family Interaction*. New York: Praeger, 1988.

Stern, Harriet W. "Family Trouble Center." *Law and Order* (March 1991): 72–75.

Valentine, Anne. *The Role of Law Enforcement Officers in Combating Domestic Violence*. Bloomington, Ind.: Indiana Coalition Against Domestic Violence, 1985.

348

DEALING WITH JUVENILES: OUR NATION'S FUTURE

CHAPTER *13*

INTRODUCTION

"Each professional working with children must understand children, their behavioral patterns and psychological development, and their changing emotional needs as they mature, seek independence, and acquire sexual appetites," says Juvenile Judge Emeritus Lindsay G. Arthur (1990, p. x). Just who is a juvenile? This is determined by state statute and the legal age set forth therein.

All states have specified an age below which individuals are subject to the juvenile justice system. This age varies from state to state and even within parts of the justice system itself in some states. For example, some state statutes specify that their juvenile courts have jurisdiction over all individuals under eighteen years of age, but that the juvenile correctional facilities have jurisdiction over all those under the age of twenty-one who were committed to a correctional facility before their eighteenth birthday.

---

*A **juvenile** is a person not yet of legal age. In three-fourths of the states, juveniles are defined as youth under the age of eighteen.*

According to the Bureau of Justice Statistics (1988, p. 79), criminal courts gain jurisdiction at ages ranging from 16 to 19, as summarized in Table 13.1.

According to the same source (p. 79), forty-eight states, the District of Columbia, and the federal government have also established a minimum age at which a juvenile can be transferred to criminal court by judicial waiver, as summarized in Table 13.2.

Do You Know

- Below what age most states consider a person a juvenile?
- What *parens patriae* is?
- How the juvenile justice system differs from the adult justice system?
- What was established in the *Gault* decision?
- What the welfare model and the justice model are?
- What reforms have been proposed for the juvenile justice system?
- What categories of children are included in the juvenile court's jurisdiction?
- What percentage of children are living in poverty?
- Who the *shadow children* are and what problems they may pose for law enforcement?
- How police departments deal with missing children reports?
- What status offenses are?
- What *decriminalization* of status offenses refers to?
- Who usually enters juveniles into the justice system?
- What alternatives police officers have when dealing with juveniles?
- What programs have been successful in dealing with juveniles?

TABLE 13.1.
Ages at Which Criminal Courts Gain Jurisdiction Over Youth

Age	States
16	Connecticut, New York, North Carolina
17	Georgia, Illinois, Louisiana, Massachusetts, Missouri, South Carolina, Texas
18	Alabama, Alaska, Arizona, Arkansas, California, Colorado, Delaware, District of Columbia, Florida, Hawaii, Idaho, Indiana, Iowa, Kansas, Kentucky, Maine, Maryland, Michigan, Minnesota, Mississippi, Montana, Nebraska, Nevada, New Hampshire, New Jersey, New Mexico, North Dakota, Ohio, Oklahoma, Oregon, Pennsylvania, Rhode Island, South Dakota, Tennessee, Utah, Vermont, Virginia, Washington, West Virginia, Wisconsin, and federal districts
19	Wyoming

Source: Bureau of Justice Statistics

TABLE 13.2
Minimum Ages at Which Juveniles May Be Waived to Criminal Court

Age	States
No specific age	Alaska, Arizona, Arkansas, Delaware, Florida, Indiana, Kentucky, Maine, Maryland, New Hampshire, New Jersey, Oklahoma, South Dakota, West Virginia, Wyoming, and federal districts
10	Vermont
12	Montana
13	Georgia, Illinois, Mississippi
14	Alabama, Colorado, Connecticut, Idaho, Iowa, Massachusetts, Minnesota, Missouri, North Carolina, North Dakota, Pennsylvania, South Carolina, Tennessee, Utah
15	District of Columbia, Louisiana, Michigan, New Mexico, Ohio, Oregon, Texas, Virginia
16	California, Hawaii, Kansas, Nevada, Rhode Island, Washington, Wisconsin

Source: Bureau of Justice Statistics

Arthur notes that "Children are not small adults. Legally, they are infants. . . ." He suggests that the classic function of the police is to "protect the safety of children and the public and investigate the behavioral facts."

The dual role of protecting both children and the public and of investigating behavioral facts is a great challenge facing not only juvenile officers, but any police officer who interacts with juveniles in any way. The aspect of protection in dealings with juveniles has its roots in the common law of England.

The Evolution of Our Juvenile Justice System

In English common law, the king, through his chancellor, was a substitute parent for abandoned, neglected, and dependent children under a doctrine called *parens patriae*. In the United States, each individual state replaced the king in this responsibility.

*The doctrine of **parens patriae** allows the state to assume
guardianship of abandoned, neglected, and "wayward"
children.*

Under this doctrine, the state is to act toward the children entrusted in its care as
a loving parent would. This is very different from the punitive thrust behind the
adult justice system.

As noted by Abadinsky (1987, p. 482), early laws "provided the basis for the
state to intervene in the cases of children who were neglected or in need of supervision, as well as those who committed crimes. The philosophy embodied in these
statutes was that of *parens patriae*." New York State law included the first statutory
definition of juvenile delinquency: "children who shall be taken up or committed as
vagrants, or convicted of criminal offenses where the judge thought they were the
'proper objects' for such treatment."

The Illinois Juvenile Court Act of 1899 established the first juvenile court in the
United States. This court's primary purpose was to "save" children from becoming
criminals. The state, as substitute parent, was to help children, not punish them.
This resulted in several important differences in terminology and procedure from
the adult system, summarized in Table 13.3.

The juvenile justice system, under parens patriae, *is intended to
help children, not to punish them.*

Although a separate system is created for youths, they are entitled to most of the
rights of adults as a result of the historic *In re Gault* decision (1967). In this case,
fifteen-year-old Gerald Gault was charged with making an obscene phone call. At his
hearing, the complainant was not present, no one was sworn in, no attorney was
present, and no record of the proceedings was made. A second hearing also had no
complaining witnesses, sworn testimony, counsel, or transcript. At the end of the
hearing, the judge sentenced Gault to the State Industrial School until age twenty-one.
Gault received a six year sentence for an action for which an adult would probably have
received a fine. As noted by Drowns and Hess (1990, pp. 217–218), "The United
States Supreme Court overruled Gerald's conviction on the grounds that:

- Neither Gerald nor his parents had notice of the specific charges against
  him.
- No counsel was offered or provided to Gerald.
- No witnesses were present, thus denying Gerald the right of
  cross-examination and confrontation.
- No warning of Gerald's privilege against self-incrimination was given to
  him; thus no waiver of that right took place.

Speaking for the Court, Justice Fortas said:

*Where a person, infant or adult, can be seized by the State, charged and
convicted for violating a state criminal law, and then ordered by the State to
be confined for six years, I think the Constitution requires that he be tried in*

TABLE 13.3
The Language of Juvenile and Adult Courts

Juvenile Court Term	Adult Court Term
Adjudication: decision by the judge that a child has committed delinquent acts.	Conviction of guilt
Adjudicatory hearing: a hearing to determine whether the allegations of a petition are supported by the evidence beyond a reasonable doubt.	Trial
Adjustment: the settling of a matter so that parties agree without official intervention by the court.	Plea bargaining
Aftercare: the supervision given to a child for a limited period of time after he or she is released from training school but while he or she is still under the control of the juvenile court.	Parole
Commitment: a decision by the judge to send a child to training school.	Sentence to imprisonment
Delinquent act: an act that if committed by an adult would be called a crime. The term does not include such ambiguities and noncrimes as "being ungovernable," "truancy," "incorrigibility," and "disobedience."	Crime
Delinquent child: a child who is found to have committed an act that would be considered a crime if committed by an adult.	Criminal
Detention: temporary care of an allegedly delinquent child who requires secure custody in physically restricting facilities pending court disposition or execution of a court order.	Holding in jail
Dispositional hearing: a hearing held subsequent to the adjudicatory hearing to determine what order of disposition should be made for a child adjudicated as delinquent.	Sentencing hearing
Hearing: the presentation of evidence to the juvenile court judge, his or her consideration of it, and his or her decision on disposition of the case.	Trial
Juvenile court: the court that has jurisdiction over children who are alleged to be or found to be delinquent. Juvenile delinquency procedures should not be used for neglected children or for those who need supervision.	Court of record
Petition: an application for a court order or some other judicial action. Hence, a "delinquency petition" is an application for the court to act in a matter involving a juvenile apprehended for a delinquent act.	Accusation or indictment
Probation: the supervision of a delinquent child after the court hearing but without commitment to training school.	Probation (with the same meaning as the juvenile court term)
Residential child care facility: a dwelling (other than a detention or shelter care facility) that is licensed to provide living accommodations, care, treatment, and maintenance for children and youths. Such facilities include foster homes, group homes, and halfway houses.	Halfway house
Shelter: temporary care of a child in physically unrestricting facilities pending court disposition or execution of a court order for placement. Shelter care is used for dependent and neglected children and minors in need of supervision. Separate shelter care facilities are also used for children apprehended for delinquency who need temporary shelter but not secure detention.	Jail
Take into custody: the act of the police in securing the physical custody of a child engaged in delinquency. The term is used to avoid the stigma of the word "arrest."	Arrest

Source: From *Crime and Justice in America: A Human Perspective,* by Leonard Territo, James B. Halsted, and Max L. Bromley, West Publishing Company, 1992, p. 539. Reprinted by permission of West Publishing Company.

accordance with the guarantees of all provisions of the Bill of Rights made applicable to the States by the Fourteenth Amendment. Undoubtedly this would be true of an adult defendant, and it would be a plain denial of equal protection of the laws—an invidious discrimination—to hold that others subject to heavier punishment could, because they are children, be denied these same constitutional safeguards. I consequently agree with the Court that the Arizona law as applied here denied to the parents and their son the right of notice, right to counsel, right against self-incrimination, and right to confront the witnesses against young Gault. . . ."

The Gault *decision established that juveniles have the right to counsel, the right to be notified of the charges against them, the right to confront and cross-examine witnesses, and the privilege against self-incrimination.*

With a juvenile justice model emphasizing the welfare of the child and the *Gault* decision granting youth the due process guaranteed in the adult justice system, some critics felt the juvenile justice system had gone too far. As noted by Springer (1986, p. 33): "It is time that we recognize the impossible double bind our juvenile judges are placed in when they, judicial officers, are commanded to diagnose the 'problem' of some young offender, when in most cases it is obvious that the criminal youth does not have a problem—he or she *is* the problem."

The Welfare Model v. The Justice Model

The concept of "helping" youths who are members of violent gangs and who engage in heinous crimes is very difficult for police officers and others within the system to accept. It has, in fact, led to a call for reform of the juvenile justice system. An advocate of such reform, Springer (pp. 2–3), says:

The first step in doing justice for juveniles is to revise juvenile court acts throughout the country so that when juvenile courts deal with delinquent children, they operate under a justice model rather than under the present treatment or the child welfare model. By a justice model is meant a judicial process wherein young people who come in conflict with the law are held responsible and accountable for their behavior.

In a **child welfare model,** *the courts operate with the best interests of the youth as the main consideration. In a* **juvenile justice model,** *the courts hold youths responsible and accountable for their behavior.*

Springer (p. 3) suggests:

The juvenile court should be maintained as a special tribunal for children, but when dealing with criminal misconduct, the emphasis and rationale of the court must be changed to reflect the following:

- *Although young people who violate the law deserve special treatment because of their youth, they should be held morally and legally accountable for their transgressions and should be subject to prompt, certain, and fair punishment.*
- *Except for certain mentally disabled and incompetent individuals, young law violators should not be considered by the juvenile courts as being "sick" or as victims of their environments. Generally speaking, young criminals are more wrong than wronged, more the victimizers than the victims.*

Juvenile court in session. Proceedings are much less formal and are nonadversarial, but they can still be frightening to youngsters.

- Juvenile courts are primarily courts of justice and not social clinics; *therefore, emphasis in court proceedings should be on the public interest rather than on the welfare and treatment of the child* [*italics added*].
- *To adopt a justice model is not to rule out or diminish the importance of rehabilitative measures employed by juvenile courts. Disapproval of, and punishment for, the wrongful act is probably the single most important rehabilitative measure available to the court.*

Our current juvenile system is treatment or welfare focused. Some argue it should be replaced with a juvenile justice system whereby youth who commit serious crimes are held accountable and punished for those acts.

This is not the only aspect of the justice system that is being challenged. Another area is that of the juvenile court's jurisdiction.

The "One-Pot" Jurisdictional Approach

Another aspect of our juvenile justice system's evolution is that, from the beginning, it was designed to deal with not only "wayward" children—that is, juvenile delinquents, whose "crimes" could range from talking back to their parents to murder—but also with children who were abandoned, abused, or neglected. Early laws, in effect, equated being poor with being criminal. As Springer (p. 45) notes,

"One of the major failings in the juvenile court system is what can be referred to as the 'one-pot' jurisdictional approach—putting poor, rebellious, and criminal children in the same jurisdictional pot. . . . All three kinds of children were thought to be the products or victims of bad family and social environments; consequently, it was thought, they should be subject, as wards of the court, to the same kind of solicitous, helpful care." This "one-pot" approach continues to be true in the 1990s.

*Juvenile court's jurisdiction includes children who are neglected or abused, those who are status offenders, and those who commit serious crimes, called the **"one-pot"** jurisdictional approach.*

Police officers need to recognize that not all youth they deal with are breaking the law. As Territo et al. (1989, p. 539) note: "A substantial number of contacts occur just because juveniles are out and about—which brings them to the attention of officers on patrol. Because juveniles often move in groups, they seem more suspicious and more difficult to control. And because they tend to congregate at shopping plazas, street corners, fast-food operations, and video arcades, they may be the object of complaints requiring police attention."

Children Who Are Poor, Deprived, or Neglected

Recall from Chapter 12 that an estimated four or five million children are neglected or physically abused each year, with an additional two million vulnerable as runaways or missing. According to Reed and Sautter (1990, p. 3): "Nearly one-fifth of America's youngest citizens still grow up poor; often sick, hungry, and illiterate; and deprived of safe and adequate housing, of needed social services, and of special educational assistance. . . . More than 12.6 million youngsters—nearly 20 percent of all children under the age of eighteen—are poor. Thus one in five American children goes to bed hungry or sick or cold."

One-fifth of America's children are living in poverty.

Reed and Sautter (p. 3) also note: "More than 10,000 children in the United States die each year as a direct result of the poverty they endure. . . . Nearly one-fourth of U.S. children lack medical, nutritional, and early-learning assistance. Thus many poor children are needlessly condemned to physical and psychological deficiencies for the rest of their lives."

This bleak picture is extended to include homelessness which, say Reed and Sautter (p. 5), is a "distressing by-product of the new poverty that plagues this nation." They cite U.S. Department of Education estimates:

- 220,000 school-aged children are homeless.
- 65,000 of these children do not attend school.

- 186,000 more children are "precariously housed," living on the verge of homelessness.

Other distressing facts related to youth come from the House Select Committee on Children, Youth, and Families 1989 report, *No Place to Call Home: Discarded Children in America,* which concludes that by 1995 nearly a million children no longer living with their parents will cause serious problems for the school" (Reed and Sautter, p. 6). It is logical to assume that these children may also cause problems for the juvenile justice system.

In addition, say Reed and Sautter (p. 6), "From 1985 to 1988, the number of children born with drug exposure quadrupled, reaching 375,000 in 1988." As noted by Rist (1990, p. 1): "The initial wave of crack babies, born after crack cocaine hit the streets in the mid-1980s, are kindergarten age today. . . . Children prenatally exposed to crack cocaine, says one psychologist, are kids wired for 110 volts, living in a 220-volt world. . . . Crack babies are irritable, tremulous, and difficult to soothe for at least the first three months."

Rist (p. 1) notes that Douglas Besharov, former director of the National Center on Child Abuse, has called these crack babies a potential "bio-underclass—a cohort of children whose combined physiological damage and extreme socioeconomic disadvantage could foredoom them to a life of permanent inferiority."

---

*Crack babies have been labeled **shadow children** by some.*

According to Rist, "Cocaine-exposed children tend to react in one of two ways [to noises, voices, instructions]. They withdraw completely, or they become wild and difficult to control."

Status Offenders

A special category of offenses has been established for juveniles, designating certain actions as illegal for any person under the age specified by the state; these actions are under the jurisdiction of the juvenile court.

Status offenses *are violations of the law applying only to those under legal age. They include curfew violations, drinking alcoholic beverages, incorrigibility, smoking cigarettes, running away from home, and truancy.*

Status offenses are considered illegal acts simply because of the age of the person committing them. Frequently, it is status offenses that bring young people into contact with police officers, often in a very negative manner. Sometimes the consequences of negative labeling and perhaps confinement with more criminally inclined youth can result in status offenders becoming involved in crime.

Of all referrals to juvenile court, 17 percent are for status offenses (Bureau of Justice Statistics, 1988, p. 95), which break down as follows:

- Running away— 28%
- Ungovernability— 28%
- Truancy and curfew violations— 21%
- Liquor violations— 23%

Most current definitions of juvenile delinquency would include status offenses. Kaplan (1984, p. 13), for example, says that **juvenile delinquency** refers to "any of a number of (1) behaviors (2) performed by young people (3) that are violations of laws applicable to young people's behavior." However, a trend that may change this predominant definition began in 1961 when California became the first state to separate status offenses from the delinquent category. California was followed by New York, Illinois, and Colorado. In addition, the American Bar Association Joint Commission on Juvenile Justice Standards voted in 1977 to eliminate uniquely juvenile offenses from the legal definition of delinquency, saying that the juvenile delinquency liability should include only such conduct as would be designated a crime if committed by an adult.

---

*Several states and the American Bar Association have made a case for **decriminalization** of status offenses, that is, not treating them as criminal offenses.*

Whether states decriminalize status offenses or not, police officers should clearly differentiate when they are dealing with simple delinquent (status offenses) behavior and criminal delinquent behavior (crimes regardless of age).

More Serious Offenders

According to the Bureau of Justice Statistics (1988, pp. 78–79), most referrals to juvenile court are for property crimes (46%), followed by offenses against the public order (21%), crimes against persons (11%), and drug offenses (5%). The specific breakdown for each category is as follows:

- *Crimes against property:* larceny 47%, burglary 25%, vandalism and trespassing 19%, motor vehicle theft 5%, stolen property offenses 3%, and arson 1%.
- *Offenses against the public order:* drunkenness and disorderly conduct 23%; contempt, probation, and parole violations 21%; sex offenses 6%; weapons offenses 6%; and other offenses 44%.
- *Crimes against persons:* simple assault 59%, aggravated assault 20%, robbery 17%, forcible rape 2%, and criminal homicide 1%.

Although juvenile arrests for violent crimes make up less than 1 percent of the total number of almost 10 million arrests for violent crimes (Sullivan, 1988, p. 159), the problem is serious. As noted by Pindur and Wells (1988, p. 194): "Nearly 2,000 juveniles are arrested each year on murder charges, and approximately 4,000 are arrested annually for rape. . . . Chronic, serious juvenile offenders often 'fall through the cracks' of the [juvenile justice] system because efforts are not coordinated."

The Police Response

The challenges facing police officers dealing with juveniles are immense. These challenges may be compounded by officers own (either conscious or subconscious) stereotyping of youth. As noted by Russell and Beigel (1990, p. 157):

> *Most police officers come into contact with juveniles only when they have indulged or are indulging in antisocial behavior. Because of this limited range of contacts, officers may perceive most children as either delinquent or potentially delinquent. Although common sense tells us this is not true, it is sometimes easy for police officers to develop negative attitudes toward those juveniles they must encounter.*

Police officers are charged with handling not only those engaged in delinquent behavior, but also those who are neglected, abused, missing, or runaways and those who are just "hanging out."

Neglected and Abused Children

When police are called to deal with a child neglect or abuse case, their primary responsibility is the immediate protection of the child. In many cases, the child is taken into protective custody and placed in a foster home, as discussed in Chapter 12.

Missing Children

When police are called to deal with a missing child report, their responsibility is less clear. Many departments lack specific procedures to deal with missing children calls. In addition, significant variation exists in the initial response to such calls. According to Forst (1990, p. 59), a policy on responding to a call might instruct officers to obtain the following: physical description, description of clothing and jewelry, amount of money carried, possible destination and places frequented, and why the reportee thinks the person is missing. A picture and the signature of the reportee should also be obtained.

Many jurisdictions also have policies as to when the information must be entered into the NCIC system. In California, for example, a 1986 law requires that a child's name be entered into the NCIC system within four hours if the child is under the age of twelve.

Runaways

Running away—that is, leaving home without parental permission—is a status offense. Usually, however, police are more interested in locating and returning the runaway than in entering the youth into the juvenile justice system. According to Drowns and Hess (1990, p. 150):

> *Generally no police investigation, social service inquiry, or school inquiry is conducted to determine the reasons these children left home, were truant because of this absence, or why they continue to run away.*

Running away is a predelinquent indicator, but its value often is not recognized by the parents, police, school, social agencies, or the courts. . . .

Because children run away for many reasons, police must be sensitive in their treatment of runaways. Police must treat different runaways differently to account for their age, sex, family social order, paternal makeup (original, adopted, or foster), or who represents control. . . .

If police dispositions are to be effective, the family must recognize the early signs of maladjustment in children. Running away is the most visible indicator of a possible future felon.

Youths Who Are "Hanging Out"

"Hanging out" behavior is well known to most police officers. It is an important part of youth development. According to Russell and Beigel (1990, pp. 161–162):

During adolescent development, teenagers acquire much of their personal identity from peer groups. In fact, peer groups are often more influential in shaping adolescents' behavior than parents, teachers, and other adults.

They also tend to prefer their [peers'] company and often hang out in large groups around businesses, shopping centers, and so on, causing problems that lead to citizen complaints. Police spend many hours breaking up minor disturbances and dealing with obnoxious behavior.

Sometimes the youths have been drinking and are belligerent and unreasonable, making the problem even more difficult. How police officers deal with such situations can make the difference between a peaceful resolution of the problem or a violent confrontation. The following are suggestions from the Law Enforcement Training and Information Network (LETIN, 1986) for handling boisterous teenage crowds:

1. Decide whether backup or medical assistance should be called for before leaving the patrol car.
2. One officer should "hang back" in a protected position with a good view of scene.
3. One officer should approach to within eight to ten feet of the crowd's edge.
4. Ignore youngsters who are doing the most talking; ignore the ringleaders.
5. Tip the balance of power by calling two or three youngsters at random, separating them from the crowd, and engage them in a separate conversation or interview.
6. Maintain eye contact with two or three youngsters when addressing the crowd, and always:
   a. Be direct and brief.
   b. Avoid judgmental remarks.
   c. Avoid reference to the citizen complaint.
   d. Make "I" statements, such as "I expect you to disperse in one minute."
   e. Make fact-based descriptive statements, such as "I see about twenty-four people and that's too many."

Teens "hanging out" in Newport, Rhode Island, during America's Cup Race week. Their presence may deter customers from entering the store.

7. Establish some degree of one-to-one trust and communication. Say what you expect the crowd to do without describing the consequences of failure to do so. If there is no response, describe what you intend to do and be fully prepared to back up what you have said. Never make empty threats.

Youths Who Are Breaking the Law

"The police officer," according to Territo et al. (1992, p. 538), "is usually the first representative of societal authority and the criminal justice system to come in contact with a youthful offender. According to the President's Commission on Law Enforcement and the Administration of Justice, 'Contacts with police are the gateway into the system of delinquency and criminal justice.' "

Of the 80–90 percent of children under the age of eighteen who commit some offense for which they could be arrested, only about 3 percent are apprehended (Sullivan, 1990, p. 159). This is largely because of the great amount of discretion held and exercised by police officers. Police may ignore simple transgressions such as a curfew violation, or they may take juveniles "into custody." (remember from Table 13.3 this is *not* an arrest). Options open to police officers, according to Territo et al. (1989, pp. 539–542), include the following:

- Warn and release. In minor offenses, police may simply warn the youth not to repeat the behavior and that to do so will result in official action.
- Release and report. Although the youth is released, an official report on the incident is filed.
- Release to parents, with either a warning or an official report. The usual criteria for filing a report is whether the youth poses a threat to public safety.

- Refer to a community agency—known as **diversion.** This will depend on department policy, the availability of appropriate programs, and police awareness of community resources. Typical police referrals are to youth service bureaus, special school programs, boys clubs, the YMCA, community mental health agencies, and drug programs.
- Refer to juvenile court. Depending on the jurisdiction, police officers can issue a citation or make a formal report to juvenile intake or the juvenile court and release the youth to the custody of parents or guardians.

Police officers who deal with juveniles may warn them, with or without an official report; turn them over to their parents, with or without an official report; refer them to a social agency; or refer them to juvenile court.

How police resolve matters involving juveniles depends on the officer's individual discretion as well as the specific incident involved. The most common procedure is to release juveniles, with or without a warning, but without making an official record or taking further action. When officers decide to deal with status offenses in their own way—usually by ignoring them—this is sometimes referred to as **street justice** or **station adjustment.** However, in such instances, the police may miss an important chance to intervene in a young person's life at a critical time of crisis. At least some social agency in the community should be notified if the police do not have the motivation or the resources to follow up as a result of the contact. This type of referral would be in keeping with problem-oriented community policing.

When a record or report is made, many police departments use a standard form such as that shown in Form 5 in Appendix B. The options exercised by the police and the usual outcome are illustrated in Figure 13.1.

Of all youth referrals to court, 84 percent are from law enforcement.

Remaining referrals to court come from parents, relatives, schools, probation officers, other courts, social services, and other services.

Research conducted in Flint, Michigan, found that police officers in the foot patrol program dealing with complaints about "rowdy" juveniles took several different actions (Belknap et al., 1986, p. 16): made a referral to social services, counseled the teenagers, counseled the parents, reassured the complainants, tried to get people to empathize with each other and see each other's side, gave orders, threatened arrest, and made an arrest.

This same research (Belknap et al., pp. 9–12) identified five role-identity orientations police officers used in dealing with rowdy teenagers:

- Peacekeeper and problem solver—trying to get everybody to get along and understand the other person's viewpoint.
- Competent law enforcer—stays within the law, obtains proper evidence to make a case.

FIGURE 13.1

Procedures of the Juvenile Justice System

Source: *From Report of the Task Force on Juvenile Justice and Delinquency Prevention* by the National Advisory Committee on Criminal Justice Standards and Goals, Task Force on Juvenile Justice and Delinquency Prevention, Washington, D.C.: U.S. Government Printing Office, 1976, p. 9. Reprinted with permission of the U.S. Department of Justice.

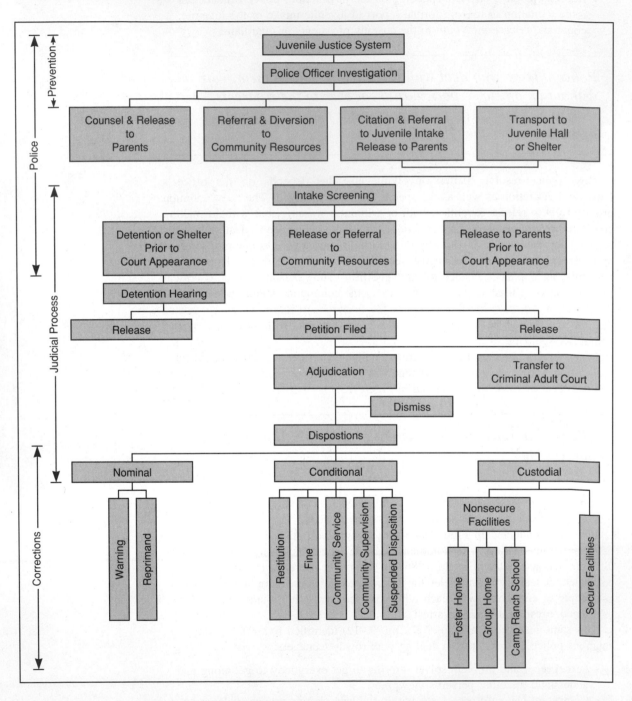

- Authority figure—possibly intimidating, advises the teenagers to leave or else.
- Friend or peer—jogs with the kids, talks to them but not down to them, lets them know "you're human with your own needs," explains the situation.
- Knight in shining armor—here to save the day. Everything will be fine. Call again if the problem recurs.

Legal Procedures When Dealing with Youth: The Uniform Juvenile Court Act

How police officers deal with juveniles they have taken into custody may be influenced by the Uniform Juvenile Court Act. This act was passed in 1968 by the National Conference of Commissioners on Uniform State Laws. Although not legally binding on the states, the act does provide guidelines for dealing with youth. The purpose of the act is to provide for the care, protection, and development of youth, without the stigma of a criminal label, by a program of treatment, training, and rehabilitation, in a family environment when possible, as well as to provide a simple judicial procedure and simple interstate procedures.

Although called a court act, specific provisions have direct relevance for police officers dealing with juveniles, defined as individuals under the age of eighteen.

Custody and Detention

Police can take children into custody by court order if they have "reasonable grounds to believe that the child is suffering from illness or injury or is in immediate danger from his surroundings . . . or to believe that the child has run away. . . . The taking of a child into custody is not an arrest. . . ." Section 14 deals specifically with the detention of juveniles:

A child taken into custody shall not be detained or placed in shelter care prior to the hearing on the petition unless his detention or care is required to protect the person or property of others or of the child or because the child may abscond or be removed from the jurisdiction of the court or because he has no parent, guardian, or custodian or other person able to provide supervision and care for him and return him to the court when required, or an order for his detention or shelter care has been made by the court pursuant to this act.

After police have taken a juvenile into custody, they should either release the juvenile to their parent or guardian, take them before a judge, take them to a detention or shelter, or to a medical facility if needed. The parent or guardian and the court are to be notified in writing "with all reasonable speed."

Section 16 of the act specifies where delinquents can be held:

A delinquent can be detained only in (1) a licensed foster home or a home approved by the court; (2) a facility operated by a licensed child welfare agency; (3) a detention home or center for delinquent children which is under the direction or supervision of the court or other public authority, or of a private agency approved by the court; or (4) any other suitable place or facility, designated or operated by the court.

Youth in custody. Are these children headed for a lifetime of crime, or can they be rehabilitated?

Delinquents are *not* to be put into a jail or other adult detention facility unless no other option is available; they are put into a room separate from the adults when their detention in an adult facility is necessary for their own safety or that of the public.

Police Records and Files

Section 55 of the Uniform Juvenile Court Act stipulates that:

Law enforcement records and files concerning a child shall be kept separate from the records and files of adults. Unless a charge of delinquency is transferred for criminal prosecution, the interest of national security requires, or the court otherwise orders in the interest of the child, the records and files shall not be open to public inspection or their contents disclosed to the public.

Juvenile records may be sealed if:

- Two years have elapsed since the final discharge of the person.
- Since the final discharge the juvenile has not been convicted of a felony, or of a misdemeanor involving moral turpitude, or adjudicated a delinquent or unruly child, and no proceeding is pending seeking conviction or adjudication.
- The juvenile has been rehabilitated.

Fingerprinting and Photographing Children

Section 56 of the Uniform Juvenile Court Act specifies that law enforcement officers can take fingerprints of children fourteen years and older involved in the crimes of murder, nonnegligent manslaughter, forcible rape, robbery, aggravated assault, burglary, housebreaking, purse snatching, and automobile theft. However, children's fingerprint files must be kept separate from adult files and should not be sent to a central state or federal file unless national security demands it. The fingerprints are to be removed from the file and destroyed if the youth is adjudicated not delinquent or if the youth reaches the age of twenty-one and has not committed a criminal offense after becoming sixteen.

If police officers find latent fingerprints during a criminal investigation and have probable cause to believe a particular youth committed the crime, they may fingerprint the youth, regardless of the youth's age. If the comparison is negative, the youth's fingerprint card is to be destroyed immediately.

Section 56 also stipulates that children should not be photographed after being taken into custody unless the police have a judge's consent. A photograph release form such as that shown in Form 6 in Appendix B can be used.

Programs Aimed at Youth

Police also may become involved in various kinds of programs aimed at youth. Many such programs are educational and are intended to be preventive.

Educational Programs

One of the best known and most effective educational programs is the **Drug Abuse Resistance Education (DARE)** program. Aimed at fourth and fifth grade students, the course consists of seventeen one-hour sessions designed to help children resist the peer pressure that frequently plays a role in initial drug experimentation. The course is geared to reach students before they have had their first contact to use and buy.

The specialized curriculum teaches students the life skills of assertiveness, self-esteem, handling peer pressure, and how to respond to drug-using situations. Learning these skills properly helps students with their ability to say NO to drugs. A side benefit is that police officers involved in the program are seen as resources and friends rather than as enforcers of the law. As one officer said, "The best thing we accomplished was to let the students know that police officers are their friends, that they are approachable and have their best interests in mind."

In addition to the curriculum, DARE-related specialty items and gifts are often used, including bumper stickers, T-shirts, pencils, rulers, folders, book covers, and large frisbees. Such items, imprinted with the "Just say NO to drugs" DARE slogan, help keep the message fresh in students' minds.

Williamson County, a rural area outside Austin, Texas, has developed a program called, Don't Choose Crime. This program teaches children from prekindergarten through twelfth grade to avoid drugs and delinquency. Included in the program are coloring books for younger students, bookmarks bearing a list of crimes and their penalties, book covers, and posters. According to Briscoe (1990, p. 92): "Since 1988, more than 23,000 students have participated in a presentation. The county probation department has distributed 300 posters to schools and business, and more than 16,000 bookmarks and bookcovers to private and public schools. More than 4,500 birthday cards have been distributed to twelfth grade students warning them that, under Texas law, adulthood begins at age 17."

Another highly successful educational program is one focused on preventing sexual assault. As Fanton (1987, p. 47) says, "Any officer who's had the experience of dealing with a weeping, battered child sexual assault victim is likely to agree that doing something to prevent the sexual assault is a good approach." In one program, conducted by Deputy Sheriff Deborah Stauffler, three one-hour sessions are conducted for students ranging from preschool up to third grade. The three things "Officer Debbie" stresses are:

- Say No.
- Get away.
- Tell someone.

She also teaches students that "private parts of the body are covered by a swimsuit" and teaches them the proper names for these body parts. Officers presenting such programs should be aware that a sexual assault disclosure by a child during the session may take place and be prepared to deal with such a disclosure.

According to Fanton (p. 67): "Universally cited guidelines to assist law enforcement agencies interested in sexual assault prevention include avoiding scare tactics and making the point that the assault can be perpetrated by someone known to the child." He stresses that:

Police officers are in a position to make contributions in sexual assault prevention for a variety of reasons. Most of them have seen the results of assaults and have no problem accepting the fact that sexual assault is "for real" and does happen. Safety lessons presented in schools by police officers are a long standing tradition, and with such a good track record, school officials are likely to welcome a sound preventive program by law enforcement. Finally, the kids are likely to believe what a law enforcement officer has to tell them.

This sentiment is echoed by Anne Cohn, Executive Director of the National Committee for Prevention of Child Abuse (Fanton, p. 67): "Because you are a law enforcement official, you have tremendous authority, a tremendous power with children, and thus you have an ability to get concepts across to them. . . . Children will tend to believe you more and take more seriously what you have to say."

Other Programs

Several other programs whose orientations are less educational have also been instituted by police departments to help deal with problem youths.

One of the most common programs is a police-school liaison program. In such programs a police officer, uniformed or not, is assigned to a school and works with students and staff within that school. Often such officers deal with the predelinquent and early delinquent youth with whom, under traditional programs, law enforcement would not become involved. The dual goals of most police-school liaison programs are to prevent juvenile delinquency and to improve community relations.

Other well-known programs found throughout the country are the Officer Friendly program and the McGruff police dog ("Take a bite out of crime") program. The McGruff program focuses not only on crime prevention and safety, but also helps youth contribute positively to the community.

Explorer Posts within police and sheriff departments are another popular way to interact positively with youth. Explorers wear uniforms similar to law enforcement officers and learn several skills used in law enforcement, including firearms safety, first aid, and fingerprinting.

In Jefferson County, in southeastern Texas, the juvenile detention center has instituted a foster grandparent program. Says Briscoe (1990, p. 92): "Even children who are sometimes hostile and aggressive work calmly and quietly in the presence of a foster grandparent."

Marion County, Indiana, has several dispositional alternative programs for youth in trouble, including the following programs (Payne and Lee, 1990, pp. 103–104).

Project Challenge. A six-week program aimed at breaking the behavior cycles leading youths into trouble. It includes a three-week wilderness camp encouraging youths to trust themselves and their peers in addition to family and vocational counseling.

Ivy Tech. Part of Indiana's technical school system. It offers vocational education, including skills such as auto mechanics, welding, and computer usage, to functionally illiterate youth in trouble with the law.

Run, Don't Run. A program developed jointly by Indianapolis Police Department and the Marion County Sheriff's Department for youth who have literally run from encounters with law enforcement officers. The program seeks to establish respect between young offenders and law enforcement officials. Youth learn how fleeing, resisting, and striking police officers influences the officers' actions.

Visions. Designed for the serious first referral or repeat offender. Youths spend one night in the juvenile detention center, receive a morning lesson about the

Officer participating in the Drug Abuse Resistance Education (D.A.R.E.) program. This program stresses assertiveness and learning to say "no" to drugs.

juvenile justice system, and then take a tour of the Indiana Boys/Girls School and the Marion County Jail.

Operation Kids CAN (Care About Neighborhoods).   Youths on probation clean up the neighborhoods.

Garden Project.   Youths and their parents plant vegetables and flowers during the summer and work on craft projects in the winter.

Paint It Clean.   Youths associated with destructive gang activities are required to paint over gang graffiti in local neighborhoods, parks, and buildings.

Summer Youth Program.   Youth get a chance to go canoeing, horseback riding, camping, hiking, caving, and take field trips to the Indiana Amusement Park.

Brown (1991, p. 6) describes two programs aimed at youth:

The Kops 'n Kids program [endorsed by the IACP in February 1991] brings officers and children together—not to deliver antidrug or anticrime speeches—but to have fun. The officers visit schools with their motorcycles and police dogs and demonstrate how they perform. They also form running clubs to teach the children about training and physical fitness. . . .

In the "Adopt-an-Officer" [Greeley, Colorado, Police Department] numerous officers have volunteered to be "adopted" by fourth and fifth graders in a local elementary school. The children and officers share meals and exchange letters and cards; the children also visit the police station. The program's goals include establishing positive role models; conveying the impression that police officers are friends; and desensitizing students, peers, and families to law enforcement personnel and uniforms.

Summary

A juvenile is a person who is not yet of legal age. In three-fourths of the states, juveniles are defined as youth under the age of eighteen.

The juvenile justice system has several important differences from the adult system. The doctrine of *parens patriae* allows the state to assume guardianship of abandoned, neglected, and "wayward" children. The juvenile justice system, under *parens patriae,* is intended to help children, not to punish them. The system is also influenced by the *Gault* decision, which established that juveniles have the right to counsel, the right to be notified of the charges against them, the right to confront and cross-examine witnesses, and the privilege against self-incrimination.

In a child welfare model, the courts operate with the best interests of the youth as the main consideration. In a juvenile justice model, the courts hold youths responsible and accountable for their behavior.

Our current juvenile system is treatment or welfare focused. Some argue it should be replaced with a juvenile justice system whereby youth who commit serious crimes are held accountable and punished for those acts. Juvenile court's jurisdiction includes children who are neglected or abused, those who are status offenders, and those who commit serious crimes, called the "one-pot" jurisdictional system.

One-fifth of America's children are living in poverty. Among them are hundreds of crack babies, often labeled shadow children.

Status offenses are violations of the law applying only to those under legal age. They include curfew violations, drinking alcoholic beverages, incorrigibility, smoking cigarettes, running away from home, and truancy. Several states and the American Bar Association have made a case for decriminalization of status offenses.

Police officers who deal with juveniles may warn them, with or without an official report; turn them over to their parents, with or without an official report; refer them to a social agency; or refer them to juvenile court. Of all youth referrals to court, 84 percent are from law enforcement.

Application #1

As an officer with the Mytown Juvenile Bureau, you have noted some inconsistent handling of juvenile offenders that have caused the juvenile court authorities to worry about youngsters not receiving due process when taken into custody by police. You call together a group, including citizens and youth, to rectify the situation by making a statement of need for juveniles and the ultimate purpose in their apprehension. Based on that group discussion, establish a policy to standardize procedures for handling juveniles.

Instructions.   Use the form from Appendix A to formulate a policy that provides guidelines to police officers in handling juveniles. Include in the policy those guidelines necessary for processing juveniles taken into custody for various reasons. The policy and procedure should include searching, questioning, and transporting juveniles. Necessary reports should be highlighted and dispositions clearly specified. A visit to the local police department or sheriff's office may help determine what to include in the policy and procedure.

Application #2

Use the form from Appendix A or create your own form to make policies and procedures regarding photographing and fingerprinting juveniles taken into police custody. Remember that state law is an important factor in who can be photographed and fingerprinted and under what circumstances. Check state statutes and then clearly specify this information.

An Exercise in Critical Thinking

Juvenile court is without jurisdiction after the minor attains legal age. The Children's Code provides that proceedings, as set forth by most states, may be commenced in court only against persons under eighteen. Waiver of juvenile court jurisdiction and certification of a juvenile to stand trial as an adult is a critically important stage of the juvenile process. The juvenile justice system is treatment focused, intended to help children, not to punish them. Serious juvenile crimes require handling that follows policies and procedures used in the investigation of crimes committed by adults.

D.F.B.'s parents and two younger siblings were killed with an axe on February 18, 1988. D.F.B., age 16, was a sophomore in high school and had discussed killing his family with friends. D.F.B. and several friends also prepared a "hit list" of others to be terminated. Several friends testified, however, that this list was merely a joke.

D.F.B. had no history of delinquent behavior. He had, however, been depressed for several years. D.F.B. expressed fear of his father, but masked the depression with jokes and quick wit at school. Some school reports indicate D.F.B. was depressed when his brother left home (or was ousted) in the fall of 1987. Two good friends moved away in the same year. D.F.B. twice attempted suicide, once in June 1987 and again in September.

There were twenty-two wounds upon D.F.B.'s father's body, nineteen upon the body of his mother, eight upon the body of his sister, and nine upon the body of his brother.

After his family was killed (sometime around 3:00 A.M. on February 18), D.F.B. obtained cash and purchased groceries. He cut and dyed his hair and then slept in a culvert. He was arrested the following day at the post office while talking on the telephone with a friend. D.F.B. was placed in the custody of the county sheriff.

1. Should D.F.B. be referred for adult prosecution?
   a. Yes, for there is probable cause to believe D.F.B. committed murder in the first degree, and there is evidence that D.F.B. is not amenable to treatment.
   b. No, because D.F.B. is only sixteen years of age.
   c. No, because D.F.B. has no history of prior delinquent acts.
   d. No, because although these acts were criminal, they were actions that came from extreme emotional disturbance during puberty when a body is not matured, and such acts will not be repeated as D.F.B. has now run out of family (which was the singular focus of his anger).
   e. No, because police should always use the least restrictive alternative for dealing with any type of juvenile problem.
2. If the county sheriff had known of D.F.B.'s disturbed emotional state of mind prior to the murders, what action might the police have taken?
   a. Initiate a treatment program (patterned along the lines of informal probation).
   b. Attempt a deterrence program (athletic, recreational, and club activities).
   c. Voluntary referral to appropriate community agencies.
   d. Establish a counselling service to give one-on-one talks to youths.
   e. Only deal with mandatory referral to mental or public health agencies under statutory authorization to make such referrals (e.g., to detoxification programs).
3. Because of the vulnerability of juveniles, greater safeguards are needed, such as:
   a. Greater intrusions than are normally allowed under the Fourth Amendment for adults should be allowed to protect juveniles from damaging home environments.
   b. Stronger mandates must be allowed for juvenile treatment programs.
   c. Juveniles should not be permitted to waive constitutional rights on their own.
   d. More restrictive means should be allowed to protect juveniles from themselves (in the instance of suicide).

e. Juveniles should receive a totally different set of safeguards than adults in preliminary investigations (e.g., stop and frisk), questioning, search and seizure, and the arrest process.

Discussion Questions

1. What are the advantages and disadvantages of a separate system of justice for juveniles?
2. A major principle of English common law is *parens patriae*. Is this philosophy viable in today's society?
3. Should the police be responsible for status offenses or should some other agency such as the welfare department be given the options of dealing with youth who commit these offenses?
4. What is "individualized" justice and what role has it played in the development of the juvenile court in the United States?
5. Would our society be better off if we treated juveniles like adults in the justice system? Explain.
6. Is the status offender like or different from the delinquent? Do status offenders "get worse"; that is, do their offenses escalate into more serious offenses?
7. Should juvenile offenders be subjected to capital punishment?

Definitions

Can you define the following terms?

child welfare model   one-pot jurisdictional approach
DARE   *parens patriae*
decriminalization   shadow children
diversion   station adjustment
juvenile   status offenses
juvenile delinquency   street justice
juvenile justice model

References

Abadinsky, Howard. *Crime and Justice: An Introduction*. Chicago: Nelson-Hall Publishers, 1987.

Arthur, Lindsay G. "Foreword," pp. ix–x. In *Juvenile Justice* by Robert W. Drowns and Kären M. Hess. St. Paul, Minn.: West Publishing Company, 1990.

Belknap, J.; Morash, M.; and Trojanowicz, R. *Implementing a Community Policing Model for Work with Juveniles: An Exploratory Study*. East Lansing, Mich.: National Neighborhood Foot Patrol Center, School of Criminal Justice, Michigan University, 1986.

Briscoe, Judy Culpepper. "In Texas: Reaching Out to Help Troubled Youth." *Corrections Today* (October 1990): 90–95.

Brown, Lee P. "Making the Problems of Youth a National Priority." *The Police Chief* (June 1991). 6.

Bureau of Justice Statistics. *Report to the Nation on Crime and Justice*. U.S. Department of Justice. Washington, D.C.: U.S. Government Printing Office, 1988.

Drowns, Robert W. and Hess, Kären M. *Juvenile Justice*. St. Paul, Minn. West Publishing Company, 1990.

Fanton, Barrie. "Preventing Sexual Assault." *Police* (August 1987): 47–67.

Forst, Martin L. "Law Enforcement Policies on Missing Children." *Law and Order* (June 1990): 57–60.

Kaplan, Howard B. *Patterns of Juvenile Delinquency*. Beverly Hills, Calif.: Sage Publications, 1984.

Law Enforcement Training and Information Network (LETIN). *Training Guide: Dealing with Adolescents*. Volume 2, Cassette 10, 1986.

Payne, James W. and Lee, Joe E. "In Indiana: A System Designed to Accommodate Juveniles' Needs." *Corrections Today* (October 1990): 100–106.

Pindur, Wolfgang and Wells, Donna. "An Alternative Model for Juvenile Justice." In *Criminal Justice 88/89,* John J. Sullivan, ed. Guilford, Conn.: The Dushkin Publishing Group, 1988.

Reed, Sally and Sautter, R. Craig. *Children of Poverty: The Status of 12 Million Young Americans–Kappan Special Report*. Bloomington, Ind.: Phi Delta Kappa, June 1990.

Rist, Marilee. "The Shadow Children: Preparing for the Arrival of Crack Babies in School." Research Bulletin. Phi Delta Kappa Center on Evaluation, Development, and Research, July 1990, No. 9.

Romig, Dennis A.; Cleland, Charles C.; and Romig, Laurie J. *Juvenile Delinquency: Visionary Approaches*. Columbus, Ohio: Merrill Publishing Company, 1989.

Russell, Harold E. and Beigel, Allan. *Understanding Human Behavior for Effective Police Work*. 3d ed. New York: Basic Books, 1990.

Springer, Charles E. *Justice for Juveniles*. Office of Juvenile Justice and Delinquency Prevention. Washington, D.C.: U.S. Government Printing Office, 1986.

Sullivan, John J., ed. "Facts about Youth and Delinquency." In *Criminal Justice 88/89*. Guilford, Conn.: The Dushkin Publishing Group, 1988, p. 159.

Territo, Leonard; Halsted, James; and Bromley, Max. *Crime and Justice in America*. St. Paul, Minn.: West Publishing Company, 1992.

Case

In re Gault, 387 U.S. 1, 87 S.Ct. 1428, 18 L.Ed.2d 527 (1967).

GANGS AND DRUGS: TWO NATIONAL THREATS

INTRODUCTION

Gangs and drugs are often intimately related to each other and to crime and violence and public fear. FBI Director William Sessions (1989, p. 11) says: "Our nation is facing the greatest law enforcement crisis in its history. It is a crisis of drug trafficking and drug use—and the enormous amount of violent crime caused by drugs."

The problem is exceedingly complex. Not all gangs deal with drugs, and not all who use drugs commit crimes. Law enforcement officers must maintain objectivity and refrain from stereotyping gang members and drug users and pushers. They must know how to deal with gangs effectively and how to do their part in the war on drugs.

Do You Know

- What illegal activities gang members often engage in?
- What the first step in dealing with a gang problem usually is?
- How gangs might be identified?
- How gang problems might be dealt with?
- How criminologists have categorized street gangs?
- What are critical elements in an illegal drug buy?
- Why the sale and use of illegal drugs is difficult for police to investigate and prosecute?
- How to avoid a charge of entrapment?
- What the predominant approach to the drug problem in the 1980s was?
- What the predominant approach to the drug problem in the 1990s is?

The Gang Problem

The *gang* label has been applied to various groups, from the "Spanky and our gang" little rascals of the 1920s to the leather-clad, violent, drug-using outlaw motorcycle gangs of the 1950s and 1960s. People often talk about getting their "gang" together. Belonging to a gang is certainly not a crime. Most people belong to groups or organizations. But when a gang engages in violence or crime, it is a law enforcement problem.

Gang members often engage in vandalism, arson, shootings, stabbings, and other kinds of violence.

Recognizing a Gang Problem

Many communities are blind to local gang activity. The Office of Juvenile Justice and Delinquency Prevention (OJJDP) held a conference for nineteen metropolitan cities where youth gangs were just beginning to emerge. Experts from Los Angeles, Chicago, and Miami provided the teams attending the conference with a national perspective on how they were dealing with the gang problem. Kramer, of the Los Angeles Police Department, cautioned that "denial and apathy in far too many communities, including Los Angeles, have resulted [in] and contributed to inertia and inaction" (Bryant, 1989, p. 4). He stressed that the first step in overcoming the gang problem is to overcome "the political denial that gangs exist in your community."

The first step in dealing with a gang problem is to recognize it.

In Bellingham, Washington (daytime population 120,000, permanent population 50,000), for example, a Los Angeles Crip member and two Black Gangster Disciples organized a rap singing group and began recruiting youth into their gang. According to Pierce and Ramsay (1990, p. 24): "The gang began to declare its existence with graffiti on downtown business walls, park buildings, and even police vehicles." They openly displayed their colors, tattoos, and gang logos on T-shirts. When law enforcement recognized the threat posed by the gang, they increased their enforcement measures, arresting over twenty-five members on felony charges. The gang's response was frightening (p. 24): "In response to heightened enforcement measures, gang-related graffiti increased markedly and became revenge-oriented. Police and sheriff's department vehicles were vandalized with gang graffiti threatening officers' lives, and the 911 dispatch center received phone threats concerning the killing of police officers."

When the community became involved in preventing gang activity, some success was finally achieved. As Pierce and Ramsay (p. 25) stress: "Most significantly, the community has accepted the fact that gangs could — and have — come to Bellingham. That acceptance is critical to the development and coordination of efforts to combat continued gang expansion; single law enforcement measures will be inadequate without community involvement. The successes achieved to date are rooted

Graffiti—the newspaper of the streets. It is likely that the wall will soon have several additions to this message unless the graffiti is promptly removed.

in a strong community desire to avoid gang victimization.'' Once the problem is recognized, the specific gang, individual members, and any illegal activities must be identified and investigated.

Identifying Gang Members

Gang members take pride in belonging to their specific gang and will make their membership known in various ways. Many gang members have street names, called **monikers.** Often more than one gang member has the same moniker. They frequently use hand signals. The color of clothing can also be an indication of gang membership. For example, Bloods are identified by red or green colors. Crips are associated with blue or purple bandanas or scarves.

Gang members identify themselves by their names, clothing, sign language, and graffiti.

Most gangs establish a specific area, their **turf,** that they mark with **graffiti** and will defend to the death. They control their turf through intimidation and violence. Police officers can learn much about gang activity if graffiti appears in their jurisdiction. Graffiti may list gang member's names, often in order of authority. The most graffiti will appear in the center of the turf area. If graffiti is crossed out or overwritten, it is often the challenge of a rival gang. If gang symbols are written upside down, this graffiti is usually written by a rival gang and is a great insult to the gang it depicts. Gang members caught crossing out a rival's graffiti are usually severely beaten or even killed.

The Vice Lords use the following symbols in their graffiti:

- Cane—staff of strength.
- Circle—360 degrees of knowledge that blacks ruled the world in the past and will again do so.

A gang summit. Mike Concepcion (seated), a co-founder of the Crips gang; popular rapper, Tone Loc (right); and other rappers talk with the press calling for a truce in gang violence before taping a music video with the same message at the Nickerson Gardens housing project in the Watts section of Los Angeles. The stars are lending their talents to a record whose proceeds will go to Project Build, a local anti-gang organization.

- Crescent Moons—the splitting of the Black Nation into two parts, one West, one East.
- Fire—the Black Nation's true knowledge being suppressed and their inability to reach knowledge because of the fire's heat.
- Gloves—purity.
- Hat—shelter.
- Pyramid—the mystery of the pyramid constructed by black people. The three corners represent physical, mental, and spiritual knowledge.
- Rabbit—swiftness.
- Star—the eye of Allah, watching over his people.
- Sun—the rising of truth in the Black Nation.

These symbols are often personalized and may appear in various combinations (see Figure 14.1).

Recording Information

An effective records system is critical in dealing with any gang problem. Ruester (1989, pp. 41–42) describes the following as essential information gathered by Los Angeles County:

> *Gang member's names, nicknames, physical description (including tattoos),*
> *territories, mothers' maiden names, tactics, condition of probation. . .*
> *whether the gang has a speciality, like car theft, as well as partial license*

FIGURE 14.1

379

CHAPTER 14
Gangs and Drugs:
Two National Threats

Typical Vice Lord Markings Documented In Minneapolis, Minnesota.
Bear in mind that these markings are often personalized and may appear in
various combinations. Watch for repeated code and image patterns.

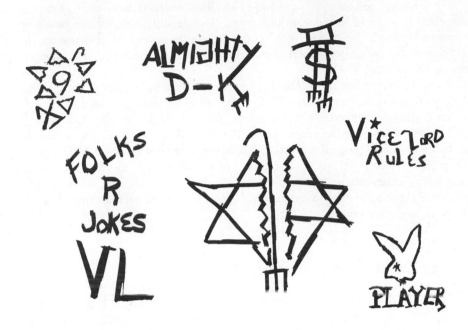

plate numbers and other aids to cross-checking. Each gang is coded as to
which jurisdiction "owns" it.

The importance of records is echoed by Jackson and McBride (1985, pp. 97–
103), who see information as an essential tool for law enforcement and recommend
that the following information be recorded and filed alphabetically by name:

- Number of active and associate members.
- Type of gang (street, motorcycle, car club).
- Ethnic composition.
- Territory and boundaries.
- Hideouts.
- Type(s) of crime(s) usually committed.
- Method of operation.
- Choice of victims (illegal aliens, aged).
- Members who fill leadership roles.
- Members known to be violent.

Photographs and information on vehicles are also important parts of the records on
gangs.

Investigating Illegal Activities of Gangs

The same procedures used in investigating any other kind of illegal activity apply
to investigating the illegal activities of gangs. Information and evidence must support the elements of specific offenses and link the gang members to those offenses.

It is often difficult to obtain information about a gang's illegal activities because the gang members will stick together, and they will intimidate the people living and working within their turf. Business people and residents alike are usually fearful of telling the police anything, believing the gang will cause them great harm if they do.

If a neighborhood canvass is conducted and information is received, it is important that the canvass not stop at that point. This would implicate the house or business at which the canvass was terminated as the source of information. In addition, more information might be available from a source not yet contacted during the canvass.

As noted by Jackson and McBride (p. 118), ''Crime scenes that involve gangs present elements that are unique.'' Often the scene is part of a chain of events. When a gang assault occurs, for example, often a chase precedes the assault, considerably widening the crime scene. If vehicles are involved, the assault is probably by a rival gang. If no vehicles appear to have been involved, the suspects are probably local, perhaps even members of the same gang as the victim. This frequently occurs when narcotics, girlfriends, or family disputes are involved. Evidence obtained in gang investigations is processed in the same manner as evidence in any other crime.

A Systemwide Strategy to Deal with Gangs

Bryant (1989, p. 4) describes an eight-step process called *IDENTIFY,* developed by the OJJDP to involve not only law enforcement but schools, courts, parents, and community leaders:

- *Identify the problem:* Specify the problem and the target location. Determine who is creating the problem, the specific nature of these activities, and where and when the problem is most intense.
- *Define the system components:* Determine which agencies in the community own the problem and have the authority and responsibility for solving it.
- *Enumerate policies, procedures, practices, programs, and resources:* Specify the existing agency policies and practices that address the problem, and resources that are or could be used to address the problem.
- *Needs clarification:* Compare information on the nature and extent of the problem with existing resources to determine additional policy, procedures, practices, and program and resource needs.
- *Target strategies:* Identify the policies, procedures, practices, and programs and integrate them into a coordinated strategy to respond to the problem.
- *Implementation plan:* Prepare a plan that defines the objectives, tasks, and resources to be dedicated by each participating agency for implementing the strategy.
- *Focus agency responsibilities:* Identify the specific activities of the strategy to be performed by each participating agency, define the role and responsibilities of each agency in implementing the activities, and ensure accountability.
- *Yell:* Each of the agencies should monitor and assess the implementation of the strategy, and make adjustments as needed (yelling as necessary to ensure adjustments are made).

The OJJDP suggested several other ways to combat the gang problem, including the following.

To combat a gang problem:

- *Gather information.*
- *Do not tolerate graffiti.*
- *Target hard-core gang leaders.*
- *Consolidate major gang-control functions.*

St. Paul, Minnesota, illustrates how a hard-core gang leader might be targeted. In December of 1989, forty-four-year-old Ralph "Plukey" Duke and four others were convicted of drug charges. A Naegele-donated billboard on St. Paul's East side bears a message other gang members will hopefully not soon forget (see photo). Much publicity has also been generated by the confiscation of Duke's car and its subsequent conversion into a police car.

Gang diversion is the approach used in Austin, Texas. To combat the onslaught of graffiti and violence caused by mobile youth gangs, the police department and concerned citizens formed a group called Citizens Helping Austin Neighborhood Gang Environment (CHANGE). The unique goal of this group, according to Benson (1990, p. 66), was "to encourage the gangs to call a truce among themselves

A billboard on Seventh St. in St. Paul's East Side bidding "Good-bye" to Ralph "Plukey" Duke, a drug dealer who was convicted of drug charges and is serving a life sentence without parole. The blue billboard was a public service message against drug use.

long enough to meet and discuss their differences.'' The approach was successful, and gang members have been able to work out many of their differences. Since the program has been operating, drive-by shootings have decreased dramatically, as has the amount of graffiti. The reduction in graffiti is due in large part to the willingness of local businesses to let gangs use their walls for murals. Gang members are challenged to make their neighborhoods the most attractive in Austin. According to Benson (p. 68), ''One gang cleaned up their neighborhood one weekend. It took seven garbage trucks to haul it out.''

CHANGE also channels the energy and aggression of gang members into competitive sports. The police department hosts a double-elimination softball tournament twice a month. Austin City Council member Robert Barnstone says of this approach (Benson, p. 68), ''. . . it was a lot harder to shoot at somebody that you have tried to put out at second base.''

Another approach to dealing with gangs is to *consolidate* those divisions within a department who deal with aspects of the gang problem. In studying Ohio gangs, Dr. Huff (Bryant, 1989, p. 5) found that police success in dealing with gangs was due in large part to combining its four major gang-control functions of prevention, intelligence, enforcement, and investigation (usually performed by four different divisions) into a Youth Violence Crime Section. The result was that all officers in the section were able to recognize all gang members on sight.

Recently, according to the Associated Press (1992, p. 7A) headlines, the FBI has brought ''spy catching skills into war against gangs.'' As a result of the breakup of Communist regimes in Eastern Europe, the FBI is sending 300 agents formerly assigned to counterintelligence there to thirty-nine cities in the United States to help deal with gang problems. The article notes:

The FBI brings some important tools to the gang front, including broader powers to use wiretaps and seize drug dealers' property, an ability to prosecute under federal laws on extortion, racketeering and interstate crime, and longer prison terms for some crimes.

Gangs and Drugs

According to Donahue (1989, p. 1), administrator of the OJJDP: ''The escalation of youth gang violence has left many communities virtually unprepared to provide an adequate response to a growing national dilemma. Much of this violence is drug-related, spurred on by the illegal, yet enormous, profits drug dealers earn.'' Donahue suggests that, ''The fierce circle of drugs, profits, and violence threatens the freedom and public safety of citizens from coast to coast. It holds in its grip large jurisdictions and small ones, urban areas and rural ones.''

The Metropolitan Court Judges (1988, p. 45) note that, in the mid-1980s, youth gangs from Los Angeles, Miami, Chicago, Detroit, and New York became ''major criminal entrepreneurs in the supply of illicit drugs.''

At this conference, the consensus was that illegal gang activity was growing worse in cities with chronic gang problems as well as in those cities where the problem was just beginning. In Los Angeles, the number of gangs increased 71 percent from 1985 to 1988, as did the percentage of gang-related homicides. Gates and Jackson (1990, p. 20) say that more than 450 street gangs with memberships exceeding 36,000 are active in Los Angeles and that 800 gangs with memberships exceeding 75,000 members are active in Los Angeles County. During 1989, 1,112 drive-by shooting incidents accounted for 1,675 victims, 50 percent of whom were "not remotely associated with any form of gang activity."

As noted by Sessions (1990, p. 17): "In Los Angeles, criminologists have divided youth or street gangs into two general categories: cultural and instrumental."

Cultural gangs *are neighborhood-centered and exist independently of criminal activity.* ***Instrumental gangs*** *are formed for the express purpose of criminal activity, primarily drug trafficking.*

Police conflicts with most cultural gangs center around turf. The youth gangs mark out a specific territory using graffiti and then defend this territory ferociously, even to the death.

Certain gangs that began as cultural gangs, especially such gangs as the Bloods and the Crips, have evolved into instrumental gangs. Says Kramer, Los Angeles Police Department (Donahue, p. 3): "These [instrumental] gangs are transporting L.A.-style gang activities from South Central Los Angeles to regional suburban areas nationwide." He suggests that the primary motive of these instrumental gangs is monetary: "With an estimated $130 billion exchanged nationwide by drug dealers in 1987, it's easy to see why gangs have become involved in the narcotics trade."

According to Hill of the Drug Enforcement Administration (DEA) (Bryant, 1989, p. 3), although members of L.A. gangs have been identified in all 50 states: "There is no organization. There is no head person in Los Angeles or San Diego or San Francisco telling a gang member to go from Los Angeles to your town, U.S.A." They go partly because of an oversupply of drugs and dealers in California and partly because of the aggressive law enforcement there. The lure of greater profits and less police harassment draws them to other cities. The fact that these gangs are not organized makes it more difficult for law enforcement to deal with the problem.

The Metropolitan Court Judges Committee (1988, p. 45) points out that domestically grown marijuana, clandestine laboratory-produced methamphetamine and PCP, and domestically manufactured crack/cocaine "opened the floodgates for serious youth participation in the huge profits available through illicit drug trafficking." They summarize the growing involvement of gangs in the drug business as follows:

The Crips and Bloods of Los Angeles, the Miami Boys of south Florida, the Jamaican Posses of Florida and New York, and the Vice Lords of Chicago are among the gangs who entered the field on a large scale. They followed on the heels of long-time marijuana and methamphetamine supply activities conducted by motorcycle gangs for a number of years. They are being mimicked by white-youth-dominated Stoner, Skinhead, neo-Nazi, and satanical cult groups.

The committee says the gangs consciously exploit the juvenile justice system, taking advantage of its paternalistic approach to youthful offenders. Although convicted youths can be certified to adult court, most states stipulate that the offender must be over the age of fifteen. Even should a youth be certified to adult court, most judges are reluctant to sentence youth under the age of eighteen to adult correctional facilities.

The Jamaican Posses are another kind of gang closely associated with drugs and violence. According to Charles Sarabyn, of the Bureau of Alcohol, Tobacco, and Firearms (ATF), the Jamaican Posses are comprised primarily of adults and are "very organized," "very transient," and "very violent." Sarabyn estimates that more than forty posses with an estimated 10,000 members are operating in metropolitan areas throughout the country and that 1,400 homicides committed between 1985 and 1988 have been attributed to the posses. The DEA estimates that the posses are responsible for 40 percent of the crack/cocaine business in the United States.

A more recent problem gang is that known as "home invaders." Burke (1990, p. 23) characterizes home invaders as "young Asian males (typically in their twenties, although the oldest known member is forty) who work in groups of two to nine members." These gang members know that Asian businesspeople mistrust banks and often keep large amounts of cash and jewelry at home. According to Burke, the robberies are usually committed in the evening when the victims are likely to be home. The robbers rely on intimidation and fear of retaliation to gain possession of the victims' valuables. He concludes that "home invaders are traveling across the country, leaving a trail of terrorized victims. It is the responsibility of police managers and community leaders to identify these gang members and take the necessary action to minimize the potential harm to the community."

The Drug Problem

Gangs are not the only faction involved in dealing drugs. Organized crime is also heavily into this area as are some "reputable" businesspeople. In fact, the illicit drug trade, according to Blank (1988, p. 27), "is probably the fastest-growing industry in the world and is unquestionably the most profitable. . . . The global drug trade may run up to $500 billion a year, more than twice the value of all U.S. currency in circulation. The American market, the world's biggest for these drugs, produces annual revenues of at least $100 billion at retail."

Further, this drug trade has created, says Blank, "a breed of shadowy billionaires who seem as canny in business as they are vicious." Blank (p. 38) concludes: "America's war on drugs is long on rhetoric and short on effectiveness. Busting drug dealers, as a Washington analyst puts it, 'is like trying to put General Motors out of business by knocking off used-car dealers.' "

The Police Response

Moore and Kleinman (1989, p. 1) suggest that when dealing with the drug problem, police should consider four strategic questions:

- What goals might reasonably be set for drug enforcement?
- What parts of the police department engage the drug problem and to what effect?
- What role can citizens' and community groups usefully (and properly) play in coping with the problem?
- What basic strategies might the police department consider as alternative attacks on the problem?

Moore and Kleinman (p. 2) also outline the main threats to community security posed by the drug problem:

- The violence associated with street-level drug dealing—THE most pressing threat.
- The close link between drug use and street crime.
- Drug use undermines the health, economic well-being, and social responsibility of drug users.
- Drug trafficking threatens the civility of city life and undermines parenting.
- Police can accomplish little by themselves.
- In committing officers to attack drug trafficking and drug use, the department risks corruption and abuses of authority.

For each identified threat, a corresponding goal can be stated (p. 2):

- Reduce the gang violence associated with drug trafficking and prevent the emergence of powerful organized criminal groups.
- Control the street crimes committed by drug users.
- Improve the health and economic and social well-being of drug users.
- Restore the quality of life in urban communities by ending street-level drug dealing.
- Help to prevent children from experimenting with drugs.
- Protect the integrity of criminal justice institutions.

To meet these goals, police often use simple drug buys, undercover operations, and raids.

The Simple Drug Buy

Many police departments use plainclothes police officers or informants to make drug buys which are watched by a surveillance team. Often these buys are taped to provide further evidence of illegal activity. In addition, the surveillance team can step in if trouble develops and the plainclothes officer or informant needs help. Such buys are also useful because they can provide leads to the suspect's other customers and associates as well as to where the supply is coming from. Often it is best to simply watch and wait, continuing to make buys and to gather information rather than to make an immediate arrest.

Even "simple" buys must be carefully prepared for to avoid charges of entrapment. The person making the buy must be searched and then given the buy money. After the transaction, the buyer must again be searched and the drugs taken as evidence. Police Science Services (1977a, p 4) lists several important points to remember about drug buys:

1. Drug dealing is a victimless crime. Both buyer and seller try to keep their transactions secret. This severely limits the value of conventional investigative techniques. Buys are used to fill the gap.
2. A buy occurs when an undercover agent and/or an informant attempts to purchase drugs from a suspected dealer.
3. When the operation succeeds:
   a. The agents and/or informants can testify to the transaction.
   b. They may get leads to the location of the suspect's stash.

    c. They may acquire evidence for a warrant to search the suspect's base of operations.

    d. They may gather information about the suspect's customers, accomplices, and source of supply.

4. A buy operation takes place in three well-defined stages:
    a. Preparations for the buy.
    b. The buy itself.
    c. Steps needed after the buy to process evidence and information.

5. Informants are often used and may sometimes be essential. Nevertheless, they cannot be trusted completely. They may supply false information, they may reveal your plans to criminals, and they may set you up for a robbery or an ambush. Always check informants carefully before using them.

6. Evidence in buy cases is subject to severe legal restrictions. These must be kept in mind at all times.

7. Try to avoid any action that may give a seller an excuse to claim that he or she was entrapped.

8. Agents and informants may be robbed or ambushed. Take every precaution that can minimize these risks.

9. Learn all you can about the situation as a whole before you make your plan.

10. Security is vital. The slightest leak can ruin the operation and endanger the agent.

11. Record all bills that are to be used for the buy.

12. The backing of a surveillance team is highly desirable. It can both protect the agent and secure additional evidence.

13. Make a careful plan. Try to cover every contingency.

14. Thorough briefing is essential, but brief each participant on a need-to-know basis.

15. When a surveillance team is involved, arrange a set of signals.

16. Search any informant and his or her vehicle just before starting.

17. During the buy, stick to the plan as closely as possible. Any deviation increases the risk and decreases the chance of obtaining admissible evidence.

18. The agent should control the situation and refuse to accept suggestions made by the seller.

19. The agent should make the buy himself rather than let the informant do it.

20. Try to secure all available information about the location of the stash. If the seller goes somewhere to get the drugs, a member of the surveillance team may be able to follow.

21. Warn sellers of their rights as soon as you arrest them. Then search them to recover the buy money and any other evidence.

22. Also search the informant.

23. Test the drugs and weigh or count them. Take every possible precaution to protect their integrity and to maintain the chain of custody.

24. Debrief everyone who took part.

25. Make an operational report and a detailed financial report.

Sometimes drug buys are much more sophisticated and complex. Such buys often involve carefully planned undercover operations.

One primary approach to dealing with the drug problem is through undercover operations. In such operations, police officers assume a fictitious identity and attempt to infiltrate a drug ring or a drug-dealing gang or to pose as a buyer of drugs.

DEA Special Agent Moriarty (1990, p. 44) stresses that: "The negotiation skills of undercover narcotics officers are among the most critical elements contributing to their operational success, as well as their personal safety and survival." This is especially critical when the officer must negotiate a "high-stakes illegal arrangement" such as a drug buy. He suggests that the negotiations conducted by an undercover narcotics officer are similar to those used by a hostage negotiator and require similar communication skills. In the case of the undercover agent, however, the innocent victim whose life may be saved is the agent: "The officer is literally negotiating for his own life, and he is usually alone with his adversary at the time."

To successfully negotiate, undercover agents need as much *information* as possible about the sellers and their needs. Agents often consider that money is the main objective of drug dealers, but security is often even more important. This can be seen in drug dealers' insistence on controlling all aspects of the transaction, especially the location. Moriarty (p. 46) suggests that undercover officers may get dealers to compromise their security by directing negotiations toward issues such as consistent quality and ease and security of future transactions: "The skilled undercover negotiator will use a suspect's failure to contest the location and conditions of the actual deal as an agreement to meet his own requirements."

Another critical factor in undercover negotiations is *time*. Most drug dealers want to conduct their business as rapidly as possible, keeping the amount of time they have the drugs in their possession to a minimum. Undercover agents can also give the impression of being in a hurry to conduct business, perhaps by having an airline ticket with an impending departure time printed on the envelope jutting from a pocket. Despite the time press to conduct the transaction, it must also be remembered that the passage of time builds trust. Says Moriarty (p. 46), "Experienced undercover officers are in almost unanimous agreement that nothing will instill greater trust in a trafficker than shutting a negotiation down and walking away."

Information and time are critical elements in an illegal drug buy.

Another critical aspect of the buy is how the **flashroll,** the buy money, is managed. Special DEA Agent Wade feels that undercover narcotics officers who are injured or killed while on assignment have usually mismanaged the flashroll. Wade (1990, p. 49) suggests that: "The best way for a new undercover agent to learn to handle flashrolls is to watch how a streetwise drug trafficker handles his product. The dealer continually strives to keep purchasers off balance, never letting them know where the drugs are until the last minute—often after the money has been observed."

Wade (p. 48) also cautions that: "The most dangerous time during the scenario is when the drugs and money are in the same place." Grave risks also occur when the flashroll is *not* present. In such instances, undercover agents may not be as on guard as they should be because they feel they are not at very much risk.

If the flashroll is present, agents should allow the dealer to count the money. There is little point in having it on hand if this is not part of the plan. If the agent cannot come up with the full amount requested, it is sometimes a good tactic to simply explain to the dealer that cash is temporarily short. According to Wade (p. 48): "This is an excellent ruse since traffickers are convinced that the police have all the money in the world, and that no undercover police officer would ever admit to having insufficient funds to make the purchase." Such an admission can do much to strengthen the agent's cover.

Undercover agent safety can be maximized, according to Wade (p. 50) by following these basic axioms of flashroll management:

1. Never flash the money twice unless absolutely necessary.
2. Always move the flashroll as soon as possible after it has been displayed, thereby severely limiting the subject's access to the money.
3. Never move to a second location with the flashroll in your possession.
4. Take pains to ensure that the dealer is not inadvertently tipped that the money will be flashed.

Police Science Services (1977b, p. 4) lists the following points to remember when conducting an undercover drug assignment:

1. Undercover operations are used as an investigative technique to gather information and collect evidence.
2. Agents may penetrate gangs or cultures associated with crime. They also gain evidence by making deals involving such things as bribery and drugs.
3. The agent normally assumes a fictitious identity. His chief function is to see and hear. He does not normally take positive action.
4. As undercover work involves high risks, it must be planned with care. Everyone connected with the operation needs to understand his or her role in detail.
5. Agents need a taste for the work and a natural aptitude. They should also have courage, intelligence, and resourcefulness. Female agents require higher qualifications than men, as they run greater risks.
6. The agent must blend in with the places where he is to work and the people with whom he will associate.
7. Each agent must assume the role of a specific individual. He needs a name, a character, and a cover story with complete background data.
8. The agent's clothes and equipment must include everything that fits the role—and nothing that is inconsistent with it.
9. When possible, plant corroboration for the agent's cover story in advance.
10. Make contact by degrees when time permits.
11. Listening is better and safer than talking.
12. Expect to be challenged. If you are:
    a. Know your cover story inside out.
    b. Answer a question with a question.
    c. Attack is often the best defense.
    d. Use the big lie technique. Stick to your story no matter how preposterous it is.

13. When you must work with an informant, check him out in every possible way—and never trust him completely.
14. Notes and written reports are risky. Telephone reports if you can. When a report must be written, get rid of it at once.

15. As most criminal deals are conducted secretly, the only way to get evidence of them may be for an agent to take part. Such operations are often complex. They must be planned and executed with great care.
16. The agent must be strictly controlled by his supervisor and must keep in close touch with him. The agent should have an emergency phone number to use if he gets into trouble. Surveillance teams are often used, both to protect the agent and to act in concert with him.
17. Agents must avoid dangerous situations whenever possible. Women and liquor always involve major risks.
18. An agent should also insist on controlling his contacts with a suspect.

The sale and use of illegal drugs is difficult to investigate and prosecute because sellers and buyers are willing participants.

Entrapment

Whether a sophisticated undercover operation or a simple drug buy is involved, care must be taken to avoid a charge of entrapment. **Entrapment,** as stated in Chapter 5, occurs when a police officer (or other government official or person acting on behalf of the police or government) entices someone to commit a crime the person would not normally commit. Repeated requests to buy drugs are sometimes considered to be entrapment.

In *Hampton v. United States* (1976), Hampton was convicted of selling heroin to DEA agents. The question before the Court was if a government informant supplies heroin to a person who then sells it to government agents, is this entrapment? The Court said No; Hampton was "predisposed" to deal in drugs. This view agrees with the majority opinion on entrapment, focusing on the behavior of the defendant rather than on that of the officers involved. States vary, however, as to whether they support the majority or the minority view. The minority view focuses on how officers or their agents conduct themselves.

To avoid charges of entrapment, those making the buy, be they plainclothes officers, informants, or undercover agents, should make more than one buy. The more buys made, the weaker the entrapment defense.

Making several drug buys will protect against a claim of entrapment.

Drug Raids

During the 1980s, drug raids also made frequent headlines. Tanklike vehicles, SWAT teams, and sophisticated weaponry have all been involved in drug raids. During such raids, communication is usually critical. According to Wallace (1990, p. 33), radios that can provide speech encryption greatly enhance officer safety. He

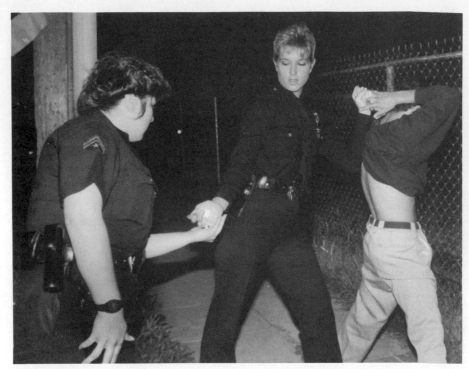

A Los Angeles police officer hands another officer a marble-sized piece of rock cocaine found on a teenage member of a local gang during a 1,000+ police task force crack down on drug dealing and street violence.

notes that "today's drug dealers have sophisticated scanners and programmable radios to eavesdrop on law enforcement communications. Using speech encryption radios, team members can communicate among themselves and with the base station with assurance that no one can descramble their conversations." This capability, says Wallace "can mean the difference between the success or failure of a drug raid, and the life or death for tactical team members."

In combatting the drug problem, law enforcement in the 1980s focused on undercover operations and sophisticated raids. In the 1990s, law enforcement is focusing on enlisting and educating the public and targeting street-level sales.

Combatting Street-Level Narcotics Sales

As noted by Cushing (1989, p. 113): "Every junkie knows of several locations where narcotics can be purchased, and is usually eager to give up this information to avoid prosecution. But the narcotics trade has expanded to the point where even law-abiding citizens can tell the police where dope is being sold."

Citizens do know where drug dealing is going on. If they can be encouraged to report these locations, police can concentrate their efforts on those locations receiving the most complaints. Cushing stresses that often police officers want to go higher than the street pusher, but that they should avoid this temptation. If information regarding someone higher up is obtained, it should be given to the narcotics unit for follow-up. The main purpose of the street-level raids is to respond to citizen complaints and to let them see that their complaints are being acted on—that arrests are being made.

This same philosophy was behind the creation of Tampa's QUAD Squads in which the city was divided into quadrants patrolled by special squads. The acronym soon came to stand for "Quick Uniform Attack on Drugs," which was its purpose—to very visibly free the streets of drug dealers. Says Korzeniowski (1990, p. 83): "Involvement is the key. . . . Every officer in a QUAD Squad has a beeper. They give out their number to citizens in their quad as they get involved. Anyone can call in, even anonymously if they wish." The officers are usually able to respond immediately.

After a QUAD Squad makes an arrest at a given location, they are often able to set up a reverse sting, arresting those who come to buy drugs thinking this is still the place to get them.

A similar approach is used by the Patrol NET (Narcotics Enforcement Team) Bureau in Suffolk County, New York. According to Rau (1990, p. 42): "The Patrol NET Bureau was created to immediately and significantly confront high-visibility drug problems. . . . Arrests are made contemporaneously with transactions by designated 'take down' teams."

St. Michaels, Maryland (population 1,300), tackled their drug-dealing problem by bringing in a new chief of police who was committed to addressing the problem. The new chief trained the six patrol officers in how to aggressively seek out and arrest those dealing drugs. As noted by Hoffmann (1991, p. 102), "Pressure and some big-city tactics applied on the out of town dealers and local users showed some success." The St. Michaels Police Department convinced the Rotary Club to buy them a surveillance telescope, which they used to take photographs of drug deals from a distance. In addition, grant money was obtained to open a daycare in a three-bedroom unit in one of the housing complexes that was formerly a problem. The daycare was geared to area children and offered crafts, recreation, and tutoring with alcohol and drug awareness messages integrated into the daily routine.

A highly visible project of the daycare is their "Cookie Kids" project. Weekly, children wear T-shirts which proclaim, We Sell Cookies, Not Drugs. The children do, indeed, bake and sell cookies to local stores.

Decatur, Georgia (population 19,000), used a similar targeting approach for its drug problem. According to Harris and Hudson (1991, p. 45):

The first phase of Decatur's drug strategy was increased street-level enforcement activities in targeted areas. Phase II was an extensive undercover investigation at a motel that served as a haven for numerous drug dealers. A housing project was the scene of Phase III, an undercover operation with informants and undercover agents. The fourth and current phase involves continuing street-level enforcement and investigation in target areas.

As noted by Harris and Hudson (p. 47): "Decatur has realized the proven worth of a planned, methodical enforcement concept. Officials feel their key to success is the continuation of a 'one neighborhood at a time' approach, concentrating all resources to eliminate one problem before moving to another." Other factors behind the success of the Decatur program are a highly supportive city administration and designating one person to coordinate the drug enforcement activities and deal with intelligence information.

Community Empowerment Policing (CEP)

Closely related to the preceding efforts are those efforts focused on Community Empowerment Policing (CEP). According to Fulwood (1990, p. 50), Chief of the Metropolitan Police Department in Washington, D.C.: "The fight against drugs is going to be won at the neighborhood level, community by community, and that police departments must work closely with these communities if we are to be successful." Community Empowerment Policing takes the concept of neighborhood- or community-oriented policing further, advancing it to a new level. It focuses on building crime-free neighborhoods by (Fulwood, p. 50):

- Organizing community-based crime prevention activities neighborhood by neighborhood.
- Increasing law enforcement's accountability to local communities by allowing neighborhood-level input in the development of police operational policy.
- Ensuring greater supervisory accountability at the neighborhood-patrol level.
- Focusing city resources within neighborhoods to address the identified causes of specific types of crime.
- Developing juvenile delinquency prevention and early intervention activities.
- Keeping the community updated on the results of police operations in their neighborhoods.

Public Housing and the Drug Problem

"The reality of the 1990s," says Weisel (1990, p. ix), "is that few public housing residents are untouched by the drug problem." Weisel notes that:

The residents may be drug abusers, or may be buyers or sellers of drugs. They may be willing or unwilling accomplices to the drug trade, or they may be beneficiaries of benevolent drug dealers. They may look up to drug dealers as successful role models, or, more frequently, they may be fearful onlookers or innocent viewers of drug activity in their community.

To deal with the drug problem in public housing projects, police officers need to understand the workings of their local public housing authorities or agencies (PHAs) managing these complexes. Officers need to work at establishing a relationship with the PHAs and at overcoming the occasional disbelief of management and residents that the police truly want to help. Once this is accomplished, Weisel (p. 74) suggests the following key steps in solving problems in public housing:

1. Fact-finding mission.
   a. Identify key players.

Co-Op City in the Bronx, New York. Basketball is popular in this city housing project, the largest in the United States.

    b. Learn about each organization.
    c. Determine what programs are in place and the level of participation.
2. Preliminary identification and analysis of problem.
    a. What is the problem and for whom? Police, residents, housing personnel, mayor, etc.
    b. What information verifies there is a problem and how severe is the problem?
    c. Does one problem mask another problem?
3. Develop a dialogue with key players.
    a. Bring everyone abreast of progress.
    b. Enlist support; mobilize community.
    c. Assess resources; build a coalition.
4. Develop a strategy.
    a. Collect more information if necessary.
    b. Refine problem definition with input from the coalition.
    c. Develop goals and objectives.
    d. Review what strategies and tactics are being used elsewhere.
5. Select and implement a response.
    a. Coordinate a response with all available resources.

  b. Specify roles for each player.
  c. Determine a time frame.
  d. Tap other resources, such as schools, utilities, and social services.
6. Evaluate progress.
  a. Was the problem improved or changed?
  b. Redefine objectives.

Various specific strategies have been used to tackle the drug problem in public housing. Often efforts focus on improving the physical environment: limiting entrances, improving lighting, fencing projects, requiring a pass card to gain entrance to the housing, and keeping trash collected.

Efforts may also focus on removing offenders, strengthening enforcement and prosecution efforts, enforcing lease requirements, and seizing assets. Or they may focus on reducing the demand, focusing on the buyers of the drugs rather than the sellers either through sting operations or through educational programs, youth diversion programs, or treatment programs.

Another strategy is to work on improving communications by using community surveys and tip lines and by improving communications between narcotics investigators and patrol officers.

Legislation as a Tool in the War on Narcotics

As noted by Clede (1990, p. 75), "Congress has given government the power to finance the war on drugs by seizing the drug traffickers' illegally obtained assets." This includes cars and weapons as well as cash. According to Wallace (1990, pp. 34–35), assets confiscated in one Lincoln County raid in 1989 exceeded the Mississippi Bureau of Narcotic's $5 million annual operating budget. Among items that have been seized are airplanes, vehicles, radio transmitters with scanners, telephone scramblers, paper shredders, electronic currency counters, assault rifles, and electronic stun guns.

Recent legislation such as Drug Abatement Statutes are also helping in the war on drugs. Such legislation makes it much easier to shut down crack houses and clandestine drug laboratories.

Drug Abatement Statutes declare any property where illegal drugs are used or sold to be a public nuisance.

In addition to being concerned with those who deal in drugs, police officers need to be prepared to manage those who use them.

Recognizing Individuals Using Illegal Drugs

Police officers must be able to recognize when a person is probably under the influence of drugs and must also be aware of the dangers the person might present. Table 14.1 summarizes the primary physical symptoms, what to look for, and the dangers involved in the most commonly used drugs, including alcohol.

Students at Minneapolis North High check out Duke's 1988 Calloway Corvette, valued at $65,000 and confiscated by police when Duke was convicted of drug dealing. The car has been outfitted with a light bar on top and police decals on the doors and is used in education programs to discourage youth from using drugs.

Summary

The first step in dealing with a gang problem is to *recognize* it. Once the problem is recognized, police need to identify gangs and their members. This is not difficult as most gang members identify themselves by their names, clothing, sign language, and graffiti. Gang members often engage in vandalism, arson, shootings, stabbings, and other kinds of violence.

To combat a gang problem: gather information, do not tolerate graffiti, target hard-core gang leaders, and consolidate major gang-control functions. Cultural gangs are neighborhood-centered and exist independently of criminal activity. Instrumental gangs are formed for the express purpose of criminal activity, primarily drug trafficking.

Frequently gangs and drugs are integrally related. Police often use simple drug buys, undercover operations, and raids to combat the drug problem. Information and time are critical elements in an illegal drug buy.

The sale and use of illegal drugs is difficult to investigate and prosecute because sellers and buyers are willing participants. Making several drug buys will protect against a claim of entrapment.

In the 1980s, law enforcement focused their efforts in dealing with the drug problem on undercover operations and sophisticated raids. Law enforcement's focus in the 1990s is on enlisting and educating the public and targeting street-level sales.

Application #1

The Chief wants you, the new commander of the narcotics squad, to establish some policies and procedures regarding drug buys. The present guidelines are obsolete, unsuited to modern, sophisticated narcotics squad operations. He instructs you to

TABLE 14.1

Common Symptoms, What to Look for, and Dangers of Commonly Abused Drugs

Drug Used	Physical Symptoms	Look For	Dangers
ALCOHOL (beer, wine, liquor)	Intoxication, slurred speech, unsteady walk, relaxation, relaxed inhibitions, impaired coordination, slowed reflexes.	Smell of alcohol on clothes or breath, intoxicated behavior, hangover, glazed eyes.	Addiction, accidents as a result of impaired ability and judgment, overdose when mixed with other depressants, heart and liver damage.
COCAINE (coke, rock, crack, base)	Brief intense euphoria, elevated blood pressure and heart rate, restlessness, excitement, feeling of well-being followed by depression.	Glass vials, glass pipe, white crystalline powder, razor blades, syringes, needle marks.	Addiction, heart attack, seizures, lung damage, severe depression, paranoia (see Stimulants).
MARIJUANA (pot, dope, grass, weed, herb, hash, joint)	Altered perceptions, red eyes, dry mouth, reduced concentration and coordination, euphoria, laughing, hunger.	Rolling papers, pipes, dried plant material, odor of burnt hemp rope, roach clips.	Panic reaction, impaired short-term memory, addiction.
HALLUCINOGENS (acid, LSD, PCP, MDMA, Ecstasy psilocybin mushrooms, peyote)	Altered mood and perceptions, focus on detail, anxiety, panic, nausea synaesthesia (e.g., smell colors, see sounds).	Capsules, tablets, "microdots," blotter squares.	Unpredictable behavior, emotional instability, violent behavior (with PCP).
INHALANTS (gas, aerosols, glue, nitrites, Rush, White out)	Nausea, dizziness, headaches, lack of coordination and control.	Odor of substance on clothing and breath, intoxication, drowsiness, poor muscular control.	Unconsciousness, suffocation, nausea and vomiting, damage to brain and central nervous system, sudden death.
NARCOTICS Heroin (junk, dope, Black tar, China white) Demerol, Dilaudid (D's), Morphine, Codeine	Euphoria, drowsiness, insensitivity to pain, nausea, vomiting, watery eyes, runny nose (see Depressants).	Needle marks on arms, needles, syringes, spoons, pinpoint pupils, cold moist skin.	Addiction, lethargy, weight loss, contamination from unsterile needles (hepatitis, AIDS), accidental overdose.
STIMULANTS (speed, uppers, crank, Bam, black beauties, crystal, dexies, caffeine, nicotine, cocaine, amphetamines)	Alertness, talkativeness, wakefulness, increased blood pressure, loss of appetite, mood elevation.	Pills and capsules, loss of sleep and appetite, irritability or anxiety, weight loss, hyperactivity.	Fatigue leading to exhaustion, addiction, paranoia, depression, confusion, possibly hallucinations.
DEPRESSANTS Barbiturates, sedatives, tranquilizers, (downers, tranks, ludes, reds, Valium, yellow jackets, alcohol)	Depressed breathing and heartbeat, intoxication, drowsiness, uncoordinated movements.	Capsules and pills, confused behavior, longer periods of sleep, slurred speech.	Possible overdose, especially in combination with alcohol; muscle rigidity; addiction, withdrawal and overdose require medical treatment.

Source: From 1991 "Drug Education Guide," The Positive Line #79930. Positive Promotions, 222 Ashland Place, Brooklyn, N.Y. 11217.

look at the previous general orders, policy and procedure bulletins, and to upgrade the operations.

Instructions. Use the form in Appendix A. Identify the problems and needs. Specify what the policy is, why it is needed, and what the police department's responsibility is.

In this set of policies and procedures, concentrate on only drug *buy* procedures. Include the preparation, intelligence, surveillance, the buy money procedures, what to do during and after the buy, what to do when making arrests and processing evidence, and what the report should contain.

397
CHAPTER 14
Gangs and Drugs:
Two National Threats

Application #2

In conjunction with the preceding drug buy policy and procedures, also establish policy and procedures regarding undercover officers infiltrating gangs and narcotics peddling operations. Identify any requirements to be met by potential undercover officers and how specific groups will be infiltrated. What role officers will play, the clothing and equipment they might wear, and how they are to work with a surveillance team should be included. Also include how agents might control challenging situations, how to make a good impression when first contact is made, and how to accumulate the information necessary to the operation. Also include tips on how officers can maintain self-control. Female agents may operate differently than males, so a separate section regarding female undercover agents might be very useful.

Research the assignment by contacting narcotics officers and also police departments or federal agencies that might offer insights into narcotics operations.

An Exercise in Critical Thinking

To deal effectively with gang problems, identify gangs and their members, gather and record information about major gang activities, and investigate illegal activities. Evidence must support specific offenses and link gang members to those offenses. The majority of illegal gang activity is involved in the narcotics trade. Drug buys must be carefully prepared to avoid charges of entrapment and illegal search and seizure. Community involvement in preventing gang activity can achieve success.

On July 8, 1988, Mike O'Brien came to an apartment building with five minors to purchase marijuana from a minor who lived in the complex. A group of minors (gang members) were also present in the parking lot for the same purpose. A number of the youths congregated around O'Brien's car, a classic 1966 Chevrolet Impala which O'Brien was in the process of restoring.

Fred Fidel (a member of a rival neighborhood gang) pulled into the parking lot and attempted to pull his vehicle partway into the limited space next to O'Brien's car, almost hitting it. Although none of the building's tenants were assigned designated parking spaces, Fidel habitually parked in the spot directly adjacent to the spot in which O'Brien had parked and in which many of the youths were standing. Although other parking spaces were available, Fidel pulled up to the spot where the youths were standing and repeatedly honked his horn. At that time, O'Brien told Fidel, "If you scratch my car, I'll kick your ass."

Fidel got out of his car, entered into an altercation with O'Brien, and pulled out a knife, brandishing it back and forth in front of O'Brien. O'Brien initially backed away as Fidel walked toward him. Fidel got back into his car and attempted to pull further into the parking space. Fidel then got out of his car, leaving it in such a position that O'Brien would be unable to move his car to leave.

As Fidel walked toward the building, O'Brien went toward him, advising Fidel that he was blocking O'Brien's car and offering to move it for him. During this second confrontation, Fidel again pulled out his knife. O'Brien told him to "back off; everything is cool." Fidel, however, grabbed O'Brien by the shirt with one hand as O'Brien tried to remove himself from Fidel's grasp and thrust the knife into O'Brien's chest with his other hand.

O'Brien was interviewed by police on the scene, but he bled to death before medical care could be administered. When Fidel was questioned by police, he at first denied possessing a knife or knowing anything about the stabbing. After a few minutes, he changed his account of the event and claimed self-defense.

1. Given the conflicting testimony between the members of the gang and Fidel, is there sufficient evidence to arrest Fidel for second-degree felony murder?
   a. Numerous witnesses give probable cause to believe that Fidel committed felony murder, and therefore Fidel should be arrested.
   b. Because the only witnesses are juvenile gang members whose testimony is suspect, prosecution will be nearly impossible; therefore, Fidel's testimony should be recorded, but he should not be arrested.
   c. As Fidel clearly was outnumbered and likely felt insecure, he probably wanted only to intimidate O'Brien; so there is insufficient cause to arrest Fidel for second-degree felony murder.
   d. Because of the intended purchase of drugs, Fidel can be arrested for first-degree intentional murder.
   e. Because it is Fidel's word against the gang's, both negate each other, leaving insufficient evidence for arresting and convicting Fidel of second-degree felony murder.

Discussion Questions

1. How might possible changes in the juvenile justice system be a deterrent to juveniles joining gangs?
2. How is youth violence escalating on the streets today? What are some reasons for it?
3. What role can citizens and community groups usefully play in coping with the drug problem?
4. What must officers consider when establishing a fictitious past for a cover story as an undercover agent?
5. As an undercover agent, if someone asks you if you are a "narc," how do you respond? What attitude will protect your safety?
6. Why have women been more successful than men in undercover operations?
7. What are some unobtrusive signals surveillance team members can use to cover such various situations as when the buy has been completed, when help is needed, and so on?

Definitions

Can you define the following terms?

cultural gang	instrumental gang
entrapment	moniker
flashroll	turf
graffiti	

References

Associated Press. "FBI Brings Spy Catching Skills Into War Against Gangs." *Star Tribune* (January 16, 1992): 7A.

Benson, Carol. "Gang Diversion." *Law and Order* (August 1990): 66–68.

Blank, Jonas Bernard. "The Drug Trade." *Fortune* (June 20, 1988): 27–29, 32, 33, 36–38.

Bryant, Dan. "Communitywide Responses Crucial for Dealing with Youth Gangs." Office of Juvenile Justice and Delinquency Prevention, Washington, D.C.: U.S. Government Printing Office, 1989.

Burke, Tod W. "Home Invaders: Gangs of the Future." *The Police Chief* (November 1990): 23.

Clede, Bill. "Drug Raid." *Law and Order* (November 1990): 74–75.

Cushing, Michael A. "Combating Street-Level Narcotics Sales." *The Police Chief,* (October 1989): 113–116.

Donahue, Terrence S. Editorial comment on "Communitywide Responses Crucial for Dealing with Youth Gangs," Office of Juvenile Justice and Delinquency Prevention, Washington, D.C.: U.S. Government Printing Office, 1989.

Fulwood, Isaac, Jr. "Community Empowerment Policing." *The Police Chief* (May 1990): 49–50.

Gates, Daryl F. and Jackson, Robert K. "Gang Violence in L.A." *The Police Chief* (November 1990): 20–22.

Harris, Wesley and Hudson, Criss. "A Small City's Approach to a Big Drug Problem." *Law and Order* (June 1991): 45–48.

Hoffmann, John. "Dealing with Crack in a Small Town." *Law and Order* (March 1991): 101–104.

Jackson, Robert K., and McBride, Wesley D. *Understanding Street Gangs.* Sacramento, Calif.: Custom Publishing Company, 1985.

Korzeniowski, George. "Tampa's QUAD Squads Attack Crack." *Law and Order* (July 1990). 81–85.

Metropolitan Court Judges Committee Report. "Drugs—The American Family in Crisis: A Judicial Response, 39 Recommendations." Reno, Nev.: Court Judge Committee 1988.

Moore, Mark H. and Kleinman, Mark A. R. "Perspectives on Policing: The Police and Drugs." National Institute of Justice, Washington, D.C.: U.S. Government Printing Office, September 1989.

Moriarty, Mortimer D. "Undercover Negotiating: Dealing for Your Life." *The Police Chief* (November 1990): 44–47.

Pierce, Donald and Ramsay, Todd G. "Gang Violence . . . Not Just a Big-City Problem." *The Police Chief* (November 1990): 24–25.

Police Science Services. "Drug Buys." Niles, Ill.: Police Science Services, 1977a.

Police Science Services. "Undercover Operations." Niles, Ill.: Police Science Services, 1977b.

Rau, Kenneth. "Patrol NET in Suffolk County." *The Police Chief* (May 1990): 42–43.

Ruester, Jim. "L.A. Fights Gang Crime with Unusual Weapon." *Law and Order* (September 1989): 41–42.

Sessions, William S. "Gang Violence and Organized Crime." *The Police Chief* (November 1990): 17.

Sessions, William S. "Public Support Needed for Victory Against Drugs." *The Police Chief* (September 1989): 11.

Wade, Gary E. "Undercover Negotiating: Flashroll Management." *The Police Chief* (November 1990): 48–51.

Wallace, James R., interview with. "Mississippi Bureau of Narcotics Employs Voice Guard Radios in War on Drugs." *Law and Order* (1990): 33–35.

Weisel, Deborah L. *Tackling Drug Problems in Public Housing: A Guide for Police.* Washington, D.C.: Police Executive Research Forum, 1990.

Case

Hampton v. United States 425 U.S. 484, 96 S.Ct. 1646, 48 L.Ed.2d 113 (1976).

EMERGENCY CALLS: WHEN DISASTER STRIKES

CHAPTER 15

INTRODUCTION

Emergencies may be natural or caused by people. Natural emergencies include floods, tornados, hurricanes, fires, tidal waves, landslides, avalanches, blizzards, leaking natural gas, and earthquakes. Emergencies caused by people include fires, hazardous materials spills, and bomb threats. Emergencies may involve individuals, neighborhoods, communities, counties, or even larger areas.

Every police department is expected to deal effectively and efficiently with all types of emergency situations. Those departments not prepared to do so may not only fail to protect property and life, they may also face expensive, time-consuming lawsuits as well as adverse political decisions.

> *Police departments should have predisaster plans for those emergencies likely to occur within their jurisdictions.*

Do You Know

- What emergencies a police department should plan for in advance?
- What should be included in a predisaster plan?
- What an ICMA survey found to be the two major difficulties during disasters?
- What the "pulse" of the government's response to an emergency is?
- What posttraumatic stress disorder is, and why it is important to police officers who respond to emergency calls?
- What emergency conditions require special considerations?
- What the prime consideration in any emergency is?
- What the two posthurricane "killers" were for South Carolina?

Predisaster Plans

Every department should have a carefully formulated, periodically updated emergency plan. What is included will depend on the types of emergencies that can be anticipated for a given jurisdiction. Jurisdictions in Minnesota, for example, would need to include responses for blizzards, an emergency situation not normally relevant for jurisdictions in the southern states.

Unanticipated emergencies should, however, also be included. For example, blizzardlike conditions virtually paralyzed parts of Georgia and Florida in 1989, precisely because this kind of weather condition was not expected in that part of the country.

Predisaster plans should include:

- *What emergencies to prepare for.*
- *What needs to be done in advance (supplies on hand, agreements with other agencies, etc.).*
- *What specific functions must be performed during the emergency and who is responsible for performing them, including outside organizations and agencies who might help.*
- *What steps need to be taken to restore order after the emergency is ended.*
- *How the response is to be evaluated.*

The plan should *not* be developed solely by top management, but rather should be developed by those who would be involved in implementing it. This would include government officials, fire department personnel, health care personnel, and the like.

To limit loss of property and lives, Kemp (1989, pp. 172–173) suggests the following guidelines for emergency plans:

- Account for known hazards in the emergency plan.
- Place most emergency responsibility on employees who live in or near the jurisdiction.
- Use current job titles and organizational structures to avoid confusion.
- List current and back-up phone numbers for the emergency response team as well as phone numbers for back-up personnel.
- List actual tasks rather than functional responsibilities; for example, do not simply say ''evacuate the area,'' list specific steps to be taken in the evacuation and who is responsible for taking them.
- Centralize all responsibilities, both at top management and department level, and clearly specify them as well.
- Clearly specify the functions of the emergency operations center (EOC). Carefully delineate the delegation of authority and individual duties at the EOC.
- Make provisions to temporarily waive certain building codes and zoning laws so temporary housing or mobile homes can be used on residential sites during an emergency.

- List available community resources, including names and locations of hospitals, social service agencies, physicians, nurses, and equipment.
- Conduct simulated disaster exercises.
- Establish a mutual-aid agreement with a neighboring jurisdiction.

The emergency plan should identify the levels of emergencies that might occur and the level of response required. Many jurisdictions use a three-level approach, with Level 1 including minor events that can usually be handled by on-duty personnel. A Level-2 event is a moderate to severe situation that requires aid from other agencies and perhaps even other jurisdictions. A Level-3 event refers to catastrophes in which a State of Emergency is proclaimed and county, state, and even federal assistance is requested. In such instances, the National Guard is often called on for help.

Unfortunately, many police departments place emergency management on a low priority, feeling that such emergencies are unlikely to happen in their jurisdiction. Nonetheless, as noted by Kemp (p. 171), most citizens expect their police departments to:

- Alert citizens in advance of a disaster.
- Quickly and accurately assess the magnitude of an emergency.
- Keep citizens properly informed of the situation.
- Safely evacuate dangerous areas.
- Move citizens to a safe place.
- Provide for a rapid restoration of services.
- Give assistance in the form of recovery services.
- Mitigate the impact of future emergencies.
- Be able to protect life and property adequately.

A 1983 survey by the International City Management Association (ICMA) (Kemp, p. 172) found that few communities seemed properly prepared for crisis situations or disasters even though 83 percent of the cities and 90 percent of the counties did have a formal emergency management plan. Only 81 percent of the cities and 73 percent of the counties felt their technology was sufficient to effectively deal with emergencies.

According to an ICMA survey, communication and coordination are the major problems during disasters.

This same survey found that local governments reported over $16 billion in property losses, 2,490 deaths, and 9,161 injuries from disasters between 1970 and 1983.

The Emergency Operations Center

The emergency operations center helps reduce the two main problems during disasters: communications and coordination. During times of disaster, it is imperative that government "not only continue to function, but that it do so in a precise and coordinated manner" (Iushewitz, 1990, p. 33). A key to effective emergency management is the emergency operations center (EOC).

A police dispatcher conveying instructions to officers in the field. Communications are essential during emergencies.

*The **emergency operations center** is the "pulse" of the government's response to an emergency.*

The San Bernardino County, California, Emergency Management Plan (p. 33) defines the role of the EOC as "the focal point for the coordination of all disaster response within this county's area of responsibility." It states that the EOC's primary functions are "the collection and correlation of all disaster-related data, coordination between key personnel, development of informed decisions to guide disaster response and recovery, and the primary communications and information link between all jurisdictions involved and all emergency response elements" (p. 33).

The specific location of the EOC will depend, in part, on the emergency being dealt with. Often an existing site in a government building works well. Ideally, the center is located close to police, fire, and government officials.

Iushewitz (p. 34) suggests that: "Whatever the physical location, the layout of the center must allow for close, continuous interaction by the EOC's staff in a nerve center (the operations room), and a range of 50–80 square feet should be allowed for each person." The key goals of this center are (p. 34):

- Information and intelligence gathering and analysis.
- An expanding EOC organization to handle the workload, both real and projected.
- Centralized allocation of resources to handle the situation.
- Planning for long-term support for manpower and the public.

Russell and Beigel (1990, pp. 258–259) identify four phases in most emergencies:

- The warning period.
- The impact period.
- The immediate reaction after impact.
- The period of delayed response.

The Warning Period.   Usually as much warning as possible is desirable. It may, however, have an adverse effect on some individuals who may panic and become totally helpless, as though the emergency had already occurred. Their panic may be transmitted to others.

The Impact Period.   People react differently when the emergency is actually happening. According to Russell and Beigel (p. 258): "The initial impact will almost always be stunned inactivity. . . . For about the first fifteen minutes, no one will be able to act effectively.

The Immediate Reaction After Impact.   The period immediately following the disaster is the most crucial from the standpoint of rescue operations. Effective performance can save property and lives.

The Period of Delayed Response.   Once the immediate danger is past, those who were functioning effectively may cease to do so, and vice versa. Russell and Beigel (pp. 260–261) suggest that: "Most people, though they may be somewhat overwhelmed initially, do manage to perform adequately after the first hour of impact." Studies by the Disaster Research Center of over 100 disaster situations identified several facts, in sharp contrast to popular beliefs held by the public, the media, and public officials, summarized in Table 15.1 (Michelson, 1984, p. 36.

TABLE 15.1
Common Misconceptions About the Public's Reaction to Disaster

Myth	Fact
People will panic.	They do *not* panic. In fact, getting them to evacuate is a bigger problem.
People are unable to cope.	People react in an active, helpful manner.
Local organizations are overwhelmed and unable to perform effectively.	The destruction in relation to total resources is quite low.
Antisocial behavior (i.e., looting) is commonplace.	Looting and so on are rare in disaster situations.
Community morale is low in stricken areas.	Community morale is generally high.
Firm measures are needed to prevent personal and social chaos.	Coordination is more essential than firm measures.

Source: From "Disaster Myths," by R. Michelson, in *The Police Chief,* May 1984, p. 34.

Guidelines for Dealing with Emergencies

Every emergency will present a unique challenge to responding officers. Nonetheless, several guidelines can help assure the most effective response possible at each phase of the disaster.

Before the Emergency

- Be prepared. Be proactive. Anticipate the immediate problems and the personnel likely to be needed to deal with them.
- Identify the equipment and resources required, and make certain they are either available or immediately accessible.
- Establish and maintain good relationships with the media. They are among the first on the scene of emergencies and have a job to do. They can be invaluable in getting messages out to the general public and keeping panic to a minimum. They can also be a terrific liability if a good relationship does not exist.
- Establish a system so that police officers can know that their own families are safe during an emergency.

During the Emergency

- Take time to assess the situation. Do not make the situation worse by acting without thinking.
- Do not broadcast a general call for help. Carefully but quickly assess what is needed and call for that.
- Keep the channels of communication open and the information flowing as required to those who need it.
- Keep as many options open as possible. Avoid ''either/or'' thinking.
- Do not get sidetracked by personal, individual requests for help, but rather focus on the ''big picture,'' routing individual requests to the appropriate source of assistance.
- Accept the fact that the police cannot do everything. The emergency manager must prioritize and delegate responsibilities quickly. Mistakes will probably happen.
- Involve key personnel as rapidly as possible. Do not let other agencies shirk their responsibilities.
- Keep top city officials fully informed of progress and problems.
- Assure that someone is tending to ''normal'' business.

After the Emergency

- Get back to normal as soon as possible.
- Expect that victims of the disaster or emergency may have very emotional reactions, including posttraumatic stress disorder. This is also true of the officers who dealt with the disaster or emergency.
- Also expect that lawyers will get into it. *Document* everything that was done.
- Evaluate the response after the situation has returned to normal. Look upon ''mistakes'' as the ''least effective alternative'' as well as learning

opportunities. However, as May (1990, p. 99a) cautions: "Nothing should be written down during these critiques that you wouldn't want to discuss in court if the material is subpoenaed." Modify emergency-preparedness plans as needed based on what was learned.

An important consideration following a disaster is to conduct a **critical-incident stress debriefing (CISD).** Such a debriefing should be conducted by a professional mental health practitioner twenty-four to forty-eight hours after the incident. Sooner than twenty-four hours is likely to be ineffective as the full impact may not yet be felt. These debriefings should be mandatory to avoid anyone feeling it is not "macho" to attend.

Restoring Order

When emergencies have been controlled and their urgency has diminished, police services are still needed. The constant threat of looting and malicious damage will continue until the area again becomes functional and the residents return to their homes or emergency workers are no longer present.

Following any disaster or emergency situation, there is usually a steady flow of curiosity seekers that will usually taper off as interest diminishes. This may take several hours, days, or weeks, depending on the magnitude of the disaster. It may take several weeks for the area to return to normal. In the meantime, police personnel will still be needed. Extra police may be required for several weeks to prevent further damage and looting, but a gradual phaseout should be conducted rather than allowing an abrupt return to normal duty.

Identifying Fatalities

A comprehensive disaster plan should include how fatalities will be identified. As noted by Sessions (1991, p. 8): "The positive identification of disaster fatalities is an important humanitarian service. . . . It is also of untold value in settling estates and insurance claims." Help in identifying fatalities is available through the FBI Identification Division's *Disaster Squad*. Sessions (p. 8) notes that, "Since its formation in 1940, the Disaster Squad has identified more than 3,600 fatalities by fingerprints, palm prints, or footprints." They have helped in such disasters as the volcanic eruption of Mount St. Helens, in the 1978 mass murder-suicides at Jonestown, Guyana, and in the 1986 space shuttle explosion. They also provided assistance during Operation Desert Storm. Their free identification services are available twenty-four hours a day, seven days a week.

In addition to cost-free fatality identification services offered by the Disaster Squad, the FBI provides assistance to law enforcement and civic agencies in formulating emergency response plans.

Posttraumatic Stress After Large-Scale Disasters

Many soldiers who were in the Vietnam war suffer what has been called **posttraumatic stress disorder (PTSD).** According to the American Psychiatric Association

(1980), this disorder refers to developing characteristic symptoms following a psychologically traumatic event generally outside the range of human experience. The symptoms include:

- Reexperiencing the event, either while awake or in recurrent dreams.
- Detachment and lack of involvement, diminished interest in formerly important activities, detachment from other people.
- At least two other of the following symptoms not present before the event:

  - Hyperalertness.
  - Sleep disturbance.
  - Guilt about surviving when others did not.
  - Memory impairment or trouble concentrating.
  - Avoiding activities that remind the person of the event.

Not only do many disaster victims experience PSTD, so do many of those involved in helping them, especially if deaths have been especially gruesome or have involved children. Police officers *are* susceptible to PSTD and should have support groups available to them.

Posttraumatic stress disorder (PSTD) is a debilitating stressful reaction to a traumatic event; PSTD may last for months or years. It can be experienced not only by victims, but also by those who help the victims.

The likelihood of PSTD occurring in responding police officers can be reduced, according to May (1990a, pp. 97–99), by having contingency plans which require them to mentally rehearse probable disaster situations, thus lowering their anxiety. It can be further reduced by practicing these plans, by assigning each officer a specific task, maintaining order during the emergency, by requiring that they get some break periods during the emergency if it lasts longer than ten hours, and by having a thorough debriefing following the emergency.

Special Considerations in Specific Kinds of Emergencies

Just as general guidelines can be specified for emergencies, general guidelines and considerations can be made in advance for specific kinds of emergencies, reducing the loss of property and lives.

In addition to general predisaster plans, contingency plans should be made in the event of floods, plane crashes, explosions, fires, hurricanes, earthquakes, hazardous material spills, bomb threats, and actual bombings. In all such emergencies, saving lives is of top priority.

Floods

A flood, although damaging and usually predictable, demands a coordinated response and implementation of a previously thought out plan. Normally police will assist residents and merchants in the affected areas to evacuate their homes and their businesses.

As soon as a police department receives notice of an impending flood, the regular and reserve officers are usually called to duty. In some instances, they may be put "on alert" or standby in case they are needed.

During an evacuation and while there is an emergency "in progress," the police must seal off the affected area to prevent looting and vandalism.

A system where special passes can be issued to residents who have legitimate business in the area should be set up. All persons not living in or having business in the flood area should be excluded.

Plane Crashes

A plane crash carries very heavy responsibilities because loss of life is usually associated with the crash. Upon notification of a plane crash, the police department must notify the Federal Aviation Administration (FAA) who have jurisdiction and responsibility for such investigations. The National Transportation Safety Board (NTSB) also has jurisdiction if a death is involved. In the case of a military aircraft, the military service involved must be notified. The security of the aircraft and its scattered parts then becomes the responsibility of the military police.

The initial responsibility of the police department is to seal off the area surrounding any parts that may have been separated from the plane. Frequently, other jurisdictions may become involved as parts of the aircraft may be found several blocks or miles away from the main crash site. If large numbers of people are injured, the ambulance services and the fire department rescue units may become overburdened. When this occurs, the hospital may send several of its staff members to the scene to assist. Police officers must provide easy access to and from the scene for those hospital personnel.

The crash of Avianca Flight 052 in Long Island, New York, in 1989 illustrated several factors to be considered in responding to plane crashes. In this crash, the airplane had run out of fuel, so there was no explosion or fire, and several passengers and crew members survived the crash. According to Maher (1990, pp. 39–43), the Nassau County Disaster Plan identified who was to be notified as well as what procedures should be followed. Radio cars from all eight precincts and the Highway Patrol Bureau were dispatched to the scene along with all available police ambulances and their fire department counterparts. Heavy rescue equipment was also ordered to the site.

A **triage** area that was located where the victims could be separated according to the severity of their injuries was established for survivors. Immediate medical needs were attended to, and victims were stabilized and then transported to medical facilities. A morgue area for those who died in the crash was also established where bodies were photographed, tagged, and transported to the Nassau County medical examiner's facility. Luggage and other personal effects were gathered into a central area and guarded.

At a critique of the emergency response held soon after, both police and fire personnel were concerned about the number of well-meaning citizens who came to

A section of a United Airlines DC10 stands among emergency vehicles after crashing at the Sioux City Airport while trying to make an emergency landing. Coordination among the various emergency vehicles responding is critical.

help but who almost completely blocked access to the crash site. Nonetheless, according to Maher (p. 43): "The crash proved that the department's disaster plan is a viable, valuable tool, albeit in need of some minor changes."

Explosions

Explosions may be accidental or purposeful. Accidental explosions may result from earthquakes, natural fires, plane or train crashes, or natural gas leaks. Purposeful explosions include those caused by arsonists and by terrorists. Department policies and procedures should be developed for dealing with explosions of all types.

Fires

Fires are usually the primary responsibility of the fire department, although some police departments have a combined service. Such departments have trained their officers to assist fire fighters in case a need arises. One responsibility of the police is to protect fire fighters from harassment. Some sections of cities are plagued with spectators who taunt the fire fighters and try to disrupt fire fighting. In these cases, police officers must give them protection and also direct attention to controlling spectators and protecting fire equipment and regulating traffic drawn to the fire.

Police officers must facilitate the rapid flow of emergency equipment and personnel as well as protect unattended fire fighting equipment.

Officer escorting a resident from her burning home. Some victims' possessions are entirely destroyed, and they must be guided to appropriate community assitance.

Hurricanes

Many of the emergencies already discussed may occur during a hurricane, including flooding, fires, explosions, accompanied by looting and vandalism. The experience of Charleston, South Carolina, in dealing with Hurricane Hugo in September of 1989 provided some valuable lessons for law enforcement as described by Greenberg et al. (1990, pp. 26–43). One key lesson was that evacuation should be ordered as early as possible and that shelters should be periodically evaluated for their ability to withstand damage.

Supplies were obtained before the storm hit, including hip boots, chain saws, flares, extra caution signs and barricades, and crowd-control equipment. Provisions were also made to obtain extra gasoline and water. Department assets were protected by moving horses and unneeded police vehicles to safe locations, taking boats out of the water and securing them indoors, and testing and sandbagging the emergency generator.

Communications were critical during the planning stage as well as during and after the hurricane hit. Cellular telephones were used by emergency personnel, and a bank of telephones was set up to provide information to people calling in.

Because of the advance warning, several measures were taken to prevent problems during the evacuation. For example, provisions were made for towing stalled vehicles off the road, but no further. If accidents occurred, drivers were given white forms to complete and sent on their way. Traffic was kept moving by allowing no one to return to evacuation areas except in extreme emergencies.

A Howard Johnson's hotel located along an evacuation route displayed on its large, lighted message sign: "If you can read this, you are going the wrong way." Local radio and television stations cooperated fully.

Personnel were stationed at predetermined safe locations to seal off areas. They were also in position to rapidly enter the evacuated area as soon as it was safe to prevent vandalism and looting as well as to provide a psychologically reassuring presence for the citizens of the area.

According to McClinton (1990, p. 35): "As a result of effective contingency planning and a proactive posture taken by public safety officials prior to Hugo's onslaught, fewer than 60 fatalities were left in the wake of the storm [considered this country's most costly natural disaster]. . . . In the early stages of response and recovery, it was clear that professional skills, untiring dedication, and innovative techniques were sufficient to meet public safety needs."

A significant problem for the police department following the hurricane was that they had used their entire year's overtime budget in just two weeks. The biggest problem, however, was not, as might be expected, the cleanup. The biggest problem was the massive paperwork required by the Federal Emergency Management Administration (FEMA) in order for the city to be reimbursed for expenses resulting from Hugo.

The posthurricane "killers" for South Carolina were the overruns in overtime and the excessive paperwork.

Earthquakes

While floods and hurricanes can usually be predicted, earthquakes strike with no warning. Areas in which earthquakes are likely to occur must have preestablished plans to deal with such emergencies. Included within these plans should be measures to deal with collapsed buildings and bridges, downed power lines, fires, explosions, injuries and deaths. As in other kinds of emergencies, traffic problems, vandalism, and looting must also be anticipated.

These problems were well illustrated in the California Bay Area earthquake which struck in October of 1989 just as the World Series was about to begin. Fortunately, some 60,000 fans were at Candlestick Park rather than on the freeways on their way home, and, because of the World Series, extra patrol officers were on duty. Nonetheless, destruction and death were widespread.

The response was coordinated by the California Highway Patrol (CHP). According to Rubin (1990, p. 50), their "marching orders" were to: "get the survivors, if any, out; locate and identify the victims and vehicles caught between the upper and lower decks of the fallen freeway; monitor the recovery of the bodies of all the victims."

One of the greatest problems was communications. The 911 system went out and cellular phones came to play a key role in maintaining communications. More than 2,000 portable phones were brought in from around the country. The highway patrol coordinated the efforts of planes, helicopters, and fixed-wing aircraft. Police officers erected thousands of feet of construction fence around the area to allow rescuers room to work and to prevent looting.

A command center was established in a trailer 100 feet from the collapsed section of Interstate 880. Here bits of information were fed into a computerized geographic

Police officers escorting a Marina district resident through the rubble of her apartment to salvage what she can. Many of the buildings in San Francisco severely damaged by a 6.9 earthquake face demolition as they have been determined to be structurally unsafe.

information system (GIS) which mapped and identified every area and neighborhood that needed immediate assistance. As noted by Tyler (1990, p. 42), vital information could be placed, moved, and updated on the map. In addition, the system could retrieve information from outside data bases such as the Registry of Motor Vehicles, making identification of damaged cars faster. Access to information from the Department of Public Works made for faster response to downed power lines.

As with the administrators who dealt with Hurricane Hugo, the administrators dealing with the Bay Area earthquake found that the paperwork required by the FEMA was tremendous, but essential. According to one captain, the weakest part of his department's disaster plan was dealing with the paperwork required by FEMA (LEN, December 15, 1989, p. 10).

Hazardous Materials (HAZMAT) Incidents

Another emergency situation police must be prepared to deal with involves hazardous materials (**HAZMAT incident**): derailed trains, tank trucks overturning, chemical-laden trucks involved in accidents, and bombs and bomb threats. Despite preventive efforts such as those described in Chapter 10, accidents will happen.

With an increasing number of hazardous materials in commercial use in the 1990s, the likelihood of officers being called to a spill of such materials has increased significantly. According to Hildreth (1991, p. 93): "In today's world of complex and exotic chemicals, even a Ph.D. in chemistry can't always predict what will happen when different chemicals are mixed, even different brands intended to do the same thing.'' Hildreth (p. 96) notes, ''Nationwide, it is estimated that over 1,000 new hazardous materials a year are produced, and more than 180 million shipments of hazardous materials are made annually in the United States.''

In addition, federal legislation dealing with hazardous materials affects every police officer in the United States. As noted by Hermann (1991a, pp. 269–270), ''the far-reaching OSHA enactment of emergency response regulations . . . deal with mandatory training'':

First responder awareness level. First responders at the awareness level are individuals who are likely to witness or discover a hazardous substance release and who have been trained to initiate an emergency response sequence by notifying the proper authorities of the release. They would take no further action beyond notifying the authorities of the release. First responders at the awareness level shall have sufficient training or experience to objectively demonstrate competency in the following areas:

1. *Understanding of what hazardous materials are, and the risks associated with them in an incident.*
2. *Understanding of the potential outcomes associated with an emergency created when hazardous materials are present.*
3. *Ability to recognize the presence of hazardous materials in an emergency.*
4. *Ability to identify the hazardous materials, if possible.*
5. *Understanding of the role of the first responder awareness individual in the employer's emergency response plan including site security and control and the U.S. Department of Transportation's* Emergency Response Guidebook.
6. *Ability to realize the need for additional resources, and to make appropriate notifications to the communication center.*

According to Hermann (1991b, p. 271): ''Every police car, fire truck and emergency service vehicle in the nation should now have a copy of the new U.S. Department of Transportation's (DOT) *1990 Emergency Response Guidebook (ERG90).*'' This valuable resource includes two pages illustrating all DOT placards, in color, with a numbered guide, a list of who to call for assistance, as well as the following for each class of chemicals or chemical compounds (Hildreth, 1991, p. 99):

- Potential hazards to fire and explosion and what will trigger these reactions.
- Potential health risk from exposure to the substance.
- Immediate emergency action to be taken even before fire, explosion, or exposure.
- Immediate steps to be taken if fire, explosion, exposure, spill, or leak does occur.

Another resource is CHEMTREC, which stands for Chemical Transportation Emergency Center, a public service of the Chemical Manufacturers Association. Through its emergency toll-free number, (800)424-9300, CHEMTREC provides information on a product's known hazards and what to do and not do in case of a spill, fire, or exposure to the substance. CHEMTREC operates twenty-four hours a day, seven days a week. As noted by Hildreth (p. 98):

CHEMTREC can provide immediate advice by telephone for the on-scene commander at a HAZMAT emergency, and then its personnel will promptly contact the shipper of the hazardous material(s) involved in the incident for

detailed assistance and relay an appropriate response back to the on-scene
incident commander. In some situations, a segment of the chemical industry
or even a company may have a HAZMAT team that will respond.
CHEMTREC can alert such teams when they exist.

In addition to being familiar with the resources available to them, officers should
have a plan for responding to such calls. One such basic response plan is described
by May (1990b, pp. 85–86):

1. Report the incident as a possible hazardous materials accident. Give exact
   location, approach route, and request assistance.
2. Stay upwind and upgrade.
3. Isolate the area of nonessential personnel.
4. Avoid contact with liquids or fumes.
5. Eliminate ignition sources.
6. Rescue the injured—only if prudent.
7. Identify the material(s) involved and determine conditions.
8. If necessary, initiate an evacuation.
9. Establish a command post.

It is also recommended that officers have binoculars in their vehicles so that they can
read the placards and markings on trucks or railroad cars which have been involved
in accidents. Because the danger of explosion, fire, or toxic fumes is always
present, officers should stay as far away as possible but also need to try to identify
what the truck or railroad car was transporting.

Dealing with a hazardous materials incident is another area where teamwork is often
essential. Hildreth (1991, pp. 96–97) describes the State of Minnesota's team effort:

> *Several state agencies have the responsibility for dealing with a HAZMAT*
> *incident. For example, four cars belonging to the Department of*
> *Transportation, Department of Agriculture, and the Pollution Control Agency*
> *are specially equipped to respond to HAZMAT incidents.*
>
> *[The state of] Minnesota also equipped a hazardous materials response van*
> *and trailer. Personnel from seven state departments and divisions are trained*
> *to respond with this equipment. The primary state entities given this*
> *responsibility are the Health-Emergency Medical Services Section, Public*
> *Safety-Fire Marshal Division, Department of Natural Resources, and the*
> *Department of Public Safety Division of Emergency Management. Before*
> *being assigned to the state HAZMAT team, all personnel successfully*
> *completed basic and advanced hazardous materials response tactics training.*

Bombs and Bomb Threats

Any business or establishment can be the victim of a bomb threat or bombing.
Among the most common targets are airlines, banks, educational institutions, government buildings, hospitals, industrial complexes, military installations, office
buildings, and utilities.

According to Higgens, Director of the Bureau of Alcohol, Tobacco and Firearms
(ATF) (1990, p. 16):

> *Bombings and bombing attempts in the United States rose from 1,103 in 1985*
> *to 1,699 in 1989—a 54 percent increase. During the past five years,*

bombings caused 176 deaths, 1,167 injuries, and property damage exceeding $57.9 million. The motive in eight of ten incidents was vandalism or revenge. Homes, vehicles, and businesses were primary targets, accounting for 63 percent of all incidents. Three-fourths of the violators chose simple but deadly devices, usually pipe bombs loaded with black, smokeless powder or bottles of flammable liquid.

The growth of bombing crimes was most volatile among drug traffickers [up 1,000 percent in the last three years].

Higgens (p. 16) notes that the picture is not as bleak as it might seem because of the "quiet revolution in the investigation of bombing crimes." He suggests that: "Thousands of local, state, and federal officers—many trained by ATF—form a growing cadre of bomb investigators on duty throughout the United States." He gives as an example of the team approach to investigating bombings the work of the ATF National Response Team (NRT), which has a 50 percent solution rate. In a North Dakota case they investigated, five guilty pleas resulted. The bomb investigation team included the Kenmore, Marshal, and Minot city police departments, the North Dakota Highway Patrol, the Air Force Security Police, the Border Patrol, and the ATF. Says Higgens: "Criminals who terrorize with explosives face a new reality in the dawn of the twenty-first century—that law enforcement officers become better each day at flushing bombers from covers. These officers, agents, scientists, and technicians work as a team while preserving jurisdictional integrity. . . . Continued success by investigators will lead to a point where a bombing is considered by most would-be lawbreakers to be a crime not worth the risk."

Several underground newsletters give detailed instructions on how to make bombs using common materials such as lead pipe filled with black powder, caps screwed on both ends, and a fuse.

Although 98 percent of bomb threats are hoaxes, the threats are costly, emotionally charged, and may be dangerous if people panic. Having a well-established procedure to handle a bomb-threat call is imperative. It should be written, kept in plain view of those who answer the phone, and practiced. If a threat is received, the person who receives it should know exactly what to do. According to Hess and Wrobleski (1992, p. 202), receivers of bomb threats should:

- Keep the caller talking as long as possible.
- Try to learn as much as possible about the bomb, especially when it will go off and where it is located.
- Try to determine the caller's sex, age, accent, and speech pattern, and whether he or she is drunk or drugged.
- Listen for any background noises.
- Immediately notify the appropriate person(s) of the call.

Some organizations have a form such as that in Appendix B to be completed by any individual who receives a telephoned bomb threat.

It is critical that individuals who answer telephones know who to report a bomb threat to. This person then determines what action to take. Alternatives include ignoring it, searching for the possible bomb, or evacuating the premises. No matter what alternative is selected, the police should be called.

If a bomb is found, the police should be prepared to deal with it themselves or know who they can call to deal with it. If a military installation is close by, their bomb demolition team may help. The following procedures are suggested by Fisher (1979, pp. 320–321), to be followed when a suspicious object or bomb is located:

FIGURE 15.1
Sample Bomb Threat Form
Source: From *Introduction to Security,* 4th ed., by G. Green and R. C. Farber,
Stoneham, Mass.: Butterworth Publishers, 1987. Reprinted with permission of
Butterworth Publishers.

```
General Services Administration        Date: _____
            Region 8                   Received        Ended

                                       Time of
   BOMB THREAT INFORMATION             Call: _____
EXACT WORDS OF CALLER:
_____
_____
                        (Continue on reverse)
QUESTIONS TO ASK:
1. WHEN IS BOMB GOING TO EXPLODE? _____

2. WHERE IS BOMB RIGHT NOW? _____

3. WHAT KIND OF BOMB IS IT? _____

4. WHAT DOES IT LOOK LIKE? _____

5. WHY DID YOU PLACE BOMB? _____

DESCRIPTION OF CALLER'S VOICE:              TONE OF VOICE
    ☐ Male     ☐ Female
    ☐ Young   ☐ Middle-Aged   ☐ Old   _____

ACCENT _____        BACKGROUND NOISE _____

IS VOICE FAMILIAR?                     IF "YES", WHO DID IT
                                       SOUND LIKE? _____
☐ Yes.  ☐ No.
ADDITIONAL COMMENTS:
_____

Name of Person Receiving Call         Organization & Location

Home Address                          Office Phone

                                      Home Phone
```

1. Doors and windows in the vicinity of the bomb should be opened to reduce
   shock waves in the event of an explosion.
2. All available fire extinguishers should be readied and in position to combat
   any fires caused by the explosion.
3. If time allows, highly flammable objects and liquids should be removed from
   areas immediately surrounding, or otherwise endangered by the bomb.

4. The bomb should be surrounded with sandbags or similar shock-absorbing objects, such as specially constructed bomb blankets. One of these blankets can cover an area of up to sixteen square feet.
5. Valuable and irreplaceable documents, files, and other papers should be taken from the endangered area.

Many police departments are using bomb-sniffing dogs with great success. Such dogs are trained to move quietly and to not bark when a bomb is located, but rather to simply "point" to it.

Summary

Police departments should have predisaster plans for those emergencies likely to occur within their jurisdictions. Such plans should include what emergencies to prepare for; what needs to be done in advance (supplies on hand, agreements with other agencies, etc.); what specific functions must be performed during the emergency and who is responsible for performing them, including outside organizations and agencies who might help; what steps need to be taken to restore order after the emergency is ended; and how the response is to be evaluated.

According to an ICMA survey, communication and coordination are the major problems during disasters. These problems can be reduced by having an emergency operations center (EOC). The EOC is the "pulse" of the government's response to an emergency.

Any particularly devastating event can have long-range emotional effects, including posttraumatic stress disorder (PSTD), which is a debilitating stressful reaction to a traumatic event. The PSTD may last for months or years. It can be experienced not only by victims, but also by those who help the victims.

In addition to general predisaster plans, contingency plans should be made in the event of floods, plane crashes, explosions, fires, hurricanes, earthquakes, hazardous material spills, bomb threats, and actual bombings. In *all* such emergencies, saving lives is of top priority.

The posthurricane "killers" for South Carolina were the overruns in overtime and the excessive paperwork. This will probably hold true for most other large-scale disasters as well.

Application #1

As the newly appointed emergency management officer, you are asked by your chief to establish a policy and procedure that will be adequate to handle bomb threats received by local public or private schools. Who will you involve as you formulate this policy and procedure?

Instructions.   Use the form in Appendix A to develop your policy and procedure directive. The policy should state that it identifies the procedures to be used if a bomb threat is received by a public or private school.

Remember that any information must be relayed immediately to the responding officers. Make sure that the principal has a plan for the instructional staff and that maintenance personnel know their responsibilities. Include in the procedures what to do if a suspicious object is found. Spell out the specific responsibilities of fire department and police department personnel.

As emergency management officer, you are also asked to review the portion of the department's policy and procedure directive that refers to natural disasters likely to occur in your area.

Instructions. Keep in mind who will need to be involved in carrying out the procedures and include them in the planning.

An Exercise in Critical Thinking

Communication and coordination are the major problems during disasters. Upon arrival at an emergency, take time to assess the situation and call for needed help. Involve key personnel as rapidly as possible. Keep the channels of communication open and keep other officials informed of progress and problems. Do not get sidetracked by singular problems, but keep in mind the overall situation, and consider various possible options for action. In all emergencies, saving lives and attending to medical needs are top priority. And after the emergency, remember to carefully document everything that was done because of probable litigation.

On July 8 at 3:35 A.M., two police officers received a call reporting a multiple-car accident on the eastbound lanes of Interstate Highway 94 three miles east of Twin Lakes at the crossing of the Kinnickinnic River. There were patches of fog approaching the area, reducing visibility in the location of the collisions to 100 feet. Seven vehicles had collided. Four were in the ditch to the right side of the road; one was on the left shoulder facing toward the ditch; one was on the right shoulder with the front left tire four feet into the right lane; and one vehicle was straddling the two lanes with its front tire in the right lane and its back tires in the left lane.

1. As no headlights of approaching traffic can be seen:
   a. Both officers should leave their squad cars, with lights flashing as warnings and survey damages to vehicles and injuries to persons.
   b. One officer should stop all approaching traffic at a point west of the patches of fog while the other officer surveys the scene in order to call for the appropriate assistance.
   c. One officer should act as an emergency manager and prioritize and delegate responsibilities.
   d. Immediately broadcast a general call for help—obtain ambulance and medical help, wreckers, and clean-up assistance, then stand aside to direct traffic.
   e. The first to arrive on the scene should attempt to give first aid to individuals requesting help, and the second should begin an investigation to see if gross misdemeanors for aggravated driving violations are in order.
2. If one person is observed leaving the scene of the accident:
   a. The second officer to arrive should pursue, arrest, and place that individual in the back seat of the squad car for later interrogation and sobriety tests.
   b. The first officer to arrive should call for K-9 backup to track down the individual for interrogation.

    c. Both officers should ignore this departure unless the individual appears to pose a threat to others. After the initial traumatic shock, this person will probably recover emotional balance and return without coercion.

    d. Action should be taken only if the emergency manager assesses it to be necessary and timely.

    e. Request an ambulatory survivor who is physically able to chase down and bring this individual back to the scene of the accident.

3. In addition to three injured persons who were removed in ambulances and two who were given medical attention but not hospitalized, Reginald Jones was found slumped behind the wheel of the vehicle that was found in the middle of the highway. Others testified that they had braked and swerved to miss his vehicle, which along with the poor visibility caused the onset of the multiple-vehicle collision. One officer walked up just as Jones was about to be removed from the vehicle by ambulance attendants. The attendants turned Jones over to the officer, who noticed indications of intoxication. Jones refused to take road sobriety tests, stating the officer had no right to ask him because an acquaintance named ''Arel'' had been driving the car all evening until it stalled at the spot where police found it. Jones did not request council with an attorney.

    a. Jones should be arrested for an aggravated driving violation.

    b. Insufficient evidence exists for Jones to be tested or arrested.

    c. Only if other witnesses can corroborate that no other person was in the vehicle with Jones should he be interrogated.

    d. If Jones can give ''Arel's'' full name and address, then he should be released; otherwise, he should be arrested and interrogated.

    e. As Jones has provided officers with a prime suspect who has caused the entire emergency, he should be arrested, searched, handcuffed, and taken to police headquarters for interrogation.

Discussion Questions

1. What types of emergencies are most likely to occur in your community? Least likely?
2. Assume that the potential for flooding exists in your community. What type of training would you recommend for the police department?
3. What should be the foremost concern of police officers when dealing with a natural disaster?
4. In dealing with a bomb threat, what are the most important considerations?
5. How might the media be of help during an emergency situation?
6. Who might your community call on for help in the event of a Level-3 emergency?
7. Have you ever been involved in an emergency situation yourself? How well was it handled? What could have been done differently?

Definitions

Can you define the following terms?

critical-incident stress debriefing (CISD)	posttraumatic stress disorder
emergency operations center	predisaster plan
HAZMAT incident	triage

American Psychiatric Association. *Diagnostic and Statistical Manual III*. Chicago IL, 1980.

Clark, Jacob R. "It's Police vs. Mother Nature: Hurricane, Earthquake Put Agencies to the Test on Two Coasts." *Law Enforcement News* (December 15, 1989): 6–7, 9–10.

Fisher, A. J. *Security for Business and Industry*. Englewood Cliffs, N.J.: Prentice-Hall, 1979.

Greenberg, Reuben, et al. "The Lessons of Hurricane Hugo: Law Enforcement Responds." *The Police Chief* (September 1990): 26–33.

Hermann, Stephen L.

    a. "Developing a Hazardous Materials Enforcement Capability." *Law and Order* (January 1991a): 266–270.

    b. "U.S. DOT's New HazMat Emergency Response Guide." *Law and Order* (January 1991b): 271.

Hess, Kären M. and Wrobleski, Henry M. *Introduction to Private Security*. 3d ed. St. Paul, Minn.: West Publishing Company, 1992.

Higgens, Stephen E. "Bombs and Bombers: Past and Future." *The Police Chief* (December 1990): 16.

Hildreth, Reed. "Are You Ready? In the Right Circumstances, Otherwise Harmless Chemicals Can Become HAZMAT Problem." *Law and Order* (March 1991): 93–100.

Iushewitz, David. "Returning to Normalcy: The Role of the E.O.C." *Law and Order* (May 1990): 33–34.

Kemp, Roger T. "Emergency Management." In *The Encyclopedia of Police Science*, William G. Bailey, ed. New York: Garland Publishing, 1989.

Maher, George F. "The Tragedy of Avianca Flight 052." *The Police Chief* (September 1990): 39–43.

May, William A.

    a. "Posttraumatic Stress After Large-Scale Disasters." *Law and Order* (March 1990a): 97–99.

    b. "Responding to Hazardous Materials Incidents." *Law and Order* (October 1990b): 85–87.

McClinton, James L. "The Lessons of Hurricane Hugo: Expecting the Unexpected." *The Police Chief* (September 1990): 34–38.

Michelson, R. "Disaster Myths." *The Police Chief* (May 1984): 36.

Rubin, Hal. "Quake Response." *Law and Order* (February 1990): 50–53.

Russell, Harold E. and Beigel, Allan. *Understanding Human Behavior for Effective Police Work*. 3d ed. New York: Basic Books, 1990.

Sessions, William S. "Emergency Response: Identifying Fatalities." *The Police Chief* (September 1991): 8.

Tyler, Susan. "Computer Assistance for the California Earthquake Rescue Effort." *The Police Chief* (February 1990): 42–43.

WORKING WITH OTHERS: COOPERATIVE EFFORTS

CHAPTER 16

INTRODUCTION

The police do not and cannot operate in a vacuum. They must interact with those they have sworn to serve and protect. They will deal with the citizens of their community as individuals as well as in groups. Police officers will be most effective if they interact and cooperate with social and educational agencies and other organizations within the community. As noted by Brown (1990, p. 8), 1990 president of the IACP, "At the heart of policing is a requirement for understanding between the police and the citizens they are sworn to protect. Put simply, police officers must be a *part* of the community, not *apart* from it." This has been a recurring theme throughout this text.

In the past, police departments have recognized the importance of the community and have instituted community relations programs. Some departments even have a separate division in charge of community relations, closely associated with crime prevention efforts.

Do You Know

- How effective foot patrol appears to be?
- What the goals of the Guardian Angels are?
- What civilianization refers to?
- How citizens become involved with crime prevention?
- How our population is changing?
- What special populations the police must learn to interact with?
- What the purpose of a citizen review board is?
- What agencies police departments interact with?
- What privatization refers to?
- How the police interact with the press?

Community Relations and Crime Prevention: A Brief History

According to Greene, (1989, p. 349): "Over the past forty years, the police-community relations movement has evolved from early one-way, police-to-community-resident communications programs, to action programs emphasizing community responsibility for crime prevention and self-protection."

In the 1960s, tensions between the police and citizens were great. The police were seen as insulated from the public, and a definite "them v. us" mentality existed. As a result, many departments instituted public relations programs aimed at enhancing the police image. They sponsored a variety of programs such as Officer Friendly programs in the schools, open houses at the police station, and the like.

Crime prevention programs such as Block Watches were instituted, but most were more "symbolic than substantive" (p. 350). The involvement of citizens in crime prevention programs legitimized the idea that citizens might contribute to combatting neighborhood crime. They became, in effect, eyes and ears for the department but had little effect on policy or decision making.

Many departments sought to help citizens understand police work better by instituting ride-along programs where citizens accompanied officers in their patrol vehicles and observed first-hand the functions officers perform. Many police departments also began experimenting with team policing in an effort to bring their officers more in touch with specific areas in the jurisdiction and to give them more of a sense of belonging.

The late 1970s and early 1980s, according to Greene, saw team policing and community crime prevention efforts giving way to an emphasis on getting officers out of their patrol cars and back on the beat (that is, foot patrol), and on community

A Neighborhood Watch notice posted in a Washington, D.C., neighborhood informs residents of a crime committed that day. Such programs are common throughout the United States.

policing. Says Greene (p. 355), "While community crime prevention is still quite active nationally, foot patrol and community-oriented police strategies have currently captured the imagination of the local police and the public."

Foot Patrol and Community Policing

Foot patrol was discussed in Chapter 9, but its contribution to community policing and its role in efforts to decentralize the police organization are also of relevance in this chapter.

Experiments with foot patrol conducted in Newark, New Jersey; Flint, Michigan; Oakland, California; Houston, Texas; Boston, Massachusetts have yielded similar results.

Research indicates that foot patrol programs improve public relations between the police and the community but do not affect crime rates.

Skogan and Pate (1987, p. 19) report on a foot patrol and community policing program in Newark:

The evaluation indicates that, where the program was solely in the hands of the police, the area did not seem cleaner and the level of public drinking, street harassment, gang activity, open drug use, vandalism, and the like does not appear to have declined. However, there is substantial evidence that the community policing version of the program may have had more positive consequences. . . . Fewer of those who were interviewed in the community policing area rated social disorder or physical decay as "big problems," and they felt safer and less worried about personal and property victimization.

Frankel (1990, p. 12A) describes the work of one officer involved in New York City's community policing efforts:

Jeff Christopher is a policeman in Harlem whose recent achievements include replacing a piano destroyed at a junior high school, getting the sanitation department to remove refrigerators dumped in a street, and shepherding 177 neighborhood kids to a concert.

He also spent four weeks crawling through back alleys and on rooftops, putting together information that became the basis of a bust netting 12,000 vials of crack, $63,000 in cash, guns, and a drug kingpin.

Christopher is a three-year veteran of a program called community policing—a cross between a cop walking the beat and a social worker.

This combination of police officer and social worker is also evident in the problem-oriented policing (POP) approach used in San Diego, California. According to Burgreen and McPherson (1990, p. 51): "Patrol officers are becoming knowledgeable about the communities they serve, and they are developing previously untapped resources to solve problems that have plagued the community for over twenty years. . . . They use a simple problem-solving model to facilitate the exchange of information between public and private agencies and community groups, and to follow up on action by those who become part of the problem-solving process."

As noted by Cummings (1990, p. 63), problem-solving policing involved three elements:

First, problems must be defined in very specific terms. Second, information about the problems must be collected from sources outside the police agency, not just from internal sources. Finally, police agencies must engage in a broad *search for solutions, including various alternatives to the criminal justice process.*

Closely related to community policing and problem-oriented policing is the *crime-specific planning* approach. According to Cummings (p. 63), "While similar to problem-oriented policing in its process, crime-specific planning is more specific in that it approaches criminal justice problems by considering underlying problems that are categorized by the type of offense." It includes considering each of the following factors (p. 63):

1. Seriousness of the offense.
2. Frequency of occurrence.
3. Public concern.
4. Impact on the community.
5. The drain on resources of the criminal justice system.
6. The susceptibility of each crime to control.
7. Whether the crime is one of opportunity or calculation.
8. The degree of concentration required to develop plans for the perpetration of the crime.
9. The modus operandi and other discernable patterns.
10. The violent characteristics that may be present.
11. The property that may be taken or damaged.
12. The victim's response.
13. The community's response.
14. The system's response.
15. The actual target.
16. Characteristics of the target.
17. When the target is attacked.
18. How the target is attacked.
19. Where the target is located in the environment.
20. The number of potential targets in each area.
21. The accessibility of the targets.
22. Transportation patterns surrounding the targets.
23. Offender characteristics.

Such modifications in policing have come largely in response to the need to provide more services with the same or diminished resources. Police cannot combat crime and preserve the peace in a vacuum. As aptly noted by Greene (1989, p. 365): "Resources for crime control have dwindled over the years. At the same time, public demand for police services has increased. While citizen involvement in community-police programs is no cure-all for the problems of crime and social disorder, it is essential for the maintenance of democratic values. Furthermore, law enforcement agencies can hardly continue to exclude the clients and producers of police service from the policies and decisions affecting the 'quality of life' in American communities."

This sentiment is shared by Trojanowicz and Carter (1990, p. 11): "It would be naive to suggest that community policing is a panacea that can heal all the wounds in any community. But it has demonstrated its ability to make people feel safer and improve the overall quality of community life." In some instances, citizens get quite involved in working with the police to make their neighborhoods safer. One way is through private citizen patrols.

Private Citizen Patrols

Neighborhood Watch programs and other citizen efforts to protect themselves and prevent crime may result in the formation of private citizen patrols. The best known citizen patrol group is the Guardian Angels. According to Clede (1990, p. 37), the Guardian Angels have approximately 5,000 individual members and have expanded into 67 cities as well as into Canada, Mexico, and England. The activities the Guardian Angels engage in vary from community to community, but most focus efforts on:

- Increasing citizen awareness of crime through community education.
- Promoting active participation in crime prevention programs.
- Enhancing neighborhood security.

The Guardian Angels seek to fight crime, enhance feelings of security, and provide positive role models for young people.

Unlike other citizen groups, according to the National Council on Crime and Delinquency (1989, p. 383), the Guardian Angels is a national organization whose major purposes are:

to be a visual deterrent to crime, to increase citizens' feelings of safety, and to provide positive role models for young people. In contrast to most citizen patrols examined, the Angels will intervene if they encounter a crime in progress, although physical intervention is viewed as a last resort to be used only to protect others from harm.

In some communities, the Guardian Angels are welcomed by the police and work well with them. In others, they present a problem. Clede (1990, p. 39) says, "Police in the nation's largest cities, New York, Los Angeles, and Chicago, are far from enthusiastic about the Angels. In Houston, Atlanta, and Minneapolis, law enforcement authorities have found them to be an asset." He further suggests: "Where a group has a working relationship with police, they seem to be quite effective. Where they don't have police cooperation, their effectiveness appears limited."

Each police department must examine the role of the Guardian Angels should the group come to their community and decide what type of interaction to foster. Most Guardian Angel groups have an informal working relationship with the local police. The police may support them through such functions as training and providing data on crime and related information.

Other citizen groups have also been effective in supplementing police patrol. Texarkana, Texas, for example, has a group called Awareness of Crime in Texarkana (ACT), which consists of citizen patrols. Bennett (1989, pp. 367–368) quotes a police captain working with the program: "We cannot be everywhere. We need the

Guardian Angels on patrol talking to two teens. This citizen patrol group has approximately 5,000 members located throughout the United States.

eyes and ears of the citizenry to call and tell us about something suspicious going on. We'll go after that location and we'll investigate.''

Another successful Neighborhood Crime Watch program that works effectively with the police department is that of Evanston, Illinois, a Chicago suburb. This program uses a crime information hotline and two products: the Digital Announcer and Delegate, by Northern Telecom. The Digital Announcer, an audio playback system, is designed for repetitive telephone inquiries. It can store messages up to 8.5 minutes long. Special messages are recorded for each of the four sections into which Evanston, for purposes of the Neighborhood Crime Watch program, is divided. The messages include the block number, crime, time and date it was committed, and any description of the suspect available as well as a crime tip. The following is an example of a typical message (Grausso, 1989, p. 38):

Hello. You have reached the Crime Information Line for Blocks X and Y, for the week of January XY. There was a house burglary in the 200 block of McDaniels at an undetermined time last week. Entrance was gained by forcing the door. There was a house burglary on the 200 block of Dodd on Friday between 9:15 and 11:15 in the evening. The offender gained entry through an unlocked window. If you know anything about either of these crimes, please call us at 866–5040. The burglary rate was up slightly last week. Remember, deadbolt locks can prevent burglaries. If you have not had a security survey of your home or apartment, please call us at 866–5019, and we will schedule one. Talk to you next week.

The Delegate stores messages up to one minute long on chips, not tape, so no rewinding is needed after each call. This message can be accessed by the community at large rather than only by a specific area of the community. Its messages announce the Crime Prevention Unit's hours of operation and explain the services it offers. Special messages are also often included. According to Grausso (p. 37):

Together, the two units [Digital Announcer and Delegate] offer Evanston's residents weekly recorded messages detailing specific incidents in specific locations. The Digital Announcer provides crime information to the Neighborhood Watch program's block captains, while the Delegate serves the general public.

As one officer involved with the program said (Grausso, p. 39):

Typically, Citizen Watch Patrols gain support when something hot is going on. After you make the arrest, interest subsides. Here, the crime-line helps keep the interest level up. It complements the Neighborhood Watch program—helping to make for a tighter knit and better informed, crime-conscious community.

Bennett (1989, p. 368) says that police need not worry about such groups becoming vigilantes except under certain conditions: "When the members are drawn exclusively from a clique; when their activities are unregulated by any umbrella organization; and when patrols become dull." Nonetheless, tension often exists between police departments and citizen groups.

Vigilante groups can also make mistakes, especially when emotion in the community is running high. In October, 1991, such an unstructured group in Kansas City, Missouri, apprehended a young male who resembled a composite drawing of a suspect being shown on television. This suspect had forcibly abducted four young females on separate occasions from school bus stops and sexually molested them. The self-appointed group severely beat the young man, inflicting some permanent injuries, only to learn later that he was innocent of the crimes in question.

Another problem can occur, as noted by McPherson and Silloway (1985, p. 63): "When citizens take the lead and preclude law enforcement, or activities do not correspond with police opinions, officers feel threatened."

In addition to private citizen patrol groups, some communities have turned to using civilians in what has traditionally been thought of as police work.

Civilianization

Some departments have encouraged citizen interaction by bringing more civilians into their actual police work. Many police departments have begun using citizen volunteers in a variety of ways. In other instances, they are hired for specific law-enforcement-related tasks, greatly increasing the potential effectiveness of the agency. As Goldstein puts it (1990, p. 21):

The police must do more than they have done in the past to engage the citizenry in the overall task of policing. In a field in which resources are so

*often strapped, the potential of this relatively untapped resource is enormous.
The police have erred in pretending for all these years that they could take
upon themselves—and successfully discharge—all of the responsibilities that
are now theirs. A relatively small group of individuals (whether 10 in a
community of 5,000 or 28,000 in a city, such as New York, of 7.5 million),
however powerful and efficient, simply cannot meet those expectations. . . . A
community must police itself. The police can, at best, only assist in that task.*

Civilianization of law enforcement is one cost-effective way to capitalize on the
numerous and varied capabilities of citizens. Many routine tasks performed by
police do not require their expertise nor their special authority and arrest powers.
Administrators, report writers, dispatchers, animal control officers, and jailers are
among those who could be civilians rather than sworn officers.

Civilianization refers to the practice of hiring citizens to
perform certain tasks for the police department.

Although many police departments do not feel citizens should become directly
involved in fighting crime, most do believe citizens should take some responsibility
for crime prevention and protecting themselves from potential risks as much as
possible.

Crime Prevention Programs

Many crime prevention programs have been operating for decades. Programs such
as Neighborhood Block Watches and Operation Identification are well known
throughout the country. So are programs featuring residential and commercial security checks and programs helping citizens become attuned to self-protection so as
to lessen their risks of being victimized. School-based programs such as DARE and
the sexual abuse programs described in Chapter 13 are also common across the
country.

Among the newer, more innovative crime prevention programs are those using
high technology to deter auto thefts. The Auto Theft Bureau (ATB) reported that
nearly 1.3 million Americans were victims of auto theft in 1988, and an additional
2.7 had either the contents or valuable auto parts stolen from their vehicles. With
the exception of their homes, vehicles are the most valuable items most citizens own.
Consequently, programs to deter auto theft can do much to improve community/
police relations.

The use of computerized chips to deter auto theft or to assist in retrieving stolen
vehicles was described in Chapter 11. Another innovative program is the CAT
program, developed three years ago by the New York City Police Department. The
acronym stands for Combat Auto Theft. It is a relatively simple program in which
police place a special decal inside the back window of vehicles registered with the
program. This decal authorizes police to stop the vehicle if it is observed being
driven between 1 A.M. and 5 A.M., peak auto theft hours. Would-be car thieves who
know about the program are unlikely to steal a vehicle displaying the decal.

Participation in the program is completely voluntary. Participants sign a consent form stating that they do not normally drive their vehicles between 1 A.M. and 5 A.M. and that, if the vehicle is being driven during that time, it can be stopped by the police. According to Hildreth (1990, p. 93), New York's three-year-old program has registered 37,326 cars, of which only 67 have been stolen.

Citizens become involved in crime prevention by participating in Neighborhood Watch programs, Operation Identification programs, security checks, school programs such as DARE and sexual abuse prevention programs, as well as programs to deter vehicle theft.

Goals for Crime Prevention Programs

Many crime prevention programs fail to live up to their expectations simply because they have not established realistic goals and objectives. The National Crime Prevention Institute (NCPI) (1986, p. 163) presents an example of a city of 100,000 who set as their crime prevention objective, *to stabilize the incidence of residential burglary throughout the city.* The activities they undertook to achieve this objective are summarized in Table 16.1.

With the impressive community response detailed in Table 16.1, it is easy to see how dismayed the department was to find that residential burglary *increased* by 61 percent that year. The reasons, according to the institute, might be that increased public awareness often results in an increased tendency for citizens to report crime, creating a statistical anomaly rather than an actual increase in crime. In addition, the institute's program affected only a small portion of the entire jurisdiction while the entire jurisdiction's burglary rates showed up in the statistics. The problem may not have been in the types of efforts, but in the expectations; that is, the stated objective was a "severe overreaching of the Crime Prevention Unit's capability during that year." The institute suggests that the activities planned for the year should more reasonably have been statements of objectives and could be worded as follows:

- To stabilize the incidence of residential burglary in forty selected neighborhoods through the establishment of Neighborhood Watch groups.
- To reduce the incidence of residential burglary as compared to the citywide average for 250 selected homes through security surveys and for 700 homes through Operation ID enrollment.
- To generate requests for crime prevention services through public presentations.
- To increase the reporting of residential burglary through a citywide public-awareness campaign.
- To obtain agreement from key public and private officials to work together on the drafting of a building security code.

Such direct, specific, and measurable goals set the groundwork for a program whose effectiveness can be fairly evaluated.

TABLE 16.1
Crime Prevention Goals, Efforts, and Effects

Planned Activity	Measured Activity	Measured Impact
Establish and sustain 40 new neighborhood groups.	Established 57; CPU staff meets about once a month with each group.	None of 600 participant households burglarized (daily burglary reports).
Conduct 250 residential security surveys.	Conducted 538 surveys.	Burglary 0.9% in surveyed homes, v. 1.6% citywide: surveyed victims apparently did not follow recommendations: local sales of "improved" security hardware doubled.
Enroll 700 new Operation ID participants.	Enrolled 1,056 new participants.	Burglary 0.4% compared to 1.6% and some attempts aborted because of marked property.
Conduct 200 public presentations.	Conducted 136.	A specific CP service was subsequently requested by 80% of participants.
Disseminate public information.	Utilized the following: ■ radio/TV announcements ■ newspaper articles ■ talk shows ■ carton stuffers ■ Welcome Wagon	Some services requested as a result, staff concluded that "it helps."
Establish patrol focus in high-crime residential areas.	Provided weekly crime activity report to Patrol Division. Maintained pin map (burglary) in Patrol Squad Room.	Report was "useful." Pin map was "marginal."
Draft a security code for adoption by city.	Not drafted but key actors "educated."	"Education" process working OK; first draft expected next year.

Source: Adapted from *Understanding Crime Prevention,* p. 163. National Crime Prevention Institute, Stoneham, Mass.: Butterworth Publishers, 1986. Reprinted with permission of the National Crime Prevention Institute, School of Justice Administration, University of Louisville. Mass.

Interaction with Individual Citizens

The most significant interaction police officers have is their one-on-one involvement with individual citizens. As our society becomes more diverse, as discussed in Chapter 1, it is critical that police officers understand the differences in individuals that they will encounter. Citizens within communities are extremely varied. Some differences such as age, sex, socioeconomic conditions, and educational levels, have been recognized and dealt with in community relations programs. Of increasing concern in today's society is the diverse and growing elderly population. Other differences are less commonly acknowledged and are often much more difficult for police to deal with on an individual basis. These differences include people newly arrived in the United States who speak little English, people with disabilities, mentally disabled people, and the homeless.

Our population is becoming older, minorities are increasing, we have growing numbers of illegal immigrants, thousands of mentally ill individuals have been deinstitutionalized, the homeless population is growing, and the gap between the "haves" and the "have nots" is widening.

As stated by Trojanowicz and Carter (1990b, p. 9): "Today's challenge is to find new ways for law enforcement to contribute to making the United States a place where all people have an equal chance to secure a piece of the American dream for themselves and their children."

The Elderly

In the past ten years, the number of Americans 65 years old and older has increased by approximately 23 percent (Exter, 1989). According to Manning and Proctor (1989, p. 1D), the first wave of "baby boomers" will turn 50 in 1996, beginning a "senior boom" in the United States. By 2010, one-fourth of our population will be 55 or older.

One problem associated with the elderly population is Alzheimer's disease, introduced in Chapter 2. Some 2.5 million American citizens have Alzheimer's. According to the Alzheimer's Disease and Related Disorders Association (1987, p. 5) the symptoms of this disease include:

Gradual memory loss, impairment of judgement, disorientation, personality change, decline in ability to perform routine tasks, behavior change, difficulty in learning, loss of language skills, and a decline in intellectual function.

Alzheimer's disease can cause several behaviors that might bring the person into contact with the police. Victims of this disease may become hopelessly lost. Often they will not remember where they live or where they were going. They may become confused, uncooperative, or even combative when questioned. Their fidgeting may be misinterpreted. As noted by the Alzheimer's Disease Association, the victim "who zips and unzips his pants or unbuttons her blouse in public may simply

Officer talking with an elderly citizen. As our population ages, officers must understand the needs and concerns of the elderly.

be fidgeting." These people also have limited impulse control and if clothing is too warm or is uncomfortable, they may simply take it off.

Sufferers of Alzheimer's may forget to pay for an item in a store and then be accused of shoplifting. Or they may misplace their purses or billfolds while shopping and then accuse store personnel of stealing. Alzheimer's victims may lose their cars, may forget that they drove somewhere and report their cars stolen, may have an accident and leave, actually forgetting that the accident happened, or they may simply keep driving. Some victims have been located hundreds of miles from home, with no recollection of having driven there. As noted in Chapter 2, the Alzheimer's patients' propensity to wander, their confusion and inability to answer questions, or their driving behavior may be mistakenly interpreted as intoxication.

Victimization, real or imagined, is another major problem. According to the A.D. Association (1987, p. 10):

> *People afflicted with A.D. are easy prey for con artists, robbers, and muggers. They may come to the attention of the police as a result of legal actions such as eviction, repossession, and termination of utility service due to forgetfulness or inability to make payments.*
>
> *On the other hand, patients may inaccurately believe they have been victimized by friends and family, as well as strangers. This may result in reports of crimes which did not happen.*
>
> *Also neighbors may report screaming and yelling at night, especially in A.D. patients who live alone. "Kidnap" or "adult abuse" reports may result from caregivers' attempts to limit an A.D. patient's behavior in public.*

The Police Response.   Police need to be familiar with the symptoms of Alzheimer's Disease and have strategies for dealing with these people whom police are likely to encounter in increasing numbers. Specific suggestions for communicating with Alzheimer's patients were given in Chapter 2.

In addition to being able to interact effectively with Alzheimer's sufferers, police officers might also develop crime prevention programs for senior citizens. Such programs can do much to lessen the risk of senior citizens' being victimized. The elderly should have their social security checks deposited directly in the bank, should not keep large amounts of money on their person or in their homes, and should give up their purse or billfold if approached by a robber.

Minorities

Just as our population is becoming older, it is also shifting in its racial balance. Trojanowicz and Carter (1990b, p. 6) state: "According to demographers, in less than 100 years, we can expect white dominance of the United States to end, as the growing number of blacks, Hispanics, and Asians together become the new majority." In fact, by 2010, according to Schwartz and Exter (1988, p. 42): "More than one-third of all American children will be black, Hispanic, or Asian."

The significance of these figures is made apparent by Trojanowicz and Bucqueroux (1990, p. 242) who note: "Race is a volatile criminal justice issue because of:

- The alarming rates of victimization many minority groups endure.
- The disproportionate number of minorities arrested and incarcerated.

- The debate about how best to promote minority hiring and promotion in police departments.
- The role of race as a common factor in police brutality.
- The concern that racially motivated incidents and attacks are on the rise.
- The worrisome emergence and growth of new militant groups, such as the Skinheads, who openly advocate violence against minorities.''

The Police Response.   One effective approach to dealing with minority problems is community policing. As Trojanowicz and Bucqueroux (1990, p. 243) state: ''While community policing is no panacea that can erase all minority concerns, it can make valuable contributions toward easing racial tensions and addressing minority crime concerns.'' It does this in several ways, including the following:

- Takes all crime and disorder problems seriously in ways that empower rather than alienate law-abiding citizens.
- Allows the opportunity to gather broad, in-depth information about racial incidents and the possible arrival and activities of troublesome groups.
- Allows the opportunity to carefully screen complaints on such crimes as vandalism and assault for signs of racial or ethnic elements.

In addition, say Trojanowicz and Bucqueroux (p. 245): ''Community policing is a dramatic way to provide full-fledged law enforcement in a new and highly personalized form. It offers the promise of directly addressing racially motivated police brutality and excessive use of force by breaking down the *us against them* mindset—a profound shift in the way the police and the public interact.''

Non-English-Speaking Immigrants

As noted by Raymondo (1988, p. 43), between 2.5 and 3.5 million illegal immigrants entered the United States in 1980. It has been estimated that the number of illegal immigrants is growing at a rate of 100,000–300,000 a year.

Often these non-English-speaking immigrants cluster together in relatively poor neighborhoods where crime rates are high. As Trojanowicz and Carter (1990b, p. 8) caution: ''The police, perhaps even more so than the population at large, must guard against stereotyping. Some newcomers may be too timid to interact widely in their new communities; yet, they may contact the police. The police, therefore, have a tremendous responsibility because those first impressions matter.''

In addition, many new immigrants come from countries where the police are feared rather than respected. The police in those countries keep secret files and have broad arrest powers. They may brutalize citizens, force confessions from them, or simply imprison them without any ''due process.'' In fact, due process may be a concept heretofore unknown to these new immigrants.

Further, many new immigrants will become victims, especially of violent crimes. Again, their fear of the police will work against them as they are unlikely to report the crimes or to assist the police in investigating them. As noted by Trojanowicz and Carter (p. 9): ''The primary challenge for law enforcement will be to find ways to meet their needs with special concern for their racial, ethnic, cultural, and religious diversity.''

The Police Response.   One obvious step toward effectively interacting with non-English-speaking immigrants is to recruit officers from among their ranks,

Another step is to carefully consider law enforcement policies toward illegal immigrants. It is natural that illegal immigrants will not want their presence known to any official of the community for fear they will be turned over to the Immigration and Naturalization Service (INS). In one border town, the chief of police has made it department policy not to inform INS about undocumented residents unless they are involved in committing a crime.

The Mentally Disabled

It is highly likely that police officers will also interact with individuals who are **mentally disabled,** that is, people who are mentally ill or mentally retarded. According to Murphy (1989, pp. 1–8): "One in ten persons suffer from some type of mental illness. There are between one and four million seriously mentally ill people in this country who require hospitalization or who have had a major psychosis for one or two years.

Mental retardation is often cited as our country's fourth leading disabling condition with an estimated 3 percent of the U.S. population, or some six million individuals, classified as mentally retarded.

Historically, mentally ill individuals were locked away from society in insane asylums. Long-term institutionalization or hospitalization was the norm. Likewise, mentally retarded individuals were placed into special schools, usually hidden away from society. In the mid-1960s, however, this changed and a massive deinstitutionalization movement occurred, placing mentally disabled individuals into the community, but without the support they formerly had. Many have become homeless, as discussed later in this chapter. Police officers should understand the differences between mental retardation and mental illness, as summarized in Table 16.2.

According to Murphy (1986, pp. 183–184), **mental illness** is in most cases "a temporary disorder during which an individual has difficulty coping with life's stresses and problems. The disorders can fluctuate in seriousness, can usually be reversed or alleviated, and can strike a person at any time." **Mental retardation,** in contrast, is permanent and is diagnosed when the following three criteria are met (p. 195): "(1) significant subaverage general intellectual functioning, (2) resulting in, or associated with, deficits or impairments in adaptive behavior, (3) with onset before the age of eighteen."

The police often become involved with mentally disabled individuals because the police are often the only twenty-four-hour, seven-day-a-week, visible assistance. When citizens, friends, or relatives feel threatened by the bizarre behavior of a mentally disabled person, they are likely to call the police. In addition, mentally ill individuals may call the police to report "incidents" resulting from their mental illness, for example, a paranoid person calls to report that someone is following him. As noted by Murphy (1989, pp. 1–11), the behaviors police most frequently encounter when called to manage mentally ill persons are:

- Bizarre, unusual, or strange behavior.
- Confused thoughts or action.
- Aggressive actions.
- Destructive, assaultive, or violent behavior.
- Attempted suicide.

TABLE 16.2

Differences between Mental Retardation and Mental Illness

Category	Mental Retardation	Mental Illness
Intellectual functioning	Retardation refers to subaverage intellectual functioning.	Mental illness has nothing to do with IQ. A person who is mentally ill may be a genius or may be subaverage intellectually.
Social adaptation	Retardation refers to impairment in social adaptation.	A mentally ill person may be very competent socially but may have a character disorder or other aberration.
Time of onset	Retardation usually is present at birth or occurs during the period of development.	Mental illness may strike at any time.
Prognosis	In mental retardation, the intellectual impairment is permanent but can be compensated through development of the person's potential.	Mental illness is often temporary and in most cases is reversible. It is not a developmental disability.
Behavior	A retarded person can usually be expected to behave rationally at his operational level.	A mentally ill person may vacillate between normal and irrational behavior.
Presence of violence	A retarded person will not be violent except in those situations that cause violence in non-retarded persons.	A mentally ill person may be erratic or even violent.
Services needed	A mentally retarded person has a learning disability and may use the services of educators, psychologists, and vocational therapists.	A mentally ill person may utilize the services of psychiatrists, psychotherapists, or psychologists.

Source: Adapted from *Special Care: Improving the Police Response to the Mentally Disabled,* by Gerard R. Murphy. Washington D.C.: The Police Executive Research Forum, 1986. Reprinted by permission of the Police Executive Research Forum.

The Police Response

Murphy's curriculum guide, *Managing Persons with Mental Disabilities,* (1989) includes comprehensive definitions and illustrations of specific types of mental illness and degrees of retardation with which all police officers should be familiar. It also includes the following suggestions for police responses to specific types of mental disability.

Handling Persons with Mental Illnesses. (pp. 4–8 through 4–10.) General guidelines for handling mentally ill persons include:

- Gather as much information as possible before arriving on the scene.
- Be discreet and avoid attracting attention.
- Be calm, avoid excitement, and portray a take-charge attitude.
- Remove as many distractions or upsetting influences from the scene as possible—this includes bystanders and disruptive friends or family members.

- Gather as much information as possible from helpful witnesses, family members, and friends.

When officers first arrive, they should introduce themselves and explain the reason for their presence. They should be alert to any potential for violence. If violence occurs, the mentally ill person should be given a chance to calm down. "It is better that the officer spend fifteen or twenty minutes waiting and talking than to spend five minutes struggling to subdue the person." Officers should *not:*

- Abuse, belittle, or threaten.
- Use inflammatory words.
- Lie or deceive.
- Cross-examine the person.
- Dispute, debate or invalidate the person's claims.
- Rush or crowd the person.
- Be a "tough" guy.
- Let the person upset or trick them into an argument.

Handling Mentally Retarded Persons.
(pp. 4–13 through 4–15.) Recognizing mental retardation is the first step in dealing with it effectively. Often those who are retarded are adept at camouflaging their disability from the casual observer. Guidelines for handling mentally retarded persons include the following:

- Arrange for a quiet, private setting.
- Avoid asking rapid-fire questions or attempting to unnerve or intimidate the person. Speak slowly, use simple language, repeat if necessary, be patient, and avoid questions that require only a "yes" or "no" response.
- Be aware of the person's reluctance to discuss the matter.
- Be aware of the person's attempts to please others.
- Be firm and purposeful.
- If possible, use visual aids, pictures, or diagrams.

Handling Suicide Attempts.
(pp. 4–15 through 4–17.) "Dealing with a suicidal person requires a calm, matter-of-fact, but genuine concern for the person and is best accomplished through communication. . . . The best way an officer can help the person is to discuss the person's problems, the suicide plan, and realistic alternatives." Guidelines for dealing with suicide attempts include the following:

- Obtain necessary personal data immediately (name, age, phone number, address, place of work, names and phone numbers of family and close friends).
- Bring the subject of suicide into the open. Ask such specific questions as: Are you thinking of killing yourself? How are you going to kill yourself? Do you have the means to kill yourself? When? What time of day?
- Remove the means.
- Notify and meet with significant others.
- Offer realistic hope.
- Establish a specific plan of action.

Making Referrals.
(pp. 3–4 through 3–8.) "Officers should be able to determine when someone needs referral to mental health professionals and should know how to gain access to those resources" (p. i). They should know what the proce-

dures for formal commitment are for individuals who pose a threat to themselves or to others.

The Gap between the "Haves" and the "Have Nots"

The gap between those at the top of the educational and economic ladder and those at the bottom is widening. McCord and Wicker (1990, p. 30) suggest that: "An underclass of Americans—those who are chronically poor and live outside society's rules—is growing." This is largely due to our society changing from an industrial-based society to an information-based one where more and more jobs rely on education and technology than on labor in its classic sense. As noted by the Tofflers (1990, p. 3): "When many of our grandfathers came to this country, speaking a foreign language and knowing nothing of American culture, their intelligence didn't count for much in the job market. What employers mostly wanted was muscle. Millions at the bottom of the pile were able to find work because they had muscle. . . . Today this is becoming impossible." They go on to note that:

> It is simple-minded to blame crime on poverty. There are plenty of societies in which poverty does not produce crime. But it is equally witless to assume that millions of poor, jobless young people—not part of the work-world culture and bursting with energy and anger—are going to stay off the streets and join knitting clubs.

The Police Response.   Many of the youth programs discussed in Chapter 13 might also help keep youth on the side of the law, out of gangs or doing drugs. Explorer posts where youth can routinely interact with police in a positive way, sports competitions sponsored by police departments, and community service opportunities for youths who do get into trouble with the law are other avenues for positive interaction with youth living in poverty.

In addition, police must view those of all ages who live in poverty as still worthy of respect and assistance from the police when needed. Among those living in poverty are the growing numbers of homeless people.

The Homeless

The homeless, some three million people who are sleeping on the streets, comprise an ever increasing social problem in the 1990s. As noted by Grossman (1987, p. 38), "In communities where sleeping on the streets is against the law, what begins as a social problem becomes a problem of criminal justice." Further, the homeless are frequently *victims* of crime and violence. Law enforcement is responsible for protecting the homeless from those segments of society who would take advantage of them. Another problem involves the fact that those who advocate for the homeless sometimes break the law—for example, by taking over unoccupied private homes as well as unoccupied public buildings and demanding that these buildings be made into shelters for the homeless. On the other hand, countless numbers of citizens do not want people sleeping in their parks. They cite problems such as littering, stealing, drinking, doing drugs, and public urinating and defecating. In general, communities simply don't want to have the homeless around. Citizens clamor to their city council to pass laws against sleeping in the street. And

Officers talking to a homeless person. In some jurisdictions, being homeless is a crime. What began as a social problem becomes a law enforcement problem.

when city councils oblige, the social problem becomes a law enforcement problem. Grossman (p. 42) describes the problems faced by Miami police officers where such legislation exists. Approximately 6,800 people were arrested for sleeping on the streets, many of them repeatedly, costing the department approximately $2–2.5 million. One Miami police sergeant, while stressing that most of the homeless people are more likely to be victimized than to commit crimes, says (p. 42):

> *You get the guy who is ex-special forces or ex-marine . . . walking around the streets, he's schizophrenic, he hasn't eaten in two days, he's working in the survival instinct mode, and you've got a very dangerous individual on your hands.*

Almost half the homeless *are* veterans, primarily from Vietnam, but certainly not all homeless people fit the preceding description. The next largest group of homeless people are the mentally ill who were deinstitutionalized in the 1960s and 1970s. Many of these individuals can become confused and violent. The problem has worsened since 1980 with more than 2.5 million units of low-income housing disappearing, along with the closing of many large mental institutions. According to Lamar (1988), the number of such institutions has gone from 560,000 to 143,000.

Lamar also notes that more than two million people will be homeless sometime during the year, one-third of whom will be families with children and one-fourth of whom will have jobs—the working poor. Lamar also says that one-third of the homeless are mentally ill.

The homeless pose a dual problem for police according to Trojanowicz and Bucqueroux (1990, p. 241): "There is a fear of crime by the general population, and people are more afraid of potentially menacing strangers loitering nearby than they are of being murdered. . . . The second concern is the alarming rates of victimization that the homeless suffer." This is especially true of the very young and the very old. Chandler (1988) states that children in shelters for the homeless are often targets of sexual abuse and that according to a study of elderly homeless in Detroit, half had been beaten, robbed, or raped the previous year.

These homeless people "inspire an anguished mix of feelings that include fear, guilt, revulsion, and shame." The change in public attitudes toward the homeless is illustrated in three major cities which have toughened regulations on panhandling, sleeping in public places, and other behavior associated with the homeless. As noted in *Insight* (p. 22), "While the plight of the homeless remains at the top of the nation's urban agenda, the public's sense of guilt appears to be giving way to exasperation. Responding to an unmistakable shift in public attitudes, officials in San Francisco, New York, and Washington, three of the most staunchly liberal cities in the nation, have adopted policies that now are as much attuned to the concerns of the average voter as to the demands of the homeless advocacy groups."

In New York, police are enforcing new regulations that prohibit lying down on floors or benches in Pennsylvania Station or Grand Central Terminal, panhandling, fighting, or disrobing and urinating or defecating outside toilet facilities.

In San Francisco, new laws have displaced as many as 350 homeless who formerly camped in the Civic Center Plaza. In Washington, D.C., the city council overturned a 1984 right-to-shelter law that was costing the city $40 million a year.

Because they have no home, most have lost the privilege of voting. Because they have no home, most cannot simply pick up the phone to call for help when needed. As noted by Trojanowicz and Bucqueroux (1990, p. 242): "Just because the homeless have no votes, no PAC money, and no telephone should not mean they are excluded from police priorities. Their complex dilemma requires more than crisis intervention, and this is yet another niche where community policing offers unique opportunities to make a positive difference."

Possible Police Responses

Police must first see the homeless as individuals and as possible victims and then do all they can to protect them from victimization. Community policing is one means of helping to accomplish this. Police should also be aware of what kinds of assistance are available for the homeless and make this information known, including helping them to obtain services.

Understanding Self and the Image Projected

Police officers must be sensitive to individual differences among the citizens of their jurisdictions. In addition, they should also be aware of their own beliefs, possible prejudices, and insecurities in dealing with certain types of individuals, and the image they are presenting to the public.

Specific suggestions for improving one-on-one citizen contact are given by the IACP:

- Use a polite, unexcited, or calm reasoning approach whenever possible. Try to be impersonal from two points of view: (1) Remember the authority you wield is that of the people and not yours personally, and (2) try to remain detached and not take as a personal insult or affront the reaction of people to your authority.
- Be businesslike and self-assured, not showing anger, impatience, contempt, dislike, sarcasm, and similar attitudes.
- Size things up as accurately as possible before making the contact. Be open-minded in evaluating the facts.
- Once you have the straight story, make your decision based on the policies and procedures under which you work, and take decisive action.
- Offer explanations where advisable, but do not be trapped into arguing.
- Be civil and courteous.
- Show by your demeanor that you are not looking for, and you do not expect, any trouble.
- Try to avoid giving people the impression that your presence constitutes a threat—either physical or psychological.

Citizen Review Boards

Citizen review boards are perceived by many citizens and civic groups as a legitimate means of interaction and cooperation between the police and the public it is sworn to serve and protect.

The need for careful scrutiny of police conduct has been universally accepted in the United States. A U.S. Commission on Civil Rights report (1981, p. v) says that police conduct requires ''continuous, thoughtful examination'' because ''police officers possess awesome powers . . . and exercise their powers with wide discretion and under minimal supervision.''

Police departments need a complaint and disciplinary procedure to ensure that complaints against officers or staff are effectively investigated and dealt with.

Neither of the preceding suggest, however, that citizen review boards are necessarily the means to accomplish careful monitoring of police work. Several municipalities, however, do feel that citizen review boards can serve this function.

Such review boards have been tried in several jurisdictions and have met with varied success. They are generally opposed by police departments, however, according to Fyfe (1985, pp. 76–87), for the following reasons:

- They impinge on the authority of the police chief. Such review boards could erode police authority in other areas as well.
- They single out police from other municipal employees.
- They use lay people with little knowledge of police work. Is it appropriate to investigate and review professional conduct by those not a part of the profession?
- They tend to polarize the police and the rest of the city.

Fyfe notes that many communities have highly unrealistic expectations of what citizen review boards can accomplish. He suggests that the typical course of action is for a citizen to make a complaint against a police officer, the police officer to deny the charge, and the board to find no conclusive evidence either way.

Citizen review boards usually function to evaluate or judge
police performance and behavior.

Interaction with Other Agencies

Previous chapters have emphasized the need for a team approach to certain police problems, including dealing with emergencies. Ideally, *most* aspects of law enforcement would be a joint effort. Brown (1990, p. 8) notes: "Community policing also requires the involvement of agencies other than the police—social services, education, clinics, businesses, employment offices, trash collection—anyone involved in community service.

Police may work with schools, colleges and universities,
clinics, hospitals, churches, social services, victim-assistance
programs, civic groups, and various city agencies involved
with human services.

By working with various agencies in concert with residents, the police chief can take a leadership role, proactively resolving chronic community problems. Frankel (1990, p. 12A) suggests that officers involved in community policing "use their influence on the municipal bureaucracy to solve problems, such as poor lighting and boarded-up houses, that can reduce fear, if not crime."

During emergencies, such interaction and cooperation can be critical in reducing the loss of property and lives. The agencies and organizations that should be "connected" will vary from community to community.

Crime Prevention through Environmental Design (CPTED)

As noted by Horne, (1991, p. 27), CPTED "seeks to integrate natural approaches to crime prevention into building design and neighborhood planning." This proactive approach to crime prevention depends on the cooperation of security specialists, architects, the police, and builders. According to Crowe (1981, p. 9): "The proper design and effective use of the built environment can lead to a reduction in fear and the incidence of crime, and an improvement in the quality of life."

Interaction and Cooperation with Private Security

According to Mangan and Shanahan (1990, p. 18), "Private security has emerged as a major player in the safeguarding of Americans and their property." Evidence of this is presented by Trojanowicz and Bucqueroux (1990a, p. 131):

- There are now almost twice as many people employed in private security as there are public police.

- In addition to for-profit prisons that house adults, we are also seeing a tremendous surge in the number of private initiates that handle juvenile offenders.
- U.S. companies now spend an estimated $250 million each year on private undercover drug investigations of their employees.
- Litigants in civil suits can now choose to hire a private rent-a-judge-and-jury to settle claims, virtually bypassing the public courts.
- The federal Trademark and Counterfeiting Act of 1984 gave businesses expanded powers to protect their property and profits, including the right to conduct independent investigations, obtain search warrants, seize evidence, arrest suspects, and pursue private criminal justice prosecutions.

Privatization of law enforcement refers to the trend toward hiring private for-profit and nonprofit corporations to assume roles once almost exclusively the province of public law enforcement.

The Hallcrest Report, "Private Security and Police in America," released in 1985, surveyed police attitudes on transferring police responsibilities to private security companies. According to Bottom (1986, p. 13), "In general, police executives said, Yes, police will be happy to yield: burglar alarm response (57%); incident report completion for insurance purposes (68%); preliminary investigation (40%); and misdemeanor incident reports (45%)."

Bocklet (1990, p. 54) says of the same report: "The study recommended that private security resources could contribute to cooperative, community-based crime prevention and security awareness programs. . . . The study recommended police and private security share crime prevention materials, specialized security equipment, expertise, and personnel." How well public and private security agencies work together will depend in large part on how well they can communicate with each other and on how well the goals of each can be complimentary rather than competitive.

Private security is here to stay. Indeed, much overlap exists with police officers moonlighting as private security officers and private security officers using their jobs as stepping stones into the law enforcement profession. Many of the top security directors have been recruited from public law enforcement. Little is to be gained by competing; much to be gained from cooperating.

Interaction and Cooperation with the Press and Media

As noted by Kobel (1988, p. 1): "In police jurisdictions throughout the United States, police become angry, adversarial, and uncooperative with the press for a variety of reasons, including press criticism of the police agency, inaccurate reporting, publication of sensitive information, lack of press sensitivity, or the betrayal of an officer's trust."

Such need not be the case. Garner (1989, p. 34) says, "A police administrator can gain as much benefit from the media as they can from you. What they have to offer, in many instances, is publicity for your agency and to a lesser extent, yourself. With a little understanding, that publicity can be positive and make your organization look good. The secret to success is honesty and approachability.'' Other keys to success in dealing with the media include the following:

- Having a clear policy on what information is to be released to the press and what is not.
- Treating all reporters fairly.
- Being as sensitive to the need for the privacy of victims and witnesses as to the need of the public to know what is going on.

Some larger departments have a public information officer who is the only one authorized to release information to the media. Other departments allow those officers involved in specific cases to be interviewed by reporters interested in the cases. Media organizations should be told who their contacts will be.

Police departments must balance the public's ''right to know'' and reporters' First Amendment rights to publish what they know with the police's need to withhold certain information and to protect the privacy of victims and witnesses.

Referring to this balancing act, Kobel (1988, p. 13) quotes Police Chief Paul Annee of Indianapolis: ''A police chief has to know that there is a right to know on behalf of the public, and the press are the ones who carry out that right. You have

Police officer being interviewed by the local media. In some departments, every officer is considered a public information officer. Good working relationships between the police and the media can benefit both.

to have a respect for that. That doesn't mean you cave in to everything the press wants, but you have to come to a mutual respect for each other's duties and responsibilities.''

A Look Ahead

This final chapter has stressed the importance of interaction with other individuals, groups, agencies, and organizations. Such interaction is important in almost all police operations: patrol, traffic, dealing with crime and violence and domestic violence, dealing with juveniles, dealing with gang members and drug dealers, and handling emergencies. Cooperative efforts are a key to maximizing resources and accomplishing the mission of each law enforcement agency.

Summary

Working with others in a cooperative effort to improve the quality of life has involved community policing as well as civilianization. Community policing is proactive and often includes increased emphasis on foot patrol. Research indicates that foot patrol programs improve public relations between the police and the community, but they do not affect crime rates. Citizen patrol may also be involved in community policing efforts. Citizen patrols such as the Guardian Angels seek to fight crime, enhance feelings of security, and provide positive role models for young people.

Civilianization refers to the practice of hiring citizens to perform certain tasks for the police department. Citizens may also become involved in crime prevention by participating in Neighborhood Watch programs, Operation Identification programs, security checks, school programs such as DARE and sexual abuse prevention programs, as well as programs to deter vehicle theft.

Police officers must also deal with citizens one-on-one and must be aware of the great diversity existing within their jurisdictions. In addition, they must be aware of the on-going changes in our population. Our population is becoming older, minorities are increasing, we have growing numbers of illegal immigrants, thousands of mentally ill individuals have been deinstitutionalized, the homeless population is growing, and the gap between the ''haves'' and the ''have nots'' is widening.

Another way in which some citizens feel they should become involved is through the citizen review board. Citizen review boards usually function to evaluate or judge police performance and behavior.

Individual citizens are not the only ones police officers need to interact and cooperate with. Most communities have several agencies and organizations who can assist police departments in their missions. Police may work with schools, colleges and universities, clinics, hospitals, churches, social services, victim-assistance programs, civic groups, and various city agencies involved with human services.

Most communities also have private security agencies that can help make the community safer. Privatization of law enforcement refers to the trend to hire private for-profit and nonprofit corporations to assume roles once almost exclusively the province of public law enforcement.

Finally, it is important that police departments be able to balance the public's ''right to know'' and reporters' First Amendment rights to publish what they know with the police's need to withhold certain information and to protect the privacy of victims and witnesses.

447
CHAPTER 16
Working with Others:
Cooperative Efforts

Application #1

You have been elected director of the local Neighborhood Watch program and, as the police representative, are asked to develop a procedure for residents to follow should they be either a victim of, or a witness to, a crime.

Instructions.   Use the form in Appendix A to develop a plan to be used as a model for other Neighborhood Block Watch captains. This procedure should simplify reporting for a civilian living in the block and specify procedures for possible apprehension of suspects by citizens. Include what resources are available, what types of crimes are committed, how often, and evaluate the impact of crime on the neighborhood. Also formulate specific tactics to be used and provide feedback to dispel any rumors to those participating.

Application #2

As an investigator supervisor appointed to administer the internal affairs division of the police department, establish a policy and procedure to investigate complaints against police officers.

Instructions.   Use the form in Appendix A to develop the policy and procedure. Include such matters as subpoena powers of the division as well as whether the complaints against the officers occurred while they were on or off duty. Include the role of the chief of police in the procedure, if any. After its investigation, should the internal affairs division make a recommendation for guilt or innocence or for suspension or reinstatement?

An Exercise in Critical Thinking

Police interaction and cooperation with citizens and organizations may not affect crime rates, but cooperative efforts do improve public relations between police and the community. Although enforcement efforts may be well intended, they must nonetheless primarily protect the rights of all and be directed towards developing sufficient evidence to find probable cause in suspected criminal actions. Citizen assistance is often needed.

In May of 1988, Brown County Police Department received a tip from an informant that a Glen Lieder would receive controlled substances from California by UPS. Although police did not inform UPS of the suspected contents of the package, they told UPS to be on the lookout for a package addressed to Lieder coming from California.

On January 25, such a package arrived at UPS. On its face, the package did not violate any UPS policy. The UPS called the police, stating that the package would be held until the police came to the UPS facility. Upon arriving, the police asked UPS to determine who sent the package. In the process, UPS discovered that the supposed sender did not exist at the return address and that the zip code on the return address did not match the city on the return address.

The police told UPS manager Keith Jones that they believed the package contained cocaine. Jones told the police he was authorized by his superiors to open the package if it contained illegal substances because UPS has a policy against transporting contraband. Under this policy, UPS will open any package it believes to contain illegal substances.

The police then brought in a specially trained dog to see if it could detect illegal substances by sniffing the package. The dog failed to detect illegal substances. However, based on the suspicions of the police, Jones decided to open the package in the presence of the police.

A search warrant allowing the police to open the package was neither sought nor issued. The police did not specifically request that Jones open the package, nor did they assist him in the endeavor. The package did contain cocaine.

Based upon the informant's tip, the suspicious origin of the package, and the cocaine in the package, the police obtained a warrant to search Lieder's home. Both Lieder and Kimberly Tessmer were present at Lieder's home during the execution of the police warrant. Tessmer's purse was opened and searched, and the police found cocaine in it. Additional drugs were found in Lieder's home. Both Lieder and Tessmer were placed under arrest and charged with violating various state laws against the possession and sale of drugs.

1. Will the trial court find that there is sufficient evidence to find probable cause to search Lieder's home and Tessmer's purse?
   a. No, for the mere receipt of a package from California through UPS certainly has no criminal implications.
   b. Yes, for there was a tip that Lieder was going to receive a package containing cocaine from California through the mail or UPS.
   c. Yes, because the return address on the package was incorrect and nonexistent, thus arousing probable cause.
   d. Yes, simply due to the fact of the arrival of a package at a UPS station.
   e. Yes, because of the actual contents of the package.
2. Is there sufficient evidence to prosecute either Lieder or Tessmer?
   a. Yes, due to the informant's tip, the suspicious origin of the package, the cocaine in the package, and the warrant to search Lieder's home.
   b. Only Lieder can be prosecuted because he was the recipient of the package.
   c. Both Lieder and Tessmer can be prosecuted, but only on the evidence gained during the search of the home and purse.
   d. Neither will be prosecuted because the warrantless opening and search of the package addressed to Lieder was a public search in violation of Lieder's constitutional rights.
   e. Only Tessmer will be prosecuted because the purse is incontrovertibly hers.

Discussion Questions

1. What is the role of the community in developing policies and procedures?
2. How does your community view the role of police officers? How do police officers view their roles?
3. What is the value of foot patrol as opposed to vehicle patrol?

4. Is there such a thing as crime prevention, or is it a myth to give citizens a feeling of being secure and protected from harm? What are the advantages and disadvantages of crime prevention programs?

5. What is your attitude toward homeless people? Is it compassionate, or do you feel the streets should be rid of such people?

6. Community policing addresses a need to focus on solving community problems in a creative new way. Is this possible or is community policing merely a rehash of old attitudes?

7. Do you think citizens ought to get involved in formulating policy? If so, to what extent? What are the advantages and disadvantages of citizen involvement?

Definitions

Can you define the following terms?

civilianization	mental retardation
mentally disabled	privatization
mental illness	

References

Alzheimer's Disease and Related Disorders Association. "Victim, Not Criminal: The Alzheimer Sufferer." Chicago, Ill.: The Alzheimer's Disease and Related Disorders Association, 1987.

Bennett, Georgette. *Crime Warps, The Future of Crime in America.* New York: Anchor Books, 1989.

Bocklet, Richard. "Police-Private Security Cooperation." *Law and Order* (December 1990): 54–59.

Bottom, Norman R., Jr. "Privatization: Lessons of the Hallcrest Report." *Law Enforcement News* (June 23, 1986): 13, 15.

Brown, Lee P. "The Police-Community Partnership." *The Police Chief* (December 1990): 8.

Burgreen, Bob and McPherson, Nancy. "Implementing POP: The San Diego Experience." *The Police Chief* (October 1990): 51–56.

Chandler, Michele, " 'Disturbing' Plight of Homeless Elderly Studied." *Detroit Free Press* (December 22, 1988).

Clede, Bill. "Guardian Angels: Bane or Blessing?" *Law and Order* (December 1990): 37–39.

Crowe, Timothy. "An Ounce of Prevention: A New Role for Law Enforcement." *FBI Law Enforcement Bulletin* (October 1981): 19.

Cummings, D. Brian. "Problem-Oriented Policing and Crime-Specific Planning." *The Police Chief* (March 1990): 63–64.

Exter, Thomas. "Demographic Forecasts–On to Retirement." *American Demographics* (April 1989).

Frankel, Bruce. "Police in NYC Walk to New Beat." *USA Today:* (November 26, 1990): 12A.

Fyfe, James J. "Reviewing Citizens' Complaints against Police." pp. 76–87. In *Police Management Today, Issues and Case Studies,* James J. Fyfe, ed. Washington, D.C.: International City Management Association, 1985.

Garner, Gerald. "Working with the Media: Winning at the Interview Game." *Law and Order* (May 1989): 34–37.

Goldstein, Herman. *Problem-Oriented Policing.* New York: McGraw-Hill, 1990.

Grausso, Tony. "On Patrol in Suburban Chicago: The Digital Announcer & Delegate Help Evanston's Crime Watch Program Curb Neighborhood Crime." *Law and Order* (September 1989): 36–39.

Greene, Jack R. "Police and Community Relations: Where Have We Been and Where Are We Going?" pp. 349–365. In *Critical Issues in Policing: Contemporary Readings,* Roger G. Dunham and Geoffrey P. Alpert, eds. Prospect Heights, Ill.: Waveland Press, 1989.

Grossman, Amy. "Homelessness in America." *Police* (August 1987): 38–42, 58–60.

Hildreth, Reed. "The CAT Program." *Law and Order* (May 1990): 93–94.

Horne, Peter. "Not Just Old Wind in New Bottles." *The Police Chief* (May 1991): 24–29.

Insight. "The New Drift in Homeless Policy." (August 6, 1990): 22–24.

International Association of Chiefs of Police (IACP). "Improving the Officer/Citizen Contact. Training Key 94." (n.d.)

Kobel, Richard. "The Pen v. the Sword: Do Police Determine the Rules and Tone of Press Relations?" *Law Enforcement News* (July 31, 1988): 1, 6, 13.

Lamar, Jacob V. "The Homeless: Brick by Brick." *Time* (October 24, 1988): 34–38.

Mangan, Terence J. and Shanahan, Michael G. "Public Law Enforcement/Private Security: A New Partnership?" *FBI Law Enforcement Bulletin* (January 1990): 18–22.

Manning, Anita and Proctor, David. "Senior Boom: The Future's New Wrinkle." *USA Today* (January 31, 1989): 1D.

McCord, Rob and Wicker, Elaine. "Tomorrow's America: Law Enforcement's Coming Challenge." *FBI Law Enforcement Bulletin* (January 1990): 28–32.

McPherson, Marlys and Silloway, Glenn. "Planning to Prevent Crime." In *Reactions to Crime,* Dan Lewis, ed. Beverly Hills, Calif.: Sage Publications, 1985.

Murphy, Gerard R. *Managing Persons with Mental Disabilities: A Curriculum Guide for Police Trainers.* Washington, D.C.: Police Executive Research Forum, 1989.

Murphy, Gerard R. *Special Care: Improving the Police Response to the Mentally Disabled.* Washington, D.C.: Police Executive Research Forum, 1986.

National Council on Crime and Delinquency. *Crime and Delinquency.* Beverly Hills, Calif.: Sage Publications, 1989.

National Crime Prevention Institute (NCPI). *Understanding Crime Prevention.* Stoneham, Mass.: Butterworth Publishers, 1986.

Raymondo, James C. "How to Count Illegals, State by State." *American Demographics* (September 1988): pp. 42–43.

Schwartz, Joe and Exter, Thomas. "All Our Children." *American Demographics* (May, 1988): pp. 42–43.

Skogan, W. and Pate, A. "Reducing the Signs of Crime: Two Experiments in Controlling Public Disorder." Paper presented at the annual meeting of the American Political Science Association, Chicago, Ill., August, 1987.

Toffler, Alvin and Toffler, Heidi. "The Future of Law Enforcement: Dangerous and Different." *FBI Law Enforcement Bulletin* (January 1990): 2–5.

Trojanowicz, Robert and Bucqueroux, Bonnie.
a. *Community Policing, A Contemporary Perspective.* Cincinnati, Ohio: Anderson Publishing Company, 1990.
b. "The Privatization of Public Justice: What Will It Mean to Police?" *The Police Chief* (October 1990): 131–135.

Trojanowicz, Robert and Carter, David L. "The Changing Face of America." *FBI Law Enforcement Bulletin* (January 1990): 6–12.

Policies and Procedures Sample Form

Name of Agency:	Date Issued:
Procedure Directive No.:	Page ___ of ___
Effective Date:	
Subject:	
Goal:	
Policy:	

Policies and Procedures Form continued on the next page.

Policies and Procedures Sample Form continued

Policy No.: _____   Page ___ of ___ _____

Procedures: _____

_____

_____

_____

_____

_____

_____

_____

_____

_____

_____

_____

_____
Chief of Police

Sample Forms

FORM B-1   Edina Police Department Offense Report

Race Code:
B - BLACK
W - WHITE
I - INDIAN
A - ASIAN
U - UNKNOWN

EDINA POLICE DEPARTMENT
OFFENSE/REPORT
MN0270600

COMPLAINT NUMBER

OFFENSE, INCIDENT

SUPP

DATE OCCURRED | TIME OCCURRED | LOCATION OF OCCURRENCE

DATE RECEIVED | TIME RECEIVED | OFFICER(S) | APPROVED BY

VICTIM | AGE | ADDRESS | BUSINESS PHONE | HOME PHONE

COMPLAINANT | (F) | (M) | HOME ADDRESS | BUSINESS PHONE | HOME PHONE

SUSPECT | (F) | (M) | HOME ADDRESS | BUSINESS PHONE | HOME PHONE

SUSPECT DESCRIPTION | SEX | RACE | DOB | HEIGHT | WEIGHT | BUILD | HAIR | EYES

ISN | MOC | COMPLEXION | BEARD | MUSTACHE | DRIVERS LICENSE #

ISN | MOC | CLOTHING DESCRIPTION

ISN | MOC

VICTIMS/SUSPECT'S AUTO — MAKE AND DESCRIPTION

LICENSE NUMBER | STATE OF ISSUE | SERIAL NUMBER | COLOR

LOSS DESCRIPTION | (INCLUDE SERIAL #S) | RECOVERED $ | STOLEN $

DATA ENTRY: CJRS _____ POSSE _____

Data Privacy Requested: ☐ Yes ☐ No

HC 6282 (3/88)
Hennepin County   **LAW ENFORCEMENT INITIAL COMPLAINT REPORT**

REC'D BY:

DAY:	S	M	T	W	T	F	S

"ECE" - Use only when optional line is omitted.   "ECI" - Use only when optional line is included.

MESS. KEY   CONTROL NUMBER (OCA)   CONT. AGENCY NCIC IDENT. (CAG)

E C /

M N 0 2 7 0 0 0 0 /

L NBR   DATE REPORTED (RPD)   TIME RPD (TRP)   LOCATION GRID NBR (LGN)   PLACE COMMITTED (PLC)

2 / / /

Reported By: _____   Phone Nbr: _____

Address: _____

Complainant: _____   Phone Nbr: _____

Address: _____

L NBR	HRD	SQUAD OR BADGE # (SBN)	TIME ASIG. (TAS)	TIME ARR. (TAR)	TIME CLR. (TCL)
O P T	3 /		/	/	/

L NBR	ISN	MOC	MCS	ISN	MOC	MCS
4	01 /	/	* /	6	03 /	/
5	02 /	/	/	7	04 /	/

HRD Codes
P - Phone
R - Radio
A - Alarm
I - In Person
V - Visual
M - Mail
T - Other

* If multiple lines are to be entered, a slash (/) must follow each line except the last.

Incident Description: _____
_____
_____

OFFICER/SQUAD ASSIGNED: _____   SUPERVISOR APPROVED: _____

ADDT'L. REPORTS: ☐
ENTERED C.J.R.S. ☐

455

MINNEAPOLIS POLICE DEPARTMENT
ARREST/CITATION REPORT

NUMBER: ARREST _____ OF _____	REPORT TYPE: □ ORIGINAL □ SUPPLEMENT	CASE CONTROL NUMBER:	PRECINCT:	DATE AND TIME OF ARREST:

ADDRESS OF ARREST:

NAME OF BUSINESS OR LOCATION:

PRISONER'S NAME (LAST, FIRST, MIDDLE):

DATE OF BIRTH:

HOME PHONE NUMBER: ( )

HOME ADDRESS (CITY, STATE AND ZIP CODE):

EMPLOYER/SCHOOL NAME AND ADDRESS:

OCCUPATION/TITLE:

CITY/STATE OF ORGIN:

NICKNAME/ALSO KNOWN AS:

EMPLOYER/SCHOOL PHONE: ( )

RACE: □ WHITE □ BLACK □ NATIVE AMERICAN □ ASIAN □ PACIFIC ISLANDER □ HISPANIC

SEX:

HEIGHT:

OFFICER(S) USED FORCE: □ YES □ NO

MEDICAL TREATMENT: □ YES □ NO

BUILD: 01 = □ LIGHT   02 = □ MEDIUM   03 = □ HEAVY   04 = □ OBESE

NATIONALITY:

DRIVER LICENSE STATE AND NUMBER:

IF JUVENILE - PARENT/GUARDIAN NAME:

PARENT/GUARDIAN ADDRESS:

PARENT/GUARDIAN PHONE: ( )

ARREST TYPE

ARREST CODE	CODE	ARREST CHARGES (MPLS P.U. & WT REQUIRE ORIGINAL CCN #)	STATUTE/ORDINANCE NO.	CITATION/ORIGINAL CCN #
00 = STATUS OFFENSE				
10 = PC				
20 = PC PICK UP				
30 = WARRANT				
40 = OTHER				
01 = PETTY MISD				
02 = MISDEMEANOR				
03 = GROSS MISD				
04 = FELONY				

ARREST DISPOSITION:
B □ BOOKED (COUNTY)   M □ BOOKED (MPD)   C □ CITED/RELEASED   D □ DETOX (ADULT/JUV)   H □ HOSPITALIZED   J □ BOOKED (JUV DET)   W □ HEALTH/WELFARE

REPORTED BY (OFFICER/CITIZEN):

DATE/TIME OF REPORT:

□ CITIZEN'S ARREST □ C/A FORM ATTACHED □ SUPPL/STATEMENT

ACTUAL ARRESTING OFFICERS:

EMPLOYEE NUMBER(S):

SQUAD NUMBER:

NPI: □

DESCRIPTION TABLES (USE AS MANY AS APPLY)

EYE COLOR	R/L HANDED	HAIR STYLE	HAIR LENGTH	FACIAL HAIR	COMPLEXION	TEETH	APPEARANCE	SPEECH	PERSON WORE
1 = □ BROWN	1 = □ RIGHT	1 = □ STRAIGHT	1 = □ SHORT	1 = □ NONE	1 = □ LIGHT	1 = □ NORMAL	1 = □ DIRTY	1 = □ REGIONAL	1 = □ GLASSES
2 = □ BLUE	2 = □ LEFT	2 = □ CURLY/WAVY	2 = □ MEDIUM	2 = □ UNSHAVEN	2 = □ MEDIUM	2 = □ BROKE/MISSING	2 = □ NEAT	2 = □ FAST	3 = □ MASK
3 = □ HAZEL	3 = □ BOTH	3 = □ AFRO/NATURAL	3 = □ LONG	3 = □ FUZZ/WHISKER	3 = □ DARK	3 = □ CROOKED	3 = □ DRUNK/DRUGGED	3 = □ SLOW	4 = □ GLOVES
4 = □ GREEN	4 = □ UNKNOWN	4 = □ JERI CURL	4 = □ RECEDING	4 = □ MOUSTACHE	4 = □ ACNED/ POCKMARKD	4 = □ DECAYED	4 = □ VIOLENT	4 = □ FOUL	5 = □ EARRINGS
5 = □ BLACK		5 = □ UNKEMPT	5 = □ BALD/ BALDING	5 = □ SIDEBURNS	5 = □ RUDDY	5 = □ BUCK TEETH	5 = □ NERVOUS	5 = □ SLURRED	6 = □ NOSE RING
6 = □ AQUA	INJURY TYPE	6 = □ BRAIDED		6 = □ BEARD	6 = □ TANNED	6 = □ SILVER TOOTH	6 = □ APOLOGETIC	6 = □ EASTERN	99 = □ OTHER
7 = □ VIOLET	1 = □ APPARENT BROKEN BONES	7 = □ PONY TAIL	HAIR COLOR	7 = □ FU MANCHU	7 = □ FRECKLED	7 = □ GOLD TOOTH	7 = □ FRIENDLY/GENTLE	7 = □ SOUTHERN	
99 = □ OTHER	2 = □ POSSIBLE INTERNAL	8 = □ PUNK/MOHAWK	1 = □ BROWN	8 = □ GOATEE	8 = □ MULATTO	8 = □ DIAMOND TOOTH	8 = □ VULNERABLE ADULT	8 = □ FOREIGN	
	3 = □ SEVERE LACERATION	9 = □ DIRTY/GREASY	2 = □ BLOND	99 = □ OTHER	99 = □ OTHER	9 = □ INLAID DESIGN	9 = □ DISTURBED	9 = □ LISP/STUTTER	
	4 = □ APPARENT MINOR INJ.	10 = □ DYED/PAINTED	3 = □ BLACK			10 = □ BRACES	10 = □ GAY/TRANSVESTITE	10 = □ NASAL	
	5 = □ OTHER MAJOR	99 = □ OTHER	4 = □ RED			99 = □ OTHER	11 = □ SUSP GANG MEMBER	11 = □ GRUFF/RASPY	
	6 = □ LOSS OF TEETH		5 = □ GREY				12 = □ SUSP BIKER	99 = □ OTHER	
	7 = □ UNCONSCIOUSNESS		6 = □ WHITE				13 = □ FRIGHTND/SHOCKED		
			99 = □ OTHER				99 = □ OTHER		

FEATURE(S)	1. HEAD/ NECK	2. ARMS/ HANDS	3. LEGS/ FEET	4. TORSO	DESCRIPTION OF FEATURE:
INJ LOC					
SCARS					
MARKS					
TATTOO					
DFRMTY					

NARRATIVE (NOTE: ARREST REPORT IS PUBLIC INFORMATION - SUPPLEMENT Ø):

CONTINUED ON REVERSE SIDE

MP-5829 Rev. 4/90

457

ARREST TYPE (CONTINUATION)

ARREST CODE	CODE	ARREST CHARGES (MPLS P.U. & WT REQUIRE ORIGINAL CCN #)	STATUTE/ORDINANCE NO.	CITATION/ORIGINAL CCN #
00 = STATUS OFFENSE 10 = PC 20 = PC PICK UP 30 = WARRANT 40 = OTHER				
01 = PETTY MISD 02 = MISDEMEANOR 03 = GROSS MISD 04 = FELONY				

NARRATIVE (CONTINUATION):

ADDITIONAL ARRESTING OFFICERS:	EMPL #(S):	SQUAD #:
ADDITIONAL ARRESTING OFFICERS:	EMPL #(S):	SQUAD #:
ADDITIONAL ARRESTING OFFICERS:	EMPL #(S):	SQUAD #:

458

STATE OF MINNESOTA
COUNTY OF _____

STATE OF MINNESOTA _____) SS.
COUNTY OF _____)

_____ COURT

_____ OF _____

**APPLICATION FOR SEARCH WARRANT AND
SUPPORTING AFFIDAVIT**

_____ being first duly sworn upon oath, hereby makes application to this Court for a warrant to search the (premises) (motor vehicles) (person) hereinafter described, for the property and things hereinafter described.

Affiant knows the contents of this application and supporting affidavit, and the statements herein are true of his own knowledge, save as to such as are herein stated on information and belief, and as to those, he believes them to be true.

Affiant has good reason to believe, and does believe, that the following described property and things, to wit:

459

(are) (will be)
(at the premises) (in the motor vehicle) (on the person) described as :

situated in the ——————— of ——————— ,County of ——————— ,and State
of Minnesota.

This affiant applies for issuance of a search warrant upon the following grounds:
(Strike inapplicable paragraph)
1. The property above-described was stolen or embezzled.
2. The property above-described was used as means of committing a crime.
3. The possession of the property above-described constitutes a crime.
4. The property above-described is in the possession of a person with intent to
   use such property as a means of committing a crime.
5. The property above-described constitutes evidence which tends to show a crime has
   been committed, or tends to show that a particular person has committed a crime.

The facts tending to establish the foregoing grounds for issuance of a search warrant are as follows:

A nighttime search is necessary to prevent the loss, destruction or removal of the objects of the search because:

An unannounced entry is necessary (to prevent the loss, destruction or removal of the objects of the search (and) to protect the safety of the peace officers) because:

WHEREFORE, Affiant request a search warrant be issued, commanding _____ (a) peace officer(s), of the State of Minnesota, (to enter without announcement of authority and purpose) (in the daytime only) (in the daytime or nighttime) to search the hereinbefore described (premises) (motor vehicle) (person) for the described property and things and to seize said property and things and keep said property and things in custody until the same be dealt with according to the law.

_____
Affiant

Subscribed and sworn to before me this
_____ day of _____ , 19 _____

_____
Judge of _____ Court

461

STATE OF MINNESOTA
COUNTY OF _____

_____ COURT

OF _____

SEARCH WARRANT

TO:
(A) PEACE OFFICER(S) OF THE STATE OF MINNESOTA.

WHEREAS, _____ has this day on oath, made application to the said Court applying for issuance of a search warrant to search the following described (premises) (motor vehicle) (person):

for the following described property and things:

WHEREAS, the application and supporting affidavit of _____ (was) (were) duly presented and read by the Court, and being fully advised in the premises.

462

NOW, THEREFORE, the Court finds that probable cause exists for the issuance of a search warrant upon the following grounds: (Strike inapplicable paragraphs)

1. The property above-described was stolen or embezzled.
2. The property above-described was used as a means of committing a crime.
3. The possession of the property above-described constitutes a crime.
4. The property above-described is in the possession of a person with intent to use such property as a means of committing a crime.
5. The property above-described constitutes evidence which tends to show a crime has been committed, or tends to show that a particular person has committed a crime.

The Court further finds that probable cause exists to believe that the above-described property and things (are) (will be) (at the above-described premises) (in the above-described motor vehicle) (on the person of _____).

(The Court further finds that a nighttime search warrant is necessary to prevent the loss, destruction, or removal of the objects of said search)

(The Court further finds that entry without announcement of authority or purpose is necessary (to prevent the loss, destruction or removal of the objects of said search) (and) (to protect the safety of the peace officers).

NOW THEREFORE, YOU

THE PEACE OFFICER(S) AFORESAID, ARE HEREBY COMMANDED (TO ENTER WITHOUT ANNOUNCEMENT OF AUTHORITY AND PURPOSE) (IN THE DAYTIME ONLY) (IN THE DAYTIME OR NIGHTTIME) TO SEARCH (THE DESCRIBED PREMISES) (THE DESCRIBED MOTOR VEHICLE) (THE PERSON OF _____) FOR THE ABOVE-DESCRIBED PROPERTY AND THINGS, AND TO SEIZE SAID PROPERTY AND THINGS AND (TO RETAIN THEM IN CUSTODY SUBJECT TO COURT ORDER AND ACCORDING TO LAW) (DELIVER CUSTODY OF SAID PROPERTY AND THINGS TO _____ .

BY THE COURT:

Dated _____ 19 _____ .

_____
JUDGE OF _____ COURT

STATE OF MINNESOTA
COUNTY OF _____

_____ COURT

OF _____

RECEIPT, INVENTORY AND RETURN

I, _____ ,received the attached search warrant

issued by the Honorable _____ , on _____ ,19___ , and have

executed it as follows:

Pursuant to said warrant, on _____ ,19___ , at _____ o'clock ___ m., I

searched the (premises) (motor vehicle) (person) described in said warrant, and left a true and correct copy of

said warrant

(with) (in) (at) _____

I took into custody property named in said warrant and listed below:

_____

_____

_____

_____

_____

_____

_____

_____

(I left a receipt for the property and things listed with the warrant as set forth above.)

(None of the items set forth in the search warrant were found.)

I shall (retain) or (deliver) custody of said property as directed by Court order.

_____, being first duly sworn, upon oath, deposes and says that he has read the foregoing receipt, inventory and return and the matters stated are true and correct, except as to such matters stated therein on information and belief, and as to those, he believes them to be true.

_____
Signature

Subscribed and sworn to before me this
_____ day of _____ ,19 _____

_____
Notary Public, _____ County, Minn

My commission expires _____

465

FORM B-5 Juvenile Report Form

W – WHITE B – BLACK I – NATIVE AMERICAN	J – JAPANESE C – CHINESE O – OTHER	PERSON CHARGED 1. ARRESTED, HELD FOR PROSECUTION 2. SUMMONED/NOTIFIED OR CITED	SS-STATE STATUTE OR-ORDINANCE TT-FEDERAL TITLE OT-OTHER	SUPP

COMPLAINT NUMBER	POLICE DEPARTMENT JUVENILE REPORT	OFFENSE, INCIDENT, CHARGE

DATE OCCURRED	TIME OCCURRED	LOCATION OF OCCURRENCE

DATE RECEIVED	TIME RECEIVED	OFFICER(S)	APPROVED BY

NAME OF BUSINESS	ADDRESS	PHONE

VICTIM/COMPLAINANT (LAST) (FIRST) (MIDDLE)	HOME ADDRESS	PHONE

DEFENDANT (LAST, FIRST, MIDDLE)	STREET ADDRESS, CITY, STATE, ZIP	CTY.	PHONE

PSN	D.O.B.	AGE	HEIGHT	WEIGHT	EYES	HAIR	COMPLEXION	SEX	RACE	D.L. NO.

MOTHER'S NAME (LAST, FIRST, MIDDLE)	STREET ADDRESS, CITY, STATE, ZIP	BUSINESS PHONE	HOME PHONE

FATHER'S NAME (LAST, FIRST, MIDDLE)	STREET ADDRESS, CITY, STATE, ZIP	BUSINESS PHONE	HOME PHONE

CHILD LIVES WITH: ☐ Parents ☐ Mother ☐ Father ☐ Other, who?	SCHOOL NAME	GRADE

DISPOSITION OF PROPERTY	DATE/TIME PARENTS NOTIFIED	NO. OF PRIOR CONTACTS	LIQUOR INVOLVED ☐ Yes ☐ No

MIRANDA GIVEN ☐ Yes ☐ No	DOES JUV. ADMIT OFFENSE ☐ Yes ☐ No	ATTITUDE:	RELEASE INFO, DATE: TIME:	BY WHOM: TO WHOM:

IF VEHICLES INVOLVED, MAKE, YEAR, MODEL	COLOR	LICENSE	STATE

REGISTERED OWNER, OR DRIVER, IF SAME AS DEF: LEAVE EMPTY	ADDRESS	CITY	STATE

ACCOMPLICES: (LAST) (FIRST) (MIDDLE)	2. (LAST) (FIRST) (MIDDLE)	3. (LAST) (FIRST) (MIDDLE)

ASSOCIATES: (LAST) (FIRST) (MIDDLE)	2. (LAST) (FIRST) (MIDDLE)	3. (LAST) (FIRST) (MIDDLE)

ISN	UOC	STATUTE CHARGED	ARREST DISPOSTION	CODE
ISN	UOC	STATUTE CHARGED	ARREST DISPOSTION	CODE
ISN	UOC	STATUTE CHARGED	ARREST DISPOSTION	CODE

STATEMENTS: _____

_____

_____

_____

OTHER SELF-REPORTED DELINQUENT ACTS: _____

_____

_____

_____

COMMENTS: _____

_____

_____

TO: JUVENILE COURT JUDGE - _____ COUNTY

FROM: _____ RE: _____
                Police Department   Juvenile   D.O.B.

THE ABOVE NAMED JUVENILE IS CURRENTLY IN CUSTODY AND UNDER
INVESTIGATION   IT IS REQUESTED THAT WE BE ALLOWED TO TAKE A PICTURE
OF SAID JUVENILE FOR THE FOLLOWING REASONS:

THE NEGATIVE, IF ANY, AND ALL PRINTS WILL BE RETAINED BY OUR JUVENILE
DIVISION IN ITS SEPARATE RECORDS UNTIL SUBJECT IS EIGHTEEN YEARS OF
AGE AND AT THAT TIME ALL NEGATIVES AND PRINTS WILL BE DESTROYED.
NO ONE WILL BE PERMITTED TO RECEIVE OR TO MAKE COPIES OF THE
NEGATIVE OR PRINTS EXCEPT OUR POLICE DEPARTMENT. VIOLATIONS OF THE
FOREGOING ARE A MISDEMEANOR, OR CONTEMPT OF COURT, OR BOTH.

_____
                                                                Chief of Police

_____
By: Date

For the court

_____
                                        Judge/Referee   Date

Original: Police Department
Copy: Clerk of Juvenile Court

absolute issue an issue with only two sides, viewed as either/or, black or white. (7)

absolute privilege no exceptions; the information or testimony cannot be received (see *privileged information*). (3)

active listening is concentrating on the message as well as the intent and feelings of the message. It involves attending skills, encouraging or motivational skills, and reflecting skills. (2)

active voice the subject of the sentence names who performed the action, for example, "I fired a shot." This is in contrast to the passive voice, "A shot was fired." (4)

aerobic training physical training aimed at strengthening the cardiovascular system. (8)

agility the ability to react quickly and easily. (8)

anaerobic training physical training aimed at strengthening the muscles of the body. (8)

arrest officially taking a person into custody to answer criminal charges. Arrest involves at least temporarily depriving the person of liberty and may involve the use of force.

Automated Fingerprint Identification System (AFIS) uses a computer to identify a limited number of likely matches for a latent fingerprint. (11)

awareness spectrum describes an officer's level of awareness, ranging from condition white, environmental unawareness, to condition black, panicked/blacked out/perhaps dead. Ideally, officers will be at condition yellow: alert but relaxed. (8)

balance neuromuscular control, the muscles and nerves working together to perform various movements. (8)

battering use of physical, emotional, economic, or sexual force to control another person. (12)

Blood Alcohol Concentration (BAC) represents the weight of alcohol in grams per milliliters of blood. (10)

body composition ratio of fat to lean tissue in the body. (8)

broken windows metaphor broken windows that go unrepaired in a neighborhood make a statement that no one cares enough about the quality of life in the neighborhood to bother fixing little things that need repair. (1)

burnout refers to a person who is "used up or consumed by a job," made listless through overwork and stress. The person lacks energy or has little interest in work. (8)

case tie one criminal case is linked to another case through fingerprints. (11)

chain of possession documents who has had control of evidence from the time it is discovered until it is presented in court. (11)

child welfare model society's attempt to help youths who come in conflict with the law. (13)

chronological order starts at the beginning and goes straight through in time to the end. (4)

civil actions lawsuits for a perceived wrong against an individual for which restitution is sought in civil court. (6)

civil disobedience intentional breaking of a law to prove a point or to protest something. (11)

Civil Rights Act states that anyone acting under the authority of the law who violates another person's constitutional rights can be sued. See also *Section 1983*. (6)

civilianization the practice of hiring citizens to perform certain tasks for the police department. (16)

*Note: The number in parentheses indicates the chapter in which the term is discussed.

469

code of ethics a statement setting forth accepted standards of behavior for a profession. (7)

cognitive interview technique puts witnesses mentally back at the scene of an incident and encourages them to tell the whole story without interruption. (3)

collective deep pocket suing every possible individual and agency involved in an incident thereby creating a pool of defendants from which astronomical financial judgments can be collected. (6)

common promise refers to the promises made by all officers when they take their oath of office. (7)

communications process consists of sending a message from one source to be received by another. (2)

community policing involves empowering citizens to help local law enforcement provide safer neighborhoods. It usually includes an emphasis on foot patrol. (1)

concise brief, not wordy. (4)

conclusionary language nonfactual language that contains assumptions, for example, ''The man was nervous.'' (4)

concrete language is specific rather than abstract, for example, ''180 pounds'' compared to ''heavy.'' (4)

conditional privilege the official information privilege, that is, the information can be received but the source of the information can be protected. (3)

conscience the ability to recognize right from wrong and to follow one's own sense of what is right conduct. (7)

crimes against persons offenses in which physical contact with the victim occurs, including assault, murder, rape, and robbery. (11)

crimes against property offenses in which no physical contact with the victim occurs, including arson, auto theft, burglary, and larceny/theft. (11)

criticality index measures the frequency and importance of physical activities performed by police officers. (8)

cross-training alternating between different forms of exercise. (8)

cruising driving around and around a predetermined, popular route, usually through the heart of a town or city; a social activity of teenagers. (10)

cultural gang neighborhood-centered groups of youths that exist independently of criminal activity. (14)

curtilage a house and the area immediately surrounding it. (5)

D.A.R.E. Drug Abuse Resistance Education Program, a school program aimed at teaching fourth and fifth grade students to say no to peer pressure to use drugs. (13)

decriminalization making status offenses noncriminal matters. (13)

differential police response strategies vary the rapidity of response as well as the responder, based on the type of incident and the time of occurrence. (9)

directed patrol uses officers' discretionary patrol time to focus on specific department goals. (9)

discovery crime the criminal act is completed and the suspect has left the scene before the crime is noticed, in contrast to *involvement crime*. (9)

discretion the freedom to act or decide a matter on one's own. (1)

discretionary acts those actions officers perform using their own judgment. Policies and procedures for the acts leave decisions up to the officers. (6)

diversion referring a juvenile out of the justice system and to some other agency or program. (13)

DNA fingerprinting uses the unique genetic structure of an individual for identification. Blood, hair, and other body tissues and fluids may be used in this process. (11)

drug recognition expert (DRE) specially trained individual who can determine if someone is under the influence of drugs. Also called *drug recognition technician*. (10)

drug recognition technician (DRT) see *drug recognition expert*. (10)

due process (of law) the fundamental idea of American justice. It requires notice of a hearing or trial that is timely and that adequately informs the accused persons of the charges, gives the defendant an opportunity to present evidence in self-defense before an impartial judge or jury and to be presumed innocent until proven guilty by legally obtained evidence. (5)

elder abuse includes physical and emotional trauma, financial exploitation, and general neglect of individuals over the age of 65. (12)

emergency operations center (EOC) the location from which personnel operate during a natural disaster or other type of emergency. (15)

encephaloendorphins relaxants released by the brain during exercise that help to reduce stress. (8)

endurance the capacity for continued exertion over prolonged periods as well as the ability to withstand pain, distress, and fatigue for extended periods. Also called *stamina*. (8)

enforcement index suggests that for each fatal and personal injury accident, between twenty to twenty-five convictions for hazardous moving violations is effective traffic enforcement. (10)

entrapment an action by the police (or a government agent) persuading a person to commit a crime that the person would not otherwise have committed. (5) (14)

epilepsy disorder of the central nervous system in which a person can have recurrent seizures. (2)

ethics the study of human conduct in the light of moral principles. It deals with standards of honesty, fairness, and integrity in behavior. (7)

exclusionary rule established that the courts cannot accept evidence obtained in illegal searches and seizures, regardless of how relevant the evidence is to the case (*Weeks v. United States*, 1914) (5)

exigent circumstances circumstances surrounding an emergency situation in which no time is available to secure an arrest or search warrant. (5)

external audience readers outside the agency, including news media, insurance company agencies, service agencies, judges, juries, lawyers, and the interested public. (4)

eye-hand coordination neuromuscular control of the eye and hand, with both working together to perform various functions, for example, shooting. (8)

feedback some indication that a message is or is not understood; how an individual or group responds to a message. (2)

felony syndrome obtaining complete information on only felony cases, deeming them to be "real" police work. (4)

field inquiry the unplanned questioning of a person who has aroused a police officer's suspicions. (3)

first person uses the pronoun *I* rather than the third person, *this officer*. (4)

flashbang a device that explodes with a loud bang and emits a brilliant light, used by police as a diversion. (11)

flashroll buy money in a drug deal. (14)

flexibility mobility of the joints, the ability to "bend without breaking." (8)

forensic hypnosis seeks to establish facts for judicial purposes (as opposed to therapeutic or clinical purposes). (3)

frisk a brief patdown following a stop to determine if a person is armed. (5)

general order used to announce changes in policies, procedures, or regulations. (1)

goal a broad, general intention. (1)

good faith believing one's actions are just and legal. (5)

graffiti symbols and slogans written on walls and sides of buildings, often by gang members to mark their turf. (14)

gratuities material favors or gifts in return for a service, such as a tip for service in a restaurant. (7)

HAZMAT incident an incident involving hazardous materials. (15)

horizontal audience fellow officers on the same level in the organization and holding similar positions. (4)

hydroplaning when the tires of a moving vehicle actually ride upon the surface of water in the roadway as a skier would behind a boat. (10)

illusionary correlation effect faulty thinking in which it is believed that, because one event followed another, the first event caused the second. Also called the fallacy of *post hoc, ergo propter hoc*. (2)

implied consent a law stating that those who request and receive driver's licenses agree to take tests to determine their ability to drive. Refusal will result in revocation of the license. (10)

informant a human source of information in a criminal action whose identity must be protected. (3)

informational probable cause communications from official sources, statements from victims, and information from informants that lead an officer to suspect that a crime has been, or is about to be, committed. (5)

instrumental gang groups formed for the express purpose of criminal activity, primarily drug trafficking. (14)

interrogation the questioning of suspects from whom officers try to obtain facts related to a crime as well as admissions or confessions related to the crime. (3)

interview the planned questioning of a witness, victim, informant, or other person with information related to an incident or a case. (3)

in the presence refers to what an officer perceives through the senses, not to proximity. (5)

involvement crime the victim and suspect confront each other, in contrast to *discovery crime*. (9)

justice model see *juvenile justice model*. (13)

juvenile a person not yet of legal age, usually under the age of eighteen. (13)

juvenile delinquent a young person whose actions violate laws that apply to young people's behavior. (13)

juvenile justice model a judicial process in which young people who come in conflict with the law are held responsible and accountable for their behavior. (13)

libel defamation of another's character; false statements that tend to humiliate a person and degrade that person in the esteem of others. (6)

litigious highly likely to sue. (6)

malfeasance acts of misconduct; also called *misfeasance*. (6)

malicious prosecution a proceeding instituted in bad faith without any probable cause in the belief that the charges against the defendant can be sustained. (6)

mental fitness a person's emotional well-being, the ability to feel fear, anger, compassion, and other emotions and to express them appropriately. This also refers to a person's alertness and ability to make decisions quickly. (8)

mentally disabled one who is mentally ill or mentally retarded. (16)

mentally ill a person who is unable to function in society, to cope with life's stresses and problems. Although usually a temporary disorder, it can be more serious and require hospitalization. (16)

mentally retarded a person with significant, subaverage general intellectual functioning resulting in, or associated with, deficits or impairments in adaptive behavior, with onset before the age of eighteen. (16)

mere handcuff rule a policy stating that, in the interest of officer safety, all persons arrested and transported shall be handcuffed. It disregards the fact that handcuffing *is* a form of force and should be used only if the situation warrants. (5)

ministerial acts duties prescribed by law as part of the tasks of an administrative office. (6)

Miranda warning a statement of a suspect's rights when that suspect is being questioned: the right to remain silent, to talk to an attorney, and to have an attorney present during questioning, the attorney to be provided free if a suspect cannot afford one. (3)

misfeasance acts of misconduct; also called *malfeasance*. (6)

mission an organization's reason for existence, its purpose. (1)

mission statement written statement of an organization's reasons for existence or purpose. (1)

moniker a gang member's street name. (14)

moral principles set ideas of right and wrong that form the basis for ethical behavior. (7)

narcoterrorism drug cartel's use of terrorists to attack those who attempt to disrupt drug-related activities and to involve terrorist organizations in the sale and distribution of drugs. (11)

nonfeasance failure to take action with the result being injury or damage to another person. (6)

non sequitur something that does not follow or make sense. (2)

nonverbal communication includes the eyes, facial expressions, posture, gestures, clothing, tone of voice, proximity, and touch. (2)

objectives specific activities to accomplish a goal. (1)

observational probable cause what an officer sees or hears that makes him reasonably believe that a crime has been or is about to be committed. It includes suspicious conduct, being high on drugs, associating with known criminals, a criminal record, running away, presence in an unusual place or at an unusual time, presence in a high-crime area, presence at a crime scene, failure to answer questions, failure to provide identification, providing false information, and physical evidence. (5)

"one-pot" jurisdictional approach using the same system to deal with youths who are neglected or abused, are status offenders, or who commit serious crimes. (13)

parens patrie a doctrine allowing the state to assume guardianship of abandoned, neglected, and "wayward" children. (13)

participatory leadership allows officers to influence decisions affecting them and seeks to form a cohesive team. (1)

Part I Index Offense FBI's classification for serious crimes, which includes arson, assault, auto theft, burglary, larceny/theft, murder, rape, and robbery. (11)

Part II Index Offense FBI's classification for less serious crimes. (11)

past tense written as though everything has already happened, for example, uses *was* rather than *is*. (4)

patdown a brief feeling of a person's outer clothing to determine if a weapon is present. Also called a *frisk*. (5)

physical fitness the general capacity to adapt and respond favorably to physical effort. (8)

plain view evidence that is not concealed, that is, easily seen by officers while performing their legal duties. (5)

police operations those activities conducted in the field by law enforcement officers as they "serve and protect." They usually include patrol, traffic, investigation, and general calls for service. (1)

policy a guiding principle or course of action. (1)

post hoc, ergo propter hoc faulty thinking in which it is believed that because one event followed another, the first event caused the second. Also called *illusionary correlation effect*. (2)

posttraumatic stress disorder (PTSD) a reaction to a violent event that evokes intense fear, terror, and helplessness; a debilitating stressful reaction to a trauma that may last for months or years. It can be experienced by not only victims, but also by those who help the victims. (3) (15)

power toughness, durability, and vigor; the explosive force which moves the body suddenly or which propels some object independent of the body. (8)

predisaster plan preparing for anticipated and unanticipated emergencies *before* they occur. (15)

preliminary investigation the on-the-scene interviews of victims and witnesses, interrogations of suspects, and search of the crime scene itself. (11)

primary victim one who actually is harmed. (3)

privileged information information that does not need to be divulged to the police or the courts because of the existence of a special relationship such as that between spouses or between lawyers and their clients. (3)

privitization the trend toward hiring private for-profit and nonprofit corporations to assume roles once almost exclusively the province of public law enforcement. (16)

probable cause the fact that it is more likely than not that a crime has been committed by the person whom a law enforcement officer seeks to arrest. An officer's probable cause to conduct an arrest depends on what the officer knew *before* taking action. (5)

problem-oriented policing (POP) a proactive approach to patrol and policing that focuses on problems to be solved rather than incidents to be responded to. (9)

procedural law deals with process or *how* the law is applied. (5)

procedure step-by-step instructions for carrying out department policies. (1)

proportionate assignment area assignments are determined by requests for service based on available data. No area is larger than the time it takes a car to respond in three minutes or less. (9)

punitive damages money awarded by a court to a person who has been harmed in a particularly malicious or willful way with the person who has done the harm paying the damages. (6)

readability results from two factors: short sentences and short, familiar words. (4)

reader-friendly writing avoids police jargon and communicates in plain, simple language. It is written as it would be spoken, and it considers who the audience is. (4)

regulation a rule governing the actions of employees of the city, including police department personnel. (1)

relative issue an issue with a range of options, neither black nor white but several shades of gray. (7)

response time the time elapsed from when the need for police arises and when they arrive on the scene. (9)

scandal-reform cycle a response to problem solving that occurs when the behavior of an organization is changed due to extreme pressure resulting from some negative behavior. It is reactive. (7)

scofflaws drivers with at least three unpaid parking tickets. (10)

secondary victim one who is not actually harmed but who suffers along with the victim—a spouse or parent, for example. (3)

Section 1983 the Civil Rights Act stating that anyone acting under the authority of the law who violates another person's constitutional rights can be sued; the legal authority for most lawsuits against law enforcement officers and agencies. (6)

seizure a sudden, uncontrolled event or episode of excessive electrical activity in the brain. See also *arrest*.(2)

selective enforcement assigns officers to areas identified as having high numbers of traffic law violations or high accident rates. (10)

shadow children children whose mothers used crack while pregnant. (13)

slander spoken defamation of another's character; false oral statements that tend to humiliate a person and degrade that person in the esteem of others. (6)

soilcake dirt and grime caked under the fenders of a vehicle. (10)

stamina the capacity for continued exertion over prolonged periods as well as the ability to withstand pain, distress, and fatigue for extended periods. Also called *endurance*. (8)

station adjustment when police officers decide to deal with an offense in their own way—usually by ignoring it. Also called *street justice*. (13)

status offenses violations of the law applying only to those under the legal age. These include curfew violations, drinking alcoholic beverages, incorrigibility, smoking cigarettes, running away from home, and truancy. (13)

Stockholm syndrome in a hostage situation, refers to the process of transference, with the hostages feeling positive toward their captors and negative toward the police and the captors returning these positive feelings. (11)

stop brief detention of a suspicious person by law enforcement officers for questioning. (5)

stop and frisk situation one in which law enforcement officers briefly detain a suspicious person for questioning and pat the person's outer clothing to assure that they are not armed. (5)

street justice when police officers decide to deal with an offense in their own way—usually by ignoring it. Also called *station adjustment*. (13)

strength toughness, durability, and vigor; the ability to exert force with the hands, arms, legs, or body. (8)

stress strain; physical, cognitive, and/or emotional response to a situation that is perceived to negatively affect future health, happiness, or security. It can be positive or negative. (8)

substantive law deals with the content of what behaviors are considered crimes; defines the elements of crimes and the punishments for each. (5)

survival triangle consists of mental and physical preparedness, sound tactics, and weapon control. (8)

third person uses the pronoun *he* or the phrase *this officer*. (4)

tort a civil wrong, the equivalent to a crime in criminal law. (6)

totality of circumstances includes an individual's age, mentality, education, nationality, and criminal experience as well as the reason for the arrest and how it was explained to the individual being arrested. In an interrogation situation, it also includes whether basic necessities were provided and the methods used during the interrogation. (3)

triage prioritizing, sorting out by degree of seriousness, as in medical emergencies. (14)

turf the territory claimed by a gang, often marked by graffiti. (14)

Uniform Crime Report (UCR) the FBI's national crime reporting system, published annually as *Crime in the United States*. (11)

vertical audience officers higher up in the agency who use reports as a basis of further action or upon which to base a decision; includes supervisors. (4)

vicarious liability makes others specifically associated with a person also responsible for that person's actions. (6)

witness a person other than a suspect who has information about an incident or another person. This person may be a victim, a complainant, an accuser, an informant, an observer of an occurrence, a scientific specialist who has examined physical evidence, or a custodian of official documents. (3)

Author Index

Subject Index

Gault decision, 351–353
    privilege against self-incrimination,
        353
    right to confront witnesses, 353
    right to counsel, 353
    right to cross-examine witnesses,
        353
    right to notification of charges, 353
"general adaptation syndrome", 198
general failure to protect, 144
general orders, 20, 22, 23
    defined, 20
    sample, 22
generalized tonic clonic seizures, 49
geographic information system (GIS),
    297
gestures, hand, 39
getting ready for patrol, 247–248
glass, 295
goals, 15–16, 21, 22–23, 27, 231,
    431
    crime prevention, 431
    defined, 15
    directed patrol, 231
    discretion, 27
    guidelines for writing, 22–23
Golden Rule, 172
golf cars, 241
golf-cart patrol, 237
good faith, 111, 139, 150, 152
graffiti, 377
Graham v. Connors, 113
grand mal seizures (See generalized
    tonic clonic seizures)
gratuities, 168–169
Guardian Angels, 427
guidelines, 22–23, 113, 192–193,
    311–312, 402–403, 406–407,
    437–438
    dealing with emergencies,
        406–407
    emergency plans, 402–403
    goals, 22–23
    handling mentally ill persons,
        437–438
    handling mentally retarded
        persons, 438
    handling suicide attempts,
        311–312, 438
    listening, 45
    policies, 22–23
    procedures, 22–23
    pulse-rate, 192–193
    use of force, 113
guiding principles, 14

H
hair, 294
Hallcrest Report, 444
Hampton v. United States, 128, 389
hand gestures, 39
hand signals, 377
handcuffs, using in making an arrest,
    113–114, 142
handheld computers, 262
handling mentally ill persons,
    437–438
handling mentally retarded persons,
    438
handling suicide attempts, 311–312,
    438
hands, 41–42
"hanging out", 359–360
"Haves" and "Have Nots," gap
    between, 439–441
hazardous materials, 273, 413–415
    CHEMTREC, 414–415
    Emergency Response Guidebook,
        414
    incidents (HAZMAT incidents),
        413–415
    transportation of, 273
hazards of patrol, 224
head position, 40
hearing impaired, communicating
    with the, 47–48
heel-to-toe straight line walk test,
    267
Hepatitis B (HBV), 213–214
high-intensity emergency lighting
    plan (H.E.L.P.) cars, 241
"home invaders", 384
homeless, 439–441
    children, 440
    community policing, 441
    elderly, 441
    mentally ill, 440
    veterans, 440
    victimization of, 439–441
homelessness, 355–356
homicide (See murder)
horizontal audience, 92
Horizontal Gaze Nystagmus (HGN),
    267
horse patrol, 237, 242–243
hostage situations, 308–311
    dispatcher as negotiator, 309–310
    flashbangs, 310
    stalling, 310–311
    Stockholm syndrome, 309
    strategies, 308

housing, public, 392–394
human rights, 303
hurricanes, 411–412
husband abuse, 336
hydroplaning, 276
hypnosis, forensic, 76

I
IDENTIFY, 380
identify, failure to, 145
identifying fatalities, 407
identifying gang members, 377–379
    clothing, 377
    colors, 377
    graffiti, 377
    names, 377
    sign language, 377
ignition interlocks, 270–271
illusionary correlation effect, 38
image projected by police, 441–442
immediate reaction after impact, 405
immigrants, non-English-speaking,
    435–436
impact period, 405
implied consent, 268
importance of legal arrests, 108–112
importance of patrol function, 224
In re Gault decision, 351–353
"in the presence", 107
incidents, 232
inconsistency, 26
incorrigible, 356, 357
indicators of physical fitness,
    184–185
    agility, 184, 185
    balance, 184, 185
    body composition, 184, 185
    endurance, 184, 185
    flexibility, 184, 185
    power, 184, 185
    strength, 184, 185
ineffective communications, 35
infections, protecting against,
    213–214
informant, 61–63, 129
    Adams v. Williams, 62
    defined, 61
    ethics, 63
    nonpolice undercover, 129
    reliability, 61–62
    Terry v. Ohio, 62
information, privileged, 60–61
information summary chart, sample,
    59
informational probable cause, 108

Photo Credits